COLLINS BRITISH
BIRDS

COLLINS BRITISH
BIRDS

John Gooders

Paintings by
Terence Lambert

and by
Norman Arlott

Collins
St James's Place, London

William Collins Sons & Co Ltd
London • Glasgow • Sydney • Auckland
Toronto • Johannesburg

First published in Great Britain 1982
© in the text John Gooders 1982
© in the paintings Terence Lambert 1982
© in additional text and illustrations William Collins
Sons & Co Ltd 1982
ISBN 0 00 219121 0
Filmset by Jolly & Barber Ltd, Rugby
Colour reproduction by Adroit Photo Litho Ltd,
Birmingham
Printed and bound in Great Britain by William Collins
Sons & Co Ltd, Glasgow

CONTENTS

7 Preface

9 Introduction

16 Identification *Peter Grant*

22 Songs and Calls *Eric Simms*

30 Habitats *Ian Prestt*

38 Nests and Nesting *Jim Flegg*

47 Food and Feeding *Philip Burton*

54 Range and Distribution *Colin Harrison*

64 Migration and Movements *Robert Spencer*

72 The Birds

337 Rare Birds

354 Introduced and Escaped Birds

358 Ornamental and Domesticated Birds

361 Where to Watch Birds

376 Birds and the Law *Richard Porter*

378 Societies and Useful Addresses

378 Bibliography

380 Index

PREFACE

For the past 30 years or so, British and Irish ornithologists have been looking outwards towards Europe, the western Palearctic and, progressively, the world. This growing internationalism has, in fact, resulted in an actual dearth of books on the birds of these islands. Yet British and Irish ornithology has not stood still. We know so much more about our birds in virtually every way than we did 30 years ago. At the same time, our avifauna has changed quite dramatically. The result has been the need for a well-produced and fully up to date account of our birds, a concept that has guided the preparation of this book. There is, however, a great deal more to a book than the text and paintings, and both author and artist are conscious of the debt they owe to a host of helpers. Norman Arlott painted the smaller, 'field guide' illustrations, as well as the rarities, introductions and ornamentals. In Peter Grant, Eric Simms, Ian Prestt, Jim Flegg, Philip Burton, Colin Harrison, Robert Spencer and Richard Porter we were able to gather a team of acknowledged experts to describe the most important aspects of British and Irish bird-life. We would like to thank Malcolm Gipson for designing the book, and, together with Todd Slaughter, for preparing the maps. Finally, we are delighted to acknowledge the help and hard work of the team at William Collins. To all, as well as to those whom failing memory omits, we are most sincerely grateful.

INTRODUCTION

Birds are fascinating, absorbing, interesting, compelling, intriguing, distracting, maddening, but seldom boring. Many reasons, intricate and obscure, have been propounded to explain the fascination of birds to man. Some wax lyrical about bird song, about colour and beauty of form. Others speak of their diversity, or the intricacy of their structure and power to body-weight ratio. Yet in essence we are all fascinated by birds because they can fly. It may be a matter of jealousy, tied up with the freedom of the air, or simply that we envy birds their international mobility. Ultimately, however, our reasons are far more simple and direct. We are fascinated by birds because they fly away before we get a good chance to see them properly and, because of their mobility, we never know what we shall see around the next corner. This leads to a remarkable skill: the ability to put a name to a fast-moving bird that is in view for only a fraction of a second. And an activity: the ceaseless exploration and search for new or unusual species. By virtue of a number of diverse factors, Britain and Ireland are uniquely situated for the enjoyment of the skill of identification and the activity of seeking the unusual. In this lies the peculiar 'Britishness' of our birds.

Britain and Ireland are offshore islands only recently separated from the landmass of Continental Europe. Five thousand years ago man could walk between Dover and Calais, thus facilitating colonization and communication. The breaching of the link made these more difficult, both to our benefit and annoyance. Surprisingly enough, and for all their mobility and aerial mastery, birds too have been intimidated by this narrow barrier of water. It is a strange function of islands that while they invariably support fewer species than adjacent mainland areas, they nevertheless have a high rate of endemism, that is, species found nowhere else. Britain and Ireland do not suffer from this apparent dichotomy. There are only two endemic species – Scottish Crossbill and Red Grouse – both of which are only dubiously separated from their mainland cousins, the Parrot Crossbill and Willow Grouse.

By adapting to the specific conditions in which they find themselves, all creatures are changed by the evolutionary process which chooses the most suitable to reproduce its genes. Under conditions of isolation, populations, including Scottish Crossbills and Red Grouse, became differentiated from their mainland ancestors to form subspecies and ultimately full species. In the case of the Scottish Crossbill, the irregular irruptive behaviour of all populations of Continental Crossbills must have led to the colonization of the old forests of Scot's pine and the subsequent adaptation over time of the most suitable bill for extracting seeds from the cones of this tree. The result is a bird roughly intermediate between the Continental Crossbill and Parrot Crossbill.

The Red Grouse, too, stems from Continental stock. The Willow Grouse is very similar in plumage and ecology, but it has white wings all the year round and moults to a full white 'ermine'-type plumage in winter. The milder, frequently snowless, winters of Britain and Ireland make white plumage a definite disadvantage and white wings unnecessary. Thus our bird has lost both – presumably to its advantage.

Sometimes regarded as a species in its own right, the Red Grouse is generally recognized only as a well-marked subspecies of the Continental Willow Grouse. Britain is thus left with only the Scottish Crossbill as an endemic species

Offshore islands

Being islands, or rather an archipelago of islands, Britain and Ireland have somewhat fewer species than the adjacent Continent and only two endemic ones to compensate. But being surrounded by water does have advantages. Seabirds that feed over the open seas to the north, east and west are drawn to our shores to find safe breeding sites – they come in their hundreds of thousands, making these islands the European stronghold of breeding seabirds. The Austrian or Greek ornithologist, for example, has plenty of exciting birds in woods and mountains, but is dependent on photographs in books or on television films for his experience of a seabird colony such as Skomer, Handa, Noss or Marwick Head.

We also, by virtue of the surrounding seas and particular nature of our coastline, have some of the finest estuaries in the world. The Wash, Morecambe Bay and the Ribble are outstanding by any standards and, with the tide coming and going, are home to hundreds of thousands of wildfowl and waders. They come from breeding grounds to north and east and are as dependent on our salt marshes for their continued existence as on the remote bogs of Siberia where they lay their eggs.

In the United States the American Birding Association (ABA) publishes annual totals of birds amassed by 'lister' members – a 'lister' is more or less the same as a 'twitcher' in Britain but both would respond to the name 'birder'. To compare the achievements of, say, a resident in Wyoming with one in Virginia, totals are given as a percentage of a State's total avifauna. Not surprisingly, listers resident in inland States regularly notch up over 90 per cent of the possible avifauna. Those working coastal States, with a larger proportion of migratory species, may do rather less well. But birders in Britain and Ireland can expect no better than 60 per cent, simply because these islands attract so many highly irregular vagrant birds. Of the total 495-odd birds that have been recorded, no less than 111 have occurred fewer than ten times. This makes Britain and Ireland an ideal centre for those hoping to see an extreme rarity or even, with luck and skill, a new bird for the national list.

Within Britain and Ireland this unpredictability of birds varies considerably. A good spot in, say, Shropshire may produce a predictable avifauna, but with always the chance of some off-course waif gracing one of the meres. In contrast, Fair Isle boasts a huge list of birds that have occurred on only a handful of occasions. Not surprisingly Fair Isle, and places like it, attracts more birders than Shropshire. This high level of vagrancy is, then, one of the major attractions of 'British' birds and the prime reason for the development of birding as a major passion in these islands. But it is not the only one.

By virtue of their ability to fly, birds are more mobile than most other animals. They are thus much quicker to respond to environmental change. The effect is twofold: birds may abandon a part of their range with remarkable speed, but they may also be quick to colonize or recolonize. During the present century Red-backed Shrike, Wryneck and Woodlark have all declined dramatically in southern England, whereas Redwing, Fieldfare and Temminck's Stint have colonized from the north. These changes have been attributed to a small, but nevertheless significant, decline in average summer temperatures. So while it was becoming too cold in the south for one group, it was becoming sufficiently cool for a group of basically Scandinavian species to move in from the north. Such an arrangement has an obvious appeal to the neat-minded, but there has also been a colonization of southern species extending their ranges northwards to reach Britain. Serin, Cetti's Warbler, Firecrest, Black Redstart, Little Ringed Plover and Mediterranean and Little Gulls have all become established during the past 50 years, despite the cooler summers. Alongside them have come species that formerly bred with us but which, due mainly to human interference, ceased to do so during the last century. Among this group can be numbered Avocet, Bittern, Black-tailed Godwit, Ruff, Black Tern and Savi's Warbler.

The Little Ringed Plover colonized Britain from 1938 onwards and was one of the first new arrivals during the present century

More and more birds

In fact, there are more species of bird breeding regularly in Britain now than there have been for over 100 years – yet still they come. Shore Lark, Lapland Bunting and Purple Sandpiper have all bred for the first time within the last few years and bird-watchers spend much time in speculation about future colonists. The favourite is the Fan-tailed Warbler, which has recently spread from its stronghold in the western Mediterranean. It is poised across the Channel and will surprise everyone if it does not soon breed in southeastern England. Perhaps the Red-rumped Swallow, confined only 20 years ago to Mediterranean coasts but now spreading rapidly northwards through France, will soon follow.

It is attractive to think of nature as somehow being in balance. But it is not. Nature is dynamic, constantly changing, constantly adapting. In attempting to deal with change species are born, while others fail to change and are lost. Only five species have been lost and have failed to

return to these islands in historical (since 1600) times. Cranes and Spoonbills once bred among the great marshes of the Fens, but succumbed to drainage. Today Cranes are only irregular visitors, while Spoonbills tease the watchers of Minsmere by staying late into the spring, but never settling to breed. The Great Bustard once roamed the Brecks and the chalkland plains of the south, but was gone before the middle of the last century. White-tailed Eagles, often called Ernes, were once more numerous than Golden Eagles, but being confined to the coasts were easier to find and shoot than their inland-dwelling cousins. Both Great Bustard and White-tailed Eagle are currently the subjects of reintroduction schemes that may or may not succeed. Finally there is (or was) the Great Auk, eliminated in the first half of the last century not only as a British bird, but also for all time. The Great Auk has gone, never to return.

British birds is thus a dynamic story. Species coming, going, colonizing, becoming extinct and recolonizing. Some are adapting to the enormous and progressive changes being wrought on our countryside, others are clearly failing and face the danger of decline and local extinction. To the ornithologist such changes are utterly fascinating; to the conservationist they present both wonderful opportunities and immense headaches; to birders they offer the ever-present chance of the thrill of a lifetime. Imagine being the first to discover the nest of the Fan-tailed Warbler in Britain. Imagine also the difficulties of the author, artist and editors of this book in attempting to give an accurate impression of the lives of our birds at a moment in time. We have tried to be as up to date as possible, but even while we were working a totally new species was accepted, had to be written up and, of course, be painted. Others were added to the British and Irish List for the first time and still others have been accepted back on the List as recolonizers.

Regular and vagrant

The birds in this book have been divided into three groups. The main text from pages 72 to 336 includes full accounts of all those species that breed, winter or pass through these islands regularly. Among them are all of the birds that one could reasonably expect to see, a total of 249 species. Secondly, there are those that may turn up from time to time but which cannot, in any sense of the word, be called regular. These are the rarities and vagrants described from pages 337 to 353. Finally on pages 354 to 360 are the introduced and escaped species, and the ornamental and domesticated ones. Of course, nothing is static and birds presently in one category may easily merit inclusion in a different one within a matter of a few years, or in extreme cases a few months. The American Laughing Gull was not admitted to the British List until the 1960s, but has now been seen over 20 times. Ring-billed Gulls were unknown until the 1970s, but no less than seven were recorded in 1979. In these cases the change has probably not been on the part of the birds, but in the increasing number and skill of birders. Formerly overlooked among the masses of gulls, these species are now deliberately searched for.

Few real rarities now escape the net of enthusiastic observers and even fewer are missed as a result of misidentification. Our knowledge of the often fine distinctions between closely related species is being progressively honed. The small American 'peep' still causes problems, as do the dowitchers; but our understanding of the often confusing immature plumages of gulls is at least on a sound footing and warbler identification has never been better. Often we are searching for very fine distinctions, but distinctions that nevertheless exist. Field guides, generally available since the mid-1950s, are still prone to make pro-

Poised on the brink of colonization, the Fan-tailed Warbler has spread northwards across the Continent to reach the Channel coasts of France during recent years

nouncements such as 'indistinguishable in the field', whereas what is meant is that no one has yet worked out the criteria. What were once LBJs (Little Brown Jobs) now turn out to be Blyth's Reed, Marsh, Paddyfield and Booted Warblers. In this area it is difficult to predict what will happen in the future, but recent correspondence in the literature has pointed out the diagnostic features by which the Asiatic Pin-tailed Snipe may be distinguished from the Eurasian Snipe. So perhaps that species may eventually turn up or, rather, be identified for the first time.

The order of birds

These, then, are the categories of 'British birds' that have been used in the structure of this book. Within each category the birds are arranged in systematic or scientific order – that is, according to their relationships one to another, starting with the oldest and finishing with the youngest in evolutionary terms. This is not the place to debate the accuracy of such listings, let alone their validity, though it is important to note that such subjects are debated. The fact remains that there is general agreement on the order in which birds should be listed, based on that proffered by Dr Alexander Wetmore and thus known as the Wetmore Order. This order has been revised and updated extensively, but still remains the basis of all serious bird books. This book follows the order (based on Wetmore) and names published in the journal *British Birds*. As a point of interest, the author disagrees with many of the names, particularly vernacular names, used by this body.

The scientific order may, at first, appear confusing to someone new to birds. Surely, he argues, it would be much more useful to arrange the birds alphabetically, starting with Albatross and Avocet and ending with Whitethroat and Yellowhammer. Alternatively, could not birds be arranged according to size, colour or habitat? In various books over the years birds have been arranged just so. All suffer from one grave disadvantage – closely related and therefore similar birds are scattered randomly through the work. The great advantage of the scientific order, even to the layman, is that birds of a similar kind are grouped together. Thus someone seeing a thrush-like bird can turn to the thrushes via the index and see within a page or two the bird he or she has observed. If it is not there, it should be nearby. In this system it may be awkward to find the woodpeckers, for example, but once found all woodpeckers are grouped together.

The scientific basis of the systematic order is the class. Thus all birds are placed in the class Aves, to be differentiated from the class Mammalia, class Insecta and so on. Next, birds are grouped into orders. Thus we have the order Charadriiformes (the waders, gulls, etc.), the order Gaviiformes (the divers) and so on. Next comes the family, e.g. Charadriidae where we find the sandpipers, the 'shanks' and the phalaropes. Next comes the genus, and within the Charadriidae we have the genus *Tringa*, genus *Calidris* and so on. Finally there is the

Pied Wagtail – one of the few subspecies confined to Britain and Ireland that may be identified in the field

species, and within the genus *Tringa* we have *nebularia* (Greenshank), *glareola* (Wood Sandpiper) and so on. These last two, the generic and specific names, are combined to give each species a binomial Latin name. Latin because that was the international language at the time of the system's invention by the great Swedish scientist Carl von Linné, who even Latinized his own name to Linnaeus. The Greenshank is thus *Tringa nebularia*, the Wood Sandpiper *Tringa glareola*. The whole system is rather like a pyramid or genealogical chart.

Class	:	Aves
Order	:	Charadriiformes
Family	:	Charadriidae
Genus	:	*Tringa*
Species	:	*nebularia*

Within the birds there is one class; 29 orders; 157 families; 2,102 genera; and 8,600 or so species, but the basic unit is the species.

In scientific circles, as well as in many a nineteenth-century handbook, species are themselves frequently broken down into subspecies or races. These may be very interesting, for many can be regarded as species in the making, but most cannot be distinguished in the field and others are determinable only with the aid of a large collection of skins for comparison. They are thus the preserve of the museum worker. For reference each subspecies is given a Latin trinomial. The Yellow Wagtail that occurs in Britain and Ireland, for example, is a yellow-headed green-backed bird quite different from the Blue-headed Wagtail of the adjacent Continent. It is given the trinomial name *Motacilla flava flavissima* whereas the Blue-headed Wagtail is *Motacilla flava flava*. The last of the three Latin names is the subspecific name and where it is the same as the specific name, such as *flava flava*, it is called the nominate subspecies or race. The Yellow Wagtail is one example of a subspecies that can easily be identified in the field. Another is the Pied Wagtail *Motacilla alba yarrelli*, as is the western Lesser Black-backed Gull *Larus fuscus graellsii*, but these are exceptions. Most subspecies cannot be identified in the field and are, therefore, of little concern to the birder.

Coverage

Every bird classed as regular in Britain and Ireland is allocated a page of text and illustration. Some are given fuller treatment over two pages on the basis of outstanding interest, whereas others are treated to extra pages facilitating their comparison with other species. The Yellow Wagatil complex is thus spread over two pages, because each subspecies can be recognized in the field. The raptors, or diurnal birds of prey, are the subject of a special plate because they are most often seen, and best identified, in flight. The text follows a uniform pattern and is divided into sections such as identification, breeding, range and so on for ease of reference. The length of such sections is inevitably variable. Some birds are easily identified, others are more difficult. Some have a complex summer and winter range, others are resident. Virtually all British and Irish breeding and wintering species are mapped. Those that are not are highly localized and their distribution is fully described in the text. Some species, mainly those that are regular passage migrants, are mapped on a European or world scale to show their origins and/or destinations.

Each species has been painted in an attitude that captures the character of the bird. Each has been caught in action. Such plates are quite different from the usual 'field guide' type of illustration where birds are shown in poses that exhibit their salient identification points to facilitate comparison. The paintings in this book pick out more readily how we actually see birds. In real life birds do not stand or perch neatly so that we can pick out their field marks. If they did, field identification would lose much of its appeal. But to help identification many species are also illustrated in 'field guide' form showing adult and immature, male and female, breeding and nonbreeding plumages. They are also illustrated in flight, if that is the way they are usually seen in the field.

A topographical section, pages 361 to 375, describes and maps the major areas of bird interest in Britain and Ireland. Within these pages all the usual sites that are frequented by birders are featured, though such is the unpredictable quality of birds that they may be enjoyed anywhere. Effectively it is the areas where others have watched birds, rather than where birds are found, that emerge. Thus, while some areas are more enjoyable and productive than others, interesting birds can and do turn up in the most unlikely of places.

With their comfortable hides, habitat creation and management programmes, the reserves of the Royal Society for the Protection of Birds offer ideal bird-watching. Anyone who is interested in birds should join the RSPB at the earliest opportunity. Apart from free entry to reserves, the Society publishes an excellent magazine, free to members. It has a flourishing network of members' groups that offer meetings, outings and opportunities to meet fellow bird-watchers and is ideally suited to anyone wishing to learn about birds. The RSPB, as well as the other major bird organizations in Britain and Ireland, is listed on page 378.

Active management has replaced simple protection of good bird habitats in recent years. Artificial lagoons and careful control of water levels may produce outstanding bird reserves that can be viewed from comfortable, well-sited hides

IDENTIFICATION

Peter Grant is one of Europe's leading authorities on bird identification, and has written and illustrated many articles on some of the trickier identification problems. He has been a member of the *British Birds* Rarities Committee since 1971, and its chairman since 1977

The ability to put a name to a bird is the key to enjoyable bird-watching and the natural desire to improve that ability is one of its main appeals.

Most beginners identify birds by thumbing through a field guide looking for an illustration that matches what has been seen. By this method common species which have a particularly distinctive shape, behaviour or coloration can quickly be learned. Limitations, however, will soon become apparent. Frustratingly, it is the exception rather than the rule for a bird to come close or to stay still long enough for its features to be noted and, in any case, many species are confusingly similar, especially in immature or female plumages.

To the newcomer, the skill of the expert can be daunting. What appears to be just a speck in the distance, or an almost subliminal flash disappearing into a bush, is instantly named. Such skill draws on knowledge and experience acquired over many years, but it is still all too easy for the beginner to feel disheartened. It is soon apparent that there is more to proficient identification than can be learned from studying the illustrations and descriptions contained in field guides. While there is no substitute for experience, there are still several techniques that provide an important background on which identification skill can be built.

Idea of 'jizz'

Most species can be identified by one or more distinctive features. These are its field marks, and they fall into four main categories: size and shape, coloration and plumage pattern, behaviour, and voice. The so-called 'jizz' of a bird is a bird-watching term for the total look or personality of a species – its own unique combination of field marks.

Size: Estimate the bird's size; this is easier if there is some familiar species alongside for comparison
Shape: Is it similar to some familiar species? If not, what does it most resemble and how does it differ?

Bill: Is it long or short, thick or thin, curved or straight? Again, compare it to some well-known common species

Familiarity with jizz will increase with experience, enabling identification to be made more quickly and at a greater distance.

An important first step in bird identification is to know what sort of field marks to look for. Confronted by an unfamiliar bird that cannot be readily identified on the spot, acquire the habit of first noting its most striking field marks. Then mentally run through a check list of other potential field marks, examining all parts of the bird's plumage and structure. Too many beginners produce descriptions that note only a single apparently obvious and dominant field mark, little realizing that such marks may be shared by several species. A dull brown bird with yellow legs may be a number of different species, and even noting its similarity to a Redshank will not eliminate them all. The technique of noting all marks will ensure that as many identification clues as possible are recorded, some of which could be crucial. Because the bird is unknown it is impossible to know which marks are vital.

There are innumerable examples of individual behaviour which are diagnostic of a particular species or group, and which form an important part of their jizz: the hovering of a Kestrel, tail-wagging of the wagtails, the flicking upwards of one wing of the Pied Flycatcher, and the nervous tail-shivering of the Redstart are just a few examples. Some species habitually form flocks outside the breeding season, whereas other species remain solitary throughout the year. It is unlikely, for

Wings in flight: Are they broad or narrow, long or short, angled or straight?

Tail: Is it long or short, square, forked or pointed?

Wing pattern in flight: Note bars, tips, underwing coverts, etc.
Tail pattern: Note terminal or subterminal bars, outertail feathers, rump, etc.

Flight: Does it flap like a thrush, glide like a gull or soar like a Buzzard?
General coloration: Note the pattern and coloration of the upperparts, underparts, wings and tail
Patches of colour: Note the position of these as precisely as possible
Eye, bill and legs: Note colour of each
Pattern: Note eye-stripe, crown stripe, supercilium, moustachial stripes, etc.
Wing pattern when perched: Note coloration and bars, etc.
Ground movement: Does it hop like a House Sparrow, shuffle like a Dunnock, walk like a Starling or run like a wagtail?
How and where does it feed? Among foliage like a warbler; on open mud or beach like a wader; or on the ground like a thrush or pipit? Does it dive under the water from the surface like a grebe or plunge in from the air like a tern?

example, that a flock of red-breasted birds will be Robins, simply because these birds remain solitary and highly territorial virtually throughout the year. It is important to get to know which species to expect in which habitat, as this too can narrow the identification choice. For example, the three regular British pipits are of similar appearance, but one seen in open woodland is almost certainly a Tree Pipit, one seen in open, treeless country is likely to be a Meadow Pipit, while one frequenting rocky shores is a Rock Pipit. Another important consideration is the time of year at which the bird is seen. While many species are resident in Britain throughout the year, others can be expected only at certain seasons. Get to know which species are resident (such as the Robin, Meadow Pipit and Dunlin), which are winter visitors (such as the Brambling, Rock Pipit and Sanderling), and which are summer visitors (such as the Spotted Flycatcher, Tree Pipit and Greenshank).

All species have their own songs and call notes, which are invaluable identification aids. The experienced bird-watcher uses his ears as much as his eyes to identify birds – probably as many as two-thirds of his identifications are made by recognizing songs and calls. The recognition of bird voice is essential, but it is one of the most difficult skills to acquire.

After locating the origin of an unfamiliar call note or song, write down a description of it at once: liberally use such adjectives as loud, piercing, thin, fluty and so on. If the flight call of a Snipe sounds to you like tearing paper, or a Goldcrest's song like distant tinkling bells, include such comparisons in the description. Many bird sounds can be likened to familiar or imaginary noises and such comparisons form excellent memory-joggers. The boom of a Bittern may sound like a ship's foghorn, the Yellowhammer may say *little-bit-of-bread-and-no-cheese*, and the Cirl Bunting may be similar, but without the *cheese*. Try to invent such likenesses wherever possible. Try also to imitate bird sounds for some time after they have been heard. This keeps them fresh in the mind and progress will be made towards the time when an increasing number of species can be recognized by their songs.

Fortunately, we all understand many of the terms used for the various parts of a bird's anatomy. Wings, rump, neck, legs are universally comprehensible – but to describe a bird accurately it is necessary to learn the location and all the names of the various parts of a bird's plumage. The purpose of this rather tedious task is to provide a vital base for proficient identification. With practice it will enable a precise and detailed description to be taken, essential when an unfamiliar bird or difficult-to-identify species is involved. It will encourage detailed study of a bird rather than just a superficial impression of its general appearance. And it will also enable detailed identification descriptions in the literature to be fully understood.

Behavioural clues

Topographical charts tend to be skipped over, and not only because they are complicated. Confusingly, many charts do not label all the parts of the bird and often the terminology varies from one chart to another. The charts used overleaf are complete and the terminology is that which British ornithologists are currently pressing to get accepted as standard.

All birds have the same basic plumage 'map', although the extent or prominence of a particular group of feathers may vary from one related species to another. For example, on some birds such as warblers and finches the tertials are relatively short, whereas on others such as larks and pipits they are long, reaching just short of, or even to, the tips of

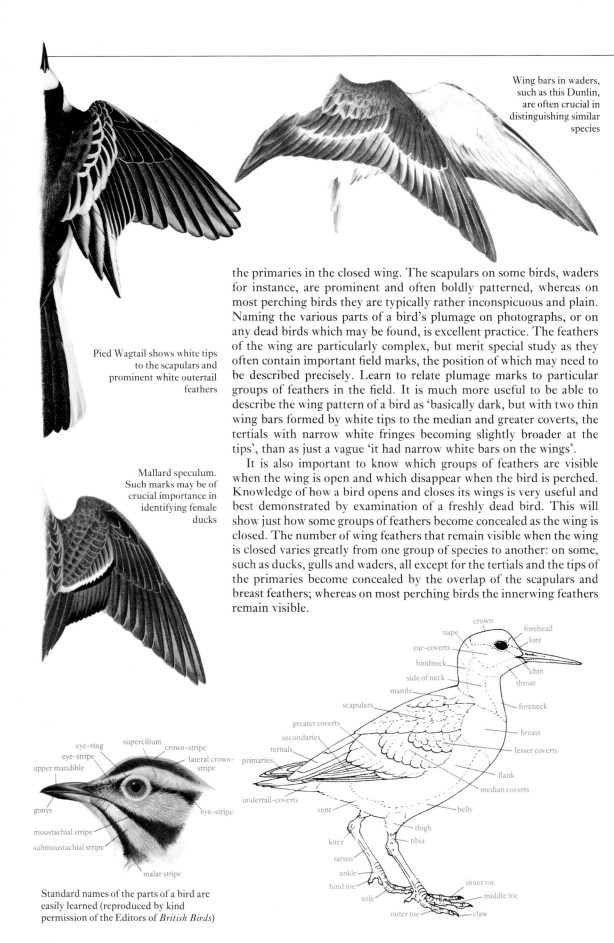

Wing bars in waders, such as this Dunlin, are often crucial in distinguishing similar species

Pied Wagtail shows white tips to the scapulars and prominent white outertail feathers

Mallard speculum. Such marks may be of crucial importance in identifying female ducks

the primaries in the closed wing. The scapulars on some birds, waders for instance, are prominent and often boldly patterned, whereas on most perching birds they are typically rather inconspicuous and plain. Naming the various parts of a bird's plumage on photographs, or on any dead birds which may be found, is excellent practice. The feathers of the wing are particularly complex, but merit special study as they often contain important field marks, the position of which may need to be described precisely. Learn to relate plumage marks to particular groups of feathers in the field. It is much more useful to be able to describe the wing pattern of a bird as 'basically dark, but with two thin wing bars formed by white tips to the median and greater coverts, the tertials with narrow white fringes becoming slightly broader at the tips', than as just a vague 'it had narrow white bars on the wings'.

It is also important to know which groups of feathers are visible when the wing is open and which disappear when the bird is perched. Knowledge of how a bird opens and closes its wings is very useful and best demonstrated by examination of a freshly dead bird. This will show just how some groups of feathers become concealed as the wing is closed. The number of wing feathers that remain visible when the wing is closed varies greatly from one group of species to another: on some, such as ducks, gulls and waders, all except for the tertials and the tips of the primaries become concealed by the overlap of the scapulars and breast feathers; whereas on most perching birds the innerwing feathers remain visible.

Standard names of the parts of a bird are easily learned (reproduced by kind permission of the Editors of *British Birds*)

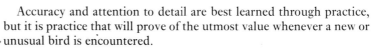

The open and closed wing of the Pied Flycatcher (top) shows the difference in appearance and even the obvious qualities of the 'field mark' from an awkward angle

Accuracy and attention to detail are best learned through practice, but it is practice that will prove of the utmost value whenever a new or unusual bird is encountered.

The value of a close study of common species cannot be over-emphasized. Start on the most common species in the garden or local area, the ones which are tame and allow a fairly close approach. Note their habitat, behaviour and calls, in particular take detailed descriptions of their plumage, practising the knowledge of bird topography by relating plumage marks to specific groups of feathers. By this approach a total familiarity will gradually be built up with common birds in their often confusing plumages – male, female, summer, winter, juvenile and so on. Get to know the different appearance of their colours and patterns in various light conditions, and the variations of one individual of the same species from another. Attention to common species is important whatever the experience of the observer; it is a continuous process by which it becomes possible to recognize them ever more quickly and at greater distance as more and more fine detail is added to the knowledge of their jizz. Such familiarity will enable the unusual to be picked out more readily. Moreover, it will make it possible to say precisely *why* it is unusual and thus preclude confusion with a common species in unfamiliar plumage or surroundings.

Joining clubs

Learning from more experienced bird-watchers will accelerate progress. Few will object to the involvement of the genuine and enthusiastic, keen to improve their bird-watching skills. Indeed, most welcome the chance to demonstrate and pass on their knowledge. Ask questions, and do not be afraid of asking the elementary. Take advice and correction constructively. There is no doubt that field experience with other more experienced bird-watchers is essential at some stage: the sooner it is arranged the better. As a start, join a local bird club or society. Most hold field trips and indoor meetings which offer an ideal opportunity for obtaining information on the best local areas and recent sightings, and provide a welcome chance to meet local experts and seek advice.

Local clubs keep a central record of ornithological sightings in their areas, collated from reports sent in by members. These form the basis for the club's annual report – a record of local bird-life that monitors populations from year to year and often forms the basis for conservation proposals should any bird-rich area come under threat of development. A study of local bird reports and bulletins shows what is usual or exceptional in the area, an important consideration when identifying birds. Send in your own records, not only because tangible use is then made of observations, but also because it forces a degree of self-censorship in identification. Knowledge that records will come under the scrutiny of local experts before being published instils a cautious approach in which only positive identifications are submitted. Self-censorship is unnecessary if you are the only judge. By not submitting records an insufficient element of caution may become part of your bird-watching, leading to incorrect identifications.

There is no doubt that the chance of discovering a rare bird is one of the excitements of bird-watching. For beginner and expert alike, however, enthusiasm must always be kept under control. An over-enthusiastic approach creates a very real danger that a rarity will be claimed when a bird has not really been seen well enough for its diagnostic characteristics to be noted with 100 per cent certainty.

Whenever a rarity is suspected, caution is the keyword. Awareness of the pitfalls of brief or distant views, and the effect of different light

Identification

conditions, should always be borne in mind. If the unusual or rare is suspected, it is much safer to assume that it is something common until it is proved otherwise: the opposite approach – 'I don't recognize it, so it must be something rare' – closes the mind to possibilities which are much more likely. Caution and self-criticism, the hallmarks of the expert, are qualities which should be fostered at all stages of bird-watching experience. Bird-watching may not be a science, or an art, but it certainly errs towards the former.

The field notebook

Always carry a notebook when bird-watching, but remember that speed is essential when taking notes on a bird. Writing a description longhand can be time-consuming – time better spent watching the bird, which may fly off at any moment. A rough sketch is a much quicker method, and there is no need for artistic skill. Practise standard outlines which show the basic topography of a perching bird, a swimming duck, a flying gull and so on, so that they can be reproduced in a few seconds in the field. The sketch does not have to be accurate in shape; its purpose is to provide a basic outline on which field marks can be quickly noted – even annotations can be abbreviated, for speed is essential. The rough, annotated sketch is then the base from which a finished description can later be compiled, a form of ornithological shorthand. Note the most obvious field marks first, then, if the bird stays in view, begin to note all its features in detail, working systematically over the whole plumage, and also noting bill shape and other structural details, calls, behaviour and habitat. Practise this on common birds, so that you are ready to handle the unfamiliar or rare when it occurs. Keep finished descriptions, which will build up into a valuable personal reference.

When confronted with a suspected rarity, the first essential is to take as detailed a description as possible on the spot: never trust the details to memory. If it is a quick view, take notes immediately after the bird has disappeared. If it stays in view, double-check all points and add extra-fine detail. When fully satisfied that everything possible has been noted, try to get other bird-watchers to corroborate the observation. This may not always be easy, but few bird-watchers will object to a phone call asking them to come to check the identification of a rarity. Later, discuss the description with other bird-watchers and consider whether all possible pitfalls have been eliminated.

Records that stand the best chance of acceptance contain a clear, precise description of the bird, as well as discussion which shows that all potential identification pitfalls have been considered. A feather-by-feather description is obviously unnecessary for a rarity of striking appearance such as a White Stork or Hoopoe. Generally it should contain sufficient detail to prove the identification, and this requires increasing detail the more subtle the species' field marks or the more confusing species there are to be eliminated. But most important, the description should be kept to details which have been noted with certainty: if there is any doubt over a particular point, this should be stated. Often an honest – if incomplete – account of the sighting is more likely to convince an official committee than an impossibly feather-perfect one.

A list of species which require a description to substantiate a sighting is published in most local reports: this varies from club to club, because what is rare in one area may be more regular in another. Records of species which are rare nationally are forwarded by the club's recorder for consideration by the *British Birds* Rarities Committee, which publishes its *Report on Rare Birds in Britain* in that journal.

Goldcrest wing showing the position of bars on open and closed wings. Attention to such detail may facilitate correct identification

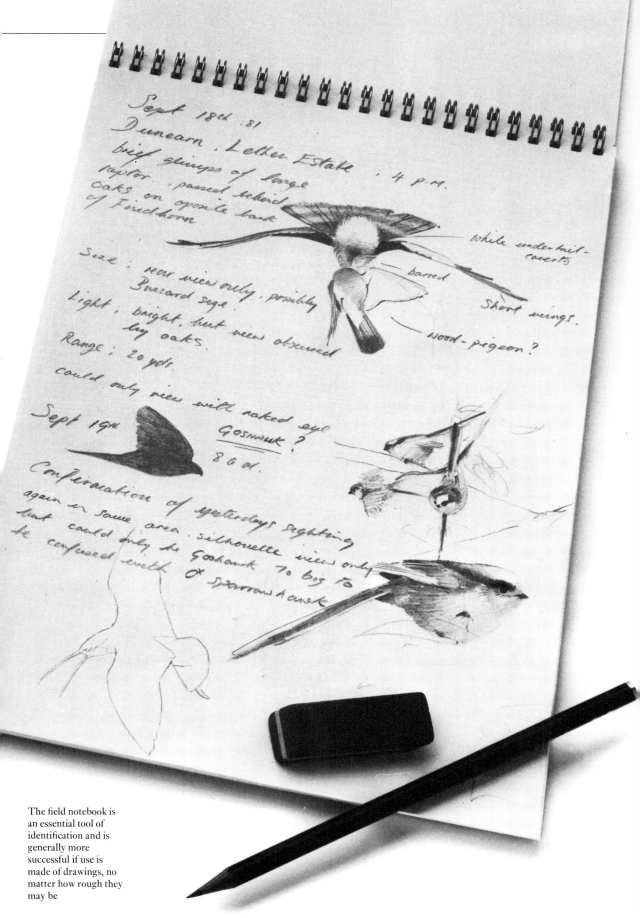

Sept 18th :81
Dunearn, Letter Estate ; 4 p.m.
brief glimpse of large
raptor, passed behind
oaks on opposite bank
of Findhorn

white under tail-
coverts

barred

Short wings.

wood-pigeon?

Size : rear view only, possibly
Buzzard size.
Light ; bright, but view obscured
by oaks.
Range : 20 yds.
could only view with naked eye
Goshawk ?
8 G ol.

Sept 19th

Confirmation of yesterday's sighting
again in same area. silhouette view only
but could only be Goshawk. Too big to
be confused with ♂ Sparrowhawk

The field notebook is
an essential tool of
identification and is
generally more
successful if use is
made of drawings, no
matter how rough they
may be

SONGS AND CALLS

Eric Simms has made well over 5,000 radio broadcasts, more than 500 television appearances, and is the author of 15 books, including an autobiography and *Woodland Birds and Thrushes* in Collins' New Naturalist series. He has served on the Council of the RSPB and is currently on the Council of the World Wildlife Fund (UK)

The song of the Robin, delivered virtually throughout the year, serves as a territorial defence and, in spring, as an advertisement for a mate. It is the first line of defence, and is followed by aggressive displays of the red breast as a second resort

For those for whom the songs of birds have a compelling attraction there is no more exciting or stimulating a time than early spring. This seasonal outpouring of song is, in fact, caused by the growing influence of hormones secreted in the birds' bodies, which can have both short- and long-term effects. The production of the hormones and the consequent growth in the amount of testosterone bring the bird into breeding condition and induce it to sing. The process may be triggered off by a number of changes in the environment such as increasing day length and light, temperature and the amount of food that the birds can find. Town Blackbirds often sing earlier than country birds and it is possible that the higher temperatures, increased light and disturbance in towns are the stimulation.

In late summer, when many songbirds moult their feathers and the energy drain on them is high, song ceases or is very greatly reduced. There may be some song or display again in the autumn, which is probably due to a revival of hormonal activity. Great Tits sing well in autumn and it is not unusual to hear bursts of song from Wrens, Robins, Song Thrushes and some of the summer migrants before their departure to the south. Stone-curlews gather in the autumn on favourite downs and indulge in quite remarkable and frenzied dances before migrating to Iberia and Africa.

The functions of song itself are rather complex, but some of them now seem clear and are reasonably well understood. In the case of a common singer such as the Robin, which has quite a loud, clear and easily recognized song, the musical outpourings in spring show that the male bird is ready to breed and in possession of a territory; is advertising for a female with which he can mate; and is imbued with a latent aggressiveness by which rival male Robins can be kept at bay. Song often acts as a substitute for actual combat between rival males which, in excess, would be detrimental to the species.

The chief characteristics of territorial songs are lack of ambiguity so that they can easily be recognized, loudness and persistence. In the Robin's song there is great variation in the linking of the different motifs or sequences of elements, but fluctuations in pitch and other characters give it the special quality of a Robin's song. The notes themselves may be audible at a distance of 200 metres or more, and an unmated male Robin may sing almost three times as long each day as a mated one, indicating that persistence is very much a part of territorial singing. Song may also form part of a display which may deter a rival or help to establish and forge a bond linking the members of a pair. In some instances the actual singing itself helps to synchronize the breeding cycle of male and female and the activities of nesting and rearing young. Blackcaps will entice females, to nest foundations they have built, with song, and the male Great Tit will also sing to attract a female to a particular nest hole.

Loudest songsters

Yet undoubtedly the loudest and clearest songs among British birds are territorial in nature. It is interesting to note that nearly all woodland birds use plenty of sound and have fairly clear, unmistakable and loud songs. In dense cover birds could mistake one another's identity, so it is vital that their songs should be different. The Chiffchaff and Willow Warbler are shrub birds which also look very much alike, but they have quite dissimilar songs. These two species of warbler cannot mistake each other when they are concealed by foliage. The Blackcap and Garden Warbler are different in plumage, but both live in woodland and to some extent share the same habitat, and their songs too are different. Great Tits sometimes have several songs and even employ calls

Song posts may be obvious or obscure. There are three birds singing in this single bush. All can be heard, but two are difficult to find

that have a similar function to song. It now seems clear that individuals with large repertoires are able to command large territories, and by the nature and quality of their songs these more experienced males are able to deter younger, more callow males from entering their domains.

Anyone walking through the countryside in spring and early summer, or waiting in the early morning light to hear the dawn chorus in a wood or garden, soon becomes aware of the extraordinary variety of sounds. The swelling chorus is composed of simple notes and calls, short uncomplicated runs of notes or phrases, and rich outpourings of great complexity and invention. Variations provide much of the delight for us as we listen to and enjoy the marvellous medley of songs and calls. A single Woodlark is capable of uttering more than 100 melodic phrases in a period of just five minutes. Yet in some birds it is difficult to separate song from call notes. Birds with comparatively simple songs such as Meadow and Rock Pipits, and even larks, can show a very close relationship between their calls and songs. There is a clear contrast between the short, repeated *jink-jink-tillee-tillee* refrain of a male Reed Bunting singing by a mereside and the richly inventive phrases and motifs of a cock Blackbird indulging in a highly relaxed and experimental evening performance from a suburban television aerial.

Inherited songs

It seems that with many species of songbird the individual inherits some characters of its full song but has to learn the rest. It was shown many years ago that the Chaffinch has to learn much of his song and in the early stages of his singing the male will use call notes as well. If one listens carefully to the song of the Chaffinch it can be seen that it falls into three parts: for example, *chip-chip-chip-chip . . . cherry-erry-erry . . . tchip-tcherweeoo*. A young male Chaffinch, even before he can actually sing himself, may acquire something of the first phrase and even become aware that the flourish at the end is necessary. The terminal phrase *tchip-tcherweeoo* can only be acquired by learning during a few weeks in the young bird's first spring when it starts to sing and compete with other male Chaffinches. In this way a community pattern of songs can be established with the young males learning from the adults the more complex rhythms and terminal endings; it seems that young Coal Tits learn in a similar way. The Blackbird also has to learn a great deal of his song. He will practise and experiment with his material, shifting it around, making mistakes in his delivery and even correcting them. A young Blackbird also has to listen to other singers more experienced than himself and so build upon their performances. Each individual singer remains distinctive and can be recognized by his song, but some of the more forceful and compelling phrases may survive in a community for a number of years. These 'dialects', which can be traced in Blackbirds and Chaffinches, and probably in Whitethroats, Wrens and Cuckoos, may be recognized by the character and length of phrases, the number and order of particular variations, and by the rhythms and inflections in the performances.

Territorial songs are often uttered from conspicuous positions or 'song posts', so that it is quite a common sight to observe a Mistle or Song Thrush singing from a perch high in a tree, or a Blackcap flitting about the canopy of a tall ash tree as he sings his fluent phrases. This habit provides a proper display for the singer and advertises him very well. Birds that seek cover, such as a Nightingale in a bramble brake or a Sedge Warbler in a dense patch of waterside vegetation, sing particularly loudly. Each species of bird differs to some extent in the way it exploits its song or conspicuous singing post, or both, to proclaim its species, sex, status and needs.

Some kinds of bird resort to a special song flight to make themselves more conspicuous. Although many species occasionally sing in flight, there are several others which frequently do so. The Tree Pipit utters its shrill song as it nears the peak of an aerial climb from some tree-top perch, while the rest of its song is delivered as the bird 'parachutes' down with raised wings like a descending paper aircraft. The typical

The roding Woodcock flies low over its territory uttering a distinctive note that acts as a 'song'

song flight of the Meadow Pipit above its breeding moor may last for up to half a minute, while the Rock Pipit's powerful notes are heard against the roar of the breaking sea. The way these rather special aerial performances are linked with the habitats in which the birds live is particularly well illustrated by the Skylark, for no other British bird has brought the technique of the song flight to such a peak of perfection. Rising vertically into the wind on rapidly beating wings, the male climbs quickly into the air. At the end of the ascent he remains in his fixed and chosen spot in space before beginning to rise and fall and then drift around in a wide circle over his territory lying far below him. For minutes on end the notes pour out in a breathless, hurried way as the bird responds to the stimulation of other rival Skylarks nearby.

Several other species reinforce their vocal declarations of territory with song flights, but they tend to be far less dramatic than the sustained and superb performance of the Skylark. The Greenfinch embarks upon a strange and hesitant 'butterfly' flight, and the male, singing his medley of twitters, *chow-chow-chow*s and musical notes, wavers, banks and floats from the top of one tall tree to another, or back to his original perch. Siskins have a dancing song flight over the canopies of coniferous trees and Redpolls utter their rippling calls and protracted *eez* notes in a special fluctuating and gliding flight. Both thus make themselves much more conspicuous in their rather arboreal habitat. In the high Grampians and in its Arctic home the Snow Bunting, a contrasting study in black and white, rises 7–10 metres in the air with wings extended, utters a brief musical warble and then descends on angled wings. The now rare Dartford Warbler declares his territorial rights above the low gorse bushes by singing a scratchy little warble in a jerky, dancing flight.

Birds sing in a variety of different aerial zones. The Skylark (top) is totally aerial, while the Tree Pipit (above) 'parachutes' to a perch. The Whitethroat (below) has a bouncing song flight and returns to the same low perch

Types of song

The territorial songs of British birds fall into three main groups. The first consists of nonmusical and somewhat social kinds of song, not always very strongly motivated territorially, such as those of the Linnet or Starling. The last species rambles on for quite long periods, continuously mixing a few rather unclear musical notes or phrases with rasping, wheezing, clucking, stuttering sounds, bouts of rhythmical bill-clicking and imitations of other bird species, train sirens, car horns and even crying infants. The second group of songs is formed from the monotonous nonfree repetition of notes or patterns of notes. In birds such as the Grasshopper and Savi's Warblers there are sustained repetitions of one element; the former's reeling trill may conceal up to

1,400 double notes in a minute while the latter may reach almost 2,000. In this group are the Willow Warbler, Robin, Wren and Redwing, although all these species can create irregular and inexact combinations of elements. The third and final group of singers includes some of our finest performers, such as the Blackbird, Mistle Thrush, Song Thrush and Garden Warbler, which all engage in continuous songs freely composed and consequently often of varying length and rhythm.

Birds that do not inherit all the components of their songs and are capable of free composition are sometimes extremely good mimics. Mimicry stamps an individual bird with a special character and may even ensure its selection by a female who may regard it as an older, more experienced bird. In fact, about 30 different kinds of British bird have been known to use imitations. Some of the best mimics are the Skylark, which sometimes specializes in wader imitations, the Marsh Warbler, which has been known to copy more than 100 other species, the Red-backed Shrike, the Sedge Warbler and even the Great Tit.

There are other kinds of song besides that associated with territory, however. Some species have rallying and nest-invitation songs, while others employ quiet courtship songs to entice females. Robins, Blackbirds and Song and Mistle Thrushes also indulge in a soft, inward and sometimes barely audible singing with their bills closed. This 'subsong' is clearly related to full territorial song, but the notes are less well defined, more rambling, less pure and range more widely in pitch. The uttering of subsong probably indicates that the performers have a rather low but climbing hormone rate. In the autumn it may just be practice by young birds. Woodland birds such as the Hawfinch and Bullfinch have quiet utterances without a high territorial content which help to cement the pair bond. Even the Raven and other crows have strange warbled subsongs of their own. Known for their harsh caws, kronks, rattles and screams, these utterances sometimes have a curiously appealing quality. The Rook has a Starling-like subsong, the Jackdaw a bubbling one, the Magpie a warbler-like series of notes and the Jay a crooning gurgle.

Vocal chords

The organ of voice in man and other mammals, and in some amphibians as well, is the larynx – the upper part of the windpipe or trachea which modulates the voice. A pair of elastic bands known as the vocal chords, which can be stretched, vibrate in the airstream that flows through the throat. In birds the vocal organ is quite different. It is called the syrinx, or lower larynx, and is located in the lower end of the trachea. It is enveloped by an air sac which can produce tones and it also possesses membranes that can vibrate and whose tension can be altered by muscles. The air pressure in the sac and the broncheal tube sets the membranes in motion. The sounds of mammals are produced during the exhalation of air and with songbirds it seems that a similar process is involved. It is from the syrinx that the pure melodies of the Blackbird and Nightingale emerge, as well as the raucous scream of the Jay or the harsh notes of Heron and Crow. Many small passerine birds with elaborate songs may be equipped with up to seven pairs of muscles that control the membranes, while larger nonpasserines such as divers, grebes and auks may have no more than three and are able to produce only simple and uncomplicated sounds such as honks, caws and rattles. Yet in their way the wailing cries of divers, echoing across a loch and reflected from a nearby mountainside, are some of the most evocative and beautiful sounds in the whole of nature.

In more highly developed birds there is clearly a complex sound-producing system by which the sounds produced by the syrinx can be

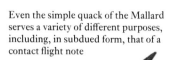

Even the simple quack of the Mallard serves a variety of different purposes, including, in subdued form, that of a contact flight note

modulated by the oral cavity and the bill and tongue. In Reed Warblers there may be double or even more complicated systems whereby birds can simultaneously utter low tones and high trills.

Some birds, however, are not able to exploit sound in the complex way songbirds do and have to resort to using calls, sometimes elaborately combined, or even mechanical devices. A few species make instrumental sounds that are received by other birds exactly as if they were vocalizations. One of the best known of these performances is that of the Snipe. This small wading bird climbs up into the air in the spring above its marshy breeding territory and then suddenly plunges earthwards with its tail fanned out and its wings half closed. As the bird descends, the air rushes over the tail and vibrates the two outer feathers, which are extended at an angle to the rest, producing a strange tremulous bleating sound. Indeed, on some northern moors the Snipe is known as the 'heather-bleater'. This aerial display, which has a similar function to song in proclaiming territory, advertising for a female and reinforcing the pair bond, is repeated over and over again. Although it is chiefly carried out by the male, some females will also 'bleat' and the sound can be heard by night as well as by day. There are several other examples of instrumental sound. Both Great and Lesser Spotted Woodpeckers will peck or drum rapidly – at rates of a score or more blows in under a second – at dead branches and other natural resonating surfaces.

Woodpigeon in display flight involving diving and wing clapping

Snipe drumming – the stiff outertail feathers create a bleating sound

Great Spotted Woodpecker drumming, another nonvocal territorial sound

Other species may use bills, wings and feathers. Some gamebirds such as Pheasant, Red Grouse and Ptarmigan flap their wings during display, while Lapwings use their noisy wing beats to supplement their calls and dramatic tumbling spring display flights. In spring Woodpigeons will clap their wings loudly during a display flight around their selected nesting tree and Feral Pigeons will do the same over busy city streets. Sound is often reinforced with postures and movements of the body. Whooper Swans greet each other with raised wings and lifted heads as well as with loud calls. The amorous Blackcock at his communal lek struts about with tail fully spread and wings drooping, and then, as he utters his display call or crow, he lifts up his head and may even jump in the air.

Some of the birds found in Britain and Ireland that are not equipped with the more complex vocal mechanisms of the true songbirds may use song substitutes or displays in addition to purely instrumental sounds. These species indulge in clear and unmistakable vocalizations that serve to declare territorial rights and advertise for or retain mates. Pigeons and doves coo and moan besides having aerial displays, Nightjars churr away at dusk at a rate of 1,900 notes a minute, owls hoot during the night, and Cuckoos call and bubble over fields, moors and along woodland fringes. Among wading birds are some of the loveliest and most intriguing song substitutes imaginable. There are the glorious drawn-out notes and bubbling trills of the Curlew, the high titterings

Songs and Calls

The yelping calls of the Redshank are an effective warning of danger and a characteristic sound of springtime marshes, where it may alert birds of a wide variety of species alongside which it lives, such as Little Grebes

of the Whimbrel, the musical creakings of the Black-tailed Godwit, the amphibian-like croaking of the Woodcock as he flies or 'rodes' between the trees, the purring trill of the Dunlin, the Woodlark-like notes of the Wood Sandpiper, the yodelling of the Redshank, the rich modulations of the Greenshank and the mournful ripple of the Golden Plover – all these delivered in various kinds of song flight. They serve as song substitutes proclaiming territory and announcing identity, sex, status and the need for a mate. The male Stone-curlew has a nuptial display in which runs of three-syllable notes are built up into a fantastic and wild crescendo of sound as the calls rise in pitch and accelerate in their delivery.

Uses of calls

Call notes in birds have a wide range of purposes and seem to be of genetic origin. The responses to them also seem to be innate. Calls tend to be short and rather simple in their acoustic make-up. Unlike song they are concerned with everyday affairs such as giving immediate and clear warning of danger, keeping in touch with one another, searching for sources of food, revealing hostile and aggressive intentions, showing care and attention for the young and even betraying fear or distress. The speed of response in birds is very high indeed and they can resolve sounds ten times faster than humans. They locate them by achieving a binaural comparison of differences in their phase, intensity and arrival time. In this way some birds can perform highly synchronized duets in which contributions from two birds are combined or moulded into a single pattern. This kind of duetting is rare in temperate parts of the world, but it seems to occur with Little Grebes where trilling duets form part of the courtship ritual.

Research has been carried out into the vocabularies of a number of British birds and it would appear that 20 separate or basic calls are about the upper limit to the number essential for survival. The Blackbird, however, has seven basic calls, the Nuthatch 12, the Wren 13 or 14, the Chaffinch and Whitethroat 14 each, while a single Great Tit has been observed to employ 40 different sounds. In the case of the Great Tit and the Chaffinch, which may expand its basic list of 14 notes to at least 21, both birds are able to express shades of intensity or what might be called 'moods'. A male Great Tit can reveal a range of intensity in its aggressive moods from a simple uncertainty to actual and vigorous attack. There can be quite a gradation in the intensity of messages between birds and some may widen their vocabulary by improvisation, or by borrowing utterances from their neighbours.

Some of the more important calls are those of anxiety and alarm. A Blackbird foraging in a comparatively strange or rarely visited part of its territory will give vent to a slightly anxious, soft *tchook-tchook* which will soon change to a quicker, higher and louder *mik-mik-mik* if the bird should become seriously alarmed. The sudden appearance of a cat or human will bring a rapid resort to flight and a fast, penetrating rattle of notes that degenerate into a high scream. Alarm notes need to be loud and unmistakable so that they will ensure an immediate response and effective action. To give warning of enemies the Blackbird also employs a thin high *see* which is pure in tone and with such an ill-defined start and finish that it is very difficult to locate. It provides warning of the presence of a hawk to other Blackbirds, but it does not give away the caller's exact place of concealment. A number of other quite common birds such as the Chaffinch also use high, pure-toned warning calls for aerial predators.

Threatening and aggressive calls are widely used by birds, especially during territorial fights and in encounters with enemies. The Mistle

Continuous honking is characteristic of most species of geese in flight and the means by which the skeins keep in contact

Thrush will boldly harass and attack a dog, cat or even human intruder when busy nesting, mobbing its enemy with rapid screeches and croaking sounds. The Arctic Tern will readily carry out airborne attacks on human visitors to its domain, striking their heads savagely and often drawing blood, while uttering calls that advance from an anxious *kee* to a menacing machine-gun-like chatter as the bird attacks. One can often hear alarm and aggressive notes when birds discover an owl roosting by day, and Blackbirds, Song and Mistle Thrushes, tits, Wrens, Robins and Jays will all announce their discovery of the previously hidden enemy with loud mobbing notes. Many birds, in fact, will scold and threaten in the presence of an intruder. The hiss of the cob swan with his cygnets and the similar hiss of the Great Tit or Wryneck, sitting on its nest in a hole, all serve to act as deterrents. Sometimes when a bird is caught by a predator or even handled by a human it will utter shrill calls of alarm or fear, and bird ringers know how Starlings, Song Thrushes and Blackbirds in particular may respond to handling with quite agonizing distress calls.

Contact calls

Birds, and in particular sociable ones, often need to remain in contact with each other when they are flying, moving in the dark, or feeding in densely wooded habitats or even very open ones. Many birds use a contact call which serves in mated pairs as an enquiry as to the whereabouts of the other member of the pair. If no answer is immediately forthcoming the enquiry may be repeated by the first bird. A mixed party of birds such as tits, Goldcrests, Treecreepers and woodpeckers foraging through a winter oak wood use contact calls for identification and to preserve the individual foraging space demanded by each member of the group. Similarly, a flock of wading birds on a beach or mud flat call continuously as they search for food – sounds such as the liquid *tuli* of Ringed Plover, the fluctuating triple whistle of Grey Plover, the dry twittering of Turnstone or the *chreep* of Dunlin.

We become, perhaps, most aware of contact calls when birds are travelling in flocks and seeking to keep together. The contact calls of wildfowl in the winter, from the buglings of Whooper and Bewick's Swans to the honks, barks, babbles and clangour of wild geese and the lovely slurred whistles of drake Wigeon, are some of the most exciting and evocative of all bird vocalizations. On many occasions birdwatchers may first become aware of birds above their heads by the sounds of their calls. They may be Swallows, martins and Swifts on the wing, Skylarks, Meadow Pipits, Chaffinches and Redwings migrating by day, and even Sandwich Terns, Redpolls and Grey Wagtails crossing over the centre of a city. Contact calls are vital for night migrants and so Redwings and other thrushes as well as many kinds of wading bird can be heard calling in the dark as they travel on their unseen way.

Each species of bird uses a recognizable set of calls which can be identified immediately by its mate or young. Even in dense and highly populated tern and Gannet colonies it seems that recognition between members of a pair or between them and their young is achieved through an understanding of the amplitude of sounds. Amplitude is the amount of change in sound pressure, which is related to changes in the intensity of power of the sound. Embryo chicks, while still inside the egg, may come to recognize the individual nature of the sounds made by their own mothers long before hatching takes place. The embryos of some ducks can identify their mothers at least five days before they are due to break out of their shells, while young Guillemots also master a special call from the parent while still inside the eggshell. In some species of gamebird the embryos will 'talk' to each other and

Prior to hatching, and often before the eggshell is cracked, the chick will call to its parent and elicit a response

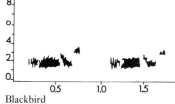

Blackbird

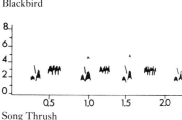

Song Thrush

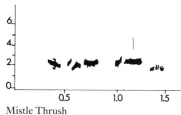

Mistle Thrush

Sound spectrographs are a highly efficient visual method of showing the differences between bird songs. Like reading music, they are difficult to understand at first

these multiple conversations ensure mutual stimulation and the hatching of the chicks at about the same time. They then evacuate the nest site in company and in the shortest possible time. In this way the female is not delayed at the nest while she waits for late chicks to hatch out. A great deal still has to be discovered about this fascinating aspect of bird vocalization and learning.

People hear bird sounds differently. Some may even have deaf spots in their range of hearing without actually being aware of it. An aural sensitivity test soon discloses them. Many of us use words to describe the bird sounds that we hear and to provide a phonetic rendering, despite the obviously subjective nature of the enterprise. For example, the creaking notes of the Scottish Crossbill's subsong could be rendered *crrook-crrok*, *yeek-yeek*, *ip-ip-yureek-yureek*, and *grrr-grr*. Although these onomatopoeic renderings are not entirely satisfactory, they represent a convenient way of expressing bird sounds in a paper or book. There is, of course, no real substitute for a tape recording which can be replayed many times, slowed down, put through a waveband analyser which shows the amplitude in decibels, or converted into a picture on a cathode-ray oscilloscope, sonagraph or melograph. But on occasion it may still be useful to record the character or lilt of a song or call using words, phrases and even onomatopoeic expressions and verse. A Song Thrush may declaim *cheerio-cheerio* or *Peter-Peter*, a Mourning Dove *Noah! Pay me!*, a Chestnut-sided Warbler *I-wish-to-see-Miss-Beecher*, a Yellowhammer *a-little-bit-of-bread-and-no-cheese* and a Woodpigeon *coos-Taffy . . . take-coos-Taffy . . . take-coos-Taffy . . . take* with variants. Leach's Petrel has a call that can aptly be shown in the rhythm of *call-up-a-sailor*, *call-up-a-crew*.

Various attempts have been made to produce a graphic notation for bird sounds to show pitch, time and loudness both through musical and verbal methods. None are really satisfactory, and simple sonagrams, which are produced when a bird's utterances are analysed electronically through a sound spectrograph or sonagraph, are valuable guides to songs and calls. There are also many good bird-recordings now commercially available. But it is not always possible to use a tape recorder, and for many people the use of words and expressions will continue to play a regular part in the way that the sounds and calls of birds are reported.

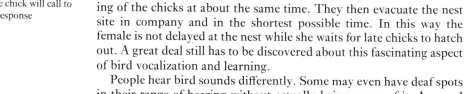

HABITATS

Ian Prestt is Director of the Royal Society for the Protection of Birds. A keen naturalist from early youth, he joined the Nature Conservancy in 1956. Following work on the effects of pesticides and other pollutants on birds, he was appointed Deputy Director Central Unit on Environmental Pollution in 1971. A Fellow of the Institute of Biology, he became Deputy Director of the Nature Conservancy Council in 1973 and was appointed Director of the RSPB in 1975

Birds, in contrast to man, are specialized and fixed in their habits and are unable to exert any deliberate influence over their surroundings. They possess a degree of physical tolerance in relation to the different seasons and can seek temporary shelter from sudden changes of weather, but in the advent of extreme conditions such as prolonged frost and snow or fierce heat and drought it is impossible for them to exist. Should their food supply fail they will starve. For their survival they are therefore highly dependent on the continued existence of an appropriate environment providing tolerable climatic conditions, an adequate supply of food and suitable breeding sites. This association of essential conditions constitutes their *habitat*.

The adaptations of different species of birds to particular habitats have evolved over thousands of years and can be seen in their form. Wading birds have long legs, short toes and fine, mud-probing bills. Diving birds have webbed feet placed well back on streamlined bodies, with sharp, often hooked or serrated bills for snapping and holding live fish. Predatory birds have large, strong wings for swift flight or soaring, sharp talons for grasping prey and hooked bills for killing and tearing. Perching birds have a well-developed hind toe to grasp branches and short, rounded wings and large tail to allow fast flight through thick foliage. Each group is highly specialized and well adapted to exploit particular conditions. The greater the specialization, however, the greater the dependence on a particular niche and the less flexibility to meet changing conditions should the need arise.

Habitat factors

Distinct habitats exist in different parts of Britain as a result of various combinations of environmental factors. These factors range from major long-term effects such as climate, altitude and substrata, to more local influences such as shelter, aspect and past and present management. Thus, while all uplands in Britain are exposed and inhospitable, those in the north of Scotland are more so and remain snow-covered for much of the year because of the severe northern winters. A sea cliff subjected to salt spray for much of the year will carry different vegetation to an inland crag on the sheltered side of a mountain. Animal and plant communities inhabiting dry, mineral-rich limestone plateaux are distinct from those on poor, acidic rocks. The short, open vegetation of a heavily grazed and regularly burnt common contrasts markedly with the scrub and woodland of one allowed to develop totally naturally.

Habitats change as a result of long-term or sudden natural events, alternating seasons and man's influence. Generations of weathering by wind and frost can transform a jagged summit into a rolling moor. A sudden landslide can replace a turf-covered slope with boulder scree. Arctic tundra during the summer is waterlogged and teeming with insect- and bird-life, while in winter it is frozen solid and devoid of active life. An oak wood which has existed for many thousands of years may be felled in the course of a few months, the ground ploughed and transformed into a field of barley.

Because of their great mobility, birds are able to exploit widely separated areas of similar habitat which may be suitable for only part of the year. Most of Britain's insectivorous birds, the thousands of Swallows, martins and warblers that are such a familiar sight during the summer, have to migrate to Africa to survive our winter. Huge flocks of wading birds, ducks and geese which inhabit our estuaries through the winter travel north to upland Britain or even further to Iceland, Greenland or elsewhere beyond the Arctic Circle to breed. Winter thrush flocks of Fieldfares and Redwings are driven south from

Aerial mastery enables the Swallow to exploit a seasonal abundance of flying insects in the Northern Hemisphere. In a sense, its habitat is thus the air through which it moves

Scandinavia by the onset of cold weather. These migrations between outliers of habitat provide a regular seasonal pattern to the movement and distribution of birds in the British Isles. Shorter, more local movements occur within Britain when birds are forced to move during severe weather if snow or floods obliterate their usual locality. These movements, with the longer seasonal migrations, provide a continually changing pattern in the distribution of bird species and their numbers.

The British countryside has been profoundly affected by man's activities. His influence has been so pervasive that today the term natural can only be applied to the remotest parts of the highest mountains and inaccessible stretches of coast. Elsewhere the natural scene has been modified to a greater or lesser degree by his industrial, agricultural or leisure activities. Where his influence has been less severe the term seminatural is appropriate.

There are four major seminatural habitats found in Britain: the coast, freshwater lakes and rivers, uplands, and woodland. Two other major, but extensively managed, habitats are represented by lowland farmland and urban areas. Each of these major habitats can be subdivided into smaller but distinguishable parts, each providing slightly different conditions which favour certain of the species associated with the habitat.

The range of opportunities for birds afforded by woodland can be used to illustrate the subdivisions within a major habitat and the use made of these by different bird species. Any area of reasonable size covered with trees represents a piece of woodland habitat. The species of birds living in woods are known. The separation into pure coniferous or deciduous woodland immediately increases the chances of finding certain of these species in one rather than the other. The Coal Tit, Goldcrest and Crossbill favour conifers, while woodpeckers, Hawfinch and Nuthatch prefer broadleaved trees.

Each can be further subdivided. Some species, for example the Spotted Flycatcher, prefer more open conditions and are attracted to glades, rides and woodland borders. Others, such as the Great Spotted Woodpecker, feed on the trunks of older trees and so will avoid

Such is the variety of the British and Irish landscape that even a small area may boast a huge range of distinct habitats. Moorland, cliffs, seashore, estuary, woods and agricultural land can all be seen below

crowded areas of young trees and scrub. The Blackcap, however, nests close to the ground, so is associated with dense parts of woods containing a good understorey of bramble and rhododendron. Even different parts of a single tree can be of importance to different species. Rooks will nest in the uppermost branches, the Mistle Thrush at a junction of a bough with the main trunk, while the Green Woodpecker will hollow out a nest inside the main trunk and the Woodcock nest at the tree base. This large number of different niches within each major habitat reduces competition and allows maximum exploitation of the environment.

Coasts

Britain's extensive and highly varied shoreline, adjacent to rich, shallow seas, represents a habitat of enormous importance to birds. For example, almost three-quarters of the European populations of the Gannet and Guillemot nest on our shores. While man's influence has been overriding in some industrial areas and at popular tourist beaches, there are still long stretches of relatively unspoilt coast. These support seabird breeding colonies and wintering sites for waders and wildfowl of international importance.

For many species of seabird which spend the winter at sea, such as Puffin, Razorbill, Manx Shearwater and Storm Petrel, remote offshore islands or inaccessible cliffs adjacent to the sea are essential for breeding. These provide nest sites on ledges or in crevices, relatively safe from human disturbance and predators and within easy reach of feeding grounds. A single stretch of sea cliff has its different niches. Black Guillemots will occupy boulders at the foot, Cormorants penetrate caverns and caves, Kittiwakes build their nests on narrow ledges against sheer faces and Puffins burrow in grassy slopes near the top.

Other species, notably terns, wildfowl and waders, favour flatter parts of the coast. Once again variations offer a range of choice. Where there is a long, shallow, shelving coast, vast areas of mud flats exposed at low tide provide rich feeding grounds for mud-probing species such as Redshank and Oystercatcher. At the upper reaches are salt marshes, shingle banks and sand dunes. Salt marsh is particularly valuable for geese and Wigeon during the winter, shingle banks are used by nesting Ringed Plovers and Little Terns, while the larger Common and Sandwich Terns and Shelduck prefer the sand dunes.

Coasts with adjoining deeper water support important wintering populations of sea ducks and divers. Species such as Great Northern and Black-throated Divers move to these waters from northern breeding localities alongside flocks of wintering Scoters and Long-tailed Ducks.

Though usually found in small groups, divers may gather in quite large mixed rafts along suitable coasts in winter

Fresh water

High rainfall and the uneven form of the land ensure that substantial amounts of persistent freshwater habitats are widely distributed in Britain. Our oceanic climate protects most of the country from long periods of hard frost and droughts are exceptional, so only rarely are these freshwater habitats unavailable.

Precipitation gathers in small upland lochs or gushes down torrents to larger lakes in the valleys before travelling along deeper, slow-

flowing rivers to the sea. Some lowland areas contain natural meres and marshes with areas of open water. Streams originating in peaty catchment areas over sour rocks are initially deficient in minerals and support little life. Enrichment usually increases as they pass through fertile lowland agricultural regions.

Extensive boggy plateaux and small lochans at high altitude carry only small populations of a few species of bird. Some, such as Greylag Goose and Common Gull, are able to find sufficient food in the immediate vicinity, while others, such as Red-throated Diver, fly to the coast or nearby larger lochs to feed.

Dashing torrents and waterfalls provide suitable niches for Grey Wagtail and Dipper, which give way to Common Sandpiper and Kingfisher as streams broaden into small rivers with deeper pools linked by shallows. As they become still larger and the pools deeper, Red-breasted Merganser and Goosander are added to the list of species.

Lowland meres and park lakes are usually richer in nutrients and carry more varied and numerous bird populations, particularly where extensive reed beds and waterside meadows have survived. In the heart of the reed beds there are unusual and exciting species such as Bittern and Bearded Tit, alongside commoner Reed and Sedge Warblers and Reed Bunting. Mallard, Teal, Coot and Water Rail nest in the reed fringes and a little further out on isolated islands and tussocks are to be found Black-headed Gull and the Great Crested Grebe with its floating nest.

Large, semicanalized rivers are not particularly suited for breeding birds unless the banks are well vegetated and undisturbed. They provide valuable sources of food for the Heron and commoner ducks, while Moorhens and Mute Swans usually find enough cover along the banks to raise a brood.

Uplands

Most of our uplands are situated in the north and west of Britain. They vary from steep, largely bare, unstable peaks and cliffs to vast rolling areas of open moorland buried under deep layers of peat and poor vegetation. Although termed seminatural and now apparently stable and well established, most have been significantly altered by man's activities. Before the advent of agriculture and industry, they would have been tree-covered up to the 600 metre contour. With rare exceptions, these upland forests have been cleared and suppressed by a long-established regime of burning and grazing which made woodland regeneration impossible. Moderate burning and light grazing improves heather moorland, which will be replaced by grass heath under more intensive treatment.

Few birds live at the extreme altitudes of the summits of the highest mountains. The hardy Ptarmigan and Golden Eagle are the exceptions. At lower altitudes, Raven, Peregrine and Ring Ouzel occupy the crags and Golden Plover, Dunlin, Red Grouse and Curlew are common in the heather. Smaller birds include Meadow Pipit, Twite and Wheatear. Along the moorland fringes, associated with remnant woodland and patches of scrub and gorse, other species appear, including Tree Pipit, Whinchat and Black Grouse.

In some regions hillside Cuckoos are numerous, parasitizing in particular the nests of Meadow Pipits. The Meadow Pipit also forms an important prey species for the Merlin, the smallest British raptor. The Hen Harrier and diurnal Short-eared Owl prefer open upland areas for hunting, taking small mammals as well as birds. The Lapwing is numerous in semicultivated grassland at the moorsides.

While the total list of bird species associated with uplands in Britain

One of the most particular, or specialized, of our birds, the Dipper is confined to fast-running streams and, therefore, mainly to the north and west

is not large, and their populations often small and scattered, upland regions now preserve a unique and important element of our avifauna. They are of special importance as the breeding stronghold for many of our larger wading birds, gamebirds and birds of prey, as well as a few characteristic smaller migrants such as Wheatear and Ring Ouzel.

Woodlands

Following the slow retreat of the great ice sheets of the last ice age, Britain was invaded by forests. At first they were principally of birch and pine, but with continuing improvement in climate and ground conditions these were gradually replaced by a range of broadleaved deciduous species, in particular oak. Eventually, apart from high mountain tops above the tree line and extensive areas of marshland, Britain became carpeted with trees. Into these great forests came the progenitors of what was to become our native inland bird fauna. This woodland habitat was so important during the formative period of our natural history that woodland species predominate to this day, long after much of their habitat has been destroyed.

The clearance of forests began with the development of agriculture and was completed by that of industry, to an extent that today Britain is one of the least wooded countries in Europe. Fortunately part survived, either because of its value to industry or because it provided outstanding hunting estates. More recently commercial forestry has been encouraged, but much of this takes the form of alien conifers planted in dense stands of uniform age which are less attractive to birds. Hedgerows, parks and gardens provide conditions similar to woodland and valuable additional sites for woodland species. Southern oak woodland on rich soils, with trees of different ages interspersed with glades and clearings and penetrated by streams, encourages the

The quickening pace of agricultural change has radically altered the face of Britain during the last 40 years. Woodlands have been felled, uplands ploughed, hedges ripped out, ponds filled in. Along the way opportunities for birds have been lost and their numbers reduced

richest bird-life in Britain. This includes large birds such as Tawny Owl, Sparrowhawk, Jay, Rook and Woodcock, medium-sized species such as Mistle Thrush and Great Spotted Woodpecker, and numerous smaller birds including many species of finch, tit and warbler. Moreover, unlike other habitats, woodlands support large populations throughout the year.

Northern conifer plantations generally carry fewer species, but some of these are uncommon and give added importance to these forests. The most spectacular is the huge, grouse-like Capercaillie, but Scottish Crossbill and Crested Tit are equally exciting inhabitants of these remote forests.

Farmlands

Medieval agricultural settlements included open ground with remnant blocks of woodland nearby. Gradually individual farm holdings replaced communal systems, and small fields with hedges, copses and shelter belts were established over most of lowland Britain. More recently, particularly in southern and eastern Britain, this pattern has begun to change again with the advent of more intensive methods of cultivation involving massive machines and chemical fertilizers and pesticides. Hedges have been removed to produce larger fields, ponds have been filled in as milkherds are replaced by arable land, marshes drained and streams piped underground.

The majority of birds present on farmland are there because remnants of natural habitat have been preserved by chance within the agricultural system. Familiar woodland birds such as Song Thrush, Blackbird, Robin and Chaffinch are found in hedgerows and copses, Mallard and Moorhen live on farm ponds and Lapwing and Snipe in marshy remnants in field bottoms.

Others, strong flyers such as Rook, Jackdaw, Woodpigeon and Starling, are able to take advantage of food provided by farmland, but return to nearby woodland to nest in more natural habitat. Farmland also provides an important food resource for migratory species such as Golden Plover and wild geese, though the latter may as a result become a pest in some areas.

Today's farmer is not only highly mechanized, but has turned the farm into a sort of rural factory

Certain species are particularly suited to farmland and have benefited by its creation. The most important of these are the Barn Owl, which hunts almost exclusively over farmland and nests in farm buildings or hedgerow trees; the Grey Partridge, which nests at field sides and feeds on cropland; the Skylark, which particularly favours grazed chalk downs; and the Yellow Wagtail, associated with grazed, lush water meadows.

Built-up areas

As with farmland, many of the birds that inhabit our towns and cities are only there because these offer remnants of natural habitat. Suburban gardens and allotments with trees, shrubs and hedges, for example, provide habitat resembling degraded woodland, and so long as disturbance is not excessive they can hold surprisingly high numbers of some of the commoner, more adaptable, woodland species such as Robin, Blackbird, Dunnock and Blue Tit. In less densely populated suburbs they may be supplemented by less usual species including Great Spotted Woodpecker, Greenfinch and Coal Tit.

Certain species, however, have become dependent on the urban habitat to an extent that they are commoner there than anywhere else. The House Sparrow is the prime example, being almost entirely reliant on man's presence for its continued survival. Likewise the migrant Swift and House Martin are now almost exclusively town breeders, the former nesting in holes and attics in towers or under tiles in house roofs and the latter building its inverted mud dome under eaves. Another familiar town dweller is the Feral Pigeon, a descendant of the cliff-dwelling Rock Dove domesticated initially to provide food in pigeon lofts and then as a racing bird.

City parks with mature trees and ornamental lakes also attract birds from the countryside. Mallard, Coot and Moorhen are regular park lake birds and Tawny Owls hunt suburban back gardens, even nesting in artificial boxes provided for them. Kestrels are a familiar sight in cities, hovering over waste land, rubbish dumps and even railway sidings and deserted factories. They now regularly nest in old buildings, chimneys and on ledges of tall buildings. This variety of birds in urban areas has enabled an interest in bird protection to be developed in the townsman as well as the more traditional countryman.

Britain is a small, densely populated country, dependent on industry and agriculture for prosperity. Little truly natural habitat remains. However, seminatural habitats have existed for a long time and still

Old buildings often have holes suitable for nesting and roosting owls. Modern structures of concrete and metal are unforgiving in their efficiency

retain many of the characteristics of the natural habitats they replaced, in that they provide equally valuable opportunities for wild birds. These habitats have undergone gradual modifications as new land management techniques developed. No doubt further developments are yet to come, but too many changes coming too frequently will eventually destroy the integrity of such areas. Most conservationists would put preservation of habitat as the major task ahead of them.

Creating habitats

Certain changes are inevitable, but with the application of the knowledge and experience that now exists it is possible to preserve, and even to create, new ornithological interest. The construction of water storage reservoirs in lowland areas is a good example. If carefully planned, with parts zoned for conservation and kept free from disturbance, they can attract populations of waterbirds into regions where none existed. In East Anglia the careful landscaping and protection of old sand and gravel workings have encouraged species such as Great Crested Grebe, Little Ringed Plover, Common Tern and Little Grebe. Almost three-quarters of the countryside is farmland, so it is important to integrate bird habitats with modern agriculture. To help achieve this, the Farming and Wildlife Advisory Group (FWAG) was established. It now has over 30 county committees of farmers and conservationists, whose aim is to achieve good output while at the same time to preserve important features such as old hedges, ponds, copses and meadows. Certain activities cannot be modernized and become derelict, but may still present opportunities for bird-life. Thus old slate quarries in north Wales provide excellent cliffs and caves for Raven, Chough and Peregrine. The important point is to ensure that the conservation potential of all operations is identified and developed.

The most constructive action that can be taken to preserve habitat is to acquire and manage it as a nature reserve. Britain now has many reserves which include both official sites (the National Nature Reserves and the Local Nature Reserves) established by the Nature Conservancy Council and local authorities respectively, and those belonging to voluntary bodies (the Royal Society for the Protection of Birds, the County Naturalists' Trusts and the Wildfowl Trust). Although in total these only account for a small percentage of the land surface of Britain, their importance far outweighs their size because they represent examples of the richest habitats, which can then be fully protected and managed to the benefit of all wildlife.

The importance of reserves is well illustrated by the RSPB's Minsmere reserve on the Suffolk coast. In 1979 this became the first British nature reserve to be awarded the Council of Europe's Diploma. Prior to the Second World War, the area had been reclaimed for agriculture and its ornithological interest was minimal. During the war it was allowed to revert to uncultivated land and was reflooded. After the war, the Society took it over and started intensive management. Now it holds the most important Avocet breeding colony in Britain, a high proportion of Britain's Bitterns, several pairs of Marsh Harrier, and large numbers of ducks, waders, gulls and terns.

It is classified as a Grade I site of international importance and is on the British list of wetland sites included in the Ramsar Convention for the protection of wetland sites of international importance. The Society has constructed hides so that each year thousands of visitors and students can watch the birds without disturbing them or damaging the site. Reserves such as this illustrate dramatically the wide variety of birds a rich habitat can contain and the fundamental importance of habitat to conservation.

The use of heavy machinery on farmland has revolutionized the business of drainage

Dr Jim Flegg became a professional ornithologist when he joined the British Trust for Ornithology as Director in 1968. In 1976 he rejoined the Agricultural Research Council and is now head of the Zoology Department at East Malling in Kent, where he divides his time between nematodes and bullfinches as fruit pests. He has published numerous articles and books, and is a regular broadcaster

Guillemot

Ringed Plover

Red-backed Shrike

Dunnock

Eggs vary not only in size, but also in shape and colour. In some cases such variations are easily explained. In other cases they remain a mystery

About 150 million years ago, as the fossil record shows, prototype birds developed as an offshoot of the then dominant reptile stock. Unlike mammals, however, birds have retained the reptilian egg as the means of reproduction and as a protective capsule for the fertilized ovum as it develops through to hatching. Clearly, as the method has endured millions of years, in evolutionary terms the egg must be considered highly successful.

Flight, although not unique to birds, can probably be considered as their most important feature. The ability to fly effectively, with high manoeuvrability and allowing ample scope for the diverse lives birds lead, has inevitably brought with it some constraints to bird anatomy. The need for lightness is one of the most important of these. Imagine the difficulties for a female bird, burdened for a considerable time with a slowly maturing foetus (or group of foetuses) of a mammalian type, remorselessly increasing in weight until birth. A series of eggs, each rapidly produced within a protective shell, laid within an additionally protective nest and then incubated by the parents, is an extremely effective evolutionary strategy to solve this problem.

There can be no simple judgement as to whether bird reproduction, using eggs, is 'better' or not than the mammalian pattern of a foetus developing within its mother. Each has its apparent advantages and its hazards seen through human eyes, but each has been tailored by a process of adaptation and evolution to be the most effective for its particular purpose.

With the great range of bird sizes – from hummingbirds to Ostriches – variation in egg size between species would be a logical expectation, but the relationship of body size to egg is not so simple. Broadly speaking, the smaller species lay proportionately larger eggs. For example, the Blue Tit egg is about 1 cm long and weighs just over half a gram, about 5 or 6 per cent of female body weight, whereas the Ostrich egg is about 17 cm long with a capacity getting on for $2\frac{1}{2}$ litres, but weighs about 1,400 grams, only 1 per cent of the female's body weight.

Egg coloration

Perhaps the most striking feature of eggs is their enormous range of colours, especially apparent when large numbers are seen on display in museums. In some cases the colours and patterns have a clear purpose. The eggs of the Ringed Plover, with blackish spots on a sand-coloured background, are ideally camouflaged. The typical Ringed Plover nesting site is a sandy beach with flecks of dark seaweed and broken shell among the grains of sand. In other cases, this purpose seems contradicted. The Dunnock is an inconspicuous bird, its plumage a tweedy mixture of browns and blacks well suited for camouflage, especially for the incubating bird sitting on a nest built of dried grass and concealed low in dead grass and bracken. The eggs, however, are the brightest of sky-blues and almost painfully conspicuous against the dark background of the nest, which must render them highly vulnerable to predators when left uncovered.

Many of the hole-nesting birds, such as owls and woodpeckers, seem to lay whitish eggs, and it is thought that the pale colour may help the returning bird to locate the eggs in the sudden gloom as it enters the nest chamber from the bright daylight outside. In the crowded circumstances of nesting colonies, variations in shade and pattern may help the individual bird to recognize its egg: this would be particularly true in species such as the Guillemot, where an actual nest is nonexistent and birds lay their single eggs side by side on sea-cliff ledges. In other species – the Tree Pipit and the Red-backed Shrike are the most striking examples – the wide range of rich colours exhibited within each species is more difficult to explain. Sadly, this colour variation was of great attraction to egg collectors, and the dreadful toll they took is a major factor in the decline of the once-common Red-backed Shrike to its present near-extinct status in Britain.

The colour pigments are added after the eggshell has been created and as the egg is passing down the oviduct. Some of these pigments are derived from bodily waste products, for example from broken-down blood corpuscles. Spots and squiggles – a feature of many eggs – are added from special secretory cells. Their shape depends very much on the movements of the egg within the oviduct.

Territory

The complete reproductive cycle in birds conveniently starts with the formation of territories. For most small birds winter is a time of hardship when communal feeding and roosting occur to exploit food resources and conserve energy to best effect. As the days lengthen and the temperature rises, hormone secretions change, causing striking alterations in behaviour patterns. In the Robin, the sexes are difficult (if not impossible) to distinguish. In winter, each sex maintains a small feeding territory and reacts aggressively to any other Robin. As spring advances, the male retains his aggressive mood but the female becomes more cautious and subdued, abandoning her territorial aspirations. This more submissive reaction on her part leads initially to her acceptance in what has enlarged to become the male's breeding territory, and ultimately to pair formation and, after a ritualized pattern of song and display, to mating.

In birds perhaps more strikingly than any other animals, well-developed voice production coupled with a wide range of plumage colours have given rise to an extraordinary array of displays, from the simple bowing and chirruping with shivering wings of the House Sparrow to the frenzied upside-down cascade of noise and dazzling filamentous plumes of the birds of paradise in New Guinea.

Birds defend a territory by singing and display. Even the repetitive *chirrup* of the House Sparrow is an effective territorial defence

Courtship feeding of the female Blue
Tit by the male not only helps to cement
the bond between the pair, but also helps
to form the eggs inside her

For some species, such as the Rook,
occupying the nest and starting repairs
may commence well before winter is out

For the male, tempting and retaining a mate, and the protection of his territory, are of paramount importance. Song and posture, displaying aspects of the plumage to most striking effect, are his major tactics in achieving these goals. The vocal capabilities of songbirds are exploited to the full in spring and summer, and in spring, too, plumage is in its best condition for display. For many of the larger birds, such as ducks, the plumage attains its full magnificence rather earlier, in the winter, when pair formation takes place.

For the female, finding a mate and being fertilized is clearly of prime importance, but in addition she must get into good condition for the rigours of the breeding season as early as possible. Here the male may help. The production of eggs is an energy-intensive process. A female Blue Tit may increase in weight by about 50 per cent in the three weeks before laying starts. Much of this stored weight is used to produce the daily egg (with a normal clutch size of 10–15 eggs) and to see her through the early days of incubation when she will not be able to leave the nest for long to feed. It seems most probable that 'courtship feeding' – once thought to be a behavioural gesture helping to cement the pair bond, as does the gift of a box of chocolates from human husband to wife – aids her in this. The extra caterpillars presented by the male to his eager, wing-fluttering female may have an important effect on her ultimate physical state.

The size and indeed the purpose of territory varies. In some cases, such as the Golden Eagle, the territory may be expected to supply the food needed by the parents and their one or two youngsters: no easy task in the harsh terrain of the mountains, hence the vast territory size of 100 sq. km. or more. For many small songbirds it seems that the possession and defence of a territory must be an important asset, but while the nest will normally be located within the territory, relatively rarely, however, can the birds involved and their growing brood be totally self-sufficient within this defended area. Although a number of theories have been advanced, it is difficult to reach a clear conclusion as to a territory's main purpose. The territorial demands of apparently similar species may differ greatly, and within a single species such factors as the nature of the habitat and the population density of the bird concerned can be seen to have an effect.

Clearly, self-sufficiency cannot be a factor in determining the size of the minute territory surrounding the nests of colonial seabirds such as the Gannet. Here, fishing for food is in bountiful seas shared with myriad other seabirds, and the critical factors that determine the spacing of nests at about two beak-thrusts apart are probably security from disturbance, pilfering of nest material and harassment of parents and chicks by neighbours.

In some larger birds, such as the Golden Eagle, Peregrine and Raven, the enormous territories may contain several ancestral nest sites available for use in different seasons. Even after a territory has been vacant for some years (as has recently been the case following deaths associated with DDT pollution in Scotland), the new inhabitants tend to select these same ancestral crags when recolonizing the area and nest building. In colonial birds such as Rooks, Herons or Kittiwakes the pattern is broadly similar. The nests survive from season to season, needing only refurbishing before the eggs are laid. In general, older-established pairs tend to hold the most desirable sites (often with the largest and most secure nests) in the centre of the colony, while junior birds have to make do with nests near the edge of the colony.

There are, however, a number of limitations to the use of egg laying for reproduction. Eggs are fragile and thus need protection from breakage; to develop, they need meticulously controlled warmth maintained over a considerable period, so they benefit from protection and insulation from adverse extremes of climate; and the eggs, and the young hatching from them, are in general particularly vulnerable to predators and unable to defend themselves, so the construction and concealment of the nest must give a degree of physical protection. These, then, are the main functions of the average nest.

Usually, within each territory, there will be a number of nest sites suitable for that particular species. In some cases, such as the Wren, the male does the bulk of the heavy construction work on several nests – each well concealed and domed, with a side entrance – before the pair together decide on one particular nest and put the finishing touches to it (largely by adding a soft, warm lining). In a similar way, the male Lapwing will form several 'scrapes', scuffing hollows in the ground using his feet and belly, in suitable areas of field or grassland, before the final site is selected and a lining of dried grasses added.

In many other small birds, it seems that the female plays the major role in deciding where the nest will be, and subsequently in the actual construction work. In such cases it should be remembered that the male is not indolently standing by in a chauvinistic way, but that he retains the important task of safeguarding the territory, which demands continual alertness.

Nest types

The simplest nests are those where the egg or eggs are laid directly on the ground. Any apparent vulnerability of such a site to predators may be reduced by physical factors – for example, the Guillemot laying on exposed but often inaccessible cliff ledges – or by the concealment provided by the coloration of the eggs and, subsequently, the down of the nestlings. In many waders – Lapwing, Oystercatcher, Ringed Plover and so on – and gamebirds, such as Pheasant and partridge, this camouflage is staggeringly effective, and the human observer, certain though he may be that he knows where a chick has crouched, must be extremely careful not to tread on it. Such camouflage is only effective when the chick is stationary, and is accompanied by a behaviour pattern in which it responds instantly to the warning cries of its parents and will not move until a predator is actually on top of it. Many wader nests of this type may appear superficially simple, just scrapes in the ground, whereas they do have a structure and may even be ornamented. One wader nest was found to contain over 1,000 small pebbles, pieces of shell and flotsam and jetsam.

This simple nest is further developed by other waders and by many ducks and gulls. Dead vegetation, flotsam and jetsam are gathered into a mound, with a depression at its centre containing the eggs. Such structures are usually built on terrain subject to changing water levels and offer extra protection against flooding and consequent chilling of eggs or young. The floating nest of many waterbirds is a natural progression from this. The Little Grebe's nest, a raft of iris leaves and waterweeds, is loosely anchored to nearby vegetation and can rise and fall naturally with floodwater. Such a nest survives more successfully than those of Coot or Moorhen, fixed firmly in the reeds or on an overhanging bough. There is an additional advantage for specialist waterbirds such as the grebes, which have legs set near the rear of their streamlined bodies, as a floating nest is easier to scramble on and off.

Practical protection is offered by the cup-shaped nest used by the majority of birds, particularly the small and medium-sized songbirds. The eggs cluster naturally at the base of the cup, safe from physical disturbance by wind and from the eyes of predators. The cup is usually lined with dried mud, fine grasses or rootlets, moss, hair, fur or

Camouflage of eggs and chicks of ground-nesting species such as Ringed Plover is highly effective, and of crucial importance to their survival

feathers, all offering excellent thermal insulation for eggs and young. The basic structural pattern of such nests is the same, even when the size varies from a few centimetres in diameter (Chaffinch) to a metre or more (Golden Eagle). An outer framework of stouter grasses or twigs (or even branches) is lodged in a suitable fork in a tree. Finer materials are woven into the inside of this structure until the central cup is ready to receive its insulating lining. Sometimes such nests may be 'decorated' on the outside with nearby plant material, and many Chaffinch nests have small lichen fragments woven into the outermost layer, making them masterpieces of camouflage in the angle of branches.

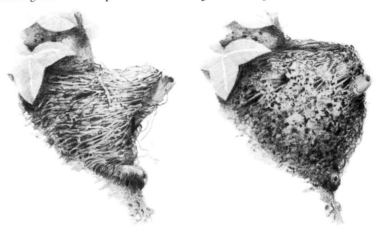

Taking a natural feature and utilizing it as a basis for a nest is comparatively commonplace. Few species produce as natural-looking a finished structure as the Chaffinch

Domed nests are extensions of the cup pattern, offering a totally enclosed cavity to protect eggs and young. The cobweb, hair, lichen and moss, flask-shaped nest of the Long-tailed Tit has the additional advantage that it is amazingly flexible, and can thus accommodate the brood as it grows up. Other tits, owls and the Jackdaw and Stock Dove seek the protection of natural cavities in old trees, cliff faces and buildings. Such protection may be rather more apparent than real, as several predators (especially weasels) are well able to climb and track down the squeaking young, and Great Spotted Woodpeckers will on occasion hack their way into nest boxes to consume the young tits inside. The woodpeckers excavate their own nest holes in standing trees, and Sand Martins and Kingfishers, for example, dig out nest burrows in suitable sandy soils.

In the tropics, the pendent woven nests of the various species of weaverbird demonstrate the most sophisticated pattern of nest building, but nearer home, the mossy swinging hammock of the tiny Goldcrest, or the basketwork nest of the Reed Warbler, incorporating a number of supporting reed stems and withstanding gales and, quite regularly, the unwanted weight of a young Cuckoo, are equally good examples.

Pattern of egg laying

In the course of evolution, a number of patterns of egg laying have emerged in various bird families. As with the egg 'versus' foetus debate, there is no clear 'better' or 'worse' method: each has evolved to be effective in particular circumstances. For example, in Britain the majority of Blue and Great Tits depend on the caterpillars of the winter moth (which occurs predominantly on oak trees) to feed their young. These caterpillars occur in enormous numbers, but only for less than a month in early summer. To match this situation, the vast majority of British Blue and Great Tits are single-brooded, laying just one clutch of eggs, normally somewhere between eight and 15 in number. Laying and hatching are timed to a nicety in most years, with the young at their most demanding at the time that the caterpillars reach maximum size. In marked contrast to this almost literal 'all eggs in one basket' are the majority of small and medium-sized garden birds, producing usually two or three clutches (sometimes more in a good summer), each of four to six eggs, allowing them to exploit a food supply which occurs at moderate levels throughout the summer, rather than in a single, short-lived glut. In each case, the appropriate food supply, in each type of ecological niche, is most effectively exploited.

Larger birds may not have time or available food supplies to form more than one or two eggs, or to raise the young successfully afterwards, so in general food seems the dominant factor determining clutch size. Perhaps the best example of this is the Short-eared Owl, which is largely dependent on voles as a food supply. Vole numbers fluctuate considerably, and when they are low the owls may lay only one or two eggs, or none at all. If voles are abundant, then the clutch size may reach double figures: a very effective birth-rate control mechanism. Food supply can also strongly influence the timing of the breeding season, as in the case of the tits. The Crossbill, with its highly specialized feeding technique, is largely dependent on the seeds within pine cones, which may mature at almost any time of year. In consequence, it is possible to find Crossbills sitting on eggs in winter – even with snow on their backs – because they are taking advantage of a localized abundance of food. In the same way, Ravens depending largely for food on placentas from the late-winter birth of hill-farm lambs, and on the carrion produced by the casualties of lambing in such severe weather, now start breeding even in February despite the climate at that time in the hills.

Cuckoo's secret

The incubation period – the time taken for the fertilized embryo to develop and then break out of the eggshell – varies considerably. Generally speaking, larger birds have longer incubation periods than smaller ones. Most songbirds incubate their eggs, starting when the clutch is complete, for about two weeks. As an adaptation to its mode of parasitism, Cuckoo eggs often hatch in only 11 or 12 days, giving the young Cuckoo a chance to shoulder its foster parents' own eggs out of the nest before they hatch. Ascending the size scale, gulls and ducks incubate for about three weeks, geese a month, the Mute Swan 35 days, and longest of all, the Golden Eagle and the Gannet, each incubating for about 45 days.

The blind, naked instinct by which the young Cuckoo seeks to rid the nest of companions is one of the strangest adaptations among birds

The females, and occasionally also the males, of most songbirds have a 'brood patch' which develops at the start of the nesting season. The belly sheds its down feathers to expose an oval patch of skin, wrinkled and very rich in superficial blood vessels. It is the body heat transmitted by the blood in these that incubates the eggs, and when a bird is settling down, with cautious shuffles, to begin brooding, it is to ensure that all the eggs are positioned beneath the brood patch and within the remaining breast feathers, which serve as a coverlet. Some seabirds such as the Gannet lack a brood patch to warm the egg and use the blood vessels in their large webbed feet, which are carefully folded over the egg beneath the sitting bird.

Often the female will do all, or almost all, of the incubation, leaving the nest only briefly to feed and drink. Sometimes the male takes a larger share, but only very exceptionally, as in the Red-necked Phalarope, will he assume total responsibility for hatching the eggs and raising the young. This unequal split of incubation is one reason why, in many birds, the plumage of the female is superficially drab, but in practice provides effective camouflage for her during the hazardous period of incubation. In contrast, it can be argued that the male needs his more colourful plumage both to attract a mate and to defend his territory to best effect. Interestingly, in the Red-necked Phalarope, where the domestic roles of male and female are largely reversed, it is *she* who is brighter and who takes the leading part in display.

Synchronized hatching

In most small birds, the eggs in a clutch all hatch within 24 hours of one another, but in larger birds, where eggs are laid at two-day (or more) intervals and where incubation starts as soon as the first egg is laid, the eggs will hatch at similar intervals. This gives rise to a considerable discrepancy in size between the young, especially in owls, where in years when clutches are large there may be a two-week difference in age and size between the oldest and youngest chick. This offers the owls facility for a further measure of effective birth control, for should the food supply diminish for any reason, oldest may eat youngest and so on. Although distasteful in human terms, this is a very effective mechanism to ensure that at least a few youngsters fledge successfully, rather than having whole broods perish from starvation.

The young birds emerge from the egg slowly, using a small calcareous 'egg tooth' on the tip of the beak to cut through the egg membranes and fracture the shell. This 'tooth' is lost soon after hatching. Most songbirds hatch naked, blind and helpless (so-called 'nidicolous' species) and develop into fledglings within the confines of the nest – a process usually taking two or three weeks depending on the weather, but two months or more in the Golden Eagle and over three in the Gannet.

Many larger birds – especially gamebirds, gulls, ducks and waders – hatch with their eyes open, with an effective covering of warm and

Shelduck with day-old chicks. The ducklings leave the nest soon after hatching and can feed and swim instinctively

Chicks of finches, like other passerines, hatch blind and naked and spend a lengthy period of growth in the security of the nest

camouflage-patterned down, and with well-developed legs. These 'nidifugous' young (literally 'fleeing the nest') scamper about and often feed for themselves as soon as the down is dry, remaining under the alert guardianship of one (in the ducks) or both parents until they can fly. In the Shelduck and Eider, large crèches of young may gather under the protection of a couple of adult females.

Once nidicolous young leave the nest, they continue to need parental care and training in feeding techniques for several days, or weeks in the case of the owls. In some nidifugous species such as the Moorhen the fledged young of the first brood may help to feed their brothers and sisters in later broods.

The nestling stage is a time of considerable risk. The young are noisy and inexperienced, and may easily attract the attention of a predator. As their parents have to spend almost all the daylight hours in ceaseless attempts to keep them well fed, after the first couple of days they are brooded less and less often (for warmth) by the female. In consequence they are more vulnerable to cold, and particularly to heavy rain or hailstorms. In the Swift, a specialist insect feeder and thus particularly prone to food shortage during spells of bad weather, the young have evolved a technique to improve survival in lean times. Unlike most small nestlings, which quickly chill and die, young Swifts reduce their body metabolism: heart and respiration rates drop and body temperature slowly falls. The chicks enter a torpor – in effect a short-term hibernation. As the weather improves and insect food again becomes available, so (like reptiles) they warm up and begin to grow again.

The division of feeding labour between the sexes varies widely according to species. Most drakes pay little or no attention to their brood from as early as the completion of the clutch, leaving it all to the duck. In the Sparrowhawk, the male is so much smaller than the female (and takes much smaller prey) that as their brood grows, so the female has to shoulder more and more of the burden. In most other birds, however, the male plays a part that may reach 50 per cent.

Wastage concept

Often, large broods will contain one or two weaklings – runts – which will survive only in years when food is plentiful. Returning parents, under pressure from hungry young to supply sufficient food, usually push their beakful into the widest gape emerging furthest from the huddle of young in the nest. This is usually one of the strongest chicks, and no attempt is made to give extra support to weaklings. In this way the fittest survive, rather than risking the whole brood being weakened and lost in order to try to save the runts.

To most harassed parent birds the upturned yellow-rimmed gape of the nestling, together with hunger squeaks, is sufficient stimulus to feed the young. Many songbirds also have a recognizable pattern of spots within the mouth to help prevent confusion. The young Cuckoo, with its particularly wheedling cry and rich orange-crimson gape, seems able to overcome these identity barriers and few food-carrying

The red spot on the lower mandible of the Herring Gull is pecked at by the chicks to elicit food from the adult

parents can apparently resist the urge to feed a nearby Cuckoo fledgling, no matter how unlike their own young it appears. In some other cases sophisticated ritual behaviour patterns have developed which must be gone through before the chick is fed. Best-known is the Herring Gull, where the chick must peck at the conspicuous red spot on the yellow lower mandible of the beak. This elicits the feeding response from its parent, which disgorges the contents of its crop.

To human eyes, birds seem to go to a lot of trouble through the spring and summer, and lay a lot of eggs. How effective is the avian reproductive system in maintaining population numbers? Two case histories will serve as examples. The Fulmar, a seabird in size and plumage reminiscent of a gull but actually a petrel, may take nine years to reach maturity, and even then will only lay a single egg each year. But Fulmars live for 30 years or more, and to maintain the population level the pair need only raise two chicks to adulthood in this period. When food supplies are good, as they have been over the last century, this maintenance level is easily exceeded. Hence the dramatic spread of this species, with its apparently very restricted reproductive capacity, right round the coasts of Britain from its single remote stronghold on St Kilda in 1872.

The second, the Blue Tit, is a more familiar bird, but exemplifies a markedly different approach. On average, each pair may raise ten young. We know from studies of ringed birds that adult mortality from year to year is about 50 per cent, which means that (again on average) a pair is made up of one adult and one young bird breeding for the first time. Thus of the ten young at the end of the summer only one need survive through until the next breeding season to maintain population numbers – leaving scope for (to us) a staggering 90 per cent juvenile mortality. We know from ringing studies that losses to weasels and to Sparrowhawks can each reach a seemingly high 30 per cent, but this *still* leaves a slack of 30 per cent to allow for other hazards.

Examined closely, the avian reproductive system is far from uniform in pattern: it is a whole gallery of masterpieces of effective adaptation to needs and possibilities. Although undeniably conservative in its tendency to overproduction, it certainly allows enough flexibility to tide birds over most troubles and to maintain population levels in all but the most extraordinary circumstances, and even then recovery can be swift. Clearly, if further evidence is required, the abundance and variety of birds in all habitats is clear proof of their success.

FOOD AND FEEDING

Dr Philip Burton is a Principal Scientific Officer at the British Museum (Natural History) Sub-department of Ornithology, Tring. He is a specialist on feeding adaptations in waders, and is a well-known author and accomplished bird painter

Flight enables birds to exploit a vast range of habitats and ways of life, but it has not been achieved without sacrifice. Conversion of the forelimbs into wings has denied birds their use as an aid in feeding, while the need for lightness of construction has brought about the loss of teeth and imposed severe constraints on size and body form. Birds have overcome these difficulties by refining and developing the jaws, tongue and neck in many subtle ways, with the result that these have the most varied structure of all the main parts of the body.

Most people are familiar with some of the different shapes of birds' bills – the conical bill of a sparrow, the hooked bill of an eagle or the broad, flat bill of a duck, for example. However, the bill is only the visible part of the jaw system: to understand how it works, one must also consider the parts that are concealed from view. An important difference between birds and mammals concerns the upper jaw. In birds, this is hinged where it joins the cranium by a thin strip of flexible bone and therefore it can move up and down relative to the rest of the skull. Like all other mammals, man only moves the lower jaw in opening the mouth, but for birds this action involves both jaws. This has various advantages. For instance, when a bird lines up its head to take a piece of food the jaws will open equally on either side of the line of sight, so that no compensation is needed as the head is moved to seize it. Another advantage is that each jaw is pivoted at a different point. This enables the upper and lower jaws to be positioned at various angles relative to each other. The amount of independence varies from species to species. Some, for instance the Wryneck, have a great capacity to move upper relative to lower, while others, such as ducks, have a system of ligaments or joints ensuring that the movement of the two jaws is closely coupled.

Independent jaws

The lower jaw or mandible is capable of some surprising movements. Instead of being composed of a single solid element as it is in mammals, the lower jaw of birds consists of several bones inherited from reptilian ancestors, and in some species these are capable of movement in the middle region. Some birds which occasionally need to swallow very large objects are able to bend the jaw outwards at this flexible point. In Nightjars this outward bending takes place automatically as the jaws are opened, so that there is plenty of leeway to scoop up the moths and other insects which the birds hunt in flight.

The tongue and neck also show many adaptations for various methods of feeding. Most spectacular of tongue specializations are those of the woodpeckers, which can extend the tongue far beyond the bill to pick grubs from their tunnels in rotten wood. However, the tongue itself is extremely small. The extra length is gained by elongating the supporting skeleton which, as in all birds, consists of a single rod extending back from the tongue to join two flexible 'horns' which curve around behind the skull. In some woodpeckers the horns are so long that when at rest they run for some distance down the neck before bending up again to extend right over the crown. The neck itself varies greatly in length and in the number of vertebrae – from 14 or 15 in passerines and other small birds to 23–25 in swans, whereas most mammals have only seven. The S shape which the neck assumes in all birds is a result of its division into three main regions. The front one only bends downwards, the middle one only upwards and the rear one to some extent in both directions. In herons and darters there is an exaggerated 'kink' in the middle of the neck which can act as a trigger for an explosively rapid forward thrust of the head to seize prey at quite remarkable distances.

Willow Tits have short stubby bills ideally suited to hacking through seed cases

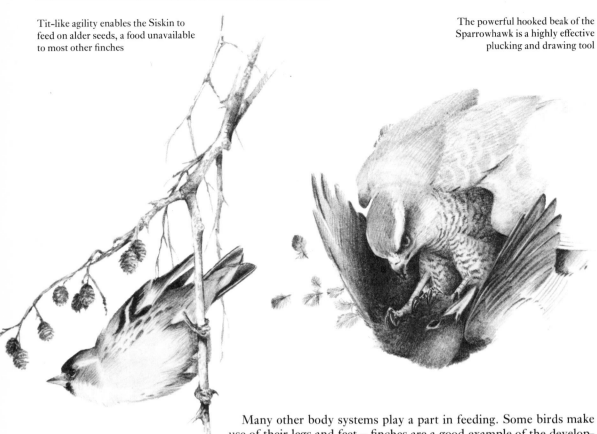

Tit-like agility enables the Siskin to feed on alder seeds, a food unavailable to most other finches

The powerful hooked beak of the Sparrowhawk is a highly effective plucking and drawing tool

Many other body systems play a part in feeding. Some birds make use of their legs and feet – finches are a good example of the development of this behaviour. Some, such as Chaffinch, Brambling, Hawfinch and Bullfinch, do not use their feet when feeding. Others, including Greenfinch, Linnet and Twite, use them to hold an object still. But the greatest coordination is shown by those species which are agile in feeding on fine twigs or stems, such as Goldfinch, Siskin, Redpoll and Crossbill. These are able to consume food such as catkins by pulling them up with the bill and then anchoring them with the toes. By far the most important use of the feet, however, is shown by raptors and owls, which depend on powerful toes with long curved talons for seizing and killing prey.

Bill sensitivity

Sense organs may be developed in special ways for use in feeding. Many waders and ducks have nerve endings in their bill which are highly sensitive to vibrations and so can be used to detect the presence of buried prey or food particles in water. Snipe and Woodcock find nearly all their food in this way, continually probing mud to feel for the vibrations of earthworms and grubs. Woodcock have come to rely on this so much that their eyes play little part in feeding and serve mainly to warn of danger, being placed so that they cover a wider field of view behind the head than in front of it. Birds such as raptors, owls and aerial insect feeders, which have to pursue rapidly moving prey, generally have eyes set well to the front, giving binocular vision to help in depth and distance judgement. Owls have in addition evolved ears with a similar capacity to locate prey. In some species, such as the Long-eared Owl, the ear openings are differently placed on the right and left sides of the head, a device further improving the ability to locate sound sources.

Feeding involves more than structure and behaviour, however. It has to be seen in relation to a bird's total ecology. Like any living thing, a bird can only survive by taking in more energy from food than is expended in finding it. In the breeding season, extra energy will be required for courtship and nesting, and food must be provided for the young. The quantities involved can be enormous. A Blue Tit feeding well-grown nestlings may bring them some 50 grams of food per day – nearly five times its own body weight – as well as obtaining enough for its own needs. Winter may be equally demanding, for extra energy is required to keep warm and there are fewer hours of daylight in which to find food. Redshanks studied on an estuary in northeast Scotland needed up to 40,000 prey items per day to survive, but their ability to detect food by touch in soft mud enabled them to continue into the hours of darkness. At the other end of the scale, large birds need relatively less food and can survive for longer without it. A Golden Eagle weighing some 4–5 kilos needs on average about 250 grams per day to survive, equivalent to one Red Grouse every three days.

Famine or feast

Birds exploit food sources in various ways. They may take large numbers of small or poor quality food items which are relatively easy to find, or at the other extreme take large or nutritious foods less frequently. The former would be represented by finches feeding on plant seeds, the latter by some fruit feeders – although fruit eating as a way of life is not well developed among temperate birds because the supply is so seasonal. Predators behave in the same way. Those feeding on small insects may have to catch thousands per day to survive and expend much energy in the process. Others adopt the strategy, exemplified by shrikes and Kingfishers, of watching from a vantage point and capturing large prey less often, but using little energy to do so.

Feeding adaptations and behaviour may deeply influence the relations between individuals of a species. Outside the breeding season, a crucial decision is whether to forage alone or in parties or flocks. If food is plentiful and evenly distributed there may be no advantage in flocking, but if it is not, the formation of flocks will help birds to locate concentrations of food more quickly. It also helps in defence against predators. When the breeding season arrives, however, most birds revert to a solitary life style because isolated nests are much more difficult for a predator to find than those in colonies. Moreover, diet often changes at this time; some seed eaters among the finches and buntings feed their young at first on insects.

At one time it was fashionable to divide birds into 'beneficial' or 'harmful' species in regard to their feeding habits. Although attitudes have changed, some species can undoubtedly be considered as harmful or 'pests', although usually this is because man's activities have inadvertently created an ideal feeding situation for them. The depredations of Woodpigeons on cabbage and kale are an example of this, and such species are generally so successful that control is difficult or impossible. But there are many less clear-cut instances. Brent Geese usually winter on mud flats where their natural food is eelgrass and seaweed, but in the 1930s disease wiped out much of the eelgrass and their numbers dropped alarmingly. In 1954 they were declared a protected species, but with the cessation of shooting Brents became increasingly tame and turned to dry land habitats which they had formerly shunned. As a result they now cause considerable damage to crops in some coastal regions where they winter.

It is even harder to assess the effects of 'beneficial' species. In general the numbers of prey control the numbers of predators rather than the reverse, so it would be difficult to argue, for instance, that

Specialist feeders suffer disastrously if their particular food suddenly disappears. Brent Geese seemed doomed to local extinction when disease destroyed the eelgrass on which they depended. Only the cessation of shooting and a change of feeding habit on the part of the birds themselves saved the situation

Swallows substantially reduce the population of troublesome flies and midges. Insecticides are more effective, although they may create problems for the Swallows as well as the flies. This is not the case, however, with localized situations. A Barn Owl with an attachment to a particular set of farm buildings might significantly reduce the numbers of mice and rats there, even though its effect on the rodent population of the whole of its territory may be quite small. The distinction between 'harmful' and 'beneficial' is particularly difficult in relation to game rearing, where predators may be killed purely so that a few extra Pheasants can later be shot. Yet, paradoxically, sporting interests are responsible for the preservation of large areas of woodland.

The simpler types of feeding adaptation are best seen in birds that take small invertebrates from the ground or foliage, supplemented with some fruits and plant seeds. Thrushes, warblers and many common small birds fall into this category. Some species, however, are more specialized. Starlings feed mainly by pushing the closed bill into earth or grass roots and then opening it, making a hole from which worms or grubs can easily be extracted. Extra force for the opening action of the jaw is provided by a backward extension of the lower jaw to give more leverage and by enlargement of the jaw-opening muscles. Tits take small but often hard food items and can concentrate great force in a small area. This is possible because their upper and lower jaws can work independently, allowing them to come together only at the tip.

Insects do not necessarily stay on the ground awaiting capture, of course, and many birds have become successful at pursuing them in flight. Flycatchers wait on a perch and make only a short foray to capture an insect. This is an economical strategy since the time spent in flight is kept to a minimum, but in temperate regions the opportunities for taking insects in this way are limited and fly-catching is best exploited in the tropics. Flycatchers have broad bills to improve the chances of seizing a flying object and stiff bristles fringing the gape, perhaps to aid capture or to protect the eyes. Some fly-catching birds have a 'snap-closing' ligament which speeds the action of shutting the jaws on fast-moving prey. However, the principal aerial feeders in Britain and northern Europe are those that catch insects in continuous flight – Swallows, martins, Swifts and Nightjars. These species have a considerably shortened bill, but the breadth of the mouth is maintained by extending the gape far back into the head. The result is that many of the insects captured strike the roof of the mouth rather than the bill, and the palate bones of these birds are consequently broadened and flattened to reinforce this area.

Specialization

Among passerines, a rather specialized form of feeding has achieved great success. This can be seen in the various finches – birds adapted to seed eating, but probably including several groups of quite different ancestry. All share the same basic features of a short, more or less conical bill, powerful jaw-closing muscles and usually some form of hard ridges lining the upper jaw and palate against which to split the coats of seeds. (See also Bills of Finches, page 327.)

Chaffinches and Bramblings have the most generalized bills of British finches, feeding partly on insects and foraging entirely on the ground. The bills of Linnets and Redpolls are lightly built and not particularly specialized, but more distinctive types are seen in some of their close relatives. Goldfinches and Siskins, which feed by extracting small seeds buried deep within fruiting bodies such as teasel heads or alder cones, have relatively long, pointed bills. Greenfinches have moved in the direction of greater force, with deep bills able to deal with

Great Spotted Woodpeckers hack away the surface bark of trees to obtain access to the creatures living underneath. Sometimes they may bore considerable holes into the trunk in their quest

Sparrowhawks grasp their prey in the air with sharp killing talons

The huge gape of the Nightjar is ideally suited to scooping up large aerial moths after dark

Plunging from considerable heights, the Osprey grasps slippery fish in its serrated talons as they swim near the surface

Upending enables Mallard, and other ducks, to obtain food that would otherwise be out of reach

Oystercatchers are specialist mussel openers. Sometimes the bill is inserted to prise the two halves of the shell open before severing the adductor muscle. At other times the bird may simply smash its way through the shell to get at the animal hidden inside. The smash method is safer, for there are several examples of Oystercatchers being unable to open their bills after being trapped by a mussel. Unless the mussel can be dislodged the bird seems doomed to starvation

larger seeds. The extreme of this type, however, is found in the Hawfinch. With its huge bill, it is able to crack the seeds even of such fruits as cherries, exerting forces of up to 70 kg (150 lb) in doing so. The Bullfinch has a short, rounded bill with sharp cutting edges. Seeds from soft fruits such as rowan and blackberry bulk large in its diet, but it is primarily a specialized bud eater. Curiously, its diet also includes considerable numbers of small snails, which it treats in exactly the same way as seeds – crushing them first, then turning them with the tongue against the sharp edge of the lower jaw to shell them. Most specialized of all is the Crossbill, with an asymmetrical bill tip and jaw muscles to match. In opening pine cones, the lower jaw is forced sideways against the body of the cone while the upper holds a cone scale away to release a seed, which is then extracted by the bird's unusually long tongue.

Unique food source

Various passerines and a few other birds have learned to exploit the rich food sources hidden under bark and within decayed timber, but none approach the woodpeckers in the degree of adaptation. Two basic features are involved – a hard chisel-like bill for excavating and a long, manoeuvrable tongue. Anyone who has watched a woodpecker excavating or drumming cannot fail to have been impressed by the force of its blows, and many wonder how the skull and brain stand up to this repeated pounding. The answer lies in the jaw mechanism. Blows on the bill tip are not transmitted directly to the skull, but via the complicated lever system that moves the jaws and their muscles. This arrangement imparts resilience and spreads stresses so that they are rendered harmless.

The powerful, hooked bill of the Golden Eagle is used for tearing, not catching, its prey

Raptors and owls have strongly hooked bills for cutting and tearing their food, but the task of killing it is performed by the powerful feet with their formidable talons. The thigh and shin bones of birds of prey are long and heavily muscled while the tarsus is usually fairly short, except for bird-killing hawks which fling their long shanks and toes forward to snatch prey in flight. Bird-killing falcons such as Hobby, Merlin or Peregrine do not have such long tarsi because they strike their prey with the legs held close to the body, relying more on the hind toe as a killing weapon. Owls, and the Osprey, have a reversible outer toe, and the latter's toes are studded on the underside with numerous sharp spicules to aid in gripping fish.

Other fish eaters catch prey with the bill. Although they include several quite unrelated families, nearly all show similar modifications of skull form in which the major elements of jaws and palate lie in a more or less straight line. This brings the line of vision closer to the line of jaw action (an advantage when pursuing prey in a highly refractive medium), streamlines the head to facilitate movement through water and enables longer fish to be accommodated between the jaws. Mergansers have horny, tooth-like serrations on the cutting edges of the bill to help grasp slippery prey, and their tongues (reduced in many other fish eaters) are long and provided with backward-pointing projections.

Mergansers are specialized for feeding on fish, but their attributes are all developed from basic waterfowl features, especially the comb-like bill edges and fleshy tongue. These structures are devices for extracting food items of all kinds from water, and wildfowl vary in the extent to which they are developed. At one extreme is the Shoveler – a filter feeder whose wide bill sifts large numbers of tiny plants and animals from water with great efficiency. At the other are geese, and a few ducks such as Wigeon, which have moved back to a land habitat and use their relatively short bills for grazing. All waterfowl share one important characteristic, however: the upper and lower jaws are linked by an extra ligament that enables them to couple the action of upper and lowers jaws very closely during their rapid opening and shutting movements as they feed.

Stabbers and probers

One group, the waders, have a highly developed and refined form of upper jaw structure. The main feature of this is the very long slit-like nostril, separating the edges of the jaw into thin, bony struts which can be moved relative to the rest of the bill, so transmitting the force of the jaw muscles further forward. In the most highly adapted waders, the whole basal half or more of the upper jaw is rigid, and bending occurs only in a narrow flexible region near the tip. This permits a Snipe, for example, to open the bill tip underground to grasp a worm, so saving much unnecessary effort in overcoming the resistance of the soil. The tip of the upper jaw can also bend down and back to push food up the bill, aided by the long tongue. This action is extremely rapid and can only be shown by high speed photography. Curlew are also long-billed, with a bending zone near the tip, but the bill is strongly reinforced with bone. This is needed because they probe in hard earth, using the curved tip in vigorous exploratory movements. However, the bill has become so robust in structure that there is no room for a long tongue, and the whole prey has to be dragged out before it can be swallowed in a series of head tossing movements.

Other remarkable jaw adaptations among waders include the up-turned bill of the Avocet, which takes small aquatic creatures by swinging it from side to side through water, and the chisel-like one of the Oystercatcher. This is provided with an extension of the horny material covering the jaws to give a tool for gaining entry to the shells of sizeable molluscs such as cockles and mussels. It can be done either by severing the adductor muscle which holds the two halves of the shell together or simply by smashing a way in. Individuals learn one method or the other early in life and stick to it; the bills of 'hammerers' can be recognized by the amount of wear and tear they show compared to the 'stabbers'.

Birds are equipped in very different ways to deal with their particular favoured food. By a careful and thoughtful examination of their structure it is often possible to deduce how, where and on what they feed. In the case of highly specialized feeders such deductions are quite obvious, in others recourse to observation of the living bird may be required to confirm a guess.

Oystercatchers have blunt, probing bills powerful enough to break an entry into the hard shells of mussels

Flexible, and with a sensitive tip, the bill of the Snipe is a lengthy probe ideally suited to soft mud

Swung from side to side, the awl-like bill of the Avocet sifts tiny creatures from the surface of marshy lagoons

Longest of all, the probing bill of the Curlew reaches food items that are out of reach of other waders

RANGE AND DISTRIBUTION

Colin Harrison is a professional ornithologist at the British Museum (Natural History) Sub-department of Ornithology, Tring. He has studied and written on such diverse aspects of birds as nests and eggs, behaviour, plumage patterns, distribution, and the bone structure of modern and fossil birds

Because Britain is a group of islands we tend to think of British birds as an entity, a kind of island fauna like those of oceanic islands. In reality we are merely the fragmented ends of extensive habitat zones that extend across Eurasia and in some instances across the land areas of the whole Northern Hemisphere. Most of Britain forms the western extremities of two major vegetative zones, the temperate broadleaf forest zone and the boreal birch and conifer zone. We are spared any uniformity of habitat that might have resulted from this because a number of other factors modify this basic pattern.

High ground alters habitat by producing areas with cooler conditions more typical of northerly zones, and our northern mountain regions have high areas of tundra-type habitat. Further south high ground may carry sparse scrub, open grassland and moors. Such montane areas also have the fast-flowing streams and rivers preferred by some birds such as Dippers and Grey Wagtails; while low-lying areas contribute swamp and fens, lakes, lagoons, slow-moving rivers and estuaries with their characteristic bird-life.

Superimposed on these broader topographical variations are other local differences contributed by the geological structure. An extensive range of tilted geological strata extend across Britain and these have been eroded away to form a complex topography of ridges and valleys with a wide range of rocks and soils, increasing the variety of plants and insects and helping to establish many different microhabitats that assist the survival of a large number of bird species.

Another factor that helps to maintain the wide variety of bird-life in Britain is the existence of the North Atlantic Drift current or Gulf Stream. This pushes a great wedge of warmer ocean waters northeastwards in the North Atlantic, along the west European coast, around Britain and towards the northern tip of Scandinavia. It creates a rich source of food for seabirds and attracts many species that may appear along the British coasts. In addition the large number of birds feeding

in these waters need breeding sites adjacent to the source of food. Many congregate for this purpose on the coasts of Britain, with nesting colonies of auks, Gannets and Fulmars on cliffs and rocky islands, terns on the flat shores and gulls on both.

The borders of the shallow muddy seas, and the larger estuaries, are also rich in food, mainly small invertebrates. They provide a feeding ground for many birds, including large numbers of waders that feed here on passage or as winter residents.

This warm sea current, and the mainly easterly moving weather systems of the Atlantic, help to modify the general climate of Britain and the western seaboard of the European mainland. Winters tend to be warmer than in eastern Europe and summers cooler, and both are usually wetter. This weather does not suit all birds and a number of species widespread in eastern Europe are absent from the western side. However, it does allow the west to provide a refuge for many species in hard weather when both ground and open water freeze in the east, and terrestrial and aquatic birds can still find food by moving westwards. It also allows species to be resident in the west that are migrant in the east.

These are the natural factors that have helped to make Britain part of the ranges of a wide and varied avifauna. In the last few thousand years, and more particularly in the last few hundred years, they have been modified, sometimes to a significant degree, by man, and this in turn has affected the range and distribution of the birds. In his attempts to control and use the land, man has drastically altered the vegetation and sometimes changed the nature of the soil and the life that it will support, and the natural drainage. The effects of this were probably already becoming apparent to some degree even while the vegetation was beginning to re-establish itself after the ice ages.

Man's most significant act was to destroy, over large areas, both forest and scrub and to create grassland and areas of arable cultivation. He also killed birds for food, and some because they were seemingly harmful to his interests. In the early stages his work was most apparent as the maintenance of cleared areas in a mainly forested country, but in more recent times this has changed to a pattern of small cleared areas

Being islands surrounded by rich cold seas, Britain and Ireland attract hosts of breeding and visiting seabirds. Gannets (far left) have their world stronghold here: Great Shearwaters visit every autumn from the Southern Hemisphere

with borders of trees and shrubs. This creates a kind of extended forest edge habitat. It is the bird species that exploit this habitat successfully that have thrived best in association with man, and most common garden birds belong to this group. Birds that were intolerant of man's close approach, from the Dalmatian Pelican and Great Bustard, both now extinct in Britain, to the still-extant Stone-curlew, suffered most.

Separation from the Continent

In the main these factors have helped to maintain or increase the variety of birds occurring in Britain. To set against this there is one event which restricted the range of some birds and partly impoverished our fauna in comparison with that of the nearby European mainland. This was the opening up of the sea channel between Britain and the rest of Europe during the post-glacial period.

Though they breed commonly along the Channel coast of France, Crested Larks have proved quite incapable of colonizing England, only 33 kilometres away

The result of this severance of Britain from mainland Europe was to prevent many plants and animals from extending their slow post-glacial colonization as far as these islands. In theory the short sea-crossing should not have deterred the birds, but in practice such a barrier may be surprisingly effective in some instances. In particular it affects the forest birds. At present, on crossing from mainland Europe to Britain, one loses five of the eight woodpeckers and five of the ten owls as breeding species, and on crossing to Ireland one loses the remaining three woodpeckers and two more of the owls.

There appear to be about 22 species of landbird that breed in western Europe and might have been expected to extend their breeding range across the Channel, but fail to do so. They include such varied species as Black Kite, Crested Lark, Great Reed Warbler and Ortolan Bunting. We may suspect that this separation from the rest of Europe has deprived us of about a tenth of our possible breeding birds. Ireland lacks 64 of the breeding species occurring elsewhere in the British Isles; nearly a third of the total. However, an absence of some suitable habitats and the slight difference in climate might play as large a part in creating this difference as does a failure to cross a further water barrier.

Post-glacial spread

The final opening up of the Channel occurred about 5,000 years ago, some 3,000 years after the approximate end of the last glaciation. During the glacial periods most birds had moved south to avoid the cold conditions, in many instances into refuge zones fragmented by seas and mountain ranges. Here some speciation and subspeciation could have occurred in isolated populations. The post-glacial spread back into northern regions seems to have been slow and probably linked with the re-establishment of vegetation. The forest birds appear to have moved back from two main refuge areas. One was in the Mediterranean region, the other and larger refuge area was in eastern Eurasia. The latter refuge appears to have given rise to a larger number of species and for some of these the successful colonization of Europe involved not only a northward movement but in addition a considerable westward extension of range. It seems likely that a number of these species arrived in eastern Europe too late to make the Channel crossing.

In other respects the effects of this island isolation have been slight. In some instances, the British population of a more widespread species may show some degree of difference from mainland Continental birds in colour and measurements. This has been attributed to such a separation, which might also have been aided by still earlier population isolation during the various glaciations of the ice age. When James Fisher reviewed this subject he listed 39 species for which British subspecies had been named on the basis of such differences. However, in most instances there is a gradual variation in colour and size of individuals throughout the range of these species. The British population exhibits the extreme endpoint of such variation, which might have been slightly enhanced during separation. For example, our birds tend to be darker in colour; our Chaffinch and Jay have more chestnut; and English Coal Tits are more yellow than their Continental counterparts, with Irish Coal Tits yellower still.

Species in the making

Two of the birds have become more specialized in isolation and are sometimes regarded as full species. One, the Red Grouse, diverged from the ancestral Willow Grouse, adapted to a heather habitat instead of willow and birch scrub, and lost its white wings and wholly white winter plumage. The other, the Scottish Crossbill, is linked with the Scots pine on which it feeds, and its Continental counterpart is the Scandinavian Parrot Crossbill. Apart from these, the other distinctive birds we may regard as typically British are the Pied and Yellow Wagtails, subspecies of the Eurasian White and Blue-headed Wagtails respectively, and now almost entirely confined to the British Isles.

Isolation during glaciation may have been responsible for the evolution of a group of our species in regions to the north of Britain at a much earlier date. It has already been mentioned, in connection with forest birds, that the distribution of some appears to indicate the origin of some species in refuges during the Pleistocene ice ages. A small group of species is centred on the northwestern extremity of the Palearctic, with some closely related species more widespread throughout the latter region. This group may have speciated in an area northwest of the main ice sheets. The species include Barnacle Goose, Pink-footed Goose, Lesser Black-backed Gull, Golden Plover and possibly Razorbill and Broad-billed Sandpiper.

In the broad vegetation zones of the Palearctic, and in the smaller areas of more specialized habitat within these zones, the general distribution of birds is controlled partly by the presence of suitable conditions for feeding, sheltering and breeding, and partly by climatic tolerance. Birds which find suitable conditions all the year round will be present all the time, although there may be local movement of individuals from one place to another. Many of the insect-eating birds will be unable to find sufficient food in winter. These tend to take advantage of the abundant insect-life available in summer, and having nested they move south to more favourable wintering areas. However, for some birds nesting in more northerly regions, Britain may seem a hospitable area in which to spend the winter; while others from similar regions need a still milder wintering area and pass through to more southerly habitats.

We can therefore group our native birds in various categories based on the periods of the year during which they occur in Britain. These categories are necessarily a little artificial and arbitrary. A reference to a species as 'resident' may conceal a more complex situation. From detailed studies we know that in some species which occur in Britain all the year round, some individuals may remain in the same area at all times while others move around locally in what may sometimes be

Being piratical, Arctic Skuas must follow the seasonal movements north and south of the terns on which they depend

regular seasonal movements, such as the passage of the Curlew from the uplands in summer to the coastal areas in winter. Still others of a normally resident species may nest in Britain but move out of the country in winter; and some from overseas parts of the species' range which have a more severe climate may join the residents in Britain, while others from such regions pass through to other wintering areas. In apparently resident species such as the Kestrel, Oystercatcher, Robin and Blackbird individuals referable to all four different groups may occur. However, this does not invalidate the general usefulness of the main categories in indicating the likely pattern of occurrence and the general status of a species.

Residents

Residents are species that breed in Britain and are present in some areas at all times of the year. Some 141 species are in this category. Of these 141 species, individuals of 61 also occur as summer visitors only, 53 also move through as passage migrants, and 73 species acquire additional individuals as winter visitors – all of which indicates the complexity of the situation. As already indicated, being resident does not necessarily imply lack of movement within Britain. Resident seabirds such as gulls, auks, divers and some ducks may be found along the shore or offshore in winter rather than at their breeding places; and inland-breeding waders move to muddy shores and estuaries.

Among the resident birds the Red Grouse and Scottish Crossbill are unique to Britain. The others are mainly those that are also resident on parts of the European mainland, and some have a still wider distribution. Some, such as Wren, Treecreeper and Redpoll, occur both in Eurasia and North America. Many others range across the Palearctic; but birds such as the Woodlark, Crested Tit, Robin and Dunnock are peculiar to Europe. One group of our residents, including Green Woodpecker, Blue Tit, Dartford Warbler and Cirl Bunting, appears to have been confined to southwest Europe by the end of the ice age and has only spread from there to a limited extent.

The Shelduck and Cormorant are warm temperate species that extend their range northwards up the Atlantic coast, probably aided by the warm North Atlantic Drift current; while others such as the Eider, Dunlin, Golden Plover and Snow Bunting extend into Britain from the opposite direction, originating in more arctic areas.

Summer visitors

Summer visitors are birds that are present in summer, breeding in Britain, but migrate, typically to warmer areas, in winter. Some 68 species are found in this category. Since many of them also breed outside Britain to the north and northeast, their numbers are usually augmented in spring and autumn by birds on passage.

The typical summer visitors are the insectivorous birds which tend to be present from April to September and then migrate to winter quarters in Africa, mostly south of the Sahara Desert. Being migrants, summer visitors are not deterred by moderate water barriers and most of them occur in suitable areas across the Western Palearctic. Some go further still, and the Wheatear, which winters in Africa, ranges in the breeding season from Greenland, across Eurasia and the Bering Sea to Alaska. In some species the winter quarters extend further north in western Europe, and individuals of such species as Chiffchaff, Blackcap and Firecrest may also occur in winter along the English south coast.

Northern areas that offer little in winter may be utilized in summer, typically by birds such as waders for which this may represent the southern limit of their breeding range. Greenshank, Wood Sandpiper

By taking advantage of the summer flush of small fish, Little Terns are able to breed around our shores. In winter such fish are unavailable and the birds must move elsewhere to winter

and Whimbrel nest in northern Scotland and are only passage migrants in most of Britain. We are at the extreme northern limits of the range of a few other species such as Quail, Hoopoe and Golden Oriole, which occur across the Continental mainland but are rare breeders with us and may not appear at all in cold summers. Both terns and the skuas that often steal food from them are summer visitors, moving southwards along the Atlantic coasts after breeding; while the Manx Shearwater and the petrels disperse into the oceans from their breeding colonies in search of better feeding grounds.

Though they breed both to north and south, Great Grey Shrikes are only autumn and winter visitors to Britain and Ireland

Winter visitors

Winter visitors are birds that breed and summer elsewhere but come to Britain in winter to take advantage of the milder climate, the greater likelihood of ice-free water and unfrozen ground, and food such as seeds and berries. There are 29 species that limit their visits to winter, but the fact that there are another 99 species in other categories, the majority of them resident, in which additional birds come to Britain as winter visitors, indicates our importance as a refuge area at this time of the year.

The majority of the 29 species breed on arctic islands or the tundra bordering the Arctic Ocean. Nearly a third of these are waders. Some of them, geese in particular, breed on tundra well to the northeast of us and must travel southwest to reach Britain. Red-necked Grebe, Smew, Great Grey Shrike and Waxwing are birds of more forested regions, and come to us in winter from a more easterly direction, from Scandinavia and northern mainland Europe. The Great Northern Diver, which comes to us from Greenland and Iceland, was originally a species of the North American avifauna and made a post-glacial extension of range northwestwards across the North Atlantic.

Passage migrants

Passage migrants are birds that pass through Britain regularly on migration but breed and winter elsewhere. They occur either in spring or autumn, or at both seasons. Although individuals of at least 160 species in various other categories regularly occur on passage, only 11 species are regarded as solely passage migrants in Britain.

Three are large oceanic shearwaters from the Mediterranean and the southern oceans, merely passing our shores. Most of the others nest to the north of Britain. Grey Phalarope, Pomarine and Long-tailed Skuas and Sabine's Gull breed on arctic tundra and pass along our coasts on passage. Temminck's Stint comes from Scandinavia, and the Icterine Warbler and Ortolan Bunting breed through southern Scandinavia and mainland Europe. The Kentish Plover is a cosmopolitan coastal species of more southerly origin but ranging north to Denmark. It usually occurs on passage in southeast England where it has bred in the past and now does so once more.

Vagrants

Vagrants form the largest group of species in these categories. They are birds which occur intermittently or as very rare strays, some recorded only once. At any time they form a minute proportion of the total population, but at least 224 species are known to have occurred on one or more occasions in Britain and come within this group, nearly doubling the final total of species on the British List.

As a group of offshore islands the British Isles are in an advantageous position for attracting vagrants. Most vagrants are badly off course, shifted from their accustomed routes and regions by winds and bad weather. For many transatlantic migrants Britain is the first landfall they see. For Continental birds being drifted westwards Britain is the last solid land before they are lost in the Atlantic. Many sea and land birds follow coastlines when on the move, and Britain has long coastlines and is likely to be encountered by anything moving along the seaboard of Europe or between the western Atlantic and Arctic Oceans.

Although mainly from east or west, vagrants to Britain appear to come from all directions. Some 63 of the vagrant species are from North America, the majority of them occurring in autumn. They are mostly migrants within their native ranges. Many are small songbirds and were probably significantly aided in passage by the predominantly eastward-moving weather systems of the Atlantic; but the stronger-flying ducks and waders may well have managed without such help. The Atlantic Ocean itself has contributed the Black-browed Albatross, six more species of shearwater and petrel, and a frigatebird. From the Arctic there are such species as the Ivory Gull and Ross's Gull, White-billed Diver, Steller's Eider and Arctic Redpoll.

Just occasionally an albatross will cross the equatorial doldrum belt to reach the Northern Hemisphere. A Black-browed Albatross did so in the 1970s and set up a partnerless home in the Shetlands

One of the ornithological events of the century was the establishment of a breeding pair of Snowy Owls in the Shetlands in the 1970s

The majority of bird species of northern and central Europe also occur as vagrants when not in other categories. The exceptions are mainly sedentary forest species, but the list does include such localized ones as the Wallcreeper and Alpine Accentor. Birds which have been extending their range into northeastern Europe, such as the Scarlet Rosefinch, Red-flanked Bluetail, Arctic Warbler and Yellow-breasted Bunting, also occur as vagrants in Britain. There are fewer species from southeastern Europe and the Mediterranean region. In view of the small number from the latter region that reach Britain it is perhaps surprising that there have been several of probably North African origin, including the Cream-coloured Courser, Desert Warbler and Trumpeter Finch.

Steppe conditions appear to encourage vagrancy, and a number of such species from the southeast have appeared as vagrants, including Pallid Harrier, Sociable Plover, Pallas's Sandgrouse, White-winged Lark and Rose-coloured Starling. The least expected vagrants are those originating further east still – in eastern Siberia. These birds appear to be mainly migrants – thrushes, warblers and buntings – and may have been deflected by abnormal weather conditions; but even so, the distance and direction of movement which brought them to Britain is unexpected.

Irruptive species

These five categories represent the main division of British birds on the basis of their occurrence in the British Isles. A subsidiary group, which is not wholly confined to any one of these but is usually linked with the vagrants, consists of irruptive species. In regions of extensive and relatively uniform habitat with a small number of bird species present, each containing a large number of individuals, problems arise if there is significant fluctuation in the food available. When shortage occurs there is a tendency for the birds affected to spill over into surrounding regions where they may not normally occur. Sometimes they are only present for a brief period, but in some instances they invade in large numbers, at times appearing to colonize new areas and disappearing gradually over several years.

In tundra regions there are irregular fluctuations in the abundance of small rodents. When a scarcity occurs after years of plenty, Snowy Owls, Rough-legged Buzzards and sometimes Gyrfalcons and Hawk Owls may take part in eruptive dispersal. From northern forest regions Waxwings, Crossbills and Nutcrackers are typical eruptive species when seed or berry crops are poor, but other species such as tits and Jays may also be involved. The third region is the Russian steppes. The best-known species from here is Pallas's Sandgrouse, which in the late nineteenth and early twentieth centuries briefly extended its range right across Europe to Scotland, but the Rose-coloured Starling also erupts from here and, as mentioned earlier, a high proportion of steppe species occur as vagrants in the west.

Introduced species

Reference has also been made to man's tendency to destroy and exterminate birds, but there have been a few attempts to make amends by reintroductions and introductions of birds from overseas. Large birds were always vulnerable, and the Capercaillie, exterminated in Britain in the seventeenth and eighteenth centuries, was successfully reintroduced to Scotland in the nineteenth century; while currently there are attempts to re-establish the White-tailed Eagle in western Scotland and the Great Bustard in Hampshire.

Although there have been grave warnings about the introduction of alien species, with the Rose-ringed Parakeet which is just maintaining a clawhold in southeast England quoted as the awful example, the surprising fact is that hardly any of the many species released from time to time have found a niche for themselves. The successful species are mainly gamebirds and waterfowl which tend to have considerable long-term encouragement.

The common Pheasant has been introduced at intervals over 900 years, and the Red-legged Partridge in the eighteenth and nineteenth centuries. The latter may yet suffer in competition with the recently released and closely related Chukar Partridge. Another recent introduction of uncertain success is that of the Bobwhite Quail. Of the many pheasants introduced, the Golden Pheasant has succeeded in a few localities and the Lady Amherst's Pheasant may persist in one area. There appear to have been vacant niches for forest waterfowl, now filled in part by the Canada Goose and Mandarin Duck, and more recently the Ruddy Duck has spread from captive stock to occupy the deeper lakes and reservoirs. The only successful nonsporting bird, the Little Owl, was introduced from across the Channel in the nineteenth century and has colonized as far as southern Scotland.

Grouping our birds into categories gives the present status of a species an erroneous air of permanence and stability. Over decades there are long-term fluctuations in climate, with alternating warmer and cooler phases of varying intensity and with longer variations

Rose-ringed Parakeets have escaped from captivity and established themselves in the wild in southeast England. Their apparent success has yet to face the challenge of a really severe winter

superimposed on these, and the distribution of birds is affected accordingly. Over the same period changes in man's activities may affect vegetation and food supply. The distribution of bird species is therefore fluid, with a constant advance and retreat of the apparent limits and variations in population density.

An effect of the cool weather cycle of the past few decades is apparent in northern Scotland. A range of species that at one time were found together no nearer than mid-Scandinavia now occur here. Great Northern Diver, Goldeneye, Gyrfalcon, Temminck's Stint, Snowy Owl, Shorelark, Redwing, Fieldfare, Bluethroat and Lapland Bunting have all bred or attempted breeding here in recent years. Lesser Spotted Woodpecker and Wryneck have also invaded, apparently from Scandinavia; the latter arriving in the north when the English population has all but died out in the extreme southeast. There is less evidence of loss of southerly species at this period, although the southern populations of Wryneck, Red-backed Shrike and Woodlark have markedly decreased. Yet at the same time Cetti's Warbler has moved in from the southeast and established itself, and the Fan-tailed Warbler is approaching our southern limits. In the 1950s the Collared Dove completed its movement right across Europe by colonizing Britain. The overall picture shows that in the long term, now as in the past, bird distribution in Britain must be seen as dynamic and not static; but while the main trends are clear, the details are confusing.

Information base

The information that enables us to comment with confidence on the occurrence and distributional changes of species comes from the great mass of data collected by bird-watchers. The official list of British birds is compiled and monitored by the Records Committee of the British Ornithologists' Union. The updated list is published at intervals, the last appearing as a book in 1971. The Rarities Committee set up by the journal *British Birds* critically examines sight records sent in by bird-watchers, and an Irish Records Panel examines records from Ireland. The British Trust for Ornithology is a voluntary body set up to gather and organize amateur observations. It has increasingly concerned itself with the difficult task of monitoring not just the occurrence but the population changes of native birds. The Common Bird Census – regular counts of a series of small areas of land – has made it possible to establish an index for various commoner species and to study the annual fluctuations in the numbers of birds present. The success of this scheme has encouraged the setting up of similar schemes to monitor birds on estuaries and along inland streams and rivers.

Conspicuous birds with obviously increasing or fluctuating populations have always attracted attention. Herons and Great Crested Grebes have been counted at intervals for nearly half a century, and in more recent times seabirds such as Fulmars, Gannets and more particularly Kittiwakes have all received attention. In addition to these intermittent counts, a large number of single surveys of species have been made, usually of breeding birds.

We have a reasonably accurate picture of the general distribution of birds in Britain. Surveys such as these, together with the broader population studies such as the total count of British seabirds in Operation Seafarer in 1969, and the production of the *Atlas of Breeding Birds in Britain and Ireland* in 1976, all help to establish and clarify the less certain picture of the occurrence and frequency of birds within their distributional range, and to provide a better basis for understanding the complexities of our avifauna.

Cool weather cycles may bring birds that breed to the north southwards to colonize Britain. The Lapland Bunting has shown a tendency to stay on in Scotland and has recently bred for the first time

MIGRATION AND MOVEMENTS

Robert Spencer has had a lifelong interest in bird migration, and since 1954 has been employed by the British Trust for Ornithology, where he is head of the Ringing and Migration section, and Director of Services. He has been Secretary General of the European Union for Bird Ringing since its foundation in 1963. He has travelled widely in pursuit of birds, his journeys including two expeditions to the northern edge of the Sahara to study migration

Abundant around towns and villages for the brief months of summer, Swifts move southwards to Africa to ensure a year-round supply of insects

The more we learn about bird movements the more difficult it becomes to define migration in a single broadly applicable phrase. The concept that a migrant has – as it were – a *return* ticket is widely accepted, and it is also said that migration is regular as to season and direction of movement. At the opposite extreme, however, are those species such as the Pheasant, which spends its entire life within a few square kilometres. Between the orthodox migrant on the one hand and the sedentary species on the other are a whole range of movement types which are fundamental to the continuation of bird-life. Migration in all its manifestations can be seen primarily as a response to seasonal variations in the availability of food.

During the summer our skies are filled with myriads of flying insects, for which the term 'aerial plankton' has been coined. They may be present hundreds of metres above the earth, and represent a vast potential food supply: a source which is indeed exploited – by members of the swallow family, by Swifts, and to a lesser extent by flycatchers. This profusion of insects is a summer phenomenon. Mild days in winter may see the appearance of small columns of insects, but not in such numbers and not regularly enough to support a wintering population of fly-catching birds. Thus such species are total migrants, spending the hard months south of the Sahara where they can be assured of a winter-long food supply. It is, however, a supply that must be shared with the various African species of swifts and swallows, and so it is advantageous for them to spend the summer in the north temperate latitudes and the northern winter in the tropics.

Empty wastes

We find a similar situation among the birds that breed in the high Arctic, where spring may start in June and winter arrive in early September. Between those dates the empty wastes may offer abundant food, endless daylight in which to seek it, few predators and little or no disturbance by man – in short, ideal conditions for raising a family. Knot and Brent Goose are two species that take advantage of these riches. On the other hand, midwinter in these high latitudes offers endless dark, low temperatures and thick snow cover. Migration permits the exploitation of brief summer plenty, coupled with winter temperatures further south which may be no lower than July temperatures in the Arctic.

For Knot and Brent Goose summer and winter quarters are discrete, so that the birds have to travel at least 1,600 kilometres from one to the other – the extreme form of migration. In contrast, consider the Robin. A glance at a distribution map reveals that Robins spread as far north as central Sweden and Finland, and as far south as North Africa. In winter they leave the colder parts of their range and crowd into the milder, more southerly parts. This kind of pattern, which is fairly common among European landbirds, has been described as a change in the centre of gravity of the population: a useful metaphor. But the Robin demonstrates a second important point. All Swifts, and for that matter all Brent Geese, migrate because to stay put would be to die. Not all Robins migrate. Those from northern and eastern Europe have to do so while the two or three months of snow cover render life intolerable. Iberian Robins, however, have no reason to move in winter: all of them can afford to stay where they are. In southern England most Robins are sedentary, whereas a significant proportion of the Scottish population move, some into Ireland and others to southern England or France. Those that remain in the north of Scotland are the most northerly wintering members of the species. Here is yet another variant, known as partial

migration. The population is thinned out by the departure of a proportion of the birds, and if the winter proves to be hard those individuals
that have migrated will stand a better chance of survival. A mild winter
will mean better survival for the individuals that have stayed behind,
for migration itself is not without risks. Song Thrush, Lapwing and
Pied Wagtail are all partial migrants in Britain: they are species for
which the pros and cons of migration, in our present climate, are finely
balanced, and are an extremely interesting example of the plasticity
of nature.

Vertical migration

Bird-watchers who have walked the Pennines or the northern moors
in summer will know that the most ubiquitous species is the Meadow
Pipit. Whether heather or grass moor, one is seldom out of sight and
sound of the species, and our uplands clearly support a huge breeding
population. Winter is a different story. At 400 metres above sea level,
and even more so at 600, the snow can lie for days or even weeks on end.
In short, these highlands are not a hospitable winter domain for the
Meadow Pipit, some individuals of which seek safety in migration to
Iberia, acting as typical partial migrants. Those that remain in Britain
must nevertheless leave the highest ground for the plains and the coast.
Theirs is an altitudinal migration, but on a very modest scale. In the
great mountain ranges of the world some species may descend 3,000
metres for the winter. Such movements may not be regular as to
direction, but are certainly seasonal, and made in response to a seasonally variable food supply.

Man has been aware of bird migration for at least 2,000 years but the
study of it spans less than the last 150 years, with most of the important
discoveries coming in the twentieth century. One of the most influential
study techniques, developed at the end of the last century, has been the
marking of birds with individually numbered metal rings, each one

The whole population of Brent Geese
leaves its breeding grounds in the Arctic
to winter in milder climates, including
the coasts of Britain and Ireland

Ringed Swifts are invariably found dead, though systematic retrapping in their wintering areas would produce a much higher rate of recovery and consequent increase in information

Light alloy rings placed around the tarsus and bearing a serial number and address are the most effective method of marking birds in large numbers for migration studies

bearing a return address. When the ringed bird is 'recovered' – whether found dead, shot or rescued from the greenhouse – two points in its life are fixed: the date and place of ringing and the date and place of recovery. From such recoveries we know that the Swifts which breed in Britain winter in the eastern portion of the Congo Basin in East Africa, whereas British Swallows winter in South Africa. Of course, it was already known that in winter there are European Swifts in East Africa and European Swallows in South Africa. In these cases, the contribution of bird ringing has been to define in some detail the winter quarters of particular populations. In the process of doing so, ringing has produced evidence that those migrants which survive for several years may return each winter to the same, fairly restricted locality. Presumably the survival value of this is that increasing familiarity with its winter home enables a bird to exploit the food resources there more efficiently, especially when such resources are limited.

Sometimes, the results of bird ringing allow us to look at a species in a new light: even to decide that it is not really the kind of migrant we thought it was. The Redwing, a species familiar to all bird-watchers as a regular winter visitor to Britain, is a case in point. We know that it breeds over northern and eastern Europe, so it seems reasonable to regard it as a migrant whose summer and winter ranges overlap. Birds ringed in Britain in winter may be recovered in Britain, France or Iberia in the same winter. Recoveries in summer are from within the known breeding range. But recoveries in subsequent winters may be not only in western Europe, but also in Italy, on almost any of the Mediterranean islands, in the Levant, or around the Black Sea. If migration is defined as regular as to season and *direction*, the Redwing is not the migrant we have always thought it to be. Individual northern European Redwings may from year to year seek winter survival almost anywhere in southern Europe or southwestern Asia. The species is thus better regarded as a winter nomad, wandering wherever it finds berries rather than in a set direction. The same is apparently true of the Fieldfare and Brambling, although birds ringed in Britain do not penetrate so far to the east in subsequent winters.

Nomads

Nomadism is thus another concept in the examination of bird movements. It can be seen as one of nature's responses to an unpredictable food supply. Among landbirds it is particularly associated with desert areas such as central Australia, where flocks of Budgerigars wander erratically in search of areas where rain has fallen and breeding is therefore possible.

A form of nomadism is also characteristic of many seabirds at a certain stage of their lives. Whereas songbirds are relatively short-lived and must settle down to the business of raising a family when they are scarcely a year old, many seabirds have potential lifespans of 15, 20 or even 30 years. Their approach to parenthood can therefore be leisurely. For example, some Fulmars do not breed until they are nine years old. Their early years are spent wandering at sea and some may penetrate the Davis and Denmark Straits and visit the Grand Banks off Newfoundland during their adolescent travels. It is not known why they should disperse so widely during the years when they have no responsibilities or timetable to observe. However, if they do leave home waters they are not competing for food with adults of breeding age or newly fledged, vulnerable juveniles.

Some seabirds are conventional migrants in that they commute regularly between a summer and winter home range. Roseate Terns winter in West Africa. Sandwich Terns also winter mainly along the coasts of West Africa, with smaller numbers reaching Angola and South Africa. Storm Petrels, which breed on rocky islands off the north and west coasts of Britain and Ireland, winter at sea to the west of Namibia and South Africa. Arctic Terns travel still further south, reaching the edge of the Antarctic ice pack. An Arctic Tern ringed in Britain has been recovered on board a Japanese whaling ship in the Antarctic seas, while another recovery was reported at an even greater distance, in Australia.

Atlantic loop

Some species of shearwater have movements that combine elements of nomadism and regular migration. Great Shearwaters, which breed in the South Atlantic on islands such as the Tristan da Cunha group, set off northwards at the end of the southern summer, working their way up the western Atlantic. At about the latitude of Labrador some turn eastwards, to be recorded off our westerly headlands in autumn, before finally moving southwards through the eastern Atlantic to reach their island homes for the start of another breeding season. In the sense that they have no winter home, but are constantly on the move, they are nomadic, yet their wanderings are predictable as to season and direction, which is characteristic of strict migrants. Wilson's Petrel also reaches the North Atlantic in winter.

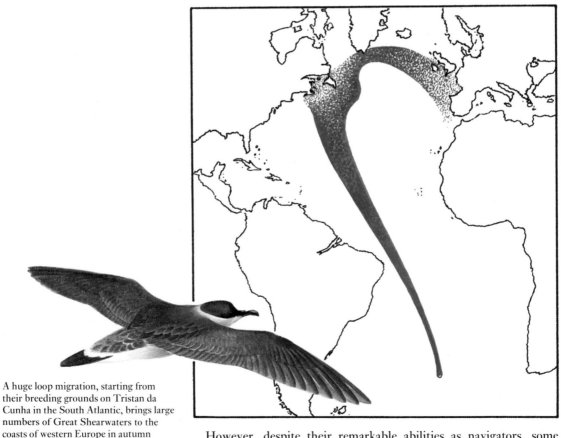

A huge loop migration, starting from their breeding grounds on Tristan da Cunha in the South Atlantic, brings large numbers of Great Shearwaters to the coasts of western Europe in autumn

However, despite their remarkable abilities as navigators, some birds do get lost. Amongst the smaller species it must be assumed that each year hundreds of thousands get blown off course, perhaps to end their lives in mid-ocean. For example, in December 1927 a flock of Lapwings reached Newfoundland, where the species is a very rare vagrant. As one of the flock had been ringed in Cumbria it is probable

Westerly movements of Lapwings across Europe have, on occasion, led to birds wandering out over the Atlantic and eventually reaching the eastern seaboard of North America

that they left Britain for Ireland on what was a very characteristic cold-weather movement for this species but, overshooting their target, were forced to complete a huge flight before making a landfall. Because of the prevailing westerly winds, such east to west vagrancy is uncommon. On the other hand, vagrant North American shorebirds reach Europe every autumn, being recorded most frequently in the southwest of Ireland. Even quite small American landbirds occur every year in tiny numbers, though it is known that they are capable of hitching a lift for part of the journey by joining a steamer. One of the most remarkable examples of this was observed aboard the RMS *Mauretania* in October 1962. During the voyage no fewer than 130 individual birds of 34 species were recorded on board the ship. Most of them joined the ship on the second day out; many died, but some survived the journey.

Unaided journeys

For a long time small New World species were not admitted to the official list of birds occurring in Britain, on the grounds that they could not make the journey unaided. Nowadays the belief is that, given favourable winds, many species are capable of making the journey unaided, and so all are given the benefit of the doubt.

That small vagrants should arrive from the west is remarkable in view of the forbidding waters of the Atlantic which all must cross, yet if we take distance into account it is possible to argue that the most spectacular journeys are those performed by the vagrants which reach our shores from eastern Siberia. No better example of this could be found than Pallas's Warbler, a tiny species weighing 5–7 grams. The western limit of its breeding distribution lies at about longitude 85° East, or roughly as far east as Mount Everest, and its wintering home lies in Southeast Asia. Yet almost every autumn a few of these tiny waifs are recorded, mainly on the east coast, after a journey of perhaps 8,000 kilometres in the wrong direction. They come with such regularity, sometimes in small parties, or in association with other species native to the Asian heartlands, that it is difficult to dismiss them simply as lost. It has therefore been suggested that a failure in their orientation mechanism causes them to set off on a course 180° out, that is, northwestwards rather than towards the southeast, but hypotheses of this nature are almost impossible to prove.

One sad fact has to be accepted for virtually all long-distance vagrants, small or large: it is most unlikely that any of them succeed in finding their way back across the thousands of kilometres of their wandering. Effectively they might as well be dead, for they are unlikely to meet a mate of their own species. It is a number of years now since a vagrant seabird, a Black-browed Albatross from the South Atlantic, first turned up at a Scottish Gannet colony. It has joined the Gannets each breeding season since then, evidently finding them company, and even building a nest. To date only one case is known of vagrants meeting up in the alien world of their adoption and then breeding. These were a pair of Spotted Sandpipers, the North American form of the British Common Sandpiper, which in 1975 were found in the Scottish Highlands with a nest containing four eggs. Unfortunately the nest was deserted, perhaps because of bad weather or trampling cattle, and so what might have been the start of an Old World colony never reached the crucial stage.

Vagrancy in birds arises as a result of navigational error, bad weather, or a combination of the two. It is abnormal, counterproductive and must almost always result in a shorter lifespan for the individual concerned. The word 'individual' is important, for another class of movement involves the periodic and somewhat erratic wanderings of

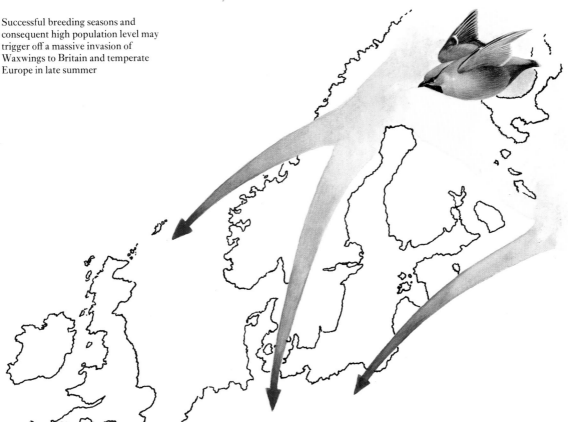

Successful breeding seasons and consequent high population level may trigger off a massive invasion of Waxwings to Britain and temperate Europe in late summer

large numbers of birds. This phenomenon has been termed 'invasion migration', but in so far as it does not occur annually and is not necessarily in the same direction, the use of the term seems inappropriate. It is also known by the terms 'eruption' and 'irruption', depending on whether one's viewpoint is the country of departure or the country of arrival, and is perhaps best thought of as being analogous to the well-known movements of lemmings. Eruptions, indeed, have much in common with lemming movements, often being roughly cyclical and associated with population size in relation to the available food supply. In Britain the two best-known irruptive species (*irruptive* because they come *into* Britain) are the Crossbill and the Waxwing. Neither species arrives with great regularity. Crossbill irruptions are associated with the failure of the conifer cone crop, and typically such immigrants tend to reach Britain in July and August. Thus they are apparently moving out of their breeding grounds before food becomes short, although the mechanism of this is not fully understood. They probably have an innate tendency to move, for very small numbers of Crossbills are recorded in the Scottish islands in years when no proper irruption develops. For the bird-watcher, further confusion may arise because after big invasions pockets of Crossbills may linger to breed in Britain. Sometimes these are one-off events, but as a result of past invasions we now have well-established breeding populations of Continental Crossbills in various parts of the country, notably the Brecks of East Anglia, the New Forest and Dumfries.

Waxwings, whose staple diet is the berry of the rowan or mountain ash, tend to irrupt more frequently than the Crossbill and although several years may pass without any arrival, it is not unusual for them to come in consecutive years. Their movements, like those of the Crossbill, are associated with failure of the food supply and the irrupting birds are most frequently recorded in Britain in November and December.

Pallas's Sandgrouse formerly erupted from its Siberian breeding grounds and even stayed on to breed as far west as Scotland. A reduced population makes such occurrences highly unlikely in the future

Waxwings, however, do not attempt to remain and breed in their temporary winter home, and it used to be believed that, like lemmings, erupting birds faced a premature death at the end of the journey. Nowadays there have been recoveries of ringed birds (including Waxwings) to suggest at least the possibility that a proportion of eruptive travellers survive and eventually return to their natal area.

The list of species which erupt, regularly or occasionally, is a long one and includes such exotic names as Pallas's Sandgrouse (which last appeared in significant numbers as long ago as 1908), Nutcracker, Rough-legged Buzzard and Snowy Owl (obliged to move when the lemming harvest fails), and even such everyday species as Great Spotted Woodpecker, Jay, Coal Tit and Redpoll. The list could probably be extended still further, for the Redpoll, like some other small seed-eating finches, seems to occupy a middle position between eruption and nomadism, moving every year but sometimes arriving in large numbers and at other times in small.

If migration can be defined as being something which is regular as to season and direction, then 'moult migration' is an interesting specialized example of it – the best-known example in Britain being the Shelduck. At the end of the breeding season Shelduck migrate, not, as most other species do, to more favourable winter quarters, but to a communal moulting ground off the coast of West Germany in the Heligoland Bight. There, on the Grosser Knechtsand, some 100,000 birds, the larger part the entire population of northwest Europe, gather between August and October apparently for the sole purpose of moulting. A small secondary moulting flock of 3,000–4,000 assembles in Bridgwater Bay in the Bristol Channel, and recently rather smaller gatherings have been detected in the Firth of Forth and on the Wash. The gatherings last no longer than is necessary for the flocks to complete their annual moult, after which their 'autumn' migration comprises a leisurely return to their breeding grounds, so that the pattern of movement is not associated with escaping the rigours of winter.

Tradition

'Tradition' plays a large part in the lives of many wildfowl. They use traditional wintering grounds and *en route* halt at traditional staging posts. It is not absolutely clear why the tradition of communal moulting has developed in some species (it is not confined to the Shelduck; for instance, Goosanders congregate in a fjord system in northern Norway), but it is probable that, being flightless and therefore more vulnerable, they gain a sense of security from being with others of their kind.

There is a different kind of moult migration, regular as to season and direction, which is apparently associated with food availability. The Pink-footed Geese breeding in central Iceland provide an excellent example. In late spring the geese, which have wintered in the northern half of Britain, gradually assemble on their traditional breeding grounds in the heart of Iceland. Unlike small songbirds, geese do not breed as yearlings so that the population which assembles on the breeding grounds consists of breeding pairs and prebreeders. At this stage in their lives the prebreeders have no useful contribution to make, yet were they to spend the summer there, they would be competing for food with the parents and their progeny. They thus undertake a further flight to northwest Greenland where they moult, and in so doing help to ensure that the maximum amount of food is available to fully mature pairs for the vital business of raising healthy families.

In recent years bird ringers have established that Canada Geese breeding in northern England also have a moult migration in which the nonbreeding birds fly to the Beauly Firth in northeast Scotland. This is interesting partly because the Canada Goose is a species originally introduced from North America as an ornamental waterfowl but now behaving as a genuine wild species, but also because even during the few years in which the phenomenon has been studied it has been seen to be extending gradually to birds breeding further and further south in Britain.

Migration research is a growing science, and a number of the facts presented here were unknown even a few years ago. Theories are proposed to account for observed facts and, generally speaking, are accepted until they are disproved. Writers in the earlier years of this century were particularly attracted by the possibility of drawing migration route maps, and there was a protracted debate between the protagonists of 'narrow front' migration and supporters of 'broad front' movements. The former, observing rather narrow streams of migrating birds passing given points, concluded that the birds really were following a route. Their opponents argued that migration occurred on a broad front, perhaps of several hundred kilometres, rather than in a narrow stream.

Four million birds

In the autumn of 1960 a team of amateur ornithologists kept a daily watch on the skies over London, on weekdays for just an hour or two before work. In practice they found that almost anywhere in London they could look up and detect migrants passing over. Indeed, it was calculated that in 50 days a possible four million migrants traversed London's skies. It is highly improbable that a major migration *route* passes over London, and radar has established time and again the reality of broad front migration. No matter where one lives in Britain, there will be times when migrants are likely to be passing overhead.

Yet narrow front migration does occur, at least with certain species, whenever the configuration of a landscape – coastlines, broad escarpment-flanked valleys, high ranges – makes it 'sensible'. The broad-winged birds of prey, for example, prefer to soar rather than flap, and everywhere on their migratory journeys seek out the shorter sea-crossings, for the lift-giving thermals do not occur over water. Thus narrow streams of raptors and White Storks may be seen crossing the Straits of Gibraltar and the Bosphorus on passage to and from their winter quarters in Africa. In a similar way many birds of prey leaving Scandinavia pass over Falsterbo, where there is the shortest crossing from Sweden to Denmark. It is like sand passing through an hour glass: narrow front migration at its most spectacular.

Most species may at some place or time be observed in narrow front migration. From the tip of western promontories one may observe migrating seabirds streaming past in narrow line ahead. Departing summer visitors track down the rocky peninsula of Portland Bill, thus reducing their more dangerous overwater flight by a few kilometres. The narrower arm of land enfolding the mouth of the Humber at Spurn Point exerts such an influence on approaching migrants that the movement along it is southwards in spring and autumn alike.

High mountain ranges tend to canalize passing migrants, especially when, as is the case with the Alps and Pyrenees, they stand athwart the desired direction of flight. Birds passing from France into Spain must, like car drivers, skirt the mountains by the narrow coastal routes or else wind up a long valley, climbing to reach the coll at the end. For hundreds of years Woodpigeons migrating through the Pyrenean passes have been netted for food as they slipped low over the colls. More recently, the Swiss have discovered that a vast migration of songbirds passes over the Col de Bretolet.

White Storks rely on rising air to create lift during long migrational journeys. As such thermals do not occur over water, the birds concentrate at narrow sea crossings such as Gibraltar and the Bosphorus

Some 250 birds occur in these islands with a sufficient degree of frequency to merit the title 'regular'. Some breed with us, some winter every year, while others pass through in spring, autumn, or both. Such birds are quite clearly 'British or Irish' even though they may be more widespread, more numerous, and even easier to see the other side of the Channel or further afield. The Snowy Owl, for example, is one of the rarest of 'regular' birds, while the recolonizing but still distinctly scarce Osprey has a virtually world-wide distribution. Nevertheless, these birds are 'British or Irish' in a way that some off-course American or Siberian waif is not. It is this group of regular species that form the core of this book and which are illustrated and described in detail in the pages that follow. The choice of such birds is almost automatic, though inevitably there are borderline cases between the regular and the rare. Some may dispute individual cases, but if we have erred it is on the side of inclusion rather than exclusion. Thus every bird that the reader is likely to see in Britain and Ireland is included. Each is described under standard headings. Except where stated a male of each species in summer plumage is illustrated in colour, often with a female alongside, in a typical natural pose. Throughout we have used smaller illustrations to show extra plumages and characteristic field marks to advantage, and thus to facilitate identification of every species.

Almost every regular species occurring in Britain and Ireland is mapped. Summer distribution is shown in yellow, winter in blue, while residents are shown in green. In the case of particularly scarce visitors, a more informative map of Europe or of the world is substituted or added to show their area of origin

THE
BIRDS

Red-throated Diver

Gavia stellata (Pontoppidan)

Goose-like diving bird that spends the summer at remote lochs and the winter on inshore seas. The red throat patch makes for easy recognition in summer, but in winter all divers look very similar and the thin, upturned bill is then the best feature

Population: about 750 pairs; several thousand winter

Thin uptilted bill and pale upperparts aid winter identification

Like other divers the Red-throated swims low in the water, often with back awash. It has a streamlined shape and the sharply pointed and comparatively thin bill is always held uptilted. In summer the head and neck are dove-grey, the throat marked with a broad triangular patch of rust-red and the hind crown and nape with a pattern of black and white transverse stripes. The back is dark slate-grey with some fine white flecking, the underparts whitish. In winter the crown and hindneck become grey flecked with black, shading gradually into a white throat and foreneck. The back is heavily speckled with white. In flight, and like other divers, the Red-throated has a humpback appearance with the neck held lower than the body. It is usually solitary in summer, but sometimes forms quite large winter flocks. 53–58 cm (21–23 in).

Voice: The song is a high, wailing, far-carrying call; also has a duck-like *kwuck*.

Habitat: Small lochs in wild open country with or without islands, but always within reach of the sea or a large loch for feeding. In winter frequents inshore waters.

Reproduction: The nest is close to the shore of a small loch, often on an island with a slipway to the water created by the birds' clumsy movements on land. It consists of a mound of available vegetation, and the 2 olive eggs are spotted with black and laid in late May. The female takes the major share of the incubation which lasts 24–29 days and starts with the first egg. The down-covered youngsters take to the water soon after hatching and are cared for by both parents. They fly after 6 weeks. Single-brooded.

Food: Mostly fish of whatever species of the appropriate size are available. Dives for about 60 seconds.

Range and Distribution: A circumpolar breeding distribution in the tundra zone. In Europe it is confined to Iceland, Ireland, Scotland, Sweden, Norway and Finland. It winters on coasts of the North Sea, the Atlantic south to Portugal and in the Mediterranean. In Britain and Ireland it is confined to the northwest from Arran to Shetland, and in Donegal. It is most plentiful in Shetland.

Movements: Leaves breeding grounds to winter at sea. Immigrants from Scandinavia haunt all British and Irish coastlines except the extreme north.

Black-throated Diver

Gavia arctica (Linnaeus)

Typical diver that is well marked in
summer plumage and confusingly
like the other species in winter. It
falls neatly between the Great
Northern and Red-throated in size,
but is best identified by bill shape

Population: about 200 pairs; several
hundred winter

More substantial
bill, not uptilted like Red-throated's,
is key to winter identification

In summer the whole of the head and hindneck are dove-grey. The
sides of the neck and upper breast have a series of vertical stripes
broken by a bold black patch on the throat. The back is dark slate-grey
with 2 oval patches of square white spots on the folded wings. In winter
the crown, hindneck and upperparts are slate-grey, and the long,
evenly tapering bill is the best field mark. This is neither as heavy as the
Great Northern's, nor uptilted like the Red-throated's. It chooses large
lochs in summer where it both nests and feeds, rather than commute to
sea like the Red-throated. 58–68 cm (23–27 in).

Voice: A deep *kwow*; the song is a high-pitched wailing.

Habitat: Large lochs, usually with islands, with a plentiful supply of
fish. In winter resorts to coastal waters.

Reproduction: Nests beside the water's edge, usually on an island.
The nest may be a simple scrape with a few bits of vegetation, or a
considerable mound, depending on availability. The 2 eggs are laid in
early May and are olive-brown spotted with black. Incubation, by both
sexes, commences with the first egg and lasts 28–29 days. The chicks
leave the nest soon after hatching and are tended by both members of
the pair until they fly at 8 weeks. Single-brooded.

Food: Fish predominate, with crustaceans and molluscs also important.
Species vary according to availability, but usually smaller fish are
taken. Dives for up to 2 minutes, but 45 seconds is average.

Range and Distribution: Circumpolar, though absent from Iceland
and Greenland. In Europe it breeds throughout Scandinavia eastwards
across northern Russia, and winters on most coasts including the
eastern Mediterranean. In Britain it is confined to the wildest and most
remote parts of the Highlands and islands, but it also breeds in
Galloway. Absent from Orkney and Shetland.

Movements: Leaves breeding grounds for the winter. Scandinavian
birds winter along Scottish coasts and on east and southeast coasts of
England. Scarce elsewhere and decidedly rare in Ireland.

Great Northern Diver

Gavia immer (Brünnich)

A large diver, with a proportionately large black bill, that is a regular winter visitor and which bred in Britain in 1970. Adult in winter shown

Population: occasionally 1 pair; several hundred may winter

Similar to Black-throated in winter, but much heavier bill usually apparent. Distinct spangled upperparts in summer

Sheer size would seem to preclude confusion with our other 2 divers, but size is notoriously misleading, especially over featureless seas. In summer the head and neck are dark bottle-green, appearing black at any distance, broken by a small patch of black and white stripes at the base of the chin and another larger one at the side of the neck. The back is dark slate-grey covered with large square spots. The bill is massive, pointed and much heavier than the Black-throated's. In winter the Great Northern is dark slate-grey above, with white on chin, front of neck and underparts. 68–81 cm (27–32 in).

Voice: Loud wailing cries and chuckles in summer; also a barking flight call.

Habitat: Large lakes, with or without islands, in remote, mostly uninhabited tundra or forest. In winter frequents sea coasts.

Reproduction: The nest is a simple scrape with little or no lining, though a quite large mound may be created in some circumstances. It is situated on an islet or promontory within easy distance of water. The 2 olive-brown eggs are laid from late May and are incubated by both sexes, commencing with the first egg, for 29–30 days. The chicks take to the water soon after hatching where they are tended by both parents for 12 weeks before they can fly. Single-brooded.

Food: Mainly fish, but with considerable quantities of molluscs and crustaceans. Dives for up to a minute, though it may submerge for much longer periods to escape danger.

Range and Distribution: Ranges across northern regions of North America from the Aleutian Islands to Newfoundland, and to Greenland and Iceland. In Europe it is a winter visitor to the coasts of Scandinavia, Britain and Ireland, and to the Channel coast of France. In Britain it was first proved to breed among the Inner Hebrides in 1970 and it regularly summers in Shetland.

Movements: Presumed Icelandic birds winter along the coasts of Scotland, Ireland and southwestern England. Elsewhere it occurs in small numbers.

Little Grebe

Tachybaptus ruficollis (Pallas)

A buoyant, dumpy aquatic bird that dives easily with the infuriating habit of disappearing completely when disturbed

Population: 10,000 to 20,000 pairs

Summer adult (foreground), winter (behind). Bold colours are lost in winter, but truncated shape precludes confusion with other grebes

In summer the Little Grebe, or Dabchick, is a brown-grey bird marked by rich chestnut sides and front to the neck. The crown and face are virtually black, but with an area of bare yellow skin at the gape. In winter it loses these colours and becomes a grey-brown bird best identified by its shape. The rear end of the body terminates vertically, whereas other small grebes tend to be more rounded or even sloping at the tail. They are usually found singly, though some favoured waters may attract quite high numbers to form loose flocks. When disturbed they will dive and emerge only under cover of dense vegetation where they are able to control their buoyancy and project only head and neck above the water's surface. 27 cm (10½ in).

Voice: A *whit-whit*, and a typical, high-pitched rippling trill.

Habitat: From small ponds and pools to large lakes, canals, slowly moving rivers, ditches and dykes, all with a strong growth of emergent and aquatic vegetation. In winter it may resort to sheltered estuaries and reservoirs.

Reproduction: The nest is a mound of plants built up above the water level, usually among dense emergent vegetation. Though nests have been recorded as early as February, April is the normal start of the breeding season. The 4–6, sometimes 2–10, eggs are white, but they soon become stained brown. Incubation, by both sexes, starts with the first egg and lasts 19–25 days. The chicks are striped in buff, brown and black, and leave the nest soon after hatching. They are often carried on their parents' backs when small and they fly after 44–48 days. Double-brooded, with an occasional third clutch.

Food: Small fish, especially sticklebacks, but also aquatic insects and their larvae, and crustaceans. Dives for 10–25 seconds.

Range and Distribution: Found over huge areas of the Old World from southern Sweden to South Africa, and from Iberia to Japan and Papua New Guinea. It is a summer visitor to northern and eastern Europe and to much of central Asia. In Britain and Ireland it is widespread, though thinly distributed in hilly districts.

Movements: Resident. Some Continental birds winter.

Great Crested Grebe

Podiceps cristatus (Linnaeus)

A beautiful aquatic species that was severely reduced by nineteenth-century plume hunters, but which has increased and spread under protection during the present century

Population: 5,000 pairs

The Great Crested Grebe is a magnificent and fascinating bird. The back is dark grey, the flanks buffish, the belly and foreneck white. It is, however, the beautiful head plumes that formerly endangered the species. From a white face they extend over the cheeks in a bright orange-red and are boldly tipped with black. The black of the crown extends to form an erectile crest. Much is made of this finery in the extraordinary courtship rituals. In winter the plumes are lost and it becomes a long-necked grey and white bird, with a dark line through the lores bordered above by a white supercilium. In the similar, though rarer, Red-necked Grebe the black of the crown extends to the eye. The bill is pink. Great Crested Grebes are frequently gregarious birds, forming breeding colonies at some waters and gathering into winter flocks. In flight they show considerable white in the wing. 48 cm (19 in).

Voice: A variety of strange calls including a *kar-arr*, a groaning, and a trumpeting bark.

Habitat: Large shallow waters with growth of emergent vegetation, usually in lowlands, but occasionally at some altitude.

Reproduction: Remarkable courtship in which the pair perform an elaborate series of movements, many of which make great use of the head plumes. They shake their heads, swim towards each other with necks low on the water's surface, bow, present weed to each other and so on. The nest is a mound of aquatic vegetation placed among reeds,

In the 'weed ceremony' the pair approach each other with necks low in the water and finally rise, treading water, turning their bills full of weed from side to side

on the bottom in shallow water, or floating anchored to an overhanging bush or to emergent vegetation. A neat cup holds the 4, occasionally 3–6, white eggs which are laid from May onwards. Incubation, commencing with the first egg, is performed by both sexes for the 25–29 days that the eggs take to hatch. When leaving the nest the sitting bird pulls vegetation over the clutch. The decaying mass of nesting material creates heat and forms an effective incubator even when the adults are not sitting. The chicks hatch over a period of several days and are boldly striped in downy plumage. They are frequently carried on the parents' backs and are fed and tended until they fly at 12 weeks. Sometimes double-brooded.

Food: Fish, insects and their larvae, crustaceans and molluscs are all important, as is vegetable matter. They also consume quantities of feathers. Dives average less than 30 seconds.

Range and Distribution: From Spain across Europe north to southern Sweden, to Siberia and western China. Also in isolated areas of Africa south of the Sahara and in Australia and New Zealand. Large areas of Siberia and Asia are deserted in winter, birds moving south within that continent. In Britain and Ireland the population has increased from 32 pairs in 1860 to about 5,000 pairs today. It is widespread in England, Wales and lowland Scotland, but absent from the southwest and from much of the southern half of Ireland.

Movements: Some winter movements, especially away from smaller lakes. Birds then gather on reservoirs and large estuaries, and are particularly numerous in the southeast.

Summer adult (foreground), winter (behind). Plumes and bold colours are lost in winter, but white area above eye remains

Red-necked Grebe

Podiceps grisegena (Boddaert)

An attractively marked grebe, a little smaller than the Great Crested, that usually occurs in Britain and Ireland only in dull winter garb. Adult in winter shown

Population: several hundred winter

Breeds in eastern Europe: moving south and west in winter to Britain and adjacent coastlines

Summer adult has distinct red foreneck with peaked crown

In summer the crown is black extending to the eye and terminating in a small crest or tuft. The sides of the head and chin are white, the neck a deep chestnut-red. The back is slaty-brown, the flanks grey and brown. Though some autumn birds still have remnants of this plumage, most visitors are clothed in various shades of grey. However, the black cap still extends to the eye, that of the Great Crested terminates in a white line above the eye, and usually the white face is bordered below by a grey neck. The bill is yellow with a black tip. They usually winter in coastal bays, though individuals may also be found inland on reservoirs. 43 cm (17 in).

Voice: A wailing song in summer; usual call note is a *keck*.

Habitat: In summer frequents quite small, marshy waters with much emergent vegetation; in winter found along coasts and in estuaries.

Reproduction: The nest is a mound of vegetation floating among emergent vegetation, but it may also rest on the bottom. The 4–5, occasionally 2–7, white eggs are laid at the end of April and incubated by both sexes for 22–25 days. The striped chicks leave the nest soon after hatching and are tended by both parents for 8–10 weeks before flying. Families tend to remain together for an extended period. Single-brooded.

Food: Predominantly aquatic insects and their larvae, also fish. Average dive lasts 30 seconds.

Range and Distribution: Circumpolar, but with significant gaps in central Siberia, in eastern North America and western Europe. Sporadic distribution in Europe outside Russia, eastwards from Denmark and southeastwards to Yugoslavia and the Black Sea. Winters along the coasts of southern Scandinavia and the North Sea.

Movements: Winter visitors are regular on the east coast from the Firth of Forth to the Channel. Scarce elsewhere and decidedly rare in Ireland and northern Scotland. Occasionally on London reservoirs.

Slavonian Grebe

Podiceps auritus (Linnaeus)

**A beautiful, small grebe marked
with bushy head tufts in summer
that are responsible for its North
American name of Horned Grebe. It
has bred in Scotland since 1908, but
its exact whereabouts are still kept
secret. Adult in winter shown**

Population: 37 to 51 pairs; several
hundred winter

Summer adult has bold golden tufts
extending from eye to nape

This grebe is clothed in summer in a startling mixture of bright
chestnut and black; in winter it becomes grey and white. The head
is black with 2 'horns' of bright orange-chestnut extending from the
lores, through the eye, to form bushy tufts at the rear of the crown. The
neck is chestnut as are the flanks. The back is black. In winter the
chestnut neck and horns and the black face are lost and it is separated
from the similar Black-necked Grebe by having a white, not grey, neck
that extends upwards behind the eye. In summer they are colonial,
nesting alongside Black-headed Gulls in some areas. 33 cm (13 in).

Voice: A long trill, together with a variety of other calls on the
breeding grounds.

Habitat: Large open waters with some growth of emergent vegetation,
often surrounded by barren moorland. Winters on sea coasts, but
regular on some inland reservoirs, particularly in autumn.

Reproduction: Territorial, but also invariably colonial. Nests are
often situated close together, frequently near that of a Black-headed
Gull. It consists of a mound of rotting vegetation anchored to some
emergent plants in shallow water. The 4, sometimes 3 or 5, white eggs
are laid from mid-May onwards and the female takes the larger share of
the incubation, which lasts 22–25 days and commences before the
clutch is complete. The chicks leave the nest soon after hatching and
are cared for by both parents, though the female may become pre-
occupied with a second nest.

Food: Mainly aquatic insects and their larvae, obtained by diving for
an average of 30–35 seconds; also takes small fish and crustaceans. In
winter takes mainly fish.

Range and Distribution: Circumpolar, though absent from eastern
North America and Greenland. In Europe it breeds in Iceland, Scotland and in parts of Norway and Sweden, and winters along the coasts
of Norway and Denmark, the North Sea and the Channel. Also in
Yugoslavia. In Britain it is confined to Scotland where in 1978 it bred
at 17 lochs. The main colony is in Inverness-shire and, even today,
suffers from illegal egg collecting.

Movements: Winter visitor to all coasts in small numbers, also regular
at London reservoirs.

Black-necked Grebe

Podiceps nigricollis (Brehm)

Beautifully coloured black and gold in summer, in winter the Black-necked Grebe becomes a dull grey bird with little to distinguish it. Adult in winter shown

Population: 13 to 15 pairs; several hundred winter

Summer adult marked by a fan of golden plumes over ear coverts

Summer plumage is black above and white below, separated by a variable line of chestnut on the flanks. The head and neck are black and a plume of feathers extends from the lores to the eye before fanning out over the 'ears'. In North America it is called the Eared Grebe. In winter the back and crown are slate-coloured with grey-white underparts and neck. This whitish area extends upwards in a comma behind the dusky ear coverts and, together with the fine uptilted bill, is the best means of separating the Black-necked from the otherwise similar Slavonian Grebe. It is generally colonial, though in Britain numbers are very small. 30 cm (12 in).

Voice: A variety of notes including some chattering and a low *poo-eep*.

Habitat: Shallow lagoons and lakes with luxuriant growth of emergent vegetation and comparatively little open water. In winter frequents coasts and large inland waters including reservoirs.

Reproduction: Builds a mound of decaying vegetation, usually in colonies often in association with Black-headed Gulls, among dense aquatic vegetation. The 3–4, occasionally 2–8, white eggs are laid from mid-April and incubated by both sexes for 20–21 days, starting with the first egg. The striped chicks leave the nest soon after hatching and are tended by both parents, sometimes together with the young of neighbouring pairs. Fledging may be as short as 21 days. A second brood is sometimes reared.

Food: Insects and their larvae, together with crustaceans, molluscs, amphibians and small fish. Frequently feeds on the surface.

Range and Distribution: Found in western North America, in Europe eastwards across Russia to central Siberia, in Turkey and Iran. In Britain it may nest anywhere conditions are suitable, but the main area is in the eastern lowlands of Scotland. A thriving colony that numbered 250 pairs in 1932 at Lough Funshinagh in Co. Roscommon was destroyed by drainage in 1934.

Movements: Birds pass through regularly in early autumn, frequenting inland reservoirs. In winter it is found along the coasts of southeast England and at a few other regular places elsewhere.

Fulmar

Fulmarus glacialis (Linnaeus)

A grey, gull-like petrel that flies shearwater-fashion on stiff wings and spends most of life roaming the oceans. It has increased dramatically over the last 100 years and has spread around our coasts from its original Hebridean base

Population: 300,000 pairs

Though gull-like in coloration, this is a typical petrel in structure and behaviour. The upperparts and wings are dove-grey, darker on the primaries. The head and underparts are pure white. The head is large and the neck thick, giving a bull-nosed effect that is particularly apparent in the air. It flaps its wings frequently, but stiffly as a whole, not stroking the air like a gull. At cliff breeding sites it can be picked out at considerable distances by its distinctive shape and method of flying. The bill is short and yellow, and marked by a typical petrel tube-nose on the upper mandible. Birds from the far north occur in a dark, as well as a typical, phase. They are sooty-grey all over, including the underparts, and can occasionally be seen in British and Irish waters. Fulmars are gregarious, forming colonies on sea cliffs and often gathering in large numbers around trawlers hauling their nets. 47 cm ($18\frac{1}{2}$ in).

Voice: A typical *ag-ag-ag-aar*, plus various grunting and growling notes at breeding sites.

Habitat: Open oceans, coming to sea cliffs to breed, but also occupying old ruined buildings and crags, occasionally some distance inland.

Reproduction: Though presumed young birds prospect new sites in summer they do not breed until they are 7 years old. Established birds occupy nesting sites very early in the year, and some even return in November. The single white egg is laid from mid-May onwards in a simple unlined hollow or rock ledge on a cliff, a wall, or on the ground in a ruined croft. It is incubated by both sexes for 55–57 days, each bird sitting for 4–5 days at a time. The chick is covered with grey down and is fed for 46–51 days by both parents prior to flying. Single-brooded. Disturbed or threatened Fulmars, both adult and nestling, eject oil from their mouths in a powerful jet that makes clothes smell for days. The fledgling spends several years at sea before returning to land to breed.

Food: Squid and fish, but also offal and waste from fishing and whaling activities.

Range and Distribution: Circumpolar in the high Arctic with populations both in Pacific and Atlantic. In Britain and Ireland it was confined to St Kilda until 1878 when Foula was colonized. Since then it has spread to every suitable sea cliff.

Movements: British and Irish birds range right across the Atlantic outside the breeding season.

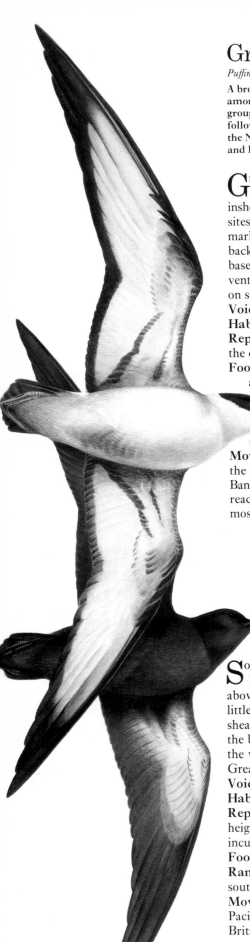

Great Shearwater

Puffinus gravis (O'Reilly)

A brown shearwater that breeds only among the islands of the remote Tristan group in the South Atlantic, and which follows a huge loop migration into the North Atlantic, bringing it to British and Irish shores in autumn

Great Shearwaters are not difficult to identify if good views are obtained. However, they are oceanic birds that seldom come close inshore, though they are recognized every year from major sea-watching sites, particularly in the west. They are brown above and white below, marked by a dark chocolate cap separated from the lighter wings and back by an almost complete white collar. There is a light patch at the base of the uppertail and a smudge of dark on the underparts near the vent. They fly in typical shearwater fashion, turning from side to side on stiff wings. Usually gregarious. 46 cm (18 in).

Voice: Gull-like cries.

Habitat: Remote islands; open oceans.

Reproduction: Nests in burrows, laying a single white egg towards the end of the year.

Food: Fish and squid taken by plunging or diving; also takes fish waste and will approach boats and even take fish offered from the hand.

Range and Distribution: Breeds only on Nightingale Island (2 million pairs), Inaccessible Island (150,000 pairs) and Gough Island (600,000 pairs) in Tristan da Cunha. A single pair was discovered in the Falkland Islands in 1961.

Movements: Moves away from the Tristan group after breeding to the coasts of South America, working northwards to reach the Grand Banks off Newfoundland by early summer. Some then move eastwards, reaching Britain, Ireland and Iberia from August to October. They are most numerous off Rockall and southwest Ireland.

Sooty Shearwater

Puffinus griseus (Gmelin)

A dark brown shearwater, with pale wing linings and more angled and flapping flight than most of its relatives. Breeds in the Southern Hemisphere, making huge loop migrations into the North Atlantic and North Pacific

Sooty Shearwaters can be found offshore along most British and Irish coasts in late summer and autumn. They are dark brown above and below and have pale, whitish wing linings. The feet project a little beyond the tail and the wings are held more at an angle than other shearwaters. The flight is often purposeful, less 'shearwatering', and the birds can be confused with a dark phase skua. However, they lack the white wing flashes of those species. They are not as gregarious as Great Shearwaters, but often occur with them. 41 cm (16 in).

Voice: Screams and gull-like cries.

Habitat: Isolated islands; otherwise pelagic.

Reproduction: Nests in burrows, often well inland at considerable heights. A single white egg is laid in November or December and incubating birds perform 4–6 day stints. Single-brooded.

Food: Squid, crustaceans and fish taken by shallow dives.

Range and Distribution: Islands off southern South America and southeastern Australia, and around New Zealand.

Movements: Performs huge migrations, taking it into the North Pacific as far as the Aleutians and North Atlantic as far as Iceland. In Britain and Ireland it occurs off most coasts in August and September.

Manx Shearwater

Puffinus puffinus (Brünnich)

A boldly pied bird that flies in typical 'shearwatering' fashion, showing first its black upperparts and then white underparts as it flies on stiff, often motionless, wings low over the water

Population: 300,000 pairs

Named from the Isle of Man, where as early as 1014 it was recorded breeding, the Manx Shearwater is locally abundant in a few areas of the coastal west. It is, however, a typical oceanic bird, coming to land only to breed and then, for reasons of safety, only under a cloak of darkness. It is black above and white below, the black extending well below the eye. In our waters it can be confused only with the extremely rare Little Shearwater *Puffinus assimilis*. A western Mediterranean subspecies, the so-called Balearic Shearwater *Puffinus puffinus mauretanicus*, is brown above and buff-grey below and lacks the contrast of the typical birds. It is an annual, if scarce, visitor to the Channel. 35 cm (14 in).

Voice: Generally silent at sea. At breeding sites utters a variety of cries, wails, screams and raucous howls that, being produced at night, have given rise to many a ghost story.

Habitat: Mainly uninhabited islands, though also island mountain tops and mainland cliffs; otherwise pelagic.

Reproduction: Nests in a burrow excavated in soft turf, or in natural holes among boulders and screes, often at considerable altitudes and occasionally some distance from the coast. The single white egg is laid in early May and incubated by both sexes in spells of 1–4 days for 47–55 days, with the male taking the first spell. The chick is brooded for 7 days and thereafter deserted during the day. It is fed every 1 or 2 days at night for 59–62 days and is then deserted. It remains in the burrow for a further week and then makes its own way to sea. These are clumsy birds on land and considerable toll is taken by Great Black-backed Gulls, particularly of youngsters as they fledge. Most birds breed at 5–6 years old. Single-brooded.

Food: Small fish, squid, crustaceans and fish offal taken by plunge-diving and from the surface.

Range and Distribution: A series of colonies extending from southern Iceland to the Mediterranean. Britain and Ireland are the world stronghold with a third of the population breeding among the mountain-top screes of the Isle of Rhum. Also found on islands off New Zealand, Hawaii and Baja California.

Movements: Our birds range right across the Atlantic with a regular migration to the eastern coasts of southern South America. The western Mediterranean subspecies moves out into the Atlantic, and some regularly wander north to Channel coasts, particularly to Cornwall from July to October.

Storm Petrel

Hydrobates pelagicus (Linnaeus)

Black, sparrow-sized seabird with a prominent white rump that flies low over the sea and comes to its few remote breeding stations only under cover of darkness. As a result it is exceedingly difficult to observe

Population: 50,000 pairs, or several times that number

An all-black bird with a faint grey bar across the folded wing which forms a neat wing bar in flight. The tail is square cut, and the rump a prominent white. There is also a pale bar on the underwing across the wing linings. The Storm Petrel flits low over the water and has a fluttering feeding flight in which the legs are held dangling below. It picks small items of food from the surface, and regularly follows in the wake of ships. 15 cm (6 in).

Voice: Silent, except at breeding stations where it utters a purring *arrr-r-r-r*, a rapid *wick-wick-wick* and a *terr-chick* in aerial chases.

Habitat: Uninhabited islands and remote and inaccessible mainland promontories; otherwise pelagic.

Reproduction: Nests in a burrow, which it may excavate itself, or in a side chamber of a rabbit or Puffin burrow. Alternatively it occupies crevices among rocks and dry-stone walls. It is colonial. The single white egg is laid between mid-June and mid-July and incubated for 38–50 days by both sexes in spells of 1–5 days. The male takes the first spell. The chick is fed and brooded for 6–7 days and then fed most nights until it is about 50 days old. It fledges some 2–3 days after its last feed. A quarter to half of the eggs laid produce fledged young. Single-brooded.

Food: Small crustaceans, squid and fish picked from the surface of the sea, frequently at night.

Range and Distribution: Breeds at a chain of colonies extending from Iceland to Sicily in the Mediterranean, but the greatest concentration is in Scotland and western Ireland with 2 notable colonies, both of which are in Co. Kerry, at Inishtearaght (20,000 pairs) and Inishvickillane (10,000 pairs).

Movements: Outside the breeding season Storm Petrels range northwards to Norway, throughout the eastern Atlantic south to the Cape of Good Hope, and in the western Mediterranean.

Leach's Petrel

Oceanodroma leucorhoa (Vieillot)

A Starling-sized, all-black seabird with a white rump and notably forked tail. Otherwise very similar to Storm Petrel, but decidedly rarer and even more difficult to see

Population: several thousand pairs

Forked tail difficult to observe at sea, but bounding flight and pale grey wing bar separate from similar Storm Petrel

The difference in size between this and the Storm Petrel is of little use in a featureless sea. They are very similar in plumage, black above and below and with a light bar extending across the wing in flight. Both have white rumps, though in the present species this is more crescent-like in shape rather than rectangular, and there is also a greyish central stripe cutting the white in two. The distinctly forked tail of Leach's, however, separates the species immediately. Leach's does not follow ships in the manner of the Storm Petrel and is generally encountered singly or in small parties. Flight is highly erratic and it does not patter over the water's surface as do so many storm petrels. 20 cm (8 in).

Voice: An *r-r-r-r* purring note, and a repeated chattering of 8 notes.

Habitat: Isolated, uninhabited islands; at sea, but tends to remain nearer land than other storm petrels, usually over the continental shelf.

Reproduction: Nests in colonies in banks and beneath rocks, and occasionally in rock crevices. Several pairs may share a communal entrance hole. The male alone excavates the nest and the single white egg is laid at the end of May. The male takes first stint of incubation, which is then shared in spells of 1–6 days for 41–42 days. The chick is brooded for 5 days and then fed every night by both parents. It fledges after 63–70 days, but is not deserted. Single-brooded.

Food: Planktonic molluscs and crustaceans, small fish and some offal picked from the surface in flight.

Range and Distribution: Found along the Pacific coast of North America from the Aleutians south to Mexico; along the western Atlantic in Newfoundland and adjacent parts of Canada; and in Iceland, Faeroes, Norway and Scotland. Scottish colonies at St Kilda, Flannan Islands, North Rona and Sula Sgeir; with breeding elsewhere only irregular. It has bred in Ireland on several occasions and may still do so.

Movements: Ranges over most of the North Atlantic outside the breeding season.

Gannet

Sula bassana (Linnaeus)

Huge white bird with black wing tips that flies on long stiff wings, and finds its food by diving spectacularly headfirst into the sea from great heights. Forms dense colonies and has been the subject of continuous population monitoring for 70 years

Population: 140,000 pairs

The adult Gannet is a goose-like bird (it was formerly called the Solan Goose) with long pointed wings that flies over the waves in shearwater fashion. It is white above and below with a distinctive wash of yellow on the head, and with large black wing tips. In flight the pointed tail balances the head and neck to produce a cigar-like shape. The bill is steel-grey, heavy, and sharply pointed. Immatures are black speckled with white, and become progressively whiter over 4 years before assuming full adult plumage. They are gregarious outside the breeding season, and are most often seen in small parties moving in line like geese. Huge numbers may, however, gather around a fishing vessel as the nets are hauled, disposing of discarded fish. 90 cm (36 in).

Second year bird (above) and first year bird. Adult plumage is adopted over a 4 year period during which variable patches of dark slate-brown remain

Voice: Mainly silent at sea; at colonies utters a loud *urrah*, a groaning *oo-ah* and a soft *crok-crok*.

Habitat: Uninhabited islands and stacks, also mainland cliffs. Some colonies are cliff-based, others on flat-topped holms.

Reproduction: An elaborate series of ritualized displays includes bowing, preening and head-pointing. Nesting begins in April with eggs laid at the end of that month or in May. The nest itself is a conical structure made of piled-up seaweed bound together with droppings. A neat cup on the top is lined with grasses and feathers and the single pale blue egg is incubated for 42–46 days by both sexes. Unlike the majority of birds, the Gannet lacks a brood patch and incubates by placing its webbed feet on the egg. The chick is brooded for the first 2 weeks after hatching and is fed by both parents by regurgitation until it fledges after 84–97 days. Single-brooded. Gannets nest closely side by side, the size of each territory being roughly the area the sitting bird can reach with its bill. There is thus a remarkably even distribution over a Gannetry that is discernible from a considerable distance. Birds alighting in the wrong place, as well as wandering chicks, are attacked mercilessly by the owners of territories they pass through, and for this reason disturbance must be kept to an absolute minimum once the chicks have hatched.

Food: Fish up to 30 cm in length captured by diving from the air. Dives vary from 5 to 20 seconds and prey is swallowed whole as the bird surfaces.

Range and Distribution: Confined to the North Atlantic with colonies around Newfoundland, Iceland, Britain and Ireland, Norway and Faeroes, and islands in the Channel. The British and Irish population represents about 70 per cent of the world total. St Kilda is by far the largest, with 40 per cent of the British and Irish total. Once decimated by direct human predation, the population continues to increase under protection and new colonies are still being established.

Movements: Outside the breeding season Gannets range over both sides of the North Atlantic, southwards to Florida in the west and Gambia in the east. They are generally absent from areas between.

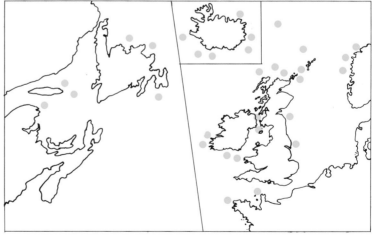

World distribution of North Atlantic Gannet

North Atlantic Gannetries:
total in pairs with date of census

Rouzic, Sept Iles, Brittany	2,500 (1967)	
Ortac, Channel Isles	1,000 (1969)	
Les Étacs, Channel Isles	2,000 (1969)	
Great Saltee, Co. Wexford	155 (1969)	
Bull Rock, Co. Cork	1,500 (1970)	
Little Skellig, Co. Kerry	20,000 (1969)	
Grassholm, Dyfed	16,128 (1969)	
Bempton, Yorkshire	18 (1969)	
Scar Rocks, Wigtownshire	450 (1969)	
Ailsa Craig, Ayrshire	13,054 (1969)	
St Kilda, Outer Hebrides	52,000 (1969)	
Flannan Isles, Outer Hebrides	16 (1969)	
Sula Sgeir, Outer Hebrides	8,964 (1969)	
Sule Stack, Outer Hebrides	4,018 (1969)	
Hermaness, Shetland	5,894 (1969)	
Noss, Shetland	4,300 (1969)	
Bass Rock, East Lothian	8,977 (1969)	
Runde, Norway	383 (1971)	
Mosken, Lofoten, Norway	77 (1971)	
Nordmjele, Norway	65 (1971)	
Syltefjord, Norway	44 (1971)	
Mykinesholm, Faeroes	1,081 (1966)	
Westman Islands, Iceland	5,315 (1960)	
Eldey, Iceland	15,000 (1962)	
Raudinupur, Iceland	34 (1961)
Stori Karl, Iceland	63 (1961)
Skrudur, Iceland	314 (1961)
Mafadrangur, Iceland	100 (1962)
Cape St Mary's, Newfoundland	c3,000 (1969)
Baccalieu Island, Newfoundland	351 (1969)
Funk Island, Newfoundland	2,987 (1971)
Anticosti Island, Quebec	144 (1969)
Bonaventure Island, Quebec	21,215 (1966)
Bird Rocks, Quebec	3,353 (1969)

Total: 194,500 pairs

Often goose-like in flight, but distinguishable in all lights by its prominent pointed tail

Cormorant

Phalacrocorax carbo (Linnaeus)

Large black seabird that swims low in the water and has a strangely primitive and serpentine look. It dives for fish, but soon becomes waterlogged and has to hang out its wings to dry in the wind

Population: about 8,000 pairs

The Cormorant appears black at any distance, though a closer approach reveals a metallic green sheen to the feathers that, bordered with black, produces a scaled effect. The bill is yellowish; the feet large, palmated and black. In summer the adult has a bold white patch on the face and a neat circular white patch on the flank. The latter is lost, the former reduced, in winter. Immatures are brown above, buffy below. They are generally gregarious, nesting in colonies and flocking in winter. Small groups often fly goose-like in line and indeed Cormorants are similar to geese in flight. They find their food by diving from the surface and are considered an enemy by fishermen. Among British and Irish birds only the Shag is similar, but that is a smaller bird and lacks any areas of white. 90 cm (36 in).

Voice: Silent except at breeding sites where it utters a large range of raucous calls with much individual variation.

Habitat: Coastal waters, particularly over rocky shorelines; also inland on reservoirs, floods, rivers and backwaters. Prefers coastal sites in Britain and Ireland.

Reproduction: The nest is sited on sea cliffs or among rocks on offshore stacks and islets; usually colonial. The 3, occasionally 2–5, pale blue eggs are laid from early April and incubated by both sexes for 30 days, beginning with the first egg. The chicks are born naked and are remarkably serpentine. They are fed by both parents for 50–60 days before fledging. Single-brooded.

Food: Entirely fish obtained by diving for 15–60 seconds. Prey is brought to the surface and may be thrown into the air before being swallowed whole.

Range and Distribution: Found over huge areas of the world from eastern Canada through Europe and Siberia to Japan, through China and India, in Australia and New Zealand, and over much of Africa. In Britain and Ireland it is primarily coastal with most birds frequenting the rocky western coastlines. It is all but absent from the Isle of Wight to Flamborough Head.

Movements: Dispersal around coasts in winter rather than true migration.

Shag

Phalacrocorax aristotelis (Linnaeus)

Large black seabird similar to, but noticeably smaller than, the Cormorant, with a tufted crest in summer. It has the same serpentine qualities as its larger relative and the same habit of 'hanging out' its wings to dry

Population: 30,000 pairs

At any distance the Shag is an all-black bird that sits low in the water, often with its back awash. A closer approach reveals a green metallic sheen. It dives easily and, like the Cormorant, swims underwater by using its large, totipalmate feet as paddles. At all seasons it lacks white on chin or flank and has a relatively small bill. The gape is marked by a patch of bright yellow bare skin. Juveniles are brown above and buff below like immature Cormorants. These are exclusively marine birds confined to rocky coasts, where they may form quite large colonies in particularly favoured areas. They fly with faster wing beats than the Cormorant and often form goose-like lines or V formations. 76 cm (30 in).

Voice: A loud *ar-ar*, broken by brief clicking notes.

Habitat: Rocky coasts, seldom venturing even to other shorelines and very rare inland.

Reproduction: Breeds in colonies among broken sea cliffs, especially screes. The nest is a pile of seaweed hidden in a rock cleft, usually with a second exit, and is built by the female from material brought by the male. The 3, occasionally 2–6, light blue eggs are laid from mid-March onwards and incubated by both sexes for 30–31 days, starting with the first egg. The chicks are fed by both parents for the 50–60 days they take to fledge, but are still dependent on them for a further month or so. Single-brooded.

Food: Almost entirely fish taken by diving from the surface, occasionally from the air. Average dive 40 seconds, but up to 4 minutes has been recorded.

Range and Distribution: Almost confined to Europe, breeding from the Atlantic coast of North Africa, through the Mediterranean to coastal Turkey and Cyprus. Also along the Atlantic seaboard to the North Cape of Norway and the Kola Peninsula. Absent from most North Sea coasts and the Baltic. In Britain and Ireland it breeds from the Isle of Wight westwards with only a single Shaggery on the English east coast. Highest numbers found in Scotland, particularly Shetland.

Movements: Resident, but post-breeding dispersal takes some youngsters as far as Norway and Iberia.

Bittern

Botaurus stellaris (Linnaeus)

A beautifully camouflaged, brown and buff heron found only in large reed beds where it is easily located by its booming call, but is extremely difficult to see. It is a self-effacing bird that seldom ventures into the open and only rarely takes to the air

The camouflaged plumage of the Bittern blends perfectly with the patterns created by the old dry reeds among which it lives. When surprised it has a curious sky-pointing posture that exposes the stripes on the neck and breast which resemble reeds. It even moves from side to side in an imitation of wind-caught reeds. The overall impression is of a brown bird, speckled with black and buff. The crown is black and there is a clear moustachial streak. The fine vermiculations on the back and wings are difficult to admire on the living bird, but the sharply pointed yellow bill and strong green legs and feet are obvious enough. In the air the broad rounded wings, virtual lack of tail and floppy flight are useful and really can only be confused with an immature Night Heron (see *Rare Birds*, p. 339). 76 cm (30 in).

Voice: A low, far-carrying, booming note similar to a ship's foghorn repeated 2 or 3 times. Also an *aark*.

Habitat: Large, dense reed beds wherever they may be found.

Reproduction: The nest is a heap of reeds and other vegetation built up among dense reeds and constructed by the female alone. The male may be polygamous. The 4–6, occasionally 3–7, olive-brown eggs are laid in early April and incubated by the female, starting with the first egg, for 25–26 days. The chicks are cared for by the female for 14–21 days in the nest and for a further 5–6 weeks after leaving. Single-brooded.

Food: Fish, amphibians, aquatic insects and their larvae, small birds and mammals.

Range and Distribution: Found right across temperate Eurasia from Spain to northern Japan, and also in South Africa. Winters south of this range in India, China and Mediterranean Europe. In Britain it was decimated by drainage and exterminated by shooting, and the last pair bred in 1868. However, by 1900 it was breeding again in Norfolk, by 1926 in Suffolk and it has since spread to several parts of the country west to Glamorgan and north to Lancashire. The stronghold remains East Anglia, but there has been a gradual decline in recent years.

Movements: Resident; some immigration of winter visitors from adjacent parts of the Continent to East Anglia and southern England.

Population: probably less than 50 pairs

Grey Heron

Ardea cinerea (Linnaeus)

Largest, and the only common and widespread, heron in Britain and Ireland. Spends much time standing motionless in shallow water waiting for fish to swim within reach of its dagger-like bill

Population: 6,500 to 11,500 pairs

In flight neck
is folded back
on shoulders and legs trail behind.
Wings held bowed like a gull

Long bill and legs, both yellow. The back is grey, covered with white plumes in the breeding season. The head and neck are white with a crest of black plumes extending backwards from the eye, and a broad black stripe running down the front of the neck to the breast. Remaining underparts are white. In flight the legs extend well beyond the tail, but the neck is tucked back on itself giving a typically bulky shape. The wings are bowed in the manner of a gull or Osprey and black primaries contrast with grey inner wing. 90–98 cm (36–39 in).

Voice: A harsh, far-carrying *frarnk* that is frequently uttered in flight. At the nest it claps its bill and produces a variety of discordant calls.

Habitat: Virtually all freshwater habitats, ponds, lakes, reservoirs, floods and marshes. It is found in brackish habitats on estuaries and even sometimes on open shores. Drainage dykes are particularly favoured.

Reproduction: Grey Herons breed in tree-top colonies. Many heronries are small, consisting of 1–5 pairs, but some are quite large with up to 25 pairs in a single tree. Heronries occupy traditional sites which may be used generation after generation. Sites are occupied and nests rebuilt of twigs lined with grass early in the new year and the 4–5 eggs are usually laid at the end of March. Both sexes incubate for a total of 25–26 days, commencing with the first egg. The young, which are covered with white down at hatching, leave the nest after 20–30 days, having been brooded continuously for 18 days and fed by both parents on regurgitated fish. Breeding success is variable, but 2–3 young are usually reared. Single-brooded.

Food: Predominantly fish which are caught between the mandibles, but also occasionally speared. Also amphibians, small mammals and birds, and insects. A certain amount of vegetation is taken.

Range and Distribution: Found virtually throughout the Old World from temperate Europe (it is generally rather localized in the Mediterranean) eastwards across Russia and Siberia to Japan. In Asia it extends southwards through China into India and Sri Lanka and is also present in southern Malaya and in Java. It occupies most of savannah Africa, being absent only from the Sahara and sahel zones and from the equatorial forests. It is also found on Madagascar. In Britain and Ireland it is widespread with a variable resident population in something approaching 1,000 heronries. Heronries in Scotland and Ireland tend to be smaller than those in England and Wales.

Movements: British birds are nomadic rather than migratory, with very few leaving the country.

Spoonbill

Platalea leucorodia (Linnaeus)

**A heron-like white bird, with a huge
spatulate bill, that flies with neck
held straight, bill protruding
forward and legs trailing behind.
Formerly bred, but now only a
passage and occasional winter
visitor, mainly to East Anglia**

Continental breeding distribution:
small numbers on passage

Uniquely adapted to filter feeding, the bill is long and flat, terminating in a broad flat spoon. It is scythed from side to side in
shallow water and mud to sift out the small organisms on which the
bird feeds. The plumage is all white, but with a wash of yellow on face
and lower foreneck in summer when there is also a tufted crest. The
legs are black, the bill dark horn with a paler tip. Immatures have black
tips to the outer primaries. Spoonbills are gregarious birds, feeding and
flying in small parties and nesting colonially. 86 cm (34 in).

Voice: Usually silent, but produces a quiet *huh-huh-huh* at nest.

Habitat: Shallow freshwater lagoons, but also shallow estuaries and
adjacent floods.

Reproduction: Breeds colonially among reeds, bushes or trees, sometimes in association with herons and egrets. The nest is an untidy
platform of twigs in tree nests, of reeds and other aquatic vegetation
when on the ground. The 4, occasionally 3–6, white eggs are spotted
with red-brown and laid in April or May. They are incubated by both
sexes for 21 days, commencing before the clutch is complete. The
chicks are fed by both parents for 45–50 days. Single-brooded.

Food: Insects and their larvae, molluscs, crustaceans, amphibians,
small fish.

Range and Distribution: Found from Europe and West Africa
through the Middle East to central Siberia, India and Manchuria. In
Europe it has a relict distribution with single isolated colonies scattered
about the Continent. It is most numerous in southeast Europe, and
western Europe has colonies only in southern Spain and Holland. It is
from this latter area that British birds doubtless originate. Recent years
have seen extended spring stays, particularly at Minsmere, and there is
some faint hope that the visitors may eventually breed.

Movements: Spring and autumn passage bring Spoonbills to south
and eastern England, and there are usually records of wintering from
Cornwall and southwestern Ireland.

Mute Swan

Cygnus olor (Gmelin)

Weighing up to 18 kilos, this is one of the world's heaviest flying birds. The huge size, white plumage, orange bill and aggressive behaviour make the Mute Swan one of the most familiar of all our birds

Population: over 5,000 pairs

Easily identified, and confusable only with the 2 wild swans that come to us as winter visitors, the Mute Swan is a widespread resident on waters as diverse as huge lakes and village ponds. The male (cob) is larger than his mate (pen) and his bright orange bill is surmounted by a large black knob; that of the female is much smaller. Though often gregarious, forming large colonies in several areas, small waters are defended vigorously against intruders. These are driven off by an elaborate, and beautiful, series of threat displays. Young swans are a dirty-grey buff and take several years to acquire full adult plumage. Mute Swans can be identified at a considerable distance by the characteristic serpentine angle of the neck. Bewick's and Whooper Swans hold their necks straight, have yellow bases to their bills, and frequently utter loud honking notes. 152 cm (60 in).

Voice: Hissing and other sounds; 'mute' only in comparison with other species of swan.

Habitat: Rivers and tidal estuaries, lakes, reservoirs and ponds, marshes, floods and, in winter, sheltered coasts.

Reproduction: Generally solitary, but large traditional colonies of near-domesticated birds can be found, as at Abbotsbury in Dorset. The nest is a huge mound of plant debris that may be added to year after year. It is placed near the water's edge and the 5–7, occasionally 4–12, white or light blue eggs are laid from mid-April and incubated mainly by the female. Incubation takes 35–42 days and the chicks (cygnets) leave the nest soon after hatching. They are tended by both parents and remain with the adults for several months, or until the start of the next breeding season. Single-brooded.

Food: Aquatic vegetation, frequently taken by upending. Also takes spilt grain and feeds among stubbles.

Range and Distribution: Found right across Eurasia, but only in pockets, and absent from large areas. Introduced to many other areas particularly in Europe. Also introduced to North America, Australia, New Zealand and South Africa. In Britain and Ireland it is widespread in the lowlands, but absent from most hilly districts. It has recently declined in numbers.

Movements: Resident; Scandinavian and Baltic birds migrate to winter in the Skagerrak.

Bewick's Swan

Cygnus columbianus (Yarrell)

The smaller of the 2 wild swans, with a smaller and more rounded patch of yellow on the bill. It is a winter visitor, mainly to England, that gathers into quite large flocks at a few favoured locations

Population: 2,000 winter.

Adult (foreground) and juvenile

Bewick's Swan is an all-white bird marked by a black bill, with a rounded patch of yellow at the base. The size and shape of the yellow varies enormously, with the result that individuals can be identified at regular wintering spots such as the Wildfowl Trust's refuge at Slimbridge. They fly in skeins or lines, keeping together as family parties through the winter and so enabling ornithologists to calculate breeding success. They are gregarious, gathering into large flocks at favoured feeding grounds. Thus the total British wintering population may be only 2,000, but 1,000 of these may be found at the Ouse Washes. Unlike Mute Swans, these are highly vocal birds that utter honking goose-like cries, particularly in flight. They engage in elaborate courtship displays and fights while still in winter quarters. 122 cm (48 in).

Voice: Loud honking in flight, a quieter babbling when feeding.

Habitat: Low, marshy tundra with pools and lakes; in winter frequents flooded grassland and shallow reservoir margins.

Reproduction: Usually quite sociable, with pairs breeding in sight of one another. The nest is a mound of moss and lichens constructed at the water's edge or on an islet. The 4, occasionally 3 or 5, white eggs are laid in the first half of June and incubated for 29–30 days. The chicks are tended by both parents and fly after 40–45 days. They remain as a family, migrating to winter quarters together. Single-brooded.

Food: Entirely vegetable matter – roots, leaves, shoots of aquatic vegetation, and similar on dry ground. Takes cereals where available.

Range and Distribution: Circumpolar from Novaya Zemlya right across tundra Asia to Alaska and the Canadian Arctic as far east as Baffin Island. Absent from Greenland, Iceland and Spitsbergen. It is called the Whistling Swan where it occurs in North America.

Movements: Migrates southwards to winter in Europe around the shores of the North Sea. In Britain and Ireland it is confined to a few traditional haunts, mostly in the south.

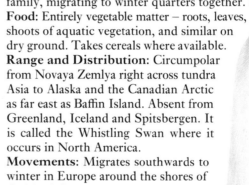

Bewick's Swan Bills

The rounded shape of the yellow on the black bill of the Bewick's Swan is the diagnostic means of separating this from our other wild swan, the Whooper. Yet a closer look shows a great deal of individual variation

As the result of an intensive feeding programme, several hundred wild Bewick's Swans have been encouraged to form a regular winter flock at the Wildfowl Trust's New Grounds at Slimbridge. Over a period of years these birds have become comparatively tame, allowing a close approach and intimate observation. Sir Peter Scott noted that individual adults varied considerably in the extent and pattern of yellow on their bills and that such patterns did not change. Thus individuals could be recognized from year to year, facilitating studies of survival rate, companionship and movements. Eight typical patterns are shown here. Though all maintain the basically rounded shape that is an aid in separating this species from the Whooper Swan, the variations are immense both in shape and, surprisingly, in colour.

Whooper Swan

Cygnus cygnus (Linnaeus)

A wild swan, with pointed yellow patch on bill, that has occasionally nested in Scotland

Population: about 5,500 birds winter

Leaves tundra breeding grounds to winter in temperate Europe

Considerably larger than the other wild British swan, the Bewick's, the Whooper has the same upright neck and a yellow patch on the bill that is pointed rather than truncated. It is generally gregarious in winter, forming small flocks rather than the larger gatherings favoured by Bewick's. It flies strongly and is highly vocal both in the air and on the ground. Young Whoopers are similar to other young swans in grey-buff plumage. The bill is similarly pink, but lacks the base of black that identifies the young Mute Swan. 152 cm (60 in).

Voice: Loud trumpeting flight calls and a clear *hoop-hoop-hoop*.

Habitat: Breeds among tundra pools and lakes; in winter frequents lakes, reservoirs and sea coasts. Whooper Swans frequently graze flooded grassland.

Reproduction: The large mound of vegetation that forms a nest is placed near the water's edge on an island or promontory. It breeds in isolation from other swans, and the 5–6, sometimes 4–8, white eggs are laid from early May depending on local weather conditions. The female incubates, while her mate remains nearby, for 35–42 days. The young are then tended by both parents which remain with them for the rest of the year, migrating as a family party. Single-brooded.

Food: Aquatic vegetation obtained by upending; in the winter also frequently feeds on farmland, taking grass, potatoes and waste cereals.

Range and Distribution: Across northern Eurasia from Iceland and Scandinavia to the Bering Sea. It formerly bred in Orkney, but is now an irregular breeder in northern Scotland. One pair produced 3 young in 1978.

Movements: Icelandic birds winter in Scotland and Ireland, while a few Scandinavian birds can be found in East Anglia. The largest numbers occur in various parts of Scotland.

Bean Goose

Anser fabalis (Latham)

A large 'grey' goose, formerly numerous as a winter visitor, but which has declined seriously and is now confined to 2 winter flocks – 1 in the north, 1 in the east

Continental summer distribution: less than 100 in Britain

Bean are typical 'grey' geese, being predominantly brown with a greyish sheen on back and underparts. The head and neck are dark brown shading lighter on breast and back. There is a narrow white line along the lower edge of the folded wing and the white tips to the coverts form a series of narrow bars across it. The undertail coverts are white, the tail white with a broad grey terminal band above. The large bill is yellow with a narrow black base, and the legs and feet are also yellow. This species is often regarded as conspecific with the Pink-footed Goose which is similarly dark-headed, but that bird has a pink bill and feet and is considerably smaller. Bean Geese are gregarious in winter, but the small numbers that now occur in Britain form only 2 regular flocks. 71–89 cm (28–35 in).

Voice: Rather quieter than other 'grey' geese – a deep *ung-unk* is the characteristic call.

Habitat: Breeds among lakes and marshes in forested country or open tundra, mostly beyond the Arctic Circle; winters on grasslands usually near water.

Reproduction: The nest is a scrape lined with mosses and lichens, with an inner lining of down. The 4–5, occasionally 3–7, whitish eggs are laid in late May or June and incubated by the female alone for 25–28 days. The chicks are tended by both parents and remain with them into winter quarters. Single-brooded.

Food: Mainly grazing on grassland, but also takes cereals and other arable crops.

Range and Distribution: From Scandinavia across northern Eurasia to the Bering Sea. Winters in Europe and the Far East in Japan and China. The Scandinavian population has been considerably reduced, accounting for the decline in winter numbers in Britain.

Movements: The large Russian population winters along the southern edge of the North Sea, particularly in Denmark and Holland. In Britain there are small flocks near Dumfries and on the Yare Marshes behind Yarmouth. Elsewhere accidental.

Pink-footed Goose

Anser brachyrhynchus (Baillon)

**Smallest of the 'grey' geese, but the
most numerous wild goose in Britain
in winter. It forms truly huge flocks
in favoured localities**

Population: about 75,000 winter

In flight shows dark neck
and pale forewing

Small, dark-headed, small-billed goose marked with a pink bill with
a broad black base, and pink legs and feet. The wing coverts are
edged with white forming a series of transverse bars across the folded
wing, with a white line extending along its lower edge. The undertail
coverts are white, and the white tail has a broad grey terminal band
above. In flight the grey forewings contrast with the dark flight
feathers, though not as pronounced as in the larger Greylag. Pink-foots
are extremely gregarious, nesting in loose colonies and forming huge
winter flocks. 61–76 cm (24–30 in).

Voice: Highly vocal, producing a cacophony of calls – *ung-unk*, *wink-
wink-wink*, etc.

Habitat: Breeds on open tundra, rocky hillsides, gorges and arctic
deltas and oases.

Reproduction: Nests on the ground in a scrape lined with moss and
down, in loose colonies starting in early June. The 4–5, occasionally up
to 8, cream-coloured eggs are incubated by the female for 25–28 days,
while her mate mounts guard nearby. The chicks leave the nest and are
taken to water immediately. They fledge at 8 weeks, but for a period
both moulting adults and young are flightless. At this time large packs
are formed. Single-brooded.

Food: Considerable seasonal variation, but always vegetable matter
depending on local abundance; cereals, potatoes and grass predominate
in winter.

Range and Distribution: Found only on the east coast of Greenland
and Iceland (75,000 birds), and in Spitsbergen (12,000 birds).

Movements: The entire Greenland–Iceland population winters in
Britain, mainly in Scotland and northwest England, arriving in October
and departing in April. The Spitsbergen population winters in Denmark,
Germany and Holland, with a few individuals reaching eastern England.
Large concentrations at Loch Leven, the Solway and at Southport.

White-fronted Goose

Anser albifrons (Scopoli)

White base to the bill and broad dark patches on belly make this one of the easiest of 'grey' geese to identify

Population: about 18,500 winter

In flight shows heavily barred underparts, though immature lacks both barring and white at base of bill

A 'grey' goose with brown plumage marked by a white line beneath the folded wing, white undertail coverts, and a grey terminal band to a white uppertail. The base of the bill is marked by a broad area of white that extends to the front of the crown to form the 'white front'. This feature can be seen at a considerable distance as can the dark, smudged bands on the belly. The legs are orange but, while the Russian White-front has a pink bill, those from Greenland have orange bills. Immatures lack the white at the base of the bill and have little or no barring below. White-fronts are typically gregarious and generally occur in a few large flocks. 66–76 cm (26–30 in).

Voice: A high-pitched *kow-lyow*.

Habitat: Tundra river banks and islands; in winter usually on flooded grassland and marshes.

Reproduction: Semicolonial, lining a scrape with mosses and down. The 5–6, occasionally 4 or 7, whitish eggs are laid in mid-June and incubated by the female for 27–28 days, while her mate stands guard nearby. The chicks are tended by both parents and migrate with them as a family party to winter quarters. Single-brooded.

Food: Grass and salting plants dominate in winter; also grazes on its breeding grounds in summer.

Range and Distribution: Breeds right across Eurasia in the far north from Novaya Zemlya to the Bering Sea, and sporadically across Alaska and northern Canada to the east coast of Greenland.

Movements: Two distinct subspecies migrate to Europe. Greenland White-fronts *Anser albifrons flavirostris* move to Ireland (8,000) with a further population in Scotland and western Wales (4,500). Russian White-fronts (6,000) winter in southern England and south Wales, but with much larger numbers in Holland and northern Germany.

Greylag Goose

Anser anser (Linnaeus)

Largest of the 'grey' geese and our only native breeding species. This is the ancestor of all domestic geese and is named after its prominent pale grey forewing

Population: Some 200 pairs breed; about 65,000 winter

Bold pale forewing contrasting with darker saddle is diagnostic of the species in flight

Considerably larger and paler than other 'grey' geese, the Greylag is grey above and below, marked with a pale line below the folded wing. It has white undertail coverts and a broad grey terminal band below a white uppertail. There are a few dark smudges on the belly, but these are never as pronounced as in the White-front. The legs and feet are pink, the large bill orange, though there is an eastern form that has a pink bill. In flight the pale grey forewing contrasts strongly with dark flight feathers. These are gregarious birds usually found in small to medium-sized flocks that roost on inland fresh waters. 76–89 cm (30–35 in).

Voice: A clanging *aahng-ung-ung*, as in the domestic goose.

Habitat: Breeds among marshes, lakes and reed beds largely in the temperate zone; winters on grasslands, estuaries, crops and lakes.

Reproduction: The Greylag forms loose colonies and builds its somewhat sparse nest on the ground on an islet, or among dense reeds. The 4–6, occasionally 3–8, creamy eggs are laid in late March or April, and are incubated by the female alone for 27–28 days. Both parents tend the young which fledge after 8 weeks, but remain in family parties well into the winter. Single-brooded.

Food: Takes a wide variety of aquatic plants as well as grass and crops. Seasonal pattern varies according to availability, but in Scotland a cycle of barley stubble, potatoes and grazing is followed.

Range and Distribution: Found from Iceland through Britain, Scandinavia and eastern Europe across Russia and central Siberia to Japan. It occupies a zone to the south of most other geese. In Britain and Ireland true native birds are found only in the Outer Hebrides, especially at Loch Druidibeg, and adjacent parts of the Scottish mainland. However, feral populations have become established in many parts of the country and have prospered under a new protective attitude. Main centres are the Scottish Solway, southern Lake District, Norfolk and the Belfast area.

Movements: The whole Icelandic population winters in Britain, mostly in Scotland, but also in northern England.

Canada Goose

Branta canadensis (Linnaeus)

A large brown goose, with a black neck and white cheek patch, that has been introduced to Britain and has prospered. In its native North America it is a wilderness bird with a well-developed migratory urge; where introduced it has become tame and resident

Far larger than other 'black' geese, the Canada's upperparts are brown delicately barred with buff; the underparts buff barred with brown. The undertail coverts are white, the tail white with a broad black terminal band. The neck and head are black with a large white patch extending from the chin over the sides of the face. Bill, legs and feet are black. Though they are distinctly aggressive toward their own kind, Canada Geese are generally gregarious. On larger waters they are colonial and congregate into large flocks to moult and winter. The first introductions remain undocumented, though it was known here as early as 1678. Certainly it has bred freely since at least the latter part of the eighteenth century. 92–102 cm (36–40 in).

Voice: A far-carrying *aa-honk* in flight; swan-like hissing at intruders.

Habitat: Marshes and lakes in wooded country in its native North America; in Britain most often large ornamental lakes, but also smaller ponds and flooded grasslands.

Reproduction: A colonial breeder on larger waters. The nest is usually placed on an islet or among woodland vegetation and consists of a scrape lined with down. The 5–6, occasionally 2–11, whitish eggs are laid in early April and incubated by the female for 28–30 days while her mate stands guard nearby. The young are tended by both sexes and fly after 9 weeks. They remain with their parents in family parties through the winter. Single-brooded.

Food: Grass together with some aquatic vegetation.

Range and Distribution: Breeds naturally over most of Canada and the northern United States, migrating south of the range in winter. Introduced to Britain and Ireland, Norway, Sweden and Finland. Swedish birds migrate to winter in Denmark. In Britain it is widespread over most of lowland England, but is rather thin on the ground in Wales and Scotland. In Ireland there is a strong population at Strangford Lough.

Movements: Resident, but a moult migration has developed since 1950, taking Yorkshire birds north to the Beauly Firth in June. Migratory in North America.

Population: about 20,000 birds

Natural range in North America

Barnacle Goose

Branta leucopsis (Bechstein)

A neat little 'black' goose marked by a bold white face that is a winter visitor from the far north. Once threatened by excessive wildfowling, it has made an excellent recovery under protection

Population: about 29,000 winter

Black neck and breast together with white face are easily seen even in flight

Small, dainty and distinctly elegant, the Barnacle Goose is a fine blue-grey on the back and wings, individual feathers being tipped with black and white to form a series of transverse bars. The underparts are white, faintly barred with pale grey. The tail is white with a black terminal band. The neck and crown are black, the face and forehead white. The Canada Goose has a similar pattern, but is larger, brown not grey, and with a much larger bill and smaller white face patch. Barnacle Geese are widely kept in captivity and frequently escape. Thus individual birds are highly suspect, for this is a gregarious species that, in favoured localities, regularly forms large, sometimes huge, flocks. 58–69 cm (23–27 in).

Voice: A dog-like *gnuk*; flocks make a more or less continuous noise.

Habitat: Arctic tundra; in winter frequents estuarine grasslands and saltings and grassy islands.

Reproduction: The nest is sited on a cliff ledge, or a crag above tundra marshes. It consists of a simple hollow, well lined with down. The 3–5, occasionally 6, whitish eggs are laid from late May and incubated by the female for 24–25 days, while her mate stands guard nearby. The goslings leave the nest soon after hatching and accompany their parents to nearby marshes. They can fly at 7 weeks, but remain in family parties into winter. Single-brooded.

Food: Mostly grass, but also seeds of salting plants and some clover.

Range and Distribution: Found on east coast of Greenland, Spitsbergen and Novaya Zemlya.

Movements: The 3 distinct populations follow different migration routes to separate winter quarters. Greenland birds fly via Iceland to winter in Ireland and the Scottish islands (population *c*. 24,000). Spitsbergen Barnacles winter entirely on the Scottish Solway (population 5,200). The Novaya Zemlya birds winter in Holland and northern Germany (population 45,000), far outnumbering the other populations.

Brent Goose

Branta bernicla (Linnaeus)

A regular winter visitor in large numbers that is marine in habit, being seldom found far from the open shoreline. Once decimated by hunting, this attractive and gregarious little goose has enjoyed a significant recovery under protective legislation. Dark-bellied (foreground) and Pale-bellied shown

Population: about 50,000 winter

Black head and neck broken only by narrow white flash, not easily observed in flight

Darkest of the 'black' geese, occurring in 2 distinct subspecies. The Pale-bellied Brent *Branta bernicla hrota* is dark brown above, black feathers being broadly fringed with brown. The underparts are mottled creamy, the undertail coverts white, and the white tail marked by a broad black terminal band. The head, neck and breast are black, ending abruptly in a bold breast band. A flash of white on the side of the upper neck is absent in first winter birds. The Dark-bellied Brent *Branta bernicla bernicla* has the same black head and neck pattern, but is darker, less brown above and much darker below, the breast band often being barely discernible. Both subspecies are gregarious and marine, and are winter visitors to Britain and Ireland that fly in wavering lines, not distinct Vs. 56–61 cm (22–24 in).

Voice: A quiet *rrouk*.

Habitat: Tundra with pools and bogs, also on rocky tundra islands. In winter haunts shorelines and estuaries with specific food plants.

Reproduction: Breeds colonially. The nest consists of a scrape lined with vegetation and down, and the 3–5, occasionally 2–8, creamy eggs are laid from mid-June onwards, usually before all the snow and ice have melted. In its typical habitat the Brent Goose has about 100 days to rear its brood. The eggs are incubated by the female for 24–26 days and the young take to the water soon after hatching. They are tended by both parents until they can fly and then remain together as a family party through autumn, winter and the following spring migration. Single-brooded.

Food: In winter takes marine *Zostera* and *Enteromorpha*; in summer various grasses and salting plants.

Range and Distribution: Brent Geese enjoy a circumpolar breeding distribution in the high Arctic – the Black Brant *Branta bernicla nigricens* of North America being a third subspecies.

Movements: Pale-bellied Brent breed in Greenland and adjacent Canadian islands and winter in Ireland (15,000). A separate population breeds at Spitsbergen and Franz Josef Land, wintering in Denmark and in northeast England (1,000). Dark-bellied Brent breed in Siberia and winter around the North Sea, including south and east England (35,000 of a total of 90,000). A few Pale-bellied occur with flocks of Dark-bellied, and vice versa.

Shelduck

Tadorna tadorna (Linnaeus)

A boldly marked white, black and chestnut duck of goose-like proportions, found mostly along the tideline, particularly on muddy estuaries. It has a lengthy moult migration and a unique crèche system of guarding its young

Population: about 12,000 pairs

Shelduck are large white ducks with a black head and neck marked by an iridescent green sheen. Two black lines run horizontally over the closed wing, and a broad chestnut band extends from the upper back across the breast. The bill is bright red surmounted in the male by a bold red, swan-like, knob. The legs and feet are pink. The female is similar, but has a smaller and less well-defined breast band, and lacks the red knob at the base of the bill. Juveniles are dusky grey-brown above and white below. Shelduck swim buoyantly, but spend much of their time feeding among the muddy ooze at the edge of the tide, swinging their bill from side to side in a sifting manner. They are territorial, but pairs may form loose colonies. At other seasons they are gregarious, and in late summer adults leave the young in the care of an 'aunt', which may find itself in charge of 50–60 youngsters, while they migrate to distant moulting grounds. 61 cm (24 in).

Voice: The calls of each sex differ considerably, those of the male being higher pitched and more whistling than his mate. A nasal *ak-ak-ak* is most commonly heard.

Habitat: Coastlines and estuaries; breeds near coast among sandy wastes and bushy broken areas.

Reproduction: The nest is usually in a rabbit burrow among grassy dunes, but can be among the roots of trees, in haystacks, holes in old buildings, and in hollow trees. The 8–15 whitish eggs are laid in May in a scanty nest with a good lining of down. The female alone incubates for 28–30 days. The chicks leave the nest soon after hatching and are escorted to the nearest water by the female, sometimes in company with the male. They are independent after 8 weeks, part of which is spent in a crèche. Single-brooded.

Food: Molluscs, especially marine snails, crustaceans and insects filtered from shallow water and soft mud.

Range and Distribution: Predominantly coastal in Europe. Widespread around the North Sea and adjacent coastlines, distinctly local in the Mediterranean. Shelduck breed in a broad belt across Eurasia from the Black Sea to eastern Siberia. In Britain and Ireland they breed around all coasts with particularly large populations in East Anglia and the Inner Hebrides.

Movements: Adults leave for moulting grounds in the Heligoland Bight in July. There is a smaller movement to Bridgwater Bay where 3,500 may gather at this time.

Wigeon

Anas penelope (Linnaeus)

A delicately marked, attractive, surface-feeding duck that is an abundant winter visitor. A gregarious bird, it maintains flock contact with a characteristic high-pitched whistling

Population: some 200,000 birds winter

White patches on inner wing are excellent field mark in flight

Female is similar to female Mallard, but distinguished by small steel-blue bill

The male Wigeon has a chestnut head, marked by a yellow forehead and crown. The breast is dull pinkish. The upperparts are grey, separated from the paler underparts by a narrow white line. There is also a white mark on the flank at the base of the black tail. The bill is small and pale steel-blue. The female is coloured in drab buffs and browns, but has the same rounded head and dainty bill of the male, making her among the easiest of female surface-feeding ducks to identify. In flight the male shows bold white patches on the upper surface of the inner wing and both sexes have a distinctly pointed tail. Wigeon are gregarious, on occasion gathering into huge flocks. They feed mainly by grazing and can often be found alongside 'grey' geese such as White-fronts that feed in the same way. 46 cm (18 in).

Voice: Distinctive, high-pitched whistled flight note *whee-oo*.

Habitat: Breeds on shores or islets in freshwater lakes; in winter frequents flooded grassland, coastal saltings and open muddy shorelines.

Reproduction: The nest consists of a scrape, well hidden among vegetation, lined with down. The 7–8, occasionally 6–10, creamy eggs are laid from the end of April onwards and incubated by the female alone for 22–25 days. The youngsters leave the nest soon after hatching and are tended by the female alone for the 6 weeks to fledging and independence. Single-brooded.

Food: Grass and aquatic vegetation, mostly marine *Zostera* and *Enteromorpha*, taken on land or from the surface while swimming.

Range and Distribution: Found across northern Eurasia from Iceland and Scandinavia to the Bering Straits. In Britain it breeds in Scotland in the Highlands, Outer Hebrides and Orkney. It has spread southwards, first nesting in England in 1897, and now breeds sporadically in southern England and East Anglia, probably as a result of escapes from wildfowl collections.

Movements: About half of the total population of northwest Europe winters in Britain and Ireland. Wigeon are found throughout the country, but with huge flocks on favoured estuaries and some 35,000 birds on the Ouse Washes.

Gadwall

Anas strepera (Linnaeus)

A somewhat undistinguished duck that, even in the male, looks like a brown female surface feeder. It was introduced to England in 1850 and has since spread

Population: about 260 pairs

Black-bordered white speculum picks out Gadwall in flight at any distance

Male (foreground) and female

Appearing brown from a distance, a closer approach reveals the male Gadwall to be finely vermiculated in greys on the body, with a brown head and a diagnostic black rear end. The female is very similar to a female Mallard. Both sexes show a clear white speculum in flight. They mix well with other ducks and are predominantly birds of inland fresh water. Being comparatively rare they do not form large flocks. 51 cm (20 in).

Voice: Male utters a single croaking note; female a Mallard-like *quack*.

Habitat: Inland fresh waters, reed beds, floods.

Reproduction: The nest is hidden among dense waterside vegetation, though it may also be among similar dry vegetation such as heather. It consists of a hollow lined with vegetation and down, and the 8–12, occasionally 7–16, eggs are washed with cream or light green. They are laid from early May onwards and are incubated by the female alone for 25–27 days. The ducklings are taken immediately to the nearest water where they are cared for by the female for 7 weeks. Single-brooded.

Food: Aquatic vegetation taken by immersing head below surface, though seldom upending.

Range and Distribution: Found in Eurasia from western Europe to eastern Siberia, and in North America. Generally breeds south of most other European ducks, but has recently spread on both continents. It is now more numerous in Iceland, colonized France in 1920, West Germany in 1930, Switzerland in 1959 and Norway in 1965. First bred in Britain in 1850 following an introduction, and has since spread to many parts of lowland England, while maintaining a stronghold in the Brecks. Colonized Scotland in 1909, probably naturally from the Continent, and Ireland in 1937.

Movements: The British and Irish population is augmented by small numbers from the Continent in winter.

Teal

Anas crecca (Linnaeus)

A tiny duck that has a distinctive green and chestnut head pattern in the male. Highly gregarious, it forms large flocks that fly with all the speed and agility of waders, turning this way and that in unison

Population: about 3,500 to 6,000 pairs; some 75,000 winter

Male (foreground) and female. Size is usually sufficient to identify, but green speculum may sometimes show

The male has a chestnut head, marked by a broad area of bottle-green extending from the eye in an inverted comma to the neck. It is bordered by a narrow line of yellow. The back is grey, the flanks a paler grey, separated by a prominent white horizontal stripe. The breast is buff, speckled with brown, and there is a triangular patch of cream on the dark undertail. At any distance the small size, dark head, flank flash and creamy spot are diagnostic. The female is mottled in browns and buffs like so many other surface-feeding ducks but, like her mate, has a green speculum and shows a wader-like wing bar in flight. Essentially gregarious, Teal form large flocks that fly with an aerial agility approaching that of the small waders. 35 cm (14 in).

Voice: Flying flocks call continuously; male has a double whistle, female a high-pitched *quack* of alarm.

Habitat: Small lakes, marshes and backwaters in summer; in winter on floods, reservoirs, estuaries and open shorelines.

Reproduction: The nest is hidden in a clump of marshland vegetation and lined with vegetation and down. The female alone builds it and incubates the 8–12, occasionally up to 15, creamy-buff eggs for 21–28 days. Breeding begins in late March in the south, but not until mid-May further north. The chicks are tended by the female and fly after 44 days. Single-brooded.

Food: Mostly aquatic seeds in winter; more animate food in summer.

Range and Distribution: Circumpolar distribution with the so-called Green-winged Teal *Anas crecca carolinensis*, which lacks the yellow border to the green head markings and the white line along the flanks, replacing the nominate bird in North America. In Europe it is absent from the southeast and southwest. In Britain and Ireland it is widespread, but decidedly scarce in the southwest.

Movements: Huge influx in autumn of Continental birds from Iceland, Scandinavia and adjacent parts of the Soviet Union. They are spread throughout the country, but with several really substantial flocks.

Small size, fast wing beats and narrow white wing bar serve to identify male Teal in flight

109

Mallard

Anas platyrhynchos (Linnaeus)

The most common and widespread of our ducks, occurring on village ponds and ornamental city lakes as well as on wild marshes and floods. The male is the familiar green-headed duck, though the species is the ancestor of most of the domestic breeds and crossbreeds that are found in western Europe. Female with chicks shown

Population: 70,000 to 100,000 pairs

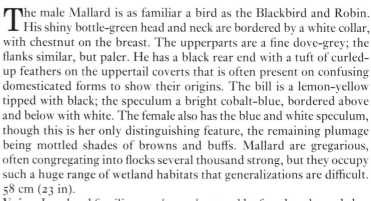

Dark neck and breast together with white-bordered speculum identify male in flight

The male Mallard is as familiar a bird as the Blackbird and Robin. His shiny bottle-green head and neck are bordered by a white collar, with chestnut on the breast. The upperparts are a fine dove-grey; the flanks similar, but paler. He has a black rear end with a tuft of curled-up feathers on the uppertail coverts that is often present on confusing domesticated forms to show their origins. The bill is a lemon-yellow tipped with black; the speculum a bright cobalt-blue, bordered above and below with white. The female also has the blue and white speculum, though this is her only distinguishing feature, the remaining plumage being mottled shades of browns and buffs. Mallard are gregarious, often congregating into flocks several thousand strong, but they occupy such a huge range of wetland habitats that generalizations are difficult. 58 cm (23 in).

Voice: Loud and familiar *quack-quack* uttered by female only; male has a *queek* note that is quieter and less raucous.

Habitat: Virtually every type of lowland wetland, from open shores, floods, lakes, village ponds, urban park lakes, to rivers and streams and even the fountains of Trafalgar Square in London.

Reproduction: Breeds virtually throughout the year, but mostly from March onwards. The nest is usually close to fresh water and is hidden among grass, bracken or bushes, sometimes in old buildings or holes in trees. The simple hollow is lined with vegetation and down and the 10–12, sometimes 7–16, pale green or bluish eggs are incubated by the female alone for 28–29 days. The brown, down-covered chicks are led to water soon after hatching and are tended by the female alone (usually) for 7–8 weeks. Single-brooded, though park and pond birds often raise a second brood.

Food: Mostly vegetable matter including many aquatic plants reached by upending. Also land plants, seeds, cereals and bread. The proportion of animate food varies according to availability, for the success of the Mallard is due in no small part to its ability to adapt to a wide variety of different foods.

Range and Distribution: Circumpolar in the northern and temperate zones, though extending southwards into Morocco, and northwards as far as western Greenland. In Europe it is absent only from the highest mountain chains and from Sicily. In Britain and Ireland it is found in every region except for the highest and most barren hills.

Movements: Eastern European and Scandinavian birds are summer visitors, wintering westwards to eastern England and Scotland. The total population may then be over 250,000 birds. British and Irish breeders are mainly resident.

Duck Wings

Male surface-feeding ducks are readily identified at rest, even at considerable range. In the air, however, their fast movements make it essential that field marks are picked out quickly and accurately. In most species a knowledge of wing pattern is particularly important

Teal: narrow white wing bar may be seen at distance even when green speculum is invisible. Extremely rapid wing beats and aerial acrobatics also serve to identify

Wigeon: bold white patch, not speculum, on inner wing is certain means of identification and most obvious field mark in flight

Pintail: identifiable by pintail and overall shape, but speculum has only 1 white border, not 2 as with Mallard. Pale inner wing also a useful feature

Gadwall: white speculum effectively separates both sexes from female Mallard, which they otherwise resemble at any distance

Shoveler: bill shape obvious even in flight, but pale inner wing with white-bordered speculum is useful feature as birds fly away

Mallard: blue (often just appears dark) speculum, bordered above and below with white, picks out at surprisingly long range

111

Pintail

Anas acuta (Linnaeus)

A rare breeder but a quite numerous winter visitor. The chocolate hood of the male is diagnostic and, in flight, the long, pointed tail is easily picked out

Population: less than 25 pairs; 24,000 winter

Male (below) and female, which is superficially similar to female Mallard, but pointed tail and smaller, bluish bill readily separate

A beautiful bird by any standards, the male Pintail has a rich chocolate-coloured hood extending to the upper throat and well down the back of the neck, divided by a vertical stripe of white. The foreneck is white, the back and flanks a finely vermiculated pale grey. There is a black line along the flanks, and the rear end is black with a white tail and white patch at the rear of the flanks. The central tail feathers are extended to a point. The female is mottled in browns and buffs like other surface-feeding ducks, but has a distinctly pointed tail. The bill is a slate-blue. In winter Pintail are highly gregarious and tend to concentrate at certain favoured locations where they may be the most abundant duck present. 56 cm (22 in).

Voice: Male utters a low whistle; female a subdued *quack*.

Habitat: Lakes, marshes, moorland pools; in winter mostly found on estuaries and inland floods.

Reproduction: Breeds semicolonially near fresh water. The nest is a hollow lined with grasses and down, often hidden among vegetation, but also sometimes in quite open situations. The 7–9, occasionally 6–12, eggs are washed with creamy-buff or bluish-green and laid in mid-April in the south to mid-June in the north. The female alone incubates for 21–23 days and the ducklings are led to water soon after hatching. Though the male may be present, it is the female that usually tends the young for some 7 weeks. Single-brooded.

Food: Variety of aquatic vegetable and animal matter obtained by upending. Much local variation.

Range and Distribution: Circumpolar in the north. Very locally distributed in Europe north of a line drawn from Boulogne to Bucharest. Much more numerous in Scandinavia and northern Russia. In Britain and Ireland it breeds annually in small numbers, mostly in Scotland and northern England, but also in the Fens.

Movements: Birds from Iceland, Scandinavia and northern Russia winter among the sheltered estuaries and floods of Britain and Ireland. They arrive from September onwards and depart by April.

Garganey

Anas querquedula (Linnaeus)

A tiny, Teal-sized duck that is a summer visitor in small numbers from Africa south of the Sahara

Population: less than 100 pairs

In flight the pale blue inner wing is a sure means of separating from Teal

Male (left) and female. The bold supercilium of the male is found in much reduced form in the female

The Garganey is the only summer visitor among the wildfowl. About the same size as a Teal, it is easily identified in all plumages in flight by its pale blue inner wing, present in both male and female. The male is a deep vinous maroon on the head with a broad slash of white over the eye. The breast and back are mottled in rich brown, with grey flanks barred with darker grey and black. The rear end is mottled brown. The long black and white feathers of the scapulars fall over the closed wing. The female is mottled brown, as are so many female surface-feeding ducks, but has a distinctive face pattern that includes a dark crown and dark lines through and below the eye. Though a gregarious species, the population of Britain and Ireland is so small that large flocks are unknown. 38 cm (15 in).

Voice: Male has a crackling call and female a short *quack*.

Habitat: Shallow fresh waters, with strong growth of emergent vegetation breaking up large areas of open water.

Reproduction: The nest is well hidden among vegetation along the margins of freshwater pools, backwaters and ditches. It consists of a depression lined with vegetation and down and the 8–11, occasionally 6–14, creamy eggs are laid from mid-April. They are incubated by the female alone for 21–23 days and the ducklings are tended by the female until they fly after 5–6 weeks. Single-brooded.

Food: Vegetable and animal matter taken from near the surface and by occasional upending. Insects and their larvae, crustaceans and molluscs are also taken, along with weeds and seeds.

Range and Distribution: Found from France eastwards right across temperate Eurasia to Kamchatka, southwards to Turkey, and north to the head of the Gulf of Bothnia. In Britain it is regular in the southeast, East Anglia and the Midlands, but sometimes occurs further north, even in Scotland.

Movements: British birds arrive in March and depart in September. They winter in the sahel zone of Africa southwards to the savannah lands of Kenya.

Shoveler

Anas clypeata (Linnaeus)

Chestnut below, and with a large spatulate bill, the male Shoveler is easily identified on the water and in the air. Male (foreground) and female shown

Population: 10,000 pairs; 5,000 birds winter

In flight the spatulate bill remains an excellent field mark, though the male has a clear chestnut belly patch

Both sexes have the large spoon-shaped bill from which the species is named and, in most circumstances, a glimpse is sufficient to identify. The male has a shiny bottle-green head broken by a bright yellow eye, bright chestnut flanks and underparts, a black rear end and a neat patch of white on the rear flanks. In flight the upperparts are predominantly white while the inner wing is conspicuously pale blue. Like other surface-feeding ducks the female is mottled in shades of brown and buff, but with the pale blue inner wing showing even at rest. The spatulate bill identifies. Shoveler are gregarious birds, feeding in small flocks and often gathering in large numbers at a favoured roost. 51 cm (20 in).

Voice: Both sexes quack; the male's being low and repeated, the female's more Mallard-like. Also a *tuk-tuk* flight note.

Habitat: Shallow freshwater pools with emergent vegetation; in winter also found on floods and estuaries.

Reproduction: The nest is constructed on a waterside site, often quite open. It consists of a simple hollow, lined with grasses and down, and the 8–12, sometimes 7–14, creamy eggs are laid from late April and incubated by the female for 22–23 days. The chicks leave the nest soon after hatching and are then tended by the female for 6–7 weeks. Single-brooded.

Food: Wide variety of plant and animal material. Feeds by surface filtering, taking large quantities of small crustaceans and molluscs, insect larvae and seeds, but also dives more than other surface feeders.

Range and Distribution: Circumpolar, but avoids northernmost tundra zone. In Europe it is sporadic and absent from large areas of the south and west. In Britain and Ireland it is confined to the eastern lowland parts of England and Scotland.

Movements: British and Irish birds migrate south to France, Spain and Portugal and are replaced in winter by immigrants from Scandinavia, eastern Europe and Russia.

Red-crested Pochard

Netta rufina (Pallas)

**A beautifully marked diving duck
with a bright rust-red head in the
male. Widely kept in waterfowl
collections, escapes are numerous,
but genuinely wild birds occur in
East Anglia in autumn**

Population: 10 to 30 in autumn
originate from adjacent parts
of the Continent

The female's chestnut crown
and pale unmarked cheeks are
excellent field marks

The large, rounded, rust-red head of the male is obvious even over
long distances. The neck and breast are black, the back brown, the
flanks white and the rear end black. The bill is bright coral-red, as are
the legs and feet. The female is similar in shape, but clothed in browns
above and buff below. There is a chocolate cap bordered by pale sides to
the head below, creating a pattern shared only with the marine female
Scoter. The small bill is slate-blue. These are gregarious birds, often
forming quite large flocks on parts of the Continent. They are decidedly
rare in Britain and Ireland. 56 cm (22 in).

Voice: Male has a wheezing call and the female a harsh *churr*; generally
silent outside the breeding season.

Habitat: Large areas of fresh water, usually with clumps and islands of
reeds; in Britain favours large reservoirs.

Reproduction: The nest is hidden deep inside cover and reached by a
tunnel through vegetation. Often sited on an island, it consists of a
mound of vegetation in wet areas and a simple hollow in drier sites, in
either case lined with down. The 6–12 creamy or light green eggs are
laid in mid-May and incubated by the female for 26–28 days. The
ducklings leave the nest soon after hatching and are tended by the
female for 6–7 weeks. Single-brooded.

Food: Predominantly aquatic plants reached by diving and upending.

Range and Distribution: Breeds in only a few major areas in Europe
including Spain, southern France, Holland, southern and East Germany, and in the Danube Delta. At some sites it may be the most
numerous duck present in summer. In Britain and Ireland escapes
have occasionally bred, and most reports refer to such birds.

Movements: Spanish and Danube birds are resident, others migrate.
Presumed Dutch birds arrive in Essex (Abberton Reservoir) in September
and may also be seen at that time elsewhere in southern England.

Pochard

Aythya ferina (Linnaeus)

A typical diving duck that sits low in the water and is marked, in the male, by a reddish-chestnut head and grey back. Usually gregarious, forming huge rafts several thousand strong on suitable waters. Male (left) and female shown

Population: 200 to 400 pairs; 45,000 winter

A grey wing bar separates from Tufted Duck in flight

A dark reddish-chestnut head and a black neck and breast that appear dark at any distance distinguish the male Pochard. The back is grey, the flanks and underparts a shade paler. The rear end is black. The bill is steel-blue, tipped and based with black. The female is brownish-grey, darker on head and neck. The crown is dark brown, and there is a grey-buff eye-ring and bridle. Pochard dive frequently and well from the water's surface and seldom venture onto land. They are usually found in dense packs and may form huge rafts in winter. In flight the wings are grey with a lighter, but not white, bar extending over their full length. They fly, like Tufted Duck, fast and direct with rapid wing beats. 46 cm (18 in).

Voice: Male has a nasal call and a soft whistle; female utters a harsh rasping croak.

Habitat: Lakes, pools and marshes with some emergent vegetation; in winter commonly found on reservoirs, lakes, sheltered brackish waters and estuaries.

Reproduction: Breeds among emergent vegetation, constructing a mound of plant material lined with down. The 6–11, sometimes up to 18, light green eggs are laid from mid-April and incubated by the female for 24–26 days. The chicks leave the nest soon after hatching and are cared for by the female for 7–8 weeks. Single-brooded.

Food: A mixture of animal and vegetable material, varying according to season and location, obtained by diving with a leap from the surface. Usually prefers waters 1–2.5 metres deep, but may upend in shallow waters. Stoneworts and pondweeds are favoured.

Range and Distribution: Found from Spain across temperate Europe, north to Scandinavia and eastwards through Russia and the Soviet Union to central Siberia. Absent from central and eastern Mediterranean. In Britain and Ireland it has expanded its range over the last 150 years, reaching Scotland in 1871 and Ireland in 1907. It remains sporadic and is most firmly established in East Anglia and the southeast.

Movements: The whole of the population from central Germany eastwards is migratory and a large population winters in Britain and Ireland. Several areas including the London reservoirs boast flocks in excess of 1,000 birds. They arrive in October and depart in April.

Tufted Duck

Aythya fuligula (Linnaeus)

A bold black and white bird with a neat crest in the male. One of the most familiar of our ducks, it is as much at home on ponds in cities as on reservoirs and lochs. Male (foreground) and female shown

Population: 6,000 to 7,000 pairs; up to 60,000 winter

Bold white bar extends right across wing in flight

The male Tufted Duck is black, with bold white flanks. On closer approach metallic purple and green sheens may be apparent, as is a crest that usually hangs limply from the hind crown. It is similar to the male Scaup, though that species has a grey back which may, however, be difficult to see at a distance. The female is a warm brown bird, lighter on the flanks, and with only a tuft instead of a crest. This is, however, sufficient to create an angular shape to the head. There is often a little white at the base of the bill, and exceptionally this may be sufficiently developed to create serious confusion with female Scaup. In flight both sexes have a bold white bar extending across the wing. These are gregarious diving ducks that often form large rafts, sometimes in association with Pochard. 43 cm (17 in).

Voice: A quiet whistle in courting male; female a soft rolling note and a crow-like croak.

Habitat: Open fresh water with depths of 3–14 metres, considerably deeper than those preferred by Pochard. Reservoirs, lakes, gravel pits, ornamental ponds; in winter also sometimes on estuaries.

Reproduction: Sometimes semicolonial. The nest is placed beside fresh water on an island in a lake or pond and consists of a grass-lined hollow well hidden among vegetation. The eggs are laid from mid-April on an inner lining of down and usually number 5–12, though up to 18 have been recorded. They are light green and incubated by the female alone for 23–25 days. The chicks are highly precocious, diving after a few hours and flying after 6 weeks, during which time they are cared for by the female. Single-brooded.

Food: Mainly animal material including molluscs, crustaceans and insects, together with plants and seeds in various proportions depending on local abundance.

Range and Distribution: Old World from Iceland across northern Europe and Siberia to the Bering Straits. In Europe abundant in the north and east, absent from Spain and most of the Mediterranean. In Britain and Ireland it is widespread, but thinly distributed in the hilly districts of the west and north.

Movements: British and Irish birds disperse, but do not emigrate. They are joined in winter by birds from Scandinavia and Russia and then form substantial rafts on many inland waters.

Scaup

Aythya marila (Linnaeus)

The marine equivalent of the Tufted Duck and similarly marked, though with a grey not black back. It may gather in enormous flocks in sheltered bays where mussels are abundant. Male (left) and female shown

Population: 1 or 2 pairs; 20,000 winter

Bold white wing bar, as in Tufted Duck, but grey back distinguishes

Scaup are sea ducks that form large winter rafts over favourite feeding grounds. The male is black on head and chest, though a close approach reveals a bright metallic-green sheen. The back is a finely vermiculated grey, the flanks white, the rear end black. The female is similar to the female Tufted Duck in grey-brown plumage, but has a large area of white at the base of the bill and a more smoothly rounded (not tufted) head profile. Both sexes show a prominent white wing bar in flight. 48 cm (19 in).

Voice: Female has harsh *karr-karr*; male a *coo*, but audible only at very close range.

Habitat: Freshwater lakes and pools among tundra and moors; in winter essentially marine, being found in sheltered bays as well as occasionally inland on reservoirs.

Reproduction: Usually colonial. The nest is a hollow with scant cover near a freshwater pool, lined with down. The 6–15, occasionally up to 17, eggs are laid from late May onwards and are light greenish in colour. They are incubated by the female for 26–28 days and the chicks leave the nest soon after hatching. They are tended by the female, though the male is sometimes present, and fly at 5–6 weeks. Single-brooded.

Food: Omnivorous, food obtained by diving from the surface. Molluscs, especially mussels, form a significant proportion of winter food, though grain is also scavenged from distillery outfalls.

Range and Distribution: Circumpolar, breeding from Iceland and Scandinavia across the tundra zone of the Soviet Union to Alaska and northern Canada, but not in Greenland. It occasionally breeds in Britain, mostly in Orkney.

Movements: Winters at mouth of Baltic, in North Sea and around coasts of Britain and Ireland. There are large flocks in the Firth of Forth and Solway areas. They arrive in October and depart in March, mostly for Iceland, Scandinavia and Russia.

Eider

Somateria mollissima (Linnaeus)

An attractive, mainly black and white, strongly built sea duck, found close inshore at all seasons. It is usually gregarious and in summer forms dense colonies that are 'farmed' to produce the famous Eiderdown

Population: 15,000 to 20,000 pairs; some 50,000 birds winter

White inner wing, back and neck form diagnostic shape above; underparts black

The male Eider is a truly beautiful bird. Black and white at a distance, a close approach reveals a wash of pale green on the hind crown, and a tinge of pale pink on the breast. The otherwise white head has a black mask that extends through the eye. The back is white, the flanks and rear are black with a circular spot of white on the rear flank. The bill is silvery, and heavily triangular from a sloping forehead. It is a chunky, robust-looking bird that dives long and well, and looks particularly heavy in flight. The female shares this build, but is heavily camouflaged in bars of brown and black. She has the same triangular head shape as her mate, the bill extending upwards in a point toward the eye. Eider are colonial breeders and gregarious at all seasons of the year. 58 cm (23 in).

Voice: A loud cooing in the male, and a raucous call in the female. Spring flocks during the courtship period are particularly noisy, the calls carrying for long distances.

Habitat: Dunes and other coastlines, sea islands, or on nearby lakes, rivers and marshes.

Reproduction: The nest is a hollow lined with vegetation and a thick mass of down. In Iceland, where Eiderdown is farmed, the first nest lining is taken and the duck plucks another from her breast. The 4–6, occasionally 3–10, light grey-green eggs are laid from May onwards and incubated by the tight-sitting female for 27–28 days. When she leaves the nest the down lining is pulled over the eggs to prevent chilling. The chicks leave the nest soon after hatching and are taken to water, usually the sea, where they are tended by the female for 8–10 weeks. Single-brooded.

Food: Molluscs and crustaceans obtained by diving for up to a minute at a time (maximum 78 seconds). Mussels figure prominently in the diet, but crabs are also dealt with expertly.

Range and Distribution: Circumpolar along arctic coastlines, though absent from much of the Siberian coast. In Europe it breeds along all coasts of Scandinavia, Iceland, northern Britain and Ireland and here and there in Denmark and Holland. In Britain it breeds on all Scottish coasts, but in England only at Walney Island, the Farnes and in the northeast. Also along the north coast of Ireland.

Movements: Native birds are joined in autumn by immigrants from Denmark and Holland, with the largest concentrations in the Firths of Forth and Tay.

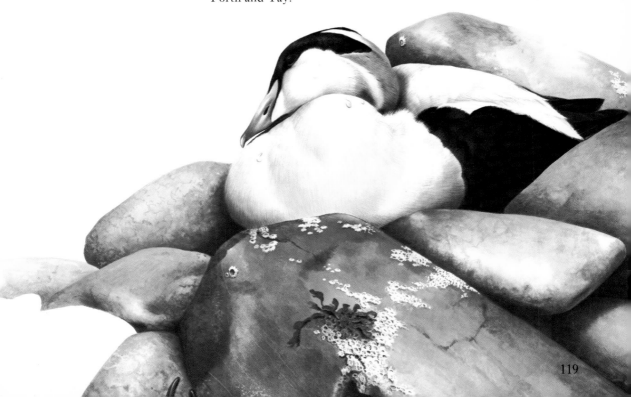

Pointed tail and black and white
'saddle' pattern distinguish

Long-tailed Duck

Clangula hyemalis (Linnaeus)

An attractive, though scarce, winter visitor, this sea duck has distinctive summer and winter plumages. It rarely comes close inshore and, though gregarious, flocks are seldom large. Male (foreground) and female shown

Population: over 4,000 winter

Leaves Scandinavian breeding grounds to winter around North Sea

At all seasons the male has 2 long, pointed tail feathers that make up a quarter of its overall length. In winter the male is a white bird with broad black stripes over back and uppertail, extending forward to join a broad black breast band. The area around the eye is grey, becoming darker, almost black, just below the cheek. In flight the wings are dark, the body white with what looks like a pair of black braces on the back. In summer the head, neck and breast are black, with the face patch silvery-white. The back is mottled brown, the flanks white, and the tail and streamers black. At all times this is a slim, graceful bird. The female lacks the tail streamers and thus appears rather chunky. She has the head and neck white in winter, marked by a dark crown and a comma of dark below the ear coverts. The back and breast band are mottled brown and black, and the flanks are white. In summer the face and flanks are washed with grey. Male 53 cm (21 in) including tail feathers; female 41 cm (16 in).

Voice: Noisy and garrulous with a range of melodic calls unique among wildfowl. Their supposed similarity to chanting Red Indians is responsible for the species' North American name of Old Squaw.

Habitat: Arctic tundra pools and deltas as far north as there is ice-free land; also on islets in lake and sea.

Reproduction: The nest is a hollow lined with down and hidden among scant vegetation, and the 5–9, occasionally up to 11, yellow-green eggs are laid from late May onwards, into July in the extreme north. They are incubated by the female for 23–25 days and the chicks are taken to water soon after hatching. Broods may combine, and the young fly after after 5 weeks. Single-brooded.

Food: Crustaceans and molluscs obtained by diving from the surface; also takes some berries and other plant material in summer.

Range and Distribution: Circumpolar in high Arctic as far north as ice-free land can be found, including the north coast of Greenland. In Britain breeding has been claimed and suspected in the past.

Movements: Winters along coasts of Norway, the southern Baltic, Holland and northern Britain.

Common Scoter

Melanitta nigra (Linnaeus)

An all-black sea duck, usually seen some distance offshore in dense packs flying low over the sea, and frequently disappearing on landing among the waves

Population: less than 200 pairs; about 35,000 winter

Leaves tundra to winter around shores of North Sea and Atlantic coasts

Male (right) and female. The dark brown cap and unmarked cheeks of the female, as well as the lack of white in the wing, distinguish from Velvet Scoter

The male Scoter is simply an all-black sea duck with a strong patch of orange-yellow on the bill. The female is a brown and buff bird barred on the flanks, with a chocolate crown, and pale grey sides to the face. Only other species of scoter are at all similar, but the Velvet Scoter has white in the wing and the rare Surf Scoter white on the head. These are gregarious birds forming dense rafts that seldom come really close inshore. The secret when observing such packs in flight is to watch for the white in the wing that identifies a Velvet Scoter among the flock. 48 cm (19 in).

Voice: Male has a plaintive piping; the female a harsh growling.

Habitat: Open tundra vegetation with lakes or pools; in winter essentially marine, though individuals may enter river mouths and even visit inland reservoirs.

Reproduction: The nest is usually near a freshwater pool or lake, but occasionally some distance away from water. It consists of a hollow lined with vegetation and down. The 6–9, sometimes 5 or 10, creamy eggs are laid from the end of May onwards and incubated by the female alone for 27–31 days. The chicks are taken to water and cared for by the female for 6–7 weeks before flying. Single-brooded.

Food: Molluscs, especially mussels, obtained by diving, sometimes in mass dives by a flock. Average dive 40 seconds.

Range and Distribution: From Scandinavia right across northern Eurasia to the Bering Straits and western Alaska. Also isolated populations in Iceland, Newfoundland, northern Canada and in western Ireland and north and western Scotland.

Movements: Flocks winter off British and Irish coasts, but mostly off the east coasts of Scotland and England. Summer moulting flocks of males may be very large, but have not been properly counted.

Velvet Scoter

Melanitta fusca (Linnaeus)

An all-black sea duck, very similar to the Common Scoter, but with a white speculum that is usually visible only in flight. It is a winter visitor in small numbers. Male (foreground) and female shown

Population: 2,000 to 5,000 winter

Breeds through tundra zone: winters along North Sea and Atlantic coasts

Male in flight: both sexes show white in the wing

The male is all black except for a small patch of white beneath the eye and a white speculum that can be seen only at close range. In flight, and when wing-flapping on the water's surface, this becomes a sure means of identification. The bill is orange-yellow like that of the Common Scoter, but is also substantially larger. The female is similar to the female Common Scoter in shades of brown. She has the same white wing flash as the male, but also a much darker head with 2 lighter patches on the side of the face. Like their more common relatives, they spend their time offshore, often in flocks and frequently in company with that species. They dive well and are similar in habits. 56 cm (22 in).
Voice: Less vocal than Common Scoter, but varied calls include croaks and growls, as well as whistles.
Habitat: Generally found more often in wooded country than the Common Scoter and breeds along the banks of freshwater pools and lakes, and on offshore islands. In winter frequents salt water, usually some distance offshore.
Reproduction: The nest is a hollow lined with plants and down, and the 7–10, occasionally 6–11, cream-coloured eggs are laid from late May onwards and incubated by the female alone for 27–28 days. The ducklings are taken to water soon after hatching and cared for by the female for 4–5 weeks. They become independent about 2 weeks before they can fly. Single-brooded.
Food: Mainly molluscs, obtained by diving from the surface for up to 65 seconds. Mussels are the dominant item where available.
Range and Distribution: Virtually circumpolar from Scandinavia across northern Eurasia to Japan and Kamchatka; and from Alaska across northern Canada to Hudson Bay. Absent from eastern Canada, Greenland and Iceland. In Britain breeding was suspected in Shetland in 1945, but there are no confirmed records.
Movements: Velvet Scoter winter along the east coasts of Scotland and England, with a few elsewhere. Much larger numbers winter off the coast of Norway and at the mouth of the Baltic.

Goldeneye

Bucephala clangula (Linnaeus)

A black and white diving duck, with a curiously triangular-shaped head that is recognizable over long distances. Though a rare, perhaps increasing, breeding bird in Britain, it is mainly known as a plentiful winter visitor. Male (right) and female shown

Population: about 15 pairs; 12,500 winter

Harlequin black and white pattern of upperparts in flight

Appearing black and white at any distance, the male Goldeneye has a dark glossy-green head marked by a white spot between bill and eye. The eye is 'golden', but this is not a prominent field mark. The back is black; the wings white marked with transverse bars of black. The flanks and underparts are also white. It is, however, the curiously peaked and extended triangular shape of the head that is so characteristic of this species. The female also shares this strange head shape, but her head is brown, the back grey and the flanks washed with grey-buff. Though seldom forming large flocks, these are generally gregarious birds that dive easily from the surface and are as much at home on large fresh waters as on the sea, though the largest numbers are found on estuaries. 46 cm (18 in).

Voice: Silent outside breeding season; male has harsh *zeee-zeee*, female a screeching call. Whistles wings loudly in flight.

Habitat: Breeds by lakes and ponds in thickly forested country; in winter frequents estuaries and coasts, also large inland reservoirs.

Reproduction: Elaborate courtship displays in late winter and spring. The nest is placed in a natural hole in a tree, often some distance from the ground, but also in large woodpecker holes, nest boxes or even on the ground in rabbit burrows. The cavity is lined with down and the 6–11 pale blue-green eggs are laid from April onwards depending on latitude. The female incubates for 27–32 days and the chicks throw themselves to the ground soon after hatching and are led to water and cared for by the female for 7–8 weeks. Single-brooded.

Food: Molluscs, crustaceans, insect larvae with some small fish and aquatic vegetation.

Range and Distribution: Circumpolar from Scandinavia across the boreal zone of Eurasia to Kamchatka, to Alaska, Canada and Newfoundland. Absent from Greenland and Iceland. In Britain it first bred in 1931, but was then sporadic until 1970. It now nests each year in the Scottish Highlands, mostly in nest boxes.

Movements: Scandinavian Goldeneye winter in Britain and Ireland, though the only really large flocks occur in the Firth of Forth. They arrive in October and depart in April.

Smew

Mergus albellus (Linnaeus)

Smallest and arguably the most attractive of the sawbill ducks, the drake Smew is a beautiful white bird with black markings. It is a rare visitor to our coasts and inland reservoirs, but with the endearing habit of turning up in small flocks to the same locations year after year

Continental summer distribution: 150 winter in Britain

Male in flight shows similar pattern to that of Goldeneye, and other sawbills

Male (foreground) and female. Females and immatures have maroon crown, grey back and are of almost grebe-like appearance

The adult male is a white bird with a black mark extending from the lores to enclose the eye. It extends to the hind crown in a narrow line. Other narrow black lines extend over the back, along the flanks and form a breast band. The flanks are finely vermiculated grey, and the tail is dark grey. The female and immature male, referred to jointly as 'redheads', are grebe-like in appearance. They have a maroon crown above white cheeks, and are grey above and paler on the flanks. In flight Smew show much white on the wings. They are generally gregarious and remarkably traditional in their choice of winter haunts. 41 cm (16 in).

Voice: A hoarse grunting or rattling; quiet outside breeding season.

Habitat: Well-wooded country with pools and lakes in summer; in winter frequents sheltered coasts and inland waters.

Reproduction: An elaborate courtship display by the male. Nests in tree holes lined with down. The 6–9, occasionally 5–14, creamy eggs are laid from mid–May and incubated by the female alone for 30 days. The chicks throw themselves to the ground and are led to water by the female. She alone cares for them during the 10 weeks they take to fly. Single-brooded.

Food: Insects and their larvae in summer; at other times mainly fish obtained by diving from the surface.

Range and Distribution: From northern Scandinavia across the boreal zone of Eurasia to the Bering Straits. There is an isolated breeding area at the northern end of the Caspian Sea.

Movements: Winters in Europe, the Caspian, and around Japan and adjacent Pacific coasts. In Britain it is present from November to April, mostly in southeastern England, and especially at some of the London reservoirs. Scarce elsewhere and rare in Ireland.

Red-breasted Merganser

Mergus serrator (Linnaeus)

A boldly crested sawbill duck that is predominantly coastal in winter. The thin, pointed bill is quite unlike that of any other duck, except for the Goosander which is more frequently found on fresh water. Male (foreground) and female shown

Population: about 2,000 pairs

White inner wing and dark back separate from similar Goosander in flight

Male is an easily identified sawbill duck with a long, thin red bill that is heavily serrated for gripping fish. The head is bottle-green, with a ragged crest that forms 2 distinct tufts at the rear of the crown. The neck is white with a broad brown- and black-flecked breast band below. The back is black, separated from the vermiculated grey flanks by a broad white line. It sits low in the water, when its attenuated shape is reminiscent of a diver. The female has a rusty head, forming 2 tufts that extend from the hind crown, and a rusty hindneck that merges with a white foreneck, and is thus very similar to the female Goosander. In that species, however, the white foreneck is sharply demarcated and the crest droops to a single point. The back is grey, the flanks a warm buff-grey. This is a generally gregarious bird found in small parties, except in late summer when quite large flocks may gather in estuaries. 58 cm (23 in).

Voice: Generally silent outside breeding season. Male then utters various wheezing and purring notes; the female harsh croaking and rasping ones.

Habitat: Mostly rivers, pools and backwaters in wooded country; in winter seeks sheltered bays and estuaries.

Reproduction: Nests on the ground among roots, boulders or in a burrow. The nest is lined with vegetation and down, and the 7–12, occasionally up to 21, buffish eggs are laid from mid–May and incubated by the female for 31–32 days. The ducklings are led to water soon after hatching and are cared for by the female. The young of several nests may band together in the care of a single female. They fly after 59 days. Single-brooded.

Food: Mainly fish obtained by pursuit from surface, and by diving using wings as well as feet. Salmon are an important prey inland, though crustaceans are the dominant item at sea.

Range and Distribution: Circumpolar in tundra and boreal zones, from Ireland across northern Europe to Scandinavia, the Soviet Union, south to Japan in the Pacific, and from Alaska across Canada to Greenland and Iceland. In Britain and Ireland it has expanded its range notably over the past 100 years, breeding in England for the first time in 1950 and in Wales in 1953. It is now widespread in the Lake District and is colonizing the Pennines.

Movements: British birds move to coasts in winter and are joined by immigrants from Scandinavia and Iceland. More numerous in the north, it is also scattered around most coasts.

Goosander

Mergus merganser (Linnaeus)

Largest of the sawbill ducks, this species is more often found on fresh water in winter than the Red-breasted Merganser. The male is attractive in black and white, though a close approach will reveal a dark bottle-green head and a fine pink wash to the flanks and underparts. Male (left) and female shown

Population: 1,000 to 2,000 pairs; some 4,000 winter

In flight, white inner wing and back, marked with black stripe, distinguish from Red-breasted Merganser

Goosanders have the typical long, thin serrated bill of the sawbill ducks, ideally suited to grasping slippery fish, and bright coral-red in colour. The head of the male is curiously elongated and rounded, and a shiny dark green. The back is black and the breast and underparts white, with a pale pink wash. Like the other sawbills he shows a white inner wing in flight. The female is similar to the female Red-breasted Merganser with a rust-coloured head, but has a sharply demarcated white throat and a crest that forms a single drooping point. Goosanders form flocks outside the breeding season and, though the largest numbers are found on salt water and estuaries, many winter inland. Their depredations on trout and salmon are tempered by their taking also the enemies of those fish. 66 cm (26 in).

Voice: Silent except while breeding. Male has a variety of croaking calls; female utters harsh cackles.

Habitat: Upper stretches of rivers and mountain lakes in wooded country. In winter favours estuaries and large lakes and reservoirs.

Reproduction: Nests in tree holes, crevices among rocks or in nest boxes. The nest is lined with down and the 7–14 creamy eggs are laid from mid-March onwards. The female incubates for 32–35 days, and the chicks leave the nest after a couple of days to be led to suitable water. They are cared for by the female for 5 weeks. Single-brooded.

Food: Fish obtained by diving from the surface, using only the feet for propulsion. Trout and salmon are dominant items, but eels can be locally important.

Range and Distribution: Circumpolar from Britain through Scandinavia right across northern Eurasia to Alaska and Canada. In central Asia it extends southwards and reaches Tibet. In Britain it was first proved to breed in 1871 and has since spread throughout the Highland region. Also found in the Border Hills extending into the Lake District and northern Pennines, which are now its stronghold. First bred in Ireland and Wales between 1968 and 1972.

Movements: Migratory over most of its range, though British birds may make only local movements. Scandinavian immigrants join our birds in winter.

Honey Buzzard

Pernis apivorus (Linnaeus)

A broad-winged, Buzzard-like bird that soars on barred drooping wings, and an extremely rare summer visitor to southern England. It lives on a diet of bees and wasps and has special feathering to protect it against stinging attacks

Superficially similar to the Buzzard, this is a slimmer and more elegant bird, with a longer tail marked with 2 bars near its base, a longer neck and smaller pigeon-like head, and an underwing that is usually heavily barred, but with 2 prominent bars. The shape and proportions in the air are more important to a correct identification than plumage features. While soaring its wings droop from the body – those of the Buzzard are held in a shallow V – and it has a unique butterfly-like display flight in which the wings are flapped overhead. Its exact whereabouts in Britain have always been a closely guarded secret and even today many observers do not report this species to national ornithological organizations. Easily overlooked. 51–58 cm (20–23 in).

Voice: A high-pitched *piha*, often trisyllabic in the male.

Habitat: Broadleaved or mixed woodland intersected by areas of open heath or agricultural land; but also pure conifer woods on occasion.

Reproduction: Arrives in May and displays immediately. The nest is placed high in a tree, frequently using an old nest of another species as a base. It is constructed of twigs by both sexes, and the 1–3 whitish eggs are blotched with reddish-brown. Incubation, mainly by the female, starts with the first egg and takes 30–35 days. The young are fed by both parents for 40–44 days. Single-brooded.

Food: Wasps, especially grubs, together with bees and honey; also takes small mammals and the eggs and young of small birds. Hunts on the ground.

Range and Distribution: From central Iberia through Mediterranean and temperate Europe to Scandinavia, Russia and central Siberia. Also southwards through the Caucasus. In Britain the stronghold is in the New Forest. Pairs have also bred in Norfolk and the north Midlands in recent years, but the British population remains less than 15 pairs.

Movements: Migratory, wintering in Africa. Breeding birds arrive in May and depart in September. Virtually a vagrant elsewhere.

Red Kite

Milvus milvus (Linnaeus)

An elegant slim-winged raptor, with a distinctly V-shaped rusty tail, that has given its name to a children's plaything, and which was persecuted to the brink of extinction during the last century. The Kite's gradual recovery is a saga of bird protection

Hanging motionless on the wind over some wooded ridge, the Red Kite is one of the easiest raptors to identify. In flight the wings are long and angled; the tail long, forked and a pale rusty-red. Distinct white patches mark the base of the outer primaries on the underwing. At rest the reddish underparts can be seen, together with the greyish streaked head and upper breast. The flight is light and agile, almost gull-like in quality. It hangs on updraughts, but soars equally easily. At one time it was widespread in Britain and even took over the urban scavenging niche occupied on the Continent and elsewhere by its relative the Black Kite. The slaughter of all birds of prey, following the introduction of the shotgun and the subsequent overprotection of gamebirds, eliminated it from many areas of England and Scotland and its rarity then attracted the collectors of stuffed specimens. By 1900 there may have been as few as 12 birds left, concentrated in a remote area of central Wales. The build up to 34 pairs in 1978 was the result of active protection by a small body of dedicated Welsh conservationists. 61 cm (24 in).

Voice: High-pitched mewing *wee-oo, wee-oo*.

Habitat: Wooded hills and open country with copses and stands of trees; in Wales in oak woods along valleys.

Reproduction: The nest is built high in a tree on the base of an old nest of Buzzard, Raven or other large bird. It is constructed of twigs, often decorated with rubbish such as rags or polythene. The 2–3, occasionally up to 5, white eggs are blotched with reddish-brown and laid from mid-April onwards. Lost clutches are only rarely replaced. The eggs are incubated mainly by the female, commencing with the first egg, for 28–30 days. The chicks are covered with down and are brooded and fed by the female on food supplied by the male. Later the female also brings food. They fly at 45–50 days, but return to the nest for a further 14 or so days. Single-brooded.

Food: Rabbits and small mammals, carrion, and other animals.

Range and Distribution: Mediterranean and temperate Europe eastwards to western Russia and northwards to southern Sweden. Also in North Africa, Turkey and the Caucasus. In Britain it has spread outwards in Wales, and may breed in Devon.

Movements: British birds are mostly resident. Elsewhere an extremely rare vagrant.

Population: some 34 pairs

Marsh Harrier

Circus aeruginosus (Linnaeus)

A medium-sized, long-winged and long-tailed bird of prey that alternately flaps and glides low over marshy reed beds

Population: the 1977–8 total of 16 nests was the best this century

Male (left) and female (right). Female is chocolate-brown with pale creamy head and forewings. Lacks white rump of other female harriers

The Marsh Harrier is a splendid bird that exhibits a large range of different plumage patterns according to age and sex. In the air it shows long narrow wings that are alternately flapped and then held in a shallow V as it glides. The tail is long and narrow and the feet and legs often dangle below. The male is smaller, but in all plumages this is a much larger bird than the other harriers. The adult male is a brown bird with a pale creamy head, a broad patch of grey on the inner wing and a grey tail. The female is uniformly brown with pronounced cream head and shoulder patches. Immatures may be all brown, but then pass through several plumage changes before becoming adult at 4 years. 48–56 cm (19–22 in).

Voice: Usually silent outside breeding season; male utters a plaintive *kwee-oo*, female a thin whistle.

Habitat: Large reed beds with areas of open water; but will frequent all manner of swamps, together with heaths and argricultural land while hunting.

Reproduction: The nest consists of a mass of reeds and other vegetation, placed over water among dense reeds. The 4–5, occasionally 3–8, eggs are palest blue and laid from mid-April onwards. Incubation, by the female alone, takes 33–38 days during which she is fed by the male. Some males may support 2 females on a single marsh. The chicks are fed by the female on food brought by the male, though as they grow older both parents hunt. Fledging takes 35–40 days, but the chicks return to the nest for a further 14 days. Single-brooded.

Food: Opportunistic, snapping up birds, small mammals and amphibians as available. Also takes eggs and young of other birds.

Range and Distribution: Found from North Africa right across temperate and Mediterranean Europe north to southern Sweden, through Russia and Turkey, central southern Siberia to Manchuria. Britain is on the edge of the species' range and it is more or less confined to East Anglia where, during its chequered history, it was once down to 2 pairs.

Movements: Most British birds probably emigrate along the Atlantic coast of France and southwards. They are replaced by Continental birds in small numbers in East Anglia and the southeast.

Hen Harrier

Circus cyaneus (Linnaeus)

A long-winged, long-tailed bird of prey, grey in the male, brown in the female, that flies near the ground and glides with wings held in a shallow V. From its stronghold in Orkney and the Outer Hebrides it has spread through mainland Scotland and northern England to Wales, and increased dramatically in Ireland, this century

The typical low method of flying, with bouts of flapping interspersed with gliding, is characteristic of all harriers. The male is dove-grey above with black wing tips and a white rump band. The throat and chest are grey, the remaining underparts white. The female is quite different, clothed in browns above, and buff streaked with black below. In this she is very similar to the female Montagu's, but has a larger white rump patch and always appears more stockily built and slightly broader-winged than that species. They are often jointly referred to as 'ring-tail' harriers; one seen in winter is bound to be a Hen Harrier, one in southern England in summer is more likely a Montagu's. 43–51 cm (17–20 in).

Voice: A high-pitched *kee-kee-kee*.

Habitat: Open moors and marshes, bogs, heather-clad hillsides, young forestry plantations.

Reproduction: The nest is built on the ground by the female, though the male may help, from late April onwards. It consists of twigs or reeds lined with grasses and the 4–6 eggs, occasionally up to 12, are incubated by the female for 29–39 days. The chicks are fed and cared for by the female for the first 14 days, food being provided by the male and presented to the female in a spectacular mid-air food pass. The young fly at 37 days. Single-brooded, but some males are polygamous.

Food: Young rabbits and other small mammals, birds and their young up to Lapwing in size, all taken on the ground by surprise cruising.

Range and Distribution: Circumpolar, found over huge areas of the Northern Hemisphere and with a closely allied species, or even subspecies, in South America. Found throughout temperate Europe from southwestern Spain to northern Scandinavia, eastwards across Russia and Siberia to Manchuria; from Alaska across Canada and most of the United States. In Britain and Ireland it reached a desperately low level by 1900, but during the present century it has increased and spread, and now breeds over much of Scotland, northern England, north Wales and especially southern Ireland.

Movements: Internal movements, with some birds leaving the country. An influx of Continental birds in September is mainly passage, though some do stay on to winter in coastal and moorland areas.

Population: 500 to 600 pairs

Female is heavily barred in shades of brown

Montagu's Harrier

Circus pygargus (Linnaeus)

A lightly built harrier; grey in the male, brown in the female; fast declining as a breeding species and that may soon be extinct in Britain. Though climatic change and direct persecution are probably responsible, the overactive attentions of bird-watchers may cause its demise

Generally lighter in build than the Hen Harrier, the male is grey above, lacks a distinct white rump, and has a black transverse bar across the inner wing in flight. The throat and breast are grey, the remaining underparts white boldly streaked with chestnut. The female is very similar to the female Hen Harrier, but has a smaller white rump patch and is less heavily built. Montagu's have the typical low flap-and-glide harrier flight and are summer visitors to Europe, in parts of which they are abundant. In Britain they are on the edge of their range and at an all-time low. 41–46 cm (16–18 in).

Voice: A shrill *kek-kek-kek*.

Habitat: Generally in drier areas than the other British harriers, though frequents marshes and reed beds, as well as moorland on occasion. Dry heaths and young conifer plantations are preferred habitats.

Reproduction: The nest is built on the ground by the female from May onwards and the 4–5, occasionally up to 10, eggs are pale blue and incubated by the female alone for 27–30 days, commencing with the first egg. The total incubation period may thus be up to 40 days, during which the male brings food to his mate. The chicks are fed and cared for by the female, the male bringing food; and the young fly at 35–40 days. Single-brooded.

Food: Variety of animal matter including small mammals, birds and their eggs, reptiles, amphibians and even large insects.

Range and Distribution: From Iberia and North Africa right across temperate Europe north to Denmark and southern Sweden, Russia, the Caucasus and northern Iran to central Siberia. In Britain numbers are very small, no more than 6 pairs, with most nesting in the southwest, though in some years none breed at all.

Movements: Migratory throughout its range, birds wintering in Africa south of the Sahara, and in southern Asia. British birds arrive in April and depart in September: they are most regular in the south.

Adult female

Goshawk

Accipiter gentilis (Linnaeus)

A large, round-winged, long-tailed hawk that is once again breeding in Britain after an absence of many years. This recolonization began in the late 1960s and has been attributed almost entirely to escapes from falconry and to introductions

Population: 18 pairs

Though both are larger than the Sparrowhawk, there is a substantial difference in size between the small male and the larger female. In plumage and shape both sexes are similar to the female Sparrowhawk and a small male may be confused with a large female of the commoner bird. Except during their soaring territorial flights in early spring, these are birds of dense forest which are self-effacing and easily overlooked. They hunt in typical *Accipiter* fashion, flying fast among the trees in large areas of woodland, a habitat that has increased considerably in Britain in recent years. The adult is a slate-grey bird above, marked by a pale greyish supercilium. The underparts are white closely barred with black. The undertail coverts are white and the tail broadly barred. The underwing is heavily barred. Immatures are buff below and streaked with black. Sheer size should be sufficient to identify most Goshawks. 48–61 cm (19–24 in).

Voice: A harsh *gek-gek-gek*, and a Buzzard-like *hi-aa*.

Habitat: Large areas of mature woodland.

Reproduction: Soaring display flight occurs in March and April. The nest is placed high up in the major fork of a tree and constructed of twigs, lined by the male with fresh, leafy twigs or conifer branches. Occasionally an old nest may be reused, but an established pair will have alternative sites within their territory. The 2–3 pale blue eggs are laid in April and incubated by the female, who is fed on the nest by the male. The chicks hatch after 36–41 days and are cared for and fed by the female on food brought by the male. The nest lining is frequently renewed and the young fly after 45 days. Single-brooded.

Food: Mainly larger birds than those taken by the Sparrowhawk.

Range and Distribution: Circumpolar in the Northern Hemisphere, breeding right across Eurasia and North America in the temperate and boreal zones. Found throughout Europe, though generally declining. In Britain it bred in Scotland last century and sporadically elsewhere since, including a small population in Sussex. From 1968 onwards it has bred regularly, increasing and spreading and reaching a total of 18 pairs in 1978. Most are in Scotland in the Highland and Border areas, but the north Midlands of England now have an established population. This colonization is due almost entirely to the escape of falconers' birds, about 50 per cent of which are lost.

Movements: A rare vagrant to south and eastern England from the Continent and British breeding grounds.

Sparrowhawk

Accipiter nisus (Linnaeus)

An agile little hawk that flits easily among trees in its pursuit of small birds. Once widespread and numerous, but the pesticide fiasco of the late 1950s decimated the population; recovery is now evident. Female shown

Population: about 20,000 pairs

Male (left) and female (right). Male is smaller and heavily barred rust-red below. In flight long tail and rounded wings apparent in all plumages

Confused with the Kestrel by the layman, this is the nonhovering small bird of prey, most often seen soaring and wheeling over woodland, or slipping easily among the trees. The male is smaller than his mate and distinctively marked. The upperparts are steel-blue-grey, the underparts narrowly barred with rust. The tail is broadly barred and the underwing barred concentrically. The female is darker above, with a clear, light supercilium, and heavily barred with brown below. Both sexes have long tails, like a Kestrel, but the wings are broader and more rounded, rather than sharply pointed as in that little falcon. Sparrowhawks are woodland birds specializing in taking small birds as prey, but they will also hunt more open areas where trees offer the chance of a surprise attack. 28–38 cm (11–15 in).

Voice: Quite vocal in summer; a *kek-kek-kek*, but also variations on *keu*.

Habitat: Mixed and coniferous woods, but also around hedgerows.

Reproduction: Nests high in a tree, often using the old nest of another species as a base, where an untidy mass of sticks lined with fresh leafy twigs is built by the female, with some help from her mate. The 4–5, occasionally 2–7, white eggs are blotched with reddish-brown and laid from April onwards. They are incubated by the female alone, starting before the clutch is complete. The chicks hatch after 32–35 days and are tended by the female, who feeds them on food brought by the male for the first few days. Thereafter both parents bring food and the young fly 32 days after hatching. Single-brooded.

Food: Mainly small woodland birds.

Range and Distribution: A huge range right across temperate and Mediterranean Europe, Turkey and Russia, eastwards through Siberia to Japan. Also in the mountains of North Africa and the Himalayas. In Britain and Ireland the population crashed as a result of secondary poisoning by pesticides in the late 1950s and early 1960s, so that large areas of the country were completely devoid of Sparrowhawks. A gradual recovery under protection and pesticide bans has made the Sparrowhawk much more common and widespread again and it can be found throughout Britain except for Highland hills, the Outer Hebrides, Orkney and Shetland.

Movements: British and Irish birds are mostly resident. Winter visitors from the Continent arrive on the east coast in October and, while some pass through, others stay until March or April.

Raptors in Flight

Most birds of prey are dully clothed in shades of brown and buff and are notoriously difficult to separate at rest. In the air, however, each species has either a characteristic shape or mode of flight that make it far easier to identify

Osprey: white below with dark patches at the carpal joint; dark above. Long narrow wings that are sharply angled in flight, together with basic coloration and association with water, produce a gull-like impression

Buzzard: highly variable plumage, but identified by broad wings, small head and short broad tail quite different to Golden Eagle's. When soaring wings held in shallow V

Rough-legged Buzzard: pale underwing with dark carpal patches; white tail with broad black terminal band; and dark belly separate from Buzzard. Frequently hovers and soars on flat wings

Kestrel: most often seen hovering. This habit, together with long, sharply pointed wings, separates from Sparrowhawk, though both birds have long barred tails. The most common of our birds of prey

Peregrine: purposeful, fast and dramatic flight on long scythe-like wings. Dark grey above and closely barred below, with bold dark moustachial patch. Usually kills in flight after dramatic high-speed stoop

Merlin: small moorland falcon. Male grey above, female streaked in browns. Fast darting flight, long wings and shorter tail separate from Kestrel. Habitat and season usually distinguish from Hobby

Hobby: summer migrant. Highly aerial falcon, dark above and heavily streaked below. Feeds by hawking for insects, soaring on long angled wings superficially similar to a Swift's

Osprey

Buzzard

Rough-legged Buzzard

Kestrel

Peregrine

Merlin

Hobby

Golden Eagle

Honey Buzzard

Red Kite

Hen Harrier

Goshawk

Sparrowhawk

Golden Eagle: huge majestic brown bird with long, broad wings and marked by prominent head, large bill and substantial tail. Overall shape more angular than Buzzard. Confusable only with another species of eagle

Honey Buzzard: similar to Buzzard but has longer tail, more prominent, almost pigeon-like, head, and boldly barred underwings. When soaring, wings have definite and diagnostic droop

Red Kite: long and narrow angled wings, together with long, deeply forked red tail, are easily picked out. Soars easily, but most often seen hanging motionless above valley woodlands

Hen Harrier: pale grey male marked with black wing tips and white rump. Similar Montagu's Harrier has narrow black bars across secondaries and less pronounced white rump

Goshawk: like huge Sparrowhawk, though small males may be confused with large females of that species. Generally less dashing. Wings more rounded and tail proportionately shorter

Sparrowhawk: often confused with Kestrel, but rounded wings usually a good feature. Fast, soaring flight interspersed with diving and circling is so characteristic that it may be identified at quite enormous distances

Buzzard

Buteo buteo (Linnaeus)

A medium-sized, broad-winged
hawk with short broad tail and small
head, most often seen in soaring
flight with wings held in a shallow V

Population: 8,000
to 10,000 pairs

Buzzards are remarkably variable and best identified by shape. They are chunky, heavily built birds, brown above, streaked and barred below; at rest undistinguished, in the air the shape and flight attitude are diagnostic. The body is usually dark, the broad tail barred throughout its length and terminating in a single broad band. The wing linings are darker than the flight feathers, which have a variable amount of transverse barring. The outer flight feathers have light bases forming distinct pale patches towards the tips of the wings. Dark carpal patches are often evident. However, the broad-winged shape, the insignificant head and the short, broad tail are more important than plumage distinctions, as is the characteristic shallow V of the wings when soaring. Where there is a dense population of Buzzards, several may be seen soaring together in a thermal. 51–56 cm (20–22 in).

Voice: A loud mewing while soaring, *pee-ooo*.

Habitat: Heavily wooded country, usually with adjacent farmland, often in hilly or broken terrain; also crags and mountainsides.

Reproduction: The nest is placed in the major crotch of a tree in a wood or isolated copse. It consists of a pile of sticks lined with fresh, leafy twigs. In moorland areas it may also be placed on a crag or cliff and, just occasionally, on the ground. The 3–4 eggs, occasionally 1–6, are laid in April or May and are white blotched with chestnut. They are incubated for 33–35 days by both sexes and the chicks are tended by the female for the first few days and fed by her on food brought by the male. Thereafter both sexes bring food for 40–45 days. Single-brooded.

Food: Rabbits and other small mammals, carrion including dead lambs, as well as a wide variety of birds, reptiles and amphibians.

Range and Distribution: Found right across the Palearctic, from Iberia north to the tree line in Scandinavia, eastwards through Siberia to Japan. In Britain it was abundant, particularly in the west, until myxomatosis decimated the rabbit population in 1955. The subsequent decline was hastened by poisoning from the persistent chemicals used in sheep dips as the desperate Buzzard population turned to carrion in their efforts to survive. The ban on use of these chemicals in 1966, and the return to health of the rabbit, have enabled the Buzzard to increase and spread once more. It is now widespread in Scotland, the Lake District and especially Wales and the southwest, where it finds conditions ideal. A small population exists in the north of Ireland, and there are signs of the Buzzard spreading in the south and Midlands.

Movements: British birds are mostly resident, but there is some passage and wintering of Continental birds on the east coast.

Rough-legged Buzzard

Buteo lagopus (Pontoppidan)

A Buzzard-like winter visitor from the far north in variable numbers, depending on the productivity of its breeding grounds and the autumn food supply. Frequently hovers and soars on 'flat' wings

Population: highly variable; uncommon winter visitor

Usually distinguished from the common Buzzard by plumage rather than shape, which is similar. This species is generally paler and has a white tail above and below, with a prominent black terminal band. The belly is dark, contrasting with the very light underwing, which is marked by prominent dark carpal patches. The head and neck are invariably pale. Though it has narrower wings than the common Buzzard, this is a fine point. However, it can be picked out at a distance by its high, hovering flight and by hanging on the wind. When the bird is soaring its wings are held slightly kinked, but flat, not in a V like the common Buzzard. In winter it may gather in some numbers in suitable areas. 51–61 cm (20–24 in).

Voice: Generally silent in winter; in summer the call is a high-pitched repeated *mee-ow*.

Habitat: Tundra, and barren mountains beyond the tree line; occasionally woodland edges; in winter mainly coastal marshes and other open country.

Reproduction: The nest is placed on a crag or cliff ledge, though also in a tree. It consists of sticks, lined with leafy twigs or moss, and the 2–3 eggs, up to 7 in productive years, are white blotched with chestnut and laid from the end of April onwards, depending on local conditions. Incubation, which is shared and commences with the first egg, lasts 28–31 days and the chicks are tended by the female and fed on food brought by the male. The young fly at 41 days. Single-brooded, with weaker chicks usually dying and being eaten by their siblings.

Food: Lemmings on breeding grounds. In years when these rodents reach plague proportions, Rough-Legged Buzzards lay more eggs and rear more young. Also grouse, voles, rabbits and small birds.

Range and Distribution: Circumpolar in tundra and boreal zones. From southern Norway right across Eurasia to Kamchatka and the Bering Straits, and through Alaska and most of Canada.

Movements: Irruptive, depending on food supply and population levels. In Britain it is a winter visitor, sometimes in good numbers, to the east coast of Scotland and England. Scarce elsewhere and rare in Ireland.

Breeds from Scandinavia eastwards: highly variable population and distribution

Golden Eagle

Aquila chrysaetos (Linnaeus)

Largest of British birds of prey, the Golden Eagle is easily distinguished from all other birds. It is truly majestic, with a prominent head in flight that is quite unlike the almost headless appearance of the much smaller Buzzard

Population: about 250 pairs

Broad wings, massive head and large tail are apparent in flight

Large, solitary birds that occupy huge territories among the wildest of country, principally in the Scottish Highlands and islands. Adults are all brown, marked by a light golden colour on the nape and a bright yellow cere. The legs are heavily feathered and sheer size is usually sufficient to identify the bird. In flight they glide effortlessly over hillsides, turning around crags and rocks in the hope of surprising prey. They frequently soar, rising high in the sky on huge, broad wings that show distinct 'fingering' at the tips, and which are held flat. The head is always prominent. Immatures are similar, but have a white tail broadly tipped with black. Golden Eagles are resident and usually have 2 or 3 nest sites within their huge and remote territories. 75–88 cm (30–35 in).

Voice: Usually silent; a *twee-oo*, and a thin yelp.

Habitat: Rugged mountain moorland, with or without trees; also elsewhere in their range in lowlands and marshes.

Reproduction: Several nest sites are used in rotation. The nest is a huge conglomeration of sticks, frequently the result of several years of occupation, placed on a buttress or cliff, or in a tall tree. It is lined with fresh leafy twigs, and the first of the 2, occasionally 1 or 3, eggs is laid in late March. These are white, blotched with chestnut, and are incubated by the female, sometimes also by the male, for 43–45 days, starting with the first egg. The eaglets are brooded by the female and fed by her for 40 days on food brought by the male. They fly at 63–70 days, though usually only a single youngster survives. Single-brooded.

Food: Grouse, Ptarmigan, hares, sheep carrion, even occasional sickly lambs, but only in areas that are overstocked.

Range and Distribution: One of the most widespread of the world's birds, being found throughout the Northern Hemisphere from the arctic wastes of Alaska, throughout North America to Mexico, through the mountains of Europe and North Africa, Turkey and Iran, Russia and through Siberia to the Himalayas and Japan. Though it formerly bred in England and Wales it was drastically reduced during the era of uninformed game protection and disappeared from many traditional haunts. The respite provided by 2 world wars and the consequent decline in gamekeepers' activities aided an increase that has been maintained in recent years by a more enlightened and protective attitude. It now breeds throughout the Highlands and islands, and, since 1969, in the English Lake District.

Movements: Sedentary; rare vagrant away from breeding areas.

Osprey

Pandion haliaetus (Linnaeus)

A spectacular bird of prey that feeds by plunging feet-first into water to catch fish. Exterminated in Britain during the collecting mania of the last century, it has since re-established itself in Scotland and is continuing a slow spread

Population: about 20 pairs

At rest the Osprey is a brown bird with a long neck (for a raptor) and a remarkably small white head. In flight, the white underparts become more apparent and are quite distinctive with dark carpal patches and a pronounced breast band. The angled, gull-like wings facilitate identification, even at a considerable distance. It frequently hovers and plunges feet-first both into fresh and salt water. Loaded with a substantial fish, it often has difficulty in rising from the surface. It is a summer visitor to northern and eastern Europe. 51–58 cm (20–23 in).

Voice: A brief cheeping.

Habitat: Lakes, rivers and sea coasts.

Reproduction: Birds arrive in April and construct or renew a nest of sticks built atop a tree or cliff. In some parts of the Osprey's range quite low bluffs, crags and ruins may be used, and it will even take to an artificial platform such as a cartwheel mounted on a pole. The female performs most of the construction, while the male gathers most of the materials. The 3, occasionally 2 or 4, eggs are cream blotched with chestnut and are incubated by both sexes for 35–38 days, the female taking the larger share. The chicks are tended by the female and fed by her on food brought by the male. Later both sexes bring food and the young fly after 51–59 days. They require considerable practice to develop their fishing techniques. Single-brooded.

Food: Fish of a wide variety of species, including trout, pike, roach and carp according to availability.

Range and Distribution: Virtually cosmopolitan, occurring on all the world's great landmasses except South America. Particularly widespread in North America and Eurasia, though eliminated from many areas of temperate Europe including Britain, where the last pair bred at Loch an Eilean in the Spey Valley in 1916. In 1955 a pair bred at nearby Loch Garten and has done so every year since, under the watchful eye of the RSPB. There are now about 20 pairs, all in the Highland region.

Movements: British birds arrive in April and depart in September. On migration through the country they are joined by Scandinavian birds and, in autumn, may remain off-passage at fish-rich waters throughout the country, and especially at English reservoirs.

Kestrel

Falco tinnunculus (Linnaeus)

A long-winged, long-tailed falcon, most often seen hovering over open farmland and, more recently, along motorway margins. The Kestrel is by far the most common and widespread of our birds of prey. Female shown

Population: over 100,000 pairs

Male (right). In all plumages long pointed wings and long tail are surest means of identification

In shape the Kestrel is quite unlike any other British or Irish bird of prey. Its size and long tail distinguish it from all species except the Sparrowhawk; and its long, sharply pointed wings as against the rather broad, rounded wings of that hawk are usually sufficient for accurate identification. The habit of hovering, head down, in its search for food is characteristic. The male has a grey head marked by a clear black moustachial streak, and a grey tail with a broad black subterminal band. The back is deep rust, spotted with black; the underparts a warm cream, spotted in streaks of black. The primaries are black and the cere and feet pale yellow. The female is similar in build and habits, but the grey of the male is replaced by brown barred or streaked with black. Kestrels feed by pouncing on their prey on the ground from their hovering flight, quite unlike the wheeling aerobatics of Sparrowhawks, which seize prey after a wild dash through woodland. 34 cm ($13\frac{1}{2}$ in).

Voice: A high-pitched *kee-kee-kee-kee* in the breeding season.

Habitat: Farmland, heaths, moors, marshes, parks, woodland edges, suburbs and city centres.

Reproduction: The nest is placed in a variety of situations from cliff ledges and crags to old buildings and the disused nests of other birds, as well as holes in trees. It is a simple hollow with little or no nesting material and the 4–5, occasionally up to 9, eggs are covered with a mottling of brown and laid from mid-April onwards. The female performs most of the incubation which lasts 27–29 days, starting with the first egg. For the first few days after hatching the female broods and feeds the young on food provided by the male. Thereafter both parents bring food until the young fly at 27–39 days. Single-brooded.

Food: Mainly small mammals, but in city centres these birds, like Tawny Owls, have adapted to a diet of House Sparrows.

Range and Distribution: Found over large areas of the Old World, from Europe and North Africa across Eurasia, through the Middle East to India, China and Japan. Also throughout sub-Saharan Africa apart from the equatorial forest belt. In Britain and Ireland it is common and widespread, being absent only from Shetland and most of the Outer Hebrides. Scarce in the Fens due to lack of nesting sites.

Movements: Most British Kestrels are resident, though some, from the north in particular, move southwards into northern France and south from there to Iberia. An immigration of Continental birds occurs on the east coast in autumn, but after that they mix with local birds and, while some winter, others pass through further south.

Merlin

Falco columbarius (Linnaeus)

A splendid, long-winged, fast-flying little falcon, found on moorland in summer and marshes in winter. Its speed and aggressiveness belie its size and it is capable of downing prey as large as itself. Female shown

Population: less than 1,000 pairs

Male (perched left) and female (right)

The male has a blue-grey crown, back and tail, the latter marked with a broad black subterminal band. The head is greyish with faint dark moustachial streaks and a prominent pale supercilium. The chest is creamy, becoming more rufous on the belly, and heavily streaked with black. The feet, legs and cere are yellow. The female is similar in size, shape and plumage pattern, but brown above and with a tail that is broadly barred throughout its length. At rest the folded wings reach almost to the tip of the short tail and, in flight, the long, angled wings scythe purposefully through the air. It is a small-bird specialist, which finds the Meadow Pipit ideal prey over most of its British and Irish range. 27–33 cm (10½–13 in).

Voice: A high-pitched *ki-ki-ki-ki*.

Habitat: Open moors, often of heather, bogs, young forestry plantations, but usually at some altitude; in winter prefers coasts with marshes and water meadows.

Reproduction: Nests most frequently among rank old heather, utilizing a simple bare hollow in the ground. Occasionally, old tree nests of other species are used. The 5–6, rarely 7, eggs are mottled brown all over and are laid from May onwards. They are incubated mainly by the female for 28–32 days, starting before the clutch is complete, during which the male provides his mate with food. The chicks are brooded and cared for by the female and fed by her on food brought by the male for the first few days after hatching. After that both parents bring food until the young fly at 25–30 days. Single-brooded.

Food: Small birds, augmented by the occasional small mammal or insect; wide variety of species recorded, though Meadow Pipits often feature prominently.

Range and Distribution: Circumpolar, breeding from Iceland across Scandinavia, northern Russia and Siberia to the Bering Straits; Alaska, across Canada into the northern United States in the Rockies, to Newfoundland. In Britain and Ireland it is confined to the hilly districts of the north and west.

Movements: Birds generally move to lower ground in winter, though some leave Britain for western France and Iberia. There is some immigration from the Continent in October, and also a passage of Icelandic birds.

Hobby

Falco subbuteo (Linnaeus)

A long-winged falcon, bearing a superficial resemblance to the Kestrel, but with all the grace and dash of a Peregrine. It is a summer visitor to England and feeds in the air on insects, and on Swallows, martins and Swifts

Adults are slate-grey above with a prominent dark moustache outlined against a white cheek. The tail is slate-grey, barred below, and the white underparts are heavily streaked with black. The leg feathering and undertail coverts are bright rust-red, forming a distinctive patch. At rest the long wings reach to, or beyond, the tail. In flight the overall shape is almost Swift-like, the tail being considerably shorter than that of the Kestrel, the wings longer and more sickle-shaped. The Hobby soars frequently, hawking for large insects which it consumes on the wing. Such are its powers of flight that it is able to catch the fast-flying hirundines and even Swifts. Immatures are brown above and buff below heavily streaked with black. The dark moustaches are even then an obvious field characteristic. 30–36 cm (12–14 in).

Voice: A *ki-ki-ki* and a repeated *keu*.

Habitat: Dry heathland and downs with clumps of large trees.

Reproduction: Hobbies arrive in May and lay their eggs in mid-June. An old nest of another species is used, usually situated high in a tree, often a conifer. The 2–3 eggs are covered with spots of reddish-brown and incubated mainly by the female for 28 days, starting with the second egg. The male brings food to his sitting mate and, when the chicks hatch, for her to feed the young. As the chicks grow both parents bring food; the young fly after 28–32 days. Single-brooded.

Food: Flying insects and small birds, Swallows, martins and Swifts.

Range and Distribution: Found from North Africa and Iberia across Europe, north to Finland, through Russia and Turkey in a great sweep to China and Kamchatka. In Britain it is confined to southern England and the adjacent south Midlands, where for generations it has been ceaselessly persecuted through illegal egg collecting. There is some evidence of a gradual increase, especially in the southwest, and also records from the Spey Valley in Scotland.

Movements: Leaves breeding range completely, European birds wintering in Africa south of the Sahara. British birds arrive in May and depart in August and September. Occasional birds wander away from breeding areas.

Population: between 68 and 152 pairs in 1978

143

Peregrine

Falco peregrinus (Tunstall)

One of the world's most spectacular birds. A master of flight, it kills in the air, but it has suffered a serious decline in numbers due to accidental poisoning and its popularity with Middle East falconers

Population: 350 to 400 pairs

Slate-grey above, with dark moustaches prominent against a white cheek; white below, closely barred on chest and belly. The cere, eye-ring and feet are yellow. The young are brown above, streaked not barred below, but with the broad moustachial patch of the adult. When the bird is soaring the long wings and short tail produce a characteristic outline, shared only with a few other large falcons not found in Britain and Ireland. In purposeful flight, the long wings cut easily through the air and in a folded-winged stoop the Peregrine is one of the fastest flying of all birds. They kill their prey with a blow from the hind toe, but also 'bind to' and carry it off. 38–48 cm (15–19 in).

Voice: A high-pitched *kek-kek-kek-kek*, also a *meechoo*, and other calls.

Habitat: Cliffs, both inland and along sea coasts, also occasionally in quarries and abroad even on tall city buildings.

Reproduction: The nest consists of a simple unlined hollow on a ledge, and nest sites are traditionally reused year after year. The 3–4, occasionally 2–6, eggs are covered with reddish-brown blotches, laid from mid-April, and incubated by both sexes for 28–29 days, starting before the clutch is complete; the female takes the larger share. The chicks are brooded and fed by the female for the first 2 weeks after hatching, and she continues most of the feeding, even when she herself joins the male in hunting for the brood. The young falcons fly after 35–42 days, but take a long time to learn to hunt for themselves and reach independence. Single-brooded.

Food: Mainly medium-sized birds, especially pigeons, but a wide variety of other prey is also taken.

Range and Distribution: Cosmopolitan, breeding on all of the world's major landmasses. In the Northern Hemisphere it has a circumpolar distribution right across Eurasia and North America. Also in Africa, Asia, Australasia and South America. The very serious decline in the mid-1950s was caused by accumulation of pesticides from prey; the Peregrine was virtually wiped out in North America and down to half of its normal population in Britain and Ireland. The new-found, oil-based wealth of the Middle East has brought the traditional sport of falconry within reach of a larger population and the subsequent demand puts all Peregrine populations at risk. British and Irish Peregrines have shown a slow increase in recent years.

Movements: Mainly resident, with some wandering, particularly by younger birds in autumn. Winter and passage visitors arrive in autumn.

Adult perched and flying (right): immature (left). Flying birds give an impression of enormous power

144

Red Grouse

Lagopus lagopus (Linnaeus)

A subspecies of the more widespread Willow Grouse and the object of the sport of grouse-shooting, traditionally celebrated for a few brief weeks after the twelfth of August

Population: about 500,000 pairs

Male (left) and female

This rust-red bird is artificially maintained at an abnormally high population level and is a favoured gamebird because it is easily driven over butts. It is a rich brown on the body, heavily barred with black. The wings and outer tail are black and the male sports a small red comb on the crown. The female is paler. The subspecies *Lagopus lagopus scoticus* is endemic to Britain, being replaced elsewhere by the Willow Grouse *Lagopus lagopus lagopus*, which has white wings in summer and all-white plumage in winter. Red Grouse are rather secretive on their native moors and will flush at the last moment when disturbed, flying away low over the ground and gliding on bowed wings before alighting a few hundred metres away. They form flocks in winter. 38–41 cm (15–16 in).

Voice: A distinctive *go-back, go-back*; also a repeated *kow-ok-ok-ok*.

Habitat: Open moorland with heather and usually some berry-bearing dwarf shrubs.

Reproduction: The nest consists of a hollow lined with grass and heather and the 6–11, occasionally 4–17, eggs are mottled reddish-brown. They are laid in late April or May, though nests as early as February are not unknown. Incubation, by the female alone, lasts 20–26 days and the down-covered chicks leave the nest soon after hatching. They are tended by both sexes for 12–18 days before flying, but remain together as a family until the autumn. Single-brooded.

Food: Shoots, seeds and flowers of heather, but also berries and other plants, and some insects; the latter are particularly important to the young chicks.

Range and Distribution: The species enjoys a circumpolar distribution across Eurasia and in Alaska and Canada, where it is called the Willow Ptarmigan. The Red Grouse is found only in Britain (introduced to Belgium) and is confined to the upland districts of the north and west. The population is maintained at a high level by rotational burning of heather and strict gamekeeping.

Movements: Resident.

Ptarmigan

Lagopus mutus (Moutin)

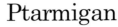

An elusive, well-camouflaged bird of the high mountain tops that bears a strong resemblance to the closely related Red Grouse, but is generally rather greyer in summer and pure white in winter. It replaces that species above the heather line. Male in winter shown

Population: about 10,000 pairs

A dumpy, short-legged, ground-dwelling bird that merges well with the broken, lichen- and rock-covered ground it inhabits. The male is mottled on head, breast and upperparts in greys, browns and blacks, but has distinctive white wings, belly and feet. There is a red wattle above the eye. The female is lighter and warmer in colour, also has white wings, a much smaller red wattle and, if anything, is even more highly camouflaged than her mate. It is remarkably easy to walk Ptarmigan territory and virtually trip over the birds before seeing them. In winter both sexes are white, the male with black on the lores, marked by a black outer tail. In intermediate plumages the grey and white body maintains the cryptic camouflage. 35–36 cm (14 in).

Voice: A repeated grating of alarm; also a croaking *uk-uk*.

Habitat: Barren mountain tops with stones and lichens mixed with dwarf vegetation. Also breeds on open, low-level tundra.

Reproduction: The nest is a hollow, often concealed among dwarf vegetation, lined with a few grasses and feathers. The 5–10, occasionally 3–12, eggs are whitish blotched with dark brown and laid from the end of May onwards. They are incubated by the female for 24–26 days and the chicks leave the nest soon after hatching. Both parents tend the young, which first fly at 10 days. They remain with the female and join up with other families to form winter flocks. Single-brooded.

Food: Vegetable matter, shoots and berries of arctic vegetation; also sometimes insects.

Range and Distribution: Circumpolar, from Iceland and Scandinavia across northern Eurasia to the Bering Straits, and across northern North America, where it is known as the Rock Ptarmigan, to the coasts of Greenland. One of the world's most northerly breeding birds. In Europe it is also found in the Pyrenees and Alps. In Britain it is confined to the high mountains of the Highlands and Inner Hebrides, though it was once more widespread and last century ranged further south, to the English Lake District.

Movements: Sedentary; some local movements to lower levels occur in winter.

From left to right: summer female, summer male, winter male. White wings separate from Red Grouse in summer

Black Grouse

Tetrao tetrix (Linnaeus)

Male called Blackcock; female, Greyhen. The male is a spectacular, medium-sized, all-black bird marked with a bright red comb, and a lyre-shaped tail that is raised vertically in display to show white undertail coverts. Male (right) and female shown

Population: 10,000 to 50,000 pairs

The all-black male is washed with shiny blue on body and tail. The wings are sooty black with 2 white wing bars. The tail is sharply divided and curls away from the centre, though in display it is raised to show the white undertail coverts. There is a bright red comb over the eye. The female is mottled and barred in shades of brown above, the lighter underparts being clearly barred with dark brown. The large, broad tail is distinctly notched. Males gather at leks to display and are so tenacious of their traditional sites that modern developments such as buildings may be ignored. Usually most active at dawn, and again at dusk. Male 53 cm (21 in), female 41 cm (16 in).

Voice: A sneezing *tchu-wai* of male; female utters a Pheasant-like *kok-kok* call.

Habitat: Moorland edges with birches or conifer plantations, mature pines with areas of undergrowth, and grassy fields.

Reproduction: Males gather at leks and display communally. Females visit the lek, are mated, and are then solely responsible for nesting and rearing the young. The nest, usually not far from the lek, is a simple hollow lined with available material and invariably hidden among vegetation. Occasionally the old nest of another species, situated low in a tree, may be used. The 6–10, occasionally 5–16, eggs are buffish, finely speckled with brown. They are laid from mid-May and incubated for 23–26 days. The chicks leave the nest soon after hatching and can fly at about 30 days. Single-brooded.

Food: Buds and shoots of trees and shrubs, as well as a variety of seeds and berries.

Range and Distribution: Breeds right across Eurasia from Britain and the French Alps to Manchuria, mostly in the boreal zone. In Britain it is confined to the hilly districts of the west and north, with a tiny remnant population in the southwest on Exmoor. Numbers are probably increasing following a marked decline in the middle of the nineteenth century.

Movements: Sedentary.

Capercaillie

Tetrao urogallus (Linnaeus)

A huge, tree-dwelling gamebird of Turkey-like proportions that was exterminated during the latter part of the eighteenth century. Present population is the result of several successive reintroductions of Scandinavian birds during the nineteenth century, aided by an extensive reafforestation programme. Male (foreground) and female shown

Population: less than 10,000 pairs

The male Capercaillie is a large bird that appears even larger when fanning its tail, Turkey-like, in display. The upperparts are pale slate-black with a brown saddle and wings. There is a red wattle above the eye, a slash of iridescent green forming a broad chest band, a touch of white at the bend of the wing and a silvery mottling on belly, undertail coverts and feathered legs. The bill is pale horn and there is a shaggy 'beard' on the chin. The overall impression is of a large, black bird. The female is camouflaged in browns above, has a rich chestnut breast and boldly barred underparts. These birds are most often seen breaking from the cover of conifers, but are nevertheless elusive. Males have a lek display system like Black Grouse. Male 86 cm (34 in), female 62 cm (24 in).

Voice: Male in display has a *tik-up, tik-up* call ending with an explosive *pop*; female utters a *kok-kok* call like that of a Pheasant.

Habitat: Mature woods of Scots pine, together with plantations of larch and spruce thinned to allow plentiful undergrowth.

Reproduction: Males gather at leks in open glades among conifers and are generally either oblivious of, or aggressive to, intruders. They strut and posture, fanning their tails to maintain their position. Females visit the lek, are mated, and are then solely responsible for the rest of the breeding cycle. The nest is a hollow hidden among the roots of a tree, but may also be in open areas with heather. The 5–8, occasionally up to 18, eggs are buffish speckled with darker tones and are incubated for 26–29 days. The chicks leave the nest the day after they hatch and fly after 14 days. Single-brooded.

Food: Shoots and buds of conifers, but also berries and seeds of a wide variety of plants. Though Capercaillies cause damage to plantations, they are usually tolerated by foresters.

Range and Distribution: From the Pyrenees and Alps right across Scandinavia and northern Europe, through Russia to central Siberia. In Britain the native birds were extinct by 1785, in Ireland by 1790. Swedish birds were reintroduced at Taymouth Castle in 1837 and subsequently at several places. It is now found throughout the Highlands including some areas north of the Great Glen in the east.

Movements: Sedentary.

Red-legged Partridge

Alectoris rufa (Linnaeus)

A compact, ground-dwelling gamebird with a distinctive pattern of black and white on the head. Introduced successfully from the Continent in 1790 and still locally known as the French Partridge or 'Frenchman'

Population: between 100,000 and 200,000 pairs

Warm vinous brown upperparts. The characteristic head pattern consists of a black stripe running through the eye continuing to form a band on the throat, and enclosing an area of white on the chin and sides of the face. The breast is streaked with black over a warm vinous pink. The flanks are white washed with lavender and heavily barred with black. The remaining underparts are a warm orange-yellow. The legs and feet, as well as the bill, are coral-red. Like the native Grey Partridge, this is a bird of open agricultural land, but it prefers drier areas than that species. 34 cm (13½ in).

Voice: A distinct *chuck-chuck-ar*, often uttered from a low perch.

Habitat: Arable land, heaths, and even coastal dunes.

Reproduction: The nest is situated in deep cover in a covert, hedgerow or among growing crops. It consists of a scantily lined hollow and the 10–16, occasionally up to 20 and exceptionally up to 28, eggs are buffish spotted with reddish-brown. They are laid from the end of April and incubated by both sexes, though a second clutch may be laid soon after, in which case the male takes charge of one, the female the other. The chicks hatch after 23–25 days and leave the nest immediately. They are tended by the female or, in the case of 2 broods, by each adult separately.

Food: Leaves, cereals, seeds and other vegetable matter, some insects and spiders in summer.

Range and Distribution: A European bird confined to Spain, France, Corsica and northwestern Italy. Introduced to Balearic Isles, Azores, Canaries and Madeira. Also introduced to Britain in 1790 and subsequently, and has now spread over most of eastern England and the Midlands, becoming scarcer in the west. Recent releases as far north as Scotland and west to the Isle of Man.

Movements: Sedentary.

Grey Partridge

Perdix perdix (Linnaeus)

The native partridge of Britain and Ireland, but a bird that has suffered a serious decline in numbers and contraction of range over the last 30 years. Coveys (flocks) are generally much smaller than in the past, and its value as a prime gamebird has been considerably diminished

Population: about 500,000 pairs

Brown, finely streaked with black and white above, grey on the breast, orange on face and throat, grey barred with light chestnut on the flanks and with a prominent dark chestnut horseshoe on the belly, this is a distinctively marked species. It is, however, most often seen flying away low over the ground and gliding on bowed wings, and is then not easily distinguished from the introduced Red-legged Partridge. It frequents open ground and is now generally found in small coveys. 30 cm (12 in).

Voice: A loud, harsh *kerric-kerric-kerric*, often uttered at dusk or well after dark.

Habitat: Arable and grassland with hedgerows or other areas of cover, also on low moors and sand dunes.

Reproduction: A simple hollow on the ground lined with grasses and hidden beneath low vegetation serves as a nest. The 9–20, occasionally up to 23, eggs are buff or brown and laid from the end of April. They are incubated by the female for 23–25 days and the chicks leave the nest soon after hatching. They are cared for by both parents and can fly, before being fully feathered, at 16 days. Single-brooded.

Food: Leaves, seeds and shoots of weeds and cereals; the young feed on insects and particularly on sawfly larvae.

Range and Distribution: From northern Spain across Europe to the head of the Gulf of Bothnia, and to Turkey, Russia and central Asia. In Britain and Ireland it is widespread, becoming thinner on the ground in the north and west and absent from large areas of Wales, the southern half of Ireland, and the Highlands and islands of Scotland. The decline in Ireland began last century and the population was nearly extinct by 1930. In Britain the decline began later and has been attributed to autumn burning and ploughing, later and wetter springs, and the widespread use of agricultural pesticides. Certainly chick mortality is very high in late springs.

Movements: Sedentary.

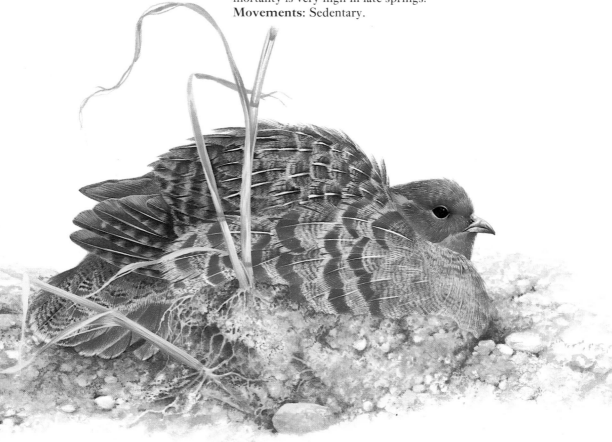

Quail

Coturnix coturnix (Linnaeus)

A diminutive, partridge-like bird, of dumpy proportions and virtually tailless appearance, that is often heard but seldom seen. When flushed its long wings and speedy flight are instantly apparent

Population: variable, but less than 1,000 pairs

Male (left) and female

Smallest of the gamebirds, brown barred with black above, and creamy below. The flanks are pale chestnut streaked with black and white, and the head of the male is marked with a black chin and throat band. However, such descriptions are virtually academic, for this is a secretive bird that is seldom seen on the ground. The usual view is of a small cigar-shaped bird, flying low over the ground on long, pointed wings, immediately after being flushed. Its presence is usually advertised by its distinctive call. 18 cm (7 in).

Voice: A repeated and rapidly uttered *quip, quip-quip*, most frequently heard at dawn and dusk.

Habitat: Cereal and hay fields, as well as rough grassland, wasteland and dunes.

Reproduction: Males are polygamous, leaving all nesting duties to the females. The nest is a simple hollow lined with grass, and the 7–12, occasionally up to 18, eggs are creamy spotted with brown and laid from late May. Incubation lasts 16–21 days and the chicks leave the nest soon after hatching. They are cared for by the female for 19 days before flying. Single-brooded, with an occasional second.

Food: Seeds of grass and cereals, some insects.

Range and Distribution: Found right across the temperate Palearctic from Iberia to Japan, southwards to North Africa, Egypt and the Himalayas. Also in the southern third of Africa and Madagascar. In Britain and Ireland it has varied enormously in numbers over the past century and a half. It is now decidedly scarce, though some years are better than others. Most Quail are concentrated in southern and central England and show a good correlation with chalklands. In Ireland it was much more numerous until the middle of last century.

Movements: Quail arrive in May and depart in September. They are total migrants (though they formerly wintered in Ireland), wintering in the Mediterranean and the sahel zone of the southern Sahara.

152
152

Ring-necked

Melanistic

Mongolian

Pheasant

Phasianus colchicus (Linnaeus)

Said to have been introduced by the Romans and certainly by the Normans, the Pheasant is a familiar sight and sound over most of Britain and Ireland. Its value as a gamebird has created a huge artificial rearing industry that continually adds to and maintains the population

Population: up to 500,000 pairs

Male (foreground) and female

The male is a large bird marked by a long, pointed tail making up half its length. It is rich chestnut boldly barred with black. The head is a dark bottle-green, usually separated from the body by a white neck-ring, though plumage varies enormously. A large red wattle around the eye covers much of the face. The female is similarly long-tailed, but paler and creamier and streaked in cryptic colours. They are generally gregarious birds, forming small parties, and are easily driven over waiting guns. As a result, and in conjunction with the development and perfection of the shotgun, the sport of Pheasant shooting has developed into a major field sport over large areas of England. Huge numbers of birds are reared annually to be released in late summer for a few brief weeks of idyllic freedom before being shot in the autumn. While the sport has protected huge areas of land and benefited much wildlife by doing so, the direct persecution of birds of prey and other so-called 'vermin' has reduced the numbers of raptors in many parts of the country. But for such continued rearing programmes, it is doubtful whether the Pheasant could survive as a British bird. In its native range, which covers a huge area through the Middle and Far East, the Pheasant has developed a variety of different plumages. Being largely resident, a great many subspecies have been described on this basis. Birds introduced to Britain and Ireland come from a variety of origins and are drawn from many distinct subspecies. Thrown together they interbreed freely and have developed a spectacular array of hybrid plumages. A melanistic form may even resemble a separate species, the Japanese Pheasant *Phasianus versicolor*. Male 76–89 cm (30–35 in), female 53–63 cm (21–25 in).

Voice: A loud *kok-kok* of the male.

Habitat: Wide variety of landforms, but usually arable land with thick hedgerows and copses, coverts and heaths; also marshes – their original Asiatic habitat.

Reproduction: Males are polygamous, females taking full charge of all nesting duties. The nest is a lightly lined hollow, and the 7–15 eggs are plain stone-brown and laid from late April. Incubation lasts 23–27 days and the chicks are tended for 12–14 days before becoming independent. Single-brooded.

Food: Varied, including both vegetable and animal matter. Leaves, berries, seeds, together with large amounts of insects, worms, slugs and other invertebrates.

Range and Distribution: From the Caspian eastwards through central Siberia to China and Burma. Introduced to most of Europe, though not northern Scandinavia or western Iberia. In Britain and Ireland it is widespread, and absent only from some of the more barren hill districts and the far north of Scotland and its islands. Population augmented every autumn by huge numbers of reared birds.

Movements: Sedentary in introduced range; some evidence of migration from extreme parts of natural range in Manchuria.

Water Rail

Rallus aquaticus (Linnaeus)

A secretive, self-effacing, marsh-dwelling bird that is more often heard than seen. Its weird cries have been likened to those of a screaming pig

Population: probably less than 4,000 pairs

A widespread bird, but one that keeps well inside dense cover and is very difficult to observe. Occasionally it wanders out into open water to reward the patient watcher. The upperparts are brown, heavily streaked with black. The head, breast and belly are a fine dove-grey, and the flanks and undertail coverts are boldly barred black and white. In flight, which is usually only a flutter of a few metres, the legs and feet dangle below. Its remarkably thin shape enables it to pass through dense vegetation with minimum disturbance. The pattern of plumage is similar to that of other European crakes, but at all times the long, pointed, red-based bill is diagnostic. The best time to see these birds is during the winter, when freezing weather may force them to seek more open conditions. 28 cm (11 in).

Voice: High-pitched squealing as well as croaks and grunts; also a repeated *kik-kik-kik*.

Habitat: Reed beds and other dense vegetation among marshes and the margins of lakes, rivers, gravel pits and bogs.

Reproduction: The nest is a substantial structure of dead reeds and other aquatic vegetation placed low down among plant debris close to, or just above, the water level. The 6–10, occasionally up to 16, eggs are buffish, thinly blotched with reddish-brown, and are laid from early April onwards. They are incubated by both sexes, the female taking the larger share, for 19–20 days, and for the first few days after hatching the down-covered chicks are brooded by one parent while the other searches for food. After that they leave the nest and are tended by both parents. Double-brooded.

Food: Insects and their larvae, crustaceans, worms, fish and even other birds, together with roots, berries and seeds.

Range and Distribution: From Iceland across temperate and Mediterranean Europe to Iran, central Siberia, Manchuria and Japan. In Britain and Ireland it is widespread, becoming progressively thinner on the ground northwards. The drainage of marshes caused a serious decline in numbers last century, for which the recent boom in gravel extraction has partially compensated.

Movements: Largely resident, though some evidence of emigration. Continental immigrants arrive in October from as far east as Czechoslovakia and, while some pass on, others spread through the country to winter.

Spotted Crake

Porzana porzana (Linnaeus)

An extremely scarce summer visitor, it is among the most difficult of birds to locate, and even more difficult to see. Best located by its characteristic call, uttered well after dark, and requiring specific outings to suitable areas at appropriate times of the day

Population: scarce, no more than a handful of pairs each year

Long-legged, thin, short-tailed bird heavily camouflaged in brown and black above, with grey underparts spotted with white on the chest, and barred black and white on the flanks. The undertail coverts are creamy-buff. The bill is yellow with a touch of red at the base, the legs and feet green. This bird is easily confused with other, even rarer, crakes, but the unbarred undertail coverts are diagnostic. It is a highly secretive, crepuscular bird that few bird-watchers have seen. It lives deep in thick cover among aquatic vegetation and is active after dark. The distinctive call is uttered when most watchers have gone home to bed, and those that have seen it have usually done so by flushing the birds after locating them by call. Such activities are extremely dangerous to rare nesting birds and are rightly discouraged. 23 cm (9 in).

Voice: The song is a clear *quip-quip-quip* repeated for long periods well after dark. It has a ventriloquial effect and has been appropriately likened to the sound of a tap dripping into a half-empty barrel of water.

Habitat: Dense aquatic vegetation along the margins of lakes, rivers and fens, but seldom in reed beds.

Reproduction: The nest is well hidden among aquatic vegetation and usually sited in a clump just above water level. It is a bulky cup with a lining of finer grasses, and the 8–12, occasionally 6–15, eggs are greenish-buff spotted with browns and laid from late May onwards. Both sexes incubate for 18–21 days and the down-covered chicks are cared for by both parents. Usually double-brooded.

Food: Aquatic insects and their larvae, molluscs, and seeds of plants.

Range and Distribution: Found throughout temperate and Mediterranean Europe eastwards to the Caucasus, Russia and central Siberia. In Britain it may be found from the Outer Hebrides to the Channel coast, but only a handful are ever heard, and breeding invariably remains unproven.

Movements: A summer visitor over most of its range, but birds do winter in western France and occasionally in southern England.

Corncrake

Crex crex (Linnaeus)

Once widespread, its voice a common sound of the countryside in summer, the Corncrake has disappeared from much of Britain as a result of changing agricultural techniques. It is seldom seen, and is best located by its characteristic call

Population: about 5,000 pairs

A well-camouflaged, dumpy but slim bird that is a summer visitor in relatively small numbers. The upperparts are streaked black and buff, the buff underparts barred with chestnut on the flanks. The wing coverts are chestnut and very obvious in flight, though flying birds are seldom seen. The head has a wash of grey and the bill is thick, stubby and, like the legs and feet, yellowish. It is a secretive bird that keeps well hidden among thick ground cover and, even when located, is extremely difficult to flush. Walked-up birds simply melt away, and the best chance of seeing one is to spend time in one of the few areas where they are still common and hope to surprise an individual along a road. 27 cm (10$\frac{1}{2}$ in).

Voice: A grating, frequently repeated *crek-crek*.

Habitat: An inhabitant not of cornfields but of moist grassland.

Reproduction: The nest is a pad of grasses well hidden among hay crops. The 8–12, occasionally 6–14, eggs are grey-green blotched with reddish-brown and are laid from the second half of May. They are incubated by the female for 15–18 days and the well-camouflaged, down-covered chicks leave the nest soon after hatching. They are tended by both parents, but are soon independent and can fly after 5 weeks. Occasionally double-brooded.

Food: Insects, worms and snails together with a smaller proportion of weed and other seeds.

Range and Distribution: From France across temperate Europe north to southern Scandinavia, eastwards through Turkey and Russia to eastern Siberia. In Britain it has declined rapidly during the present century as a result of the mechanical harvesting of hay crops earlier in the year. It still breeds over much of England, Wales and Scotland, but in very low numbers. It remains abundant in the Outer Hebrides and on Tiree in the Inner Hebrides. In Ireland it has also been reduced, though there are still healthy populations in many areas.

Movements: A summer migrant that arrives from mid-April and departs in October. Winters in Africa south of the Sahara.

Coot

Fulica atra (Linnaeus)

An all-black, aquatic bird that swims buoyantly, dives rather clumsily to resurface cork-fashion, and takes to the air after a lengthy pattering over the surface. A bare, white frontal shield is its best identification feature

Population: 50,000 to 100,000 pairs

This rotund, somewhat dumpy bird is the only all-black freshwater bird in our area. It has a white bill and a bold white frontal shield that is visible at a considerable distance. It upends and dives for its food, but its buoyancy makes it cork-like as it resurfaces. It walks well on land, when its semipalmated silver feet can be seen. Aggressive during the breeding season, in winter it often occurs in dense packs, occasionally several thousand strong on suitable waters. 41 cm (16 in).

Voice: A loud, explosive *teuk*.

Habitat: Shallow freshwater lakes, ponds, slow-moving rivers, gravel pits, reservoirs and marshes; in winter it may also occur on estuaries.

Reproduction: The nest is built among emergent vegetation and consists of a mound of debris resting (not floating) on the bottom. Coots may also build on fallen trees and among dead vegetation at the base of reeds. The 6–9, occasionally up to 15, eggs are buffish, speckled all over with black. They are laid from mid-March and incubated by both sexes for 21–24 days, starting with the first or second egg. The chicks are covered with down and are cared for by the female and fed by the male. They leave the nest after a few days, when their red heads make them easy to distinguish from the young Moorhens that often share the same water. They return to the nest or to a specially constructed brooding platform, and are independent after 8 weeks. Double-brooded, with an occasional third.

Food: Aquatic vegetation taken from the surface by upending, and by dives in up to 2 metres of water. Also feeds on grassland and takes a small proportion of animal food.

Range and Distribution: From Iceland south to North Africa, eastwards across temperate Europe and Siberia to Japan, China, Southeast Asia and India. Also in Java, New Guinea and Australia. In Britain and Ireland it is found everywhere except in hilly upland districts, Lewis and Harris, Shetland, and northern and western areas of the Scottish mainland.

Movements: Resident, though northern birds move south within Britain and Ireland. Large influx of winter visitors from as far east as Russia, arriving in October and staying until April.

Moorhen

Gallinula chloropus (Linnaeus)

A well-marked aquatic bird that swims buoyantly and walks easily, a familiar sight on rivers, marshes, village ponds and even city-centre lakes. The habit of cocking its white tail as it swims and walks makes it easily identifiable

Population: about 300,000 pairs

A sooty-black bird above with slate-grey flanks below. A white line runs horizontally below the folded wing and the undertail coverts are white and frequently cocked in a slow, rhythmic motion. The eye is red and the bird has a red comb and base to its yellow bill. Juveniles are dusky-brown, but with the same white line along the flanks and the same white undertail coverts as the adults. The down-covered chicks swim easily and are distinguished from similarly aged Coots by the lack of red on the sides of the head. Moorhens are not gregarious, though small loose flocks may be seen in winter and where nesting situations are limited in summer. It is generally rather aggressive towards its own kind. It takes to the air after lengthy pattering over the water's surface and flies, rather weakly, with its legs dangling behind. 33 cm (13 in).

Voice: A loud *kr-r-rok* of alarm.

Habitat: Freshwater margins of rivers, lakes and ponds, also gravel pits, canals and marshy reed beds.

Reproduction: The nest consists of a platform of vegetation built at the water's edge, though also at some height in adjacent shrubs and in the disused nests of other birds. The 5–11 eggs, occasionally up to 20 as a result of more than 1 female laying in the same nest, are stone-buff spotted with brown and laid from mid-March onwards. Incubation is shared between the pair and lasts 19–22 days. The down-covered chicks leave the nest a few days after hatching, and are cared for by both parents and sometimes by the young of an earlier brood. They swim easily. Double-brooded, occasionally treble-brooded.

Food: Mainly vegetable matter including seeds, fruit and leaves, as well as insects and their larvae, worms and snails.

Range and Distribution: Virtually cosmopolitan and, among the world's great landmasses, absent only from Australia. Centred on the temperate and tropical zones, and within this huge belt missing only from the deserts of Africa and Arabia. In Britain and Ireland it is widespread, but not in the hillier districts of the north and west.

Movements: Resident. Winter visitors from the Continent – Denmark, Holland, Germany and Sweden.

Oystercatcher

Haematopus ostralegus (Linnaeus)

A large, boldly pied shorebird with a thick orange-red bill and pale pink legs. Often gregarious, forming large flocks along favoured shorelines and estuaries, and frequently vociferous, uttering loud piping calls

Population: about 30,000 pairs

Black above and white below, the Oystercatcher has a white band along the folded wing that forms a prominent wing bar in flight. The eye is bright red; the long, thick bill bright orange-red; the legs pale pink. In winter there is a white half-collar on the throat. These are gregarious birds that feed along shorelines and on intertidal ooze in estuaries. They are active when the tide is at its lowest and, at high tide, resort to coastal fields or rocky roosts when they may gather in dense flocks. They have increased considerably during the present century and can now be found breeding inland along rivers and among the stony shorelines of lakes. 43 cm (17 in).

Voice: A loud, penetrating *pic-pic-pic*, also a *kleep* and a song consisting of loud piping trills.

Habitat: Predominantly coastal, frequently rocky, sandy and muddy shores, but also, in summer, along the banks of rivers and lakes.

Reproduction: The nest is a simple scrape among shingle or sand on beaches, rivers or lake shores. The 3, occasionally 2 or 4, eggs are creamy, boldly spotted with dark brown, and laid from mid-April onwards. Incubation by both sexes lasts 24–27 days; the sitting bird leaves the nest early on the approach of danger. The down-covered chicks are as well camouflaged as the eggs and leave the nest after a day or so. They are tended by both parents and reach independence after 34–37 days. Single-brooded, though lost clutches may be replaced.

Food: Predominantly molluscs, especially mussels, opened by prising the bill into the half-open shell and severing the muscle; also probes for other intertidal creatures.

Range and Distribution: Found along the coasts of northern and western Europe and sporadically along the shores of the Mediterranean. Also inland from the Caspian region eastwards into central Asia, and along the Pacific coasts of Korea and Manchuria. In Britain and Ireland, except for eastern Scotland, it was a coastal bird until the latter part of the last century, since when it has spread inland over the whole of Scotland and much of northwestern England. Increasing disturbance of beaches has reduced its numbers along the south and east coasts.

Movements: A general exodus to the coasts in autumn and some emigration of British birds to Portugal, Spain and Morocco. Large influx of Continental birds from Scandinavia as well as Iceland, with peak winter numbers building up to 200,000, about 40 per cent of the European total.

Avocet

Recurvirostra avosetta (Linnaeus)

A slim, elegant black and white bird, with long legs and a sharply upcurved bill. Once exterminated in Britain, it now breeds at 2 colonies on the Suffolk coast

Population: 150 pairs

A tall, attractive wader that feeds in shallow margins by moving its slim upturned bill from side to side with a deliberate scything motion. It is boldly pied with black on wings, crown and nape, and white elsewhere. The legs and feet are pale slate-blue, the bill black. Avocets are gregarious at all seasons, forming loose colonies in summer and flocks in winter. Being large and obvious, and with quite specific feeding requirements, they are unlikely to become firmly established anywhere without strict protection. Their success in re-establishing the species in Britain has led the RSPB to adopt the Avocet as its motif. 43 cm (17 in).

Voice: A high-pitched *kloo-it*.

Habitat: Semisaline, brackish lagoons with low islands and sloping banks for feeding.

Reproduction: The nest is a simple scrape with a few bits of vegetation added as a cursory lining. The 4 eggs are buff, variably marked with spots of black, and are laid at the end of April or beginning of May. Incubation by both sexes lasts 25–26 days and the down-covered chicks leave the nest soon after hatching. They are cared for by both parents for 4 weeks. British colonies are frequently attacked by the gulls that nest alongside them. Single-brooded.

Food: Insects and their larvae, crustaceans and molluscs sifted from shallow margins.

Range and Distribution: Found in temperate and Mediterranean Europe, though patchy distribution is probably a relict of more widespread occupation in earlier times, and from the Black Sea eastwards to Iran and eastern Asia. Also in South Africa, Egypt and the Rift Valley lakes of East Africa. In Europe large and increasing populations in Denmark and Holland undoubtedly supplied the overspill to colonize East Anglia, where strong, long-standing colonies are established at Minsmere and Havergate.

Movements: Summer visitor, with small winter flocks on estuaries of the southwest, particularly the Tamar.

Stone-curlew

Burhinus oedicnemus (Linnaeus)

The sole British member of a widespread family of long-legged, ground-dwelling birds that have brown plumage, a curiously hunched attitude and a deliberate gait. It is a crepuscular bird found only on dry open areas and has suffered a considerable decline in numbers in recent years

Population: about 500 pairs

Stone-curlews are easily overlooked. They are coloured in browns and buffs, streaked with black, and their slow, deliberate movements and tendency to be most active at dawn and dusk add to the difficulties of locating what is already a well-camouflaged bird. Once the bird is found, the long yellow legs, large yellow eye and a prominent black and white wing bar make identification straightforward. It is a summer visitor most at home on dry heaths and open downland, but encroaching scrub caused by a decline in the rabbit population following myxomatosis, and the increased ploughing of marginal land, have both contributed to a decline in a species that is now more frequently found on dry ploughed fields. It forms flocks in autumn. 41 cm (16 in).

Voice: A tin-whistle-like *coor-lee*.

Habitat: Dry heaths and downland, and similar areas when ploughed; also areas of shingle.

Reproduction: The nest is a simple scrape, often with a few odds and ends such as rabbit droppings added. The 2, occasionally 3, eggs are laid from early April and are buff, spotted and scrawled with brown, and incubated by both sexes for 25–27 days. The chicks are covered with grey down marked with 2 black stripes on the back. When danger threatens they lie prone, neck and head stretched out, and are very difficult to locate. They are cared for by both adults for about 6 weeks. Single-brooded, with an occasional second clutch.

Food: Insects and their larvae, snails, worms and some small mammals.

Range and Distribution: Found in a huge belt around the Mediterranean extending northwards to the southern Baltic and southwards well into the Sahara. Also in the Middle East, southern Russia and Siberia as far as India and Burma. In Britain it is confined to southern and eastern England where its distribution coincides with the chalk country, the Suffolk heaths and Brecks and the shingle of Dungeness. Changes in habitat have caused a serious decline in numbers.

Movements: A summer visitor that arrives in March and departs in October. Outside the breeding range it is a very rare bird indeed.

Little Ringed Plover

Charadrius dubius (Scopoli)

A smaller relative of the Ringed Plover distinguished by its different head pattern, absence of wing bar, and different habitat and call. It first colonized Britain in 1938 and has since spread successfully through England, mainly occupying recently created gravel pits

Population: over 400 pairs

Lack of wing bar in flight distinguishes from more abundant Ringed Plover

A fast-running plover, very similar to the larger Ringed Plover; brown above and white below, and marked with a broad black band across the chest. It is distinguished by another black band extending from the ear coverts through the eye, being bordered on the crown by white; by a distinctly yellow eye-ring; by flesh-coloured, not orange-yellow, legs; and by a dark, not black-tipped, orange bill. In flight the absence of a wing bar is diagnostic. A summer visitor, it first bred in Britain at Tring Reservoirs in 1938 and has since spread by taking advantage of the new habitat created by gravel extraction. Though it occurs in small 'trips' (flocks), it is less gregarious than the closely related Ringed Plover and is invariably found inland on fresh water. 15 cm (6 in).

Voice: A thin, down-slurred whistle *pee-oo*.

Habitat: Sand and shingle areas beside fresh water; on the Continent it characteristically breeds along shingle banks of rivers, but in Britain gravel pits and, to a lesser extent, reservoirs under construction are most favoured.

Reproduction: The nest is a scrape scantily lined with a few selected pebbles or pieces of grass, usually among shingle, but also on sand or dried-out mud. The 4, occasionally 3, eggs are buffish, spotted and blotched with brown, and merge perfectly with their surroundings. They are laid from late April onwards. Incubation, which lasts 24–26 days, is shared and the cryptically coloured chicks leave the nest soon after hatching and are tended by both adults. Double-brooded, though only a single brood may be reared in the north.

Food: Insects and their larvae, worms and small molluscs.

Range and Distribution: Found across the whole of Europe north to Sweden, throughout the Mediterranean, Turkey, the Middle East to Southeast Asia in the south and Japan in the north. Also in the Philippines and Papua New Guinea. In Britain it is widespread in England, except for the southwest and northwest, northwards as far as Durham. It has bred in Scotland since 1968.

Movements: A summer visitor that arrives in April and stays through to October. Scarce away from southern and eastern England and decidedly rare in Ireland.

Ringed Plover

Charadrius hiaticula (Linnaeus)

A compact little shorebird marked by a broad 'ring' of black across the breast and another through the eye. The orange legs, black-tipped orange bill and a prominent wing bar differentiate it from similar species. It has the typical plover habit of pausing between fast, pattering runs

Population: 8,000 pairs

Bold white wing bar shows clearly in flight

Common around our coasts, the Ringed Plover frequently breeds on shingle beaches and marshes and in late summer moves away to form substantial flocks at favoured estuaries, with smaller winter flocks. Summer adults are greyish-brown above and white below. Black bands across the chest and head break up the bird's outline and are an effective form of camouflage. The short bill is orange tipped with black, the legs and feet orange. In flight a bold white bar extends across the wings. In winter the black bands are partially lost, that on the breast becoming no more than a smudge at either side. In this, as well as in juvenile plumage, it could be mistaken for the rare Kentish Plover. 19 cm (7½ in).

Voice: A fluted *too-lee* and a sharper *queep*.

Habitat: Shingle and sandy beaches, but also gravel pits and reservoirs; in the north it breeds inland along shingle banks of rivers. In winter it frequents open shores, estuaries and coastal marshes.

Reproduction: Courtship consists of much aerial chasing and a bowing display in which the white outer tail is spread over the back. The nest is a scrape among sand or shingle with little or no lining. The 4, occasionally 3 or 5, eggs are buffish-grey spotted and blotched with dark brown. They are laid from late April onwards and are incubated by both members of the pair. The down-covered, well-camouflaged chicks leave the nest soon after hatching and are cared for by both parents for 25 days. Usually 2 broods, occasionally 3.

Food: Crustaceans, molluscs, insects and their larvae together with some vegetable matter.

Range and Distribution: Breeds from Britain eastwards across northern Europe, arctic Russia and Siberia to the Bering Straits. Also in Spitsbergen, Iceland and in Greenland as far north as ice-free land can be found. In Britain and Ireland it nests on all coastlines except for the southwest of England and Wales, where it is decidedly local. In northern England and Scotland it is also fairly common inland, and is becoming more frequent inland elsewhere.

Movements: Leaves inland sites and becomes mainly coastal in late summer when large flocks may form on estuaries. Some birds leave the country, but there is an immigration of Continental, Icelandic and Greenland birds to make a total winter population of 25,000.

Kentish Plover

Charadrius alexandrinus (Linnaeus)

One of only a handful of birds to be named after British localities. A typical 'ringed' plover, but in which the breast band is incomplete, only 2 smudges remaining on the sides of the chest. Male (foreground) and female shown

Cosmopolitan distribution: recent recolonist

Bold white wing bar in flight

Brown above and white below, and very similar both to Ringed and Little Ringed Plovers. However, the black head markings are much reduced compared with those species and the male has a transverse crown bar, eye-stripe and chest smudges, all quite separate from one another. There is a touch of ginger on the crown, as well as black bill, legs and feet. The female is more washed out, with the head markings much less distinct. She could be taken for a juvenile or winter plumage Ringed Plover, but not for a Little Ringed which lacks a wing bar. Though it is found on every continent, Britain lies right on the edge of the range and it is now only a very scarce breeder and rare bird of passage. 16 cm (6¼ in).

Voice: A melodic *poo-it*, also a quiet *wit-it-it*.

Habitat: Coastal shingle, sandy beaches, salt pans, dried-out marshes.

Reproduction: The nest is a scrape, with little or no lining. The 3, occasionally only 2, eggs are laid in early May and are sandy-buff spotted with black. Both sexes incubate the eggs for the 24 days they take to hatch, though in many parts of the range they have to be shaded from the sun rather than incubated and may be partially buried. The chicks leave the nest soon after hatching and are cared for by both parents. Single-brooded, apparently.

Food: Insects and their larvae, worms, crustaceans.

Range and Distribution: Cosmopolitan, found in North America where it is called the Snowy Plover, western South America, temperate and Mediterranean Europe north to Denmark, the whole coastline of Africa and the Middle East to Pakistan, Japan, China and Southeast Asia, Java and Australia. Also found inland from the Caspian eastwards through central Asia. In Britain it formerly bred in very small numbers in Kent and Sussex, and has recently done so again after an absence of 20 years.

Movements: A summer visitor to northern Europe that passes through southern and eastern England in very small numbers each year.

Dotterel

Charadrius morinellus (Linnaeus)

A rotund plover of the Arctic that breeds on the highest mountain tops and exhibits sexual role reversal in which the male performs the nesting duties. Beautifully marked in summer in brown, grey and chestnut, it becomes a rather plain grey bird in winter. Female in summer shown

Population: less than 100 pairs

In summer the Dotterel has brown upperparts, the head marked with a white supercilium. The face is white, the chest a paler dove-grey bordered below by a band of white and with a chestnut belly. This area becomes progressively darker and terminates abruptly in white undertail coverts. The head is rounded, the bill short and the legs long and yellow. The male is slightly duller and less well marked than his mate. These are gregarious birds outside the breeding season, but though they have traditional stopover places (there is a Dotterel Hall Farm near Cambridge) their plumage pattern makes them difficult to locate. Once found they are remarkably tame. 22 cm ($8\frac{1}{2}$ in).

Voice: A *wit-e-wee, wit-e-wee*, and a *ting* of contact.

Habitat: High, mountain-top plateaux with grass, lichens and moss. In the far north it breeds at sea level on arctic tundra and also, since 1961, below sea level on Dutch polders.

Reproduction: The female is the dominant partner, initiating courtship and mating and, having laid the eggs, bands together with other females and takes little if any part in nesting duties. The nest is a scrape, with some lichens and other material added as a lining, and the 3, occasionally 2 or 4, eggs are laid from late May. They are buffish, heavily blotched with dark brown. The male incubates alone for 21–26 days and the chicks leave the nest the day after hatching and are tended by the male for 4 weeks. The male performs injury feigning to distract attention from nest and young. Sometimes the female will offer some assistance. Single-brooded.

Food: Insects and their larvae, spiders, some seeds in winter.

Range and Distribution: Found from Scotland to the Bering Straits, but discontinuously and mostly in mountains. In Europe it occurs in Scandinavia, Austria, Romania and Poland. In Britain it was formerly found only on the highest Scottish mountains, but cooler springs have enabled it to colonize the Border Hills and north Wales in recent years.

Movements: European population winters south of the Mediterranean. On passage Dotterel are scarce in April and May, and again in September and October. Most often seen in East Anglia.

Golden Plover

Pluvialis apricaria (Linnaeus)

A medium-sized plover, with golden-tinged upperparts and black underparts. It loses the black and becomes somewhat nondescript in winter, when it is often found with Lapwings on grassland

Population: 30,000 pairs; some 250,000 birds winter

Gold speckled with black extends over the crown from the white forehead to the back and tip of the tail. The face, throat, breast and belly are black, bordered by a broad line of white. The southern form *Pluvialis apricaria apricaria* that breeds in Britain has a less extensive area of black and distinctly greyish sides to the face compared with the northern form *Pluvialis apricaria altifrons*, which breeds in Iceland, the Faeroes and Scandinavia. In flight the upperparts are uniform, devoid of wing bars or tail pattern. These are gregarious birds, often found inland, where they keep company with Lapwings. Huge numbers may gather on splashy meadows in winter. 28 cm (11 in).

Voice: A clear *tlu-i*, uttered as a flight call and audible at night as flocks migrate overhead.

Habitat: Grassy upland moors, but down to sea level in the far north and west; in winter grassy and other fields.

Reproduction: Aerial display on slowly beaten wings uttering a *pee-pee-yer* call. The nest is hidden among heather and is a scrape lined with variable amounts of available material. The 4 eggs, occasionally only 3, are laid from mid-April and are stone-coloured, blotched with dark brown. They are incubated by both sexes, the female taking the dominant role, for 27–28 days, and the down-covered chicks are cared for by both parents for 4 weeks. Single-brooded.

Food: Insects and their larvae, worms, spiders, as well as grass seeds and berries.

Range and Distribution: Found in Iceland, Britain and Ireland, across Scandinavia and northern Russia, also in southern Baltic States and Denmark. In Britain and Ireland it is found in the hilly districts of the north and west, with over half of the total concentrated in the Scottish Highlands.

Movements: Large influx of Icelandic and Continental birds in October. Spring departure in March and April. Birds are present on all coasts, as well as inland in most areas except for northern Scotland.

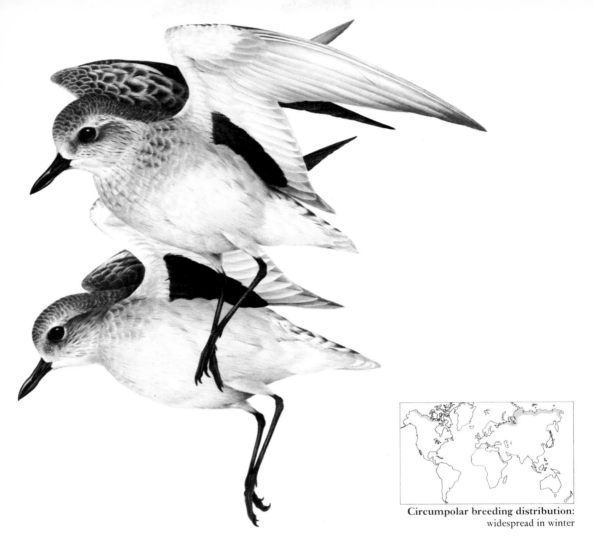

Grey Plover

Pluvialis squatarola (Linnaeus)

A winter and passage visitor from the high Arctic to our coasts and estuaries. Similar to Golden Plover, but grey above and marked by black axillaries that flash on/off in flight and by a white rump and barred tail. Adults in winter shown

Population: peak of 15,000 in autumn

In summer the Grey Plover is mottled black and white above, with solid black face and underparts bordered by a white band. It is, however, seldom seen in this plumage in Britain where, as a passage migrant and winter visitor, it is mottled grey above, with white on the belly and a grey-streaked breast. At this time it is essentially a shore-bird and best identified by the black axillaries that flash as the bird flies. It also has a white rump and barred tail. The typical plover shape, with rounded head and short bill, is easily seen. Though good numbers are found in winter, they usually form only small to medium-sized flocks. 28 cm (11 in).

Voice: A thin, whistled *tlee-oo-ee* of 3 notes.

Habitat: Open arctic tundra in the breeding season; on passage and in winter on estuaries and open muddy and sandy shores. Seldom inland.

Reproduction: The nest is a scrape, lined with lichens and moss, usually on a slight rise or ridge. The 4, occasionally 3, eggs are buffish blotched with brown and are laid from mid-June onwards. Both sexes share the incubation for 23 days and then care for the down-covered chicks. Single-brooded.

Food: Crustaceans, worms, molluscs and some seeds.

Range and Distribution: Circumpolar in far northern tundra zone, but absent from Greenland and Europe. In North America it is known as the Black-bellied Plover.

Movements: Summer visitor to breeding grounds, wintering south throughout the world southwards to Australia, Brazil and South Africa. Huge migration through western Europe only skims Britain where peak numbers occur in autumn. Slightly fewer in winter, widespread round all coasts.

Circumpolar breeding distribution: widespread in winter

Lapwing

Vanellus vanellus (Linnaeus)

One of the most common and familiar birds of our countryside, both in summer and winter. Known by a large range of local names including Peewit and Green Plover

Circles and dives on rounded wings in display

Population: about 200,000 pairs

Black above and white below at any distance, a closer approach reveals the upperparts glossed with green and bronze, and the undertail coverts as a pale orange-buff. A distinctive black breast band extends to the chin, and a thin black crest rises from the crown. In the air the broad and noticeably rounded wings flash black and white, giving rise to the most popular vernacular name. Lapwings are found over a huge range of habitats both in summer and winter. In the latter season they are gregarious and are among the most abundant birds in the country. However, a spell of frost that freezes the ground and prevents them from feeding will set them off on hard weather movements that may involve actual emigration. 30 cm (12 in).

Voice: A distinctive, somewhat plaintive *pee-wit*.

Habitat: Grasslands and marshes, arable fields, estuaries, floods, low-lying moors.

Reproduction: Courtship and territorial displays involve much flying and diving while calling. The nest is a hollow, usually well hidden among vegetation, with variable amounts of lining. The 4, sometimes 2–5, eggs are laid from late March onwards and are buffish blotched with black. At one time they were considered a great delicacy, but are now strictly protected. They are incubated by both sexes, the female playing the dominant role, and the down-covered chicks leave the nest soon after hatching. They are cared for by both parents for 33 days. Single-brooded.

Food: Insects and their larvae, worms, molluscs, spiders, crustaceans, together with smaller amounts of seeds and cereals.

Range and Distribution: Found right across Eurasia from Spain to Manchuria, northwards to Finland and Sweden, through Turkey and the Caucasus, Russia and southern Siberia. In Britain and Ireland it is widespread and abundant, but thin on the ground in western Cornwall, southernmost Ireland and parts of the western mainland of Scotland.

Movements: Many British birds are resident, but some move to Ireland and Iberia. A huge immigration of Continental birds starts in June and continues through to October when approaching a million birds may be present. Most are found inland. Hard weather movements continue throughout the winter.

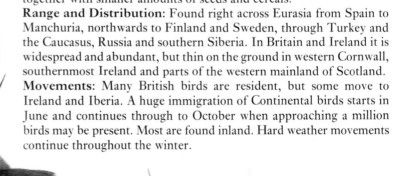

Knot

Calidris canutus (Linnaeus)

One of the globe-spanners, which breeds in the farthest north and winters as far south as Australia and New Zealand. Adults in autumn shown

Population: about 300,000 winter

Breeds on remote arctic tundra

Knot are typical waders, most commonly found on large estuaries and along rich intertidal shores. They are highly gregarious, occurring in packs tens of thousands strong where conditions are to their liking, but often being totally absent elsewhere. They are larger than Dunlin, and the grey feathers of the upperparts have broad white edges producing a scaly effect. There is a white wing bar and grey, lightly barred rump and tail. The bill is just shorter than the head, the legs are shortish and the impression is of a large-headed, dumpy bird. In summer the head and underparts are rich chestnut, the upperparts scaled brown, with some barring on the flanks. Sometimes a little reddish remains on autumn birds. 25 cm (10 in).

Voice: A deep *knut*.

Habitat: Arctic tundra; in winter and on passage frequents estuaries and shorelines; rare inland.

Reproduction: The nest is a hollow lined with lichens, often hidden beneath a clump of vegetation, among bare and stony tundra. The 4, occasionally only 3, eggs are light olive blotched and scrawled with brown, and are laid from June onwards. Both sexes probably incubate for 20–25 days and the chicks leave the nest soon after hatching. They are cared for by the male, with possibly some help from his mate. Single-brooded.

Food: Crustaceans, molluscs, worms and insects; probably more insects and even berries in summer.

Range and Distribution: Circumpolar in the highest latitudes. Alaska and islands of Canadian Arctic, Greenland, Spitsbergen, Taimyr Peninsula, New Siberian and Wrangel Islands.

Movements: The whole population migrates southwards to winter in western Europe and as far south as Africa, Asia, Australia, New Zealand and Argentina. In Britain and Ireland it is a passage migrant from late July to November and again, in spring, from March to May. Huge numbers winter on the Ribble, Morecambe Bay and the Wash. The total is over half of the European wintering population, and the majority come from Canada and Greenland, the rest from Siberia.

Sanderling

Calidris alba (Pallas)

A pale grey and white wader, found along open beaches, where small flocks run rapidly up and down with the washing of the waves picking small food morsels as they go. Adult in winter shown

Population: about 10,000 winter

Confined to remote tundra in summer: virtually cosmopolitan in winter

Sanderling can be identified at long distances by their habit of following waves up and down beaches. They are grey above and white below, marked by an area of black at the bend of the wing. In flight they show a prominent white wing bar and a Dunlin-like tail pattern with a dark central stripe. They are gregarious birds, forming small flocks around our shores. Though they will also feed among rocks in company with Purple Sandpipers and Turnstones, they are seldom seen inland. In summer, they become a warm marbled brown on upperparts and chest, with white belly and undertail coverts. The bill is thin, but shortish and, like the legs and feet, is black in colour. 20 cm (8 in).

Voice: A brief *twick* uttered as a contact note in flight.

Habitat: Along coasts or dry arctic tundra; in winter on sandy beaches and rocky shores, infrequently on estuaries and coastal marshes.

Reproduction: The nest is placed on the ground in the shelter of a tussock and is lined with leaves. The 4 eggs are olive-green spotted with darker tones of the same colour and are laid from late June. They are incubated by both members of the pair for 23–24 days. The down-covered chicks leave the nest soon after hatching and are cared for by both parents. Single-brooded.

Food: Small crustaceans, molluscs, worms; in summer also takes buds and insects.

Range and Distribution: Circumpolar in northernmost latitudes. Coasts of western Canadian islands, northern Greenland as far as ice-free land exists, Spitsbergen, Taimyr Peninsula, Severnaya Zemlya, Lena, New Siberian Islands.

Movements: Migratory, wintering from western Europe southwards throughout the world. In Britain and Ireland it is widespread on passage from August to October with a return, particularly in the northwest, from March to May. Smaller numbers winter. British birds are apparently of the Greenland and Canadian stock.

Little Stint

Calidris minuta (Leisler)

A tiny wader, similar to a Dunlin, but with a shorter bill and, particularly in autumn, a bold white V on the back. Juvenile in autumn shown

Breeds from northern Scandinavia eastwards: winters in temperate and tropical zones; 200 or more in autumn in Britain

A small wader with a short, thin bill less than the length of the head. In winter it is grey above and white below, with a variable amount of grey on the breast. In summer upperparts and breast are rich rust-brown. In autumn, the season when it most commonly occurs in Britain, there is often a hint of buff on the breast, and the upperparts are warmer grey and boldly marked with a white V. In comparison with the similarly sized Temminck's Stint, it is a chunky, more busy, more Dunlin-like bird that feeds by vigorous probing rather than delicate picking. It is also inclined to frequent coasts including estuaries and open shorelines, areas where Temminck's is seldom found. Its legs and feet are black, those of its relative greenish. Beware small North American vagrant 'peeps'. 13 cm ($5\frac{1}{4}$ in).

Voice: A *tit*, or trilled *trri-it-tit*.

Habitat: Arctic marshes near coast, but also in higher and drier areas; in winter frequents shorelines, estuaries, coastal and inland marshes.

Reproduction: The nest is a hollow, lined with leaves, often in the shelter of a small bush. The 4 eggs are light olive-green spotted with dark brown and laid from the end of June into July. They are incubated by both sexes, the male taking the greater share, and the chicks leave the nest soon after hatching and are cared for mainly by the male. Single-brooded.

Food: Crustaceans, molluscs, worms; also insects and their larvae and seeds in summer.

Range and Distribution: Found from northernmost Scandinavia along the north coast of Siberia to the New Siberian Islands.

Movements: Summer visitor to breeding range, moving south to winter in Africa, Iran and southern Asia. In Britain and Ireland it is a passage migrant, more plentiful in autumn, from August to early October, than in spring. It is most frequent in the south and east, but seldom in any numbers. A few winter in the south and west.

Temminck's Stint

Calidris temminckii (Leisler)

A diminutive wader, with a delicate picking action while feeding, that is a scarce passage migrant most frequently found inland by fresh water. After irregular and unsuccessful attempts to breed in the 1930s, it has colonized Scotland since 1969

Northern breeding distribution: colony of less than 5 pairs in Scotland

Small wader, much the same size as the Little Stint, but a more delicate Common Sandpiper-like, rather than Dunlin-like, bird. In winter upperparts are a uniform grey, the breast smudged with the same colour. In summer the plumage is a rich brown, with a white belly. The bill is thin and short, the legs yellowish-green. In flight a pale wing bar and white outertail feathers may be seen. The delicate picking of food from the water's edge, compared with the vigorous probing of the Little Stint, is characteristic. 14 cm ($5\frac{1}{2}$ in).

Voice: A *ptirr* contact note.

Habitat: Marshes and bogs among tundra, often with scrub, and mainly freshwater outside the breeding season.

Reproduction: The nest is a hollow, lined with leaves and grass, hidden among low vegetation usually in a marshy area, sometimes on an island. The 4, occasionally 3, eggs are pale olive spotted with brown, and are laid from mid-June. The male performs most of the incubation which lasts 21–22 days, and the chicks leave the nest soon after hatching. They are cared for by both parents for 15–18 days, though the female soon deserts. Single-brooded, though lost clutches may be replaced, and a second brood is not unknown.

Food: Insects and their larvae, worms.

Range and Distribution: From Scandinavia and northern Russia across Siberia to the Bering Straits. In Britain it first nested in the Cairngorms in 1934, but was unsuccessful in this and the 2 following years. Nesting was attempted in Yorkshire in 1951. The first successful breeding was in Easter Ross in 1971, after birds had been present since 1969. A small colony now exists there, and possibly elsewhere.

Movements: A summer visitor to breeding range, wintering from the Mediterranean, Africa and the Middle East to India and Southeast Asia. In Britain it is a regular autumn migrant in small numbers from August to October in East Anglia and Kent. Elsewhere scarce.

Sandpipers in Flight

Clothed generally in greys and browns, sandpipers at rest are a confusing group of mainly similar species. In the air they show distinctive patterns of wing and tail that are vital clues to their identification

Watching sandpipers along the shoreline or at some estuarine marsh is often a frustrating experience. Frequently the birds are at some distance, feeding over the huge mud banks exposed at low tide. At high water they often congregate in tight packs where, secure from disturbance, they tuck their bills beneath their scapulars and present a virtually uniform mass of brown birds. Those who would identify the individual from among the mass must take the opportunity when it is presented – noting wing and tail patterns as the bird flies. Call notes are particularly useful aids once learned

Green Sandpiper: virtually black on wings and back, contrasting with bold white rump and barred tail to form almost a House Martin pattern. Feet extend beyond tail, but not as far as in similar Wood Sandpiper, which is always paler, less contrasted, in colour. Usually solitary, haunting narrow drainage ditches, streams and freshwater marshes

Wood Sandpiper: brown across wings and back contrasting with white rump and finely barred tail produce similar pattern to that of Green Sandpiper. The present species is, however, always paler, more heavily spotted, and never appears black and white like that bird. Paler underwing is diagnostic if seen. Long legs extend well beyond tail. Sometimes solitary, but usually found in small groups frequenting open fresh marshes and floods. Like Green Sandpiper seldom found on open shorelines

Greenshank: large wader with long straight bill and long legs extending beyond tail. Upperparts dark grey without wing bar, and white rump extends up back to form a narrow V. White tail narrowly barred with black. Generally solitary or in small groups. Easily learned *tu-tu-tu* flight call quite characteristic at all times

Redshank: easily recognized brown wader speckled with white. Long red legs extend beyond tail, though not as far as Spotted Redshank's. Red base to bill. White V extends up back from narrowly barred tail. Most prominent feature is bold white trailing edge to wing, particularly apparent as it hovers yelping over intruders or predators during the breeding season

Spotted Redshank: outside breeding season a greyish wader with long red legs that extend well beyond tail. No wing bar, but white of rump extends well up back to form a V. Distinctive call. Generally found in small groups, not large flocks like so many other waders, both on passage and on its wintering grounds in Asia and Africa. Usually frequents fresh marshes and pools, although not averse to brackish areas such as estuaries. It is seldom found on open shorelines, unlike its common relative which so often associates with other waders at intertidal areas of great diversity

Golden Plover: appears dull fawn at any distance. A compact plover with short bill and large, rounded head. Lacks any distinguishing marks on rump or wings. Pale underwing. Usually gregarious, often found on agricultural land with Lapwings in winter

Grey Plover: larger and paler than Golden Plover and essentially an estuarine bird, though Golden Plovers sometimes resort to estuaries and shorelines, especially on passage. Grey Plover has white rump and narrow white wing bar, and underwing is marked by black axilliaries

Grey Plover

Greenshank

Wood Sandpiper

Redshank

Golden Plover

Spotted Redshank

Green Sandpiper

Curlew Sandpiper

Calidris ferruginea (Pontoppidan)

A passage migrant that occurs in
variable numbers, mostly in
autumn, and which must be
separated from the similar Dunlin
with care. The white rump is always
diagnostic if seen. Juvenile in
autumn shown

Remote tundra breeding grounds:
virtually cosmopolitan in winter;
100 or more in autumn in Britain

In summer plumage, rarely seen in Britain and Ireland, this is a
russet-chestnut bird below, with rich brown upperparts. In autumn
and winter it bears a strong resemblance to the Dunlin, with which it
often associates. The upperparts are grey with pale edges to the
feathers creating a scaled appearance. The underparts are white with a
buffish suffusion on the breast and sides of the head, particularly in
autumn. The tail pattern is distinctive, with a clear, square white rump
by far the simplest method of identification. Though it can sometimes
be seen at rest, it is most obvious in flight when a white wing bar also
shows. However, on the ground the Curlew Sandpiper is structurally
distinct from the Dunlin. The bill is longer and has a more pronounced
downward curve. The neck and legs are longer and the bird appears
slimmer and more elegant. Though spring birds do pass through,
autumn is the usual time to see this species, which breeds in the high
Arctic. Numbers vary year by year, with quite large flocks in some
seasons. 19 cm (7½ in).

Voice: A *chirrup* of contact in flight.

Habitat: Breeds on dry tundra as well as among marshes in river
valleys; in winter and on passage it frequents open shores, estuaries and
coastal, as well as occasionally inland, marshes.

Reproduction: The nest is a hollow hidden in a tussock of grass on an
open tundra slope and lined with a few lichens. There may be several
pairs nesting in a loose colony. The 4, occasionally 3, eggs are olive-
grey blotched with dark brown and are laid from the last week of June
onwards. Both sexes share the incubation. Single-brooded.

Food: Crustaceans, molluscs, worms, sandhoppers, insects and their
various larvae.

Range and Distribution: Found in summer only in remote north-
central Siberia, east of the Taimyr Peninsula.

Movements: Summer visitor migrating southwards to tropical Africa,
the Middle East and Asia, to Australia and New Zealand. In Britain it
is a double passage migrant, scarce in spring and far from abundant in
autumn. It is most regular in the south and east of England but also
occurs in southern Ireland, northwest England (where a few sometimes
winter) and eastern Scotland from late July to early October. Normally
scarce, but occasionally occurs in larger numbers.

Purple Sandpiper

Calidris maritima (Brünnich)

A squat, darkly coloured wader that frequents rock-strewn shorelines where it is easily overlooked. It breeds in the high Arctic, but a pair bred for the first time in Scotland in 1978

Population: perhaps 1 pair; about 20,000 winter

Breeds on tundra: winters on all ice-free coasts of northern Europe

Very dark wader with slate-grey upperparts and heavily mottled grey breast and flanks. The remaining underparts are white. Key features are a pale eye-ring and chin, a yellow base to the bill and yellow legs and feet. Though these birds may be found in a variety of coastal situations on passage, in winter they are invariably associated with masses of intertidal rocks where they hunt for food among seaweed, often in association with Turnstones. Both species are easily overlooked, though when located the sandpipers are often tame and confiding. 21 cm (8¼ in).

Voice: A repeated *tritt* flight note.

Habitat: Open tundra hillsides with rocks and growth of dwarf vegetation; in winter invariably found among intertidal rocks with pools and seaweed.

Reproduction: The nest is a hollow lined with leaves constructed by the male, and the 4, occasionally 3, eggs are light olive-green blotched with dark brown. They are laid from early June and are incubated by both sexes for 21–22 days, the male taking the larger share. The down-covered chicks leave the nest soon after hatching and are cared for by the male for 3–4 weeks. Single-brooded.

Food: Worms, molluscs and crustaceans; seeds form a substantial proportion of the diet at certain times of the year.

Range and Distribution: Circumpolar in the high Arctic regions from Iceland and mountain Scandinavia to Spitsbergen and the islands of Siberia, the Taimyr Peninsula, the Aleutian Islands, north-eastern Canadian islands and Greenland. In Britain a pair reared at least 1 young in 1978 – the first breeding record.

Movements: One of the most northerly wintering landbirds, occupying all ice-free Arctic coasts and moving southwards only to the coasts of northern Europe. In Britain and Ireland it is most numerous in the north and west, arriving in October and departing in April.

Dunlin

Calidris alpina (Linnaeus)

The most abundant and widespread of our waders, often occurring in huge flocks on favoured estuaries and shorelines. A dumpy, active little bird that probes vigorously in its search for food. Adults in winter shown

Population: between 4,000 and 8,000 pairs

In summer Dunlin are well-marked, handsome little birds with broad, brown-buff edges to the black feathers of the upperparts. The breast is buff, streaked with black, and the belly has a diagnostic bold black patch. The flanks and undertail coverts are white. In winter the black belly is lost, though it may be partially present on some adults in autumn. The upperparts are greyish-brown, the underparts buffish, with considerable streaking on the breast. The bill is longer than the head, and decurved towards the tip. The head is held hunched into the body and, in flight, there is a white wing bar and a black centre to the white rump. This is the 'basic' wader, from which all other sandpipers should be distinguished. A sure familiarity is essential to the birdwatcher. 17–19 cm (6½–7½ in).

Voice: A distinctive nasal *treep* in flight; a trilling song.

Habitat: Open grassy moorlands, lakeside marshes, upland bogs; in winter on shorelines, estuaries, floods, reservoirs and gravel pits.

Reproduction: Semicolonial, with several pairs nesting in close proximity. The nest is a cup-shaped depression lined with grasses and hidden in a thick clump. The 4, sometimes 2–6, eggs are light green blotched with dark brown, and are laid in mid-May. They are incubated by both members of the pair for 21–22 days and the down-covered chicks leave the nest soon after hatching. They are brooded by the female, but tended by both parents, though the male may leave before the young are independent at about 25 days. Single-brooded.

Food: Molluscs, crustaceans, worms, insects and their larvae.

Range and Distribution: Circumpolar, mainly in the arctic tundra zone, but extending southwards to countries bordering the North Sea. In Britain and Ireland it breeds in the Pennines and Scottish hills and islands, sporadically in Wales, Dartmoor, and northwestern Ireland.

Movements: The breeding grounds are deserted in autumn and birds move to the coasts, while a few actually emigrate. Siberian birds move to the Middle East, tropical Africa and Asia. Some 500,000 birds from Russia and further east winter.

Ruff

Philomachus pugnax (Linnaeus)

Formerly a widespread breeding bird, the Ruff did not nest in Britain for over 40 years prior to 1963. Since then it has done so annually at the Ouse Washes, where over 100 males may gather at their jousting grounds in elaborate and variable nuptial plumage. Reeve shown overleaf

Population: about 30 breeding Reeves, 4 times that number of displaying Ruffs

Outside the breeding season Ruff are undistinguished birds clothed in browns and buffs and with no prominent field marks. The male (Ruff) is considerably larger than the female (Reeve), and this difference in size is a help in recognizing birds in a flock. Both have heavily scalloped upperparts, the dark feathers having broad buff margins. The head and underparts are a uniform buffish, the legs yellow, orange or even red. However, the proportions are quite distinct. The head is small, the bill thicker than many other waders and not much longer than the head. The neck is long and the bird invariably stands upright and tall. In flight 2 white oval patches show on the rump. While the Reeve remains similarly coloured in summer, the Ruff gains a highly decorative and variable nuptial plumage. The face is bare and wattled red; 2 distinct plumes of feathers grow from the crown and an elaborate ruff surrounds the neck. This may be coloured white, black, chestnut or buff, or a variable mixture of these colours. Male 29 cm ($11\frac{1}{2}$ in), female 23 cm (9 in).

Voice: A *teuce* flight call; generally rather silent.

Habitat: Grassy freshwater floods, lake shores, marshes.

Reproduction: Males gather at lekking grounds in spring (see p. 178)

and establish territories about 30 cm across and a metre or more apart. With much bowing and jousting they raise their ruffs and crown tufts in elaborate displays every morning and evening and, over a period of time, the ground is worn bare. Reeves visit the lek for mating, sending all the Ruffs into a frenzy of display, but they invariably choose a male with a territory at the centre of the lek that seems to have to display much less than the insecure peripheral males. On occasion Reeves will virtually queue up for the attentions of a dominant Ruff. Having mated, the Reeve takes full responsibility for the rest of the breeding cycle. She creates a shallow cup among nearby grass and from mid-April onwards lays 4, occasionally 2 or 3, pale buffish or greenish eggs spotted and blotched with reddish-brown. Incubation lasts 20–21 days and the chicks leave the nest soon after hatching. Single-brooded.

Food: Insects, molluscs, crustaceans, worms, cereals; in summer mainly insects and their larvae.

Range and Distribution: From north temperate Europe, through Scandinavia and the northern half of Russia, northern Siberia to the Bering Straits. There is also a population on the Atlantic coast of France. In Britain, Ruff bred in Norfolk until 1871, but then only occasionally until 1963, when breeding was proved on the Ouse Washes. This remains the species' stronghold, but there are occasional records elsewhere including Lancashire, indicating that further expansion can be expected.

Movements: Though Ruff winter regularly at several inland and coastal sites in England, they are long-distance migrants, the bulk of the population moving to Africa on huge loop migrations. The spring return is usually further east than in autumn, and it is at the latter season that they are most numerous in Britain.

In summer males sport an elaborate nuptial plumage consisting of ruffs and head plumes. These vary from individual to individual, but are divisible into various types – white, brown, chequered and so on. There is no evidence to suggest that males with a particular ruff pattern are more successful than others, though it doubtless facilitates recognition by the individual females

Jack Snipe

Lymnocryptes minimus (Brünnich)

A winter visitor from the Arctic and Siberia that is much rarer than the similar common Snipe. It is smaller, with a far shorter bill, and has a much less erratic flight than the more abundant species

Population: several thousand winter

Breeds in high Arctic: migrates south and westwards to temperate zone to winter

In plumage pattern this is very similar to the Snipe, boldly streaked in browns and buffs above and below. It has a similar pale buff double V on the back, but a more complex and broken pattern of dark stripes on the head. It is, however, even less frequently seen on the ground than the larger Snipe, keeping to thick cover whenever possible. Identification in flight is thus crucial, but fortunately is simple. The bill of the Jack Snipe is much shorter, about the same length as the head. The tail lacks white and, when flushed, the bird does not tower and fly in zigzags like a Snipe. Instead it usually flies low and direct for a short distance before disappearing into cover. 19 cm (7½ in).

Voice: Silent, but utters a deep 'galloping' note in display.

Habitat: Marshes and bogs on tundra as well as among scrub; in winter often found with Snipe on floods and marshes.

Reproduction: The nest is a hollow lined with grass, placed on a hummock or ridge in a marsh. The 4, sometimes 3, light green eggs are spotted with dark brown and laid from June onwards. Incubation, by the female alone, takes 17–24 days and the chicks hatch in a covering of well-camouflaged down. The species, unusual in a wader, may be double-brooded.

Food: Worms, molluscs, insects and some seeds in winter.

Range and Distribution: Found from northern Scandinavia and from south of the Gulf of Finland eastwards across northern Russia and Siberia almost to the Bering Straits. A pair summered in Britain in 1975 and the species may well breed in the future.

Movements: A summer visitor to northern Europe that winters in western Europe, Africa and Asia. In Britain and Ireland it is a widespread winter visitor from August to May, with some birds certainly passing on southwards. It is nowhere numerous and definitely irregular in several parts of the country. The south and east of England are more favoured than the north and west, especially in autumn.

Snipe

Gallinago gallinago (Linnaeus)

A widespread breeding bird and abundant winter visitor to coastal and inland marshes. This well-camouflaged bird is self-effacing, but has an extraordinary drumming display flight in which the outertail feathers are beaten through the air to produce a bleating sound

Population: about 100,000 pairs

Drumming with stiff outertail feathers bleating noisily through the air in steep dive

Heavily camouflaged in stripes and bars of brown and buff, but with a prominent creamy double V on the back. The head has a boldly striped pattern, but the most noticeable feature is the long straight bill that is over twice the length of the head. In flight an area of white shows on the outertail feathers, and the bird's progress through the air is a highly erratic zigzagging. Generally gregarious outside the breeding season and in flight forms small 'wisps' (flocks). 27 cm (10½ in).

Voice: A harsh *shnarp* when flushed and a *chip-a, chip-a* song.

Habitat: Wetland sites including upland bogs, marshes and floods and even salt marshes.

Reproduction: The drumming display flight is performed by both sexes, though most frequently by the male. It consists of rising high in the air and diving with the stiff outertail feathers held outwards at an angle to 'bleat' through the air. At the end of the dive the bird will rise once more before diving, repeating the process in a wide circle around its territory. The nest is a well-lined hollow hidden in a tussock and the 4, sometimes 3, eggs are pale green or pale buff blotched with dark brown, and are laid in April. They are incubated by the female for 18–20 days before hatching, and the young are cared for by both parents. Sometimes double-brooded.

Food: Mostly worms taken by vigorous probing with the long bill, but also insects, molluscs and crustaceans, together with some seeds.

Range and Distribution: Virtually cosmopolitan, being replaced by very similar species (perhaps subspecies) in South America and Africa. Otherwise breeds from Iceland right across temperate and northern Europe, through Siberia to northern Japan and the Bering Straits. Also from Alaska, over most of Canada south to the central United States, southwards in the Rockies to southern California. Also breeds in India. In Britain and Ireland it is widespread, though a little thinner on the ground in southern and southwestern England.

Movements: Most British and Irish birds make only local movements, though there is some definite emigration. Winter visitors, together with passage migrants, arrive in September and October and are found throughout the country, except in parts of northern Scotland. Birds from Iceland and the Faeroes winter in Ireland.

Woodcock

Scolopax rusticola (Linnaeus)

A large, chunky wader that has adapted to a purely woodland existence and which is crepuscular by nature

Population: 10,000 to 50,000 pairs

Roding flight over tree tops at dusk marked by characteristic call note

Woodcock are seldom seen on the ground and even less frequently feeding. They may be flushed from their nest, but will invariably fool an intruder by producing an elaborate and convincing display of injury feigning. When they sit tight their cryptically camouflaged plumage of bars and stripes of browns and buffs closely resembles a background of dead leaves and hides them most effectively. Woodcock are best seen late in the evening when they perform a roding advertising flight accompanied by a characteristic call. Against the light their dumpy, rounded appearance is marked by broad rounded wings and a distinctive, long, downward-pointing bill. The similarity to an owl is complete except for the long bill. 34 cm (13½ in).

Voice: The typical roding call is a sharp *tsiwick* repeated with some frequency and audible at considerable distances. Also a croaking note audible only at close range.

Habitat: Mostly deciduous woods and forests, with dry areas for nesting and damp or wet ones for feeding. Also frequents mixed woods and the grassy rides of more recent conifer plantations.

Reproduction: The nest is a simple hollow, usually placed at the foot of a tree, among dead leaves. The 4, occasionally 3 or 5, eggs are greyish to buff in colour, boldly blotched and spotted with brown or chestnut. Incubation, which lasts 20–21 days, commences when the clutch is complete and is by the female alone. The young hatch in a covering of warm brown down and leave the nest immediately. Two broods are regularly raised. If threatened the female will carry her young in flight one by one between her legs to a new site.

Food: Predominantly earthworms obtained by probing with the long sensitively tipped bill. Also insects and their larvae, freshwater molluscs and some plant seeds.

Range and Distribution: Breeds from northern Spain right across Europe and Siberia to Japan. Largely absent from the Mediterranean except for Corsica, but outposts in the Caucasus, Himalayas and on the Atlantic islands. In Britain and Ireland it is widespread, being absent only from the Outer Hebrides, Shetlands, Orkneys and parts of England, notably the Fens and the southwest.

Movements: Most British Woodcock are sedentary, though there is evidence of a movement of northern birds to Ireland and southwards through England to adjacent parts of the Continent. There is an arrival of Continental birds in autumn and a return movement in spring.

Black-tailed Godwit

Limosa limosa (Linnaeus)

A large and elegant wader, beautifully marked in chestnut in summer, that has returned to breed after an absence of over 100 years. Moulting adult in autumn shown

Population: less than 100 pairs; some 5,000 birds winter

Summer (foreground): winter (flying) showing distinct white wing bar and tail band

Head, neck and breast are bright chestnut in summer, with bars of black on the white flanks and underparts. The upperparts are delicately mottled in rich brown and black, with grey and black wings. In winter it is a grey bird, darker above and lighter below. At all seasons the long bill, about two and a half times the length of the head, is only slightly upturned and has a pinkish base. The wings are mainly black with a broad white wing bar, and the tail is white with a broad black terminal band. In addition the legs are considerably longer than those of the Bar-tailed Godwit. 41 cm (16 in).

Voice: A clear *wicka-wicka-wicka* flight note, and a *pee-oo-ee* on breeding grounds.

Habitat: Breeds on rough flooded grassland, but also among bogs and marshes; in winter on marshes and estuaries.

Reproduction: The nest is a hollow lined with grasses and hidden among ground vegetation near water. The 4, sometimes 3 or 5, greenish eggs are blotched with dark brown and laid from late April onwards. Incubation, which is shared, lasts 22–24 days and the chicks leave the nest soon after hatching and are cared for by both parents until they fly at about 28 days. Single-brooded.

Food: Crustaceans, molluscs, marine worms; in summer mainly takes insects and their larvae, also earthworms.

Range and Distribution: From Iceland and temperate Europe, including France, Holland and Denmark, eastwards across Russia and southern Siberia to Kamchatka. In Britain and Ireland it was virtually exterminated by about 1830, but in 1952 bred (unsuccessfully) on the Ouse Washes and is now established at several spots in East Anglia, Kent and Somerset, and occasionally in Cumbria and Yorkshire.

Movements: A double passage migrant, arriving in Britain and Ireland from July onwards. Some birds pass on to winter south to Africa, but many winter in Ireland and in Lancashire; and increasing numbers of the Continental subspecies on the English south coast.

Bar-tailed Godwit

Limosa lapponica (Linnaeus)

The arctic equivalent of the Black-tailed Godwit, with a shorter, more upturned bill and a barred, not banded, tail. It lacks a wing bar. Adult in winter shown

Population: about 45,000 winter

Winter (foreground): summer (flying) showing lack of wing bar and narrowly barred tail

In summer the Bar-tailed Godwit is mottled brown above with chestnut below, the latter covering the complete underparts. It is, however, seldom seen in this plumage in Britain and most autumn birds are brownish above and whitish below, becoming greyer in winter. At all seasons it is best separated from the Black-tailed Godwit by the lack of a wing bar and barred, not banded, tail. However, the bill is noticeably more upturned and the legs shorter – fine points that can be discerned when the bird is at rest and not showing wings and tail. Essentially gregarious, it is much more abundant than the Black-tailed and forms dense packs at several favoured estuaries. 38 cm (15 in).

Voice: A *kirrick* flight note; a *keu-oo* on the breeding grounds.

Habitat: Marshes and bogs among tundra; in winter frequents open shores and estuaries, seldom inland.

Reproduction: The nest is a hollow on the ground, often on a ridge, lined with vegetation. The 4, occasionally only 2 or 3, eggs are greenish blotched with dark brown and laid from the end of May onwards. Incubation lasts 20–21 days and, though shared, is predominantly by the male. The chicks leave the nest soon after hatching and are cared for by both parents. Single-brooded.

Food: Crustaceans, molluscs, marine worms; in summer mainly insects and their larvae, together with earthworms. The female has a longer bill than her mate, enabling her to reach deeper food in intertidal mud and ooze.

Range and Distribution: High Arctic from northernmost Scandinavia across a narrow band of northern Siberia to the coasts of Alaska.

Movements: Winters from western Europe to Africa, Asia and Australia. In Britain and Ireland it winters on most coasts, though large numbers are concentrated at favourite estuaries, the population being about half the total of western Europe. Some birds pass through further south. Arrives from August to October and departs in spring up to the end of May.

Whimbrel

Numenius phaeopus (Linnaeus)

A smaller and scarcer version of the Curlew, with a shorter bill and a pronounced pattern of head stripes. Its characteristic call has earned it the country name of Seven Whistler

Population: less than 200 pairs

Similar to the Curlew, mottled dark brown and buff above, with buff-streaked breast and arrowed with dark brown below. A white V extends up the back in flight and the tail is narrowly barred brown and buff. It is, however, considerably smaller than the Curlew, with a proportionately smaller bill and a diagnostic brown- and cream-striped crown pattern. Though gregarious, it is seldom found in the large flocks formed by those birds. It is a summer visitor and passage migrant to Britain and Ireland, and is exceptional in winter when the larger species is most numerous. 41 cm (16 in).

Voice: Flight note is a short whistle repeated 7 or so times; in summer has a bubbling call similar to that of the Curlew.

Habitat: Moorland with grass and heather, and bogs; in winter and on passage frequents open sandy and muddy shores, estuaries, creeks and coastal marshes.

Reproduction: The nest is a hollow with a scant lining of vegetation. The 4, sometimes 3 or 5, eggs are greenish spotted with brown and laid from mid-May onwards. Incubation, which is shared between the pair, lasts 24–28 days and the chicks leave the nest soon after hatching and are cared for by both parents prior to fledging and independence at 5–6 weeks. Single-brooded.

Food: Crustaceans, molluscs, marine worms; in summer mainly insects and their larvae, but also worms and molluscs. Takes some berries in autumn.

Range and Distribution: Circumpolar, but with large gaps in various parts of its range. From Iceland and Scotland to Scandinavia and northern Russia to beyond the Urals. Then there is a gap before it is found breeding again in northeastern Siberia and Alaska. Breeds along the western shores of Hudson Bay, but no further east. In Britain it declined seriously in the latter part of last and the early part of this century and, by 1950, was more or less confined to Unst in Shetland. Since then it has increased and spread and can now be found on most of Shetland, Orkney, the Outer Hebrides and northern Scotland.

Movements: Summer visitors arrive in late April and leave again by October. They are widespread on most coasts and a few may winter in Ireland and the southwest of England. An exceptional autumn gathering occurs at Bridgwater Bay in early autumn, when up to 1,000 birds may be present at a single time.

Curlew

Numenius arquata (Linnaeus)

Largest of our waders and a familiar bird throughout the country. The very long, decurved bill and the distinctive *coor-lee* flight call make it readily identifiable

Population: 40,000 to 70,000 pairs

Basically a buff-brown bird above and below, heavily mottled and streaked with darker brown. The huge size and long decurved bill, about 3 times the length of the head, preclude confusion with all other species except the smaller Whimbrel. The legs are long and, together with the bill, enable Curlews to feed by probing deep into marshes and intertidal areas and obtain food that is out of reach of all other birds. They are generally gregarious and form large flocks on favoured feeding grounds on coasts and estuaries. They are, however, often found inland in many dry areas. 53–58 cm (21–23 in).

Voice: A distinctive *coor-lee*; also an attractive bubbling call in spring song flight.

Habitat: Grassy and heather-covered moors, peat bogs, lowland marshes and floods, and dry arable fields; in winter frequents estuaries and shorelines.

Reproduction: A display flight advertises and defends the territory during which the bubbling call is produced. The nest is a hollow among vegetation lined with plant material and the 4, sometimes 3 or 5, eggs are olive-green spotted with various shades of brown. Incubation, mainly by the female, takes 26–30 days and the down-covered chicks leave the nest soon after hatching and are cared for by both parents, later by the male alone, for 5–6 weeks before flying. Single-brooded.

Food: Lugworms, molluscs, crustaceans, fish; also insects and their larvae; berries and grass seeds are taken in season.

Range and Distribution: From Ireland and northwestern France across temperate Europe, north to Scandinavia, to Russia, and Siberia to Manchuria. In Britain and Ireland it is widespread in all upland districts with suitable habitat, but is rather sporadic in eastern and southeastern England.

Movements: Some birds migrate southwards as far as Iberia, but most stay in Britain and Ireland, where they are joined in September and October by Continental immigrants. Found on all coasts, but also inland with up to 150,000 present at peak periods.

Spotted Redshank

Tringa erythropus (Pallas)

Arguably the most beautiful of all waders. The all-black, white-spotted summer plumage, with bright red legs and red base to the bill, is unfortunately seldom seen outside the arctic breeding grounds. Adult in winter shown

Tundra breeding range: about 1,000 in autumn in Britain and Ireland

Adult in summer, a plumage sometimes seen in late spring or summer in Britain and Ireland

Spotted Redshanks are double passage migrants and scarce winter visitors to our coastal marshes. Mostly they are clothed in dull grey winter plumage, lightly spotted with white on the wings, and whitish below. The legs are red and there is a red base to the bill, but both bill and legs are longer than the similar Redshank's, which is much browner than the present species. Additionally, though the Spotted Redshank has a pale area across the wing it lacks the bold white trailing edge to the wing of the common bird. Returning adults in July appear on the east coast in full or nearly full nuptial plumage, which is all black spotted with white and with a prominent, broken white eye-ring. In flight the feet extend well beyond the tail. Usually seen singly or in small parties. 30 cm (12 in).

Voice: A loud *chu-it* flight note, instantly recognizable once learned; also a *chick-a chick-a-chick*. Song is a beautiful *noo-too, noo-too*.

Habitat: Open glades and clearings in conifer and birch woods, usually among or near marshes; in winter frequents brackish waters rather than open estuaries.

Reproduction: The nest is a hollow lined with grass, often placed near a dead branch or other mark. The 4, sometimes 3, eggs are light olive-green blotched with dark brown and laid in June. They are incubated by the male. The down-covered chicks leave the nest soon after hatching and are tended by both parents, though the female leaves before the young reach independence. Single-brooded.

Food: Insects and their larvae, crustaceans, molluscs.

Range and Distribution: From northern Scandinavia eastwards across northern Russia and Siberia in the taiga zone.

Movements: Passes through Britain and Ireland on its way to and from its winter quarters in the Mediterranean and Africa. Spring passage lasts from April to June and there is then only a short break before returning birds occur from July to October. More numerous in autumn, mainly in the south and east. Some 100 or so winter on the south coast of England, but also on the Dee in Cheshire and south-western Ireland.

Redshank

Tringa totanus (Linnaeus)

A slim brown bird, with long, orange-red legs, that is among the most widespread of our waders. Its loud far-carrying cries of alarm have earned it the nickname of 'watchdog of the marshes', to many a bird-watcher's dismay

Population: 38,000 to 48,000 pairs

A rather elegant brown wader marked with bright orange-red legs and a red base to the bill. In flight it shows a broad white trailing edge to the wing and a white rump extending up the back in a V. The tail is closely barred with brown. It can be confused with Ruff and Spotted Redshank, but both of these birds lack the white wing bar of the Redshank. It has the characteristic habit of bobbing in a deliberate way when alarmed and will fly above and around an intruder calling loudly. It is gregarious, often gathering in large flocks, but without forming the dense packs of, say, Dunlin and Knot. 28 cm (11 in).

Voice: A *tleu-hue-hue*, also a repeated *teuk* of alarm.

Habitat: Splashy floods and marshes, damp meadows, coastal marshes and saltings; in winter also frequents estuaries, intertidal shores and even rocky areas.

Reproduction: Noisy aerial display on stiff, jerky wing beats yelping loudly. The nest is placed in a tussock and consists of a well-lined hollow built by the female. The 4, occasionally 3 or 5, eggs are buffish with spots of dark brown and are laid from mid-April onwards. They are incubated by both members of the pair for 23–24 days and the down-covered chicks soon leave the nest to be cared for by both parents until they fledge after 30 days. Single-brooded.

Food: Insects, molluscs, crustaceans and worms together with some vegetable matter.

Range and Distribution: From Iceland right across Europe, though rather local in the Mediterranean and the south, northwards to the North Cape of Norway, through Russia and the Caucasus to southern Siberia, the eastern Himalayas and Manchuria. In Britain and Ireland it is widespread, though thin on the ground in Wales and absent from the southwest and from many parts of Ireland.

Movements: Mainly resident, but some birds leave the country and move southwards to Iberia and Morocco. Continental and Icelandic birds arrive from July to October and depart from March to May. Many pass onwards further south, but huge numbers winter around all coasts. Total, just under 100,000 birds.

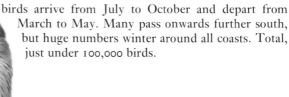

Greenshank

Tringa nebularia (Gunnerus)

A slim, elegant, slate-grey bird, with a long, slightly upturned bill and long green legs. It has a characteristic 3-note call

Population: 400 to 750 pairs

This highly attractive bird from the north is marked by long olive-green legs and a long, slightly uptilted bill. The upperparts are slate-grey-brown, becoming more contrastingly grey and black in summer. The underparts are white, lightly streaked on the breast. A white rump extends in a V well up the back and is particularly noticeable in flight. The tail is narrowly barred. The legs are longer in proportion than the Redshank's and extend beyond the tail in flight. Its call is characteristic. Usually found in small flocks in coastal areas, but also quite frequently singly inland. 30 cm (12 in).

Voice: A fluted *tue-tue-tue*, a *chip*, and a *teu-ee* on breeding grounds.

Habitat: Open moorlands with lakes and bogs, broken heather-clad hillsides among forest margins and glades; in winter estuaries and coastal marshes, inland at reservoirs and marshes on passage.

Reproduction: The nest is a hollow lined with vegetation placed near a rock or dead branch, and noted as one of the most difficult to find. The 4, sometimes 3 or 5, eggs are creamy blotched with various shades of brown and are laid from early May onwards. Incubation, mainly by the female, takes 24–25 days and the down-covered chicks leave the nest the day after hatching and are cared for by both parents for about 28 days. Single-brooded.

Food: Insects and their larvae, crustaceans, worms, molluscs.

Range and Distribution: From Scotland, through Scandinavia and northern Russia to boreal zone of Siberia east to Kamchatka. In Britain it was persecuted by egg collectors during the last century and may now be increasing. Certainly breeding is well established in the Outer Hebrides where it was irregular only 40 years ago. It now breeds over much of the Highland district, especially north of the Great Glen. A pair has nested regularly in Ireland in recent years.

Movements: A summer visitor and passage migrant that arrives in April and May and departs from July to October. A few winter in the southwest of England, in Ireland and even as far north as western Scotland. It is more numerous in autumn and is then widespread on coasts and inland. Total, about 1,500 birds.

Green Sandpiper

Tringa ochropus (Linnaeus)

A passage migrant that winters in small numbers in southern England. The plumage pattern is similar to the Wood Sandpiper's but is always much darker above, giving the impression of a black and white bird

Population: moderate numbers

Breeds in boreal zone:
migrates southwest to winter

A small, neat wader, usually encountered singly or in pairs, that shuns open shorelines and is most frequently found along freshwater dykes and small streams. The upperparts are blackish, spotted with white and with a bold white rump above a black-barred tail. There is a pale supercilium. The underparts are white, heavily streaked with black on the breast and with some barring on the flanks. The bill is thin and about one and a half times the length of the head, and the long legs are blackish. The overall impression is of a black and white bird. In contrast the Wood Sandpiper is brown and white; has a similar white rump, but less prominent tail bands; pale legs and shorter bill. The Green Sandpiper bobs its head when alarmed. 23 cm (9 in).

Voice: A *tweet-weet-weet* alarm and flight note; song is a trilling *tittilooidee* repeated.

Habitat: In summer frequents marshes and bogs in forested country; in winter and on passage found along dykes, freshwater margins, sewage works and streams.

Reproduction: The nest is usually in a tree, utilizing the old nest of another species, though it may also be hidden among tree roots or an old stump. The 4, sometimes 2 or 3, eggs are creamy spotted with dark brown and laid from mid-April onwards. Incubation, mainly by the female, lasts 20–23 days and the down-covered chicks leave the nest soon after hatching and are cared for by both sexes, though the female leaves well before they fly at 4 weeks. Single-brooded.

Food: Insects and their larvae, worms, crustaceans, molluscs, together with some plant buds.

Range and Distribution: From Scandinavia and East Germany southwards to Romania and eastwards across Eurasia to Manchuria. Also in the Caucasus. It has bred once in Cumbria in 1917, and once in Inverness-shire in 1959.

Movements: Winters in the Mediterranean, and in tropical Africa to Asia. In Britain it is a double passage migrant from March to May, and July to October. It is more plentiful in autumn, particularly in south and east England. Some birds winter in this area every year. It is decidedly scarce in Scotland and Ireland.

Waders in Flight

Like those other shorebirds, the sandpipers and 'shanks', waders are often dully coloured and remarkably similar at rest. Some are large, some small; some have long bills, some short. But virtually every wader closely resembles at least 1 other species

Separating the waders is very often a matter of eliminating 1 member of a species-pair. There are thus 2 godwits, 2 curlews, 2 stints and the Curlew Sandpiper to be separated from the Dunlin. Knowing what to look for is more than half the battle and, especially at·long range, it can almost be a battle. But the rewards in terms of satisfaction are more than justified, for these are exciting birds of wild places that perform some of the most extraordinary of all bird migrations

Ruff: during the breeding season the adult male Ruff is marked by nuptial plumes in various colours that preclude confusion with any other bird. The Reeve, and her mate in winter, are somewhat nondescript brown above and buffy below. There is a narrow white wing bar across the secondaries, but the diagnostic feature is the tail pattern. A dark centre separates 2 white ovals that are clearly visible as the bird flies away

Curlew Sandpiper: a small Dunlin-sized wader with a longer and more decurved bill; a decidedly unreliable feature, especially in flight. But longer legs protrude beyond the tail. Most obvious feature is pure white rump which most readily separates this bird from the much more numerous Dunlin, with which it frequently associates during passage periods

Black-tailed Godwit: longer both in bill and legs than the similar Bar-tailed Godwit, giving this species a slimmer and more elegant appearance at all times. A bold white wing bar extends across all flight feathers and, together with the broad black tail band, makes this one of the easiest of all waders to identify on the wing

Bar-tailed Godwit: generally a rather greyish wader, though some birds in late spring and early autumn may still retain a little of their chestnut breeding plumage. Neither as long in bill or leg as the Black-tailed Godwit, the white rump extends up the back to form a distinct V. However, by far the easiest method of separating from the Black-tailed Godwit is the absence of a wing bar and black tail band.

Dunlin: the typical small, nondescript wader from which all similar small waders have to be separated. Though both featureless and variable on the ground, when feeding or at rest, in the air the Dunlin is actually quite a well-marked bird. A clear white wing bar extends across the flight feathers and a dark-centred tail shows white outer feathers tipped with black

Turnstone: though it loses its fine harlequin pattern of colours in winter, the Turnstone in flight still presents a motley of brown and white quite unlike any other wader. The white tail and rump have broad black terminal and central bands; the wings a bold white wing bar and creamy-coloured greater coverts. The whole effect is of a somewhat dumpy, but patchy wader with a short stubby bill

Black-tailed Godwit

Bar-tailed Godwit

Ruff

Dunlin

Curlew Sandpiper

Turnstone

Ringed Plover

Ringed Plover: typical, fast-flying, small plover marked with a bold pattern of black and white bands on the breast. A conspicuous white wing bar separates from the Little Ringed Plover. The dark tail has broad white outer edges that enable the bird to be picked out easily from the flocks of Dunlin with which it frequently associates. Usually forms small flocks outside the breeding season

Curlew: largest of our waders, with huge decurved bill. Can be confused only with the summer-visiting Whimbrel, but is larger, with a longer bill, and lacks the crown stripes of that bird. Large white V extends well up back and is most prominent feature as bird flies away. Distinctive *coor-lee* call quite different from the 7-whistled flight note of the Whimbrel

Whimbrel: small version of the Curlew with similar brown plumage. Identified by pattern of stripes on crown, but also by proportionately shorter bill and legs. Buffy, streaked breast extends to belly, whereas Curlew has white belly. In flight, when size may be an unreliable feature, length of bill is as useful an identification mark as any. Generally found in small flocks, never in the great hordes of so many other shorebirds

Common Sandpiper: one of the easiest of all waders to identify. In flight the Common Sandpiper shows a bold white wing bar and characteristic pale outertail feathers. However, its mode of flight, usually low over the water, on shallow beats of its 'stiff' wings, is quite different to any other regular wader and makes for instant recognition

Little Stint: small size alone is usually sufficient to pick this bird out from the flocks of Dunlin with which it frequently associates. Most of our autumn visitors are juveniles and show a distinctive pale V on the back. A white wing bar is similar to that of the Dunlin, but the pale outer feathers create a quite different tail pattern. A shorter bill may prove an additional point of distinction

Temminck's Stint: similar in size and flight pattern to the Little Stint, but always greyer and more uniform above and marked with greyish throat and breast. Though distinguished quite easily in flight by the experienced observer, the beginner should confirm identification by a careful examination of field characteristics on the ground

Sanderling: grey wader marked with black at the carpal joints and the most prominent white wing bar of all small waders. Prefers sandy beaches and usually forms small dense packs, but a solitary bird on a marsh or estuary may present a problem for the unwary

Knot: despite its much larger size the Knot is a featureless shorebird that closely resembles a Dunlin at rest. In flight, however, it shows only a narrow white wing bar extending across the secondaries and a pale, but narrowly barred, rump and tail. This pattern is quite unlike that of the Dunlin

Curlew

Whimbrel

Knot

Sanderling

Little Stint

Temminck's Stint

Common Sandpiper

Wood Sandpiper

Tringa glareola (Linnaeus)

An elegant wader that passes
through in spring and autumn and
which, since 1959, has bred in small
numbers every year. It has brown
upperparts and a contrasting white
rump and is usually found in
freshwater habitats in small flocks

Population: between 4 and
10 pairs

Breeds in north and east:
migrates to Africa to winter

Brown upperparts and white underparts, streaked with brown on neck and breast, would seem to offer little chance of separating this from a large number of similarly plumaged waders. The Wood Sandpiper, however, is an elegant, long-legged bird that picks food delicately. It is heavily spotted with white on the back and wings and has a white rump above a lightly barred tail. The legs are always pale, often yellowish, and extend beyond the tail in flight. In the air the pattern is similar to that of the Green Sandpiper, though that species appears black above and white below. 20 cm (8 in).

Voice: A triple flight note *wit-wit-wit*, also a *chew-ew*; the song, delivered in flight, is a liquid trilling including a *tleea-tleea-tleea*.

Habitat: Marshes and freshwater margins in forest and taiga zones, but also where even a few birches surround a pool. In winter frequents marshes and lake shores, in Africa and Asia often well inland.

Reproduction: Nests on or near the ground among scrub, but also occasionally in the old nest of another species, often a Fieldfare. The nest consists of a hollow with some grass or other vegetation added and the 4, occasionally 3, light green eggs are spotted with dark brown and laid in late May or June. Incubation is shared, though the female takes the larger part, and lasts 22–23 days. The chicks leave the nest soon after hatching and are cared for by both parents, though the female deserts before they fledge. Single-brooded.

Food: Insects and their larvae, worms and some vegetable matter.

Range and Distribution: From Denmark and Scandinavia across northern Russia and Siberia to Kamchatka. Also in the Caucasus. Bred in Northumberland in 1853 and possibly 1857. After a gap of 100 years it bred in Sutherland in 1959 and after that in several parts of the Scottish Highlands.

Movements: Winters in tropical and South Africa, and from Asia to Australia. Smaller numbers also winter in the Mediterranean where there is a notable migration stopover in the Camargue with up to 50,000 birds in autumn. In Britain it is a double passage migrant, more frequent in autumn than in spring, mainly to the south and east coasts of England. Scarce in south and east Ireland.

Common Sandpiper

Actitis hypoleucos (Linnaeus)

A neat little brown wader, marked by a distinctive white wedge in front of the folded wing, that bobs continuously like a wagtail. It breeds beside hilly streams and has a strangely fluttering flight low over water

Population: about 50,000 pairs

Warm brown upperparts separated from a brown smudge across the breast by a triangular wedge of white that is an extension of the white underparts. The head is brown with a distinct pale supercilium. The *continuous* bobbing of the tail is a characteristic not shared with any other wader. The flight too is characteristic and unlike other waders. The wings are beaten shallowly and very rapidly, producing a fluttering effect low over water, and the flight ends in a glide on bowed wings. It also shows a bold white wing bar and a dark rump. These are generally solitary birds which never form large flocks; at most half a dozen may band together. They frequent hilly streamsides and often perch on a mid-stream rock like a Dipper. 20 cm ($7\frac{3}{4}$ in).

Voice: A high-pitched *twee-wee-wee* when flushed; song is a similar *kitti-weewit* repeated.

Habitat: Hill streams and upland lake shores. On passage and in winter it is found on marshes, freshwater margins and, less frequently, estuaries.

Reproduction: The nest is a hollow or scrape, lined with vegetation among open areas of shingle, or hidden among waterside vegetation. The 4, occasionally 3 or 5, eggs are buffish spotted and lined with reddish-brown. They are laid in early May and incubated by both sexes for 20–23 days. The chicks leave the nest soon after hatching and are cared for by both parents for 4 weeks, though they can fly after 3 weeks. Single-brooded.

Food: Insects and their larvae, molluscs, worms and crustaceans.

Range and Distribution: Found across Europe from Iberia to Scandinavia, through Russia, the mountains of northern Turkey and the Caucasus, to Siberia and Japan. It is replaced in North America by the similar Spotted Sandpiper *Actitis macularia*, which is a rare wanderer to our shores in autumn. In Britain and Ireland the Common Sandpiper is a widespread breeding bird mostly in the north and west. It is decidedly thin on the ground south and east of a line joining the Severn and Humber.

Movements: A summer visitor from April to August, but found on passage as late as mid-October. Widespread on coastal and inland marshes with some, at least, from Scandinavia. A few birds winter in the south and west.

Red-necked Phalarope

Phalaropus lobatus (Linnaeus)

An attractive little wader that spends most of its time swimming, and winters at sea among the southern oceans. In courtship it is the female that is the dominant partner and she is more brightly coloured than her mate. Adult in winter shown

The upperparts are slate-grey in summer, and striped with 2 buff bars that form a wide V on the back. The crown and sides of the head are slate-grey with a neat, light ring around the eye; the chin is white bordered below and behind by a prominent rust-red neck patch. The underparts are grey becoming white on the belly. The male is similar, but paler, especially in the colour of the neck patch. Both sexes have a fine, needle-like bill, and in winter become pale grey with less pronounced striping on the back, and a dark mark through the eye. The feet and bill remain dark. At all seasons these birds swim buoyantly, sitting on, rather than in, the water. In summer they spin round like a child's top to bring small food to the surface of freshwater marshes, and in winter are found offshore swimming in dense flocks on the sea. In flight they show a bold wing bar and a Dunlin-like tail pattern. Usually remarkably tame. 18 cm (7 in).

Voice: A low-pitched *whit-whit-whit* in flight.

Habitat: Freshwater marshes, small pools and lake margins with a growth of emergent vegetation; in winter at sea often far from land.

Reproduction: The nest is placed in a clump of vegetation surrounded by water and lined with grass. It is constructed by both sexes and the 4, occasionally 3, eggs are olive blotched with black and laid at the end of May. It is the female that initiates courtship and breeding, but once the eggs are laid she takes no further interest in the proceedings. The male alone incubates for 18–20 days and he tends the down-covered chicks for the 18–22 days they take to fly. Females gather in loafing flocks, though sometimes an individual will show some interest in her offspring. Single-brooded.

Food: Insects and their larvae picked from the water's surface; plankton in winter.

Range and Distribution: Circumpolar in the tundra zone, breeding from Scandinavia across northern Russia and Siberia to Alaska, northern Canada, Greenland and Iceland. In Britain and Ireland by far the largest numbers breed in Shetland. The species also breeds in Orkney, Outer Hebrides, Tiree and at a single spot on the Scottish mainland. A substantial colony in Co. Mayo finally disappeared in the early 1970s.

Movements: Arrives on breeding grounds from winter quarters from mid-May onwards. Shetland birds are seldom present before this date. Passage is mainly offshore, though in autumn a few may be found around our shores between August and early October.

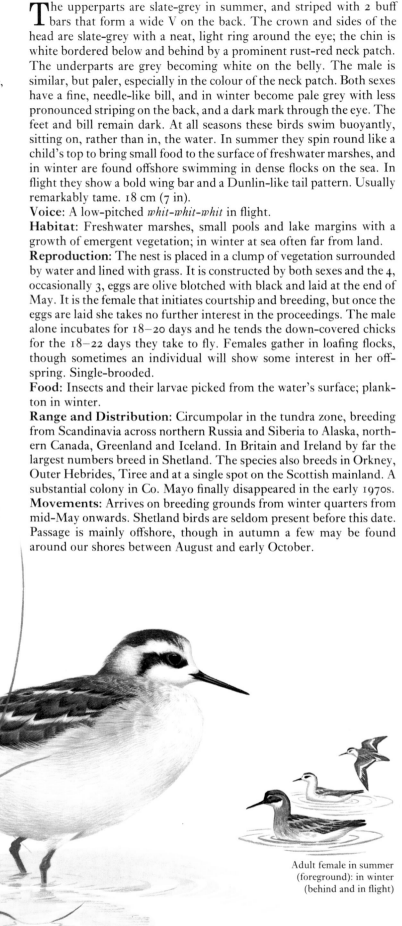

Adult female in summer (foreground): in winter (behind and in flight)

Adult female in summer (foreground):
in winter (left and flight)

Grey Phalarope

Phalaropus fulicarius (Linnaeus)

The high Arctic counterpart of the Red-necked Phalarope. Slightly larger, distinctively plumaged in summer, and sometimes storm-driven to the western approaches in large numbers in autumn. Adult in winter shown

Circumpolar in breeding season: a few thousand, at best, in autumn in Britain and Ireland

In summer the female is bright chestnut from the chin and sides of the neck to the undertail coverts. The face is white, the crown and base of the bill black. The upperparts are scalloped black and buff. The male is a similar, but duller, version of his mate. In winter both sexes become grey like the Red-necked Phalarope, but the present species is always paler grey above, has no V on the back and has a shorter and thicker bill with a yellow base. The legs are also pale and the overall impression is of a larger and stronger-built bird. Gregarious at all times, but particularly on migration and in winter. 20 cm (8 in).

Voice: Slightly higher-pitched *whit* than Red-necked Phalarope.

Habitat: Tundra deltas and pools, coastal lagoons; in winter at sea.

Reproduction: The nest is constructed by the male in a tussock, ridge or small island in a freshwater pool, from late June into July, usually close to other nests to form a small colony. The 4, occasionally 3, eggs are olive blotched with black, and are incubated by the male alone for 19 days. The down-covered chicks leave the nest soon after hatching and are cared for by the male for the 16–20 days before they fly. Single-brooded.

Food: Crustaceans and molluscs, as well as insects and their larvae; in winter takes plankton.

Range and Distribution: Circumpolar in the highest latitudes. Small numbers breed in southwest Iceland, Spitsbergen, Novaya Zemlya, and the far northeastern coast of Siberia, to Alaska, northern Canada and Greenland.

Movements: Entire population winters in southern oceans and large numbers move off the British and Irish west coasts, particularly in autumn. Storms at this season may blow hundreds or even thousands within sight of land, and occasionally inland. Peak movements are from September to November. Generally scarce away from the southwest.

Turnstone

Arenaria interpres (Linnaeus)

A chunky, thick-set wader, essentially marine in habit, that turns over stones and other debris in search of food. It has a small stout bill for the purpose and, in summer, plover-like breast and face bands. Adult in winter shown

Population: 10,000 to 12,000 in winter

Adult in summer (foreground and flying left): in winter (behind and flying right)

Though named from its stone-turning habits, the Turnstone is a catholic feeder that has even been found feeding from a corpse on the tideline. In winter it is dark brown above marked with paler edges to the feathers. The head is brown and there is a broad, smudgy breast band. The underparts are white and the legs orange-yellow. The short bill is slightly upturned and the bird has a dumpy appearance. It is most often encountered on rocky shores in company with Purple Sandpipers, though it also frequents sand and shingle. Generally gregarious in flocks of 10–50 individuals, and either hyperactive or fast asleep atop some rock. In summer the back is marked in chestnut, black and brown to form a tortoiseshell pattern, and black breast band and facial lines break up the shape in an effective camouflage. 23 cm (9 in).

Voice: A rapid *tuk-a-tuk*, and a *kititit*.

Habitat: Bare offshore islands, but also delta and river islands and sometimes on high fjells; in winter along rocky shores as well as sand and shingle estuaries and intertidal areas.

Reproduction: The nest is usually a simple scrape or hollow among pebbles or lichen-covered rocks, with or without lining. The 4, occasionally 3 or 5, eggs are pale green spotted with various shades of brown. They are incubated by both sexes for 22–23 days, starting with the first egg – unusual in a wader. The chicks leave the nest soon after hatching and are cared for by both parents, but with the male playing the more important role. Single-brooded.

Food: Molluscs, crustaceans, insects, carrion; in summer mainly insects and their larvae.

Range and Distribution: Circumpolar, but confined to coastal regions from Scandinavia, northern Russia and Siberia, the Bering Straits, Alaska and northern Canada to Greenland. In North America it is known as the Ruddy Turnstone.

Movements: Winters throughout the world along the ice-free coasts of Iceland and Norway to Australia, New Zealand and South Africa. In Britain and Ireland it is a widespread winter visitor from August to May, with only a few birds passing on further south.

Pomarine Skua

Stercorarius pomarinus (Temminck)

A heavily built, fast-flying, piratical seabird, with boldly twisted central tail streamers in summer. Scarce passage migrant to our shores

Circumpolar in summer: less than 100 in Britain and Ireland in autumn

Although the blunt, twisted tail streamers are diagnostic in spring, they are often lost or broken by late summer at which time the differences between this and the Arctic Skua can be picked out only with great care. Both species occur in 2 phases, a light and a dark, and plumage differences are slight and particularly difficult to see on a fast-flying bird careering over the waves. The Pomarine is heavier built than the Arctic and in the pale (and far more common) phase has a much more clearly marked breast band. Otherwise they are very similar and the presumption is that such skuas are Arctic until proved to be the much rarer Pomarine. Usually solitary, though small flocks are noted from time to time. Employs the usual skua harrying tactics to force gulls and terns to part with their food, though also takes carrion. 51 cm (20 in) includes 5 cm (2 in) tail extension.

Voice: A harsh *which-yew*, and other gull-like notes.

Habitat: Tundra swamps and marshes; in winter found offshore, but also in open oceans.

Reproduction: The nest is a simple unlined scrape and the 2, just occasionally 3, buffish eggs are spotted with dark brown and laid from the end of June onwards. They are incubated by both members of the pair for 27–28 days, and the chicks are cared for by both parents for 5–6 weeks. Single-brooded.

Food: Piratical attacks on gulls and terns, particularly Kittiwakes, forcing them to drop their food; also takes offal and garbage. In summer dependent on lemmings and the eggs and young of many species of birds.

Range and Distribution: Circumpolar in the tundra zone from northern Russia and Siberia to Alaska, northern Canada and eastern Greenland. Absent from Europe including Iceland.

Movements: These skuas regularly pass to the northwest of Britain and Ireland in spring and autumn on their way to and from their arctic breeding grounds. They may be seen between April and June and August and November off any coast, but are never common.

197

Arctic Skua

Stercorarius parasiticus (Linnaeus)

An elegant master flyer that gleans a
living by pursuing other seabirds to
force them to disgorge their food.
Long, sharply pointed wings are
reminiscent of a Peregrine

Population: about 1,100 pairs

Dark phase

A powerful seabird of piratical habits that is
the most common member of the skua tribe in
spring and autumn. Usually gregarious, this species occurs
in both light and dark phases, as well as an intermediate phase which is
most common in Britain. The dark cap is separated, in the light phase,
from the dusky-brown upperparts by a white neck delicately washed
with yellow. The underparts are white. Even in the dark phase the
black cap can be picked out quite easily. In flight the white wing flashes
are never as prominent as those of the Great Skua. In summer the
2 central tail feathers are extended to form streamers, but they are
often broken off before the end of the breeding season, a fact which can
lead to confusion with Pomarine Skuas in autumn. 46 cm (18 in)
including 7.5 cm (3 in) tail extension.

Voice: A *tuk-tuk* note; and a wailing *ka-oow* on breeding grounds.

Habitat: Tundra and marshes, moorland; in winter among coastal and
open seas.

Reproduction: Breeds in loose colonies among wet or marshy land
and is generally vociferous in defence of its territory. The nest is a
hollow with little or no lining and the 2, occasionally only 1, eggs are
olive or buff, spotted with dark brown. They are laid at the end of May
and incubated for 24–28 days by both sexes, commencing with the first
egg. The down-covered chicks remain at the nest for the first few days,
but then leave to be cared for by both parents until they fly at 30 days.
They remain a family unit for a further month. Single-brooded.

Food: Forces gulls and terns to disgorge fish and other food; in
summer takes lemmings in quantity as well as eggs and young of a wide
range of birds. Also kills adults of smaller species.

Range and Distribution: Circumpolar in tundra zone from Scandinavia to northern Russia and Siberia, to Kamchatka, Alaska, northern
Canada, Greenland, Iceland and Scotland. In Britain the main breeding
area is in Shetland, but birds are also to be found in Orkney, Caithness,
the Outer Hebrides and some of the Inner Hebrides, notably the
barren Jura and Coll.

Movements: Arctic Skuas winter in the southern oceans and pass
through the Atlantic twice each year. They are widespread around our
coasts from August to October, but are scarce in spring.

Great Skua

Stercorarius skua (Brünnich)

A large, broad-winged, all-brown seabird, with bold white flashes on the wings in flight, that is fearless in its pursuit of birds far larger than itself

Population: 3,800 pairs

Prominent white wing flashes show in flight

Superficially like an immature gull the Great Skua, or Bonxie as it is called in Shetland, is a rich chocolate-brown bird, flecked all over with gingery-buff markings. The head is small and the black bill remarkably so for a predator. In flight, as well as when displaying aggressively on the ground, the wings have the boldest white flashes of any skua. The tail is square, and a close approach is required to see the 2 small notches that just break its smooth outline. These are gregarious birds, breeding in loose colonies and sometimes gathering in good numbers at favoured feeding grounds. 58 cm (23 in).

Voice: A *tuk-tuk*, a *skerr* and a loud *hah-hah-hah*.

Habitat: Near sea on moors and islands; in winter in offshore waters ranging across oceans.

Reproduction: Forms loose colonies and the nest is a simple unlined scrape, on a hillock or mound, among grass or heather. The 2, sometimes only 1, eggs are olive-grey spotted with dark-brown. They are laid from late May into June and are incubated by both sexes for 28–30 days. The chicks are brooded by the female which is fed on the nest by the male; thereafter both sexes tend the offspring for a further 30 days before they fly. The family unit is maintained for a further month. Single-brooded.

Food: Forces gulls, terns and birds as large as Gannets to disgorge fish and other food; also kills birds as large as Whimbrel and takes the eggs and young of a variety of species. Carrion locally important.

Range and Distribution: Confined to Iceland, Faeroes, Scotland and, more recently, Norway. In Britain it breeds in Shetland, Orkney, the coast of Sutherland, Outer Hebrides and St Kilda. However, over two-thirds of the British population is found on Foula. A decline in Iceland may be linked with an increase in Scotland, though this may be due to protection.

Movements: Population moves southwards to winter off west coast of Africa, and large numbers pass along the west coast of Ireland between August and October. There is a spring passage in March and April. Recorded casually from most of our coasts.

Mediterranean Gull

Larus melanocephalus (Temminck)

A pale-winged gull that has become an increasingly frequent visitor to Britain in recent years and which was first proved to breed in 1968. Adult in winter shown

Range extending northwards and eastwards: a pair breeds most years in England, up to 100 winter

Adult in summer with black (not brown) hood extending to neck

In adult summer plumage this is an easily identified gull. It has light grey wings and white primaries; a black hood broken by an incomplete white eye-ring; and red legs and bill – the latter marked by a narrow black band. In adult winter plumage the hood is lost and replaced by a smudge behind the eye. The absence of black on the underwing and in the wing tips, folded and in flight, is characteristic. However, in immature plumages this gull is easily confusable with other species, notably the Common Gull. At all times the pale eye-ring and large droopy bill are good field marks; the primaries are blacker than in the Common Gull, and a black trailing edge to the secondaries contrasts with a greyish mid-wing panel. These are generally gregarious birds, but in Britain usually occur singly with Black-headed Gulls. 38 cm (15 in).

Voice: A *kow-kow-kow* that is harsher than call of Black-headed Gull.

Habitat: Lagoons and salt pans, coastal marshes; in winter at sea, though strictly coastal in range.

Reproduction: Nests in colonies, sometimes mixed with other species. The nest itself is a thinly lined scrape in the ground, and the 3, occasionally 2, creamy eggs are spotted with black and brown and laid from late May onwards. Single-brooded. In Britain it has nested among huge colonies of Black-headed Gulls and most records concern cases of hybridization with that species.

Food: Fish, molluscs, insects.

Range and Distribution: Breeds at eastern end of Mediterranean including Greece, Turkey and coasts of Black Sea, where it is abundant. It has bred in Holland and Hungary, and at Needs Oar Point in Britain in 1968, 1976 and 1977. Hybrids have bred in other years, but these are the only 3 pure pairs to date.

Movements: Winters in Mediterranean, but some wander into the Atlantic northwards to northwestern Europe. In Britain it is a scarce passage migrant and winter visitor, mainly to English south and east coasts. Some individuals winter at the same place year after year.

Little Gull

Larus minutus (Pallas)

A tiny, almost tern-like gull that is marked with a clear, uniform dark underwing in the adult, and which has attempted to breed for the first time in recent years. Adult in winter shown

Eastern breeding population: less than 1,000 in autumn in Britain and Ireland; 1 or 2 pairs occasionally breed

Adult in summer with black hood extending to neck

Adult in summer is identified by small size, black hood extending to the nape, lack of black wing tips, uniform dusky-grey underwing and white trailing edge to upperwing. In winter the hood is replaced by a simple smudge behind the eye, but the dark underwing remains. Legs and feet red, bill black (red in summer). Immatures have a broad black W across the wings in flight, similar to that of a Kittiwake; at this age the underwing is less uniform. At all ages and in all plumages the tiny size is the first feature that is noticed. Generally a gregarious bird and, even where it is rather scarce on passage, it is normally noted in small flocks. It often feeds in the manner of a marsh tern by picking food from the water's surface. 28 cm (11 in).

Voice: A *kek-kek-kek*.

Habitat: Marshes, coastal pools and lagoons; on passage at reservoirs and along sea coasts.

Reproduction: Breeds colonially, often in association with other species of gulls or terns, among marshland with tussocks of grass or reeds. The nest is a loose structure of aquatic plants placed above water level and the 3, occasionally 2–5, light olive-green eggs are speckled with black and laid from late May. Incubation is shared between the sexes and lasts 20–21 days. The down-covered chicks are cared for by both parents and may fly after 21–24 days. Single-brooded.

Food: Small fish, crustaceans, molluscs, insects.

Range and Distribution: Found in 3 separate populations in Europe, central Siberia and eastern Siberia. In Europe it breeds eastwards from the Baltic to the Urals, and in rather isolated pockets in Sweden, Denmark, Germany, Holland and the Black Sea coast. It has bred in Ontario in Canada since 1962 and more recently in the United States. In Britain the first breeding record was at the Ouse Washes in 1975, with 2 further nests in 1978 – 1 in Norfolk and 1 at Fairburn Ings in Yorkshire. None were successful.

Movements: An increasing passage migrant and winter visitor to Britain that is most numerous in autumn when quite large flocks gather at certain favoured sites in the north and east, and along the south coast. Elsewhere it tends to be casual.

Black-headed Gull

Larus ridibundus (Linnaeus)

Most widespread and familiar of our gulls, being as common inland as it is on the coast. In summer it is resplendent in a chocolate hood, which is replaced by a dark smudge behind the eye in winter

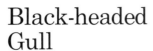

Population:
150,000 to
300,000 pairs

Easily recognized by chocolate (not black) hood (not head) in summer. Upperparts dove-grey, with tips of the primaries forming a black tip to the folded wing. The legs, feet and bill are red. In winter the hood is lost and replaced by a dark smudge behind the eye. However, the white forewing and dark underwing, both created by the colouring of the primaries, are always sure means of identification. Highly gregarious, spending entire life cycle in large groups – some breeding colonies are 20,000 pairs strong. Roosts, on estuaries and at reservoirs, in winter may consist of literally tens of thousands of birds. 36 cm ($14\frac{1}{2}$ in).

Voice: A *kwaar* and other harsh notes.

Habitat: In summer frequents marshes, moors, bogs, dunes and islands; in winter spreads around coasts and inland to sewage works, reservoirs, rubbish dumps, playing fields and agricultural land.

Reproduction: Breeds colonially. The nest varies according to the site, consisting of little more than a bare scrape among dunes, to a quite elaborate structure of vegetation in a tussocky marsh. The 3, occasionally 2 or exceptionally 5–6, pale olive eggs are blotched with black and laid from mid-April onwards. They are incubated by both members of the pair, commencing with the first egg, for 20–21 days. The down-covered chicks are cared for by both parents and can fly after 21–24 days. Single-brooded.

Food: Huge variety of food recorded, from fish and crustaceans to offal, carrion, debris and waste, insects and their larvae and so on. Presumably very little that they will not eat.

Range and Distribution: From Iceland right across temperate Europe, Russia and Siberia to Kamchatka. In Britain and Ireland it breeds mostly in the north and west of both countries. Strong colonies along coast of East Anglia but otherwise rather scarce in southern England.

Movements: Post-breeding dispersal takes our breeding birds to various parts of the country where they are joined by a huge autumn influx of Continental birds from as far away as Czechoslovakia and Russia. Some British birds winter south to Spain.

Adult in winter showing white forewing (right) and dark undersides to primaries (left)

Common Gull

Larus canus (Linnaeus)

A neat, elegant gull, roughly halfway in size between Black-headed and Herring Gulls. The combination of black wing tips with white mirrors, and small yellow-green bill are sufficient to identify. This gull is frequently found inland, often in association with Black-headed Gulls

Population: about 50,000 pairs

Though it has a 'gentle' rather than 'fierce' look, created by the small bill and head, and is rather shy, it will nevertheless pursue Black-headed Gulls skua-fashion to rob them of food. The back and wings are pale dove-grey, marked with black wing tips with white mirrors. These form a distinctive line on the underwing, quite unlike that of a Herring Gull. The head and underparts are white; the bill, legs and feet yellow-green. Immatures are marked in shades of brown, becoming grey on the mantle by their first summer. The size of the bill separates them from all the more common British and Irish gulls, but not from the Mediterranean or other rarer species. Gregarious at all seasons. 41 cm (16 in).

Voice: A high-pitched *kee-ya*, also a *kak-kak-kak*.

Habitat: Moorland marshes and bogs, lake and coastal islands; in winter frequents coasts and marshes, playing fields, reservoirs.

Reproduction: Breeds colonially, though single pairs are not unknown. The nest is a hollow lined with variable amounts of nearby plant material, but can occasionally be a quite substantial structure in a bare tree. The 3, occasionally 2 or 4, olive-green eggs are blotched with dark brown and laid from May onwards. They are incubated by both sexes for 22–27 days. The down-covered chicks leave the nest after a couple of days, but do not stray far. They are cared for by both parents and fly after 4 weeks. Single-brooded.

Range and Distribution: Northern Holarctic, though absent from eastern North America and Greenland. From Iceland to Scandinavia, south to Denmark and northern Germany, then eastwards in a broad band across Russia and Siberia to Japan, Alaska and northwestern Canada. In Britain and Ireland it is confined to the north and west, except for isolated breeding spots in England and Wales. A shingle-breeding colony continues to survive at Dungeness.

Movements: Large influx of Continental visitors from August to October spreading over all parts of the country to winter. Return movements in March and April.

First year: bill shape and size separate from other immature gulls

Herring Gull

Larus argentatus (Pontoppidan)

A large and familiar gull with a light grey back, black wing tips with white mirrors, and a red-spotted yellow bill. Its raucous, laughing cries conjure up memories of seaside holidays

Population: over 300,000 pairs

First year bird difficult to distinguish from similar-aged Lesser Black-backed Gull

Although varying considerably over its huge range, the Herring Gull of Britain and Ireland is pale dove-grey on mantle and wings. The wing tips are black with white mirrors and the head, neck and under-parts are white. The bill is yellow with a red spot near the tip of the lower mandible and the legs are pink – though in the Mediterranean and other parts of the range they are yellow. Immatures are mottled browns and buffs and decidedly difficult to distinguish from young Lesser Black-backed Gulls. These are gregarious and aggressive birds that have taken advantage of new food sources created by human wastage to increase and spread in recent years. They now nest inland in several areas as well as among the chimney pots of many coastal towns, and as a result have become decidedly unpopular. Their depredations on the eggs and chicks of rarer birds have also brought them into conflict with conservationists. 56–66 cm (22–26 in).

Voice: A loud *kee-yow*; a *gah-gah-gah* in the breeding season; and a variety of barks and mews.

Habitat: Sea cliffs, dunes, shingle beaches, roofs of buildings, some-times by inland lakes and moorlands; in winter frequents coasts, harbours, estuaries, rubbish dumps, reservoirs.

Reproduction: Breeds colonially, creating a substantial nest of veg-etation on a cliff ledge or on the ground. The 2–3 olive-coloured eggs are blotched with black and laid from late April onwards. Incubation, mostly by the female, lasts 25–33 days and the down-covered chicks are cared for by both parents for 30 or so days. Single-brooded.

Food: Omnivorous and opportunistic. Fish offal and refuse, as well as more natural foods such as fish, crustaceans, molluscs, worms. Also takes small birds, eggs, chicks and small mammals.

Range and Distribution: Circumpolar from Iceland across Scandi-navia, northern Russia and Siberia to Bering Straits, Alaska, Canada and the northern United States. Also breeds in Mediterranean, north-west Africa, and from the Black Sea to the Caspian and central Siberia. This vast range actually extends right around the world in the north

temperate zone and, as one would expect, there is considerable geographical variation. Indeed, what is simply a darker form in, say, Siberia or North America, actually becomes a separate species with the Lesser Black-backed Gull in Europe. In Britain and Ireland it breeds around all coasts except for East Anglia northwards to Flamborough Head. Largest numbers are in the north and west.

Movements: Immigration of winter visitors from Continent in September and October, staying through to March or April. British and Irish birds mainly resident, though some wander as far as France.

Lesser Black-backed Gull

Larus fuscus (Linnaeus)

About the same size as the Herring Gull and decidedly smaller than the similarly dark-backed Great Black-backed Gull. Migratory, mainly wintering well south of its breeding haunts

Population: unknown, but 50,000 or more pairs

Variable upperparts, so that a light Lesser Black-backed may be similar to a dark Herring Gull. Even the legs, which are normally yellow but sometimes pink, can cause confusion with the other species. In general, however, the Lesser Black-backed is dark slate-grey above with black wing tips marked with white mirrors. The head and underparts are white, streaked with black in winter. The bill is yellow with a red spot near the tip of the lower mandible, and the legs are yellow. In the Scandinavian subspecies *Larus fuscus fuscus* the back may be virtually black. Immature Lessers are distinguishable from young Herring Gulls only with the greatest of care. These are gregarious birds that breed colonially and migrate and winter in flocks, often in company with other gull species. 53–56 cm (21–22 in).

Voice: A sharp *kyow*, also a variety of barking calls.

Habitat: Flat-topped islands, sand dunes, moors and upland lakes; in winter and on migration frequently found inland on playing fields and reservoirs, but also on coasts and marshes.

Reproduction: Breeds colonially. The nest is a well-lined structure placed on the ground. The 3, occasionally 1 or 2, eggs are olive-buff spotted with black, and are laid from the end of April onwards. They are incubated by both members of the pair for 25–29 days, and the chicks are cared for by both parents for 35–40 days. Single-brooded.

Food: Much more natural food than the Herring Gull and feeds less often from offal or on rubbish tips; fish, worms, molluscs, crustaceans and insects according to availability.

Range and Distribution: Found from Iceland and northwestern France eastwards along the coasts of the North Sea to Scandinavia and northwest Russia. In Britain and Ireland it is found along the south, west and north coasts, but is absent from much of the east coast of England and from the resort areas of the south. Over a third of the total breed at Walney Island. Breeds inland in hilly districts.

Movements: Most birds leave Britain and Ireland moving southwards to winter along the coasts of Iberia to West Africa. These movements also include some dark-backed Scandinavian birds, particularly in the southeast. An increasing number are remaining to winter in Britain and Ireland.

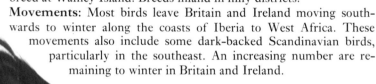

First winter similar to same-aged Herring Gull

Iceland Gull

Larus glaucoides (Meyer)

A scarce winter visitor to northern Scotland. Similar to larger Glaucous Gull, but with smaller bill and more buoyant flight. Iceland Gull shown above

World distribution: no more than 50 winter in Britain and Ireland

Glaucous Gull

Larus hyperboreus (Gunnerus)

A sparse winter visitor that is as large as a Great Black-backed Gull, but which is pale grey above with white primaries completely devoid of wing-tip pattern. Glaucous Gull shown below

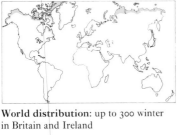

World distribution: up to 300 winter in Britain and Ireland

Pale grey mantle and wings with white primaries lacking black on tips. Yellow bill with red spot near the tip, but head and bill are decidedly small. The feet are pink. In all plumages this species is similar to more widespread Glaucous Gull. The smaller bill is an important distinction. First winter plumage is buff with cream primaries; the second winter virtually white all over. 56–66 cm (22–26 in).
Voice: An *ack-ack-ack* of alarm; shriller calls than Herring Gull's.
Habitat: In winter frequents coasts and harbours.
Reproduction: Colonial, building a large nest of mosses and grass. The 2–3 eggs are buff spotted with rufous-brown and laid in June. Single-brooded.
Food: Varied; fish, offal, rubbish and carrion.
Range and Distribution: Found in Baffin Island, Greenland, but not (despite its name) Iceland.
Movements: Reported annually in northern Scotland and Cork.

The pattern of pale grey wings and white primaries, lacking black on the tips, is common to both Glaucous and Iceland Gulls, but this species is larger, with broad wings and a massive head and bill. In immature plumages, only the tip of the bill of this species is dark. 64–81 cm (25–32 in).
Voice: Herring Gull-like shrieks and barks.
Habitat: In winter frequents coasts, nearby rubbish tips and lagoons.
Reproduction: Mostly colonial, building a substantial nest of mosses and grass. The 2–3, occasionally 1 or 4, olive-buff eggs are blotched with dark brown and laid from mid-May onwards. Incubation, which lasts 27–30 days, and care of the young are shared between the sexes.
Food: Carrion and offal, and virtually anything animate.
Range and Distribution: Circumpolar in highest latitudes.
Movements: Winter visitor to east and west coasts. Seldom inland.

Great Black-backed Gull

Larus marinus (Linnaeus)

A huge, slow-flying, black-backed bird, with a massive head and powerful bill. It is a considerable predator of other seabirds

Population: 22,000 pairs

Mantle and wings of this gull are as black as the wing tips, whereas those of the only other black-backed species, the Lesser Black-backed, are noticeably lighter. However, the present species is much larger, with a large head and a particularly long and thick bill. Like other large gulls the bill is yellow with a red spot near the tip of the lower mandible, and the legs and feet are pink. Nevertheless a single large gull can still cause problems, though if there is any doubt about an individual being a Great Black-backed – then most probably it is not. 64–79 cm (25–31 in).

Voice: A short *owk*, and a gutteral *uk-uk-uk*.

Habitat: Generally more marine than other gulls, being most numerous on coasts and frequently seen far out at sea: islands and islets, sea cliffs, coastal banks and shoals.

Reproduction: Colonial or singly, usually on some eminence overlooking a large seabird colony, but separate from it. Builds a substantial nest of available materials, and the 2–3 olive-green eggs are spotted with dark brown and laid from mid-April. Incubation is shared between the sexes and lasts 26–30 days. The chicks are covered with down, and are cared for by both parents for the 50 days before they are able to fly. Single-brooded.

Food: Variable, but adults, nestlings and eggs of seabirds are particularly important in summer; also fish, crustaceans, worms, molluscs, small mammals and much carrion.

Range and Distribution: Confined to the North Atlantic where it is found along the eastern seaboard of Canada as far south as New York in recent years, as well as inland at Lake Huron; Greenland, Iceland, Britain and Ireland, and all Scandinavian coasts. In Britain and Ireland it is found along most coasts except for the south and east from the Isle of Wight to the Firth of Tay. Over two-thirds of the total breed in Scotland. The recent increase and spread has been attributed to climatic changes, a decline in persecution and the increase in food due to human waste.

Movements: A few British birds wander south to Iberia. Immigration of winter visitors from Iceland and Scandinavia from August until October brings many birds to our shores. They return in March and April.

Adult (foreground)
and immature in
second summer

208

Kittiwake

Rissa tridactyla (Linnaeus)

A delicate, long-winged gull that spends most of its life well out to sea and comes to land to breed in noisy throngs along our sea cliffs. Huge increase in numbers in recent years following drastic decline due to shooting last century. Adult (right) and juvenile shown

Population: nearly 500,000 pairs

A grey and white gull marked by a neat yellow bill and black legs. In flight the long wings show well and are marked with 'ink-pot' tips of black, with no white mirrors. In immature plumage a bold black W extends across the wings and there is a black mark extending over the nape as well as a black terminal band to the V-shaped tail. These are essentially pelagic birds that spend most of their year well out at sea. They are great wanderers, making regular transatlantic crossings, and gather around our sea cliffs in enormous concentrations to breed. Unlike most gulls, they build a substantial and well-constructed nest. 41 cm (16 in).

Voice: A distinctive and loud *kitti-mark*, repeated and uttered in chorus at noisy breeding colonies.

Habitat: Steep sea cliffs, open oceans, sometimes at freshwater pools near the coast for bathing.

Reproduction: Colonial; the nest is a well-constructed and solid mass of vegetation worked outwards from a narrow crevice in a sheer sea cliff or cave. It is built by both sexes, which may fly considerable distances to gather suitable materials. The neat hollow, or shallow cup, holds the 2, rarely 1 or 3, buffish eggs spotted with various shades of brown. They are laid in late May and incubated by both sexes for 25–30 days. The chicks are cared for and fed by both parents for about 43 days before flying. Single-brooded.

Food: Small fish, crustaceans and molluscs taken from the surface in flight, by picking or by tern-like diving.

Range and Distribution: Circumpolar, but absent from large areas of northern Canada and Siberia. Widespread in North Atlantic and North Pacific. In Britain and Ireland it breeds on all coasts, but mainly in the north and west where large cliffs are found. Over three-quarters of the population breed in Scotland, including 128,000 pairs in Orkney. Current increase of 50 per cent every 10 years. Along low-lying coasts even piers or shingle beaches may be used.

Movements: Wide-ranging over open oceans; occasionally blown inland by autumn storms.

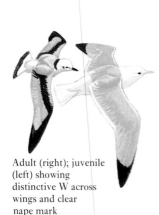

Adult (right); juvenile (left) showing distinctive W across wings and clear nape mark

Sandwich Tern

Sterna sandvicensis (Latham)

Largest of our regular terns and the only one with a black bill. This is a highly gregarious and erratic bird that will desert a well-established colony without apparent reason

Population: over 14,000 pairs

Pale grey above and white below, with a black cap that terminates in a ragged crest. The bill is long, sharply pointed, and black with a yellow tip. Unfortunately this tip is often difficult to see, especially in flight, and its apparent absence may cause confusion with a scarcer species, particularly the Gull-billed Tern. The legs are short and black. It flies with deep, almost leisurely strokes of its long pointed wings, and the pronounced V in the tail can be clearly seen. In winter the forehead becomes white to beyond the eye. Sandwich Terns nest close together in colonies and are generally gregarious at all times. 41 cm (16 in).

Voice: A distinctive rasping flight note *kirr-ick*.

Habitat: Sand and shingle bars and islands, offshore grassy holms; at other times in coastal waters.

Reproduction: Breeds at traditional sites, though it will abandon such areas if disturbed. Forms dense colonies, with sitting birds virtually within touching distance of one another, and dates of egg laying and hatching are highly synchronized. The nest is a scrape with little or no lining material and the 2, occasionally 1 or 3, buffish eggs are spotted and scrawled with shades of brown, and laid from late April onwards. Incubation, which is shared, lasts 20–24 days and the down-covered young are cared for by both parents for 35 days, though they form colony creches after about 10 days. Single-brooded.

Food: Sand-eels and other small fish.

Range and Distribution: Found on Baltic, Denmark and North Sea coasts, Britain and Ireland, and northwest France; and in isolated spots

in Mediterranean, Black and Caspian Seas; on southern coasts of United States, Mexico and Bahamas; and possibly in South America. In Britain and Ireland it breeds mostly in north Norfolk with the largest colony, approaching 4,000 pairs, at Scolt Head Island. It is decidedly scarce in the western isles of Scotland and absent from Shetland.

Movements: British birds arrive from mid-March to May and depart between July and October. They move along the west coasts of Africa south to the Cape.

Adult at rest

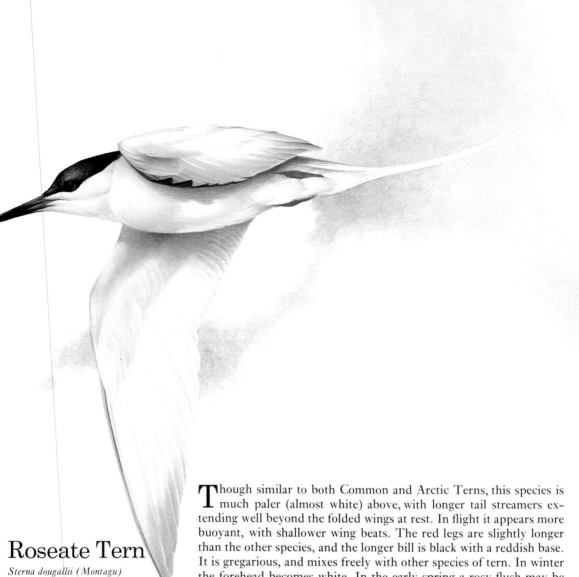

Roseate Tern

Sterna dougallii (Montagu)

One of our rarest seabirds and a very elusive species away from its breeding sites, of which no more than 6 are used regularly by any substantial number of birds

Population: about 2,500 pairs

Adult at rest

Though similar to both Common and Arctic Terns, this species is much paler (almost white) above, with longer tail streamers extending well beyond the folded wings at rest. In flight it appears more buoyant, with shallower wing beats. The red legs are slightly longer than the other species, and the longer bill is black with a reddish base. It is gregarious, and mixes freely with other species of tern. In winter the forehead becomes white. In the early spring a rosy flush may be detected on the breast. 38 cm (15 in).

Voice: An *aak* that is prolonged, and a *chuvick*; also a chattering *kekekekekek*.

Habitat: Rocky or sandy islands near or adjacent to coasts; very rare inland, winters off coasts.

Reproduction: A simple scrape in sand, or a hollow in rock acts as the nest. These are colonial birds that frequently nest among colonies of other terns. The 1–2, occasionally 3, buffish eggs are blotched with dark brown and laid in June. They are incubated mainly by the female, usually commencing with the first egg, for 21–26 days. The down-covered chicks are cared for by both parents. Single-brooded.

Food: Small fish including sand-eels taken from near the surface by diving. May also rob other terns.

Range and Distribution: Cosmopolitan; highly fragmented range in most continents of the world, from the West Indies to Australia, and Scotland to South Africa. In Europe it is mainly to be found in Britain and Ireland where nearly half formerly bred on Tern Island in Co. Wexford; but there are still regular colonies on Anglesey, on the Firth of Forth islands, and on the Farne Islands.

Movements: Arrives from the end of April and departs from the middle of July to September. Winters in the Gulf of Guinea and adjacent coasts of West Africa.

Common Tern

Sterna hirundo (Linnaeus)

Most widespread, though not the most numerous, of our terns and so easily confused with the more abundant Arctic Tern that they are often lumped together and light-heartedly referred to jointly as 'Commic' Terns

An elegant, long-winged seabird, with pale grey upperparts, white underparts, a bold black cap, short red legs, and a long, black-tipped red bill. A sure means of identification in flight is that Common Terns have a translucent inner wing, whereas in the Arctic Tern the whole wing is translucent. At rest the black bill tip is clear cut in summer, though in autumn and winter both species have black bills and white foreheads. Generally gregarious, it feeds by diving headfirst into shallow seas. 35 cm (14 in).

Voice: A grating *kree-err*, and a *kikikikik*.

Habitat: Coastal sand and shingle banks and islands, salt marshes, estuaries; but also in similar areas inland; in winter frequents coasts and lakes.

Reproduction: Colonial, but nests are often some distance apart. The nest itself is a simple scrape with little or no lining and the 2–3, occasionally 4, eggs are creamy-olive spotted and blotched with dark brown, and are laid from the end of May onwards. They are incubated mainly by the female, starting with the first egg. The chicks hatch after 20–23 days and are cared for by both parents until they fly at 4 weeks. Single-brooded.

Food: Small fish including sand-eels, crustaceans, molluscs, marine worms, insects; mostly taken by shallow dives or by picking from the surface in flight.

Range and Distribution: Virtually circumpolar but absent from western North America. Otherwise throughout Europe and across Russia and Siberia to the Bering Straits, and across eastern Canada and in the northeastern United States. There are also many isolated colonies in warmer seas including the Caribbean, the Azores, Tunisia, West Africa and the Persian Gulf. In Britain and Ireland it breeds in good numbers and is found along most coasts, but is scarce in northeastern and southwestern England, and in Wales except for Anglesey.

Movements: British birds arrive from mid–April onwards and depart between July and October. They winter along the coasts of West Africa.

Population: 15,000 to 20,000 pairs

Adult at rest and in flight – note differences from Arctic Tern

Arctic Tern

Sterna paradisaea (Pontoppidan)

A long-winged, fast-flying tern that migrates from the Arctic to the Antarctic and back every year. A summer visitor that must be distinguished with care from the similar Common Tern

Population: over 30,000 pairs

Adult at rest and in flight – note darker bill in winter (flying right)

In summer the bill is coral-red. A black cap extends from the forehead, through the eye to the nape and is bordered below by a line of white above the grey underparts, creating a plumage pattern rather similar to that of the rare Whiskered Tern. But the Arctic Tern is much more likely to be confused with the Common Tern and is distinguished by the lack of a black tip to the bill, completely white and semitransparent flight feathers and longer tail streamers reaching beyond the folded wings. In winter the bill becomes darker and the black cap is partially lost on the forehead. These are typically gregarious terns, flying on long angular wings. 35 cm (14 in).

Voice: A harsh *kee-yar*, similar to call of Common Tern.

Habitat: Sea coasts and islets, inland only along arctic rivers.

Reproduction: Colonial and particularly aggressive towards intruders. The nest scrape may be lined with a few oddments of vegetation by the female, the 2–3 eggs being laid from late May and camouflaged in buffs and browns. They are incubated by both sexes for 20–23 days and the down-covered chicks first leave the nest at about 3 days. They are fed by both parents and fly after 28 days. Single-brooded, but replacement clutches may be laid as late as July.

Food: Small fish, especially sand-eels, but also crustaceans and squid.

Range and Distribution: Circumpolar in northern latitudes as far as ice-free land extends. In Europe it breeds furthest south in Brittany, northern Britain and Ireland and North Sea coasts. Scarce in England and Wales with large colonies only in the northeast. Abundant in Scotland, but declining in Ireland.

Movements: Summer visitor returning in late April. The whole population makes huge migrations to winter in the southern oceans, with Greenland and eastern Canadian birds crossing the North Atlantic to pass along the shores of Britain, Ireland and western Europe. Some birds travel over 32,000 km a year on migration alone.

Little Tern

Sterna albifrons (Pallas)

Smallest of our terns and distinctively marked by a white forehead and yellow bill. Frequently hovers while fishing. Almost exclusively coastal in distribution

Population: 1,600 pairs

Adult at rest and flying: white forehead visible at all times

Much the smallest of our terns with distinctively fast wing beats and frequent hovering before diving after food. Upperparts are pale grey with dark wing tips. Underparts pure white. The feet and legs are yellow as is the black-tipped bill. The tail is deeply forked, but lacks streamers. A black cap extends from the lores through the eye and over the crown, but the forehead is white. Generally gregarious, but colonies tend to be strung out along beaches. 24 cm (9½ in).

Voice: A loud *kik-kik* and a sharp *kirri-kirri-kirri*.

Habitat: Sand and shingle beaches, with only a few small colonies even a few hundred metres from the shoreline. Elsewhere it has taken to nesting on flat-topped roofs of coastal buildings as its beaches have been invaded by tourists.

Reproduction: The nest is a simple scrape, mostly within a few metres of the high tide mark, lined with a little vegetation by the female. The 2−3 buffy eggs are blotched with various shades of brown and incubated by both sexes for 19−22 days. The down-covered chicks leave the nest a day or so after hatching and are fed by both parents before flying at 15−17 days. Single-brooded.

Food: Crustaceans and marine worms taken by aerial diving, also small fish. Often hunts over tidal creeks and dykes.

Range and Distribution: Virtually cosmopolitan. Breeds in United States, Central America and the West Indies, coastal Europe and inland over huge areas of western and central Asia. Also on both coasts of tropical Africa, through the Middle East and Asia to Australia. In Britain and Ireland it is widespread on most coasts, but declining numbers have reduced many colonies. Subject to much disturbance.

Movements: Summer visitor, arriving in mid-April from winter quarters in southern Europe and West Africa.

Black Tern

Chlidonias niger (Linnaeus)

Regular passage migrant and most frequent of the marsh terns. Formerly nested in eastern England and returned to breed in 1966 after an absence of 100 years. Adult in winter shown

Southerly breeding distribution: 1 or 2 pairs every few years in Britain. Regular autumn migrant

Adult in summer

Light and airy flight, typically dipping to pick insects from the water's surface, distinguishes the Black Tern from the sea terns. In summer the head and underparts are black, the wings sooty-grey with pale linings and the undertail coverts white. The tail is neatly forked, the bill and legs black. In winter (and autumn) the black is lost and the underparts are white. A black cap extends from above the eye to the hind crown, and a black smudge remains before the bend of the wing. The much rarer White-winged Black Tern is distinguished at this season by the absence of the dark smudge, a less prominent cap and other minor features. 24 cm ($9\frac{1}{2}$ in).

Voice: Usually quiet; occasional *kit* or *krew*.

Habitat: Marshes and lowland lakes and reservoirs; often coastal on passage.

Reproduction: Colonial. Builds a floating platform of materials among emergent vegetation or on a damp tussock. The 3, occasionally 2 or 4, eggs are buffish blotched with darker browns and black and laid in mid-May. They are incubated by both sexes, the female taking the larger role, and hatch after 20–21 days. The down-covered chicks remain in the nest, though active, for 14 days and are fed by both parents until they fly after 28 days. Single-brooded.

Food: Aquatic insects and their larvae picked from the water's surface in flight.

Range and Distribution: Found right across North America and from Spain across temperate Europe to Russia beyond the Urals. Bred in eastern and southeastern England until 1858 but then absent until it returned to the Ouse Washes in 1966. Intermittent breeding at this and nearby sites since then. Bred in Ireland in 1967.

Movements: Summer visitor and double passage migrant to southern and eastern England, mostly in mid-May and August. Winters in tropical Africa.

Guillemot

Uria aalge (Pontoppidan)

The typical auk that throngs our
seabird cliffs. Dark above and light
below, it stands upright on land and
flies on rapidly whirring wings low
over the sea. Badly hit by oil spills

Population: some 577,000 pairs

Exclusively marine and gregarious bird that comes to land only to
breed on tiny ledges of the most precipitous cliffs. Upperparts are
dark chocolate brown, extending in summer to cover the head, neck
and breast; underparts white. A percentage of birds, increasing with
higher latitudes, have a white eye-ring with a white line extending over
the ear coverts and are known as the 'bridled' form. In winter the
brown on the chin and breast is lost. Swims horizontally, duck-like, but
stands upright on land. Gregarious at all seasons. 42 cm (16½ in).

Voice: A growling *arrr*.

Habitat: Offshore waters over the continental shelf; seldom in open
oceans and often quite close inshore. Breeds on sheer cliffs and atop
isolated stacks.

Reproduction: Colonies are occupied at the end of the year, though
eggs are seldom laid before mid-May. A single egg is laid on an open
ledge, 'sitting' birds often packed tightly together. It is pyriform, and
shaped to spin rather than roll off into the sea. Colour and pattern are
highly variable; white, buff and blue spotted with brown and black.
Incubation by both sexes involves resting the egg on the webbed feet in
an upright, penguin-like posture. The down-covered chick hatches
after 28−35 days and is fed by both parents for 18−25 days. At this
point it flutters to the sea where it may be fed by another adult until it
flies after a further 21 days. Single-brooded.

Food: Plunge-dives from the surface using its wings for underwater
propulsion. Dives as deep as 60 metres in its search for fish, crustaceans
and molluscs.

Range and Distribution: Coasts of North Atlantic and Pacific. In
Britain and Ireland it breeds on most coasts with suitable cliffs, though
over three-quarters are found in Scotland. Absent from the Isle of
Wight to Flamborough Head. The significant decreases in southern
colonies are probably due to the serious effect of oil pollution. The
Guillemot is the most common victim of such seabird disasters.

Movements: Some movement away from colonies, with a few birds
wintering as far away as Biscay, Denmark and Norway.

From right to left:
normal adult in
summer, bridled form
in summer, adult in winter

Razorbill

Alca torda (Linnaeus)

A black and white auk, similar to the more abundant Guillemot, marked by a deep bill with a transverse white bar from which it is named. Breeds in rock crevices rather than on open cliff ledges

Population: 144,000 pairs

A typical auk, black above and white below, best distinguished from the similar Guillemot by the deep wedge-shaped bill with its white transverse bar. Like that species it loses the dark on chin and breast in winter. Immatures have a shorter, stubby bill. These are gregarious birds, but they do not crowd together on open ledges like the commoner species. Waddling and ungainly on land, the Razorbill flies on short, rapidly whirring wings. 41 cm (16 in).

Voice: A grating *caarr*; generally rather noisy at colonies.

Habitat: Inshore waters, seldom venturing far from land. Nests among broken cliffs in crevices and caves.

Reproduction: Colonies are occupied at the beginning of the year and the single egg (occasionally 2) is laid in May. Like those of the Guillemot, they are highly variable in colour, buff to green, spotted and blotched in brown or black. Incubation, which is shared between the sexes, lasts 25–35 days and the downy chick is fed by both parents for 12–14 days before it takes to the sea, usually in the company of one of the adults. Single-brooded.

Food: Fish obtained by plunge-diving from the surface and pursued underwater by using the wings for propulsion. Razorbills often feed closer inshore than Guillemots.

Range and Distribution: Coasts of North Atlantic, from northeastern coasts of United States, Newfoundland and adjacent Canada, western Greenland, Iceland, Britain and Ireland to Scandinavia. In Britain and Ireland it breeds on most cliff-bound coasts, but is absent from much of southeast and eastern England. The largest colony is at Horn Head in Co. Donegal, with 45,000 pairs.

Movements: Southern birds move southwards to Biscay and the Mediterranean. Northern birds cross the North Sea to Scandinavia.

Adult in winter

217

Black Guillemot

Cepphus grylle (Linnaeus)

A beautiful black seabird, marked by
bold white patches on the wings and
bright red feet and inside of the
mouth. Confined to the north and
west and much less common than
the other breeding auks

Population: about 8,300 pairs

Adult in summer (left)
and in winter

Easily identified by all-black plumage broken only by large, white
oval patches on the wing that are particularly obvious when the
wings are flapped. The legs and feet, as well as the gape, are a bright
coral-red. Most frequently seen in pairs and small parties at the foot of
breeding cliffs. In winter much of the black plumage is lost; the
underparts becoming white, the upperparts mottled grey. Only the
primaries and tail feathers remain black, giving the bird a black-ended
appearance. It is generally gregarious, usually forming single-species
rafts at the foot of cliffs. Frequently called by its old Norse name of
Tystie. 34 cm (13½ in).

Voice: A thin, whistled *peeee*.

Habitat: Marine, but much closer inshore than other auks; frequently
well inland on sea lochs. Breeds among boulder debris at base of cliffs.

Reproduction: Elaborate communal displays on sea involve tail-
cocking and exposing the red mouth, as well as much pursuit and
in-line swimming. The nest is a crevice and the 2, occasionally 1 or 3,
eggs are laid from early May. They are white spotted with grey and
incubated by both sexes, beginning with the second egg, for 29 days.
The chicks are fed by both parents until they fledge after 34–36 days.
Single-brooded.

Food: Fish, crustaceans and molluscs taken from the bottom in
shallow water. Plunge-dives and can remain submerged for periods
of up to a minute.

Range and Distribution: Circumpolar, mostly along arctic coasts. In
Europe also found in Iceland and Scandinavia. Confined to the north
and west in Britain and Ireland with heavy concentrations in Shetland,
Orkney and the Hebrides.

Movements: Virtually sedentary.

Little Auk

Alle alle (Linnaeus)

A tiny auk that breeds in huge numbers in the Arctic and which may be the world's most numerous bird. A scarce visitor to our shores, mainly storm-driven in autumn. Adult in winter shown

Breeds in high **Arctic** in teeming colonies: from 50 to 1,000 birds in autumn in Britain and Ireland, depending on weather

Adult in summer with black extending to throat

About the same size as a Starling, this is the smallest of our auks and of decidedly dumpy appearance. It is black above and white below with a short, stubby bill. In summer the chin, throat and breast are black with a white mark above the eye. In autumn and winter these areas are white. The wings are long for an auk and huge flocks wheel in fast flight over their breeding grounds. It usually appears singly in our waters and is most frequently observed near the shore, storm-driven in autumn. Sometimes, gales may coincide with a heavy movement of birds offshore and large numbers may be forced to find shelter. Occasionally such large numbers may be forced inland that a 'wreck' occurs. At such times birds may turn up in the most unlikely places, though most individuals involved manage to find open water in the form of reservoirs or lakes. 20 cm (8 in).

Voice: Noisy on breeding grounds, uttering a shrill, chattering *kraak-aak-ak-ak-ak-ak*.

Habitat: Breeds high on sea cliffs and on frost-shattered mountain tops, often some distance inland. Outside breeding season frequents edge of pack ice.

Reproduction: The nest is an unlined rock crevice and the single pale blue egg (occasionally 2) is laid from mid-June onwards. Incubation, shared between the sexes, lasts 24 days and the down-covered chick is fed by both parents for 21–28 days before leaving for the sea. Single-brooded.

Food: Mostly planktonic creatures, especially crustaceans, taken by diving from the surface using the wings for underwater propulsion.

Range and Distribution: High Arctic, from Greenland and Spitsbergen to the islands of northern Siberia. May still breed in small numbers in Iceland. In Britain and Ireland it is reported annually in variable numbers, mostly between November and February. Regular in Shetland.

Movements: Deserts breeding colonies and haunts the edge of the arctic pack ice. Such a wintering range does little to explain the 'wrecks' that occur from time to time on both sides of the Atlantic. What seems to happen is similar to the mechanism that triggers movements of several other arctic species, such as the Crossbill and Waxwing. A high population may force large numbers of such species southwards away from their normal wintering range in search of food, in this case bringing Little Auks to the central Atlantic storm belt.

Puffin

Fratercula arctica (Linnaeus)

Endearing and slightly comical, this gregarious little auk is marked by a bright, multicoloured bill in summer, and stands around in small groups near its cliff-top colonies

Population: 490,000 pairs

Black above and white below, the Puffin is easily distinguished even at considerable distances by its white cheeks. A closer approach reveals the strange parrot-shaped bill coloured in tones of red, orange and yellow, a red eye-ring and red legs and feet. On land off-duty birds stand around in small groups, often photogenically posing against sea thrift. On the water they appear rather dumpy, with a large head. In winter the brighter colours of the bill are lost and the cheeks become decidedly grey. Immatures have shorter, stubby bills, but never as stubby as the much smaller Little Auk. 30 cm (12 in).

Voice: A growling *arr-arr-arr* on breeding grounds.

Habitat: Generally inshore and seldom far from land at any season. Breeds on grassy cliff tops and flat grassy holms.

Reproduction: Breeding colonies, which may be huge, are occupied from March onwards. The nest is an unlined burrow, excavated by the birds themselves or taken over from rabbits. Over a lengthy period tunnelling may honeycomb a suitable site and lead to erosion and eventual self-destruction. Some birds may share an entrance hole with rabbits or Manx Shearwaters; others may use rock crevices. The single white egg (sometimes 2) is laid in May and incubated by the female, with occasional help from the male, for 40–43 days. The down-covered chick is fed by both parents for 40 days and is then deserted. Some 7–11 days later it finds its own way to the sea under cover of darkness. Single-brooded.

Food: Small fish and sand-eels taken by diving from the water's surface.

Range and Distribution: North Atlantic from the northeastern United States to Greenland, Iceland, Spitsbergen and Novaya Zemlya. Also in Brittany, Britain and Ireland, and Scandinavia. Breeds on all British and Irish coasts except for the south and east between Dorset and Lincolnshire. Serious decline in numbers at many colonies, though huge numbers remain on the Scottish islands.

Movements: Colonies are deserted in late summer with birds moving into the North Sea and along the Atlantic coasts of France and Spain, into the western Mediterranean.

Adult in winter

Rock Dove

Columba livia (Gmelin)

Ancestor of the feral town pigeon, which is now found virtually throughout the world and exhibits such a huge range of different plumages

Population: about 100,000 pairs, including feral doves

The true Rock Dove is a blue-grey bird boldly marked with 2 black bars across the wing, blackish primaries, a black terminal tail band and a neat white rump patch. The neck has a slash of iridescent green and purple. Many feral birds still exhibit this basic plumage. The Rock Dove can be distinguished from the similar Stock Dove by its wing bars and rump patch. Wild Rock Doves are now found in Britain and Ireland only on the north and west coasts where they remain a favourite prey of the much reduced Peregrine population. They frequently form flocks. 33 cm (13 in).

Voice: Same as the feral stock; a repeated *oor-roo-coo*, also a quiet *ooo*.

Habitat: Wild birds are almost entirely coastal, occupying ledges and niches in steep cliffs, often in company with cliff-nesting seabirds. Feral birds are found also in cities and towns, often gathering at tourist spots where they are traditionally fed.

Reproduction: Slow-flapping display flight, and elaborate strutting and breast-puffing by the male. The nest is placed in a crevice or rock hole, frequently deep inside a sea cave. The 2 white eggs are oval in shape and laid from April through to July. Incubation, predominantly by the female, takes 12 days and the chicks are fed on pigeon's milk regurgitated from the crop of both parents, and later on regurgitated grain. The chicks fledge after 35 days. Two or 3 broods are raised.

Food: Mainly cereals, but also weed seeds and small molluscs.

Range and Distribution: Throughout the Mediterranean southwards into the mountains of the Sahara and eastwards through southern Russia, central Siberia, the Middle East, India and Burma. There are also populations in western and northern China. In northern Europe it is confined to the coasts of Brittany and Britain and Ireland where truly wild birds can be found along the coasts of northern and western Scotland as far south as Kintyre and on the northern, western and southern coasts of Ireland. Elsewhere even coastal birds show a considerable mixture with feral stock, and on many parts of our coastline birds bearing any resemblance to the true Rock Dove may be very difficult to find. The proportion of wild-type birds increases to the north and west.

Movements: Resident, though with some local movements, and absent from some northern isles in winter.

Adult showing distinct wing bars and prominent pure white rump

221

Stock Dove

Columba oenas (Linnaeus)

A finely marked dove, superficially similar to the wild Rock Dove, but lacking that species' characteristic field marks. However, many Feral Pigeons do bear a strong resemblance to this species and should be distinguished with great care

Population: over 100,000 pairs

Basically a blue-grey bird with darker flight feathers, a broad black terminal band to the tail and a slash of iridescent green and purple on the sides of the neck. Though the tips of the wing coverts may form bars across the wing, these are never as prominent as those of the Rock Dove. The Stock Dove also lacks the white rump of that species. Usually found in small flocks, sometimes in company with Woodpigeons, but occasionally in large concentrations up to 200 strong. 33 cm (13 in).

Voice: An *ooo-roo-oo* or *ooo-woo*, with the stress on the first syllable.

Habitat: Generally distinct from the Rock Dove, though many birds are coastal and may breed in holes among cliffs. Normally inhabits woods of all types, parkland and large gardens, as well as inland cliffs and plantations.

Reproduction: Elaborate series of displays and postures like other pigeons and doves, including a slow-flapping display flight with some wing-clapping. The nest is placed in a hole in a tree, in a nest box, or in a hole among rocks or cliffs. The 2 white eggs are laid without nesting material, though sometimes twigs, grasses or leaves may form a rudimentary lining. They are laid from the end of March onwards and, beginning with the first egg, are incubated by both sexes for 16–18 days. The chicks are fed on pigeon's milk for 27–28 days by both parents and 2, sometimes 3, broods are normally reared.

Food: Grain is the predominant food, though clover, root vegetables, shoots, and leaves of peas and beans are also taken.

Range and Distribution: Found throughout temperate Europe north to southern Scandinavia and in North Africa, Turkey and Russia eastwards to central Siberia. Also in isolated regions of Tibet and the central Asian plateau. In Britain and Ireland it is widespread in the south but rather scarce in Scotland and northwestern Ireland, the colonization of the last 2 countries dating only from the latter part of last century. It is absent from much of the Highlands and islands. A recent decline in numbers has been attributed to agricultural pesticides.

Movements: Resident, but with some indication of a small, though regular, population of winter visitors from the Continent.

Adult with faint wing bars and lack of white rump

Woodpigeon

Columba palumbus (Linnaeus)

Largest, most common and widespread of our pigeons and doves, with a huge British and Irish population that is a serious menace to agriculture and which seems impervious to control

Population: 3 to 5 million pairs.

Adult showing prominent white bars across wing in flight

Woodpigeons are predominantly grey birds at any distance, though a closer approach reveals a vinous pink breast and a warm brownish-grey back. The primaries are black and the long, broad tail terminates in a broad black band. There is a slash of vinous pink and green on the neck and, in the adult, a prominent white neck mark. A white edge to the folded wing becomes a bold white bar across the wing in flight – an easily seen and diagnostic field mark. The bill is yellow and the short legs and feet pale coral. Woodpigeons are gregarious and sometimes form enormous flocks. 41 cm (16 in).

Voice: A far-carrying and distinctive *coo-coo-coo, coo-coo*.

Habitat: Woodland, copses, hedgerows, town parks and gardens. Forages over agricultural and other open land.

Reproduction: Elaborate courtship display in which bird rises high, claps its wings and descends in a gentle glide; also much bowing with tail raised high, and chest-puffed strutting. The nest is a flimsy platform of twigs placed in a tree, bush, or occasionally on a rocky ledge or building, constructed by the female from materials gathered by the male. The 2 oval white eggs are incubated by both members of the pair, beginning with the first, for 17 days. The squabs (chicks of pigeons) are fed on pigeon's milk by both sexes for 29–35 days before they fledge. Normally treble-brooded.

Food: Mainly grain, but also fruits and seeds; leaves, root crops, peas and beans, and a few worms and slugs.

Range and Distribution: Widespread over most of Europe north to central Scandinavia, eastwards in Russia to beyond the Urals, and southeast into the Middle East. Also found in North Africa. Occurs throughout Britain and Ireland except for the higher hills of Scotland, and the Outer Hebrides and Shetland where it is decidedly scarce.

Movements: Regular immigration of Continental birds in October and November; spring passage less discernible.

223

Collared Dove

Streptopelia decaocto (Frivaldszky)

A distinctive, pink and buff dove, with a neat white-edged black half-collar, that has made one of the most startling spreads and colonizations in ornithological history

Population: 30,000 to 40,000 pairs and increasing

Note long tail with white outer margins in flight

The back is a warm buff, with a pale bluish area at the bend of the wing – more obvious in some populations than others – and black primaries. The longish graduated tail has white tips to the outer feathers. The head and breast are a pinkish buff broken only by black neck markings. The bill is dark, the feet a dirty red. In flight the tail is black with a large white band at the end, and the underwing coverts are virtually white – features which help to distinguish this species from the Turtle Dove. Collared Doves will gather in large numbers at suitable feeding grounds. 32 cm ($12\frac{1}{2}$ in).

Voice: An insistent and repeated *kuk-koo-kook*.

Habitat: Usually found in association with man, particularly where grain is available. Conifers offer year-round nest sites.

Reproduction: Courtship flight consists of rising on clapped wings and gliding down with tail fanned. On the ground male bows and bobs before female, puffing up the breast and cooing insistently while hopping tail-down. The nest is a flimsy platform of twigs placed in a tree, often an evergreen. The 2 white eggs are incubated by both sexes, which also share feeding the young. Multibrooded virtually throughout the year.

Food: Grain, spilt or otherwise, and the seeds of weeds.

Range and Distribution: From the Faeroes southeastwards across Europe to the Balkans where it was confined until about 1930. The species' remarkable spread across the Continent, reaching Britain in 1955, is one of the more significant ornithological occurrences this century. It is now widespread throughout the country except in the less frequented hilly districts.

Movements: A continued movement of surplus birds northwestwards into uncolonized areas; though some British birds have been found to the south and east. There may well be a continued immigration into Britain and Ireland.

Turtle Dove

Streptopelia turtur (Linnaeus)

One of the most attractive of all the world's doves, this summer visitor to Britain is a boldly marked bird with distinctive brown edges to the black feathers of its upperparts. These give a scalloped appearance quite unlike any other British dove

Population: over 125,000 pairs

Tortoiseshell pattern on back separates from Collared Dove at all times

A grey crown with the sides of the head, breast and belly a fine vinous pink. A black and white slash at the side of the neck is distinctive. The long, rounded tail is dark, with white tips to the outer tail feathers forming a clear white band on the undertail in flight. The upperparts are scalloped black and brown. This is a generally gregarious species that, being shot throughout Mediterranean Europe, is wild and quick to take flight. It frequently gathers at corn spills and will work over cereal fields once harvested. 27 cm (11 in).

Voice: A cat-like purr: *roor-r-r* repeated.

Habitat: Primarily open ground, but nests in woods or hedgerows. Frequents agricultural land.

Reproduction: A display flight consists of a rapid climb followed by a spiralling glide on spread wings and tail. The female bobs and bows on a perch. The nest is a platform of twigs at no great distance from the ground, lined with roots or some other fine material. The 2 white eggs are laid between mid-May and the end of June and incubated by both sexes for 13–14 days. The chicks are fed by both parents on pigeon's milk for 18 days before fledging. Two broods are normal.

Food: Mainly the seeds of fumitory, but also cereals.

Range and Distribution: From Spain and North Africa throughout the Mediterranean and temperate Europe north to southern Denmark and eastwards across Russia to central Siberia and into the Middle East. Also locally in the Sahara and lower Nile Valley. In Britain it is widespread in England as far north as Yorkshire and southern Lancashire, but absent from the Pennines between and from much of Wales and the southwest. In Scotland a handful of pairs breed and in Ireland it is a scarce bird of the south and east coasts.

Movements: Turtle Doves arrive from mid-April, though the bulk of birds do not arrive until well into May. Most have departed for winter quarters in Africa by September.

Cuckoo

Cuculus canorus (Linnaeus)

A medium-sized, slim, long-winged, long-tailed bird of rather hawk-like proportions that is the only brood parasite to breed in Britain and Ireland. Young Cuckoo being fed by foster-parent Dunnock shown below

Population: between 17,500 and 35,000 pairs

When perched the Cuckoo looks dishevelled, seemingly having trouble in folding its wings properly, and with tail held at an awkward angle. In flight, the long tail and sharply pointed wings which flap in shallow beats are diagnostic. Normally grey above with black primaries, and a long graduated black tail marked with white spots. Throat and breast are grey with white underparts closely barred with black. Short legs, pointed decurved bill and bright yellow eye. Rare rufous phase of female is chestnut above and white below, barred throughout with black. All juveniles are similarly barred, but are dark brown above and white below. 33 cm (13 in).

Voice: A far-carrying, often repeated *cuck-oo, cuck-oo* uttered with bill usually closed, from a perch or when flying. Female has 'bubbling' call.

Habitat: Catholic, from woodlands through marshes and heaths to open moorland.

Reproduction: A brood parasite. Each female establishes a territory covering an adequate number of suitable foster parents' nests. Each tends to favour a particular species and lays eggs that closely resemble those of the host. From suitable vantage points she observes the comings and goings of potential hosts and notes the state of readiness of their nests. Before the clutch is complete in late May and June she lays a single egg in each nest: swooping down, picking an egg from the nest, laying her own and flying off, all within a few seconds. Usually less than 12 eggs are laid in different nests, cases of more than 1 Cuckoo in a nest are invariably the result of 2 female Cuckoos. However, cases of up to 21 eggs have been recorded from a single female. These are small for the size of the bird and vary from resembling those of a Reed Warbler through Wren, Meadow Pipit, Dunnock and Pied Wagtail to Robin. Over 50 species have played host to Cuckoos.

The egg is incubated by the foster parents for $12\frac{1}{2}$ days and usually hatches first. The young Cuckoo instinctively arches its back and forcibly ejects the other eggs or young from the nest. Alone in the nest, it is fed and brooded by its foster parents for 20–23 days. During this period the young Cuckoo grows to several times the size of its unfortunate hosts.

Food: Predominantly insects and their larvae, including hairy caterpillars rejected by most species. Also takes spiders and worms.

Range and Distribution: Breeds virtually throughout the Old World from Spain to Japan and northwards to well beyond the tree line. It is replaced in India and Southeast Asia by the closely related and remarkably similar Oriental Cuckoo *Cuculus saturatus*. In Britain and Ireland it is widely spread, and is thin on the ground only in Orkney and Shetland.

Movements: The Cuckoo arrives in Britain from the second half of April and adults leave from early July onwards. Juveniles follow soon after to about mid-September. European birds winter in Africa south of the Sahara.

In flight the Cuckoo bears a strong resemblance to a hawk or Kestrel

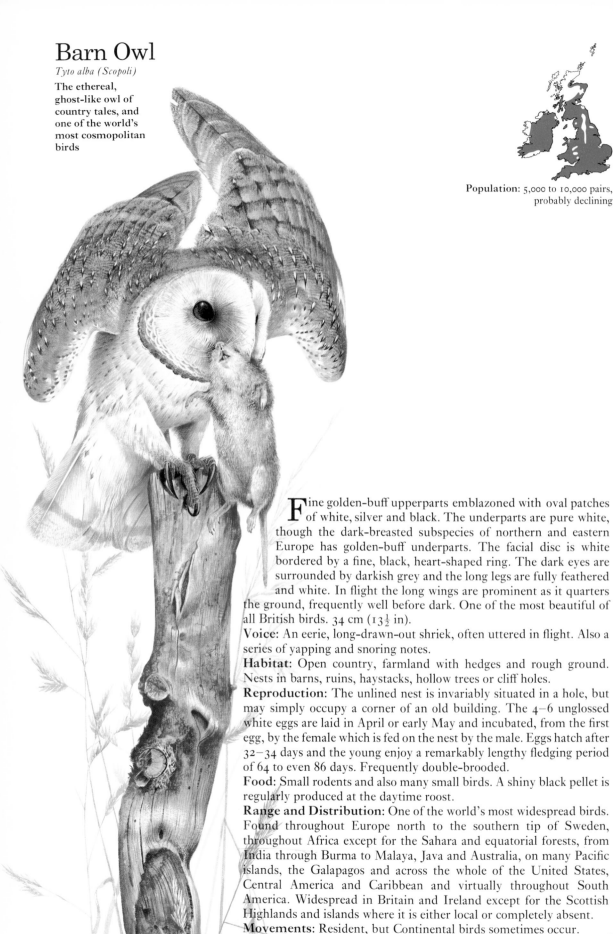

Barn Owl

Tyto alba (Scopoli)

The ethereal, ghost-like owl of country tales, and one of the world's most cosmopolitan birds

Population: 5,000 to 10,000 pairs, probably declining

Fine golden-buff upperparts emblazoned with oval patches of white, silver and black. The underparts are pure white, though the dark-breasted subspecies of northern and eastern Europe has golden-buff underparts. The facial disc is white bordered by a fine, black, heart-shaped ring. The dark eyes are surrounded by darkish grey and the long legs are fully feathered and white. In flight the long wings are prominent as it quarters the ground, frequently well before dark. One of the most beautiful of all British birds. 34 cm ($13\frac{1}{2}$ in).

Voice: An eerie, long-drawn-out shriek, often uttered in flight. Also a series of yapping and snoring notes.

Habitat: Open country, farmland with hedges and rough ground. Nests in barns, ruins, haystacks, hollow trees or cliff holes.

Reproduction: The unlined nest is invariably situated in a hole, but may simply occupy a corner of an old building. The 4–6 unglossed white eggs are laid in April or early May and incubated, from the first egg, by the female which is fed on the nest by the male. Eggs hatch after 32–34 days and the young enjoy a remarkably lengthy fledging period of 64 to even 86 days. Frequently double-brooded.

Food: Small rodents and also many small birds. A shiny black pellet is regularly produced at the daytime roost.

Range and Distribution: One of the world's most widespread birds. Found throughout Europe north to the southern tip of Sweden, throughout Africa except for the Sahara and equatorial forests, from India through Burma to Malaya, Java and Australia, on many Pacific islands, the Galapagos and across the whole of the United States, Central America and Caribbean and virtually throughout South America. Widespread in Britain and Ireland except for the Scottish Highlands and islands where it is either local or completely absent.

Movements: Resident, but Continental birds sometimes occur.

Snowy Owl

Nyctea scandiaca (Linnaeus)

A large diurnal owl that appears virtually pure white at any distance, and which bred in Britain for the first time in 1967

The male is a ghostly silver-white above and below marked only with a scattering of dark flecks on the back and crown, wing coverts, wing tips and tail. The facial disc is white with darker grey areas around the bold yellow eyes. The tip of the bill protrudes like a black tooth, as do the black talons from the white-feathered feet. The female is similar but considerably larger, and has much heavier speckling forming bars that completely cover the upperparts as well as the breast and belly. In flight the wings are long and pointed and the bird gives an impression of great power. 53–66 cm (21–26 in).

Voice: Generally silent, but produces a repeated, shrieking *know-ow* in flight; also a loud *rick*.

Habitat: Arctic tundra with rocky outcrops and slopes. In Britain frequents the highest hills and rock-strewn grassy slopes.

Reproduction: 4–9, but in lemming years up to 14, oval white eggs are laid in a depression atop a hummock and incubated, starting with the first egg, by the female alone for 32–33 days. She is fed on the nest by the male. Later both parents hunt and the young fledge at 51–57 days. Single-brooded.

Food: Lemmings, but in Britain rabbits and other small mammals. Also takes birds and even fish.

Range and Distribution: Circumpolar from the Scandinavian mountains along the tundra coasts of Russia and Siberia to Alaska, northern Canada and Greenland. Also breeds in central Iceland. In Britain it bred at Fetlar in Shetland from 1967 onwards, but by the mid-1970s only nonbreeding females were present. It may be that the much smaller males were unable to survive in such marginal conditions.

Movements: Winter visitor in tiny numbers to Shetland and other parts of northern Scotland; elsewhere exceptional. Sporadic crashes in the population of lemmings trigger off irruptions that send owls streaming south in their search for food.

Circumpolar in tundra zone:
British population up to 6 females

229

Little Owl
Athene noctua (Scopoli)

The only small, predominantly diurnal, owl to occur regularly in Britain

Population: about 10,000 pairs

Little Owls fly in a bounding fashion similar to that of woodpeckers and quite unlike that of other owls

Small size, dumpy appearance and a habit of sitting atop some post, telegraph pole or other prominent perch make this one of the most frequently observed of owls. It is a deep grey-brown above, boldly spotted with white. The underparts are white, with broad, broken streaks of dark grey-brown. A prominent facial mask is marked by dark areas around the yellow eyes, giving a remarkably 'cross' or 'frowning' look to the face. There is a dark band at the chin. Like most other owls it perches upright, and it has a bounding, woodpecker-like flight. When threatened it bobs and moves from side to side, as if to get a better look at the danger. 22 cm ($8\frac{1}{2}$ in).

Voice: A plaintive *kiu*, frequently heard by day, is the normal note. At the nest it utters a variety of chattering notes and, during the breeding season, the *kiu* note may be modulated and repeated to form a song.

Habitat: Open country, often farmland, with hedges, ruins, hayricks or other suitable nesting and hiding places. Also found in broken country where rocks fulfil the same function.

Reproduction: Most nests are occupied during May. They are situated in tree holes, pollarded willows, in walls, old buildings, hay and straw ricks, and even in rabbit burrows and cliff holes. The 3–5 white, unglossed eggs are laid in early May and incubation, mostly if not entirely by the female, takes 28–29 days. Fledging takes a further 26 days during which food is brought by the male alone at first and later by both sexes. The occasional second brood is reared.

Food: A wide variety of prey is taken, but small mammals such as mice, voles and shrews invariably form a significant proportion. Even small rabbits are not immune from attack. Small birds are frequently taken during the breeding season, as well as the chicks of larger species. Earthworms, snails and slugs and even small fish are all taken, but insects are perhaps the dominant element.

Range and Distribution: From Spain and Morocco eastwards through the Mediterranean and temperate Europe, southwards through the Middle East and as far east as northern China. It is found in southern Scandinavia, but in Britain was introduced first (and unsuccessfully) in 1842 and progressively after 1874. From centres in Kent, Northamptonshire and Bedfordshire in the 1890s it has gradually spread to cover most of England, parts of north and south Wales and to a few isolated spots in Scotland.

Movements: British birds are sedentary.

Tawny Owl

Strix aluco (Linnaeus)

The most common and widespread of British owls, with its familiar hooting call a characteristic sound of the night

Population: approaching 100,000 pairs

A chestnut-brown bird, boldly barred and streaked with buffs, blacks and whites to form a highly cryptic pattern. The breast is pale buff, heavily streaked with arrows of black-brown. A broad, rounded head has a prominent facial disc with deeply set dark eyes. Buff 'eyebrows' extend between the eyes to the bill. The tail is short and the wings broad and rounded. There is much individual variation in ground colour, from brown to grey, but all plumages are highly effective in hiding the bird from the attentions of irritating small passerines at its daytime roost. It flies on soft, silent wings after dusk and is more frequently heard than seen. 38 cm (15 in).

Voice: A characteristic *who-who-wh-whooo*, a more tremulous note *hooooooooo* and a sharp *ke-wick*, often repeated.

Habitat: Mostly deciduous or mixed woodland, but also in mature coniferous forests. It will also occupy old trees in hedgerows, copses, parkland and in city squares and churchyards.

Reproduction: Territories are established in the autumn when much calling and hooting can be heard. The male may clap his wings in display. The nest is an unlined hole in a tree or the old nest of a Crow, Magpie or Grey Heron. The 2–4 rounded white eggs are laid in March or early April and incubated, starting with the first egg, by the female for 28–30 days. The male feeds the brood for 21 days or so and the youngsters fledge after 32–37 days. Single-brooded.

Food: Predominantly small mammals such as long-tailed field mouse, field vole and common shrew. Birds, fish and other small mammals may be taken, and urban Tawny Owls have become specialist House Sparrow predators. The birds have favourite roosts and the pelleted remains of indigestible fur, feather and bones gather beneath the perch.

Range and Distribution: Breeds right across the Palearctic from Spain to China and Taiwan. It is found throughout Europe northwards to southern Scandinavia and south into North Africa from Morocco to Algeria. In Britain it is widely spread in England and Wales, but rather thin on the ground in northern Scotland. It is absent from the Fens, due to lack of suitable nest sites, and also from the Outer Hebrides, Shetland and Orkney, the Isle of Man and the whole of Ireland.

Movements: Resident; some local wandering after breeding.

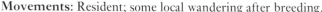

Long-eared Owl

Asio otus (Linnaeus)

A highly secretive, medium-sized owl that is notoriously difficult to locate and observe

Boldly marked in browns and buffs and heavily streaked, both above and below. A prominent facial disc is marked with a fine rim of black, and the large orange eyes are surrounded by black and separated by a wedge of buff divided by a narrow black line. Two ear tufts rise from the crown, but these are frequently held flat and inconspicuous against the head. The wings are long and the overall shape most closely resembles that of the Short-eared Owl, rather than the round-winged and more bulky Tawny Owl which shares its woodland habitat. Most regularly located and identified by call. 36 cm (14 in).

Voice: A long, low, moaning *oo-oo-oo* most frequently uttered from January to March, otherwise silent. Nests can be located by the discordant hunger note of the young, which has been likened to the sound of an unoiled hinge of a farmyard gate.

Habitat: In Britain frequents coniferous woods and especially old shelter belts and copses near open ground. In Ireland, where the competitively dominant Tawny Owl is absent, it also frequents deciduous and other woodland.

Reproduction: Display flight over tree tops includes much wing-clapping. Takes over an old nest, or sometimes a new one by evicting the owners, of Magpie, Carrion Crow or Rook, as well as squirrels' dreys. The 4–5 rounded, dull white eggs are laid in March or early April and incubated, commencing with the first egg, by the female (perhaps also the male) for 27–28 days. The young fledge after 23–24 days. A single brood is normal, but occasionally there will be 2. When disturbed at the nest a threat posture involves raising ear tufts and half-spread wings.

Food: Small mammals and birds including field vole, field mouse, bank vole, water vole, shrew and brown rat, and birds as different in size as Jay and finches.

Range and Distribution: Holarctic; from northern Spain across Mediterranean and temperate Europe and Siberia to Japan. In North America it breeds right across Canada and the United States from California to Maine. Breeds in every part of Britain and Ireland, but it is rather scarce in southwest England and Wales. There are strongholds in the Brecks and in Kerry.

Movements: Immigrant winter visitors arrive on the northern part of the east coast from Scandinavia, the Baltic and Holland in late autumn and depart mainly in April.

Population: between 3,000 and 10,000 pairs

Short-eared Owl

Asio flammeus (Pontoppidan)

A medium-sized, diurnal owl most frequently seen over marshes and hilly moorland districts

Population: 1,000 to 10,000 pairs

Harrier-like flight, systematically quartering open ground during daylight, may lead to confusion with females of those birds

Cryptically coloured in dull buffs and browns, with barring and streaking above, and bold dark streaking below. It has a prominent facial disc marked with dark around the pale yellow eyes. The small ear tufts are invisible in the field. In flight it has long wings and its method of hunting is remarkably similar to that of a harrier; indeed it shares both habitat and distribution with the Hen Harrier in the northern parts of its range. Prominent dark carpal patches, the absence of a white rump, shortish tail, and flattened owl-type face serve to distinguish it from the female Hen Harrier as it quarters and hovers over the ground. 38 cm (15 in).

Voice: A triple hooting *boo-boo-boo* and a harsh barking *keeaw*.

Habitat: Open grassy moorland, marshes, sand dunes; in winter frequents grassy marshes and grazing meadows, also adjacent arable fields and moors.

Reproduction: A slow-winged display flight with occasional wing beats and wing-clapping. The nest is a roughly lined scrape hidden among grass, heather, marram, or dead reeds. The 4–8 white eggs, exceptionally up to 14 in years when voles are plentiful, are laid in late April or early May at 2-day intervals. Incubation, by the female alone, commences with the first egg and lasts 24–28 days. The young leave the nest after 12–17 days and fly after 24–27 days. One brood is usual, though in years of vole plagues 2 may be attempted.

Food: Field voles are the principal food, but a wide variety of other small mammals such as long-tailed field mice, shrews, rats and even young rabbits may be taken. Small birds are also important items at some times and places.

Range and Distribution: Found in North and South America, across Eurasia, in the Caribbean, the Galapagos and Hawaii. In Britain it is found in most hilly and northern districts except for the Shetlands, as well as on the marshes of eastern and southeastern England. It is highly irregular in Ireland.

Movements: Birds from Norway, Finland, Germany and Iceland arrive in autumn to winter and depart again in spring. Though mostly found in the north and east, some pass through to the south and west.

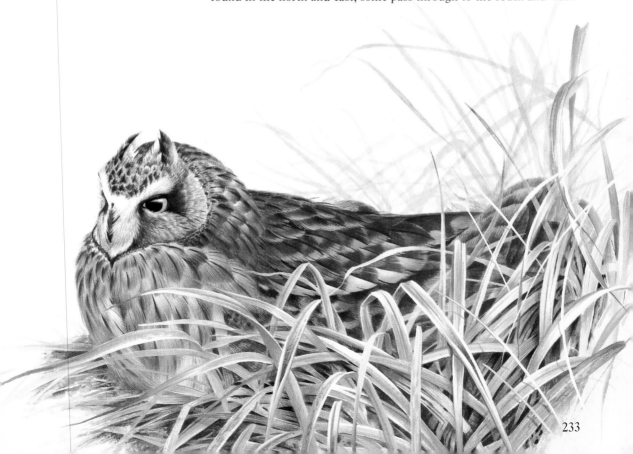

Nightjar

Caprimulgus europaeus (Linnaeus)

A highly camouflaged and semi-crepuscular bird that spends most of its day hidden on the ground among dead vegetation and emerges to hunt, owl-like, at dawn and dusk

Population: between 3,000 and 6,000 pairs

Though seldom seen in its full glory in daylight, except by bird photographers, the Nightjar is a beautiful bird. Mixtures of browns and buffs, greys and creams blend together in a series of bars and stripes to produce one of the most effective of all avian camouflages. At rest the effect is broken only by the large dark eye, but this is invariably kept closed. In the air Nightjars have an attenuated shape, with long tail and long angular wings. They are extremely manoeuvrable and change direction and hover with ease as they catch large flying insects in their huge gape. The male shows bold white patches on wings and tail. 27 cm (10½ in).

Voice: The song consists of a deep, far-carrying churring note repeated, with a ventriloquial effect as the head is turned from side to side, for minutes on end. Also a sharp *cui-ic* call note, and they frequently clap their wings in flight.

Habitat: Typically found on dry heaths with a strong growth of small trees, but also in open woodland and woodland edges, felled areas, moors, sand dunes and areas of bracken, heather and gorse.

Reproduction: Churring is produced from a bare perch from mid-May onwards, and the courtship display includes bouts of wing-clapping, particularly by the male. The 2 greyish-white eggs are speckled and blotched with yellow-brown and laid in a bare scrape, often next to a piece of dead wood. Incubation is by the female alone during the day, relieved by the male at dawn and dusk, and lasts 18 days. The down-covered young are fed by both parents until the hen begins incubating a second clutch.

Food: Large nocturnal-flying insects, especially moths. The large gape, fringed with a strong growth of rictal bristles, forms an effective funnel for hunting such prey.

Range and Distribution: Widespread throughout Europe north to southern Scandinavia and eastwards to Iran and central Asia. In Britain and Ireland it was formerly quite common, but has declined drastically during the present century. It is still fairly widespread in southern England and parts of East Anglia, but is local in the Midlands and north, and scarce in Scotland, Wales and Ireland.

Movements: Birds arrive from the beginning of May and leave by mid-August. They winter in Africa south of the Sahara to the Cape.

Swift

Apus apus (Linnaeus)

A totally aerial species that can be confused only with the swallows and martins – the hirundines. The Swift is all black, but with a whitish chin which can be seen at close range when it bulges full of food

Population: about 100,000 pairs

Compared to the hirundines this is a more angular and streamlined bird, with longer sickle-shaped wings and a thin cigar-like body that tapers towards the neatly forked tail. It is essentially gregarious and frequently flies and feeds higher above the ground than the hirundines. It glides more often, interrupted by short bouts of flapping. Swifts eat, drink, sleep, mate, gather nesting materials and preen on the wing. Once on the ground they find great difficulty in getting airborne again. 16.5 cm (6½ in).

Voice: A shrill, far-carrying screaming, often uttered by parties circling on fast-beating wings, followed by synchronized glides over their nesting colonies.

Habitat: Widespread, with concentrations over favoured feeding grounds such as marshes, reservoirs and sewage works. During the breeding season it occupies buildings, as well as cliffs which were its original nest sites, and is particularly fond of suburbs and small towns where sites are plentiful.

Reproduction: Mates on the wing. It enters lofts via ventilation grilles under the eaves of houses; or uses holes in cliffs. The nest is a rudimentary cup of feathers and grasses gathered in flight and held together with saliva. The 3, sometimes 2 or 4, dull white eggs are incubated by the female during the day, though both sexes are present at night, for 18–19 days. The chicks are fed by both parents for 35–56 days and then leave the nest and must fly and fend for themselves instantly. Single-brooded. At the end of the summer young birds spend time prospecting suitable nest sites.

Food: Insects of various species taken on the wing.

Range and Distribution: Throughout Europe, except for the mountains and extreme north of Scandinavia, eastwards through Russia and central Siberia south to Iran, and east to northern China. In Britain and Ireland it is widespread except in hilly districts and the extreme north of Scotland.

Movements: Swifts arrive at the end of April and throughout May. They leave for their winter quarters in Africa south of the Sahara by the end of August, though birds continue passing through for a month.

Kingfisher

Alcedo atthis (Linnaeus)

Often seen as only a streak of cobalt blue flying fast over some stream or river, a closer approach reveals the Kingfisher as one of the most spectacularly colourful and beautiful of British birds

Population: 5,000 to 9,000 pairs

Quite unmistakable with its bright iridescent blue upperparts barred with black on crown and wings. The back and tail are pure cobalt blue, the chin white, and the remaining underparts a bright chestnut-red. There is a patch of chestnut and white on the ear coverts. The bill is long and dagger-like, and the legs and feet short and bright red. Apart from flying it is most regularly seen perched a few feet above the water watching intently the movements of small fish below. It feeds by diving either directly from a perch or from a hover. 16.5 cm (6½ in).

Voice: A loud, shrill *cheee* or *chee-kee*, often uttered in flight.

Habitat: All types of fresh water, from ponds and canals to rivers and quite fast-flowing streams. In winter it often resorts to brackish coastal waters and marshes.

Reproduction: A slow-winged display flight with a whistling, trill-like song. The nest is usually a tunnel excavated in a steep river bank, but sometimes in a sand bank or even among the roots of a tree some distance from water. It is excavated for 50–100 cm (20–39 in) by both sexes, ending in a rounded nest chamber. The 6–7 round white eggs are laid in late April or early May on the bare earth, but fish remains quickly form a lining. Incubation by both sexes lasts 19–21 days and towards the end of the fledging period of 23–27 days the youngsters frequently come to the mouth of the burrow in their eagerness to be fed. Two broods, sometimes in the same hole, are normally reared.

Food: Fish and insects, also crustaceans and worms; dominant fish prey includes minnows, sticklebacks, stone loach, small trout and other young fish.

Range and Distribution: Breeds right across Europe from Spain to the Russian Urals, through the Middle East and Iran to India and most of Asia to Japan. It is found in the Celebes, Papua New Guinea and the Solomon Islands, and is widespread in Africa south of the Sahara. In Britain and Ireland it is widespread, though becoming rather scarce in Scotland where it is absent from large areas of the country, including all of the islands.

Movements: Mainly resident, with some wandering in winter to the coasts and even, as a vagrant, to some of the Scottish islands where it is otherwise unknown.

Hoopoe

Upupa epops (Linnaeus)

Unmistakable cinnamon-coloured bird, marked with an erectile crest tipped with black and white, and with boldly barred black and white wings. A scarce passage migrant that occasionally stays on to breed

Continental summer visitor: about 100 each spring with a few pairs staying to breed

Unmistakable and eye-catching barred pattern in flight

Large, distinctive, and with the habit of feeding openly on the short grass of lawns, there can be few Hoopoes that are overlooked. The head, neck, breast and underparts are a pale cinnamon. There is a large cinnamon crest that can be erected to form a black- and white-tipped fan, and the back and wings are boldly barred black and white. Though obvious enough at rest, the latter are particularly prominent in flight. The dark bill is long and noticeably decurved, and is used for probing industriously in the ground. 28 cm (11 in).

Voice: A far-carrying and distinctive *poo-poo-poo*.

Habitat: Open country with woods and hedgerows offering large trees with substantial holes. Also gardens, orchards, parks and olive groves.

Reproduction: The nest is a hole in a tree or stump, but also in a rock crevice, building, hayrick or nest box. The 5–8, occasionally up to 12, eggs are washed with grey, green or brown and incubated by the female alone for 16–19 days, starting before the clutch is complete. The chicks hatch over several days and thus vary considerably in size. They are fed by both parents for 20–27 days before fledging. During the nesting period droppings accumulate in the nest, creating a distinctive, if foul, smell. Single-brooded, with an occasional second.

Food: Grasshoppers, lizards, crickets and similar-sized prey.

Range and Distribution: Widespread through the Old World, from Spain to China, in India and Asia, the Middle East and Africa. In Britain it is a regular spring and autumn visitor to southern England and in suitably warm springs occasionally stays on to breed.

Movements: Northern birds migrate to winter in the Mediterranean region and in tropical Africa. Most occurrences in Britain are the result of overshooting on spring passage from March to May.

Wryneck

Jynx torquilla (Linnaeus)

A cryptically coloured, woodpecker-like bird with a shrill, repeated, far-carrying call. Easily overlooked both as a breeding bird and as a passage migrant

Population: less than 10 pairs; regular but scarce on passage

Delicately coloured in buffs, browns and greys, the Wryneck has a woodpecker-like foot construction with 2 toes pointing forward and 2 back, but it does not climb the trunks of trees like those birds. It is dark above, with mottled shades of brown and buff barred with chestnut and grey, and with 2 creamy stripes forming a distinct V on the back. The tail is barred in similar colours. Barred underparts are warm buff on throat and breast becoming paler on the belly. The head is striped in the same colours and the bill is sharply pointed. The bird can turn its head through 180 degrees, hence the name. 16.5 cm ($6\frac{1}{2}$ in).

Voice: A shrill, repeated *kee-kee-kee-kee*. The song is uttered soon after the birds arrive in April and ceases when the clutch is complete in May.

Habitat: Parkland with old trees, orchards and large gardens. Sometimes frequents woodland edges and on the Continent is also found in conifer woods.

Reproduction: The nest is situated in a tree hole, nest box or natural hole in wall or bank. There is no nesting material, though wood chips may gather on the floor of the hole. The 7–10 (sometimes 5–12) dull white eggs are laid from the end of May and incubation is shared between the pair, though the female takes the dominant role. The chicks hatch after 12 days and are fed frequently by both parents for 19–21 days. Two broods are unusual.

Food: Predominantly ants taken from the ground, but other insects and their larvae, as well as beetles, are also taken.

Range and Distribution: From northern Spain right across the northern Mediterranean almost to the Arctic Circle, eastwards across Russia and Siberia to northern Japan. Also in isolated pockets in the Caucasus, Himalayas and northern China. In Britain it has decreased dramatically in England over the last 50 years and may well become extinct in the very near future. However, Scandinavian birds colonized northern Scotland from the 1960s onwards and seem to be increasing.

Movements: Leaves Europe to winter in Africa. Continental birds regularly occur, especially in autumn, mainly on the east coast as passage migrants.

Green Woodpecker

Picus viridis (Linnaeus)

Largest, and the only bright green, woodpecker found in Britain. Its loud 'yaffling' call is a characteristic sound of woodlands wherever it occurs

Population: 15,000 to 30,000 pairs

Both sexes are bright green above with a lemon-yellow rump and a sharply attenuated tail. The underparts are a pale lemon-green, barred on the flanks and undertail coverts with green-brown. The crown is a bright crimson, inconspicuously flecked with blue. The pale yellow eye stands out from an area of black extending from the lores to the ear coverts, and a bold moustachial stripe is crimson bordered with black in the male and pure black in the female. The strong pointed bill is black and the species has the long, extendible tongue of the woodpecker family. If disturbed on the ground it will fly directly to trees with an exaggeratedly undulating flight. 32 cm (12½ in).

Voice: A loud, far-carrying, laughing cry *queu-queu-queu* called a yaffle, with a more shrill and extended version acting as a song in spring. A variety of similar calls have been described.

Habitat: Parkland, heaths and commons with plentiful trees, also in open deciduous woodland and farmland hedgerows. Scarce in coniferous woodland in the south, but extending northwards with newly maturing plantations.

Reproduction: Rarely drums like other woodpeckers. The pair excavate an oval hole in a tree trunk at varying heights from the ground, which extends downwards for 30–40 cm (12–16 in) to form the nesting chamber. A fresh hole is generally used each year and the 5–7, occasionally more, rounded white eggs soon become stained by the bare wood on which they are laid. Incubation by both sexes is from May onwards, though because of hole appropriation by other species it may not start until the end of May. The chicks hatch after 18–19 days and are fed on a regurgitated semiliquid. They fledge after 18–21 days. Single-brooded.

Food: Predominantly the larvae of wood-boring insects found by hacking away the bark of trees; also ants, caterpillars and spiders.

Range and Distribution: Almost confined to Europe where it extends throughout the Continent northwards to the southern half of Scandinavia. In central Russia it is found as far east as the Urals and is also found in the Caucasus southeast to Iran and west well into northern Turkey. In Britain it is widespread in southern England and Wales, except for treeless areas such as the Fens, but it has extended northwards into the southern Highlands of Scotland over the past 30 years. Absent from Ireland.

Movements: Resident, with occasional wandering.

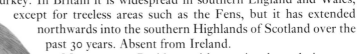

Great Spotted Woodpecker
Dendrocopos major (Linnaeus)

Most common and widespread of the 3 British woodpeckers. Male, female and juvenile are boldly pied black and white and show 2 white oval patches on the back when perched

Population: about 30,000 pairs

Males have a distinct red patch on the nape that is lacking in the female; juveniles have the whole crown red; otherwise all are boldly pied, with oval white patches on the wing. Only the Lesser Spotted Woodpecker is similar, but that species differs in habitat, size and in having a 'laddered' pattern of black and white across the back. Like other woodpeckers the Great Spotted is an extremely agile climber. 23 cm (9 in).

Voice: A sharp, often repeated *tchick*. In the breeding season the same note may be repeated into a trill. The most frequently heard sound is drumming, which is not a call at all – see below.

Habitat: Deciduous and coniferous woodland and forests, but has recently spread into suburban gardens and parks.

Reproduction: Drumming, performed by both sexes, is commonly heard during the breeding season in March and April, and less frequently in January and February. It acts as a territorial defence and is produced by beating the bill rapidly on a dead branch up to 10 times a second. The display consists of a wing-quivering flight towards the mate, chasing around branches, raising the crown feathers and spreading the tail. The nest, usually over 4 m (12 ft) from the ground, is excavated in a tree by both sexes. The entrance hole is oval and the chamber some 30 cm (12 in) deep. A few chips suffice for nesting material. The 4–7 white oval eggs are laid in mid-May to early June and incubated mainly by the female. The chicks hatch after 16 days and are fed by both parents for 18–21 days. Single-brooded.

Food: Probes into bark crevices and hacks away loose bark to get at the larvae of wood-boring insects. In the breeding season it will take the eggs and young of other hole-nesting birds.

Range and Distribution: Found right across Eurasia in the temperate and boreal zones from Spain to Japan. In Britain it is widespread wherever suitable woodland occurs and has recently increased and spread northwards through Scotland, doubtless in association with reafforestation. It is absent only from the barren wastes of Shetland, Orkney, the Outer and many of the Inner Hebrides, and much of northern Sutherland and Caithness. It is also missing from Ireland, the Isle of Man and the Fens.

Movements: Predominantly resident, but Continental birds visit in winter. Quite large irruptions can take place, bringing migrants to areas devoid of trees.

Male (foreground) and female

240

Lesser Spotted Woodpecker

Dendrocopos minor (Linnaeus)

The smallest and most elusive of our woodpeckers, the Lesser Spotted Woodpecker spends most of its time among the upper branches and canopy of woodland and is very easily overlooked

Population: 5,000 to 10,000 pairs

Male (foreground) and female

Its diminutive size, about the same as a House Sparrow, chiefly distinguishes this from the other pied British woodpecker, the Great Spotted. The upperparts are black, marked with a series of white horizontal bars across the back and wings, giving a ladder-like appearance. The underparts are white, finely streaked with black. There is a black moustachial streak that widens out to form an inverted T bordering the white cheeks and the male has a crimson crown bordered with black. The female's crown is black and both sexes have a white forehead. Its easy agility among even the twigs of the tree canopy is quite unlike any other woodpecker. 14.5 cm ($5\frac{3}{4}$ in).

Voice: A shrill *pee-pee-pee-pee* that is similar to the call of the Wryneck, but higher pitched. Also a weak *tchik*.

Habitat: Deciduous woodland, often inhabiting the same areas as the Great Spotted Woodpecker, but feeds mainly among the tree canopy where the larger species seldom ventures. Also parkland and orchards and even hedgerows with a strong growth of alder.

Reproduction: Drums on a dead branch like the Great Spotted Woodpecker, but less far-carrying and of a higher frequency than that species – up to 14–15 blows per second as against 8–10 of the Great Spotted. Excavates a hole up to 20 m (65 ft) from ground with an oval entrance. Both species excavate the nest chamber and share in incubating the 4–6 white eggs for 14 days. The chicks are fed by both parents for 21 days before fledging. Single-brooded.

Food: Mainly the larvae of wood-boring insects, but also caterpillars, spiders, ant grubs and even berries.

Range and Distribution: Right across temperate and boreal Europe and Asia from Spain to Japan with outposts in North Africa, southern Turkey, the Caucasus and northern Iran. In Scandinavia it extends north to the tree line. In Britain it is widespread in England and Wales and has increased and spread recently with the arrival of Dutch Elm disease. Records in Scotland are well north of the English range and may be the result of a potential colonization by Scandinavian birds. Absent from most of Scotland and Ireland.

Movements: Resident.

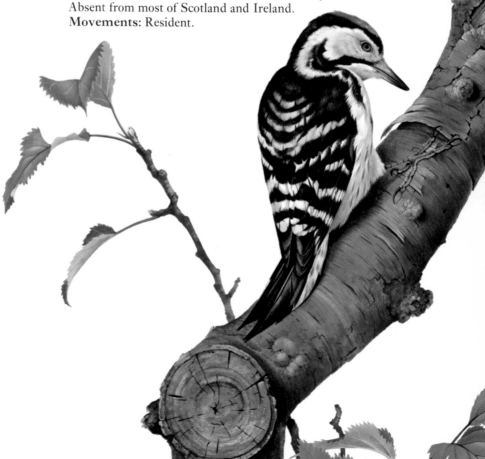

Woodlark

Lullula arborea (Linnaeus)

A typical lark clothed in subdued browns and creams, and streaked both above and below. Recent decline linked with habitat destruction and changing climate

Population: 200 to 450 pairs

Similar to the more common and widespread Skylark, but occupying a different habitat, and distinguished by a shorter tail lacking white outer feathers, supercilia that meet at the nape and a neat black and white mark just below the bend of the folded wing. The Woodlark is generally a solitary bird that perches freely on small trees and shrubs. It is a magnificent songster, but is unfortunately a fast-declining species in Britain. 15 cm (6 in).

Voice: Varied and melodic song with liquid phrases broken by a pleasant trilling; also a liquid *toolooeet*.

Habitat: A mixture of dry, broken or sloping ground with short-cropped grass, together with areas of longer grass with scattered trees or bushes. Fences serve as adequate song posts on open heathland.

Reproduction: Male's song flight consists of rising to considerable height on butterfly-like wings and circling and hovering while singing. The final descent is silent. The nest is placed on the ground and consists of a neat cup built by both members of the pair and hidden among grass or heather. It is constructed of grasses and lined with finer material, including hair. The 3–4 eggs are grey-white finely spotted with reddish-brown and are laid from the end of March onwards. Incubation by the female alone lasts 13–15 days and the young are fed by both parents before fledging after 11–12 days. Two broods are usual and 3 not uncommon.

Food: Mostly insects and their larvae, but with seeds forming a significant part of the diet in autumn.

Range and Distribution: Predominantly European, extending northwards to southern Sweden and Finland, eastwards into European Russia and southwards into Turkey and the Middle East. Also found in North Africa. In Britain (as elsewhere in northern Europe) it has suffered a serious decline and is found locally only in southern England, particularly in the southwest and among the Brecks of East Anglia. Some pairs are scattered through Wales, but it is completely absent from northern England, Scotland and Ireland. Decline may be due to agricultural change, reafforestation, and the decline of the rabbit.

Movements: Resident.

Skylark

Alauda arvensis (Linnaeus)

One of the most common and widespread of British and Irish birds and a conspicuous inhabitant of open landscapes

Population: 2 to 4 million pairs

Dull brown and buff bird, with heavily streaked upperparts and a streaked breast. The crown is marked by an erectile crest that rises to a point above the nape, but which is never as pointed nor as long as that of the Crested Lark, a possible visitor to southern England. It spends most of its time on the ground, rising before an intruder on fluttering wings. In the air it shows white outertail feathers and hovers and circles at considerable height singing continuously. During migration periods it often forms sizeable flocks, and hard weather sends it searching for a milder climate. 18 cm (7 in).

Voice: A loud clear warbling uttered from a fluttering flight high above the ground and sometimes continued for as long as 5 minutes. Also utters a rippling *chirrup* of contact. The song is regularly produced for an extended period from February to June and again in the autumn, though it may be heard throughout the year. It is the first bird to sing at dawn and the expression 'up with the lark' is thus based on fact.

Habitat: Wide variety of landforms, but mostly open country including bare moorland, downs, heaths, farmland, salt marshes, sand dunes and even mountain tops. The most widespread British and Irish bird.

Reproduction: Nests on the ground among grass or crops. A simple grass-lined cup is constructed by the female and the 3–4, occasionally 5, eggs are dull white speckled all over with olive-brown. They are laid from late April onwards and incubated by the female alone for 11 days. The chicks are fed by both parents for 9–10 days in the nest and fly some 10 days later. Double- or treble-brooded.

Food: Roughly divided between vegetable and animal matter. Seeds of weeds as well as cereals, leaves of growing root crops and clover, and worms, insects and their larvae, spiders and slugs have all been recorded. Recent damage to young drill-sown sugar beet is a cause for alarm in some areas.

Range and Distribution: Right across the Palearctic from Spain to the Bering Straits. Found from Lapland south to Morocco and in the Middle East into northern Iran. Has been introduced to Vancouver Island in Canada. In Britain and Ireland it is found in all parts of the country.

Movements: Mostly resident, but probably some local movements. From mid-September huge numbers of Skylarks enter the country via the south and east coasts. Some doubtless pass on, but many stay to winter. Spring passage is in March and April.

Shore Lark

Eremophila alpestris (Linnaeus)

A scarce winter visitor that has, on occasion, stayed on to breed in Scotland

Arctic breeding grounds: small numbers in Britain in autumn and winter

Male in winter (below) and in summer.

A skulking bird that is difficult to locate, but which is then rather tame and confiding. It spends most of the time on bare ground in small winter flocks. The upperparts are a cinnamon-buff heavily streaked on back and wings. The brown tail has black feathers on each side, with the outermost feathers white. The underparts are white, becoming buffy on the flanks. The stubby bill and legs are black. The characteristic face pattern consists of a black breast band, a black mark through the lores extending to the cheeks, and a black crown patch from which rise 2 prominent 'horns'. The rest of the face is yellow. In winter the pattern is somewhat blurred but still clearly discernible. 16.5 cm (6½ in).

Voice: A thin *tseep* or *tsee-ree*, nearer to a pipit than a lark. The song, which is produced in a song flight similar to that of a Skylark, is a high-pitched tinkling.

Habitat: Open mountain tops and tundra; in winter found on open shorelines, beaches and salt marshes, which accounts for its English name. In North America the species is, more appropriately, called the Horned Lark.

Reproduction: The nest is placed on the ground among open tundra, often near a stone, and consists of a neat grass cup lined with plant down or animal hair. The 4, occasionally 2–7, greenish eggs are speckled with yellow-brown and laid from mid-May to June. Incubation, by the female alone, lasts some 10–14 days and the chicks are fed by both parents for 9–14 days. Double-brooded.

Food: Seeds of weeds, together with insects and, in winter, crustaceans and molluscs. Shuffles close to the ground picking small items from among low vegetation.

Range and Distribution: Circumpolar, but extending southwards in North America from the Canadian Arctic islands to Central America. In Eurasia, in contrast, there are 2 distinct populations; 1 in the arctic tundra and another stretching from the mountains of North Africa through Turkey and the Caucasus into the high central Asian plateau. Winter visitor in small numbers to western Europe. In 1972 birds were found in the Scottish Highlands in summer and were proved to breed in 1973.

Movements: A winter visitor to the east coast of Britain in small numbers from late October onwards.

Sand Martin

Riparia riparia (Linnaeus)

Smaller than other hirundines and with even more dashing and erratic flight. Highly gregarious at all seasons

Population: varies from 250,000 to over 1 million pairs

In flight shows uniform brown upperparts and white underparts marked with distinct breast band

Brown above; white below broken only by a conspicuous brown breast band. The underwing is brown, and the tail marked by a neat fork. Sand Martins are the most gregarious members of the family. While Swallows breed solitarily, and House Martins in small colonies, these birds are found together in numbers at all seasons. They feed together, migrate together, roost together and breed in large, closely grouped colonies. As a result of this habit they are an excellent subject for co-operative ringing studies – being easy to catch in large numbers – and were the subject of a special enquiry in the 1960s. 12 cm ($4\frac{3}{4}$ in).

Voice: A chirrup-like twittering, a *tchurrip*, and a song that is virtually inseparable from the usual twittering.

Habitat: Invariably found near water, more so than other hirundines, and roosts in reed beds, often in company with Swallows. Nests in sandy cliffs both by the sea and inland, but is restricted by the location of suitable sites. It has increased with the excavation of ever more sand pits opening up new habitat.

Reproduction: Birds begin nesting in early May and both sexes participate in excavating a tunnel 60–100 cm (22–39 in) long in a sand cliff situated in a sand or gravel pit, sea cliff, railway cutting or bank of a river. Small colonies exceptionally breed in drainpipes and heaps of sawdust. Colony size varies from just a handful of pairs to several hundred; all are prone to cliff falls. The 4–5 unglossed white eggs are laid in a rounded chamber lined with a few feathers or pieces of straw gathered in the air. Incubation by both sexes lasts 12–16 days and the chicks are fed by both parents. Towards the end of the fledging period, which lasts 19 days, they may gather at the tunnel entrance to be fed. Two broods are normally reared.

Food: Insects taken on the wing.

Range and Distribution: Circumpolar in the Northern Hemisphere, except for Iceland and the mountains of Scandinavia. In Britain and Ireland it is a widespread breeding bird with absences due only to lack of suitable nest sites, and in the far north in the Orkneys, Shetlands and Outer Hebrides.

Movements: The whole population departs to Africa south of the Sahara in autumn, leaving by August and September. The return is detectable by the end of March, but main arrivals take place in April.

Swallow

Hirundo rustica (Linnaeus)

Most common and widespread of the hirundines and a familiar bird throughout the country. Essentially aerial, its flapping and gliding flight combined with extended tail streamers make it easy to identify

Population: less than 1 million pairs

Swallows can be aged and sexed by length of tail streamers, from left to right: adult male, adult female, juvenile

Upperparts are a dark iridescent blue, underparts creamy, sometimes with a suffusion of pale rufous. The forehead and chin are bright rust-red, bordered on the chest by a dark blue band. The wings are long and sharply angled and the tail deeply forked, marked with white 'mirrors' and with outertail feathers greatly extended – longer in the male than the female, but virtually absent in juveniles. Though Swallows nest in solitary pairs they are gregarious when feeding and migrating, and when roosting in reed beds often in association with Sand Martins. They perch freely, especially on wires on migration, sometimes in large numbers. 19 cm ($7\frac{1}{2}$ in).

Voice: A twittering *tswit-tswit-tswit*. The song is a twittering warble varying in tone and pitch, usually produced on the wing.

Habitat: Occupies virtually all habitats, though most commonly found in lowlands rich in insects. Nests in old, often disused, buildings, among cliffs and in caves. Absent from the centres of large cities. It has doubtless increased with man's accidental provision of nest sites.

Reproduction: The nest is a shallow cup constructed of mud, reinforced with grass, by both members of the pair, usually on a rafter or ledge inside a building. Globules of mud are gathered in the bill and allowed to harden in place before the next course is added. The 4–8 eggs, sometimes only 3, are white finely spotted with reddish-brown and laid from mid-May onwards. Incubation, predominantly by the female, lasts 14–15 days and the chicks are fed by both sexes. They fly 17–24 days after hatching. Double-brooded, with sometimes a third.

Food: A huge range of different insect species taken in flight.

Range and Distribution: Circumpolar in the Northern Hemisphere from Alaska throughout Canada and the United States southwards through Mexico. Breeds throughout the Mediterranean and from Iceland and Scandinavia eastwards across Russia and the Middle East to China and Japan. There is considerable geographical variation, with the colour of the underparts varying enormously. The resident birds of the Nile Valley in Egypt are a brick-red below and occasional British and Irish birds may approach such coloration. Swallows are numerous and widespread in Britain except for the highest Scottish hills.

Movements: British birds migrate through the Mediterranean to the southernmost part of South Africa.

House Martin

Delichon urbica (Linnaeus)

A boldly marked black and white hirundine with a prominent white rump patch that builds its nest under the eaves of houses and sometimes makes itself unpopular by the mess that is created

Population: 300,000 to 600,000 pairs

Though the House Martin appears pied, a close approach reveals crown and back to be dark iridescent blue. The wings and tail are black, the latter being neatly forked but lacking the streamers of the Swallow. The white rump patch appears quite square and the underparts, including the chin, are pure white. It is gregarious, forming small colonies on suitable houses and sometimes quite large colonies on other structures such as bridges. On the Continent colonies may grow to really substantial proportions with nests plastered on top of one another. It roosts in breeding colonies when many birds may be found in a single nest. Essentially an aerial feeder. 12.5 cm (5 in).

Voice: A hard *chirrup* and a high-pitched *tseep* of alarm. The song is a quiet twittering.

Habitat: Frequents suburbs and small towns where buildings provide a choice of nest sites; but also sometimes on cliffs. A nearby source of mud for nest-building is essential.

Reproduction: The nest is a globular structure built under the eaves of buildings with an entrance hole at the upper rim. The owners are frequently ousted by House Sparrows. It is constructed of mud reinforced with grass by both members of the pair, who allow each course to harden before the next is added. Mud is gathered in the bill from a pond, lake or even puddle up to 1 km away. There is a lining of soft grasses and feathers. The 4–5 eggs are white, rarely spotted with red, and laid from late May onwards. Incubation, by both sexes, takes 13–19 days and the young are fed by both parents for 19–25 days. The young of an earlier brood will sometimes help feed second and third brood nestlings.

Food: Insects taken in flight.

Range and Distribution: Throughout Europe, North Africa and the Middle East right across Russia and Siberia to Japan, with an extension southwards across central southern Asia to the Himalayas. In Britain and Ireland it is widespread except for the Scottish hills, the extreme north and the islands, where it is irregular rather than absent.

Movements: Arrives from the end of March onwards staying through to September, and to October in small numbers. Winters in Africa south of the Sahara.

247

Tree Pipit

Anthus trivialis (Linnaeus)

Typical pipit, but with a much 'cleaner' and warmer appearance than the similar Meadow Pipit

Population: less than 100,000 pairs

Upperparts olive-brown streaked with black-brown. Tail olive-brown with white outer feathers. Underparts a warm buff on the breast clearly streaked with black extending to the flanks, becoming lighter, almost to white, on the belly and undertail coverts. The chin and supercilium are creamy, and there is a prominent moustachial streak. The legs and feet are pinkish and have a short hind claw. The call and song are distinctive, as is the habit of singing in flight and returning to a prominent perch. Meadow Pipits are essentially ground-dwelling birds, but Tree Pipits perch freely. 15 cm (6 in).

Voice: A rasping flight note *teez*. The song is a musical trill uttered in display flight, culminating in a *seea-seea-seea* as the bird 'parachutes' to rest. Also produces a lesser song from a prominent perch.

Habitat: Open woods and heaths, often on sloping ground, with a plentiful growth of small trees, often conifers. Will use telegraph wires as perches, but areas of short-cropped grass for feeding are essential.

Reproduction: The nest is placed beneath a tussock or among bracken and consists of a strongly constructed cup of grasses on a moss base, lined with fine material including hair. The 4–6 eggs are remarkably variable with pink, green, grey or brown as a ground colour, speckled or blotched with darker shades. They are laid in the second half of May and incubated by the female alone for the 12–14 days they take to hatch. Fledging, during which both sexes feed the chicks, takes some 12–13 days. Sometimes double-brooded.

Food: Mainly insects, but also spiders together with some seeds, at least in winter.

Range and Distribution: From northern Spain across Europe including the whole of Scandinavia, except for the mountains, and to Russia and Siberia almost as far as the Pacific. Also found southwards to the Caucasus and western Himalayas. It is widespread in Britain, but is absent from Ireland, the Fens, parts of eastern Scotland and the Outer Hebrides, Orkneys and Shetlands.

Movements: Arrives in late April and May, departing in August and September. The whole population moves to sub-Saharan Africa.

Meadow Pipit

Anthus pratensis (Linnaeus)

Similar to the Tree Pipit, but much more widespread and numerous and, in some places, the most abundant bird. It is, however, less brown and more olive in basic coloration, producing a less warm and clear-cut appearance

Dull olive upperparts boldly streaked with black; white outertail feathers. Underparts almost white and heavily streaked with black extending to the flanks. This bird lacks the warm buff on the breast of the Tree Pipit. There is a whitish supercilium and a prominent black moustachial streak, and the legs and feet are dark rather than pink. Outside the breeding season this is a much more gregarious bird than the Tree Pipit, frequently forming large flocks on migration and in winter, when it gathers on coastal marshes and estuaries. 14.5 cm (5¾ in).

Voice: A thin *tseep*, and a *tissup* call note. Song, uttered in display flight, consists of a trill of thin *tseeps*, similar to call note and terminating in a parachute-like descent to the ground.

Habitat: Remarkable variety of open country, including upland moors, where it may be the most common bird, heaths, rough grassland, sand dunes and saltings. In winter many birds become coastal, though they are also found along the margins of inland waters and sewage works.

Reproduction: The nest is a neat cup of dry grass lined with hair, hidden in a clump of grass or heather. The 3–5 eggs are brown or grey, finely mottled with darker brown or darker grey, and are laid from mid-April onwards. Incubation, by the female alone, takes 11–15 days, and the chicks are fed by both parents for 10–14 days before fledging. Two or more broods are reared each year.

Food: Predominantly insects, but also spiders, worms and occasionally plant seeds.

Range and Distribution: Found over the whole of northern Europe with an outpost in the mountains of central Italy. In Scandinavia it ranges as far north as the arctic tundra, and is also present in Iceland and on the east coast of Greenland. It extends through northern Russia to beyond the Urals. In Britain and Ireland is widespread and often abundant, but is absent from many inland areas of the Midlands and eastern England.

Movements: Many British birds emigrate to France and Spain, but most make only local movements within these islands. Continental and Icelandic birds arrive in autumn in September and October and many pass on to winter further south. A return passage takes place in late March and April. Widespread in winter in Britain.

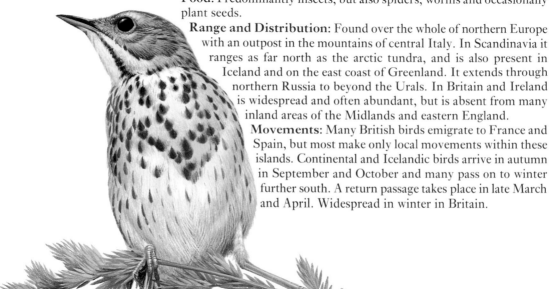

Population: over 3 million pairs

249

Rock Pipit
Water Pipit

Anthus spinoletta (Linnaeus)

Rock and Water Pipits are 2 subspecies (of 3 that occur in Britain) that are sufficiently distinct to merit separate vernacular names. They are separable in the field. Rock Pipit in summer shown

Breeding ranges of Rock Pipit (Britain and France), Scandinavian Rock Pipit (Scandinavia) and both subspecies in winter

Water Pipit: summer and winter

Three subspecies that are capable of being distinguished in the field by the careful observer, and that are also distinctive both in habitat and status:

Rock Pipit *Anthus spinoletta petrosus* breeds around the coasts of Britain and northwestern France. It is the only subspecies that breeds with us and is a darker and larger bird than the Meadow Pipit. The upperparts are olive-grey streaked with black and the outertail feathers are grey, not white. The pale-grey underparts are heavily streaked with black. It has darker legs than the Meadow Pipit and is essentially a coastal bird.

Water Pipit *Anthus spinoletta spinoletta* breeds among the mountains of southern and central Europe, but regularly winters in Britain. In summer it is grey above, with only faint streaking, and buffish unstreaked underparts. In winter it becomes darker with a streaked breast, but never as dark or as heavily streaked as the Rock Pipit. Frequents inland waters.

Scandinavian Rock Pipit *Anthus spinoletta littoralis* breeds along the coasts of Scandinavia and the Baltic and is always much browner and buffer than our Rock Pipit. Winters along coasts. 16.5 cm ($6\frac{1}{2}$ in).

Voice: A high-pitched *tsip*; song uttered in display flight like Meadow Pipit, but more melodic.

Habitat: Rocky coasts and mountain slopes; in winter along coasts and marshes, and inland at reservoirs, sewage works and watercress beds.

Reproduction: Rock Pipits breed within a short distance of the sea, hiding their nest in a rock crevice or hole in a cliff well protected by grass. The display flight is similar to that of the Meadow Pipit. The nest itself is a cup of grass lined with hair and the 4–6 greyish-white eggs are covered with ash-brown spots and laid in late April and early May. Incubation, by the female alone, lasts 14 days and the young are fed by both parents for 16 days before fledging. Double-brooded.

Food: Mainly insects, but also sandhoppers, crustaceans and seeds.

Range and Distribution: The species has a circumpolar distribution across the Canadian Arctic and southwards through the Rockies. In Europe it is confined to the coasts of Brittany, Britain and Scandinavia, with separate populations in the mountains of Spain, the Alps, the Carpathians and the mountains of Yugoslavia. Also breeds in the Caucasus, central Asia and northeastern Siberia.

In Britain it breeds around coasts from Flamborough northwards and the Isle of Wight westwards, except for Lancashire. Breeds on all Irish coasts.

Movements: Local movements bring British breeding birds to the south and east coasts where they do not breed. Scandinavian birds are regularly noted on the south and east coasts; and Water Pipits are found at inland waters in south and southwest England.

Rock Pipit (foreground) and Water Pipit, both in winter

Grey Wagtail

Motacilla cinerea (Tunstall)

In some plumages bears a resemblance to some of the Continental subspecies of the Yellow Wagtail, but large size and a proportionately longer tail, which it bobs almost continuously, serve to distinguish it

Population: 25,000 to 50,000 pairs

Male in summer (foreground) and in winter

In summer the male is dove-grey above with black wings, the primaries edged with white, and an extremely long black tail with white outer feathers. The underparts are yellow. The head is grey marked by a white supercilium and moustachial streak, and with a black chin. Females are duller and have a white, not black chin. Males in winter resemble females, but in all plumages the species boasts yellow belly and undertail coverts. It is generally solitary and does not form large flocks like other wagtails. A close association with water, where it picks its food delicately from the edge, is also a useful feature. 18 cm (7 in).

Voice: A clipped *tchip* or *titsee* call; song consists of a high-pitched *tse-tse-tse-tse-tsee-ree-ree-ree*.

Habitat: In summer along fast-flowing streams in hilly districts, but also lowland rivers in places where the water moves faster. In winter more widespread, but still never far from water.

Reproduction: The nest is placed in a shallow hole, or cleft in a rocky bank or cliff, usually close to running water. Sometimes the species occupies the old nests of other birds. It is built by the female of moss, twigs and grasses and lined with hair and wool. The 5–6 greyish eggs are marbled with brown and laid in late April or May. Incubation, almost entirely by the female, takes 12–14 days and the chicks are fed by both parents for 13–16 days before fledging. Mostly single-brooded.

Food: Predominantly insects, also water beetles, dragonfly and other aquatic larvae, and some small fish.

Range and Distribution: Breeds in suitable habitats throughout Europe east to the Russian border region and northwards to southern-most Sweden. Extends eastwards through Turkey and the Caucasus to Iran and Kashmir, and over the Tibetan plateau to occupy the eastern half of Siberia to Japan and northern China. In Britain and Ireland it is widespread, though absent from Orkney and Shetland and from much of eastern England from Yorkshire to the Thames.

Movements: Mostly resident and may suffer considerable losses during hard winters. Some movements within Britain and Ireland.

M.f. flavissima   *M.f. iberiae*   *M.f. cinereocapilla*   *M.f. feldegg*   *M.f. pygmaea*

Yellow Wagtail

Motacilla flava (Linnaeus)

A slim, elegant bird, predominantly yellow in colour, marked by a long tail, long legs and a propensity to visit shallow, fresh stillwater margins. Male **M.f. flavissima** (foreground) and female shown below

Population: about 25,000 pairs

Brown wings with broad whitish margins to the feathers, the tail dark with white outer feathers, and the underparts yellow. There is a bold supercilium. The colour of the head and back varies according to subspecies, which can be recognized in the field, though mutants resembling others occur within the range of a subspecies. British breeders have a yellow head, greenish back and are assigned to *Motacilla flava flavissima* – the Yellow Wagtail. A number of other subspecies have been recorded, especially the Blue-headed Wagtail *Motacilla flava flava*, which breeds in adjacent parts of the Continent and which sometimes does so in Britain. The characteristic, undulating, wagtail flight, together with the call, serves to separate this from related species. 16.5 cm (6½ in).

Voice: A clear *tsweep* is the flight note; song consists of a series of calls interspersed with brief warbling.

M.f. beema   *M.f. lutea*   *M.f. thunbergi*   *M.f. flava*

Habitat: Marshes, water meadows, pastures and floods, often with domestic stock; occasionally arable fields.

Reproduction: Display consists of much hovering, chest-puffing and tail-spreading. The nest is a neat cup, placed on the ground under cover of a tussock of grass. The 6, sometimes 4–7, eggs are covered with buffish speckles and laid from mid-May onwards. The female performs most of the incubation for 13–14 days, and the young are fed by both parents for 10–13 days. Often double-brooded.

Food: Insects, including caterpillars, as well as spiders and worms.

Range and Distribution: Breeds from Spain across Europe as far north as northern Scandinavia and eastwards through Russia and Turkey to Iran, Siberia, the Bering Straits and, in the New World, coastal Alaska. Over so vast a range the development of subspecies is only to be expected, but the Yellow Wagtail is clearly in process of evolution and a number of well-marked forms have been described. Each varies mainly in the colour of the head and, capable of being distinguished in the field, has been given an English vernacular name. Thus we have the Blue-headed, Black-headed and Grey-headed Wagtails, and so on. Were each subspecies to occupy a geographically distinct region a good case could be made for regarding each as a separate species, but zones of overlap and persistent interbreeding occur in many areas, producing a variety of hybrid types. Furthermore, an aberrant individual may appear hundreds or even thousands of miles from its apparent home and breed freely with the native stock. In these circumstances it is best to regard all as a single, if unstable, species – the Yellow Wagtail. The British form is widespread in England except for the southwest, but is absent from large areas of Wales and most of Scotland except for the western lowlands. It is irregular in Ireland and absent from the Isle of Man.

Movements: Winters south of its range, with European birds crossing the Sahara to West Africa where huge numbers gather at favoured areas such as Lake Chad. They arrive in Britain from mid-April and depart southwards in late September.

Males displaying yellow breast in territorial dispute

Aerial dispute at margins of adjacent territories

Actual fighting, rare among birds, but quite commonplace in the Yellow Wagtail

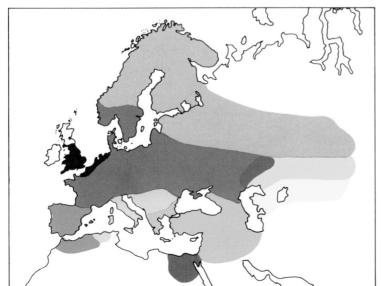

■	*flavissima*
	iberiae
	cinereocapilla
	feldegg
	pygmaea
	beema
	lutea
	thunbergi
	flava

Range of Yellow Wagtail subspecies
Being a species in a state of evolutionary flux, individuals bearing a strong resemblance to 1 subspecies may appear and breed within the range of another

253

Pied Wagtail

Motacilla alba (Linnaeus)

The familiar black and white wagtail, frequently called the Water Wagtail. Birds in Britain and Ireland are referred to a different subspecies, *Motacilla alba yarrelli*, than Continental birds – the White Wagtail *Motacilla alba alba*

Population: about 500,000 pairs

Male (foreground) and female

In the Pied Wagtail the upperparts are pure black marked with white wing bars and edges to the primaries. The tail is black with white outer feathers and is frequently bobbed. The belly and undertail coverts are white as is the face and forehead. The chin and breast have a large black bib that joins with the black back. Females are similar, but inclined to dark grey on the back. The White Wagtail is similarly marked, but has a dove-grey back. Juveniles are difficult to distinguish in autumn. Though frequently associated with water, the species has extended its habitat to a variety of dry areas. It is usually solitary, but joins in large communal roosts in trees and even inside large greenhouses where it doubtless benefits from higher temperatures. 18 cm (7 in).

Voice: A sharp *tschissick* contact call; a twittering song of repeated call notes with variants.

Habitat: A variety of open country, though not moorland, including farms, gardens and even city centres. Extends into upland districts along mountain streams.

Reproduction: An elaborate display of aerial chasing and bowing with tail erect and spread. The nest is situated in a variety of different locations, including holes in walls and banks, old sheds, among ivy on cliffs or buildings, among thatch and even hidden among the earth of roughly ploughed land. It is constructed of twigs, moss, roots, grass and dead leaves lined with feathers and wool by the female alone. The 5–6 eggs are greyish-blue spotted with pale brown and grey, and are laid in late April through to June. Incubation, mainly by the female, lasts 12–14 days and the chicks are fed by both parents for the 13–16 days they take to fledge. Double-brooded.

Food: Mostly small insects and especially flies, but also small moths and their larvae.

Range and Distribution: Breeds virtually throughout the Palearctic from Iceland to Japan, except for the extreme parts of northern Siberia. Also breeds in Morocco and Greenland. In Britain and Ireland it is absent only from Shetland. A few White Wagtails breed each year and some Pied Wagtails do so on the Continent.

Movements: While many British and Irish birds are resident there is also a considerable emigration southwards to southwestern Europe. White Wagtails regularly pass through in spring in April and May, returning from August to October. A few birds may winter.

Waxwing

Bombycilla garrulus (Linnaeus)

A delicately coloured, Starling-like, pinkish-brown bird with a crest and bold areas of colour in the wing. The Waxwing is a winter visitor to Britain in highly variable numbers depending on the prevalent conditions in its native Scandinavia

Boreal breeding range: may erupt to Britain and Ireland in numbers varying from a handful to several thousand in winter

A decidedly bulky, plump-looking bird with a rich dark brown back and pinkish-brown underparts. A curved pinkish-brown and erectile crest rises from the crown and the eye is set in an area of black extending from the base of the stubby decurved bill. There is a white flash at the gape below which is a black bib. The tail is grey shading to black and boldly tipped with yellow; the undertail coverts are rusty. The wings are tipped with yellow and white, and with red, wax-like appendages to the secondaries. It is a gregarious species that sometimes descends on a hedgerow in large flocks to devour berries. 18 cm (7 in).

Voice: A thin *sirrrrr*, but usually a quiet bird, though various other calls have been described.

Habitat: Coniferous forests of larch, spruce and pine, but also areas of scattered pines and birches. In winter frequents any area of open country that produces suitable berries in quantity, including hedgerows and gardens.

Reproduction: Breeds in Scandinavia in June, sometimes earlier or later, and the cup of conifer twigs and grass lined with reindeer moss is placed in a pine or spruce. The 4–6 eggs are grey-blue with blackish spots and incubated by the female for 13–14 days. The chicks are fed by both parents for 15–17 days. Single-brooded.

Food: Berries of various species, and in summer some insects. In winter they may take berries of privet, yew and holly, as well as rose hips and ornamental species.

Range and Distribution: Breeds in the boreal zone from northern Scandinavia eastwards across northern Russia and Siberia to Kamchatka, and into Alaska and adjacent areas of Canada.

Movements: Arrives in October and November in highly variable numbers from Scandinavia. Occasional invasions depend on the population level and on the availability of food, but many occur several years in succession after periods of virtual absence. Many birds then winter in Britain and Ireland and there is a small return movement in March and April.

Dipper

Cinclus cinclus (Linnaeus)

A rotund, chunky bird that spends all of its time alongside, in or beneath fast-flowing streams. About the size of a thrush, but with a bulkier body and short, often cocked tail that make it look somewhat larger

Population: about 30,000 pairs

Dippers are dark brown above and below, except for a bold white patch on the chin and breast bordered below by a lighter, more chestnut-coloured brown on the belly. The bill is short and pointed and the legs are quite long and strongly built. It is a streamside bird at all seasons and is seen away from water only when taking a short cut to avoid a loop in a river. It thus has a territory that may be up to 2 km long but only a few metres wide. It perches freely on rocks in midstream and feeds by picking aquatic creatures from the water's surface or by wading in and frequently submerging to pick them from the bottom. The angle of its body when feeding head-down forces water over its back and helps to keep it submerged. 18 cm (7 in).

Voice: A loud *zit-zit-zit* call note most frequently uttered in low, fast flight over water. Song is a Wren-like warble of rippling quality.

Habitat: Fast-running water, from streams to quite substantial rivers.

Reproduction: Display consists of bowing and wing-shivering by both sexes. The nest is invariably over or alongside water, in a cliff face or bank, hole in a wall, bridge, or beneath a waterfall. It is constructed by both members of the pair of grass and moss lined with dead leaves, and is cup-shaped with a canopy of moss overhanging the entrance. The 5, sometimes 3–6, white eggs are laid in March or April and incubated by the female alone for 15–18 days. The chicks are fed by both parents for 19–25 days. Double-brooded with occasionally a third, but sometimes single-brooded.

Food: Predominantly the larvae of aquatic insects, but also molluscs and crustaceans, worms, tadpoles and small fish.

Range and Distribution: Enjoys a patchy distribution through the western and southern parts of the Palearctic, mainly in hilly or mountainous districts from Spain across Europe and Scandinavia to Turkey and the Caucasus, the Himalayas and central Siberia to the Urals. In Britain and Ireland it is widespread in hilly districts but absent from southern and eastern England, the Isle of Man and Shetland.

Movements: Birds are resident in Britain and Ireland. A few Continental birds arrive in October and stay through to April, often occupying lowland streams where British Dippers do not breed. They are called Black-bellied Dippers because they lack the light chestnut area below the white bib of our birds, being dark brown instead.

Wren

Troglodytes troglodytes (Linnaeus)

Third smallest bird of our area – both Goldcrest and Firecrest are smaller

Population: up to 10 million pairs

A familiar warm brown bird, barred and mottled with shades of buff and dark brown. The stocky shape and short, permanently cocked tail are characteristic. A long, thin, slightly decurved bill is used for probing for food among walls and bank crevices. Wrens spend much of their time well out of sight (*Troglodytes* literally means cave dweller), working their way among thick ground cover, and in winter form communal roosts with up to 60 or more birds crammed into a single nest box. Their amazingly vibrant and loud voice is usually a giveaway. 9.5 cm (3¾ in).

Voice: A clear loud warbling broken by a vibrant trill that is almost wheezy, ending with a final flourishing trill. Usual call note is a hard *tic-tic-tic* that may be extended and run together. The song is uttered from prominent song posts as well as from deep within cover.

Habitat: Virtually ubiquitous; occupies a huge range of different habitats from the densest of woodland to the barest of mountain slopes. Also found in hedgerows, copses, gardens, parks, city centres, heaths, wasteland, sea cliffs and on isolated islands.

Reproduction: Sings virtually throughout the year and is generally found singly or in pairs. The domed nest is hidden in a bank, rock crevice, shed, hole in a tree, or old nest of another species. The male builds several 'cock' nests, one of which is chosen by the female and which she lines. Whatever materials are at hand are used – grass, dead leaves, moss, feathers. The 3–6, sometimes up to 16, spotted white eggs are laid from the end of April through to July and incubated by the female alone for 14–15 days. Fledging takes a little longer, 16–17 days, during which the young are fed by the female. Two broods.

Food: The young are fed almost exclusively on a diet of moth larvae. These, together with fly and other insect larvae, as well as spiders, form the diet throughout the year.

Range and Distribution: The Wren ranges right across Europe from the Lofoten Islands south to Morocco, eastwards to Russia and Turkey, through the Himalayas to China and Japan. It is found in the Aleutian Islands, southern Alaska and boreal Canada southwards into the United States in the Rocky and Appalachian Mountains. In the New World it is called the Winter Wren. In Britain and Ireland its numbers are dramatically reduced by severe winters, but in some years it is the most numerous of our birds. It nests in every corner of the country and has developed into distinct subspecies in Shetland, the Hebrides, Fair Isle and St Kilda.

Movements: British and Irish Wrens are far from being pure residents, though only a few birds wander abroad. Migrants arrive on the east coast of England in autumn and some may then pass on to France.

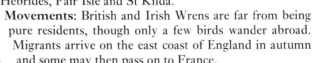
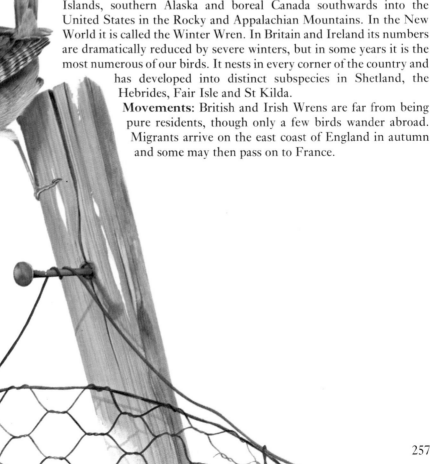

Dunnock

Prunella modularis (Linnaeus)

Sometimes misleadingly called the Hedge Sparrow, though it is unrelated to the sparrows; and in former times the Hedge Accentor, which is the best name of all for a member of the Prunellidae

Population: 5 to 8 million pairs

This is a self-effacing little bird that spends much of its time shuffling close to the ground picking up small items of food as it goes. At any distance it is rather dull, but a closer approach reveals a uniform grey throat and breast enclosing a delicately spotted brown face and chin. The upperparts are streaked black and brown with considerable chestnut on the wings. The flanks have a series of broad streaks. The neatly notched tail is dark, the bill fine and pointed. The legs and feet are invariably hidden in a semi-crouched posture as it feeds. 14.5 cm ($5\frac{3}{4}$ in).

Voice: The song is a pleasant and quite distinctive jingling warble; also utters a high-pitched *tseep* that may be extended as an alarm.

Habitat: Unlike any other accentor it occupies lowlands, including hedgerows and gardens, woodland edges, copses and open scrub. It frequently feeds beneath bird tables but does not join the hurly-burly of species above.

Reproduction: Much wing-quivering and waving between aerial chases low over the ground. The nest, of twigs with moss and grass lined with hair or wool, is built by both members of the pair and the 4–5 eggs are blue, sometimes with a few reddish spots, and laid from April to June. Incubation by the female lasts 12–13 days and the young are fed by both parents for 12 days. Two broods are normally reared, but 3 is not unknown.

Food: Mainly seeds in winter, but with insects, spiders and worms taken in summer.

Range and Distribution: Almost, but not quite, exclusively a European bird, the Dunnock ranges from northern Iberia across Europe, though avoiding the Mediterranean coastline, to the Urals. It occupies most of Scandinavia, except for the extreme north, the Crimea and northern Turkey and the Caucasus. It is found throughout Britain and Ireland, but is absent from the higher Scottish hills and the Shetlands.

Movements: British and Irish birds are resident and subject to only local dispersal. There is an immigration of Continental birds to the east coast in autumn and a return movement in spring.

Robin

Erithacus rubecula (Linnaeus)

One of the most familiar of our birds and one of the easiest to identify, the rust-red breast picking it out from almost all other species. Juvenile lacking red breast shown overleaf

Population: 5 million pairs

Khaki olive-brown upperparts extend from the crown to the tip of the tail and blend well with the woodland floor that is the Robin's natural home. The forehead, face, chin and breast are red, with the belly and undertail coverts white. Upperparts and breast are separated by a line of dove-grey. The sexes are similar, and even Robins have to tell one another by behaviour rather than any plumage distinction. Juveniles are mottled and barred in browns and buffs, though they have the characteristic upright stance and general cockiness. Encouraged by affection and food Robins become very tame and confiding, and there are many examples of them feeding from the hand and entering houses to perch on people. 14 cm (5½ in).

Voice: A characteristic and rather angry *tick*, and a *tsipp-ip*. Song a melodious warble of separated phrases, sometimes including the notes of other birds, and often with a rather plaintive *peu-peu-peu*.

Habitat: Woods and woodland edges, hedgerows, parks and gardens even in the centres of cities.

Reproduction: Highly territorial throughout the year, females having their own territory in winter. Defence consists of song and (see p. 260)

making much of the red breast to drive away intruders. Only by adopting a submissive posture is the female allowed into the male's territory. The nest is a cup placed in a roadside bank, among ivy, on a shelf in a building, in a specially erected open-fronted nest box, in an old gardening jacket or kettle or some such. The nest is built by the female of moss on a base of dead leaves, lined with hair. The 5–6 eggs are white speckled with reddish-brown and laid from the end of March onwards. They are incubated by the female for 12–15 days and the chicks are fed by her with food brought by the male. The male may take over the brood when the female lays another clutch. Two broods with an occasional third.

Food: Mainly insects and their larvae, as well as spiders and centipedes, worms, seeds of various weeds and summer and autumn soft fruit.

Range and Distribution: Throughout Europe with absences in Spain, the mountains of Scandinavia and southern Russia, but extending eastwards to central Siberia. Also in Turkey and the Caucasus and parts of North Africa. In Britain and Ireland it is found everywhere except for some of the higher Scottish hills, Shetland and northern Lewis.

Movements: Most birds are resident, but females from northern Britain move southwards to the Continent. There is also an arrival of Continental birds, particularly on the east coast in October, and many of these pass through to winter further south.

Nightingale

Luscinia megarhynchos (Brehm)

Best told by its beautiful and distinctive song, the Nightingale is a dull brown bird with a rounded rufous tail but with no other distinguishing characteristics

Population: 10,000 pairs

Warm brown upperparts and dull buff underparts. The head is devoid of marks except for a narrow creamy eye-ring. It could be confused with a Reed Warbler, but has a rufous tail; and with a female Redstart, which is smaller and has a much redder and less rufous tail. The bill is pointed and dagger-like. Nightingales are seldom demonstrative and usually remain in deep cover. They are, however, highly vocal. 16.5 cm (6½ in).

Voice: A variety of calls including a *hweet*, a hard *tac* and a grating *chaaa*. Song is remarkably varied and rich with pure liquid phrases broken by harsh *choc-choc* notes. Often sings at dusk when other birds have gone to roost.

Habitat: Deciduous woods and clumps of trees with open ground, bushes and thickets, hedgerows and other areas with densely tangled undergrowth.

Reproduction: The nest is built by the female, usually on the ground among ivy, nettles and thick grass. It has a base of dead leaves lined with grass and some hair, and the 4–5 eggs are grey-green covered with reddish speckling. Incubation by the female alone begins in mid-May and lasts 13–14 days. The chicks are fed by both parents for 11–12 days and for several days after leaving the nest. Single-brooded.

Food: Insects and their larvae, ant pupae, worms and spiders; also fruit and berries.

Range and Distribution: Found throughout temperate and Mediterranean Europe. Also in North Africa, Turkey eastwards to northern Iran and in a sweep beyond the Caspian and Aral Seas to central Asia. In Britain it is confined to southern and eastern England, barely reaching Devon, Wales and southern Yorkshire. A notable decline has occurred over the past 30 years, possibly due to habitat destruction, especially the abandonment of coppicing in many woodlands.

Movements: Birds arrive in late April and May, and depart again in August and September. Only a rare visitor to Ireland.

Bluethroat

Luscinia svecica (Linnaeus)

A neat, self-effacing little chat that occurs regularly in small numbers both in spring and autumn

Continental breeding grounds: regular in autumn in small numbers and has bred in Scotland

Rather Robin-like in posture, with deep brown upperparts broken by a prominent creamy supercilium and white underparts. In spring and summer males boast a ring of bright blue extending from the chin to the breast, which is marked below by black, white and red breast bands. The centre of the blue area has a spot of red in a northern sub-species and of white in a more southern-distributed one. Females and winter males lack this bold pattern and have a dark moustachial streak that merges with a smudgy breast band with only a little blue. The base of the outertail feathers shows as bright rust-red, easily visible as the bird plunges into cover or cocks its tail. Juveniles resemble young Robins, but are streaked rather than barred on the breast. Bluethroats keep to dark places and thick cover. 14 cm (5½ in).

Voice: A harsh *tac-tac* and a softer *hoeet*; song varied and rich with a Nightingale-like repetition of phrases, including a high-pitched metallic *ting-ting-ting*.

Habitat: Birch and willow scrub, usually in marshy locations; in winter resorts to areas of tangled vegetation with dense undergrowth, frequently near water.

Reproduction: The nest is built against a bank, hummock or base of a bush, usually on damp or swampy ground. The 5–7 eggs are pale greenish with reddish spots, but very variable. Incubation, by the female alone, lasts 14–15 days and the chicks are fed by both parents for a similar period. Single-brooded, but occasionally 2 broods are reared by the southern subspecies.

Food: Insects and their larvae, but also worms and some berries and seeds in winter.

Range and Distribution: From isolated populations in Spain and western France across temperate Europe, and from Scandinavia across northern Europe to Russia and most of the northern Palearctic region to the Bering Sea. There are also populations in the Caucasus and at a few spots in the New World in northern Alaska. In Britain it bred unsuccessfully in Inverness-shire in 1968.

Movements: It winters southwards into Africa and Asia with red-spotted birds appearing on the east coast of Britain in autumn in small numbers. Both red- and white-spotted birds are regular, but rare, in spring.

Male white-spotted form in summer (foreground) and in winter

Black Redstart

Phoenicurus ochruros (Gmelin)

A dark, sooty chat with prominent rust-red tail that colonized England in the 1930s and 1940s and found a perfect home in war-torn inner cities. Male (above) and female shown

Population: less than 100 pairs

The male is black on face and underparts, becoming greyer on the belly and white on undertail coverts. The crown and back are sooty-grey and the wings black with white margins to the inner feathers that show as a bold white panel on the closed wing. The rump and tail are rust-red, but with darker, more brownish central feathers. The bill is sharp and pointed, the feet and legs black. The female is a dull sooty-brown, darker on the wings, with a light ring around the eye. The dark underparts serve to distinguish her from the otherwise similar female Redstart. 14 cm (5½ in).

Voice: A flute-like song, *tsip* call note and scolding *tic-tic*.

Habitat: Mountain screes and rocky outcrops on the Continent, but in Britain is associated with derelict sites and more recently with industrial areas such as railway sidings.

Reproduction: Holes or ledges among decaying or dirty industrial buildings serve as nest sites. The nest itself is constructed of grass and moss lined with hair and feathers and is built by the female alone. The 4–6 white eggs are laid from early April onwards and incubated by the female for 12–16 days. The chicks are fed by both sexes for 12–19 days. Double-brooded with an occasional third.

Food: Insects and their larvae constitute the main food, but berries may be important in autumn.

Range and Distribution: From Spain north to Denmark and southern Sweden, and east through Europe to the Black Sea, Caucasus, Afghanistan and the Himalayas, western China and parts of central Asia, with an isolated population in the Moroccan High Atlas. Bred on the cliffs of Sussex in 1923, appeared in London in 1926 and colonized City bomb sites in 1942. Most urban birds are now found at power stations and gas works. Largely confined to southeast and central England, it breeds at many coastal sites, and in Cheshire and Orkney in 1973.

Movements: Breeding birds arrive in April and leave in September; most winter on the Continent. Passage migrants are present on south and east coasts north to Yorkshire from March to May, and in September and October. Most pass on to France and Spain, but some winter on south and southwest coasts.

Redstart

Phoenicurus phoenicurus
(Linnaeus)

An attractive, well-marked chat,
with a characteristic red tail that is
quivered as it perches

Population: 50,000 to 100,000 pairs

A fine dove-grey on crown and back, the male has black wing feathers broadly margined with pale brown. The rump and tail are bright rust-red but with brownish central feathers. The forehead is white extending over the eye in a truncated supercilium. An area of black on the face extends from the lores to the ear coverts and to the chin and upper breast. A warm rufous-orange extends from the breast over the flanks, becoming pale and creamy on the belly and undertail coverts. The bill is sharply pointed and, like the legs and feet, is black. In contrast the female is a dull bird, brown above and a warm cream below marked only with a rufous-red tail and with a light creamy eye-ring. 14 cm (5½ in).

Voice: Calls include a soft *hweet* and a louder *twick*; also a *hwee-tuc-tuc* of alarm. Song is a brief, varied warbling. The Redstart sometimes mimics other species.

Habitat: Wide variety of areas from woodland edges and glades to hedgerows, parkland, heaths and commons, and moorland.

Reproduction: In dry areas nests on the ground, but most frequently in holes in trees or walls. The nest itself is built by the female and constructed of grass with moss, roots and strips of bark lined with hair. The 6–7 pale blue eggs are laid from mid-May onwards and incubated almost entirely by the female for 11–14 days. The chicks are fed by both parents for 14–20 days, with the male taking sole responsibility when the female lays a second clutch. Double-brooded.

Food: Predominantly insects and their larvae, but also spiders and worms as well as berries in autumn.

Range and Distribution: Throughout Europe, except for the far north of Scandinavia and parts of the Mediterranean and Black Sea coasts. Extends across Russia to central Siberia. Also in Turkey and the Caucasus into Iran, and at a few places in the mountains of northwest Africa. Widespread in Britain, but patchily distributed in the south and east of England and in eastern and northern Scotland. Absent from the Outer Hebrides, Orkney and Shetland, and highly irregular in a few coastal areas of Ireland.

Movements: British birds are present from April to September. It is also a fairly numerous passage migrant in April and May and, more commonly, from August to October, especially on the east coast. All move on to winter in Africa south of the Sahara.

Male (foreground) and female

Whinchat

Saxicola rubetra (Linnaeus)

An open-perching, rough-ground
chat that can easily be confused with
the Stonechat.

Population: 20,000 to 40,000 pairs

Whinchat males are mottled brown and black above, with dark primary feathers broadly edged with brown and a broad white bar on the wing. The tail is black, but with bold patches of white at the outer sides of the base that are particularly noticeable in flight. There is a white supercilium that distinguishes it at once from the Stonechat, and a white moustachial stripe that encloses an area of dark brown extending from the lores to the ear coverts. The chin and breast are a rich rufous-orange fading to a creamy-white on the undertail coverts. The bill is sharply pointed and, like the legs and feet, black in colour. The female is similar but generally duller, with less contrast. The supercilium, in particular, is much less pronounced, making confusion with the female Stonechat a distinct possibility. Whinchats perch freely, usually atop a bush or other low vegetation. 12.5 cm (5 in).

Voice: A harsh *tic-tic*, also a more musical *tu-tic* and a *tza*; song is a chat-like warble often incorporating the calls of other species.

Habitat: Rough ground in a wide variety of circumstances, but with open moorland a distinct favourite. Also found in lowland rough grazing, freshwater marshes and hillside sheep pastures; and in more confined areas such as railway cuttings and embankments.

Reproduction: The nest is placed on the ground among grass or at the foot of a bush. It is constructed by the female alone of grass and moss lined with hair, and the 5–7 pale blue eggs are finely speckled with rust-brown and laid in late May or early June. Incubation, by the female, lasts 13–14 days and the young are fed by both parents for a similar period. Sometimes double-brooded.

Food: Insects and their larvae, together with spiders and worms.

Range and Distribution: From northern Spain across Europe to Russia and central Siberia. Absent from parts of the Mediterranean and from northern Scandinavia. In Britain and Ireland it is widespread, but distinctly local in the southeastern half of England and over most of Ireland. Local in Orkney and absent from Shetland.

Movements: Arrives in the latter part of April and departs for winter quarters in Africa south of the Sahara in September. Passage migrants pass through in April and May and again from August to October, and may be quite numerous on the south and east coasts at the end of August and beginning of September.

Stonechat

Saxicola torquata (Linnaeus)

A thickset, white-collared chat that perches even more upright than the similar Whinchat. Less numerous than in the past

Population: 30,000 to 60,000 pairs

Male is distinctive with black head and dark brown and black mottled upperparts with a white rump and a white flash in the wing. The dark tail is short and stumpy. The black head extends to the chin and is bordered by a white half-collar that becomes almost complete in some individuals. The breast is a bright rufous-orange fading to white on the belly. The sharply pointed bill and the legs and feet are black. The female is similar, but lacks a white collar and is less dark and more rufous throughout. Only the absence of a supercilium, a light chin and white base to the outer tail distinguish her from the female Whinchat. 12.5 cm (5 in).

Voice: A characteristic *weet-tsac-tsac* likened to the sound produced by clapping 2 stones together. The song is a rather Dunnock-like jingle of repeated double notes.

Habitat: Heaths and commons, mostly coastal in Britain but inland in Ireland, with heather and gorse, grass and bracken. Also young conifers on heather moors.

Reproduction: The nest, built by the female alone, is situated on the ground at the base of a bush or clump of gorse, and is constructed of grass and moss lined with hair. The 5–6 pale greenish-blue eggs are speckled with rusty-brown and laid from late March to June. Incubation by the female (the male may assist) lasts 14–15 days and the chicks are fed by both parents for 12–13 days. Double-brooded, with occasionally a third clutch.

Food: Mainly insects and their larvae, but also spiders and worms and occasionally seeds.

Range and Distribution: In the Old World ranges from Iberia through Europe to a line drawn from Denmark to the Black Sea, eastwards through Turkey and the Caucasus to northern Iran, the Himalayas and over the bulk of Siberia to Japan. Also found in North Africa, most of savannah Africa, Madagascar, and the southwest of the Arabian peninsula. Mainly coastal in Britain though absent in the east from much of the coast from Durham to Norfolk. In Ireland it is more widespread inland, though absent from several areas. Partial recovery in recent years from hard winters of early 1960s, but still less numerous than last century.

Movements: Some movements, particularly of northern birds within Britain, but little evidence of immigration from abroad. Some British birds cross the Channel in winter.

266

Wheatear

Oenanthe oenanthe (Linnaeus)

A compact, ground-dwelling chat that, like most other wheatears, shows a prominent white rump. Male (below) and female shown

Population: about 80,000 pairs

From crown to lower back the male is a fine dove-grey. The rump is white extending to the sides of the black-centred and black-tipped tail, a feature of crucial importance in separating this from a number of similar species that occur as vagrants in Britain and Ireland. The wings are black and a black stripe extends from the lores, through the eye to widen out over the ear coverts. The underparts are a pale orange, becoming lighter on the belly and undertail coverts. The female, like the male in winter, is much duller, being warm brown above and creamy-buff below. The tail pattern nevertheless remains diagnostic. 14.5–15 cm ($5\frac{3}{4}$–6 in).

Voice: A hard *chack* and *wheet-chack*; the song, uttered in hovering display flight or from a low perch, is a pleasant warble similar to a lark's but interspersed with harsh croaks and rattles.

Habitat: Open ground, especially moorlands, and lowlands with sufficient short-cropped grass. Also areas of coastal shingle.

Reproduction: The nest is placed in a hole in ground or wall, or beneath a clod, and consists of a cup of grasses lined with hair, feathers or wool. It is constructed by both sexes, though mainly by the female, and the 5–6 (usually 6) pale blue eggs are laid from late March to June. Incubation, again mainly by the female, lasts 14 days and the young are fed by both parents for 15 days. Single-brooded, though some southern populations may raise a second.

Food: Insects and their larvae, ants, spiders and centipedes.

Range and Distribution: Virtually circumpolar, but with a large gap between Alaska and Baffinland in northern Canada. Extends along the coasts of Greenland, to Iceland, throughout Europe, Turkey and northern Iran, eastwards across southern Siberia to the Bering Straits and Alaska. In the north it is absent only from northernmost Siberia. In Britain and Ireland it is widespread in coastal and hilly regions, but decidedly scarce south of a line drawn from Flamborough Head to the River Severn.

Movements: Arrives between March and June, returning from late July to the end of October. British birds winter in Africa south of the Sahara. Many Continental birds often arrive on the east coast in autumn, with a regular passage in late autumn of the Greenland Wheatear *Oenanthe oenanthe leucorrhoa*, which is larger with richer colouring on the breast.

Ring Ouzel

Turdus torquatus (Linnaeus)

Very similar to the Blackbird, which it replaces in hilly moorland districts, but marked with a white crescent on the breast

Population: 8,000 to 16,000 pairs

Female

The male is a bold, black bird marked on the wings with silvery margins to the feathers which are particularly apparent in flight. The underparts are black with silvery feather margins, especially on the flanks. There is a bold white crescent across the upper breast that is diagnostic. The female is less black and more silvery all over and the breast band is less distinct. The bill is yellowish, but never bright orange-yellow like that of the Blackbird. Ring Ouzels will perch freely where trees are available, both on breeding territory and on migration. They are most frequently seen, however, perching on prominent rocks or walls. 24 cm (9$\frac{1}{2}$ in).

Voice: A clear *pee-u* and a scolding *tac-tac-tac*; song consists of repeated phrases opening with a single note, interrupted by a chuckle, and culminating in the repeated opening.

Habitat: Moorland broken by cliff, gully or scree, sometimes with a few stunted bushes, at 250 metres or higher in Britain.

Reproduction: The nest is constructed of grass on a foundation of heather and earth, hidden in a gully, watercourse, sides of a track, or old moorland building. The 4–5 eggs are pale blue blotched with rust-brown and laid from mid-April to May. Incubation by both members of the pair lasts 13–14 days and the chicks are fed by both parents for a similar period. Single-brooded, though sometimes a second is reared.

Food: Insects and their larvae, worms, together with berries and fruit in autumn.

Range and Distribution: Confined to the mountain zones of Europe; to the Caucasus, Britain, Scandinavia, northern Spain and the Pyrenees, the Alps and mountains of Yugoslavia and the Carpathians. In Britain and Ireland it is found only in the hilly districts of the north and west – Dartmoor, Exmoor, Wales, Pennines, Yorkshire Moors, Lake District and Scotland. In Ireland it is a very scarce local breeding bird on moors near the coasts.

Movements: Arrives in April and stays through to September; winters in the Mediterranean. Passage migrants pass through in small numbers from March to May and from September to early November; most are presumed to be Scandinavian birds, especially on the east coast in autumn.

Blackbird

Turdus merula (Linnaeus)

One of the most numerous and
familiar of our birds, marked black
with yellow bill in the male.
Male (below) and female shown

Population: 7 million pairs

Juvenile – more warmly coloured
on breast than female

Black above and below and marked only by a yellow bill and yellow
eye-ring, the male is unmistakable. The female is warm brown
above with paler, warm rufous breast streaked and blotched with dark
brown. This breast pattern is much darker and less clear cut than those
of Song and Mistle Thrushes. The bill is dark becoming lighter, almost
yellow, at the base. Young males can be distinguished by their dark
brown, not black, wings. Blackbirds are tame and confiding as well as
highly territorial. They are evenly spaced over most of Britain, but
numbers are reduced after a severe winter. 25 cm (10 in).

Voice: A harsh and noisy rattle of alarm and a low-pitched *chook-
chook*, also a clear *pink-pink* which may be repeated for lengthy periods.
The song is fluty and varied, lacking the repeated phrases of the
Song Thrush.

Habitat: Wide variety of landforms, though presumably a woodland
species by origin. Also now found in hedgerows, copses, parks and
gardens, and from city centres to the edges of highland moors.

Reproduction: The nest is constructed low in a tree or bush, but
sometimes at a considerable height, often using a previous nest as a
base. Also placed in a shed and occasionally on the ground. It is built of
grass and mud by the female, though the male may help in the
gathering of materials. The 4–5 eggs are heavily marked with red-
brown on a bluish-green ground and laid from March onwards. The
female performs the incubation and the eggs hatch after 11–17 days.
Both parents feed the young for 12–19 days and the fledglings are split
between the pair when they leave the nest. Two or 3, sometimes 4,
broods are reared.

Food: More vegetable than animal: takes all fruits and berries as well as
seeds and grain, earthworms, a wide variety of insects and their larvae,
spiders and centipedes.

Range and Distribution: From Iberia through the Mediterranean, Turkey, northern Iran, Himalayas, Assam to China; and
northwards throughout temperate Europe to central Scandinavia and Russia. In Britain and Ireland it is absent only
from the highest Scottish mountains.

Movements: Mainly resident, though a small proportion of birds move southwards within Britain
and some venture across the Channel. There is
a large immigration of Continental birds in
October and early November, occasionally
giving rise to spectacular numbers on the
east coast. Many stay on to winter and
return in March and April.

Fieldfare

Turdus pilaris (Linnaeus)

A large gregarious thrush, and a common winter visitor that has started to breed in recent years. Fieldfares are distinctive birds similar to Song and Mistle Thrushes

Population: about 6 pairs; many thousands winter

Continental breeding distribution

Dove-grey head and rump, separated by a dark chestnut-brown saddle on back and wings. The tail is black and there is a pale supercilium. The breast is a warm orange-brown striped with black arrow-shaped markings in typical thrush pattern. The belly and under-tail coverts are white. The bill is dark, but with an orange-yellow base like a female Blackbird's. These birds often form quite large flocks that scour the hedgerows in autumn and grassy fields through the winter. They are often very noisy and frequently keep company with Redwings. Like other thrushes, they can be enticed into large gardens by fallen apples. 25.5 cm (10 in).

Voice: A harsh *cha-cha-cha-chack*, frequently uttered in flight as a contact call. Song like a weak version of the Blackbird's, with whistling and harsh notes, most commonly uttered in flight.

Habitat: Birch and pine woodland in the breeding season, often near marshes, but also among dwarf vegetation on hillsides and even in city parks. In winter frequents hedgerows, grassland and other open areas, including parks.

Reproduction: Usually nests in colonies among birches, pines or alders and in Britain in conifer plantations, woodland and moorland scrub. The nest is constructed of grass and mud and the 5–6 eggs are blue-green blotched with rusty-brown. They are laid in May and June and incubated from the first egg by the female for 11–14 days. Frequently double-brooded.

Food: Varied; berries, fallen fruit and cereals as well as worms, insects and their larvae, and spiders.

Range and Distribution: From Paris eastwards across northern Europe to eastern Siberia and northwards to the North Cape of Scandinavia. Also in Iceland and the southern tip of Greenland. Has spread westwards in recent years and continues to colonize new areas. In Britain it has nested sporadically since 1967 in Shetland, Orkney and the hills of Scotland, and through the Pennines as far south as Derbyshire.

Movements: Heavy autumn influx from September to November with birds moving through the country to winter in southwestern Europe. Many stay on and there is a return movement in March and April through the south and east.

Song Thrush

Turdus philomelos (Brehm)

Common, widespread, and a familiar bird throughout the country

Population: about 3,500,000 pairs

Upperparts a warm brown. Underparts streaked with lines of clear spots on a warm pale-orange breast that fades to white on the lower breast and belly. A faint pale eye-stripe is barely discernible behind the eye. Most easily confused with the Mistle Thrush, but is smaller; brown not grey-brown; and lacks white in the tail. Song Thrushes are comparatively tame and come readily to gardens. They have the engaging habit of breaking open the shells of snails by beating them on a rock 'anvil' or path. 23 cm (9 in).

Voice: A *sip* flight note and a *tchook-tchook* of alarm that may become a chattering call similar to a Blackbird's. Song is a flute-like whistling in which each phrase is repeated 3 or 4 times, followed by a brief pause before another phrase is similarly repeated.

Habitat: Woodland and copses, hedgerows, parks, gardens, indeed anywhere that suitable thickets or undergrowth are found adjacent to cropped ground vegetation.

Reproduction: The nest is usually placed at no great height in a bush or hedgerow, against the trunk of a tree, or among ivy or other vegetation growing over a building. It is built by the female alone, and is constructed of grass, roots, twigs and leaves lined with mud or wood pulp. The 4–5, occasionally 6, light blue eggs are spotted with black and laid from the end of March until June. Incubation, again by the female alone, lasts 11–15 days and the chicks are fed by both parents for 12–16 days. Double- or treble-brooded.

Food: Worms are pounced upon and dragged from the earth. Also takes snails and slugs as well as insects and their larvae, ants, spiders, and much fruit and berries in season. May be quite destructive of soft fruit and takes large quantities of elder, holly and yew berries.

Range and Distribution: From northern Spain through temperate Europe including Scandinavia, except for its mountain ranges, and eastwards through Russia to central Siberia. Also from the mountains of northern Turkey through the Caucasus to northern Iran. In Britain and Ireland it is absent only from Shetland and the highest Scottish hills. Numbers may be seriously reduced by severe winters.

Movements: Partly resident, but with large movements within and out of the country. Continental birds arrive on the east coast from September and, while many pass on southwards, some stay on to winter.

Redwing

Turdus iliacus (Linnaeus)

An abundant winter visitor that has successfully colonized Scotland and northern England

Population: about 10 pairs breed; many thousands winter

Like a small Song Thrush; earth-brown above and with streaked breast and flanks on a warm creamy background that becomes white on the belly and undertail coverts. A bold, creamy supercilium and a similarly coloured moustachial streak give the face a strangely 'cross' look. The vernacular name derives from a wash of rust-red along the flanks that is a continuation of the underwing coverts. Redwings are gregarious birds in winter, often forming mixed flocks with Fieldfares, that scour the hedgerows and short grassy fields. Their small size and distinctive calls make them readily identifiable even in flight. 21 cm ($8\frac{1}{4}$ in).

Voice: A thin *seeep* in flight, also an abrupt *chup* and a harsh *chittuk*. Song is a repetition of a single phrase, like a Song Thrush, but lacking the variation of that bird.

Habitat: Birch and alder woods together with young pines and willow scrub, often near water; also above the tree line and even in large gardens. In winter frequents fields and other grassland, as well as hedgerows and gardens.

Reproduction: Not colonial like the Fieldfare. The nest is constructed by the female in a tree, bush, or among the roots of a fallen tree, in a bank or even in a shed. It is a neat structure of grasses and earth and the 5–6 eggs are greenish-blue, mottled with reddish-brown, and are laid from May to July. Incubation, by the female alone, lasts 11–15 days and both parents feed the young for 10–15 days. Usually double-brooded.

Food: Insects and their larvae, worms, snails, slugs as well as a variety of berries.

Range and Distribution: From Iceland eastwards across the Baltic States, Scandinavia and the northern Palearctic to northeastern Siberia. In Britain it nested first in Scotland in 1925 and occasionally thereafter. Seven pairs were discovered in 1967 and no less than 45–55 pairs in 1970. The total population may have reached several hundred pairs by the mid-1970s, but numbers have since declined.

Movements: A huge exodus from the breeding range brings large numbers to western and Mediterranean Europe and to Britain and Ireland in September and October. Many pass on to winter further south, with a return movement mainly in March and April.

Mistle Thrush

Turdus viscivorus (Linnaeus)

The largest thrush of the region, heavily spotted, with a characteristic flight note

Population: 300,000 to 600,000 pairs

The upperparts are greyish brown, not warm brown as in the Song Thrush, and the underparts heavily speckled with large spots on a creamy, not orange, breast. The tail has white tips to the outer feathers – a feature prominent in flight, which is deeply undulating and much more woodpecker-like than the direct flight of the Song Thrush. In this it more closely resembles the Fieldfare, but lacks the distinctive plumage pattern of that bird. 27 cm (10½ in).

Voice: The characteristic flight note is a rasping chatter; also a *tuc-tuc-tuc*. Song is a flute-like repetition of similar phrases, frequently uttered in winter from the bare branches of a tall tree and from which the bird's country name of Storm Cock derives.

Habitat: Open country with hedgerows, copses and isolated clumps of trees, woodland edges, large gardens and parks. Also open moorland with walls.

Reproduction: Usually begins early in the year in February or March before leaves cover the trees. The nest is placed in a major fork and consists of a cup of grasses and mud decorated (and thus camouflaged) with moss, built by the female alone. In treeless areas the nest may be on a wall. The 4–5, occasionally 3–6, pale bluish-green eggs are spotted with rusty-brown and incubated by the female for the 12–15 days they take to hatch. The chicks are fed by both parents for 12–16 days and, after leaving the nest, by the male alone if the female begins a fresh clutch. Double-brooded.

Food: Vegetable matter, including fruit and berries, especially of yew and holly, in quantity. Also snails, worms, ants, insects and their larvae, as well as the chicks of other birds.

Range and Distribution: Right across Europe, except for the Scandinavian mountain chain and most of Norway, extending southwards to North Africa and eastwards to central Siberia. Also from Turkey through the Caucasus to northern Iran and the western Himalayas. In Britain and Ireland the Mistle Thrush has extended its range dramatically since the early eighteenth century and is now absent only from the Scottish hills, Caithness, and from Orkney and Shetland. Distinctly local in the Outer Hebrides.

Movements: Mainly resident, but some movement across the Channel. Some Continental birds arrive from September onwards.

Cetti's Warbler

Cettia cetti (Temminck)

A secretive little brown bird with an explosive voice that has colonized southernmost England in recent years

Continental range: extending and colonizing northwards

Upperparts are uniform warm brown marked by a neatly rounded tail that is frequently cocked. Underparts are whitish, warmer on the flanks, and with barred undertail coverts. It has a medium-sized bill, not dagger-like as in the Reed Warbler, and a short supercilium. The overall effect is of a more rotund bird than other similarly marked warblers, but the surest means of identification remains the voice. 14 cm (5½ in).

Voice: An explosive *cheweeoo* repeated in strident fashion. Also a similarly produced *settee* and a loud *chee*, usually uttered from inside dense cover.

Habitat: River and marsh edges with dense thickets of bushes or trees, often, but not invariably, with associated growth of reeds. Sometimes in dry vegetation near a stream.

Reproduction: Breeds in late April or early May, the female building a bulky cup-shaped nest of leaves and plant stems, slotted neatly into a fork of a low bush. The 4, occasionally 3 or 5, bright rust-red eggs are incubated by the female alone and the chicks are fed by both parents in the nest and for a considerable period afterwards. Single-brooded.

Food: Predominantly insects, but also worms together with some vegetable matter.

Range and Distribution: From Mediterranean Europe and North Africa eastwards through the Middle East to Afghanistan and northwards to southern central Siberia. An expansion of range northwards during the present century has been checked by severe winters but has continued, reaching Belgium in 1962, Holland in 1968 and West Germany in 1975. Birds first bred in Britain in 1972, though they had been suspected of doing so for some years prior, and then spread rapidly in southern and eastern England. The largest numbers are located at Stodmarsh in Kent.

Movements: Largely resident.

Grasshopper Warbler

Locustella naevia (Boddaert)

A skulking, dull brown little bird with a distinctive reeling song

Population: 25,000 or more pairs

Dull grey-brown upperparts streaked with black and faintly barred on the tail; underparts dull greyish-white with some faint streaking on the breast. There is a pale supercilium that is insignificant compared to those of other streaked marsh warblers, and the overall appearance lacks the contrast of birds such as the Sedge Warbler. Generally keeps well inside dense cover and attention is usually drawn to it by its song. 13 cm (5 in).

Voice: A reeling sound similar to the winding of a fishing reel that continues, varying only slightly in pitch, for minutes at a time. Confusable only with that of Savi's Warbler. May also produce short snatches as well as a quiet *twitt*.

Habitat: Often associated with dense marshland vegetation such as reed beds, sedges and tangled thickets; but also found on heathland and among recently planted conifers. Low, densely tangled vegetation is invariably present.

Reproduction: The nest is built on the ground, or close to it, among dense vegetation by both members of the pair. It consists of a base of dead leaves holding a cup of grass lined with hair. The 6, occasionally 4–7, white eggs are densely speckled with purplish-brown and incubated by both sexes for 13–15 days. The chicks are fed by both parents for 12–14 days. Usually double-brooded.

Food: Insects and their larvae, also spiders and woodlice.

Range and Distribution: From northern Spain eastwards across temperate Europe, avoiding many parts of the Mediterranean, to southern Sweden and Finland eastwards through Russia to central Siberia. Also in the Caucasus. In Britain and Ireland it is widespread, but with the highest population in southern and central England. It becomes very scarce in hilly districts and especially in the Scottish Highlands and islands. Absent from Shetland.

Movements: Arrives from mid-April onwards and departs southwards for winter quarters in Africa in September.

Savi's Warbler

Locustella luscinioides (Savi)

A uniformly brown bird with a distinctive reeling song

A shade larger than the Reed and Grasshopper Warblers and with warmer rufous-brown on unstreaked upperparts. Underparts are creamy-white, darker on the flanks, and the tail is long and rounded. A faint supercilium extends over the eye, and a clear white throat is often visible when the bird is singing. It is less skulking than the Grasshopper Warbler and invariably sings from a reed top or other prominent perch. 14 cm (5½ in).

Voice: Like the Grasshopper Warbler, a continuous reeling with ventriloquial effect produced by turning the head from side to side. But it is slower and at a lower pitch than that bird.

Habitat: Reed beds with small bushes, or sometimes sedges, but always in wet situations.

Reproduction: The nest is built by the female on or near the ground at the base of reeds or sedges, and consists of a cup of loosely woven marsh vegetation with a neater and more tightly constructed lining of grass. The 4–5 eggs are laid in May and are white speckled with brown. Incubation, which lasts 12 days, is by the female, though the male will feed his mate on the nest. The chicks are fed by the female, and sometimes also by the male during the latter part of the 12–14 days they take to fledge. Double-brooded.

Food: Marsh-dwelling insects and their larvae, including dragonflies.

Range and Distribution: Somewhat patchy, doubtless as a result of loss of habitat, from Spain across Europe to central southern Siberia. Has spread northwards in recent years and breeding was proved in Kent in 1960. The range has since increased and the bird now breeds in coastal Norfolk, Suffolk, Kent and Hampshire, as well as inland at Stodmarsh in Kent. Numbers, however, remain small.

Movements: Arrives in mid-April and begins singing immediately; departs for Africa in July. Away from the breeding areas it is a scarce vagrant, mainly in southeastern England.

Continental breeding distribution:
colonizing northwards

Sedge Warbler

Acrocephalus schoenobaenus (Linnaeus)

The most common and widespread of our marsh warblers

Population: about 300,000 pairs

Rich rusty-brown upperparts streaked with black. The rump is rusty-brown and the tail graduated and rounded. The crown is faintly streaked but appears dark at any distance, and there is a broad, creamy supercilium. The underparts are buffy-cream. The legs and feet are dark and the bill thin and sharply pointed. This is the 'standard' streaked warbler from which the less contrasting Grasshopper Warbler, and the decidedly rare Moustached and Aquatic Warblers, must be differentiated. Some young Sedge Warblers have a lighter crown stripe, but never one as pronounced as that of the Aquatic Warbler. 13 cm (5 in).

Voice: A rich song consisting of repeated harsh calls interspersed with some pleasant rich notes. Chattering, trills and mimicry are all involved to produce a much more varied song than that of the Reed Warbler. Also has a harsh *tuc* note that may be run together *tuctuctuctuc*.

Habitat: Much more varied than the Reed Warbler, occupying a range of habitats including reed beds, sedges and damp willow scrub, as well as dry areas such as young conifer plantations.

Reproduction: The song is frequently uttered in a bouncing display flight. The nest is located on or near the ground and consists of a deep, bulky structure of loosely woven grass, sedges and leaves with a lining of grasses, hair and plant down constructed by the female. The eggs are laid from mid-May and incubated mainly by the female for 13–14 days. The chicks are then fed for 10–12 days. Single-brooded.

Food: Insects and their larvae, also spiders.

Range and Distribution: From western France across Europe northwards into Scandinavia, and eastwards through Russia to beyond the Urals. Also in Turkey and the Caucasus. In Britain and Ireland it is widespread, though absent from most hilly and mountainous districts, and from the Shetlands.

Movements: Winters in Africa south of the Sahara and arrives from mid-April, staying on until September. Migrants are presumed to be of British and Irish breeding stock.

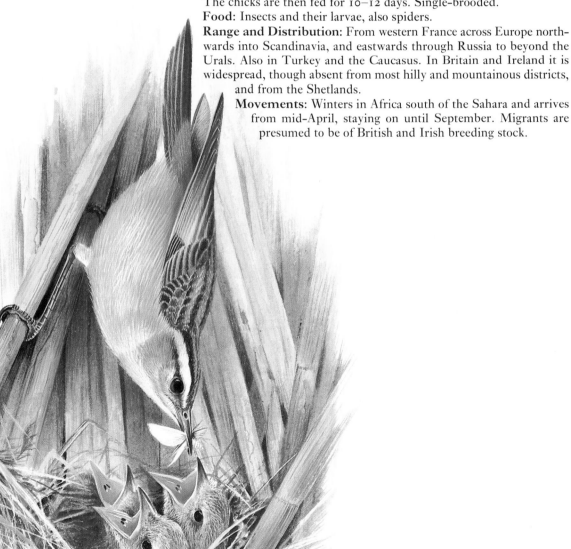

Marsh Warbler

Acrocephalus palustris (Bechstein)

A scarce summer visitor that can be distinguished from the Reed Warbler only with the greatest of care

Population: 50 to 80 pairs

Wing formula: second primary longer than fourth. Notch on second falls between fifth and sixth

Adults are olive-brown above with rump brownish or yellowish-brown, but never rufous as in the Reed Warbler. Underparts are whitish washed with creamy-buff. There is a pale indistinct supercilium. Young birds are more brown in colour with a rufous wash on the rump that makes them indistinguishable from young Reed Warblers. Even identification in the hand requires meticulous attention and measurement of wing formulae. 12.5 cm (5 in).

Voice: A strong *tchuc*. Song varied, including mimicry of a whole range of different species (over 50) which are performed to perfection. Many Reed Warbler-like sounds.

Habitat: Thickets and dense vegetation along banks of streams and ditches, also found among crops near water. Osier beds were formerly an important habitat, but are now uncut and neglected. Meadowsweet and nettles are important nest sites.

Reproduction: The nest is situated near the ground and lashed by 'handles' to the supporting stems of meadowsweet or nettle. It is a bulky structure of loose grass and plant stems lined with finer grasses and hair built mainly by the female. The 4–5 pale green-blue eggs are spotted or blotched with olive-green and incubated by both sexes for 12 days. The chicks are then fed by both parents for 10–14 days. Single-brooded.

Food: Insects and their larvae, together with spiders and, in autumn, some berries.

Range and Distribution: From northern and central France eastwards through Europe, north to southern Sweden, to the Caucasus and Russia west of the Urals. In Britain it is a decidedly scarce breeding bird. A large percentage breed in Worcestershire, but there are a few others scattered through southern England.

Movements: Arrives in May and departs in August. A vagrant away from breeding areas.

Reed Warbler

Acrocephalus scirpaceus (Hermann)

The basic marsh warbler from which other more rare species have to be distinguished

Population: 40,000 to 80,000 pairs

It is a warm brown bird above, with a noticeably rusty rump that helps to separate it from the otherwise similar Marsh Warbler. It can also be confused with Cetti's and Savi's Warblers, but easily told from the Sedge Warbler by its unstreaked back. Underparts are creamy-white, rather warmer along the flanks. The legs and feet are dark. The bill is sharply pointed and dagger-like, accentuated by a sloping forehead. There is a faint supercilium. Though other species of warbler occur in reed beds, the Reed Warbler is almost the only species confined to this habitat. 12.5 cm (5 in).

Voice: Song consists of a series of churring notes interspersed with the odd musical one – *churruc-churruc-churruc-jag-jag-jag*. Also produces a *skurr* and a *churr* as call notes.

Habitat: Predominantly reed beds, but also among rank vegetation nearby including osiers, meadowsweet and willow herb. May occur in other, even dry, areas on passage.

Reproduction: Usually breeds in loose colonies, the nest being slung around reed stems and consisting of a deep cup of reed leaves and grasses lined with softer material. The 4, occasionally 3–6, pale green eggs are heavily speckled with darker green and laid from late May onwards. Incubation, which is shared, lasts 11–12 days and the chicks are fed by both parents for a similar period. Single-brooded. Reed Warblers are one of the favourite hosts of Cuckoos.

Food: Marsh-dwelling insects and their larvae as well as spiders; in autumn may consume quantities of berries.

Range and Distribution: From the western Mediterranean, including North Africa, eastwards to southern Russia, north and south of the Caspian, to southern Siberia. In the north, it reaches southern Sweden and Finland. In Britain there has been a gradual extension westwards and northwards, but the main population breeds east of Bristol and south of Leeds.

Movements: Birds arrive from mid-April onwards and depart in late August and September. Birds observed on passage are probably mostly British with perhaps a few Continental birds here and there.

Wing formula: second primary as long as fourth. Notch on second falls above sixth

Dartford Warbler

Sylvia undata (Boddaert)

A totally resident warbler and a bird particularly vulnerable to severe winters, when its numbers may be reduced dramatically

Population: about 500 pairs, but frequently reduced to a handful

Apart from being highly localized, Dartford Warblers are also very secretive. They skulk deep in bushes and are virtually impossible to flush – indeed, often the only sign of their presence is a harsh call note. Yet in spring they may sit atop a bush in full view while singing. The male is a dark slate-grey above with a touch of rust on the wing and a long tail that it frequently holds cocked over its back. The underparts are a rich vinous chestnut marked by speckles of white on the often puffed-out chin, and fading to grey-white on the belly and undertail coverts. The eye is a piercing red. The female is similarly marked, but lighter above and below. Juveniles are buffish-brown below and, abroad, may be confused with Marmora's Warbler. In flight the wings whirr rapidly and the tail bobs up and down, but birds usually disappear into a bush fairly quickly and sustained flights are rarely seen. 12.5 cm (5 in).

Voice: Call notes are harsh and metallic – a *tchirr* and an abrupt *tuc*. Song resembles the chattering warble of a Whitethroat and is often similarly delivered in a bouncing song flight.

Habitat: Heather-covered heaths with a plentiful growth of gorse, but also in stands of pure heather if these are sufficiently mature; abroad frequents the Mediterranean maquis of dwarf shrubs and bushes on barren hillsides.

Reproduction: The nest is constructed on or near the ground among dense cover, often in gorse, and consists of a neat cup of grasses and moss, lined with hair and plant down, built mainly by the female. The male constructs insubstantial 'cock' nests. The 3–4, occasionally up to 6, white eggs are speckled with brown and laid from mid-April onwards. Incubation, by the female with some male assistance, takes 12–13 days and the chicks are fed by both parents for 11–13 days. Usually double-brooded, with an occasional third.

Food: Insects and their larvae together with spiders and some blackberries in autumn.

Range and Distribution: Confined to North Africa and western Europe from Iberia to western France, the Mediterranean coast and islands to Italy and Sicily. In Britain it is mainly to be found in Hampshire and Dorset with some numbers in Sussex and Surrey and the occasional nest elsewhere in southern England.

Movements: Resident; rare wandering individuals may have their origins in France.

Lesser Whitethroat

Sylvia curruca (Linnaeus)

An unobtrusive little warbler that skulks within dense vegetation and may be easily overlooked when silent

Population: 25,000 to 50,000 pairs

The upperparts are plain grey, marked with some brownish edges to the primaries and white outertail feathers. The Whitethroat, in contrast, has a brown back with broad rusty margins on the wing. The throat is white and the remaining underparts pinkish-cream. A black mask extends from the lores through the eye and over the ear coverts and is a diagnostic feature. The legs and feet are black, pale horn in the Whitethroat. 14 cm (5$\frac{1}{2}$ in).

Voice: Song consists of a repeated rattling on one note; call notes similar to those of Whitethroat, a hard *tac-tac* and a *charr*.

Habitat: Thick hedgerows with tall trees, copses, large gardens and conifer plantations with plenty of ground cover.

Reproduction: Does not have a song flight like the Whitethroat. The nest is usually constructed near the ground in a bush, but may be 2 metres or more up. It consists of a neat cup of twigs and grasses lined with roots and hair and is built by both members of the pair. The 4–6 white eggs are spotted with olive, laid mainly in May, and incubated by both sexes for 10–11 days. The chicks are fed by both parents for a similar period. Usually single-brooded, but an occasional second clutch may be reared.

Food: Larvae and eggs of insects including many moths, ants, spiders and even small worms. Many berries are taken in autumn.

Range and Distribution: From Britain eastwards across Europe, north to the head of the Gulf of Bothnia, and across Russia and Siberia to western China. Also southwards through Turkey to northern Iran. In Britain it is most numerous in the south and east, becoming decidedly scarce in Wales and the southwest and from Yorkshire northwards.

Movements: Arrives from late April onwards, staying through to September. Birds migrate southeastwards to winter in East Africa and the Far East. Most migrants are arriving and departing British birds. Decidedly scarce in Ireland.

Adult male

Whitethroat

Sylvia communis (Latham)

A compact warbler, most frequently found among dense hedgerows, that has declined dramatically in numbers over recent years. Female shown

Population: 500,000 to 700,000 pairs

Male has grey head, dull brown back and broadly edged rusty-brown wings. The brown tail has white outer feathers. The throat is white and often puffed out above a pale, pink-washed breast. The belly and undertail coverts are white. There is a narrow white eye-ring and the legs and feet are pale horn. The female is similar, but has a brown, not grey, head and warmer buffy underparts. Whitethroats skulk in dense cover, but much less so than the closely related Lesser Whitethroat. 14 cm (5½ in).

Voice: The song consists of a chattering uttered from a prominent perch or in a bouncing song flight; call notes include a jarring *tchurr* and a clipped *check*.

Habitat: Scrub areas of hedgerows, heaths and commons, woodland edges, conifer plantations with dense ground cover of grass and nettles.

Reproduction: The nest is built among dense vegetation, usually less than half a metre from the ground. The male constructs several rudimentary nests of grasses for the female to choose from and which she completes and lines with roots and hair. She may, however, build a fresh nest. The 4–5 eggs are pale blue or green speckled with green and grey. They are laid from early May onwards and incubated by both sexes for 11–13 days, the chicks being fed for a further 10–12 days. Double-brooded as a rule.

Food: Insects and their larvae, but ants and spiders are also taken along with fruit and berries in the autumn.

Range and Distribution: From Europe, north to central Scandinavia, and from North Africa eastwards to Turkey, Russia and central southern Siberia. In Britain and Ireland it is still a widespread breeding bird, being absent only from hilly districts, northern Scotland and much of the Outer Hebrides, Orkneys and Shetlands.

Movements: Arrives in late April, staying through to September. British and Irish birds winter in the sahel zone of Africa immediately south of the Sahara. Most passage migrants are of British and Irish origin, but some Continental birds do occur.

Garden Warbler

Sylvia borin (Boddaert)

A rather dull, uniformly grey-brown bird lacking any distinguishing features that may be confused with the warblers of the genus *Hippolais*

Population: 60,000 to 100,000 pairs.

Upperparts dull grey-brown, darker on the wings. Underparts whitish-buff. Has a *Sylvia* character, but is a somewhat bulkier bird than the typical members of the genus. The short and stubby bill separates it from the *Hippolais* warblers. This is a generally featureless bird, but it has a distinctive song. 14 cm ($5\frac{1}{2}$ in).

Voice: A *check-check* call note and a *churr*; song is a delightful warble similar to that of Blackcap, but generally quieter and lacking the higher-pitched notes of that species. Usually continues for longer, too.

Habitat: Woodland and scrub, often lacking the mature trees required by the related Blackcap, together with conifer plantations.

Reproduction: The nest is placed low in the fork of a shrub, though occasionally it can be a metre or more above the ground. It consists of a cup of grasses and moss lined with roots and hair and is built by both members of the pair. The 4–5 eggs are laid in late May or June, are white with a cast of pale buff, pink or green, blotched with darker shades of the same colour, and are incubated by both sexes for 11–12 days. The chicks are fed by both parents for 9–10 days. One, occasionally 2, broods are reared.

Food: Insects, including moth caterpillars in numbers, also worms and spiders together with many berries in autumn.

Range and Distribution: From northern Portugal eastwards across Europe, though largely avoiding the Mediterranean coast, to northern Scandinavia, Russia and the Caucasus, and central Siberia. In Britain it is widespread in the south, becoming rather thinner on the ground in Scotland. Absent from the Fens and Shetland. In Ireland it is decidedly scarce and is absent from much of the west.

Movements: Arrives from late April onwards and stays through to September. Passage migrants may be numerous on the east coast from late July to October and are doubtless of Continental origin.

Blackcap

Sylvia atricapilla (Linnaeus)

A bulky warbler that is among the easiest to identify. An exquisite songster that vies for pre-eminence with the Nightingale

Population: over 200,000 pairs

Male (left) and female

The male is grey above, darker and browner on the wings, with a distinct black crown. The underparts are pale grey becoming lighter on the belly and with a warmer wash along the flanks. The female is similar, but browner above and more buffish below, and with a distinct rust-red crown. The legs and feet are black. Juveniles are brown above and yellowish below, and males have a dark brown crown. In all plumages this species lacks the white outertail feathers that mark so many *Sylvia* warblers. In general it is an unobtrusive bird rather than a skulker, but its song frequently attracts attention. 14 cm ($5\frac{1}{2}$ in).

Voice: A sharply repeated *tac-tac* and some churring. Song is a rich warble of great variety and with many loud notes, similar to the Garden Warbler's but louder and more varied. Some regard it as even more beautiful than the Nightingale's.

Habitat: Deciduous and mixed woods with a strong underlayer of shrubs. Also found in hedgerows, thickets, coppices and gardens.

Reproduction: The nest is constructed in a bush or low down in a small tree, and consists of a neat cup of grasses built by both members of the pair and lined with roots and wool. The 5, occasionally 4 or 6, variable eggs are white, buff or pale green, spotted with similar but darker colours. They are laid in late May and incubated, from the second or third egg, by both sexes for 12–13 days. The chicks are fed by both parents for 10–14 days. Sometimes double-brooded.

Food: A wide variety of insects and their larvae, as well as significant amounts of fruit and berries whenever they are available.

Range and Distribution: From Spain and North Africa eastwards through the Mediterranean and temperate Europe, north to Scandinavia, Russia and Siberia. Also in Turkey and northern Iran. In Britain and Ireland it is widespread and numerous in England and Wales, but is becoming scarce in Scotland and is absent from most areas of the north and the Orkneys, Shetlands and Outer Hebrides except for Stornoway Castle. In Ireland it is decidedly thin on the ground and is absent from much of the west.

Movements: Birds arrive from the end of March onwards and leave through August and September. Most winter in the Mediterranean southwards into Africa, but over 2,000 may winter in Britain and Ireland, mainly in the west. There is evidence that these wintering Blackcaps are of Continental origin.

Wood Warbler

Phylloscopus sibilatrix (Bechstein)

A clean-cut yellow leaf warbler with a characteristic song and display flight

Yellowish-green upperparts, with darker wings and a tail marked with broad yellow margins. There is a strong yellowish supercilium and a darker stripe through the eye. Chin and throat are bright yellow fading to pure white on the breast, belly and undertail coverts. The legs are pale flesh-coloured. The overall yellow appearance, together with the yellow throat and white breast, make this one of the easiest of all leaf warblers to identify. 12.5 cm (5 in).

Voice: A distinct *peu* and a *whit-whit-whit*; song consists of repeated *peu* notes or a *stip-stip-stip* that is accelerated into a vibrant trill as the bird flies on fluttering wings below the canopy.

Habitat: Woodland with a thick canopy and little ground cover; numerous in the sessile oakwoods of Wales and in oaks, beeches and birches elsewhere. Sometimes also in conifers, but always mixed with deciduous trees.

Reproduction: Nests on the ground among scant cover, usually against a mound. The domed nest is built in late May, by the female alone, of grasses and dead leaves lined with hair. The 6–7 eggs are white liberally spotted with various shades of brown and are incubated by the female for 13 days. The chicks are fed by both parents for 11–12 days before fledging and for up to a month after leaving the nest. Occasionally double-brooded.

Food: Insects, their larvae and eggs picked with delicacy from among the leaves of trees; mostly small species but the caterpillars of moths are seasonally important.

Range and Distribution: From France and Italy eastwards across temperate Europe to southern Scandinavia and Russia. In the south of its range it is found at considerable altitudes in the Pyrenees, the mountains of Yugoslavia and Italy, and the Caucasus. In Britain it is most numerous in the west from Devon to Argyll, though the chalk uplands of southern England also have strong populations. Absent from much of eastern England and from the northern and western isles of Scotland. It has, however, spread northwards during the last 100 years and has colonized eastern Ireland since 1968.

Movements: Birds arrive in late April and stay through to August. As a bird of passage it is decidedly scarce at coastal observatories and most reports are assumed to be of arriving and departing British birds. Winters in tropical Africa.

Population: 30,000 to 60,000 pairs

Chiffchaff

Phylloscopus collybita (Vieillot)

Forms a species-pair with the virtually identical Willow Warbler and is best distinguished by its unique song

Population: 300,000 pairs

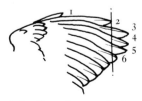

Wing formula: second primary shorter than sixth; sixth emarginated

Upperparts are olive-brown marked by a supercilium that is neither as clear nor as long as the Willow Warbler's. Underparts buffish marked with yellow on the breast. The legs and feet are usually dark, those of the Willow Warbler pale horn. Though separable by voice, and by wing formula in the hand, the Chiffchaff appears a plumper bird and generally has rather duller plumage than the Willow Warbler. 11 cm ($4\frac{1}{4}$ in).

Voice: A soft *hweet* of contact; song consists of a repetition of the 2 notes from which it is named, in random order *chiff-chaff-chiff-chiff-chaff-chaff* and so on.

Habitat: Mature deciduous or mixed woods with plentiful undergrowth. Also hedgerows, parks and heaths, and conifer plantations and coppices with some deciduous trees.

Reproduction: The domed nest is built near the ground, less frequently actually on the ground than the Willow Warbler's, of grasses, leaves and moss lined with feathers by the female alone. The 4–9 eggs are white marked with speckles and spots of brownish-purple and incubated by the female for 13–14 days. The chicks are fed, mainly by the female, for the 12–15 days they take to fledge. Double-brooded in the south.

Food: Mainly small insects, but also large quantities of moth larvae and spiders and their eggs.

Range and Distribution: Breeds right across Europe, except for southern Iberia, to northern Scandinavia, Russia and Siberia almost to the Bering Straits. Also patchily in North Africa and from northern Turkey through the Caucasus to northern Iran. In Britain and Ireland it is widespread in southern England, becoming thinner on the ground northwards and on the hills. It is absent from the Fens and over most of the Highlands and islands of Scotland.

Movements: One of the first summer visitors to arrive, from mid-March onwards; and one of the last to leave, many birds staying well into October. There is considerable passage of Continental birds in both spring and autumn and some stay on to winter each year. Most winter in the Mediterranean region.

286

Willow Warbler

Phylloscopus trochilus (Linnaeus)

Delicate little green and yellow warbler similar to the Chiffchaff and best distinguished by its song

Population: about 3 million pairs

Wing formula: second primary as long as fifth; sixth lacks emargination

Olive-brown upperparts marked by a clear supercilium that extends well beyond the eye. Underparts buffish-white washed with yellow on the breast. At all times this is a slimmer and more elegant bird than the Chiffchaff, with brighter colouring and a better-marked supercilium. The legs are usually pale horn, not black, but this is an unreliable feature on which to base identification. An active little leaf warbler that seems to be in perpetual motion feeding among vegetation. 11 cm ($4\frac{1}{4}$ in).

Voice: A quiet *hooeet* very like similar note of Chiffchaff; song is a pleasant trill of whistles on a descending scale beginning and ending quietly. Many birds sing on passage in spring.

Habitat: Less arboreal than the Chiffchaff and found in mature woodlands only in clearings and coppices. Widespread in bushy country such as heaths and commons, as well as among birches on hillsides and mountain valleys, and along streams and wet thickets. Conifer plantations are favoured in their early stages of growth.

Reproduction: Nests mostly during the first half of May. A neatly domed structure of grasses and dead leaves lined with hair is built on the ground against a hummock by the female alone. The 6–7 white eggs are spotted brown all over and are incubated by the female for 13 days. The chicks are fed by both parents for 11–12 days and for several weeks after leaving the nest. Double-brooded at least in the south.

Food: Insects and their larvae, particularly moth caterpillars; also worms and spiders and, in autumn, berries and soft fruits.

Range and Distribution: From northern Spain and western France right across Europe, except for the Mediterranean, but north to the North Cape of Norway, to Russia and northern Siberia almost to the Bering Straits. In Britain and Ireland it is abundant and is absent only from the Fens and Shetlands. Scarce in Orkney and the Outer Hebrides.

Movements: Arrives in early April and stays on into September and October. Huge numbers of birds pass through the country on their way to and from their breeding grounds to the north and east and are frequently the most numerous migrant at many coastal stations. Sometimes substantial 'falls' of birds arrive, particularly on the east coast in late August and early September.

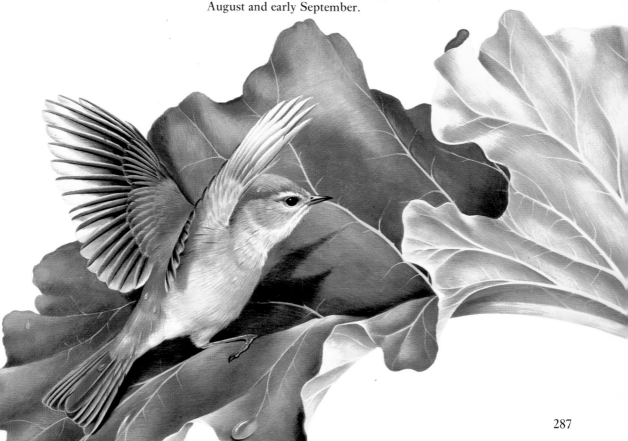

Goldcrest

Regulus regulus (Linnaeus)

The smallest British bird, a distinction shared with the much rarer and closely related Firecrest. Resembles a small leaf warbler and particularly several very rare eastern vagrants that occur in late autumn. Male (left) and female shown

Population: 1,500,000 pairs

Upperparts are olive-green. Darker wings are marked with a bold double bar and pale edges to the flight feathers. Underparts are a pale olive-buff. The crown of the male shows a distinctive slash of orange, bordered with yellow and black. There is no supercilium or other facial marking, but the eye is large and black. Females are similar, but the coronal stripe is pale yellow and lacks orange. Juveniles lack any crown markings. These are active little birds that are invariably gregarious, forming flocks that scour the canopy. They frequently hover to pick food from the underside of leaves. 9 cm ($3\frac{1}{2}$ in).

Voice: A high-pitched *tsee-tsee-tsee*; song consists of the repetition of a thin double note ending in a flourish *steeng-steeng-steeng-stichipi-steeng*. The call note is very similar to that of Coal Tit and Treecreeper.

Habitat: Mainly frequents coniferous woods, though it will spread into deciduous woods when the population is high, and is found among sessile oaks in Wales and especially in Ireland.

Reproduction: The nest is suspended from the outer branch of a conifer, is cup-shaped, and constructed of moss and spiders' webs lined with feathers. It is built by both members of the pair in late April and the 7–10, occasionally up to 13, whitish eggs are speckled with buff-brown at the larger end. They are incubated by the female for 14–17 days and both sexes share in feeding the chicks for 16–21 days. Double-brooded.

Food: Mainly insects, their larvae and eggs, together with spiders and their eggs.

Range and Distribution: From the mountain regions of Spain eastwards through Europe to Scandinavia and northern Russia. South of this it is a bird of mountains (conifer areas) in Italy, Yugoslavia and Greece, northern Turkey and the Caucasus. Also breeds in central Siberia and the Himalayas and in Japan. In Britain and Ireland it is widespread and has prospered as a result of increasing reafforestation with conifers. Has recently colonized Shetland and the Isles of Scilly.

Movements: Mostly resident in Britain and Ireland, but numbers are augmented with influxes of Continental birds in autumn, most of which pass through southwards to winter elsewhere.

Firecrest

Regulus ignicapillus (Temminck)

Jointly with the Goldcrest, Britain's smallest bird, and a regular breeder in variable numbers since 1962.
Male (right) and female shown

Population: less than 100 pairs

Continental breeding distribution

Very similar to the Goldcrest; upperparts olive-green marked with light margins to flight feathers and a bold, white double wing bar. There is a diffuse patch of pale chestnut above the bend of the wing and the crown is bright orange-red, edged with black. This coronal stripe is yellow in the female. A bold white supercilium, a black eye-stripe, and a thin moustachial streak combine to produce a face pattern that is quite distinct from the unmarked face of the Goldcrest; and the grey-white underparts combine with other features to produce a much more contrasting effect. This is a similarly active bird, however, flitting and hovering among foliage when feeding. It has colonized Britain from 1962 onwards. 9 cm ($3\frac{1}{2}$ in).

Voice: High-pitched *zit-zit*, similar to call of Goldcrest; song is repetition of *zit* notes becoming more rapid and terminating suddenly. Once learned it is easily distinguished from song of Goldcrest with its flourishing end.

Habitat: A wide variety of conifer woods, often alongside the Goldcrest. In Britain it favours Norwegian spruce, but is also found among other conifers as well as in deciduous woods with yew and holly.

Reproduction: Nests in similar sites to Goldcrest over most of Europe, but in Britain also among ivy on tree trunks and in forks of conifers. The nest is a tightly woven cup of mosses and spiders' webs and the 7–12 white eggs, often with a pink wash, are speckled with a darker, but similar, colour. They are laid in May and incubated by the female for 14–15 days. The chicks are fed by both parents for 19–20 days. Generally double-brooded.

Food: Insects, their larvae and eggs, also spiders and their eggs.

Range and Distribution: Breeds in North America in western and eastern Canada and the United States, these areas being separated by the coniferless plains of the prairies, and in southern Mexico and adjacent states of Central America. In Europe it ranges from Spain to the Russian border and is also found in North Africa and Turkey. In Britain it was first proved to breed in the New Forest in 1962 and has since spread to several areas of England south of a line drawn from the Wash to the Severn. In some areas it is locally abundant and may easily be overlooked elsewhere.

Movements: British birds arrive on their breeding grounds in late April and depart in July, though they may not leave the country. Passage of Continental birds is apparent, especially on the south coast in autumn, though in small numbers. A few birds overwinter.

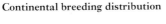

Spotted Flycatcher

Muscicapa striata (Pallas)

A small, upright-perching brown bird that makes repeated sallies after flying insects, invariably returning to the same perch

Population: 100,000 to 200,000 pairs

Leaden-brown upperparts marked on the crown with flecks of buff and with buff margins to the wing feathers. The tail is dark and neatly forked and the long wings are particularly apparent in flight. The underparts are buffish-white, neatly streaked on the throat and breast with dark brown. Though similar to female and immature Pied Flycatchers, the streaked breast and absence of white in the wings are diagnostic. Generally confiding, it perches quite openly to watch for aerial insects, which it takes often with an audible snap of its bill before returning to the same perch. 14 cm (5½ in).

Voice: Song consists of a short series of squeaky notes *sip-sip-sreet-sreet-sip*; call is a thin *tzee*. But it is not a very vocal bird.

Habitat: Woodland edges and glades, hedgerows, parkland, gardens and farmyards.

Reproduction: The nest is usually against a tree or building and is supported by ivy or similar vegetation, but can also be on ledges, branches, in open holes and specially erected open-fronted nest boxes. It is constructed of grasses and lined with feathers, hair and leaves. Both sexes participate, though the female does most of the work. The 4−5 pale blue or green eggs are blotched with red-brown and laid in the second half of May or in June. Incubation, by the female, lasts 11−15 days and she alone feeds the chicks for the first few days of their lives on food collected by the male. As they grow larger both parents participate in feeding. Fledging takes 12−14 days, but the young are fed for a similar (or even longer) period after leaving the nest. Single-brooded, with an occasional second clutch.

Food: Mainly small flies taken in flight, but also other flying insects.

Range and Distribution: Throughout Europe, except for the Scandinavian mountain chain, eastwards through Russia, Turkey and Iran to central Asia. Also in North Africa. In Britain and Ireland it breeds throughout the country except for some of the higher hills and the Outer Hebrides, Orkneys and Shetlands where breeding is at best sporadic.

Movements: Birds arrive in late April and are present into September. Though most coastal records are probably of British and Irish birds there is undoubtedly a passage of Continental birds, especially on the east coast in autumn.

Takes readily to an open-fronted nest box

Regularly returns to original perch after aerial sally

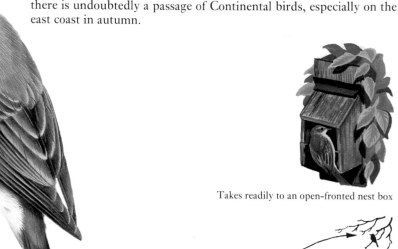

Pied Flycatcher

Ficedula hypoleuca (Pallas)

A neat black and white flycatcher that has expanded its range in Britain in recent years. Summer males are easily identified, winter males, females and juveniles may pose a problem

Population: about 20,000 pairs

In summer the male is black above marked only by a white forehead and an extensive patch of silvery-white in the wing. The underparts are pure white. The female, juvenile and winter male are brown above with blackish wings marked by less extensive areas of white. The underparts are dull white with a buffish wash on the breast. In all plumages the white in the wing and lack of streaking on the breast are sufficient to distinguish this bird from the Spotted Flycatcher. The Collared Flycatcher is similar, but has a white collar and rump in the male and, in all plumages, more extensive white on the wings. It is a very rare vagrant to Britain. 13 cm (5 in).

Voice: A high-pitched *whit* and a repeated *tic*; song is a pleasant 2-part call *zee-it, zee-it* followed by a brief trill.

Habitat: Deciduous woods, particularly with sessile oaks, usually near running water, in the valleys of hilly districts.

Reproduction: Birds tend to breed in loose colonies and the nest is situated in a hole, usually in a tree and often the old nest of a woodpecker. It may, however, be in a hole in a wall, or in a nest box. The nest itself is a loose cup of grasses, leaves, moss and lichens lined with hair and built by the female alone. The 4–7 pale blue eggs, occasionally with a few brown speckles, are laid in late May and incubated by the female for 12–13 days. The chicks are fed by both parents, though the female plays the dominant role. Single-brooded.

Food: Predominantly flying insects, but also moth caterpillars, ants and even worms. Takes berries in autumn.

Range and Distribution: Nests over much of Iberia, as well as in North Africa, but is absent from large areas of France and from Italy and southeast Europe. Extends from the Alps and Germany across northern temperate Europe to Scandinavia, northern Russia and Siberia. In Britain it is almost confined to the north and west with only a handful of pairs east of a line drawn from the Severn to the Humber. In Wales it is abundant, but in Scotland, though increasing, it is still thinly distributed and is absent from most of the islands.

Movements: Arrives in May and stays through to August. It is one of the most typical members of the arrivals of Scandinavian night migrants on the east coast in autumn.

Makes use of ordinary 'hole' nest boxes

Seldom returns to same perch after catching insect

Long-tailed Tit

Aegithalos caudatus (Linnaeus)

A tiny, gregarious, black and white bird with well over half its length consisting of an extremely long tail

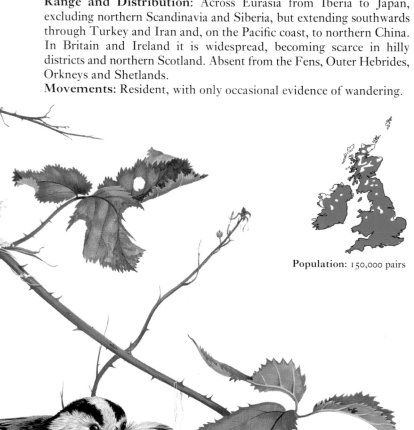

The back is black bordered by a band of deep vinous pink across the folded wing. The inner flight feathers are broadly edged white, creating a parallel bold panel. The tail is black, but the white outer webs give it a distinctly pied look. The black of the back extends to the nape and over the sides of the white crown. The underparts are white with a vinous pink wash on the belly and undertail coverts. The bill is stubby and, like the feet and legs, black. Long-tailed Tits are gregarious, usually forming single-species flocks that call continuously as they work their way through wood or hedgerow. In flight they appear as rotund little birds with the extremely long tail almost an appendage. 14 cm (5½ in).

Voice: A thin *zee-zee-zee* and a characteristic *tupp*; song consists of call notes repeated rapidly with a bubbling quality.

Habitat: Woods, hedgerows, heaths and scrub.

Reproduction: The nest is usually placed near the outside of a gorse or thorn bush, but also among brambles or high up in a tree, and consists of a ball of mosses and lichens with a hole near the top. It is constructed by both sexes and lined with feathers. The 8–12, occasionally up to 16, white eggs are sometimes speckled with reddish and are laid in late March or early April. Incubation, which is performed mainly by the female, takes 12–14 days and the chicks are fed by both parents for 14–18 days. Sometimes extra birds will participate in the nesting routine, and territory is a group, rather than an individual or pair, phenomenon. Usually single-brooded.

Food: Insects, their larvae and eggs, also spiders and some seeds.

Range and Distribution: Across Eurasia from Iberia to Japan, excluding northern Scandinavia and Siberia, but extending southwards through Turkey and Iran and, on the Pacific coast, to northern China. In Britain and Ireland it is widespread, becoming scarce in hilly districts and northern Scotland. Absent from the Fens, Outer Hebrides, Orkneys and Shetlands.

Movements: Resident, with only occasional evidence of wandering.

Population: 150,000 pairs

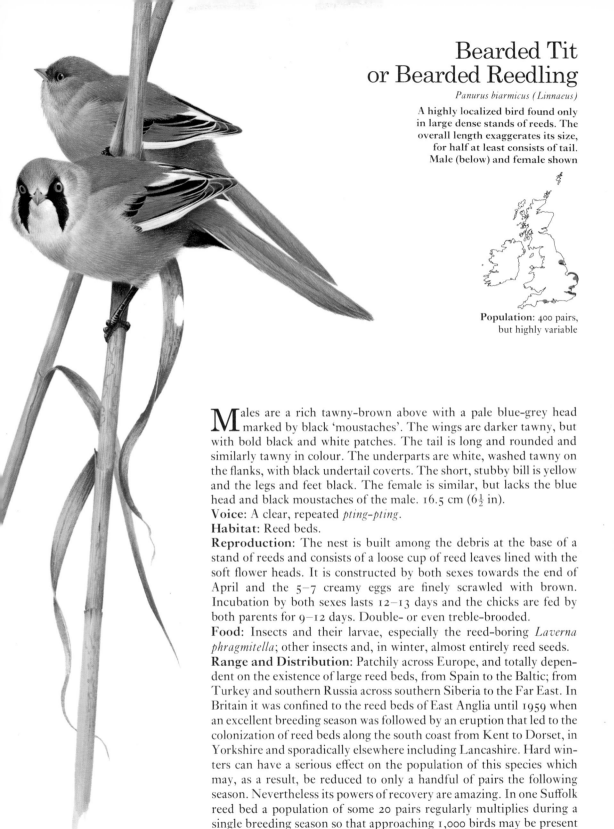

Bearded Tit
or Bearded Reedling

Panurus biarmicus (Linnaeus)

A highly localized bird found only in large dense stands of reeds. The overall length exaggerates its size, for half at least consists of tail. Male (below) and female shown

Population: 400 pairs, but highly variable

Males are a rich tawny-brown above with a pale blue-grey head marked by black 'moustaches'. The wings are darker tawny, but with bold black and white patches. The tail is long and rounded and similarly tawny in colour. The underparts are white, washed tawny on the flanks, with black undertail coverts. The short, stubby bill is yellow and the legs and feet black. The female is similar, but lacks the blue head and black moustaches of the male. 16.5 cm (6½ in).

Voice: A clear, repeated *pting-pting*.

Habitat: Reed beds.

Reproduction: The nest is built among the debris at the base of a stand of reeds and consists of a loose cup of reed leaves lined with the soft flower heads. It is constructed by both sexes towards the end of April and the 5–7 creamy eggs are finely scrawled with brown. Incubation by both sexes lasts 12–13 days and the chicks are fed by both parents for 9–12 days. Double- or even treble-brooded.

Food: Insects and their larvae, especially the reed-boring *Laverna phragmitella*; other insects and, in winter, almost entirely reed seeds.

Range and Distribution: Patchily across Europe, and totally dependent on the existence of large reed beds, from Spain to the Baltic; from Turkey and southern Russia across southern Siberia to the Far East. In Britain it was confined to the reed beds of East Anglia until 1959 when an excellent breeding season was followed by an eruption that led to the colonization of reed beds along the south coast from Kent to Dorset, in Yorkshire and sporadically elsewhere including Lancashire. Hard winters can have a serious effect on the population of this species which may, as a result, be reduced to only a handful of pairs the following season. Nevertheless its powers of recovery are amazing. In one Suffolk reed bed a population of some 20 pairs regularly multiplies during a single breeding season so that approaching 1,000 birds may be present in late summer. Doubtless it is this ability to produce young that triggers off the eruptive movements that have become such a feature of recent years.

Movements: Resident, but irruptions in good autumns bring Continental birds from Holland and elsewhere, and send our native birds off on journeys westwards to reed beds where they do not breed, but which they may thus colonize.

Marsh Tit

Parus palustris (Linnaeus)

A dully coloured, black-capped tit, very similar to the Willow Tit and best distinguished by its voice

Population: 70,000 to 140,000 pairs

Dull buff-brown upperparts marked by a black cap that extends over the eye to the nape and which is glossy rather than matt black as in the Willow Tit. Underparts a dirty grey washed on the flanks with buff; it has white cheeks and a tiny black bib. The Willow Tit has a more extensive black chin and a white patch in the folded wing. Marsh Tits join the mixed flocks of tits and other species that scour the woods and hedgerows in winter and will also join in and feed alongside other species at bird tables. 11.5 cm (4½ in).

Voice: A distinctive *pitchoo-pitchoo*; song variable, but often an extension of the call *pitchaweeoo*.

Habitat: The name is somewhat misleading, for it frequents deciduous woodland and hedgerows.

Reproduction: Pairing takes place in late winter and territories are established by calling in February or March. The nest is a hole that may be chipped away, but it is not excavated as is the Willow Tit's. It consists of a cup of moss lined with hair and feathers, and is built by the female alone. The 6–9, occasionally up to 11, eggs are white with spots of brown and are incubated by the female for 13–17 days. The chicks are fed by both parents for 16–21 days. Single- or double-brooded.

Food: Insects and their larvae; but also weed seeds and a variety of berries in winter.

Range and Distribution: From northern Spain through Europe as far north as southern Scandinavia, eastwards to Russia as far as the Urals. Also in western Turkey and in the Caucasus. A separate population exists in the east in Japan, Manchuria and northern China. In Britain it is confined to England, Wales and the Scottish Borders. It is nevertheless absent from the Fens, the Lake District, parts of Lancashire and western Wales including Anglesey. Absent also from Ireland and the Isle of Man.

Movements: Resident.

Separated from similar Willow Tit by having shiny black cap and by call note

Willow Tit

Parus montanus (van Baldenstein)

Closely resembles the Marsh Tit, with similar dull coloration and black cap

Population: 50,000 to 100,000 pairs

Dull, not glossy, black cap and pale wing panel

Buff-brown upperparts marked with a dull, not shiny, black cap extending over the eye to the nape. The white outer margins to the flight feathers form a clear pale panel on the closed wing that is never prominent in the Marsh Tit. Underparts a dull greyish-white with a warm wash of buff on the flanks, and a black bib on the chin that is considerably larger than the similar mark of the Marsh Tit. At all times the voice is the clearest and simplest means of separating the 2 species. 11.5 cm ($4\frac{1}{2}$ in).

Voice: A buzzing *eez-eez-eez*, also a thin *zi-zi-zi* and a *tchay*. Song, which is rarely heard, consists of a liquid warble that has even been likened to that of the Nightingale.

Habitat: Despite the names of the species, the Willow Tit is much more commonly found in damp and wet places than the Marsh Tit. In part this is accounted for by the Willow Tit's need for old and rotten timber in which to excavate its nest, but where such timber is found in dry deciduous woods it will readily occupy them. Willow, birch and alder woods are commonly occupied as well as hedgerows and, in northern Europe, mature spruce forests.

Reproduction: Nests in a sufficiently rotten soft tree or stump to enable the female to excavate her own hole. So crucial is this factor that ingenious bird gardeners have persuaded the species to breed in nest boxes filled with expanded polystyrene which can then be removed by the bird. The nest itself consists of little more than a lining of hair with a few feathers. The 6–9, occasionally up to 13, white eggs are speckled with brown and laid in late April and early May. Incubation, by the female alone, lasts 13–15 days and the chicks are fed by both parents for 17–19 days. Single-brooded.

Food: Insects and their larvae, spiders and some berries.

Range and Distribution: From central France eastwards across non-Mediterranean Europe northwards to northern Scandinavia, to Russia, Siberia and Japan. In Britain it is widespread in England and Wales extending northwards to southern Scotland. It is absent from the Fens, north Wales and Anglesey, northern Lancashire, the Isle of Man and totally from Ireland.

Movements: Resident.

Coal Tit

Parus ater (Linnaeus)

A distinctive little bird most abundant in conifers, but which also frequents other woods and comes readily to bird tables

Population: about 1 million pairs

Slate blue-grey upperparts with 2 white wing bars, and white tips to the inner flight feathers. The head is glossy black with a prominent white nape patch that is the most significant field mark. The cheeks are white and enclosed by a large black bib. The remaining underparts are dirty white, washed on the flanks with dull buff. It is a gregarious little bird that is often numerous among mixed tit flocks. 11.5 cm ($4\frac{1}{2}$ in).

Voice: A high-pitched *tsee-tsee-tsee*; song is similar to the Great Tit's and consists of 2 notes *tsee-choo, tsee-choo*.

Habitat: Coniferous and deciduous woods, and gardens with clumps of decorative trees.

Reproduction: The nest is in a tree hole, in a hole in the ground or bank among tree roots, or in a nest box. It consists of a neat cup of moss bound together with spiders' webs and lined with hair and feathers. It is built by the female in late April and the 7–9, occasionally up to 12, white eggs are speckled with rusty-brown. The female alone performs the incubation for 14–18 days and the chicks are fed by both parents for 16–19 days, and thereafter for a further 14 days or so. Generally double-brooded.

Food: Insects and their larvae, and spiders; also seeds, and food scraps and peanuts put out in gardens.

Range and Distribution: Found right across Europe except for some areas of the Mediterranean coast and the mountains and extreme north of Scandinavia. Also in a huge sweep across Russia and Siberia to the eastern Himalayas, China and Japan, as well as in isolated pockets in northern Iran, Turkey and North Africa. In Britain and Ireland it is widespread and numerous, but is absent from the Outer Hebrides, Orkneys and Shetlands, and from the Fens.

Movements: Resident; Continental birds occasionally 'invade' southern England, and a few may appear every year.

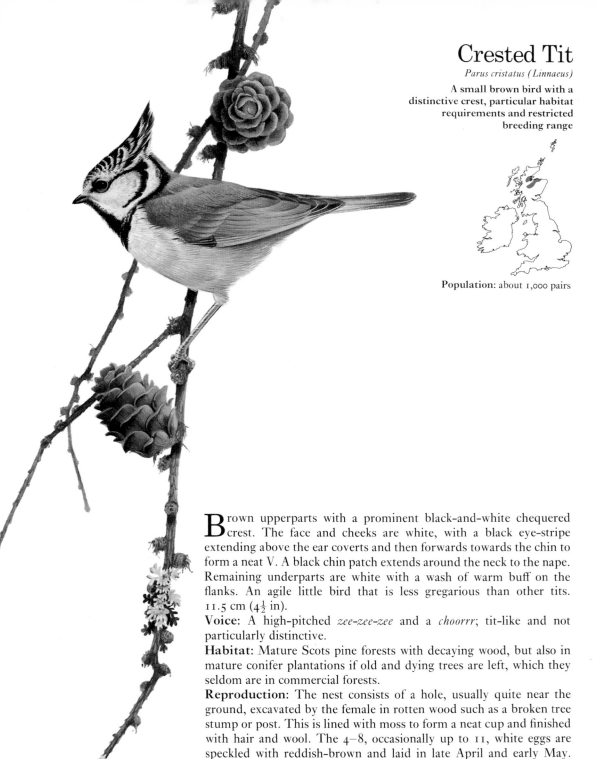

Crested Tit

Parus cristatus (Linnaeus)

A small brown bird with a
distinctive crest, particular habitat
requirements and restricted
breeding range

Population: about 1,000 pairs

Brown upperparts with a prominent black-and-white chequered crest. The face and cheeks are white, with a black eye-stripe extending above the ear coverts and then forwards towards the chin to form a neat V. A black chin patch extends around the neck to the nape. Remaining underparts are white with a wash of warm buff on the flanks. An agile little bird that is less gregarious than other tits. 11.5 cm (4½ in).

Voice: A high-pitched *zee-zee-zee* and a *choorrr*; tit-like and not particularly distinctive.

Habitat: Mature Scots pine forests with decaying wood, but also in mature conifer plantations if old and dying trees are left, which they seldom are in commercial forests.

Reproduction: The nest consists of a hole, usually quite near the ground, excavated by the female in rotten wood such as a broken tree stump or post. This is lined with moss to form a neat cup and finished with hair and wool. The 4–8, occasionally up to 11, white eggs are speckled with reddish-brown and laid in late April and early May. Incubation, by the female alone, takes 13–18 days and the chicks are fed by the female with food brought at first by the male and later with food that she helps to gather herself. Fledging takes a further 17–21 days. Usually single-brooded.

Food: Insects and their larvae; also pine seeds and berries.

Range and Distribution: From Iberia right across Europe to Russia as far as the Urals; southwards into Greece and northwards to central Scandinavia. In Britain it is confined to the Scottish Highlands and, in particular, to old forests north and south of the Caledonian Canal. Some increase and spread noted in recent years.

Movements: Resident, and thus little chance of birds colonizing the now extensive areas of conifers that exist throughout the country.

The back is a deep green, with blue wings heavily edged and barred with white. The crown and nape are bright blue, bordered with white and black bands that encircle the head to join the black bib and black eye-stripe. The cheeks are white. The remaining underparts are yellow broken on the central belly by a narrow vertical black mark. Blue Tits are gregarious and frequently gather together with other species into sizeable flocks that roam the woods and hedgerows. They take readily to gardens and are invariably the most numerous species at feeding stations. 11.5 cm (4½ in).

Voice: A high-pitched *tsee-tsee-tsee* is the usual call note and, followed by a trill, constitutes the song. Also has a characteristic *churr* note.

Habitat: Deciduous woods, hedgerows, orchards, large gardens, parks, bushy thickets, suburbs, indeed virtually anywhere with trees.

Reproduction: Nests in holes in trees, walls or in nest boxes. The hole is lined with moss and a neat cup formed and lined with hair and feathers by the female. The 7–12, occasionally up to 16, white eggs are speckled with reddish-brown and laid in early May. The female performs the incubation which lasts 12–16 days, though she is fed on the nest by the male. The chicks are fed by both parents for 15–23 days. The timing of nesting in this species depends on the appearance of abundant small green moth caterpillars on which the chicks are fed. Single-brooded as a rule.

Food: Insects and their larvae as well as spiders and millipedes; also fruit and berries, seeds, buds and food provided by man.

Range and Distribution: From Iberia and North Africa to central Scandinavia, Russia as far as the Urals, Turkey, the Caucasus and Iran. In Britain and Ireland it is widespread and is absent only from the Scottish hills and the far north, the Orkneys, Shetlands and most of the Outer Hebrides.

Movements: Resident, but with some winter wandering. Immigrants from the Continent arrive in varying numbers in autumn, with the occasional invasion in heavy numbers.

Population: over 5 million pairs

Blue Tit

Parus caeruleus (Linnaeus)

One of the most common and familiar of British and Irish birds with an ability to live easily alongside man. Readily identifiable by its blue and yellow plumage

Great Tit

Parus major (Linnaeus)

Largest of the tits and a widespread and numerous bird virtually throughout the country. Usually the most aggressive species at bird-table feeding stations

Population: over 3 million pairs

A dark bottle-green back marked on the wings with white edges to the inner flight feathers and a bold white wing bar. The base of the tail is blue and the tail itself black with white outer feathers. The crown is shiny black extending from the nape to enclose white cheeks and join a black bib. The remaining underparts are bright yellow divided down the centre of the breast by a broad black line extending from the bib. The sexes are similar, but the black chest line broadens out between the legs of the male quite noticeably. Great Tits are gregarious in winter and common members of mixed tit flocks in woods and hedgerows. They will come readily to bird tables and dominate the other tits at peanut baskets. 14 cm ($5\frac{1}{2}$ in).

Voice: Remarkably varied with up to 57 distinct calls described. Song consists of a 'saw-sharpening' *tee-choo, tee-choo*; also a *pink-pink* Chaffinch-like call; a *tchair-tchair*; and a *chi-chi-chi*.

Habitat: Deciduous woods of all types and also coniferous forests; frequently feeds on the ground and found in farms, hedgerows, parks, gardens and scrub.

Reproduction: The nest is a hole in a tree or wall, or in a nest box. It is lined by the female with moss, grass and hair, and the 8–13, occasionally up to 15, white eggs are speckled with reddish-purple and laid in late April or early May. Incubation, by the female alone, takes 13–14 days, sometimes up to 22 days, and the chicks are fed by both parents for 16–22 days. Single-brooded as a rule.

Food: Insects and their larvae, moths and bees, also spiders and worms; takes many berries and fruit seeds in winter and attacks buds in spring.

Range and Distribution: Huge range from Iberia and North Africa to northern Scandinavia, eastwards across Europe, Russia, Siberia, the Middle East, India, Java and Borneo to Japan. In Britain and Ireland it breeds everywhere except for the Scottish hills and the extreme north, and is absent from the Orkneys, Shetlands and Outer Hebrides except for Stornoway Castle since 1966.

Movements: Resident, but with some winter wandering. Continental immigrants arrive in the south and east in varying numbers, sometimes being abundant and at other times virtually absent.

Treecreeper

Certhia familiaris (Linnaeus)

An aptly named little bird that is immediately recognizable by its mottled brown plumage and tree-creeping habits

Population: 150,000 to 300,000 pairs

Striped dark brown and cream-buff upperparts with a prominent series of bars across the wing. The rump is rusty and the tail somewhat ragged and noticeably rounded. A bold white supercilium and a thin, decurved, probing bill are characteristic. Treecreepers climb with great agility upwards around the trunks of trees picking food here and there from bark crevices. When they have fully explored the feeding possibilities of one tree they drop down to the foot of an adjacent one and start over again. Though their calls draw attention to them, they are easily overlooked, and will frequently move behind a tree trunk when suspicious of an intruder. They also 'freeze' and are then virtually invisible. 12.5 cm (5 in).

Voice: A thin *tsee* contact note; song similar to call note but repeated and accelerated, *tsee-tsee-tsee-tsssi-tsee*.

Habitat: Coniferous woods on the Continent, but also deciduous woods in Britain. Indeed, it is more common in deciduous woods because of their greater age and the availability of nest sites. Also in tall hedgerows, parks and gardens.

Reproduction: The nest is placed in a tree crevice, behind loose bark, or among the broken debris of a tree trunk, though also in a stone wall, or the plank walls of a shed. It consists of a neat cup of twigs and grasses lined with bark and wool and the 6, sometimes 3–9, white eggs are speckled with red-brown and laid in April. Incubation by the female lasts 14–15 days and the chicks are fed by both parents for a similar period. Double-brooded.

Food: Insects and their larvae, spiders and their eggs.

Range and Distribution: Inhabits the boreal and alpine zones from the Pyrenees eastwards across Eurasia to Japan, with extensions southwards to the Caucasus and Himalayas. It is also found over large areas of North America from Alaska to Mexico and Newfoundland, where it is known as the Brown Creeper. In Britain and Ireland it is widespread and found in most wooded areas. It is thus absent only from the Fens, Orkneys, Shetlands and Outer Hebrides, except for Stornoway Woods which was colonized in 1962.

Movements: Resident. A handful of records of Continental birds at island bird observatories.

Nuthatch

Sitta europaea (Linnaeus)

Brightly coloured and tree-clinging like a woodpecker, the Nuthatch climbs as easily downwards as it does up

Population: about 20,000 pairs

Fine dove-grey upperparts with black primaries and white corners to the tips of the short square tail. There is a bold black eye-stripe. Chin and throat are whitish becoming heavily washed with orange-buff on chest and belly. The bill is thick, but sharply pointed, and the legs and feet strong and sharp-clawed. The Nuthatch feeds on the trunks and major limbs of large trees, clambering with great agility in every direction. Its name derives from 'nut-hack', a reference to its ability to break open nuts by hacking them with its bill after wedging them in a tree fork or crevice. 14 cm ($5\frac{1}{2}$ in).

Voice: A clear, ringing whistle *chwit-chwit-chwit*; a loud *twee* repeated several times; and a *pee-pee-pee-pee-pee*.

Habitat: Deciduous and mixed woods with old mature trees, also in hedgerows, gardens and parks similarly endowed.

Reproduction: Nests in a tree hole, old woodpecker hole or nest box, but in all cases insists on plastering the entrance hole with mud even where it is already the correct size. The nest itself is no more than a few chips of wood, bark and dead leaves. The 6–9, occasionally up to 13, white eggs are speckled with reddish-brown and laid in early May. Incubation by the female takes 14–18 days and the chicks are fed by both parents for 23–25 days. One brood, with sometimes a second.

Food: Insects and their larvae, but also large quantities of hazel nuts, beechmast, acorns and seeds. In recent years Nuthatches have learned to come to bird tables, even in suburban areas, where they compete for food with the resident tits and Starlings with considerable success.

Range and Distribution: Throughout Europe except on Corsica, where a separate species occurs, north to central Scandinavia and eastwards across the Palearctic to the Bering Straits. Also in North Africa, Turkey and the Caucasus, and India northwards and eastwards through China to Japan and Manchuria. In Britain it is widespread in the south and Wales, becoming scarcer further north as far as the Scottish border. Absent from the Isle of Man and Ireland.

Movements: Resident, with Continental birds being only exceptionally recorded.

Golden Oriole

Oriolus oriolus (Linnaeus)

A delightful black and yellow woodland bird that, despite its bright colouring, would be easily overlooked were it not for its distinctive fluty song. Scarce bird of passage in spring that regularly stays on to breed in small numbers

Continental breeding distribution: breeds in England every year in small numbers

Female

Male is golden-yellow on head, back and underparts with black wings and a black tail broadly tipped with yellow. The bill is bright red, the legs and feet black. The female is more soberly coloured in yellow-greens. This is a bird of mature woodland that is easily overlooked among the leaves of the canopy. Its clear far-carrying call is distinctive. 24 cm (9½ in).

Voice: A flute-like *weela-weeo*.

Habitat: Mature woodland, deciduous or mixed, seldom in stands of pure conifers.

Reproduction: The nest is slung between the branches of a horizontal fork high in a large tree. It is built by the female of grasses and consists of a neat cup bound to the supporting branches and lined with plant down and wool. The 3–4, occasionally up to 6, white eggs are washed pinkish and spotted with black. They are laid from May onwards and incubated mainly by the female for 14–15 days. The chicks are fed by both parents for a similar period. Usually single-brooded.

Food: Insects and their larvae in summer, but much fruit at other times of the year.

Range and Distribution: Breeds right across Europe north to Denmark and southern Finland, eastwards to central Siberia and south to India. In Britain it is a regular spring migrant to southern England that breeds in very small numbers most years. It has recently bred in East Anglia regularly, and for the first time in Scotland in 1974.

Movements: Migrates southwards and southwestwards to winter in tropical Africa and India.

302

Red-backed Shrike

Lanius collurio (Linnaeus)

An attractively marked, somewhat voracious bird that is fast disappearing as a British breeding species, though it may well be colonizing the north. Male (right) and female shown

Population: less than 50 pairs

The male is a fine dove-grey on crown, nape and rump. The back is chestnut-red shading to brown on the folded wing. The tail is long, black and marked by white bases to the outer feathers. A prominent black mask extends from the lores through the eye to the ear coverts, bordered above and below with white. The bill is stubby, but quite definitely hooked. While the same shape, the female is camouflaged in various shades of cream and brown, with particularly noticeable barring on the breast and flanks. Like other members of the family, these shrikes frequently impale their prey on thorns or barbed wire to form a larder of reserve food. 17 cm ($6\frac{3}{4}$ in).

Voice: A harsh *chack-chack* is the most common call note, but there are many others; the song is a discrete warble incorporating harsh notes and considerable mimicry.

Habitat: Commons, heaths and other bushy ground with thorns and gorse; also neglected gardens, orchards and parks.

Reproduction: The nest consists of a large cup of grasses lined with hair and wool, situated, usually in a thorn, some 1–3 metres from the ground. The 5–6 eggs are laid in late May and are remarkably variable both in ground colour and markings. They may be greenish, pinkish, buffish or virtually white and marked with brown, olive, red or purple. Incubation, predominantly by the female, lasts 14–16 days, and the chicks are fed by both parents for 12–16 days, though initially the male provides most of the food for the female to distribute. Single-brooded, though replacement clutches are not unknown.

Food: Mainly insects such as moths, mantises and particularly grasshoppers; but also a wide range of other creatures including birds up to Yellowhammer in size, small mammals, and amphibians and reptiles.

Range and Distribution: From northern Spain right across temperate Europe and Eurasia as far as Japan and China. It breeds northwards to southern Sweden and through much of Mediterranean Europe to Turkey and Iran. In Britain it has suffered a dramatic decline in recent years. Most pairs are to be found in the Brecks and coastal East Anglia with a smaller concentration in the New Forest. There is growing evidence of a colonization of Scotland by Scandinavian birds.

Movements: Arrives in May, staying through to September. Winters in East and southern Africa and can be found on passage, mainly in autumn, on the east and south coasts.

Great Grey Shrike

Lanius excubitor (Linnaeus)

Large grey and black bird that is a winter visitor to Britain. It perches upright and openly atop a bush watching for its prey

Crown and back a dull dove-grey; wings black with bold white marking; tail long, rounded and black broadly edged with white. A broad black eye-stripe extends from the large, hooked bill to the ear coverts, forming a characteristic mask that does not extend to the forehead as in the rarer Lesser Grey Shrike. The underparts are white, but tinged with pink in the Mediterranean form and in the Lesser Grey. As with many other shrikes, the Great Grey is a voracious hunter, pouncing on a variety of creatures from its bush-top watchpoint. The sexes are similar. 24 cm ($9\frac{1}{2}$ in).

Voice: Harsh *sheck-sheck* of alarm; song consists of a quiet warbling broken by harsh notes and some mimicry. This species is rarely heard in Britain in winter.

Habitat: Open heaths with scattered trees, hedgerows, commons; in breeding season frequents wooded country more than other shrikes.

Reproduction: The nest is a large cup of grasses and twigs placed at variable height in a bush or tree. The 5–7, occasionally up to 9, white eggs are laid in April, May or June according to latitude. They are washed with green or buff and speckled with reddish-brown. During the 15 days of incubation the female plays the dominant role, though the male frequently feeds her on the nest. The chicks are fed on food brought by the male for the first few days, thereafter by both parents. They leave the nest after 19–20 days. Single-brooded.

Food: Predominantly small birds, but occasionally up to Blackbird in size. Also small mammals, amphibians, reptiles and insects. Creates a larder of stored prey on thorns, even in winter.

Range and Distribution: A remarkably successful species that breeds in the temperate and boreal zones right around the Northern Hemisphere including North America, where it is called the Northern Shrike. In the Old World it breeds from northernmost Scandinavia to the southern Sahara and in northern India, but is absent from Britain and Ireland as a breeding bird.

Movements: Continental birds move into eastern Britain from mid-October onwards, many staying through till March or April. Most are confined to the east from Shetland to Kent, but some move westwards even reaching Ireland on occasion. Never numerous, but often regular at certain favoured locations year after year.

Population: a few hundred winter

Continental breeding distribution

Jay

Garrulus glandarius (Linnaeus)

A large, noisy woodland bird that can be remarkably self-effacing on occasion. Most often seen in flight when its characteristic shape and laboured wing-flapping are easily recognizable

Population: about 100,000 pairs

Vinous pink body becoming vinous grey on the back, with rounded black wings and long black tail. The wings are marked with white shafts to the primaries, white patches on the secondaries and bright blue- and black-barred primary coverts. The crown is streaked black and forms an erectile crest, and there is a bold black moustachial patch. The bill is stout and the legs long and strong. In flight it shows a prominent square white rump. Jays are usually encountered singly or in pairs, though in early spring large, noisy parties may career through the woods. 34 cm ($13\frac{1}{2}$ in).

Voice: A harsh, far-carrying *skraak*; also various other harsh notes including a *keeuw*, and a quiet, seldom heard warbling song.

Habitat: Woodland of all sorts, but particularly fond of oak woods. Also found in parks, gardens and even in the centres of large cities.

Reproduction: The nest is a neat cup of twigs and mud placed in the fork of a tree in late April or early May. It is lined with roots and hair and the 5–7, occasionally 3–10, pale green eggs are speckled with darker shades of the same colour. The eggs are incubated by the female, starting with the first egg, and the chicks hatch after 16–17 days. Both parents participate in feeding the young which fledge some 19–20 days after hatching. Single-brooded.

Food: Virtually omnivorous, taking a wide variety of vegetable matter including acorns, beechmast, nuts and berries, the eggs and young of other birds, mice, worms and insects.

Range and Distribution: Found across Eurasia to Japan, China and the Himalayas. Widespread in Europe north to the tree line and from Turkey into parts of the Middle East. In Britain and Ireland it is absent only from the treeless hills of the Pennines and Scotland, the far north, the west of Ireland, and from the Fens.

Movements: British birds are resident, but immigrants from the Continent occur in October on south and east coasts.

Magpie

Pica pica (Linnaeus)

A large black and white bird with a prominent long tail. In the field the Magpie appears a pied bird, but a closer approach shows the black areas to have a glossy green sheen with some bronze near the tip of the tail

Population: over 250,000 pairs

Upperparts are iridescent green-black extending onto the breast and broken only by a bold white patch on the wing that is particularly noticeable in flight. The belly is white. The strong bill and the legs and feet are black. At all times the extremely long tail, which makes up more than half the overall length, is the most obvious feature and, in flight, its wedge shape is apparent. Magpies are generally solitary birds, though small parties are not uncommon and fairly large gatherings may occur in winter. They are virtually omnivorous and were shot out of many game-rearing areas until quite recently. An increase has now brought them into many surburban areas. 46 cm (18 in).

Voice: A far-carrying *chak-chak-chak*, also various harsh chattering notes and a babbling spring song.

Habitat: Open country with plentiful bush and tree cover; farmland and hedgerows, woodland edges, orchards, heaths, parks and gardens even in city centres.

Reproduction: Magpies build a domed nest of twigs resembling an untidy squirrel's drey. The side entrance gives access to a neat cup of twigs, lined with mud and roots, constructed by the female from materials brought by the male. The 5–8, occasionally up to 10, pale blue eggs are speckled with grey-brown and laid in early April. The female alone incubates for the 17–18 days the eggs take to hatch and the chicks are fed by both parents before fledging after 22–28 days. Single-brooded.

Food: Insects, small mammals, fruit, berries, carrion and, in the breeding season, the eggs and young of many species of birds. Its habit of hoarding food has been extended to shiny objects, giving rise to stories of thieving Magpies.

Range and Distribution: A highly successful species that nests throughout Europe and across huge areas of Siberia and central Asia to China and the Bering Sea. It has colonized southern Alaska and extends southwards through western North America to southern California. In Britain and Ireland it is widespread and numerous and is absent only from the Scottish Highlands and islands, the Border Hills and from parts of eastern England where habitat destruction and persecution may be mainly responsible.

Movements: Resident.

Chough

Pyrrhocorax pyrrhocorax (Linnaeus)

A medium-sized, all-black bird, most frequently seen in flight high against some cliff where attention is attracted by its high-pitched cries

Population: 700 to 800 pairs

Pure black above and below, marked with an iridescent sheen visible only at close range. The bill is long, thin and decurved and, like the legs and feet, bright crimson. The large, slightly rounded tail and the broad, square-cut wings produce a distinctive flight silhouette with the tips of the primaries spread widely apart to produce a 'fingered' appearance. It is a gregarious bird given to masterly displays of aerobatics, though its highly localized and declining status make such sights unfortunately rare. 39 cm ($15\frac{1}{2}$ in).

Voice: A shrill *kyow*, more musical than the similar call of the Jackdaw; also various *kuk-kuk* notes similar to those of a gull.

Habitat: Confined to cliffs in mountainous country and sea coasts; found in quarries in some areas. Gathers on grasslands to feed in flocks.

Reproduction: The nest is constructed on a cliff ledge, often in a cave or under the shelter of an overhang, or in a rock crevice or hole. It consists of a substantial structure of twigs and grasses lined with wool and hair. The 3–4 green-washed eggs are spotted with brown and laid at the end of April or in early May. Incubation begins with the first egg and is by the female alone for 17–23 days. The chicks are fed by regurgitation by both parents for the 38 days they take to fledge. Single-brooded.

Food: Mainly ants in the breeding season, the bill being particularly well adapted to probing among short grass. Also insects and their larvae, worms, corn and carrion.

Range and Distribution: Highly fragmented from Spain and North Africa across southern Europe to Turkey, the Caucasus, Himalayas and the mountains of northern China and central Asia. In Britain and Ireland the decline of the Chough has been linked with various factors, including the severe winters of the latter part of last century and again in more recent years. Three-quarters of the total population are confined to the north, west and south coasts of Ireland. They are also found along Welsh coasts as well as in the Snowdon area where they inhabit disused slate quarries; in the Isle of Man; and on Islay and Colonsay in the Inner Hebrides.

Movements: Resident, with some local wandering along coasts.

Masterful flyer showing 'fingered' wing tip pattern

Rook

Corvus frugilegus (Linnaeus)

A large, black, crow-like bird that is invariably more gregarious than the similar Carrion Crow

Population: 1,500,000 pairs

More angular and lighter in build than similar Carrion Crow

The plumage is all black washed with a purple metallic sheen visible at close range. The legs and feet are black marked by shaggy 'trousers' and the bird walks a great deal, though with a decided waddle. An area of bare grey skin extends from the eye, over the lores to the chin in the adult; a feature that at once distinguishes it from the Carrion Crow. However, juveniles lack this patch and are thus very similar to Carrion Crows. In all plumages the thinner bill, and the lighter, more narrow-winged and angular shape of the Rook in flight are fine, but nevertheless valid, identification points. While Carrion Crows may gather into small groups they are seldom as gregarious as Rooks. 46 cm (18 in).

Voice: A variety of harsh notes, including a *caw* and *caah*.

Habitat: Farmland with large trees, woods, copses and hangers.

Reproduction: Rooks nest in traditional rookeries in the tops of tall trees. Both sexes gather nesting materials, but the female alone constructs the nest of twigs bound together with mud and lined with bents, roots, wool and other soft items. The 3–5, occasionally up to 9, eggs are laid in late March and washed in shades of green or blue-green, blotched and spotted with olive-green. The female incubates for 16–20 days, being fed on the nest by the male. Both sexes feed the young for the 29–30 days they take to fledge. Single-brooded.

Food: Mainly vegetable matter such as corn, root vegetables, berries and seeds, but Rooks also take many harmful insects and their larvae, worms, slugs, spiders and some carrion. On balance they are beneficial.

Range and Distribution: From Britain right across Europe and Asia to China, with extensions southwards to the head of the Persian Gulf and with isolated pockets in northern Spain and southern Sweden. In Britain and Ireland it is widely spread, but is absent from treeless areas as in the Scottish Highlands and islands and from London. The largest rookery is Hatton Castle in Aberdeenshire where nearly 7,000 nests have been counted. In recent years Dutch elm disease has destroyed many traditional rookeries.

Movements: Resident, with some late summer dispersal. Immigrants from the Continent, from Holland and Germany east to Russia, arrive on the east coast in autumn to winter.

Jackdaw

Corvus monedula (Linnaeus)

A small, totally gregarious crow which has increased and spread as a result of agricultural activity

Population: about 500,000 pairs

Compact, thick-necked appearance in flight

Black plumage distinguished by a grey nape extending from the ear coverts. The legs and feet are long and powerful and the bill short, stubby, but noticeably pointed. Jackdaws have distinctive calls and, in flight, have quicker wing beats and a less flapping flight than other crows. They are invariably found in flocks, often feeding in company with Rooks. 33 cm (13 in).

Voice: A clear *kyow* and *chak*, sometimes repeated in combinations.

Habitat: Jackdaws feed mostly on grassland where they pick food from the surface. They breed in a variety of different habitats including town centres, quarries, sea and inland cliffs, woods and parks.

Reproduction: Nest sites are as varied as habitats, the only essential being a crevice or hole. The birds find suitable sites on cathedrals, castles, cliffs and trees, and will take to large nest boxes. They are predominantly colonial and the nest is built by both members of the pair of sticks and twigs, lined with softer vegetation together with wool and hair. Chimneys are blocked by dropping large sticks down until they wedge to form a base platform. Huge quantities of kindling may accumulate in the process. The 4–6, occasionally 2–9, pale blue eggs are marked with variable spots and blotches of dark brown. They are laid in late April and are incubated from the first egg by the female alone for 17–18 days. The young are fed by both parents for 28–32 days before fledging. Single-brooded.

Food: Insect larvae, spiders and caterpillars, as well as worms, eggs and young of other birds and some berries and seeds.

Range and Distribution: Breeds right across Europe north to central Scandinavia and eastwards through Russia and Turkey to central Siberia. There are outposts in North Africa and the Mediterranean islands where it is decidedly more numerous in winter. Jackdaws are found in virtually every corner of Britain and Ireland, except for the higher hills and islands of northwestern Scotland. A considerable extension of range has taken place during the present century with birds colonizing and increasing in several areas.

Movements: British and Irish birds are resident with only some local wandering. Continental birds from Scandinavia and Holland arrive on the east and southeast coasts in October to winter, with some passing through further south.

Carrion Crow

Corvus corone (Linnaeus)

A large and familiar bird that occurs in 2 distinct subspecies – the Carrion Crow *Corvus corone corone* and the Hooded Crow *Corvus corone cornix* – which overlap in northern Scotland

Population: about 1 million pairs

Appearing bulky and somewhat laboured in flight, the Carrion Crow is all black with a large powerful bill. It lacks the bare face patch of the Rook and is generally found singly, in pairs or in small family parties. The Hooded Crow is more distinctly marked with pale grey underparts and wing linings, and a grey back. The head and breast, wings and tail are black. In structure there is no appreciable difference between the 2 subspecies, though they show distinct habitat preferences. Both are much smaller than the Raven. 47 cm ($18\frac{1}{2}$ in).

Voice: A rasping *kraah* that is often repeated 3 or 4 times; also utters a *keerk* call, and a honking *konk*.

Habitat: Every type of country from city centres and woodland, through hedgerows to open moorland. The Hooded Crow is more abundant in upland districts.

Reproduction: Nests high in tall trees, though also on cliffs, buildings and even on the ground among heather. The nest is of twigs bound together with mud and lined with wool and hair. The 4–6, occasionally 2–7, eggs are laid in late March or April and coloured in various shades of pale green or blue, marked with olives and browns. Incubation, which begins before the clutch is complete, is by the female alone for 18–20 days and the chicks leave the nest after a further 28–35 days. Single-brooded.

Food: Wide variety of animal and vegetable matter including small mammals, birds and their eggs, insects, worms, reptiles and amphibians, as well as grain, acorns, root crops, fruit and seeds. Also takes carrion and has, in the past, been blamed for attacks on ewes and lambs, but such attacks are rare.

Range and Distribution: Breeds right across Europe and Asia to well north of the tree line and southwards to the Nile Valley and the Persian Gulf. The Carrion Crow is widespread in England and Wales, and northwards in Scotland to the Caledonian Canal where it overlaps the range of the Hooded Crow, which is found north and west to Shetland, the Outer Hebrides and even remote St Kilda. It is, with a few exceptions in the north, the subspecies found over the whole of Ireland and is dominant in the Isle of Man.

Movements: Resident; but immigrants of both subspecies arrive in autumn from adjacent parts of the Continent.

More heavily built than Rook

Hooded Crow (above) compared with Carrion Crow

Raven

Corvus corax (Linnaeus)

A huge black bird, much larger than a Carrion Crow or Rook, with a fearsome bill

Population: 5,000 pairs

Heavy build, prominent head and bill distinguishes from other crows in flight

Entire plumage is black marked with a blue and purple metallic sheen visible only at close range. The long, deep bill is large even in comparison with the bulk of the bird, and the feathers of the throat protrude to form a 'beard'. In flight the huge size becomes even more apparent and the long tail is distinctly wedged in shape. 64 cm (25 in).

Voice: Most common call is a *pruk-pruk*; but also utters a variety of other harsh croaking notes.

Habitat: Once widespread, the Raven has been forced back into remote uplands and sea coasts where it inhabits moors and cliffs.

Reproduction: The nest, which is constructed of twigs and heather bound together with mud and lined with grass and wool, is placed on a cliff, usually under an overhang, though trees are also used, particularly in Ireland. There may be some competition for cliff sites with the Golden Eagle and, like those birds, a handful of alternatives may be used in a casual rotation. The eggs may be laid as early as February, but early March is more usual. They are highly variable in shades of pale green or blue, marked in green, brown or virtually black, and usually number 4–6. The female alone performs the incubation, commencing before the final egg is laid, for the 20–21 days the chicks take to hatch. She is fed on the nest by her mate. The youngsters are fed by both parents for the 35–42 days prior to fledging. Single-brooded.

Food: Variable, with much carrion, particularly sheep placentas, dead sheep and lambs, other mammals such as rabbits, birds and their eggs, reptiles, amphibians, insects and some crops and large seeds.

Range and Distribution: A highly successful species, the Raven has a breeding distribution that circles the world in the Northern Hemisphere. It ranges as far north as Baffinland and Greenland, and as far south as Central America and Ethiopia. In Europe it is absent from large areas of the lowlands, doubtless as a result of persecution. In Britain and Ireland this same persecution has eliminated it from most lowland areas and it is thus confined to the north and the west. On the south coast it finds a niche as far east as the Isle of Wight.

Movements: Resident, with only a little local wandering.

Starling

Sturnus vulgaris (Linnaeus)

A confiding bird, aggressively successful in its relationship with man, that has increased and spread remarkably in the last 100 years

Population: between 4 and 7 million pairs

At a glance the Starling is an all-black bird with a yellow bill and is superficially similar to a Blackbird. It is, however, smaller than that bird and is washed with shiny iridescent greens and purples in summer. It has a waddling walk, not a deliberate hop like the Blackbird, and, in winter, is heavily spotted and streaked with creamy-white both above and below. The tail is shortish and, in the air, the pointed wings and direct flight are characteristic. It is generally gregarious and forms colossal roosts in city centres, though the largest roosts, up to a million strong, are in the countryside. Starlings come regularly to gardens and usually dominate bird tables. 21.5 cm (8½ in).

Voice: A wide variety of whistles, chuckles and grating notes run together to form a discordant whistling song; a repeated *tcheer*; also effectively mimics the songs and calls of other birds.

Habitat: Frequents virtually every landform, from city centres to the wildest of marshlands; in the breeding season it occupies virtually any area that will provide a nest hole – woods, parks, towns and cities, sea cliffs, quarries and upland crags.

Adult in summer (foreground) and in winter (behind); immature (rear). Below, evening roosting flocks flight across the bare skies of winter

Reproduction: Starlings nest in a hole, usually in a tree or building, and frequently usurp those of other species including woodpeckers and Sand Martins. The nest itself is an untidy assortment of twigs, grasses, feathers, wool and other materials started by the male and finished by the female. The 5–7, occasionally 4–9, pale blue eggs are laid from mid-April and are incubated by both members of the pair for 12–15 days. The chicks are fed by both parents for 20–22 days. Frequently double-brooded.

Food: A wide variety of items are taken according to season, with mainly animate matter being consumed in summer, fruit in autumn, and other vegetable matter including seeds and berries in winter. It comes regularly to feeding stations.

Range and Distribution: Found throughout Europe, except for Iberia where it is replaced by the similar Spotless Starling, eastwards through Russia to central Asia, south through Turkey to Iran and northern India. The Starling has been introduced and has prospered in North America, Australia, New Zealand, South Africa and Polynesia. In Britain and Ireland it was a declining species, absent from most of mainland Scotland and from all but a few coastal localities in Ireland, until about 1830. Thereafter it prospered and spread, and is now found in virtually every corner of the country except for the highest Scottish hills and moors.

Movements: Huge numbers arrive on the east coast in October and November and, though some pass on, many remain to winter. It is in autumn that the largest communal roosts are found.

Tree Sparrow

Passer montanus (Linnaeus)

A neat little bird, very like the male House Sparrow but easily distinguishable. The sexes are similar

Population: 250,000 pairs

Back and wings are broadly streaked with black, brown and chestnut; the underparts are white. The crown and nape are bright chestnut, this bird lacking the grey crown of the male House Sparrow. The cheeks are white extending to the base of the nape and almost forming a collar. A black bib is much less extensive than in the House Sparrow and a black 'comma' marks the cheek. Though often overlooked, Tree Sparrows are widespread in Britain and may be found in many areas where holes are available as nest sites. They usually form loose colonies and are decidedly more rural than their more successful relatives, with which they sometimes form mixed flocks. 14 cm (5½ in).

Voice: A distinctive *tek* in flight; also a *chip* and a *chip-tchup*.

Habitat: Wooded country, hedgerows, orchards and other areas with natural holes, including cliffs. Also in old buildings, especially in Ireland, and frequently near water or the sea.

Reproduction: The nest is placed in a hole in a tree, cliff, old building or among ivy or other creepers. It is similar to that of the House Sparrow, being a domed and untidy structure of grasses lined with feathers. The 4–6, sometimes 2–9, eggs are whitish blotched with brown and laid from April onwards. Both sexes incubate for 11–14 days, and both feed the chicks for the 12–14 days they take to fledge. Two, occasionally 3, broods are reared. They take readily to nest boxes and may increase as a result of their provision in suitable habitats.

Food: Seeds and insects according to season.

Range and Distribution: Found across Eurasia from eastern Spain to Japan, China and Malaysia south to Java. In Europe it is absent from southern Greece and the boreal zone of Scandinavia. In Britain it is widespread in the drier eastern parts of the country and, though found on many of the islands, is absent from many of the hilly districts of Scotland. It is decidedly local in west Wales and southwest England and is absent from much of Hampshire. In Ireland it is a highly local coastal bird, but increasing in numbers.

Movements: Predominantly resident, but with some autumn wandering and a few proven cases of emigration.

314

House Sparrow

Passer domesticus (Linnaeus)

A chirpy little bird that would be regarded as particularly attractive were it not so common. Gregarious and bold, it inhabits all areas permanently occupied by man

Population: some 3½ to 7 million pairs

Female

Males are streaked black and brown on back and wings and are dull white below. There is a patch of deep chestnut on the nape, and the crown is dove-grey. The cheeks are white, all but enclosed by a black bib that widens out over the chest. The female is marked in browns and buffs with a clear creamy supercilium. 14.5 cm (5¾ in).

Voice: A distinct *cheep*, and a chirping song.

Habitat: Virtually wherever man has a permanent occupancy, including city centres, towns, villages, hamlets, hedgerows, farmyards and even isolated islands provided domestic stock is fed and maintained.

Reproduction: Most nests are built in holes in buildings, but in agricultural areas House Sparrows will also nest in haystacks, tree holes and nest boxes, and will even construct large untidy domed nests among bushes and cliffs. The nest consists of a cup, with or without a dome, built of straw and grasses, and a mass of rubbish including paper, polythene and cloth, lined with feathers. The 3–5, occasionally more, eggs are whitish covered with blotches of grey and are laid from May onwards, though nests can be found in every month of the year. Incubation, mainly by the female, lasts 11–14 days and both parents feed the chicks for 15 days. Three or more broods are reared.

Food: Insects during the breeding season; at other times mainly cereals in agricultural districts where huge flocks may form in late summer, and human refuse in towns and cities.

Range and Distribution: Found throughout Europe south to North Africa and the Nile Valley and north to Scandinavia. Eastwards it extends throughout the Middle East to India and Burma, and across central Asia to Manchuria. It has been introduced and spread in North and South America, Australia, New Zealand, South Africa and many other areas. In Britain and Ireland it is absent only from the highest uninhabited uplands.

Movements: Resident.

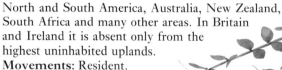

Chaffinch

Fringilla coelebs (Linnaeus)

One of the most widespread
and numerous of our birds, and
particularly well marked and
attractive in the male. Chaffinch
female (bottom) and male (middle)
shown opposite

Population: some 7 million pairs places
this among the ranks of Britain's most
abundant birds

The male is a fine dove-grey on crown and nape, deep chestnut on back, green on rump, with black wings marked by broad brown margins and 2 bold white wing bars that are particularly noticeable in flight. The dark tail has prominent white outer feathers. The underparts are a deep pink, fading to white on the belly. The bill is a bright steel-grey. The female is dull in comparison in creamy-greys, but with the same white double wing bar and white outertail feathers as her mate. Chaffinches are usually gregarious, forming large flocks in autumn and winter on agricultural land and in hedgerows and woods. 15 cm (6 in).

Voice: A distinctive *pink*, also a *tsip* of contact in flight.

Habitat: Found in a wide range of areas with trees or bushes. Most numerous in deciduous woods, but also in hedgerows, gardens, parks and bushy heaths.

Reproduction: The nest is a neat cup of grasses, camouflaged with mosses and lichens, lined with hair, and built usually by the female in April or May in a bush or tree. The 4–5, occasionally 2–8, pale blue eggs are spotted and scrawled with deep maroon and are incubated by the female for 11–13 days. The chicks are fed by both parents for 12–15 days before fledging. One or 2 broods are reared each season according to latitude and climate.

Food: Insects and their larvae, as well as spiders, are taken in summer; vegetable matter is the staple diet at other seasons. Seeds, fruit, cereals and beechmast are important.

Range and Distribution: Found throughout Europe southwards to North Africa and northwards to northern Scandinavia, extending eastwards through Turkey and northern Iran and to the Soviet Union beyond the Urals. In Britain and Ireland it is widespread and numerous except in the Outer Hebrides, Orkney and Shetland.

Movements: British birds are resident, but large numbers of Continental birds arrive on the east coast in autumn, especially in October, passing westwards through the country, often in easily observed daytime movements. The spring return takes place in March and April. Some birds probably pass on to winter elsewhere.

Brambling

Fringilla montifringilla (Linnaeus)

An attractive woodland finch that
replaces the Chaffinch in the north
and is a winter visitor to Britain and
Ireland. Male Brambling in winter
(top) shown opposite

Population: thousands winter

In breeding plumage the male is a resplendent black, orange and white bird the size and shape of a Chaffinch. In winter the black of the head and back becomes mottled with browns and a steel-coloured bill becomes dull horn. The characteristic orange underparts and the broad pattern of orange and white wing bars remain, as does the diagnostic white rump. The female is a duller and browner version of the winter male. These are gregarious birds that frequently join mixed flocks of finches along field margins and hedgerows. 14.5 cm (5¾ in).

Voice: A *tsweep*, and a *tchuck* flight note; males in song utter a rasping, Greenfinch-like *dzwee*.

Habitat: In summer frequents birch and willow in the taiga zone. In winter roams hedgerows and agricultural land, as well as broadleaved woods, especially beech.

Reproduction: Nests in a tree, usually at no great height, constructing a similar, though larger, neatly camouflaged nest to the Chaffinch. Moss, grasses, hair and spiders' webs are bound together by the female alone and decorated with bark chippings to match the surroundings. The 5–7, occasionally 4 or 8, pale blue eggs blotched with pinkish-red

are laid from mid-May onwards and incubated by the female alone for 11–12 days. The chicks are fed by both parents for a similar period before fledging. Invariably single-brooded.

Food: Moths and their larvae are taken in summer. In winter seeds and berries are the staple diet, including large quantities of grass seeds, beechmast and some cereals.

Range and Distribution: Breeds from Scandinavia eastwards across the taiga zone of Eurasia to Kamchatka, and winters to the south and west of this huge range. In Britain it has been proved to breed only once, though there are 2 cases of hybridization with Chaffinches and several records of singing males holding territories. Otherwise it is a winter visitor from Scandinavia to most areas, except for northern Scotland and western Ireland where it is decidedly scarce.

Movements: Birds arrive mainly in October and return in March and April. Some undoubtedly pass through to winter further south.

Serin

Serinus serinus (Linnaeus)

A small Canary-like finch, with a prominent yellow rump, that has extended its range northwards through Europe during the last 200 years. Male (foreground) and female shown

Continental breeding distribution: colonizing northwards, 1 or 2 pairs some years in England

A dumpy little bird with a rounded head and a tiny, wedge-shaped bill. The male is predominantly yellow, but is heavily streaked both above and below with black except on the chest, nape and rump. The female is similar, but with less yellow and heavier streaking, particularly on the breast. These are comparatively tame finches that utter a distinctive tinkling call both as a song and in winter flocks. 11.5 cm (4½ in).

Voice: A flight note *tirrillillit*, and a *tsooeet* are the most common calls; but the song is a rapid jingling of high-pitched notes.

Habitat: Orchards, gardens and olive groves, with an extension into other habitats, usually in association with man, as it has spread into temperate Europe.

Reproduction: The nest is built high in a deciduous tree (sometimes in an evergreen) and is well concealed towards the tip of a slender side branch. It consists of a neat cup of grasses, roots and moss lined with feathers and hair and is constructed by the female from March to May depending on latitude. The 4, occasionally 3 or 5, pale blue eggs are spotted and scrawled with reddish-brown and incubated apparently by the female alone for 13 days. The chicks are fed by both parents for 14 days. Double-brooded.

Food: Consists almost entirely of weed seeds.

Range and Distribution: Confined to Iberia and the Mediterranean until 1800, the Serin has since spread northwards to reach southern Sweden and Britain in recent years. The increasing frequency of records during the 1960s led to the first British breeding record in Dorset in 1967. It has bred since in southern England, but the expected colonization has yet to materialize. Devon appears to be most favoured. Elsewhere it is a very rare bird indeed.

Movements: Birds leave Britain and temperate Europe to return to their traditional Mediterranean home to winter.

Greenfinch

Carduelis chloris (Linnaeus)

A common bird, attractively coloured in greens and yellows, that is widespread and numerous in most parts of the country

Population: between 1 and 2 million pairs

The male is distinctive in a variety of greens mostly washed with pale grey, and with bold yellow flashes on wings and tail particularly noticeable in flight. The lores are dark and the bill is wedge-shaped and heavily built. The black-tipped tail is deeply forked. The male's rasping call and diagnostic slow-winged display flight are typical of many suburban areas in spring. The female is similar but, being more dully coloured, is like a greenish version of a female House Sparrow. The yellow flashes on wings and tail are less pronounced. Greenfinches flock in winter with other finches, though they also form exclusive flocks, especially to roost. 14.5 cm (5¾ in).

Voice: An unpleasant nasal *dzwee* is characteristic in spring; also a *chup* and a *chi-chi-chit* in flight. The song consists of a musical jingle of twittering notes.

Habitat: Formerly woodland edge, but now most numerous in parks, gardens, orchards, hedgerows and among young conifer plantations.

Reproduction: The song may be heard as early as January, but the nest is not begun until April. Throughout the early spring the male produces his rasping nasal call, often accompanied by a quite beautiful display flight. From some high perch he will fly, with slow deliberate movements of his wings, and tail widely spread, in a large circle before alighting and calling. This territorial flight doubtless serves to show the bright yellow on wings and tail to advantage. Certainly it bears a strong resemblance to the similar flight of the Serin that is such a feature of Mediterranean groves. Greenfinches usually nest in loose colonies. The nest is built mostly by the female and consists of a neat cup of grasses and moss, lined with hair and roots, usually placed in a fork of a tree or bush. The 4–6, occasionally 3–8, light blue eggs are spotted with black and incubated by the female for 12–14 days. The chicks are fed on regurgitated food by both sexes for 13–16 days. Usually double-brooded, but with an occasional third.

Food: Mainly seeds of weeds, but also cereals, fruit and berries with some insects and spiders added for the young.

Range and Distribution: Throughout Europe, except for northern Scandinavia, eastwards to the Urals and south to North Africa and Turkey. In Britain and Ireland it is widespread except in the higher hill districts, particularly of Scotland, but is thin on the ground in the Outer Hebrides, Orkney and Shetland.

Movements: British and Irish birds are largely resident, though some long distance movements take place in hard weather. There is also a small influx of winter visitors from adjacent parts of the Continent.

Goldfinch

Carduelis carduelis (Linnaeus)

A colourful little finch with a pleasant tinkling song and a penchant for thistles

One of the most attractive of British birds, the Goldfinch is marked by a distinctive head pattern of crimson, white and black. The upperparts are warm buff-brown, with black wings marked with white tips to the primaries and a brown golden-yellow flash across the folded wing that is eye-catching in flight. The rump is white, the deeply forked tail black. The underparts are washed with buff on chest and flanks, shading to white on the belly. The bill is more pointed and narrow than most other finches and well adapted to picking seeds from thistle heads. The male has a larger area of crimson on the face than the female. Goldfinches are gregarious birds often found in single-species flocks called 'charms'. 12 cm ($4\frac{3}{4}$ in).

Voice: A tinkling *tswit-wit-wit* that is extended into an attractive Canary-like song.

Habitat: Open areas with waste ground and scrub, dunes and marshes, agricultural margins and hedgerows, gardens and parks.

Reproduction: Nests in trees, sometimes in bushes, adjacent to open wasteland habitat. A neat cup of grasses and mosses, lined with wool and plant down, is built by the female among the outer twigs of a branch. The 4–6, occasionally 3–7, light blue eggs are speckled with dark purple and incubated by the female for 12–14 days. First clutches are laid in late April or early May and 2 or even 3 broods are reared. The chicks are fed by both parents for the 12–15 days that they take to fledge.

Food: Seeds of thistle, knapweed and teasel taken from the seed heads, or when fallen, form a staple diet largely unavailable to other species. Also takes insects and their larvae.

Range and Distribution: From the Atlantic islands eastwards through Europe and North Africa to southern Sweden, central Siberia, the Middle East and the western Himalayas. In Britain and Ireland the Goldfinch is widespread in lowland areas, becoming decidedly scarce in the Scottish Highlands and virtually absent from the islands.

Movements: Some birds are resident, but a considerable number make internal movements and many emigrate to winter in France, Iberia and even North Africa.

Population: about 300,000 pairs

320

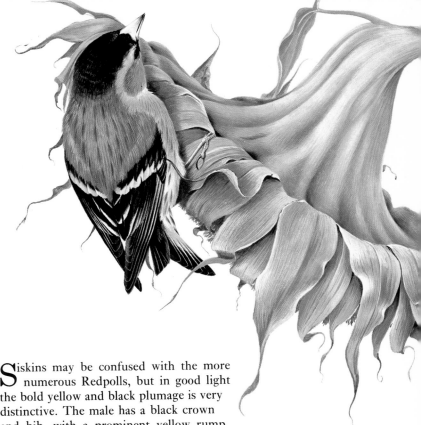

Siskin

Carduelis spinus (Linnaeus)

A distinctive yellow and black finch that feeds acrobatically among the trees canopy, but which has developed a habit of visiting gardens for peanuts in early spring

Population: about 20,000 pairs

Siskins may be confused with the more numerous Redpolls, but in good light the bold yellow and black plumage is very distinctive. The male has a black crown and bib, with a prominent yellow rump and breast and yellow in the tail margins. The back is streaked green and black and the wings are black and yellow with a bold yellow wing bar. The female is generally duller, streaked below and lacking the bright yellows and blacks of her mate. The yellow in the tail remains a clear-cut feature. 12 cm (4¾ in).

Voice: A distinctive twittering song ending in an extended wheeze; also various *tsooeet* and *tsee* notes. Highly vocal at all seasons.

Habitat: Always found among conifers in summer, especially Scots pine, but also more recently plantations of spruce. In winter particularly fond of alders and birches, but also among conifers.

Reproduction: The nest, which is built high up on an outer branch of a conifer, is notably difficult to find. It consists of a neat cup of twigs and grasses, bound together with moss and lined with wool and plant down. The 3–5, occasionally 2–6, light blue eggs are spotted with lilac and laid from late April onwards. Incubation, commencing with the second to last egg, is performed by the female for 11–14 days. The chicks are fed by the male for the first week or so while the female is brooding, but after that by both parents. Food is regurgitated. The total fledging period is 13–15 days. Double-brooded.

Food: Conifer seeds in summer, especially spruce, larch and pine, but with alder, birch and other deciduous species in winter.

Range and Distribution: Breeds across central and eastern temperate and Scandinavian Europe to beyond the Urals. Also in eastern Asia from Manchuria to northern Japan. The restricted habitat enables isolated populations to survive in mountain areas south of the main range in the Pyrenees, Sardinia, the Italian and Greek mountains, and in the Caucasus and mountains of northern Turkey. In Britain and Ireland it has prospered with the extensive planting of conifers and is now widespread in the Scottish Highlands. Elsewhere it is found rather locally throughout the country.

Movements: Though there may be some local wandering, British and Irish birds are largely resident. Winter visitors arrive on the east coast in October in variable numbers and, though some pass further south, most spread through the country to winter.

Linnet

Carduelis cannabina (Linnaeus)

An abundant, ground-feeding, wasteland bird that sometimes forms huge flocks where weed seeds are abundant

Population: about 1 million pairs

Linnets are gregarious throughout the year, nesting in loose colonies and foraging in variable-sized flocks. The male in summer is distinctively marked with a rosy red crown and breast that are largely lost in winter when he is difficult to distinguish from the female. The back is brown streaked with dark brown and the underparts are buff heavily streaked with black. The wings and tail are black, the former with brown edges to the flight feathers, and with areas of white that are particularly noticeable in flight. A continual twittering in flight attracts attention, but may be easily confused with similar calls of the Twite. 13.5 cm (5¼ in).

Voice: A *tsooeet*, and a constant twittering in flight; the song is a similar twitter mixed with some warbling and broken by a few nasal notes.

Habitat: Heaths and downs, hedgerows, wasteland and neglected corners, young conifer plantations, dunes and saltings with bushes and thick ground cover. In winter may be numerous on salt marshes, but also frequents playing fields and other grasslands.

Reproduction: Breeds in loose colonies of about 5–6 pairs, the males singing from prominent perches and in a display flight. The nest is constructed in a bush and consists of a cup of grasses and moss lined with hair and wool. The 4–6, occasionally 7, light blue eggs are spotted with purple and laid from mid-April onwards. Incubation, by the female alone, takes 10–14 days and, while she broods the young, the male brings food for the first 4–5 days. Thereafter both parents feed the young. The total fledging period is 11–14 days and 2 or 3 broods are normally reared.

Food: Predominantly weed seeds, but also seeds of some crops as well as a few insects. The chicks are fed on caterpillars, insects and their larvae, and spiders.

Range and Distribution: Breeds throughout Europe north to central Scandinavia and southwards to North Africa. In Siberia it is found beyond the Urals, extending southwards into Turkey and the Middle East. In Britain and Ireland it is widespread, except in hill country and the Scottish Highlands and islands where it is largely replaced by the closely related Twite.

Movements: Southern birds mostly emigrate in October to winter in southern France and Iberia, returning mainly in April. They are replaced by birds from the north and by Continental immigrants, many of which can be seen coasting in October and early November. Such movements can also be detected over large urban conglomerations where they cannot be confused with local birds.

Twite

Carduelis flavirostris (Linnaeus)

An undistinguished little brown finch that is the northern equivalent of the Linnet and which otherwise gathers only along coastlines in winter

Population: 20,000 to 40,000 pairs

In all plumages the Twite is a much more heavily streaked brown bird than the Linnet. Indeed, the streaking is much more akin to that of a pipit than a finch, though the dumpy shape and short, thick bill preclude confusion with those birds. The male has a vinous pink rump, but this is notoriously difficult to see in the field. This species has the same white wing and tail flashes as the Linnet and its calls are also very similar. 13.5 cm ($5\frac{1}{4}$ in).

Voice: Constant twittering in flight that is more metallic, and a *chweet* that is more nasal, than similar calls of the Linnet.

Habitat: Heather moors and grassy hillsides, usually at some altitude, but down to sea level in the extreme north. In winter frequents coasts, and may be especially numerous on salt marshes.

Reproduction: The nest is placed on the ground among heather, but also in bushes and even in stone walls. It is built by the female of grasses, lined with feathers, hair and wool, in late April and early May. The 5–6, occasionally 4 or 7, light blue eggs are spotted and scrawled with dark brown, and incubation, which lasts 12–13 days, is by the female alone. The chicks are fed by both parents for 15 days, and 1 or 2 broods are reared in a season.

Food: Seeds of weeds and grasses, especially *Molinia* grass in spring; also cereals and some insects and, in winter, the seeds of many marine species including *Salicornia*.

Range and Distribution: A bird of the high plateaux of central Asia, including Tibet, that has spread to the Caucasus and to the coastal mountains of Scandinavia and northern and western Britain and Ireland. It replaces the Linnet in the Scottish Highlands and islands, but is also found in the Pennines and in western coastal Ireland. In some areas climatic change has enabled Linnets to invade Twite habitat and mixed colonies have resulted.

Movements: While some birds are resident others move southwards to winter in coastal England where they are joined by Scandinavian immigrants that arrive in October and November and stay on until March or April. Such birds often join with Linnets to form huge flocks several thousand strong on favoured feeding grounds.

Redpoll

Carduelis flammea (Linnaeus)

An acrobatic, canopy-feeding species that is gregarious throughout the year and which has a distinctively buzzing flight note. Two males (below) and female shown

Redpolls are small brown and buff birds marked with a neat black bib and a patch of bright crimson on the crown. The male in summer has a Linnet-like wash of pink on the breast and at all seasons a vinous pink rump streaked with black. However, like the similar vinous rump of the Twite, this is notoriously difficult to see in the field. The overall impression is of a heavily streaked brown bird that feeds among the tree tops, often in the manner of a tit. 13 cm (5 in).

Voice: A buzzing, nasal flight call uttered more or less continuously; a song of trills and buzzing and a quiet *tsooeet*.

Habitat: Though often associated with conifers, and particularly with recent plantations, the Redpoll is just as at home in birch and alder woods and shows an increasing tendency to expand into hedgerows among farmland.

Reproduction: Breeds in loose colonies from late April onwards, the nest being placed in a tree usually (but not always) at some considerable height from the ground. The roughly constructed cup of twigs and grasses is lined with feathers and hair, and the 4–5, occasionally 3–7, light blue eggs are spotted and scrawled with pink and red-brown and incubated by the female for 10–13 days. The chicks are fed by both parents for 11–14 days before fledging. Sometimes double-brooded.

Food: Mainly seeds of birch and alder; some insects, eggs and larvae.

Range and Distribution: The Redpoll enjoys a circumpolar breeding distribution that includes the whole of Eurasia and North America in the northern taiga zone. It is also found in isolated pockets further south in the Alps. The taxonomy of the redpolls is complex, however, with several different forms being treated as separate species by some authorities. In Britain and Ireland there has been a considerable increase and spread due to afforestation and these birds can now be found in most parts of the country except for the Outer Hebrides, Orkney and Shetland. They are, however, decidedly local in the southern Midlands, the southwest, and the south of England.

Movements: Many birds regularly emigrate to Holland and Germany and, in some years, the exodus may include a larger part of the population. Similarly, immigrants from the Continent arrive every year in October and November, but in highly variable numbers, making the species virtually irruptive in the character of its migrations. Some birds undoubtedly move further south, but many settle down to winter in Britain.

Population: 300,000 pairs

324

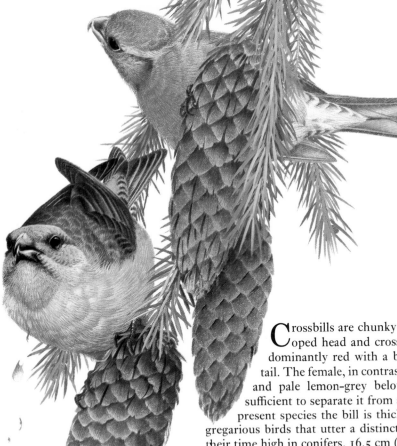

Crossbill

Loxia curvirostra (Linnaeus)

A bird of northern forests, specifically adapted to feed on the seeds of spruce, that occasionally irrupts to invade our shores and which may then settle to breed. Very similar to the Scottish Crossbill. Male (above) and female shown

Crossbills are chunky finches with a powerfully developed head and crossed mandibles. The male is predominantly red with a brown back and black wings and tail. The female, in contrast, is a dull green; dark olive above and pale lemon-grey below. The 'crossed' bill is always sufficient to separate it from all but its closest relatives. In the present species the bill is thick without being huge. These are gregarious birds that utter a distinctive flight call and spend most of their time high in conifers. 16.5 cm (6½ in).

Voice: A *chip-chip* in flight; song consists of a series of chipping, trilling and warbling notes and is the surest means of separation from the Scottish Crossbill.

Habitat: Exclusively conifers, usually feeds among spruces, but not confined to large forests.

Reproduction: The nest is sited usually quite high up in a conifer at the forest edge or in an isolated clump or windbreak. It consists of a cup of twigs with grasses and mosses, lined with fur and feathers, and may be built any time between December and July, though most birds nest in February or March. The 3–4, occasionally 2 or 5, light blue eggs are speckled with dark purple and incubated by the female for 13–16 days, commencing with the first egg. Both parents feed the chicks for the 17–22 days they take to fledge. At first the young have normal uncrossed bills and are dependent on their parents for food for a further 20–30 days. Later they gain the crossed bill of the adult. Single-brooded.

Food: Predominantly seeds of spruce together with those of other conifers; also berries and seeds, and even some insects and spiders.

Range and Distribution: Breeds right across the coniferous zone of the Northern Hemisphere with isolated populations to the south in mountainous areas. In Europe it is found from Spain to Lapland wherever large areas of conifers exist. In Britain it has bred in the Brecks and New Forest since 1910 following a huge eruption from the Continent. Recent irruptions have established populations in many parts of England and southern Scotland, aided, no doubt, by the vast increase of conifers planted during the present century. In Wales and Ireland it is a sporadic breeding bird.

Movements: Crossbills exhibit a strong population cycle that, combined with shortage of food, occasionally sends huge numbers south and west in search of conifer seeds. They thus irrupt into Britain every few years and many may stay on to breed, colonizing new areas and augmenting populations already established during previous irruptions.

Population: varies, about 3,000 pairs

Scottish Crossbill

Loxia scotica (Hartert)

Britain's only endemic bird species and virtually identical in the field to the Crossbill of the Continent. A much more substantial bill enables it to prise open the larger cones of Scots pines to extract seeds that the common bird cannot obtain. Male (below) and female shown

A large, strongly built bird with crossed mandibles that is more or less confined to forests of Scots pine. The male is red, the female dull green; both are indistinguishable from the Crossbill on plumage features. They do, however, have a much stronger bill that falls neatly between the thinner bill of the Crossbill and the huge bill of the very rare (to Britain) Parrot Crossbill. These are gregarious birds with a clear flight note that spend their lives high in conifers. 16.5 cm (6½ in).

Voice: A coarse *tyoop-tyoop* flight note; song consists of 'chips' and trills warbled together – distinctive once learned.

Habitat: Pine forests, both old Caledonian and more recent plantations.

Reproduction: The nest is placed on an outer branch of a pine, usually at some height. The base of twigs supports a neat cup of grasses and mosses lined with feathers, and is built usually in February or March. The 3–4, up to 5 on occasion, pale blue eggs are speckled with purple and incubated by the female for 13–16 days, starting with the first egg. Both sexes feed the chicks for the 17–22 days they take to fledge and thereafter until they develop the crossed mandibles that enable them to extract their own food. Single-brooded.

Food: Seeds of Scots pine; also berries and other seeds.

Range and Distribution: Confined to the Highlands of Scotland where recent plantings have enabled it to increase and spread from its stronghold in the Spey Valley.

Movements: Resident; invasions further south in Britain are not of this species.

Population: about 2,000 pairs

326

Bills of Finches

Except for the waders, no other group of British and Irish birds shows such specific adaptation to their food as the finches. Though each bird has a basically conical bill, the specific shape, size and power varies enormously. Each has adapted to a particular source of food and, by so doing, has to a greater or lesser extent eliminated competition from related birds. A variety of species with highly specific adaptations is shown, together with the food source on which they specialize

Chaffinch: dependent for its winter survival on the crop of fallen beechmast, this species also takes more insects than other finches. Its long pointed bill is ideal for picking and probing, but quite unsuited to prising open seed heads

Siskin: long, narrow pointed bill ideally suited to picking seeds from seed heads such as those of the alder. Great agility enables it to cling to, often upside down in tit fashion, and gain access to alders and birches

Greenfinch: short, broad bill ideally suited to breaking open and eating quite large seeds such as those of the sunflower. Also takes various tree fruits and cereals, and is an adept consumer of peanuts and other hard seeds provided at bird tables

Goldfinch: long, thin bill enables it to probe deep into thistles and teazles, which it clings to with considerable agility, to extract seeds. Similar to Siskin in its tweezer-like feeding method, it specializes on quite different plants

Hawfinch: massive, strong bill capable of cracking the hardest of stones including those of cherry and olive. Though it weighs only 60 grams or so, the Hawfinch can exert a force of over 45 kilos to crack seeds

Crossbill: most highly specialized of all finches, the Crossbill's overlapped mandibles force conifer cones apart to extract the seeds. Continental birds feed mainly on Norwegian spruce, Scottish Crossbills on Scots pine seeds

Bullfinch: has a large bill that is ideally suited to nipping off buds, which brings the Bullfinch into sharp conflict with fruit farmers and gardeners. Takes soft fruit which it crushes and may also deal with small snails

Bullfinch

Pyrrhula pyrrhula (Linnaeus)

A strongly built, attractive finch, generally found either singly or in pairs, that is responsible for considerable damage to budding trees and which is regarded as a serious pest in fruit-growing areas

Population: 600,000 pairs

One of the easiest of small birds to identify. The male Bullfinch has a black cap, dove-grey back, a bold white rump that is particularly noticeable in flight, and black tail and wings, the latter marked with a bold white bar. The underparts are a startling deep pink. The female is similar, though browner above, but with the underparts a vinous pink-brown. The strong, heavy bill is distinctly conical in shape and the head always appears small compared with the body. Bullfinches are invariably found in pairs and seldom form more than transitory flocks. They are never far from cover and are generally seen flitting away along a hedgerow. 14.5 cm (5¾ in).

Voice: A piping *deu*, often *deu-deu*; sings a quiet warbling song that is seldom heard.

Habitat: Tangled bushy areas including woodland edges, hedgerows, gardens, heaths, forestry plantations and, when feeding at least, is also found in orchards.

Reproduction: The nest is usually placed at no great height in a bush and consists of a simple platform of twigs with a cup of roots and hair. It is built by the female alone in late April or May and the 4–5, occasionally 6–7, pale blue eggs are spotted and scrawled with dark purplish-brown. Incubation, by the female, lasts 12–14 days and the chicks are fed by both parents, though the female broods for the first few days. The chicks fledge some 12–18 days after hatching. Two or even 3 broods are reared.

Food: Seeds, buds and fruit, though young are fed on moth and other larvae. In winter dependent on seeds, mainly ash, but when this crop is insufficient birds turn readily to the buds of fruit trees and can cause serious damage in orchards.

Range and Distribution: Across Eurasia from northern Spain to Kamchatka and Japan. In Europe the Bullfinch breeds north to northern Norway and south to Italy and the mountains of Greece. Also in the Caucasus and northern Iran. In Britain and Ireland it is widespread and is absent only from the major hill areas, northern Scotland and the Outer Hebrides, Orkneys and Shetland, and from the Isle of Man and western Ireland.

Movements: Resident, with some local movements due to winter food shortage. A small number of Continental birds sometimes arrive in the northeast in October and November.

Hawfinch

Coccothraustes coccothraustes (Linnaeus)

A large, heavily built finch with a massive head and bill that is widespread but notably elusive and difficult to find. The largest of our finches, the Hawfinch is a remarkably self-effacing bird that even keen watchers may go years without observing

Population: 5,000 to 10,000 pairs

The most prominent feature is the huge steel-coloured bill that can exert sufficient pressure to crack a cherry stone. In flight the chunky shape, large head and bill and distinctive call are enough to distinguish it from all other British birds. The crown is rich brown bordered below by a grey half-collar. The back is dark chestnut with black wings marked by a whitish wing bar and curiously shaped triangular-tipped inner flight feathers. The tail is chestnut tipped with white, the underparts warm buff-brown. The female is similar, but less brightly marked. 18 cm (7 in).

Voice: A distinctive *tic* or *tzik*; the song is a seldom-heard *tchee-tchee, tur-whee-whee*.

Habitat: Deciduous woods with plentiful fruiting trees such as wild cherry, hornbeam, wych elm and beech. Orchards of fruit trees are also favoured as are parks and large gardens.

Reproduction: The nest, which consists of a cup of twigs and roots lined with hair, is built in an apple, pear, oak or sycamore, usually at some height from the ground, in late April or early May. The 5, occasionally 2–7, pale blue eggs are marked with speckles and scrawls of dark brown and incubated mainly by the female for 9–14 days. The chicks are fed by both parents and fledge after 10–14 days. An occasional second brood is reared.

Food: Buds in spring and insects in summer, but most food consists of the hard seeds of fruit that other finches cannot utilize. Its powerful bill thus allows the Hawfinch a monopoly of certain items.

Range and Distribution: Found from North Africa across Europe, through central Siberia to Manchuria and Japan. It reaches its furthest north in southern Sweden. In Britain it is widespread in England, Wales and southern and eastern Scotland. It is absent from the Highlands and islands, from Ireland, though a pair bred in 1902, and from much of the southwest. It is, however, easily overlooked.

Movements: Mainly resident, but movement takes birds to areas, such as Ireland, where they do not breed. Perhaps some wandering from the Continent.

Lapland Bunting

Calcarius lapponicus (Linnaeus)

An arctic bird that occurs regularly in small numbers as a passage and winter visitor and which first bred in Britain in 1977. Male in summer (foreground) and female shown

Tundra breeding distribution: 1 or 2 pairs in Scotland; no more than 100 winter

Essentially a ground-loving bird superficially similar to the Reed Bunting, especially in female and immature plumages. The male in summer has a black head and breast bordered by a white line that extends to form a white eye-stripe behind the eye. The nape is a distinctive rich chestnut and the remaining upperparts are brown streaked with black. There is a touch of chestnut on the rump and the dark tail has broad white margins. The underparts are white, streaked black on the flanks. Females and immatures are similar to female and immature Reed Buntings, but have a distinctive pale coronal stripe, as well as a patch of chestnut on the nape in the female. In winter Lapland Buntings are found in small flocks among coastal marshes and saltings. 15 cm (6 in).

Voice: A clear *teeu* and a *ticky-tick-tick*; the song is uttered in flight and resembles a short version of the Skylark's warbling.

Habitat: Open tundra with rocks and dwarf vegetation, often among marshy swamps; in winter on saltings and coastal marshes.

Reproduction: The nest is placed on the ground against a hummock, and is constructed of grasses, moss and lichens lined with feathers and hair. The 5–6, occasionally 2–7, pale greenish-buff eggs are mottled all over with red-brown and laid from the end of May. The female alone incubates for 10–14 days, and the chicks are fed by both parents for 11–15 days before fledging, though they usually leave the nest before they can fly. Single-brooded.

Food: Insects and their larvae in summer; in winter grass and other seeds form the staple diet.

Range and Distribution: Circumpolar in the Northern Hemisphere, though absent from Iceland. In Britain no less than 6 different sites were occupied in 1977 and at least 2 broods were reared, constituting the first breeding record. In 1978 2 pairs bred.

Movements: A regular autumn passage of birds in the northwest of the country and on the east coast, where a few remain throughout the winter. These birds originate from Greenland.

Snow Bunting

Plectrophenax nivalis (Linnaeus)

A delightfully tame and attractive ground-dwelling bird that breeds on the arctic tundra and, in tiny numbers, on the highest Scottish hills. Elsewhere it is known as a winter visitor, often forming quite large flocks on beaches and coastal marshes. First winter bird shown

Population: 2 to 8 pairs; several thousand winter

Continental distribution

Summer male (foreground) and female. Male (lower) and female in flight

The male Snow Bunting is a handsome pied bird in summer. The head, nape and underparts are white; the back and tail black, though in flight the inner wing is also white. The female is clothed in dull browns and sandy colours that merge well with open stony country, but in flight she shows similar flashes of white on wings and tail as her mate. In winter males are similar to females, though invariably showing more white. Winter flocks feed quietly and confidingly on shingle beaches, and may be passed unnoticed. However, in the air they are distinctive and resemble nothing so much as pieces of paper being blown about in the wind. 16.5 cm (6½ in).

Voice: A clear *tweep* in flight, also a *teu*; the song is a high-pitched jingling *turee-turee-turee-turiwee*, uttered from a rock or in flight.

Habitat: Open tundra and mountain tops right to the edge of the permanent ice line; in winter haunts coastal marshes and beaches.

Reproduction: Males make much of their bold pied plumage in an elaborate courtship display and are sometimes polygamous. The nest is hidden in a rock crevice and consists of a cup of grasses and mosses lined with hair and feathers. The 4–6, occasionally up to 8, eggs are pale blue blotched with light brown, and are laid from late May onwards depending on latitude. The female alone incubates for 10–15 days and both parents feed the young for a similar period, though the female mainly broods for the first few days. The chicks frequently leave the nest for short periods before fledging. Double-brooded.

Food: Insects, especially flies and caddis, together with seeds of dwarf trees and grasses. In winter seeds predominate, though insects may be taken as available.

Range and Distribution: Breeds further north than any other small bird and enjoys a circumpolar distribution. In Europe it is found only in Scandinavia, Iceland and Scotland, which is right on the very edge of its range. It was first proved to breed in 1886 and is largely confined to the Cairngorms and some of the highest hills in the northwest.

Movements: Birds arrive from mid-September onwards and form flocks on hills in Scotland and along the Scottish and English east coasts. Some birds pass on to winter further south.

Yellowhammer

Emberiza citrinella (Linnaeus)

One of the most familiar birds of open country, with a distinctive song rendered by millions as 'a-little-bit-of-bread-and-no-cheese'. Yellow-hammers are numerous and widespread in Britain and Ireland, and the male's habit of singing his characteristic little song atop a prominent perch has earned the species a place in the countryman's heart. Male (foreground) and female shown

Population: about 1 million pairs

The impression of a yellow bird is produced by this colour on head and belly, for a closer look shows the plumage to be both more complex and more beautiful. The head is yellow marked with dark grey lines above the eye and outlining the ear coverts. The back is brown streaked with black and the wing feathers are broadly edged with rufous. The rump is bright rufous, plainly visible in flight, and the tail dark with white outer margins. The underparts are yellow streaked with chestnut on breast and flanks. The female is more subdued and streaked as are so many female buntings. However, the underlying yellow on face and crown and a rufous rump separate her from the female Cirl Bunting. Though found throughout the year singly or in pairs, hard weather and suitable feeding may create quite sizeable winter flocks. 16.5 cm (6½ in).

Voice: Distinctive song *chi-chi-chi-chi-chi-cheez*; also a hard *chip* note.

Habitat: Variety of open landscapes – heaths and commons, hedge-rows, waste ground and rough hillsides, young plantations. Yellow-hammers may resort to coastal marshes in hard weather.

Reproduction: The nest is placed on the ground at the foot of a bush or is hidden in a hedge, though occasionally it may be above the ground. It consists of a neat cup of grasses lined with hair and is constructed by the female alone from late April onwards. The 3–5, occasionally 2–6, white eggs are washed with blue or grey and finely spotted with reddish. They are incubated by the female for 11–14 days, and the chicks leave the nest some 10–14 days after hatching, though they cannot fly until 16 days. Double- or treble-brooded.

Food: Weed seeds, cereals, fruit and, in the breeding season, many insects, larvae, millipedes and other invertebrates.

Range and Distribution: Breeds throughout Europe, except for southern Iberia and the Mediterranean coastline, eastwards to central Siberia. Also in the Caucasus and northern Iran. In Britain and Ireland it is widespread and is absent only from London, the highest Pennines, the Highlands and from most of the Outer Hebrides and Orkneys. It is totally absent from Shetland.

Movements: Predominantly resident; Continental birds probably occur annually in autumn and spring, but their status is obscure.

Cirl Bunting

Emberiza cirlus (Linnaeus)

An attractive bird of sheltered country with bushes, trees and open glades that finds southern England at the very northern edge of its range. The male Cirl Bunting, despite some similarity to the more common and widespread Yellowhammer, is a distinctive bird with an unmistakable head pattern. Male (foreground) and female shown

Population: 500 pairs, but declining rapidly

Head and crown are black with a yellow supercilium and with yellow extending from the lores over the ear coverts. The back is rufous streaked with black, the rump grey, and the tail dark with white outer feathers. There is a yellow band forming a half-collar across the breast below the black chin that, in turn, gives way to a band of greenish-grey extending to the nape. The remaining underparts are yellow streaked with rufous on the flanks. The female is a rather nondescript brownish bird, streaked above and below and with some yellowish on head and belly. The grey, not rufous, rump separates her from the otherwise similar female Yellowhammer. 16.5 cm (6½ in).

Voice: The song is a prolonged and rattling jingle similar to, and confusable with, that of the Lesser Whitethroat, and similar to that of the Yellowhammer but lacking the final *cheez*. Also utters a *zip* that is repeated in a flight call.

Habitat: Warm, southern-facing sheltered valleys with good growth of hedges and trees. It is found at the foot of downlands, often near villages in and about large gardens, and also on sheltered heaths.

Reproduction: The nest is built into a thick hedge or bushy tangle, but also in a tree or on the ground. It is a neat cup of grasses lined with hair and is constructed by the female in mid-May. The 3–4, occasionally 2 or 5, pale blue or green eggs are speckled and scrawled with black and incubated by the female alone for 11–13 days. The female also feeds and tends the young, with little or no help from her mate, for the 11–13 days the chicks take to fledge. Double-brooded, with an occasional third clutch.

Food: Weed and grass seeds, cereals, berries, and insects and their larvae particularly as food for the young.

Range and Distribution: Breeds across Europe south and west of a line drawn from Birmingham to the southern Black Sea, and in Turkey. Also in North Africa and the Mediterranean islands. In Britain it is almost confined south of a line from Bristol to London, though some birds penetrate the Midlands. Most are found along the south coast with its mild winters and warm summers. Severe winters can seriously affect its numbers.

Movements: Resident.

Ortolan Bunting

Emberiza hortulana (Linnaeus)

A regular, if rare, wanderer from the Continent that occurs mainly in autumn at a few chosen sites and along the south coast. It is most frequently seen on plough where its self-effacing behaviour makes it easily overlooked

Continental breeding distribution: a handful of migrants in Britain each year

An attractive bird, the male Ortolan has a greenish head and breast marked with a yellow moustachial streak and throat. The upperparts are brown streaked with black, it has white outertail feathers, and rich orange underparts. Females and juveniles are darker and more heavily streaked above. The yellow throat pattern can usually be seen and, in all plumages, the bird has a yellow eye-ring and a pink bill. 16.5 cm (6½ in).

Voice: A thin *zit* and a stronger *tseu*; the song is rather melancholy with 6 or 7 *tseu* notes ending with another higher or lower pitched.

Habitat: Open country with low vegetation, agricultural land with hedgerows, gardens, and on passage frequently on plough.

Reproduction: The nest is placed on the ground among grass or low bushes and consists of a cup of grasses lined with hair built by the female in May or June according to latitude. The 4–6 eggs are washed with light blue, green or grey, spotted with darker tones, and are incubated by the female for 11–14 days. The chicks are fed by both parents for 10–15 days. Double-brooded.

Food: Seeds of grasses, cereals, weeds and insects and their larvae.

Range and Distribution: Found right across Europe to central Siberia, Turkey and northern Iran. Though it breeds but a short distance from the Channel coast of France it is only a rare wanderer to Britain and Ireland.

Movements: Migrates to the Mediterranean and tropical Africa to winter. Occurs in Britain at Fair Isle, north Norfolk and the Isles of Scilly in autumn, all places intensively monitored by bird-watchers, and along the south coast of England. It mostly occurs singly, but small flocks are not unknown. Usually recorded only at Fair Isle in spring.

Reed Bunting

Emberiza schoeniclus (Linnaeus)

A boldly marked, black-headed species most often associated with marshes and reed beds, but which has successfully expanded into a variety of dry habitats during recent years

Population: about 600,000 pairs

Female

M ales have a complete black hood extending from nape to upper breast, and broken only by a white moustachial streak. The lower nape is white, forming a collar between the head and the chestnut- and black-striped back and wings. The tail is broadly edged with white and the white underparts are finely streaked on the flanks. The female is a heavily streaked brown and buff bird with a light outline extending from the eye around the ear coverts, and bordered below by a black moustachial streak. Reed Buntings perch openly, and frequently feed among low vegetation and on the ground. They sing from prominent perches and are generally tame and approachable. 15 cm (6 in).

Voice: The song is an accelerated *seek-seek-seek-tisseek*; also utters a high-pitched *seep* and a *chink*.

Habitat: All manner of wetlands from reed beds to marshes and floods, but in more recent years, specifically since a high population level in 1968, it has spread into drier areas including wasteland, hedgerows, conifer plantations, dry scrub and gardens.

Reproduction: Breeds in a variety of situations, mainly wetland, among reeds and other dense vegetation. The nest is constructed on the ground or in a bush and consists of a cup of grasses lined with hair and plant down built by the female alone. The 4–5, sometimes up to 7, pale lilac eggs are scrawled and spotted with black and laid from late April. Incubation, mainly by the female, lasts 12–14 days and the young are fed by both parents for 10–13 days prior to fledging. Usually double-brooded, with sometimes a third clutch.

Food: Predominantly seeds and cereals, also insects and their larvae in summer, as well as molluscs and crustaceans.

Range and Distribution: Found over a huge area of the Palearctic from western Europe to northernmost Scandinavia, through Turkey and Siberia to Manchuria and Japan. In Britain and Ireland the Reed Bunting is widespread and is absent only from high hills and from most parts of Shetland.

Movements: Most birds are resident, though with some local movements. Continental birds arrive on the east and south coasts in autumn and, while some undoubtedly pass on further south, many stay to winter. There is a regular return migration from March to May.

Corn Bunting

Miliaria calandra (Linnaeus)

A dull-coloured, chunky little bird that has spread successfully as a result of agricultural activities, but whose distribution still remains something of an enigma

Population: about 30,000 pairs

Male in typical singing posture

The Corn Bunting is a buff bird, boldly streaked above and below with dark brown. A smudgy moustachial streak and the lack of white in the tail are the only positive distinguishing marks, but the chunky shape with a large head and substantial bill are sufficient once the bird is well known. The habit of singing, head back, from a prominent perch and the rapid jingling song are diagnostic. Corn Buntings are generally solitary birds, though some areas may be densely populated and their calls echo across the landscape. They form flocks in winter. 18 cm (7 in).

Voice: A rattling song often likened to the sound produced by jangling a bunch of keys; also a clear *chip* and a rasping *zeep*.

Habitat: Farmland, cornfields, hedgerows, heaths with gorse, short-cropped grasslands, but always with a selection of song posts.

Reproduction: Singing often starts at the beginning of the year. But the nest, which is usually on the ground but also occasionally at some height in a tree or bush, is not built until April. It consists of a cup of grasses lined with roots and hair. The 4–6, occasionally 2–7, white eggs are sometimes washed light blue or buff, and are lightly streaked and spotted with grey. Males may be polygamous, and the female alone incubates for 12–14 days and feeds the chicks for the 9–12 days they spend in the nest, which they leave before they can fly. Single- or double-brooded, though a third brood is not unknown.

Food: Weed seeds, grass, berries, cereals and wild fruit, though insects and their larvae may be seasonally important. Also takes worms, slugs and other invertebrates.

Range and Distribution: Found in Mediterranean and temperate Europe northwards to southern Sweden, through Turkey and the Middle East to the Persian Gulf and beyond. In Britain and Ireland it is found throughout the country, but is absent from huge areas. In the north and west it is primarily a coastal species, though it is also confined to the coast over much of East Anglia.

Movements: Resident, with little evidence of wandering. Some immigration from the Continent, but on a very limited scale.

RARE, INTRODUCED AND ORNAMENTAL BIRDS

There are nearly 500 birds on the British and Irish Lists, though only some 200 breed, with another 50 or so occurring on a regular basis. This leaves over 200 species that can be categorized as rare, accidental, vagrant, introduced or escaped. By virtue of a variety of factors explained elsewhere, these islands have a remarkable wealth of birds that are of rare or vagrant status. This fact is surely an important element in the attractiveness of our birds and a contributory factor in the popularity of watching them. Every time that a bird-watcher plans an outing he (or she) has the chance of encountering an unusual or rare bird. Such birds may turn up at any time or at any place, indeed it is their very 'unexpectedness' that constitutes their appeal. Over the years our avifauna has also been enriched by deliberate introductions of birds not naturally found here. Some have occupied a vacant niche, settled down and prospered; others have failed to acclimatize. In addition, there are a number of birds that may be encountered in parks and gardens, and that could be described as ornamental. Such birds often escape, bringing excitement to those before whose binoculars they appear, though disappointment when their origins are realized. All such birds are described and illustrated in the pages that follow.

RARE BIRDS

By virtue of their geographical position at the edge of a large continental landmass and their extraordinary coastline, with off-shore islands and isolated headlands, Britain and Ireland are ideally suited to attract vagrant birds from virtually all directions. Arctic birds, wandering southwards, reach our northern isles. Siberian waifs moving westwards make the North Sea crossing and recuperate along our east coast. Summer visitors to Continental Europe overshoot in spring and cross the Channel to southern England. And birds drifted out over the Atlantic seaboard of North America find their first landfall along our western shores. As a result, over half of the 495-odd species that have been admitted to the British and Irish List can be classed as irregular. Some have occurred only once, others may be almost regular in small numbers each year. All can be classed as 'rare'. Of the species that have not been included in the main section of this book, under half have occurred on less than 10 occasions. These are listed at the end of this section. The others are detailed in the pages that follow.

White-billed Diver
Gavia adamsii
Slightly larger than Great Northern Diver and similarly marked in summer and winter plumage. At all seasons, large ivory-coloured bill with prominent uptilt to lower mandible is best distinction; but some Great Northerns show similar bill-shape. 84–86 cm (33–34 in). Circumpolar distribution in Arctic; wintering off Norway; occasionally wanders south to Scottish islands, especially Shetland.

Cory's Shearwater
Calonectris diomedea
Typical shearwater, larger than Manx Shearwater with much less contrasting plumage. Grey-brown upperparts, whitish underparts, and with no sharp demarcation between cap and chin (see Great Shearwater). 'Shearwatering' flight. 46 cm (18 in). Scarce but regular visitor, mainly to southwest in late summer from Mediterranean and adjacent Atlantic.

Black-browed Albatross
Diomedea melanophris
Huge, black-backed and black-winged seabird, with wingspan of over 2 m and 'shearwatering' flight. Can be confused only with Great Black-backed Gull, but stiff narrow wings and black tailband easily distinguish. Underwing is white with broad black margins. 81–86 cm (32–34 in). Other albatrosses may enter North Atlantic but this is most regular. Individuals have joined Gannet colonies, as at Hermaness in late 1970s, others at sea. Vagrant from Southern Hemisphere.

Little Shearwater
Puffinus assimilis
Very similar to Manx Shearwater, black above and white below. Considerably smaller and with much more flapping flight. 27 cm (10½ in). Very rare vagrant to sea-watch points, mainly off western Ireland; but may be overlooked. Breeds on Atlantic islands and elsewhere around the world.

American Bittern
Botaurus lentiginosus
Similar to Bittern with mottled brown plumage and secretive habits. Slightly smaller and marked by a broad moustachial streak that widens out to form a considerable black patch on sides of neck. Also lacks black crown of Bittern. 66 cm (26 in). Rare vagrant from North America.

Squacco Heron
Ardeola ralloides
A smallish heron beautifully marked in summer with warm buff above and below, and with cascading, black-streaked head plumes. In winter becomes more drab in streaked browns. Dark grey, black-tipped bill and yellow eyes. In all plumages white wings obvious in flight. 46 cm (18 in). Summer visitor to southern Europe rarely wandering northwards to Britain.

Great White Egret
Egretta alba
Large white heron similar to much smaller Little Egret. All-white plumage with filigree plumes on back in summer. Legs and feet black; bill black, black and yellow, or pure yellow. 89 cm (35 in). Resident in southeastern Europe; very rare vagrant northwards to Britain.

Little Bittern
Ixobrychus minutus
Small, secretive heron that frequents reed beds. Male is marked by black crown, back and wings, the latter with large bold creamy-pink patches obvious when perched and in flight. Underparts pale buff-white. Female duller, browner and streaked below, but with wing patch still quite obvious. 35 cm (14 in). Summer visitor to most of Continent that is a rare vagrant to Britain. May have bred and likely to do so again.

Cattle Egret
Bubulcus ibis
A small white heron, marked in summer with warm buff on crown, chest and back. Bill pale yellow, legs darkish rust-red. In winter becomes pure white. At all times gregarious, often gathering around and perching on cattle and other large, wild and domesticated, animals to feed. 51 cm (20 in). Resident in southern Spain and Africa that has spread across the Atlantic to colonize the New World this century. Rare vagrant northwards to Britain.

Purple Heron
Ardea purpurea
Smaller than Grey Heron and generally much darker. Sides of neck and chest deep rust-brown with distinctive black stripe extending from chin to breast. Foreneck and underparts creamy, streaked black. Back and wings dark grey. Bill and legs yellowish. 79 cm (31 in). Summer visitor to Continent; scarce visitor, usually in spring, to Britain.

Night Heron
Nycticorax nycticorax
A crepuscular and gregarious heron that spends its days hidden in cover, flighting to feed on marshes at night. Adult is black on crown and back, wings are dove-grey, face and underparts white, legs yellowish. Large reddish eye. Immature grey-brown spotted with whitish and similar to but paler and smaller than Bittern. 61 cm (24 in). Vagrant from southern Europe where it is a summer visitor. A free-flying population lives around Edinburgh Zoo.

Little Egret
Egretta garzetta
A slim, elegant heron that has a much less hunched appearance than either Squacco Heron or Cattle Egret. Pure white at all seasons, with filigree plumes on chest, crown and particularly back in summer. Bill and legs black, feet yellow. Slim lines and long neck distinguish it from all European herons except Great White Egret. 56 cm (22 in). Resident in Mediterranean, partial migrant further north. Rare in Britain and seen mainly in spring.

Black Stork
Ciconia nigra
Large, well-built heron-like bird. Black upperparts and chest, glossed with bottle-green; white underparts. Large, sharply pointed red bill and red legs. Walks easily with deliberate gait and flies with neck extended forward. Frequently soars on still wings. 97 cm (38 in). A declining summer visitor to eastern Europe and southern Iberia that is a very rare vagrant to Britain.

339

White Stork
Ciconia ciconia
Large, heavily built bird, with long red legs and sharply pointed red bill. Plumage white, except for black flight feathers of wings. Usually gregarious, particularly on migration, and nests on house tops and telegraph poles. 102 cm (40 in). Summer visitor to central and eastern Europe, and Iberia, that is a rare vagrant to Britain.

Snow Goose
Anser caerulescens
Dimorphic: white phase has all-white plumage with black primaries, pink bill and dark pink legs. Blue phase has white head, remaining plumage mottled blue-black and white, tail with black subterminal band. Gregarious at all seasons. 63–76 cm (25–30 in). Breeds on arctic tundra in Canada, migrating into United States in huge flocks. Scarce, but regular, vagrant to Ireland; rare elsewhere. Beware escapes and albinistic forms of other species.

American Wigeon
Anas americana
Similar in shape to Wigeon, but male has paler whitish forehead bordered by green sides to the head, and with bold mottling on chin and neck. Also mottled in brown (rather than grey) above and below. Similar white marks on flanks, and black tail bordered by white as with European bird. Female very similar to Wigeon, but greyer on head and mantle and with white axillaries in flight. 46–56 cm (18–22 in). Rare transatlantic vagrant, but virtually annual in Ireland in autumn.

Glossy Ibis
Plegadis falcinellus
Medium-sized, dark, heron-like bird with long, decurved, Curlew-like bill. Close approach reveals purplish gloss on neck and wings, with dark iridescent bottle-green on wings. Bill and legs dark. Flies with neck extended. Gregarious. 56 cm (22 in). Summer visitor to southeastern Europe. Vagrant northwards to Britain, but beware escapes.

Red-breasted Goose
Branta ruficollis
Small, boldly marked goose with black back and wings, and black belly separated by bold white line. Black face and hind-neck and bold pattern of white-bordered chestnut patches on head, foreneck and chest. Small bill and legs slate-grey. White undertail and tail with black terminal band. 53–56 cm (21–22 in). Very rare vagrant from Siberian breeding grounds and winter quarters in southeast Europe.

Blue-winged Teal
Anas discors
Teal-sized duck marked, in the male, by dark powder-blue head with a bold white crescent before the eye. Pale blue patch on inner wing of both sexes in flight. Black tail bordered by white patch at rear of flanks. Female has bluer forewing and longer bill than similar female Garganey. 38 cm (15 in). Rare transatlantic vagrant – beware escapes.

Lesser White-fronted Goose
Anser erythropus
Similar to though slightly smaller than White-fronted Goose. Has similar black bars and smudges on belly, but white forehead extends further on crown. Yellow eye-ring, present even on juveniles, can be seen at considerable distances, and pinkish bill is decidedly smaller. 53–66 cm (21–26 in). Breeds on tundra from Scandinavia eastwards, wintering in southeastern Europe. Rare vagrant to Britain, usually in association with White-fronts.

Ruddy Shelduck
Tadorna ferruginea
Large, uniformly cinnamon, goose-like duck, closely related to Shelduck. The head is paler than rest of plumage, particularly in the female which also lacks the narrow black neck-ring of the male. Both sexes have a white then black line bordering the wing, black tail, and black bill and feet. In flight the wing coverts, above and below, form bold white patches. 64 cm (25 in). Decidedly rare visitor from southernmost Europe, but regularly escapes from wildfowl collections – all records to be treated with great caution.

Ring-necked Duck
Aythya collaris
Similar to Tufted Duck, but with peaked crown. Male has white crescent at front of greyish flanks extending upwards around the bend of the wing. Neck-ring of little value in field. Female has buffer face than female Tufted, with clear buff eye-ring and buff line over ear coverts. In flight shows grey (not white) wing bar. 43 cm (17 in). Rare transatlantic vagrant – beware escapes from wildfowl collections.

Rare Birds

Ferruginous Duck
Aythya nyroca
Sometimes called White-eyed Pochard.
Male is rich chestnut with darker back,
bold white mark below tail and yellow eye.
Female dark brown all over with similar
white rear end, but lacks pale eye. Both
sexes show white wing bar in flight. 41 cm
(16 in). Vagrant from southern and eastern
Europe, but on occasion may escape from
wildfowl collections.

Surf Scoter
Melanitta perspicillata
Similar to Common Scoter, but male
marked with patches of white on crown
and hindneck, and yellow, red and white
bill. Female dull brown with 2 distinct
pale buffy patches on sides of head similar
to female Velvet Scoter's, but lacks white
speculum of that bird. 56 cm (22 in).
Vagrant from North America, mostly to
northern and western isles.

Lesser Kestrel
Falco naumanni
Slightly smaller and lighter in build than
Kestrel; shares hovering habit, but gener-
ally gregarious in native haunts. Male dis-
tinguished by unspotted back, lack of dark
moustaches, and warmer, buffy underparts.
Female very similar to female Kestrel, but
underparts less streaked. 30 cm (12 in).
Very rare vagrant from southern Europe.

King Eider
Somateria spectabilis
Male is boldly marked in black and white
and separated from Eider at any distance
by black back. Red bill backed by bold
orange facial shield, crown pale blue, face
pale green. White line along flanks and
white spot near tail. Female like female
Eider, but with smaller, less triangular bill
extending in shorter point towards eye.
Pale buff eye-ring. 56 cm (22 in). Rare
visitor from Arctic that occurs most winters at sea in northern isles.

Black Kite
Milvus migrans
Dark, largish bird of prey similar to Marsh
Harrier. Slow, flapping flight on long narrow wings; long tail slightly forked. Generally gregarious and mostly a scavenger.
56 cm (22 in). Rare vagrant northwards
from southern Europe.

Red-footed Falcon
Falco vespertinus
A small, Kestrel-like falcon that frequently
hovers and is generally gregarious. Male
is sooty blue-black with chestnut-red leg
feathers and undertail coverts. Cere, eye-
ring and legs all red. Female is slate-grey
above broadly barred with buff; crown
and underparts a rich orange-buff lightly
streaked with black on the flanks. Black
around eye extends to form a moustache
against white cheeks. Eye-ring and legs
red. 30 cm (12 in). Rare visitor, mostly in
spring to southern England: a summer
visitor to eastern Europe.

Steller's Eider
Polysticta stelleri
Male has white head marked by 2 patches
of green. Black extending from chin and
foreneck to back and tail, with broad white
area below. Cinnamon breast and flanks
with black spot. Female uniformly dark
with pale eye-ring. Both have small bill
and rounded head. Essentially marine.
46 cm (18 in). Very rare visitor from Arctic.

White-tailed Eagle
Haliaeetus albicilla
Large, dark brown bird of prey with huge,
broad, vulture-like wings. Prominent head
and massive pale bill; strongly wedge-
shaped white tail in adult. Immatures uniformly dark, but with wedge-shaped tail.
69–91 cm (27–36 in). Formerly bred on
Scottish coasts and in process of reintroduction in Inner Hebrides; otherwise extremely rare vagrant from Norway.

Gyrfalcon
Falco rusticolus
Large, powerful falcon that occurs in 2
phases. Normally grey all over, heavily
barred and flecked with black and white.
Some birds of Greenland race are white
flecked with black mainly above. Broader
wings and longer tail, together with size,
distinguish it from Peregrine. 51–56 cm
(20–22 in). Rare visitor from Arctic in
winter, becoming scarcer.

Little Crake
Porzana parva

Secretive and elusive marsh bird, smaller than Starling, with grey underparts and brown and black streaked upperparts. Rear of flanks barred with white; similar Baillon's Crake is barred black and white. Bill yellow with red base, legs green. Female has buffy underparts barred dark on flanks. 19 cm (7½ in). Rare visitor to Britain from eastern Europe.

Baillon's Crake
Porzana pusilla

Similar in size and habits to Little Crake, but distinguished by black and white striping on rear flanks, pinkish legs and green bill. Female greyish below with similarly striped flanks. 18 cm (7 in). Rare vagrant from Continental Europe, but increasingly identified in recent years.

Black-winged Stilt
Himantopus himantopus

Boldly pied wading bird, with black wings and back. Underparts, head and neck white, but male has black crown in summer. Black bill fine and needle-like, a little longer than head. Easily identified at all seasons by extremely long pink legs that trail behind in flight. Usually gregarious. 38 cm (15 in). A scarce visitor in summer, mostly spring, that has bred on a single occasion.

Little Bustard
Otis tetrax

Stocky, ground-dwelling bird, vermiculated brown above and white below; thick yellow legs. Male in summer has striking black and white neck pattern. Flight duck-like, showing large areas of white on wings. Much smaller than closely related Great Bustard and, despite being more common, is only an exceptional visitor. 43 cm (17 in). This rare vagrant from Continental Europe breeds no further away than northern France and is thus surprisingly scarce as a visitor.

Crane
Grus grus

Large, grey, heron-like bird with black and white head and neck topped with patch of red on crown. Grey plumes cascade over tail. In flight holds neck stretched out stork-like in front. Gregarious and usually found in large flocks. 114 cm (45 in). Rare and erratic visitor that may occasionally stray to Britain in quite remarkable numbers from its traditional and narrowly defined route between Scandinavian breeding grounds and winter quarters in central and southern Spain. As with Cranes worldwide, this species is declining in numbers and may therefore become an even less frequent visitor in future.

Cream-coloured Courser
Cursorius cursor

Slim, elegant, fast-running bird of arid desert areas. Upperparts are a rich sandy-brown, underparts a paler buff. Long neck with small head and neat decurved bill; long yellow legs. Head pattern distinctive with blue-grey hind crown bordered by white and black stripes extending from eye to nape and producing a capped appearance. In flight shows outer half of upperwing black, and black underwing. 23 cm (9 in). Rare vagrant, mostly in October from North Africa, that finds sandy beaches nearest equivalent to usual desert habitat.

Great Bustard
Otis tarda

Huge, Turkey-like bird marked by rich chestnut back barred with black; white underparts, grey head and neck. Adult males have drooping white moustaches and are larger than younger males and females. In flight shows bold white areas in wing. Generally found in small parties. Male 102 cm (40 in), female 76 cm (30 in). Erratic vagrant from Continent with single birds occurring no more than every 5 or more years. However, such strays invariably stay put and are seen by considerable numbers of interested bird-watchers. Attempted reintroduction in southern England in the 1970s has had little success and may well fail.

White-rumped Sandpiper
Calidris fuscicollis
Dunlin-like wader, but with only faint wing bar. Bill short and straight, legs short and dark, wings long and extending beyond the tail when folded. Identified at all times by white rump – but see Curlew Sandpiper. 15 cm (6 in). Regular though scarce transatlantic vagrant occurring from August to November.

Collared Pratincole
Glareola pratincola
Darkish, streamlined marshland bird usually seen flying in noisy parties. Upperparts brown with dark primaries. Throat, chin and foreneck pale cream enclosed by line of black; chest brown shading to white on belly. Bill stubby and decurved with red spot at base. Legs short and black. Long pointed wings and deeply forked tail produce tern-like shape in flight, when maroon axillaries and white trailing edge to secondaries may be seen. 25 cm (10 in). Rare vagrant from Mediterranean, mostly in spring.

Lesser Golden Plover
Pluvialis dominica
Slightly smaller than Golden Plover, but longer legged and generally slimmer. Upperparts of juvenile greyer, less golden and, in flight, underwing and axillaries are dusky-grey, not white. Crown appears darkish, producing a capped appearance. 25 cm (10 in). A rare transatlantic autumn vagrant, previously overlooked.

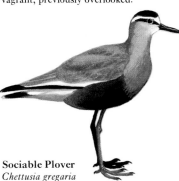

Baird's Sandpiper
Calidris bairdii
Dunlin-like wader, but always more scaly-rufous above. Long wings, extending well beyond tail when folded, produce an elongated look heightened by shortish black legs and horizontal stance. Streaking on breast produces clear-cut pectoral band. Winter birds are paler above. 15 cm (6 in). Transatlantic vagrant in autumn.

Black-winged Pratincole
Glareola nordmanni
Virtually identical to Collared Pratincole and formerly regarded as conspecific. Adult distinguished by black, not maroon, axillaries; and lack of white trailing edge to secondaries. 25 cm (10 in). Rare vagrant from east, mainly in autumn.

Sociable Plover
Chettusia gregaria
Long-legged relative of Lapwing, with distinctive summer plumage. Brown above; vinous grey on breast, bordered below by a band of rich purplish-chestnut. Crown black, white forehead and supercilium, and distinctive black eye-stripe. In flight underwing shows much white, and upper surface has white secondaries. Tail white with black subterminal band. In winter bold pattern is lost and best field marks are blackish eye-stripe and flight pattern. 29 cm ($11\frac{1}{2}$ in). Rare vagrant from southern Russia, mostly in autumn and winter.

Killdeer
Charadrius vociferus
Similar to but slightly larger than Ringed Plover, with 2 distinct breast bands and a different head pattern. Black bill slightly longer, and legs pale pink. Wedge-shaped tail longer and, in flight, is bright rufous tipped with black and white. A loud *kill-dee* call is distinctive. 25 cm (10 in). A transatlantic vagrant most likely to occur in winter.

Least Sandpiper
Calidris minutilla
Smaller than Little Stint and other North American 'peeps', with very thin bill. Feeds busily in stint-like manner. Identified only with extreme care. Dark brown above and frequently (though not always) with pale greenish legs. Distinctive *kreet* call. 14 cm ($5\frac{1}{2}$ in). Vagrant from North America, mainly in August and September.

Pectoral Sandpiper
Calidris melanotos
Like diminutive Ruff, with brownish scaled upperparts, small head on long neck, and straight bill. Upperparts marked by a double white V. Chest heavily streaked black in band terminating abruptly. Remaining underparts white. In flight shows similar, though less pronounced, tail pattern as Ruff and faint wing bar. Legs greenish. Distinctive *treep* call note. 19 cm ($7\frac{1}{2}$ in). Regular transatlantic migrant in small numbers, mostly in autumn.

Great Snipe
Gallinago media
Distinguished from Snipe with greatest of care. Plumage pattern very similar, with barring and striping in browns and creams, but larger area of white on outertail feathers when flushed. More rotund, even Woodcock-like, in shape and has shorter, thicker-based bill. Flight more direct, on bowed wings, with bill held nearer the horizontal. 28 cm (11 in). A vagrant from Scandinavia that may occur in all months outside the breeding season.

Sharp-tailed Sandpiper
Calidris acuminata
Siberian equivalent of Pectoral Sandpiper, but shorter legs and heavier build produce less Ruff-like appearance. Also differs in having dark crown marked by prominent supercilium, and with breast margins fading into pale underparts rather than terminating in a band. 19 cm (7½ in). Extremely rare autumn vagrant from Siberia.

Buff-breasted Sandpiper
Tryngites subruficollis
Distinctive Ruff-like wader with long neck and small, rounded head. Upperparts scaly-buff, underparts a uniform rich cinnamon. Bill short and straight, legs yellow, eye-ring white. No white in tail, or wing bar in flight, but white underwing contrasts with cinnamon body. 18 cm (7 in). Regular transatlantic vagrant in variable numbers, mostly in September, especially to Isles of Scilly and to southern Ireland. This is a grassland species best looked for on well-cropped sheep pastures, golf courses or similar areas. Even airfields are a favoured resting ground.

Broad-billed Sandpiper
Limicola falcinellus
Similar to Dunlin, but darker and browner above, and whiter below. Pattern of stripes on crown and back produce Snipe-like impression, heightened by long bill distinctly kinked and flattened at tip. Elongated appearance produced by short legs. Shows white outertail feathers in flight, but lacks wing bar. Generally solitary. 16.5 cm (6½ in). Rare spring and autumn visitor on passage to and from its Scandinavian breeding grounds.

Upland Sandpiper
Bartramia longicauda
Buff-brown, mottled and barred wader with long neck, small head, and thin, pointed bill. Runs plover-like over the ground. In flight long wings and extremely long wedge-shaped tail are diagnostic. Distinctive *quip-ip-ip-ip* call. 25 cm (10 in). Rare autumn vagrant from North America.

Long-billed Dowitcher
Limnodromus scolopaceus
Medium-sized, long-billed wader of Snipe-like proportions. Rich chestnut in breeding season. In autumn and winter upperparts grey, becoming darker on wings. Underparts pale grey with faint barring on sides of breast and flanks. Legs greenish and extending slightly beyond tail in flight. Bill at least twice length of head. In flight shows narrow white trailing edge to wing and white rump extending up back to form a prominent V. Tail barred black and white. Though there are 2 separate species – the other is the Short-billed *L. griseus* – over three-quarters of those that occur in Britain remain specifically un-identified. Surest means of separation is comparative width of tail bars – the dark bars being wider than the white ones in this species. Great care must be taken, however, and bill length is of little value. *Keck* call. 28 cm (11 in). Rare vagrant from North America. Short-billed species shown above, Long-billed below.

Stilt Sandpiper
Micropalama himantopus
Greenshank- or Wood Sandpiper-like wader, with rich chestnut breeding plumage. In autumn and winter is grey, with white rump visible in flight, and white underparts. Long legs, long neck and long bill, the tip decurved, produce an elegance more like a *Tringa* than *Calidris* sandpiper. The prominent pale supercilium is a good field mark. 19 cm (7½ in). Rare transatlantic vagrant, mostly in early autumn.

Marsh Sandpiper
Tringa stagnatilis
Like a small and slim Greenshank, but with darker upperparts producing a more contrasted pattern. Smaller head on long neck, and proportionately longer legs give a distinctive shape. Bill much finer, almost needle-like. In flight legs extend well beyond barred tail, and white rump extends in V up back. 23 cm (9 in). Very rare vagrant from eastern Europe during passage periods from May to September.

Greater Yellowlegs
Tringa melanoleuca
Elegant, Greenshank-like bird, greyish above and white below. Long yellow legs extend well beyond tail in flight. No wing bar and white rump is square, not extending up back in V like Greenshank's. Long, thick bill has definite uptilt. 28 cm (11 in). Very rare vagrant from North America, mainly in autumn.

Terek Sandpiper
Xenus cinereus
An elegant grey wader marked with flecks of black Greenshank-fashion on the back. Underparts white, bold supercilium. Bill long and distinctly uptilted; legs short and orange-yellow. Bobs tail like Common Sandpiper. In flight shows pale grey secondaries and rump, with white margins to the tail. 23 cm (9 in). Very rare vagrant from northern Russia, mostly in May.

Long-tailed Skua
Stercorarius longicaudus
Smallest of the skuas with correspondingly lighter, more airy, flight. Only pale phase birds now occur. Similar in coloration and plumage pattern to pale phase Arctic Skua, but usually with longer tail streamers. When streamers are broken, grey rather than brownish upperparts, size and lack of breast band are best distinguishing features. 51–56 cm (20–22 in). Regular autumn migrant offshore from August to October, mostly to the north and west coasts, though some numbers penetrate the North Sea as far south as East Anglia. Regular offshore in northern Biscay and the Channel approaches.

Lesser Yellowlegs
Tringa flavipes
Very similar to Greater Yellowlegs, but slimmer and considerably smaller. Best distinction is comparatively shorter and thinner bill – more like Marsh Sandpiper's than Greenshank's. 23 cm (9 in). Transatlantic vagrant in irregular numbers, mainly in September and October, but also in spring and summer.

Spotted Sandpiper
Actitis macularia
Considered conspecific with Common Sandpiper until quite recently. In summer boldly spotted breast is diagnostic, but in autumn and winter virtually identical to European bird. Best distinctions are more contrasting barring on wing coverts, and *teep-teep* call note. 20 cm (8 in). A transatlantic vagrant that has been identified, mainly in autumn, with increasing frequency in recent years and which bred in Scotland in 1975.

Laughing Gull
Larus atricilla
Black-hooded gull in summer, with dark grey wings and blackish primaries, not white as Black-headed Gull's. In winter has smudge of dark on hind crown and around eye. Immatures separated with care from immature Common Gull by more prominent white trailing edge to black secondaries and patchy underparts. In all plumages rather long black or dark red bill is useful feature. 41 cm (16 in). Only recently admitted to British List, but ever-increasing records since first identified in 1966 indicate that this American bird was previously overlooked. Increasing skill and a knowledge of what to look for on the part of birdwatchers have revolutionized our understanding of the occurrence of what were previously regarded as highly unlikely, or at best rare, vagrant gulls.

Solitary Sandpiper
Tringa solitaria
A greyish wader bearing a remarkable similarity to Wood and Green Sandpipers, but lacking the white rump of those birds. Long wings extend beyond tail when folded. Clear-cut white eye-ring. In flight lacks wing bar, has dark underwing, and white barred outertail feathers. 18 cm (7 in). A very rare vagrant from North America to the west in autumn.

Wilson's Phalarope
Phalaropus tricolor
Larger than other phalaropes and less inclined to swim. Distinctive breeding plumage marked with vinous black and red pattern on neck and back. In autumn and winter is pale grey above and whitish below, with fine black bill and yellow legs. In flight has white rump, but no wing bar. Lesser Yellowlegs is more spotted on back and wings. 23 cm (9 in). Rare transatlantic vagrant, mostly in September.

Sabine's Gull
Larus sabini
Delicate little marine gull with slate-grey upperparts, white underparts, and a grey hood in summer. In winter the hood is lost. In all plumages a combination of black outer primaries, white inner primaries and secondaries, and grey (brown in immature) wing coverts and back produces a marked pattern in flight. 33 cm (13 in). Regular transatlantic migrant that may be forced by prevailing weather to seek refuge along our shores from August to November.

Ross's Gull
Rhodostethia rosea
Delightful, small gull with extremely long wings and long, wedge-shaped tail giving it an elongated and horizontal appearance. Pale grey above, white below, the latter washed with pink in summer. A black necklace may persist into winter. Small black bill, legs and feet red. 32 cm (12½ in). Very rare vagrant from arctic oceans, but becoming more frequent.

Caspian Tern
Sterna caspia
Huge tern, pale grey above and white below with large coral-red bill. In summer prominent black crown and black legs, the crown becoming mottled black in winter. Underside of primaries dark. 53 cm (21 in). Vagrant to southern England, mainly from June to September.

Bonaparte's Gull
Larus philadelphia
Similar to but slightly smaller than Black-headed Gull with same pattern of white forewing and black wing tips. Distinguished in summer by slate, not brown, hood; and in all other plumages by white, not dark, undersides to outer primaries, and smaller black bill. 30–35 cm (12–14 in). A transatlantic vagrant in autumn and winter.

Ivory Gull
Pagophila eburnea
Only all-white gull when adult – but beware albinos of common species. Long wings extend well beyond square tail giving an elongated appearance. Bill yellow tipped with red; legs and feet black. Small rounded head and short bill give the bird a pigeon-like look. Immatures are boldly speckled with black and have a smudge between bill and eye. 44 cm (17½ in). Very rare vagrant from Arctic in winter.

Sooty Tern
Sterna fuscata
Large, pied tern, black above and white below, with deeply forked tail. Forehead white, crown and nape black continuous with black head and wings. Only the even rarer Bridled Tern is similar, but in that slightly smaller species there is a pale collar between crown and back. Bill and legs black. 41 cm (16 in). Very rare vagrant from tropics, mostly found dead along the tideline in summer.

Ring-billed Gull
Larus delawarensis
Very similar to Common Gull, but thicker bill has black ring near the tip on adults. Also larger with paler grey upperparts and wings, and longer legs. Immatures separated only with greatest care. 46–51 cm (18–20 in). First recorded in 1973, but since of virtually annual occurrence in spring and autumn. Presumably overlooked previously.

Gull-billed Tern
Gelochelidon nilotica
Similar to Sandwich Tern, but stockier and with a thick, heavy black bill. Pale grey above, white below, with black bill and legs. The black cap of summer becomes only a smudge behind the eye in winter. The legs are much longer than the Sandwich Tern's. Often hawks for insects over dry land. 38 cm (15 in). Variable numbers from April to September, has bred once.

Whiskered Tern
Chlidonias hybridus
Easily distinguished in summer by grey underparts with white cheeks below black cap. Bill and feet red. Beware dusky Arctic Terns in poor light. In autumn and winter looks more like typical tern than marsh tern, but tail only slightly forked. Lacks Black Tern's smudge on side of breast. Bill and feet dark; rump and nape grey. 25 cm (9¾ in). Vagrant from southern Europe in May and June, also in autumn.

White-winged Black Tern
Chlidonias leucopterus
Black head and body with white wings (lined with black) together with red bill and legs make this marsh tern not only easily identifiable, but also quite beautiful in spring. In autumn and winter similar to Black Tern, but lacks smudge on side of breast and darker back forms 'saddle' between lighter wings. Dark ear coverts almost separated from dark crown. 24 cm (9¼ in). Scarce visitor from eastern Europe in spring and especially autumn.

Great Spotted Cuckoo
Clamator glandarius
Large, long-tailed bird of similar shape to Cuckoo. Dark slate-brown above boldly spotted with white, creamy-yellow throat and breast, white underparts. Dark crown has prominent crest. 39 cm (15½ in). Very rare vagrant from Mediterranean to the west in spring and to the east in autumn.

Hawk Owl
Surnia ulula
A hawk-like owl with long tail and pointed wings that frequently hunts by day and perches openly with little fear of man. Barred underparts and flat-topped head marked by prominent black facial outline. 36–40 cm (14–16 in). Very rare vagrant from Scandinavia and North America.

Tengmalm's Owl
Aegolius funereus
Totally nocturnal owl, slightly larger than Little Owl, but brownish rather than greyish. Large head with white facial disc and prominent raised black 'eyebrows'. Distinctive white V on back. Flies in typical owl-fashion rather than woodpecker-like bounding of Little Owl. 25 cm (10 in). Rare vagrant from Scandinavia and eastern Europe, mainly in winter.

Brünnich's Guillemot
Uria lomvia
Very similar to Guillemot and distinguished only with great care by heavier bill marked with white line at gape. In dead birds the gape of the common Guillemot may swell up with lengthy soaking in sea. 42 cm (16½ in). Extremely rare vagrant from Arctic, mostly found dead along tideline.

Yellow-billed Cuckoo
Coccyzus americanus
Slim, elegant, long-tailed bird, brown above and white below. Long, graduated black tail, each feather boldly tipped with white. Base of lower mandible yellow, rusty patch on primaries prominent in flight. 28–32 cm (11–12½ in). Very rare transatlantic vagrant in autumn.

Pallas's Sandgrouse
Syrrhaptes paradoxus
Typical streamlined shape of sandgrouse marked with narrow black band across belly. Fast-flying, short-legged bird. 35–41 cm (14–16 in). Formerly an irruptive species from Russian steppes that occasionally reached us in large numbers, and sometimes stayed on to breed. No large irruptions since 1908 and only 1 record has been noted since 1909.

Scops Owl
Otus scops
Even smaller than Little Owl with proportionately smaller head and erectile ear tufts. Flies like other owls rather than woodpecker-fashion like Little Owl. Best distinguished by monotonous, endlessly repeated piping *piu* note. 19 cm (7½ in). Rare vagrant northwards from southern Europe, mostly in spring and late autumn.

Alpine Swift
Apus melba
Huge swift with correspondingly slower wing beats than common Swift. Identified by white underparts broken by narrow breast band and brown rather than black upperparts. Forms huge colonies in native range. 22 cm (8½ in). Rare vagrant from Mediterranean from April to October, with spring and autumn peaks.

Bee-eater
Merops apiaster
Boldly coloured in bright greens, yellows and chestnut. Streamlined shape, long tail and large pointed wings apparent in flight, which is masterful and agile. A liquid *quip* call draws attention to high-flying birds. Confusable only with other bee-eaters. 28 cm (11 in). Rare vagrant northwards from Mediterranean, mainly in spring. Has bred on 2 occasions.

Roller
Coracias garrulus
Turquoise-blue head and underparts, with blue flashes on wings and tail, and chestnut back A large bird, hard to overlook, that perches on prominent posts and wires and has spectacular 'rolling' display flight. 31 cm (12 in). Vagrant from Mediterranean and eastern Europe in summer, mostly May and June.

Short-toed Lark
Calandrella brachydactyla
Small, short-billed lark, with greyish or rufous upperparts and whitish underparts. Dark patches at side of breast may be distinct, but often appear smudgy or streaky. 14 cm (5½ in). Vagrant northwards from Mediterranean in spring and autumn, mainly May, and September and October.

Lesser Short-toed Lark
Calandrella rufescens
Similar to Short-toed Lark, but with more rounded head. Breast and flanks streaked, but at certain angles streaks may appear to combine to form patches. 14 cm (5½ in). Rare vagrant from Spain or Middle East to southwest (Ireland) in early spring.

Crested Lark
Galerida cristata
Large heavily streaked lark, with short tail bordered with buff not white. Prominent spiked crest obvious at all times. Distinctive liquid *til-looeet* call. Similar to Thekla Lark which has smaller bill, greyish underwing, and has not been recorded in Britain and Ireland to date. 17 cm (6¾ in). Rare vagrant across Channel from Continent to southern counties.

Red-rumped Swallow
Hirundo daurica
Rufous underparts, nape and rump distinguish it from Swallow, but the shape is also quite different. Bulky body and inward-turned tail streamers produce an attenuated, highly streamlined shape. 18 cm (7 in). Vagrant northwards from Mediterranean, but range extending northwards and occurrences may become more frequent. Most occur in April and May, though some also in autumn.

Richard's Pipit
Anthus novaeseelandiae
Large pipit, heavily streaked above and below in browns and buffs. Long legs and upright stance, more pronounced than Tawny Pipit. Distinctive *schreep* call. 18 cm (7 in). Autumn visitor from Siberia.

Tawny Pipit
Anthus campestris
Pale, washed-out pipit with buffy upperparts and paler underparts appearing virtually devoid of streaking at any distance. Prominent line of dark spots on median wing coverts. Long legs and sometimes very upright stance. Immature browner and more streaked, but never as boldly as Richard's Pipit. 16.5 cm (6½ in). Vagrant from Continent in spring and autumn.

Olive-backed Pipit
Anthus hodgsoni
Similar to Meadow Pipit, but greenish rather than olive above, and white below. Upperparts dark and heavily streaked, and yellowish breast heavily spotted with black. Clear supercilium. Displays wagtail-like bobbing of tail below horizontal when walking. 14.5 cm (5¾ in). Exceptionally rare vagrant from Russia, mostly in autumn.

Pechora Pipit
Anthus gustavi
Strong resemblance to Meadow Pipit as well as to other rare pipits. Upperparts striped black on brown and marked by 2 white lines forming a distinct V in the fashion of a Little Stint. Outertail feathers buffy. Distinct *pwit* call note repeated several times. 14.5 cm (5¾ in). Very rare vagrant from Russia and Siberia, mainly to Fair Isle in September and October.

Red-throated Pipit
Anthus cervinus
Distinctly marked with variable rust-red face and breast in summer. In autumn and winter similar to Meadow Pipit, but has darker upperparts heavily streaked with black. Streaking extends to rump and uppertail coverts. Underparts also heavily streaked. Call a thin, high-pitched *pssss*, also a sharp *chup*. 14.5 cm (5¾ in). Regular, but rare, spring and autumn visitor, mainly to Isles of Scilly and Fair Isle.

Rufous Bush Robin
Cercotrichas galactotes
Attractive, pale buff-brown chat that frequently perches quite openly, and cocks large tail in characteristic manner. Upperparts warm buff-brown with prominent creamy supercilium. Pale chestnut tail long and distinctly wedge-shaped, tipped with black and white. Underparts warm buff-cream. Long legs and dagger-like bill. Eastern subspecies darker. 15 cm (6 in). Very rare autumn visitor from Mediterranean, mostly in September.

Desert Wheatear
Oenanthe deserti
Similar to black-throated form of Black-eared Wheatear. Black mask extending to throat, black wings, but whole of tail black below white rump. Remaining plumage pale buff, lighter than most Black-eared Wheatears. Female buffish with dark wings and similar tail pattern. 14.5 cm (5¾ in). Rare spring and autumn vagrant from North Africa and Middle East.

Citrine Wagtail
Motacilla citreola
Distinct summer male has bright yellow head and underparts bordered by clear black nape and upperparts. In winter (and in the female) yellow much reduced. Immatures often lack yellow altogether; they have greyish upperparts, a distinct supercilium, white double wing bars and edges to tertials, and whitish underparts. Similar to but always paler than Pied Wagtail. 16.5 cm (6½ in). Rare autumn visitor from Russia, mainly to Fair Isle in September and October.

Thrush Nightingale
Luscinia luscinia
Similar to Nightingale, but darker above and less rufous on tail. Breast mottled with grey. Song comparable to Nightingale's, but lacking crescendo. Often called Sprosser. 16 cm (6½ in). Rare vagrant, mostly in May to Fair Isle.

Rock Thrush
Monticola saxatilis
Chunky, heavily built chat-like bird that, despite its name, frequently perches in trees. Male is slate-blue on head, neck and back, with black wings and bright chestnut-red underparts. Tail, often quivered Redstart-like, is bright rufous. Female mottled and barred brown and cream, but with similar rufous tail. 19 cm (7½ in). Extremely rare vagrant from southern Europe in May and June.

Alpine Accentor
Prunella collaris
Greyish, Dunnock-like bird, with clear band of chestnut spots along flanks and double white wing bars separated by bold area of black. A 'necklace' of black and white spots on chin may be less apparent in autumn and winter. Flight and call somewhat lark-like. 18 cm (7 in). Increasingly rare autumn and winter vagrant from mountain areas of Europe.

Black-eared Wheatear
Oenanthe hispanica
Typical slim wheatear with black mask through eye that may or may not extend to chin. Whole of wing black; tail white with black central feathers as in Wheatear, but with less black at tip. Remaining upper and under parts variable, buffish to virtually white. Female buffish with dark wings and similar tail pattern. Perches freely on bushes. 14.5 cm (5¾ in). Rare vagrant from southern Europe in spring and autumn.

White's Thrush
Zoothera dauma
Large and distinctive thrush. Boldly barred with black crescents above and below on buff-gold and white background. In flight underwing shows clear black and white striped pattern. 27 cm (10¾ in). Extremely rare vagrant from central Siberia, mostly in autumn.

Grey-cheeked Thrush
Catharus minimus
Small, Song Thrush-like bird, brownish above and whitish below, with diffusely spotted breast. Lacks a distinct eye-ring, but has greyish ear coverts. 16.5 cm (6½ in). Very rare vagrant from North America in October and November.

American Robin
Turdus migratorius
Black head and dark slate upperparts broken only by incomplete white eye-ring. Chin and throat streaked black and white. Breast, belly and flanks rufous; white undertail coverts. 22–27 cm (8½– 10½ in). Rare winter vagrant from North America.

Lanceolated Warbler
Locustella lanceolata
Similar to Grasshopper Warbler, heavily streaked black and brown above. Underparts buffish, finely streaked on breast and flanks. Keeps to dense cover. 11.5 cm (4½ in). Rare autumn vagrant from Russia and Siberia to Fair Isle.

Aquatic Warbler
Acrocephalus paludicola
Sedge Warbler-like bird, but marked by heavier black streaking above on paler buffy-cream background. Head pattern of black and cream stripes quite distinctive. Easily overlooked reed-dwelling bird. 13 cm (5 in). Regular autumn visitor in small numbers to southern England where over half are discovered in mist nets.

Blyth's Reed Warbler
Acrocephalus dumetorum
Very similar to Marsh and Reed Warblers, but brown upperparts lack either olive or rufous washes of those species. Indistinct supercilium and longer and thinner bill. 12.5 cm (5 in). Extremely rare autumn vagrant from east.

Great Reed Warbler
Acrocephalus arundinaceus
Large warbler with strident song. Similar to Reed Warbler, but much larger, with marked supercilium and long, dagger-like bill. Frequently sings atop a reed. 19 cm (7½ in). A regular visitor in small numbers, mainly in May and June.

Olivaceous Warbler
Hippolais pallida
Medium-sized, greyish-brown warbler with shortish, rounded wings and long, dagger-like bill accentuated by flat crown. Similar to Melodious Warbler, but lacks yellow or olive of that species. 13.5 cm (5¼ in). Very rare autumn vagrant.

Booted Warbler
Hippolais caligata
Smallest member of genus with typically flattened crown, but comparatively small bill. Greyish-brown above, buffy-grey below with narrow eye-ring and indistinct supercilium. Tail edged with white. 11.5 cm (4½ in). Extremely rare autumn vagrant from the east.

Icterine Warbler
Hippolais icterina
Olive-green above and yellow below and thus superficially similar to a leaf warbler, but much larger. Long, pointed bill and forehead that slopes to a rounded crown. Yellow supercilium and slate-grey legs. Distinguished from similar Melodious Warbler by longer wings and pale wing patch formed by light edges to secondaries. 13.5 cm (5¼ in). Regular spring and autumn visitor in small numbers, mainly in August and September.

Melodious Warbler
Hippolais polyglotta
Very similar to Icterine Warbler. Olive-green above, yellow below; but has shorter, more rounded wings, lacks pale wing patch, and sloping forehead and flattened crown give bill even more dagger-like appearance. 13 cm (5 in). Regular autumn migrant in small numbers from southwestern Europe, mainly to southwest Britain.

Subalpine Warbler
Sylvia cantillans
Small, Whitethroat-like warbler with characteristic habit of cocking tail. Male is slate-grey above with narrow rufous edges to primaries that are never as pronounced as in confusable species. Underparts dull pink, with prominent white moustache. White outertail feathers and undertail coverts. Female duller and browner, but with a vestigial moustache. 12 cm (4¾ in). A rare vagrant from Mediterranean from April to October, most often seen in May. Shetland has the majority of records.

Barred Warbler
Sylvia nisoria

A chunky, rather nondescript warbler, mostly seen in undistinguished immature plumage. Grey above with boldly barred underparts and yellow eye in adult. Immature with barring only on undertail coverts; but has white outertail feathers, 2 wing bars and a rather heavy bill. 15 cm (6 in). Scarce autumn migrant with Fair Isle collecting a high proportion of birds.

Greenish Warbler
Phylloscopus trochiloides

Similar to Willow Warbler and Chiffchaff, but rather greyer in colour above. A single wing bar serves to distinguish from both, and there is a prominent supercilium. Legs dark. 11 cm (4¼ in). A rare autumn visitor from August to October, some also in winter, from eastern Europe and Russia.

Arctic Warbler
Phylloscopus borealis

Superficially similar to Willow Warbler, but larger, greener above and whiter below. Distinguished by 2 wing bars, sometimes only 1, and prominent stripe through eye bordered above by bold supercilium extending to nape. Pale legs. 12 cm (4¾ in). Rare autumn visitor from August to October, mainly to Fair Isle from Scandinavia and Russia.

Pallas's Warbler
Phylloscopus proregulus

Tiny warbler nearer Goldcrest than Willow Warbler in size and appearance. Green above and buffy below, marked with crown stripe, prominent supercilium, bold double wing bar and yellow rump patch. Ever active, often hovers to pick insects from foliage. 9 cm (3½ in). Rare but apparently increasing vagrant, in October and November from central Siberia.

Yellow-browed Warbler
Phylloscopus inornatus

Similar to Willow Warbler, but even more so to Pallas's Warbler. Olive-green above with bold double wing bar and prominent supercilium. Underparts buffish on breast, whitish undertail. 10 cm (4 in). Regular autumn visitor in small numbers in September and October to Fair Isle and east coast from Siberia.

Radde's Warbler
Phylloscopus schwarzi

Large leaf warbler. Grey-brown above and buffy below, with marked creamy supercilium bordered by dark eye-stripe. Short stout bill and long, thick legs. Skulking, ground-dwelling species with deliberate actions, similar to Dusky Warbler. 12.5 cm (5 in). Rare vagrant from Siberia, mainly to east coast in October.

Dusky Warbler
Phylloscopus fuscatus

Dark brown upperparts and grey-buff underparts – otherwise similar to Chiffchaff. Prominent buffy supercilium. Often feeds on ground with Dunnock-like shuffle, generally self-effacing. 11 cm (4¼ in). Rare vagrant from Siberia, mainly to Norfolk and Scilly in October and November.

Bonelli's Warbler
Phylloscopus bonelli

Similar to Willow Warbler, but head and upper back pale grey. Underparts white. Wings and tail greenish with yellow edges to feathers, pale yellowish rump. 11.5 cm (4½ in). Rare spring and autumn vagrant to southern Britain from western Europe.

Red-breasted Flycatcher
Ficedula parva

Characteristic habit of cocking tail to expose white bases to outer feathers diagnostic in all plumages. In summer, male has bold red breast. In female, winter males and immatures breast is buffy and upperparts earth-brown. Pale orbital ring a useful field mark. 11.5 cm (4½ in). Regular, but scarce, visitor to east coast and Scilly, mainly in September and October.

Isabelline Shrike
Lanius isabellinus

Pale, sandy-coloured shrike with little difference in colour between head and back. Rump and tail rusty-chestnut. Black line behind eye. Wings brown with white bar. Underparts washed with pale pinkish. Often regarded as subspecies of Red-backed Shrike or Brown Shrike. 17 cm (6¾ in). Extremely rare vagrant to western Europe from central Asia.

Lesser Grey Shrike
Lanius minor

Similar to Great Grey Shrike, but black facial mask extends over forehead. No white on crown or back, and larger white patch in wing. Underparts washed pink, but southern races of Great Grey are pink too. 20 cm (8 in). Rare spring and autumn vagrant from the Continent, mainly seen on Fair Isle.

Woodchat Shrike
Lanius senator
Black and white shrike marked by distinctive chestnut cap and oval white patches on scapulars. Immature similar to Red-backed Shrike, but more barred and with paler scapular patches. 17 cm (6¾ in). Regular, if scarce, spring and autumn visitor, mainly to southern Britain from Continent.

Red-eyed Vireo
Vireo olivaceus
A thick-set, warbler-like bird with heavy pointed bill. Adult distinguished by grey cap, bold white supercilium and dark eye-stripe. Remaining plumage olive-grey above with some hint of green on the wing, and white underparts. Red eye useful, but not diagnostic. Immature has brown eye. 15 cm (6 in). Very rare vagrant from North America to Isles of Scilly in early October.

Parrot Crossbill
Loxia pytyopsittacus
Very similar to Crossbill and distinguished only at close range by much heavier bill and larger head. Feeds among pines more often than other species. 17 cm (6¾ in). Rare vagrant in autumn in association with Crossbill irruptions, but probably over-looked because of its similarity to the common and Scottish Crossbills, and by the comparatively fine field mark of its heavier bill. May have bred.

Nutcracker
Nucifraga caryocatactes
Large, crow-like bird with blackish-brown plumage, boldly spotted above and below with silvery-white. White undertail coverts and white tip to tail create striking undertail pattern. 32 cm (12½ in). Rare irruptive species in autumn and winter, but huge influx in 1968–9 to southern and eastern England from Russia.

Arctic Redpoll
Carduelis hornemanni
Very similar to Redpoll and frequently considered conspecific, and is part of a complex group of similar 'redpoll' species that occur in the boreal zone of the Northern Hemisphere. Generally paler with unstreaked white rump, white underparts, lighter head and double white wing bar. 13 cm (5 in). A vagrant from Scandinavia and northern Russia to east coast in autumn and winter.

Scarlet Rosefinch
Carpodacus erythrinus
Upperparts grey-brown, belly and undertail coverts white. Adult male has red crown, chin and breast, and rump. Females and immatures dull brown-grey, similar to female House Sparrow but with fine breast streaking and lacking supercilium. Pale double wing bar, conical bill. 14.5 cm (5¾ in). Scarce spring and autumn visitor, mostly to northeast and especially Fair Isle, where it is regular.

Rose-coloured Starling
Sturnus roseus
Typically Starling-like in shape, but adults have pink back, scapulars and belly contrasting with black head, wings and tail. Immatures similar to Starling, but with paler bill and greater contrast between dark wings and pale sandy-brown body. Gregarious nomadic wanderer, but may escape from captivity. 21.5 cm (8½ in). Vagrant from eastern Europe and Siberia from June to September with irruptive peaks in some years.

Two-barred Crossbill
Loxia leucoptera
Similar to other crossbills, but smaller and marked by bold white double wing bar. Male brighter red and female more yellow than other species. 14.5 cm (5¾ in). Generally associated with Crossbill irruptions. Rare vagrant to Fair Isle and east coast from July through to winter. Worth searching Crossbill flocks during an invasion, but immature and some adult Crossbills have narrow whitish wing bars.

Blackpoll Warbler
Dendroica striata
Most likely American warbler to be seen in Britain. Well marked in summer but confusing in autumn when most likely to occur on this side of the Atlantic. Upperparts olive-green, finely streaked black. Underparts yellow, finely streaked, with white undertail coverts. White double wing bar; pale yellow legs. 13 cm (5¼ in). Very rare vagrant from North America in October, mostly to Isles of Scilly.

White-throated Sparrow
Zonotrichia albicollis
Well-marked, bunting-like American sparrow that spends most of its time shuffling along ground. Head boldly striped black and white, with coronal stripe and yellow supercilium before eye. White throat patch. Upperparts striped brown and black, underparts grey. 17 cm (6¾ in). Rare vagrant from North America, usually in spring and autumn.

Little Bunting
Emberiza pusilla
Similar to female Reed Bunting, but much smaller. White underparts delicately streaked with black on breast and flanks. Ear coverts chestnut bordered with black, chestnut coronal stripe and sometimes throat. Narrow pale eye-ring. Black moustachial streak does not reach to bill. 13 cm (5¼ in). Rare vagrant from northern Scandinavia and Siberia in spring and autumn, especially to Fair Isle.

Black-headed Bunting
Emberiza melanocephala
Gives impression of being a large, slim bunting. Male has black cap, yellow underparts and collar, unstreaked pale chestnut back, and no white in tail. Female pale greyish, with yellow undertail coverts, and unstreaked underparts. 16.5 cm (6½ in). Rare vagrant from southeastern Europe from May to August.

Rustic Bunting
Emberiza rustica
Summer male has black head, marked by white eye-stripe, and white chin. Chestnut rump, breast band and streaking on flanks, and slightly peaked appearance to crown. Female and winter male may also appear crested and have chestnut streaking on chest and flanks. Bill appears large and straight. 15 cm (6 in). Rare vagrant in spring to Fair Isle, and in autumn to the same location and the Isles of Scilly.

Yellow-breasted Bunting
Emberiza aureola
Like small Yellowhammer. Male boldly marked with black face, dark chestnut crown and back, yellow underparts broken by narrow chestnut breast band and bold white wing bar. Females and immatures have yellow unstreaked breast and belly and prominent pale supercilium. 14 cm (5½ in). Rare vagrant from Finland and Russia, mainly to Fair Isle in September.

Northern Oriole
Icterus galbula
Formerly called Baltimore Oriole. Black and orange-red bird with white wing bar and white edges to inner flight feathers. Characteristic orange-red tips to outertail feathers. Female warm olive above, orange-yellow below; double white wing bar. 18 cm (7 in). Very rare vagrant from North America to southwest England and Ireland in autumn.

Birds that have occurred on less than 10 occasions, or which have not occurred within the last 50 years

Pied-billed Grebe	**Pallid Harrier**	**Forster's Tern**	**Isabelline Wheatear**	**Orphean Warbler**	**Hooded Warbler**
Podilymbus podiceps	*Circus macrourus*	*Sterna forsteri*	*Oenanthe isabellina*	*Sylvia hortensis*	*Wilsonia citrina*
Capped Petrel	**Spotted Eagle**	**Bridled Tern**	**Pied Wheatear**	**Collared Flycatcher**	**Summer Tanager**
Pterodroma hasitata	*Aquila clanga*	*Sterna anaethetus*	*Oenanthe pleschanka*	*Ficedula albicollis*	*Piranga rubra*
Bulwer's Petrel	**American Kestrel**	**Rufous Turtle Dove**	**Black Wheatear**	**Wallcreeper**	**Scarlet Tanager**
Bulweria bulwerii	*Falco sparverius*	*Streptopelia orientalis*	*Oenanthe leucura*	*Tichodroma muraria*	*Piranga olivacea*
Wilson's Petrel	**Eleonora's Falcon**	**Black-billed Cuckoo**	**Siberian Thrush**	**Short-toed Treecreeper**	**Rufous-sided Towhee**
Oceanites oceanicus	*Falco eleonorae*	*Coccyzus erythrophthalmus*	*Turdus sibirica*	*Certhia brachydactyla*	*Pipilo erythrophthalmus*
White-faced Petrel	**Saker**	**Eagle Owl**	**Hermit Thrush**	**Penduline Tit**	**Fox Sparrow**
(Frigate Petrel)	*Falco cherrug*	*Bubo bubo*	*Catharus guttatus*	*Remiz pendulinus*	*Zonotrichia iliaca*
Pelagodroma marina	**Sora Rail**	**Red-necked Nightjar**	**Swainson's Thrush**	**Spanish Sparrow**	**Song Sparrow**
Madeiran Petrel	*Porzana carolina*	*Caprimulgus ruficollis*	*Catharus ustulatus*	*Passer hispaniolensis*	*Zonotrichia melodia*
Oceanodroma castro	**Allen's Gallinule**	**Egyptian Nightjar**	**Veery**	**Snowfinch**	**White-crowned Sparrow**
Magnificent Frigatebird	*Porphyrula alleni*	*Caprimulgus aegyptius*	*Catharus fuscescens*	*Montifringilla nivalis*	*Zonotrichia leucophrys*
Fregata magnificens	**American Purple Gallinule**	**Common Nighthawk**	**Eye-browed Thrush**	**Citril Finch**	**Slate-coloured Junco**
Green Heron	*Porphyrula martinica*	*Chordeiles minor*	*Turdus obscurus*	*Serinus citrinella*	*Junco hyemalis*
Butorides striatus	**Sandhill Crane**	**Needle-tailed Swift**	**Dusky/Naumann's Thrush**	**Trumpeter Finch**	**Pine Bunting**
Falcated Teal	*Grus canadensis*	*Hirundapus caudacutus*	*Turdus naumanni*	*Bucanetes githagineus*	*Emberiza leucocephalos*
Anas falcata	**Houbara Bustard**	**Pallid Swift**	**Black-throated/**	**Pine Grosbeak**	**Rock Bunting**
Baikal Teal	*Chlamydotis undulata*	*Apus pallidus*	**Red-throated Thrush**	*Pinicola enucleator*	*Emberiza cia*
Anas formosa	**Semipalmated Plover**	**Little Swift**	*Turdus ruficollis*	**Evening Grosbeak**	**Cretzschmar's Bunting**
Black Duck	*Charadrius semipalmatus*	*Apus affinis*	**Fan-tailed Warbler**	*Hesperiphona vespertina*	*Emberiza caesia*
Anas rubripes	**Greater Sand Plover**	**Belted Kingfisher**	*Cisticola juncidis*	**Black-and-white Warbler**	**Pallas's Reed Bunting**
Harlequin Duck	*Charadrius leschenaultii*	*Ceryle alcyon*	**Pallas's Grasshopper**	*Mniotilta varia*	*Emberiza pallasi*
Histrionicus histrionicus	**Caspian Plover**	**Blue-cheeked Bee-eater**	**Warbler**	**Tennessee Warbler**	**Rose-breasted Grosbeak**
Bufflehead	*Charadrius asiaticus*	*Merops superciliosus*	*Locustella certhiola*	*Vermivora peregrina*	*Pheucticus ludovicianus*
Bucephala albeola	**White-tailed Plover**	**Yellow-bellied Sapsucker**	**River Warbler**	**Parula Warbler**	**Bobolink**
Hooded Merganser	*Chettusia leucura*	*Sphyrapicus varius*	*Locustella fluviatilis*	*Parula americana*	*Dolichonyx oryzivorus*
Mergus cucullatus	**Western Sandpiper**	**Calandra Lark**	**Moustached Warbler**	**Yellow Warbler**	
Egyptian Vulture	*Calidris mauri*	*Melanocorypha calandra*	*Acrocephalus melanopogon*	*Dendroica petechia*	
Neophron percnopterus	**Short-billed Dowitcher**	**Bimaculated Lark**	**Paddyfield Warbler**	**Cape May Warbler**	
Griffon Vulture	*Limnodromus griseus*	*Melanocorypha bimaculata*	*Acrocephalus agricola*	*Dendroica tigrina*	
Gyps fulvus	**Eskimo Curlew**	**White-winged Lark**	**Thick-billed Warbler**	**Yellow-rumped Warbler**	
	Numenius borealis	*Melanocorypha leucoptera*	*Acrocephalus aedon*	*Dendroica coronata*	
	Great Black-headed Gull	**Blyth's Pipit**	**Spectacled Warbler**	**American Redstart**	
	Larus ichthyaetus	*Anthus godlewskii*	*Sylvia conspicillata*	*Setophaga ruticilla*	
	Franklin's Gull	**Brown Thrasher**	**Sardinian Warbler**	**Ovenbird**	
	Larus pipixcan	*Toxostoma rufum*	*Sylvia melanocephala*	*Seiurus aurocapillus*	
	Slender-billed Gull	**Siberian Rubythroat**	**Rüppell's Warbler**	**Northern Waterthrush**	
	Larus genei	*Luscinia calliope*	*Sylvia ruepelli*	*Seiurus noveboracensis*	
	Royal Tern	**Red-flanked Bluetail**	**Desert Warbler**	**Yellowthroat**	
	Sterna maxima	*Tarsiger cyanurus*	*Sylvia nana*	*Geothlypis trichas*	

INTRODUCED AND ESCAPED BIRDS

The idea of keeping birds in captivity, either as decoration or for food, is as old as human history. Yet no sooner had birds been captured than they started to escape. At first it must have been a simple matter of local birds returning to nature, but as man began to wander, and later travel, he brought back some of the more exotic things, including birds, that he found along the way. Pheasants were brought back from the Far East, probably by the Romans. Turkeys were imported from the New World by post-Columbian explorers. By the nineteenth century birds were imported, dead and alive, from every part of the world. Inevitably many escaped and some settled down to breed and create feral, self-supporting populations. Over the years several have become an integral part of our avifauna, even though their origins may have been thousands of miles away. Today caged birds are kept on an unprecedented scale and in unprecedented variety. Commercial bird gardens often allow some species to fly free and at wildfowl collections it is often impossible to catch all the young ducklings even of rare and expensive species. As a result there are more exotic birds than ever flying about the countryside. Some will undoubtedly settle down, occupy a previously vacant niche, and prosper. Most will not survive. This enrichment of our bird population might, at first sight, seem welcome. But the newcomers may compete with some natural species to its detriment and, in any case, will serve to confuse the study of our native avifauna.

While some birds have colonized Britain and Ireland by escaping from captivity, others have been deliberately introduced. Some, such as the Pheasant, were never native. Others, such as the Little Owl, were here many hundreds of years ago, while others, the Capercaillie for example, were reintroductions of birds only recently lost by direct human persecution. In general such introductions, especially of totally foreign birds, are to be condemned, and we have been particularly fortunate in not having acquired a real pest as a consequence. North America has, as a result of introductions, acquired a House Sparrow and Starling problem of immense proportions. New Zealand has so many European birds that its delicate native avifauna has been partially destroyed. Elsewhere introductions have proved either a mixed blessing or a total disaster.

The birds that follow fall into a number of different categories. Some have been deliberately introduced; others have escaped and built up viable or potentially viable populations; still others have escaped and could be confused with genuine wild vagrants; while some have escaped and attempted to breed on at least 1 occasion. There remain a host of different birds wandering about the country that have simply escaped and do not fall into any of these categories.

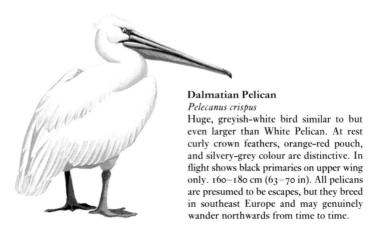

Dalmatian Pelican
Pelecanus crispus
Huge, greyish-white bird similar to but even larger than White Pelican. At rest curly crown feathers, orange-red pouch, and silvery-grey colour are distinctive. In flight shows black primaries on upper wing only. 160–180 cm (63–70 in). All pelicans are presumed to be escapes, but they breed in southeast Europe and may genuinely wander northwards from time to time.

Mandarin Duck
Aix galericulata
Delightfully attractive little duck, spectacularly marked in the male with bright orange wing fans that protrude like small sails as it swims. Bold white line through eye is bordered below by droopy crest of flame-orange. Female grey above, mottled below, with prominent pale eye-ring. 43 cm (17 in). Imported in 1747, and established feral population in 1930s. Now some 400 pairs breed in southern England, mainly in Surrey and Berkshire. Native of China.

White Pelican
Pelecanus onocrotalus
Huge, white bird with large bill, yellowish pouch and a yellow-buff mark on the breast. Similar to Dalmatian Pelican in flight with black primaries on upper wing. Under wing shows all flight feathers black – Dalmatian's are silvery-grey. Swims well and soars in raptor-like fashion on broad stiff wings. 140–180 cm (55–70 in). Presumed escape, for the species is widely kept in captivity, but genuine vagrants may occur from southeast Europe.

Egyptian Goose
Alopochen aegyptiacus
Neat, buffish-brown goose, a little larger than similarly built Shelduck. Marked by chestnut patch around eye, pale chestnut upperparts and narrow darkish neck-ring. Bill and feet pale pink. In flight black and white wing pattern with green speculum. 70 cm (27 in). Introduced in eighteenth century and established self-supporting population in Norfolk, and elsewhere in southern England. Native of Africa.

Baikal Teal
Anas formosa
Male boldly marked with harlequin pattern in black, green and buff on head. Upperparts brown with feathers cascading over grey flanks. Chest cinnamon spotted white bordered by white crescent. Black under tail. Female mottled brown with green speculum and pale creamy spot at base of bill. 41 cm (16 in). Very rare vagrant from Siberia or, more likely, escape from captivity. First recorded in 1906.

Greater Flamingo
Phoenicopterus ruber
Tall, elegant pink bird with long neck and extremely long pink legs. Bold black and roseate colour in opened wing and on bill are diagnostic, separating this from other flamingos. Generally gregarious, feeds with bill upside down. 127 cm (50 in). Invariably regarded as an escape, this is the only flamingo ever likely to appear in Britain and Ireland in a wild state. South American flamingos such as the Chilean *P. chilensis* are most frequent escapes.

Wood Duck
Aix sponsa
Boldly marked relative of the Mandarin Duck. Male has distinctive pattern of bronzy-black and white stripes on head that terminates in a drooping crest. Breast is chestnut spotted white, back a deep bottle-green, and flanks pale buff. Female duller with grey and white head pattern with crest, pale chestnut breast and flanks heavily spotted white. 43–51 cm (17–20 in). Escapes from wildfowl collections have bred, but have yet to establish a self-supporting feral population. Most in Surrey and Berkshire. Native of North America.

Ruddy Duck
Oxyura jamaicensis
A neat little stiff-tailed duck. Male is cinnamon above and below with black line along flanks, black crown and white cheeks, and stiff black tail often held upright. Stubby bill is pale blue. Female is slate-grey above, heavily barred below, with white cheeks marked by indistinct smudgy bar, and blue bill. 41 cm (16 in). Escaped from Slimbridge from 1960 onwards and spread to establish feral breeding population along Severn Valley. Native of North America.

Black Vulture
Aegypius monachus
Huge, uniformly dark bird with scrawny ruff, bare face, huge bill and powerful feet. Mostly seen in air when unmarked dark coloration and huge wings distinguish it from other vultures. 99–107 cm (39–42 in). Has escaped from captivity from time to time; no hint of wild occurrence of this increasingly rare scavenger from southern Europe.

Bobwhite Quail
Colinus virginianus
Attractive and well-marked little game-bird, smaller than partridge. Upperparts rich chestnut, underparts barred black and white. Chestnut crown, white forehead extending to supercilium, black eye-stripe extending to enclose white chin patch, form a distinctive head pattern. Best located by characteristic whistled *bob-white* call. 22–26 cm (8½–10½ in). Introduced from North America on several occasions in past 150 years. Population, not yet self-supporting, based on Minsmere, Suffolk, and Tresco, Isles of Scilly.

Reeves's Pheasant
Syrmaticus reevesii
Spectacularly beautiful bird with amazingly long tail about 3 times length of body. Male is bronzy-gold above with each feather edged with black. Chest and belly chestnut, undertail coverts black. Head white, marked by black line through eye to

Golden Pheasant
Chrysolophus pictus
A patchwork of bright colours, the male is a splendidly gaudy bird. Head and extendible cape that may cover face, both golden; back bright yellow with uppertail feathers extended in flame-red. Underparts bright red, tail a mosaic of yellow and black. Female warmish buff boldly barred on wings and tail. Male 100 cm (39½ in) in-

cluding 75 cm (29½ in) of tail: female 65 cm (25½ in). First introduced at end of last century, the species now breeds in several parts of the country with a stronghold in the Brecks, where it roosts communally in small coniferous breaks. Added to British and Irish List in 1971. Native of China.

Lady Amherst's Pheasant
Chrysolophus amherstiae
Arguably the most beautiful of all British birds, the male is bottle-green and blue on wings and back, with a train of flame-coloured feathers falling from the rump to cascade over the extended black and white tail feathers. The underparts are white and a black and silver cape can be extended over the face. Female similar to female Golden Pheasant. Male 150 cm (59 in), including 90–110 cm (35½–43 in) of tail: female 67 cm (26½ in). First attempted introduction from China at beginning of

century, now established in Bedfordshire. Shortage of females has led to hybridization with Golden Pheasant in captivity and in the wild, as a result of which females of indeterminate species breed freely with males both of Lady Amherst's and Golden Pheasants. In England habits and habitats are similar to the common Pheasant.

nape. Female rather dull, but with goldish wash to sides of head. Male 210 cm (83 in) including 100–160 cm (39½–63 in) of tail: female 75 cm (29½ in). Introduced from end of nineteenth century onwards, but so far has failed to establish viable feral population, though it must be considered likely to do so. Native of China.

Rose-ringed Parakeet
Psittacula krameri
Often, misleadingly, called Ring-necked Parakeet. A medium-sized, fast-flying green bird with long pointed wings and extended tail. Male has clear neck band of pink and black. Cannot be confused with any other British bird, but other parakeets are similar and may escape. Shrill *kee-et* call. 40 cm (16 in). Escaped in 1969 and immediately established feral breeding population in London suburbs and northern Kent. Native of India.

Introduced and Escaped Birds

Yellow-shafted Flicker
Colaptes auratus

Woodpecker-like bird with barred back, spotted underparts, black half-collar and cinnamon 'face' with black moustachial streak. Small patch of crimson on nape and bold white rump. Flies in deep undulations like woodpecker. 33–35 cm (13–14 in). One crossed Atlantic on RMS *Mauritania* and flew ashore at Cobh on 13 October 1962.

Blue Rock Thrush
Monticola solitarius

Dark, slaty-blue bird with black wings and pale eye-ring, given to perching openly on large rocks and producing flute-like warbling song. Female very dark brown, barred, particularly below, with buff. 20 cm (8 in). One on Orkney in August and September 1966 was regarded as an escape, though there seems no reason why this Mediterranean bird should not, on occasion, wander northwards to these islands in spring.

Chestnut Bunting
Emberiza rutila

Small bunting, marked chestnut on head and entire upperparts, extending to form a distinct breast band in male. Underparts sulphur-yellow. Female dully mottled in browns, with yellow underparts streaked with brown on flanks. 14 cm (5½ in). One on Foula in June 1974, but a widely kept cage bird from Siberia.

Red-headed Bunting
Emberiza bruniceps

Male is easily identified by bold rust-red face and upper breast. Crown and back green streaked black; wings and tail black; underparts yellow. Female remarkably similar to female House Sparrow, but bunting-shaped. 16.5 cm (6½ in). Escapes common in all parts of the country.

Blue Grosbeak
Guiraca caerulea

Chunky, thick-set finch with large powerful bill and long tail. Male is dark blue, marked on the wing by broad rusty edges to the inner flight feathers and 2 bold rusty wing bars. Female in dull browns with 2 bold pale wing bars. 16.5–19 cm (6½–7½ in). Two doubtful records.

Indigo Bunting
Passerina cyanea

A little smaller than a House Sparrow and with a smallish conical bill. Male is bright blue washed with a greenish tinge on flanks. Female is brown above and buff below, with 2 narrow pale wing bars. 14 cm (5½ in). Two reports of this North American species are regarded as escapes.

Painted Bunting
Passerina ciris

Small, boldly patterned finch-like bird. Male has cobalt-blue head, green back, and crimson underparts, rump and eye-ring. Female green above and yellow below. 14 cm (5½ in). Only a single record has been accepted, but this too is regarded as a probable escape.

Canary
Serinus canaria

In its natural state this is a Serin-like bird marked in greys and greens and heavily streaked above. The male has considerable yellow on head and breast, but lacks the yellow rump of the smaller Serin. Selective breeding has produced a huge range of forms in captivity. 12.5 cm (5 in). Escapes have bred on occasion.

Java Sparrow
Padda oryzivora

Delicately marked in vinous greys and buffs, but with a huge, Hawfinch-like pink bill. The head is black with a prominent enclosed white cheek patch and a red eye-ring. 16 cm (6¼ in). Escapes may have bred on occasion. An Asian species that has been successfully introduced to many parts of the world.

Pin-tailed Whydah
Vidua macroura

Distinctive pied bird marked by thick pink bill and exceedingly long black tail feathers. Female an undistinguished brown bird with heavily streaked back and pale supercilium. Male 32 cm (12½ in) including 19 cm (7½ in) of tail. Female 13 cm (5 in). A parasitic African bird that has possibly bred.

ORNAMENTAL AND DOMESTICATED BIRDS

Man has domesticated birds for thousands of years. At first, no doubt, his main motivation was food, for birds that were able to glean a living around his settlements provided fresh meat during lean times of the year. Pigeons were 'farmed' in medieval England for just this purpose and dovecotes are a memorial to this pre-refrigeration practice. Much earlier, chickens had been brought in to domestication to provide both eggs and meat. Even today their wild ancestors, the Red Junglefowl of India, will gather around a new settlement.

Slowly birds were added to the domestic scene, not because they were edible but because of their beauty and elegance. The development of art and other such pursuits may have evolved at the same time, for both are essentially the product of leisure. Ducks were particularly easy to keep and breed into strange forms. Later some of the world's most spectacular birds were added from all corners of the earth. Those that follow include most that can be seen outside specialist collections.

American Flamingo
Phoenicopterus ruber ruber
Though only a subspecies of the Greater Flamingo, this is a much redder bird than the Old World equivalent. Virtually the whole body is a rich pink in colour. 127 cm (50 in). A native of the Caribbean and adjacent South America that is kept in some numbers as ornamentation in large parks and zoos.

Lesser Flamingo
Phoeniconaias minor
Much smaller than Greater Flamingo and a warm pink in colour. Best distinguished by whole of bill and area around the eye being dark maroon. 100 cm (39½ in). An abundant, if localized, South and East African species that is kept in some parks and zoos, and which from time to time will breed and produce free-flying young. Generally a less common escape than the related Chilean Flamingo.

Chilean Flamingo
Phoenicopterus chilensis
Sometimes regarded as conspecific with Greater and American Flamingos. Has same black and pink bill, but is nearer Greater in coloration and lacks the deep pink body of the American. Red and black on wings prominent. Best distinguished by grey legs with red feet and 'knees'. 110 cm (43 in). Found only in Andean region of South America. Widely kept in parks and zoos and most frequent escape.

Coscoroba Swan
Coscoroba coscoroba
Large duck-like bird that is actually a swan, though some authorities place it with the tree ducks. All-white plumage broken only by black tips to primaries, often hidden at rest. Legs and feet pink: bill bright coral-red. Neck is short for a swan and held distinctly kinked. 75 cm (29 in). A native of southern South America that is kept in some parks and most wildfowl collections of note.

Black Swan
Cygnus atratus
Large black swan with long neck and typically graceful movements. Some wing feathers terminate squarely and are curled upwards. Primary and secondary feathers white and prominent in flight. Bill red with broad white band near tip; feet slate-grey. 127 cm (50 in). Scarce import from Australia, but becoming a regular member of wildfowl collections.

Chinese or Swan Goose
Anser cygnoides
Large 'grey' goose with prominent long neck and long bill. Legs orange; bill slate-grey. In domestic forms there is a large knob at the base of the upper mandible, and a 'keel' often develops on the breast. 90 cm (36 in). A native of northern China and Siberia.

Muscovy Duck
Cairina moschata
A dark, bottle-green duck marked by white in the wing, and a knob of bare red skin extending from the base of the bill to the eye. The body appears long and attenuate and there is a crest on the crown. Domesticated forms may be pure white, grey, or pied green and white. Male 85 cm (33 in); female 66 cm (26 in). One of the most commonly kept ornamental birds; native of Central and South America.

Black-necked Swan
Cygnus melanocoryphus
Spectacular ornamental bird. Whole body white; long, typically swan-shaped neck black; black head with white line through eye and red knob at base of slate-grey bill. Legs pink. 100 cm (39½ in). Native of southern South America and somewhat scarce even in wildfowl collections.

Domestic Duck
Anas platyrhynchos
Mallard, kept in captivity for generations, have gradually been bred into a variety of domestic forms. Some of the better known, such as the Aylesbury, are bred for eating, others such as the Khaki Campbell are bred for egg production. Even more are a purely decorative white; with 'top-knot' plumes on crown; or in a variety of different colours. 58 cm (23 in). Widely kept in every part of the country. Escapes interbreed with Mallard.

Bufflehead
Bucephala albeola
Attractive relative of the Goldeneye with green back, white underparts, and distinctly crested head boldly patterned in iridescent green and white. Female more like female Goldeneye with chocolate head and white cheek patch. 36 cm (14 in). Kept in many wildfowl collections; native of North America and extremely rare vagrant to Britain and Ireland.

Domestic Goose
Anser anser
A variety of forms all derived from the wild Greylag Goose. They vary in colour from brownish-grey to pure white, but all have neat striping on the neck. The Emden Goose has a prominent 'keel', especially in the female. 76–90 cm (30–36 in). Found in different shapes and sizes throughout the country.

Chiloe Wigeon
Anas sibilatrix
Upperparts and breast streaked black and white, with pale orange-buff on flanks, and bottle-green head marked with white around base of bill and cheek. 48 cm (19 in). Widely kept in wildfowl collections and an unusual species in that the duck is similar to the drake in plumage.

Hooded Merganser
Mergus cucullatus
The most spectacular of the sawbill family. The male is black above with barred chestnut flanks. The head and neck are bottle-green marked by a huge white crest, and the breast is white. Female resembles a small Red-breasted Merganser. 46 cm (18 in). Kept in wildfowl collections; native of North America.

Ornamental and Domesticated Birds

Great Argus Pheasant
Argusianus argus
An extraordinary bird, rivalling the Peacock in its elaborate plumage and nuptial display. Male has long tail, and long, broad secondaries that are erected to form a fan during courtship. At other times it is somewhat dull in appearance, clothed in greys and blues with chestnut on the breast. Male

168 cm (66 in) of which tail is up to 122 cm (48 in); female 61 cm (24 in). Inhabits Malaysia, Java and Borneo and is now exported only under licence. Kept in some collections.

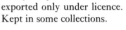

Helmeted Guineafowl
Numida meleagris
Dark blackish-blue bird spotted all over with white. Long, thin neck and pointed tail feathers create pear-drop shape to body. Small head has blue and red wattles and horny protrusion on crown. 51 cm (20 in).

Silver Pheasant
Lophura nycthemera
A finely marked decorative pheasant with silvery-white upperparts, wings and long broad tail. Underparts dark royal-blue and similarly coloured crest. Face red with bare skin. Bill silvery; legs red. Male 120 cm (47 in); female 70 cm (27½ in). Imported from native China and Southeast Asia and highly variable in colour. Well established in captivity.

Barbary Dove
Streptopelia risoria
Like Collared Dove, but smaller and creamy-buff in colour. Lacks black wing tips and dark grey in tail. 25 cm (10 in). Widely kept as a decorative species but sometimes escapes and breeds ferally.

Red Junglefowl
Gallus gallus
Ancestor of all chickens and the world's most numerous bird. Bears a strong resemblance to a Bantam and is not much larger. Has been bred into huge variety of different forms and for different purposes, including fighting, eating, egg laying and sheer decoration. Male 58 cm (23 in); female 43 cm (17 in). Widespread import from Asia.

Demoiselle Crane
Anthropoides virgo
Very attractive small crane with pale grey body marked by black neck and breast plumes, and neat white crest. 96 cm (38 in). Kept as ornamental species in some parks and bird collections; native to Middle East and Asia.

Fancy Pigeons
Columba livia
All fancy pigeons are descended from the wild Rock Dove which is also ancestor of the Feral Pigeons that inhabit our cities. 33 cm (13 in). Formerly kept both for food and decoration, a wide variety of different forms have been bred.

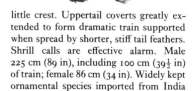

Peafowl
Pavo cristatus
Arguably the world's most decorative bird. Male is spectacular in bright royal-blue with cinnamon-rust primaries and delicate

little crest. Uppertail coverts greatly extended to form dramatic train supported when spread by shorter, stiff tail feathers. Shrill calls are effective alarm. Male 225 cm (89 in), including 100 cm (39½ in) of train; female 86 cm (34 in). Widely kept ornamental species imported from India and other parts of Asia.

Blue and Yellow Macaw
Ara ararauna
Boldly coloured bright blue and vivid yellow, this typical large parrot flies on pointed wings and has a long pointed tail. 33 cm (13 in). Free-flying birds at bird gardens may be seen screeching overhead nearby.

WHERE TO WATCH
BIRDS

One can watch birds anywhere: hundreds of thousands of observers seldom venture further than their garden or local open space. Because of the mobility of birds even a garden will, over a period of time, produce a substantial list of species and quite rare birds can, and do, appear in someone's back yard. Yet places exist in every part of the country that concentrate birds and their watchers. In some the appeal is seasonal – it is as pointless to visit a seabird colony in December as it is an estuary in June. But others have a year-round appeal. These places are really those at which watchers have observed birds, rather than those at which birds actually occur. Each year sees one or more 'new' places discovered not by birds, which had presumably used the area before, but by bird-watchers. There is thus immense scope for observers in every part of the country to discover their own particular 'good' spot. Most of the land of these islands is private and permission to enter must be sought, or the complex laws of trespass faced. In general landowners are sympathetic to birds and their watchers, but mass trespass in search of a particular species can lead to damage to fences, crops and livestock and must be avoided. For ease of reference the major areas of bird interest have been divided into self-explanatory sections.

National Nature Reserves of Major Bird Interest

The Nature Conservancy Council is an independent body financed by a grant-in-aid administered by the Department of the Environment. It manages a system of over 170 National Nature Reserves (NNRs) which have a statutory basis and that include many of the most important natural history sites in England, Scotland and Wales, although at some NNRs, by virtue of the nature of the fauna and flora, the scientific work in progress, or because of private ownership, visitors are discouraged. Those that follow have been carefully chosen as of particular ornithological interest.

ENGLAND

Ainsdale Sands, Lancs: Coastal dune area north of Formby with stands of pine. Some shorebirds, but migrants among scrub are main attraction. 492 hectares (1,216 acres). Footpaths and concessionary paths.

Braunton Burrows, Devon: Dune area at mouth of River Taw at Barnstaple Bay. Good vantage point for watching waders and wildfowl on the estuary. 604 hectares (1,492 acres). Free access subject to Ministry of Defence by-laws.

Bridgwater Bay, Somerset: Estuaries of the Rivers Parrett and Huntspill together with Stert Island. Noted as moulting ground for Shelduck and winter home of White-fronted Geese. Good waders and other birds. 2,559 hectares (6,323 acres). Permit required to visit Stert Island.

Bure Marshes, Norfolk: Broadland area with open water, reed beds and surrounding woodland including Hoveton Great Broad and Ranworth Broad. Specialities include Bearded Tit and Water Rail together with Common Tern. 412 hectares (1,018 acres). Access along nature trail gained only by boat at Hoveton Great Broad.

Castor Hanglands, Northants: Grassy fenland with oak woods offering wide range of regular birds including Siskin and Sparrowhawk. 90 hectares (221 acres). Near Peterborough. Maps at reserve entrance show accessible areas.

Hickling Broad, Norfolk: Most famous of all the Broads. Exquisite area of reed beds, mud banks and scrub with Marsh Harrier, Bittern and Bearded Tit regular, and passage waders and terns in season. 487 hectares (1,204 acres). Access, by permit from Norfolk Naturalists' Trust, via boat to various well-sited hides.

High Halstow, Kent: Woods and grazing meadows among North Kent Marshes with noted Heronry. 52 hectares (130 acres). See *RSPB Reserves* for access.

Holkham, Norfolk: Prime bird-watching area near Wells on north Norfolk coast. Open shore with wildfowl, including Brent Geese, and waders, large stand of planted pines and open scrubland beloved by migrants and their watchers. 3,925 hectares (9,700 acres). Unrestricted access except to farmland.

Leigh, Essex: Fine marshes at the mouth of the Thames with wildfowl, including Brent Geese, many ducks and waders. Permit required to visit.

Lindisfarne, Northumberland: Outstanding estuarine area with good populations of wildfowl and waders. 3,278 hectares (8,101 acres). Viewable from public roads and paths. See *Major Estuaries*.

Orfordness-Havergate, Suffolk: Famous RSPB Avocet reserve and huge shingle bank. See *RSPB Reserves*.

Rostherne Mere, Cheshire: Most famous Cheshire mere full of ducks in season. 47 hectares (116 acres). Permit for A. W. Boyd Memorial Observatory from Manchester Ornithological Society.

Saltfleetby-Theddlethorpe Dunes, Lincs: Coastal dunes, shoreline, freshwater marsh and lagoons make this an excellent birding area. Waders, terns and small migrants. 440 hectares (1,088 acres). Unrestricted access except during Ministry of Defence operations; best is Rimac entrance off A1031.

Scolt Head Island, Norfolk: Beautiful dune island with interesting shoreline. Best terneries in England. 737 hectares (1,821 acres). Free access except to terneries in season. Boat trips arranged out of Burnham Overy and Brancaster Staithe.

Stodmarsh, Kent: Fine area of lagoons and reed beds near Canterbury formed by mining subsidence. Site of colonization by several decidedly rare warblers and has Garganey and Marsh Harrier in spring. 163 hectares (402 acres). Access from village along raised footpath. Entrance to NCC car park in village.

Studland Heath, Dorset: Excellent area of heathland with large lagoon near the sea and good visiting facilities. Dartford Warbler may be seen. 174 hectares (429 acres). Easy access from Swanage with footpaths and marked trails.

Swale, Kent: Outstanding intertidal area full of geese, ducks and waders. Probably best worked via Elmley. See *RSPB Reserves*.

Tring Reservoirs, Herts: Group of small older reservoirs built to feed canals. Regularly attracts wide variety of ducks and grebes, and always has a few rarities each year. 20 hectares (49 acres). Access along footpaths via trail guide.

Thursley, Surrey: Open heathland with marshy areas and scrub woodland with variety of breeding birds including Nightjar and Woodcock. Great Grey Shrike regular in winter. 319 hectares (789 acres). Visitors are asked to keep to tracks.

Walberswick, Suffolk: Varied area on bird-rich coast with reed beds, woodland, heath and part of Blyth Estuary. Bearded Tit, Bittern and other Suffolk specialities. 514 hectares (1,270 acres). Permit required away from public paths.

Westleton Heath, Suffolk: Open heathland with scrub supporting several less common species. 47 hectares (117 acres). Access along footpaths.

WALES

Cors Tregaron, Dyfed: Large raised bog with geese in winter and a noted haunt of passing Red Kite. 768 hectares (1,898 acres). Much can be seen from public roads and path along the old railway.

Dyfi, Dyfed: Fine estuary on west coast with wildfowl and waders in season. 1,608 hectares (3,973 acres). Free access over much of area with nature trail and leaflets to guide one.

Newborough Warren, Ynys Mon, Anglesey: With excellent estuary, forest and dunes and rich bird-life. Waders a speciality, but much else besides. 676 hectares (1,670 acres). Access via rights of way only.

Oxwich, West Glamorgan: Fine area of shore backed by dunes, marshes and woods, noted as most westerly breeding haunt of Reed Warbler. Other marsh birds interesting. 261 hectares (646 acres). Access by public footpaths and nature trail to certain areas.

Skomer, Dyfed: Marvellous seabird island offering some of the best and most accessible watching in Britain. Auks, gulls and Fulmars abound. 307 hectares (760 acres). Access by boat, landing fee payable.

SCOTLAND

Beinn Eighe, Highland: Huge area of mountain and moorland dotted with lochs and some woodland. Good mountain birds with several Scottish specialities including Red-throated Diver, Golden Eagle and Crested Tit. 4,758 hectares (11,752 acres). Free access to short, and extended, nature trails.

Caerlaverock, Dumfries and Galloway: Splendid area of saltings with huge flock of Barnacle Geese and other wildfowl in winter. Adjacent Wildfowl Trust Refuge. 5,501 hec-

marsh and islands. Breeding birds include Capercaillie. 416 hectares (1,028 acres). Prior permission required for visits to mainland and for organized parties to Inchcailloch.

May, Isle of, Fife: Base of bird observatory and good colonies of cliff-breeding seabirds. 57 hectares (140 acres). Free access for day trips, accommodation available at observatory.

Monach Isles, Western Isles: Splendid isolation among multitude of breeding seabirds and other species. 577 hectares (1,425 acres). Permission to land from North Uist Estate, Lochmaddy, or from warden at Loch Druidibeg.

Morton Lochs, Fife: Fine bird haunt at all seasons with waders the speciality in summer and autumn, and wildfowl in winter. 24 hectares (59 acres). Access via public roads, and to hides with permit.

Nigg and Udale Bays, Highland: Intertidal bays near the mouth of Cromarty Firth with masses of wildfowl including Whooper Swan, and Pink-footed and Greylag Geese. 640 hectares (1,581 acres). Easily viewed via public rights of way and roads.

North Rona and Sula Sgeir, Western Isles: Remote, uninhabited islands full of seabirds including Leach's Petrel. 129 hectares (320 acres). Difficult to land and a real expedition if one wants to stay. Permission from Barvas Estate, c/o Smiths Gore, Edinburgh. Regional Officer to be informed.

Noss, Shetland: Wonderful, and easily accessible, seabird cliffs. Gannets, auks, Kittiwakes by the thousand. 313 hectares (774 acres). NCC run a ferry to the island from May to August.

Rhum, Highland: Living laboratory with many typical Highland birds and large colony of Manx Shearwaters. 10,684 hectares (26,400 acres). Permits needed to visit area away from Loch Scresort. Trail guide and handbook available. Not very suitable for the casual visitor.

St Kilda, Western Isles: Finest seabird cliffs in eastern Atlantic. Stupendous scenery with Gannets, auks, gulls and many other birds. 853 hectares (2,107 acres). Permission to stay from National Trust for Scotland, 5 Charlotte Square, Edinburgh 5. Expedition or organized tour required.

Tentsmuir Point, Fife: Sand dune area near the coast with good waders and wildfowl offshore, especially sea ducks in winter. 505 hectares (1,246 acres). Access along forest drives on foot only.

tares (13,594 acres). Access unrestricted except to sanctuary; access to Wildfowl Trust area by fee on arrival.

Cairngorms, Grampian and Highland: Wonderful high-level massif with adjacent lochs and old Scots pine forest. All the Highland specialities including Golden Eagle, Dotterel, Snow Bunting, Crested Tit, Capercaillie. 25,947 hectares (64,118 acres). Access restricted at various times between August and October. Ski lift via Loch Morlich to tops.

Craigellachie, Grampian: Lovely area of birch woods above Aviemore alive with Willow Warblers in summer and home to other interesting species. 260 hectares (642 acres). Access along paths.

Druidibeg, Loch, Western Isles: Large shallow loch and base of the native Greylag Goose. Other good birds at all seasons. 1,677 hectares (4,145 acres). Permit required during the breeding season, but birds viewable from roads.

Forvie, Sands of, Grampian: Dunes at mouth of the delightful Ythan Estuary. Noted breeding ground of terns and Eider. 1,073 hectares (2,651 acres). Access restricted in summer and autumn, but birds easily seen on Ythan from rights of way.

Hermaness, Shetland: Wonderful seabird cliffs and moors at northern tip of Unst. Stronghold of Great Skua, but also auks, Gannet, Arctic Skua and moorland waders. 964 hectares (2,383 acres). Free access, but cliffs are dangerous.

Inverpolly, Highland: Splendid remote mountain area with lochs, streams and really wild country. Divers, waders, terns and many Highland specialities. 10,856 hectares (26,827 acres). Free access at most times, but some restrictions in late summer and autumn.

Leven, Loch, Tayside: Rich lowland loch and best population of breeding ducks in Britain. Major arrival point of geese in autumn with staggering numbers at times. 1,597 hectares (3,946 acres). Access only at Kirkgate Park, Findatie, Burleigh Sands and Loch Leven Castle. See also Vane Farm, *RSPB Reserves.*

Lomond, Loch, Central and Strathclyde: Famous route to the Highlands, but worth a stop at southeast corner with good

Royal Society for the Protection of Birds Reserves

The RSPB owns or leases a network of reserves covering the country from Fetlar in Shetland to Arne in Dorset. Some, such as Havergate, Minsmere, Loch Garten and Handa, were classic birding locations before the RSPB acquired them, and by 1981 the Society was administering 81 reserves covering over 38,000 hectares (92,000 acres). Most reserves have carefully sited hides to allow birds to be seen without disturbance. Access details vary from year to year, and nonmembers may have to pay an entrance fee. Information is obtainable from the RSPB.

ENGLAND

Arne, Dorset: Fine area of open heathland famed for the most viewable Dartford Warblers in the country. Escorted tours by prior arrangement in summer; but Shipstal Point area open throughout the year.

Aylesbeare, Devon: Interesting lowland heathland on the edge of Dartmoor. Access at all times.

Bempton Cliffs, Humberside: Excellent seabird cliffs with huge numbers of gulls and auks together with 100 pairs of Gannets. Access along clifftop footpaths at all seasons; best from April to August.

Blacktoft Sands, Humberside: Good marshland area at the base of the Humber Estuary with mud flats, and reed beds with Bearded Tits. Free visiting via public footpath.

Chapel Wood, Devon: Tiny mixed valley woodland near Barnstaple with possible Buzzard. Free permits available.

Church Wood, Bucks: Mixed wood near Slough with usual birds including all 3 British woodpeckers. Free access along marked paths.

Coombes Valley, Staffs: Long wooded valley in hills above Stoke-on-Trent. Delightful stream with Dippers and Pied Flycatchers. Access, by permit only, in summer.

Dungeness, Kent: Large shingle area at famed bird site. Recent management has created freshwater lake which attracts variety of species. Noted migration watch-point with good numbers of rarities every year. Open on specific days throughout the year, access by permit.

Eastwood, Greater Manchester: Woodland near industrial area where emphasis is on introducing common birds to school parties from urban background. Access by arrangement with warden.

Elmley Marshes, Kent: Delightful area of flooded grazing alongside Swale at Isle of Sheppey. Heavy influx of waders and wildfowl in winter along with good raptor population.

Access throughout the year on specific days.

Fairburn Ings, West Yorkshire: Flooded mining subsidence next to A1 east of Leeds. Shallow fresh water with fringed edges that hold interesting birds throughout the year. Information centre and free access at all times.

Fore Wood, East Sussex: Good woodland birds at Crowhurst near Battle. Marked trails through lovely countryside allow access at all times.

Fowlmere, Cambs: Interesting wetland and surrounding countryside near Royston offering many common birds, particularly to young ornithologists. Access free at all times along marked trail to elevated hide.

Gayton Sands, Dee Estuary, Cheshire: Part of the intertidal flats of the famed Dee Estuary with hordes of waders in season. No access, but good views at high tide from car park north of Boathouse Restaurant. Beware dangerous tides.

Havergate Island, Suffolk: Stronghold of the Avocet, and excellent marshland birds throughout the year. Approached only by boat from Orford, advance permits required. Members charged for boat, nonmembers for boat and entry. A fine day's birding.

Hornsea Mere, Humberside: Large natural lake near sea north of Hull with good waterfowl throughout the year. Smew reasonably regular early in year. Access on specific days.

Langstone Harbour, Hants: Part of the finest estuary on the south coast with huge numbers of Brent Geese and other wildfowl, and monumental flocks of waders. No access, but easily seen from public road by the causeway between Langstone and Chichester Harbours.

Leighton Moss, Lancs: Excellent reed marsh near Morecambe Bay with strong populations of Bittern and Bearded Tit. Fine access and hides on specific days via permits.

Lodge, The, Beds: Heath and woods with artificial lake surrounding RSPB headquarters.

Good woodland birds with masses of nest boxes and feeders, and the opportunity to purchase all the Society's products. Access free (car park charge) except Sundays and Bank Holidays which are reserved to members.

Minsmere, Suffolk: The gem in the RSPB collection and the most famous bird reserve in Britain. Exquisite reed marsh with the 'Scrape', an artificially created lagoon full of breeding birds. Marsh Harrier, Avocet and Bittern on view – with luck. Access by permit obtainable at reserve on specific days. Free access to modern double-decker hide on beach.

Morecambe Bay, Lancs: One of Europe's top wetlands with an intertidal area of sand and mud full of waders. Good views from Hest Bank, near Carnforth, at high tide, but beware quicksand and dangerous tides.

Nagshead, Glos: Upland oak wood near Forest of Dean with typical species including Pied Flycatcher. Free access.

Northward Hill, Kent: Mixed wood overlooking excellent North Kent Marshes with noted Heronry. Good for woodland birds including Nightingale. Access at all times from High Halstow.

North Warren, Suffolk: Interesting heathland area north of Ipswich. Free access along marked trail.

Ouse Washes, Cambs: Wonderful wetland with winter wildfowl and wealth of breeding birds. Site of recolonization by Black-tailed Godwit and Ruff. Information centre and public hides available at all times. Access via Manea on western shore of Washes.

Radipole Lake, Dorset: Marvellous little marsh virtually in

the centre of Weymouth with Bearded Tit and many other species. Free access via the Swannery car park.

Rye House Marsh, Herts: Shallow water and reed swamp in the Lea Valley with excellent educational opportunities. Access restricted to certain days each week.

St Bees Head, Cumbria: Spectacular scenery and excellent seabird cliffs from April to August. Includes the only Black Guillemots breeding in England and thousands of gulls and other auks. Free access.

Snettisham, Norfolk: Pits behind seawall on eastern shore of the Wash with good wildfowl and waders and fantastic fly-past of roosting waders at high tide. Access at all times along beach to hides.

Strumpshaw Fen, Norfolk: Broadland marsh rapidly improved by careful management. Reed swamp with increasing collection of breeding birds. Access on specific days throughout the year. This is the only area in the country with regular and viewable Bean Geese at nearby Buckenham.

Tetney Marshes, Lincs: Coastal marshes south of Grimsby and a noted haunt of birds and their watchers on this coast. Good waders and migration watch-point. Visiting only by arrangement.

Titchwell Marsh, Norfolk: Fine coastal marshes, reed beds and woodland at the western end of the famous north Norfolk coast. Good waders and wildfowl and some interesting breeding birds. Reserve centre and free access to public hides.

Wolves Wood, Suffolk: Interesting deciduous wood west of Ipswich with usual woodland birds. Free access.

Fetlar

Noup Cliffs • • North Hill, Papa Westray
Marwick Head • • Cottasgarth
Hobbister • • Copinsay

Handa •

Balranald •

• Loch of Strathbeg

Insh Marshes • • Loch Garten
Killiecrankie • • Fowlsheugh
• Loch of Kinnordy

• Vane Farm

• Lochwinnoch

• Rathlin Island Cliffs

Shanes Castle •
• Castlecaldwell
• Mull of Galloway
St Bees Head •
Leighton Moss and
Morecambe Bay •
Fairburn Ings •
Eastwood •
South Stack Cliffs •
• Gayton Sands

• Bempton Cliffs
• Hornsea Mere
• Blacktoft Sands
• Tetney Marshes
Titchwell Marsh
Coombes Valley • Snettisham •
Lake Vyrnwy • Strumpshaw Fen
Ynys-Hir • Ouse Washes •
The Lodge • Fowlmere • Minsmere
Wolves Wood • North
Warren
Gwenffrwd/Dinas • Havergate
Nagshead • Rye House Island
Grassholm • Church Wood • Northward
Elmley Marshes • Hill

Chapel Wood • Dungeness •
Langstone Harbour • Fore Wood •
Aylesbeare Common • • Arne
Radipole Lake •

WALES

Grassholm, Dyfed: Classic flat-topped island off Welsh coast with huge Gannetry of more than 16,000 pairs. Landing by arrangement only, but difficult at all times due to weather.

Gwenffrwd/Dinas, Dyfed: Two areas of lovely oak wood in the centre of Kite country. Buzzard and other hill birds always on view, Red Kite a distinct possibility. Trail at Dinas always open, access to Gwenffrwd only on specific days in summer.

Lake Vyrnwy, Powys: Huge reservoir in hills with interesting wetland and hill bird populations. Easily viewed from roads and public hide at northeast corner. Information centre near west end of dam, nature trails in summer.

South Stack Cliffs, Gwynedd: Seabird cliffs beyond Holyhead with good numbers of auks. Access along public paths at all times, best April to August.

Ynys-Hir, Dyfed: Excellent marshes alongside the Dyfi Estuary with good populations of wintering wildfowl and waders, and breeding birds. Access by permit on specific days throughout the year.

SCOTLAND

Balranald, North Uist, Western Isles: Wonderful marshland and coastal reserve among the 'machair' of the Outer Hebrides. Terns and other seabirds breed along with waders including the rare Red-necked Phalarope. Visits by arrangement in summer. Phalaropes arrive mid-May.

Copinsay, Orkney: Superb little island purchased in memory of James Fisher with good populations of seabirds of 12 species. Free access at all times. Boats arranged at Skaill.

Cottasgarth, Dale of, Orkney: Interesting open moorland with Orkney specialities including skuas, Short-eared Owl and Hen Harrier as possibilities. Free access at all times.

Fetlar, Shetland: The 'green isle' of Shetland with one of the richest of seabird cliffs. Excellent seabird cliffs, and Snowy Owl usually present. Access to reserve only from May to July by arrangement.

Fowlsheugh, Grampian: Seabird cliffs with usual auks and Kittiwakes. Easily approached via cliff-top footpath, best April to August.

Galloway, Mull of, Dumfries: Seabird cliffs with free access at all times – best in summer.

Garten, Loch, Highland: Famous Osprey breeding site in delightful Scots pine woods. Information centre and hide free in summer.

Handa, Highland: Idyllic seabird island in far northwest of Scotland full of auks, gulls and Fulmars. Day visits (not Sundays) arranged via local boatman at Tarbet.

Hobbister, Orkney: Open moorland with typical Orkney species and possible Hen Harrier. Free access to area between A964 and the sea.

Insh Marshes, Highland: Marshes bordering large Highland lake in Spey Valley, well known for Whooper Swans and other winter wildfowl. Access on specific days in summer; charge to nonmembers.

Killiecrankie, Tayside: Good area of hill woodland with Highland-type birds. Access in summer by arrangement with warden.

Kinnordy, Loch of, Tayside: Interesting marshland area. Access on specific days in summer.

Lochwinnoch, Strathclyde: Attractive haunt of winter wildfowl handily situated near Glasgow. Small entrance fee to nonmembers. School parties welcomed to nature centre and the lookout tower by arrangement.

Marwick Head, Orkney: Spectacular seabird cliffs with masses of birds. Free access along cliff tops – best April to August.

North Hill, Papa Westray, Orkney: One of the best seabird colonies in Britain with more breeding species than any other. Access by arrangement with warden.

Noup Cliffs, Westray, Orkney: Fine seabird cliffs best visited in summer. Free access at all times via Noup Head lighthouse.

Strathbeg, Loch of, Grampian: Delightful coastal loch with major wildfowl interest, noted for autumn geese arrivals and huge numbers of ducks. Good for migrants. Access on specific days throughout year by arrangement with warden.

Vane Farm, Tayside: Fine visiting centre on shores of Loch Leven with good hides for autumn geese arrival and winter wildfowl. Small charge to nonmembers, school parties by arrangement. Open on specific days throughout year.

NORTHERN IRELAND

Castlecaldwell, Co. Fermanagh: Attractive deciduous woodland with good bird population and adjacent lake. Access free at all times. Boat trips by arrangement.

Rathlin Island Cliffs, Co. Antrim: Good colonies of seabirds on attractive offshore island. Access by arrangement with boatmen at Ballycastle.

Shanes Castle, Co. Antrim: Nice woodland area open in summer. Small permit fee.

Bird Observatories

A network of observatories covers much of the coastline of Britain and Ireland. There are, however, substantial gaps, notably in the west and northwest, and along the northeast coasts both of England and Scotland. Even that noted watch-point the Isles of Scilly has no officially recognized bird observatory. The reasons for such uneven coverage are partly historical and partly inherent in the very nature of observatory work.

Most observatories were established in the 1940s and 1950s as the result of the enthusiasm of individuals and groups of bird-ringers. Some became well-established and well-run organizations with their own administration and funding that continued despite changes in personnel. Others never reached this stage, and so when the initial enthusiasts (all amateurs, of course) moved on, the observatory structure broke down. Among others there have in the past been observatories at Seahouses in Northumberland, Cley in Norfolk, Walberswick in Suffolk, St Catherine's on the Isle of Wight, the Isles of Scilly and Saltee in Co. Wexford.

The initial impetus has always been the ringing of migrants and the locations chosen are such as to offer the chance of ringing these birds in numbers. At first elaborate and costly Heligoland traps – huge funnel-like structures of chicken wire – were required, but the use of mist nets has emancipated ringers and made them as mobile as the birds themselves. Many of the best sites survived this revolution, though observatories remain as varied as anyone could wish. Some are splendidly equipped small hostels offering appropriate accommodation and food. Others offer no more than a place to sleep and facilities to cook. All are self-financing.

Observatories also vary in the work they perform, but they have the regular daily counting of migrant birds in common. Their results are co-ordinated through the British Trust for Ornithology which administers the national ringing scheme and from whom details of current addresses can be obtained.

Bardsey Island: A small island some 2 km by 1 km, situated about 3 km off the Lleyn Peninsular in north Wales. It rises high in the east with farmland in the lower western part, where migrants frequently seek shelter among field walls. A variety of different birds breed, including good numbers of Manx Shearwaters on the mountain top, Storm Petrels and a few Choughs. In spring and autumn there is a good passage of birds entering the country via the Irish Sea and among them a few rarities make an appearance, sometimes attracted to the lighthouse. There is a self-catering hostel for 11 visitors that is open from March to October, and a resident warden. There is a boat from Pwllheli every Saturday.

Bradwell: Established in 1954 at the mouth of the River Blackwater on the Essex coast. Unlike most other observatories Bradwell is situated, indeed surrounded, by prime birdwatching in a variety of forms. The bird-rich estuaries and shoals that line the coast are full of waders and wildfowl virtually throughout the year, and there is thus less concentration on passerine migrants than at other sites, though these sometimes occur in numbers. Accommodation is available in a large wooden hut in 2 bunk rooms sleeping 8.

Cape Clear: Island off the southwest corner of Ireland ideally situated to attract trans-atlantic vagrants and for observing the occasionally spectacular passage of seabirds. Yet, although rarities do turn up most seasons, the actual number of American birds remains surprisingly small. The late summer movements of Great and other Shearwaters can usually be seen and other seabirds are regular. Breeding birds include Black Guillemot, Chough and genuine Rock Dove. There is a hostel for up to 10 visitors open throughout the year on a self-catering basis. Access is by bus from Cork to Baltimore and thence by boat on Mondays, Wednesdays, Fridays and Saturdays.

Copeland: A small island off the northwest coast of Northern Ireland offering good regular passage of passerine migrants and a variety of breeding seabirds including Manx Shearwater. Activities depend entirely on the enthusiasm of visitors – there is no resident warden. A hostel offers accommodation on a self-catering basis for 8 men and 4 women and is open from March to October. Access details available from the BTO.

Dungeness: One of the older-established observatories and now situated in a Victorian villa in the shadow of the nuclear power station. 'Dunge', as it is affectionately known by generations of enthusiasts, has a good reputation for producing regular numbers of passerine migrants, many of which are

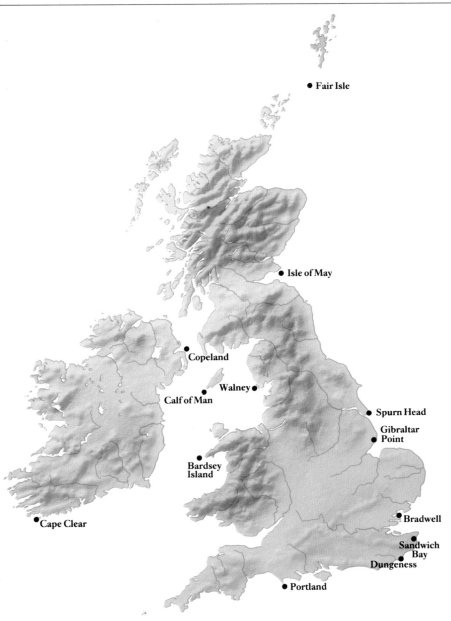

Fair Isle

Isle of May

Copeland

Walney

Calf of Man

Spurn Head

Gibraltar Point

Bardsey Island

Bradwell

Sandwich Bay

Dungeness

Cape Clear

Portland

movements of migrants through this area. There is a hostel offering accommodation for 13 visitors between March and October, and a resident warden. Access is by boat from Port St Mary or Port Erin.

May, Isle of: Small island in the Firth of Forth with a history of observation of bird migration. This is a fine island with a good population of breeding seabirds, including the 3 common auks, which regularly attracts good numbers of migrants. There is a hostel for 6 visitors, who must bring all their food with them, from April to October. No warden.

Portland: Based on the old lighthouse, this is a model for all observatories were sufficient money available. Accommodation is tasteful and comfortable, enabling up to 20 visitors to concentrate on the birds rather than on survival, as at some other notable observatories. Its geographical position is ideal for observing seabird passage through the Channel and for receiving incoming and outgoing passerine migrants. Usually produces a reasonable crop of rarities each season. Self-catering basis and open throughout the year with a resident warden. A small self-contained flat is also available for observers and their families.

Sandwich Bay: Estuarine and coastal area at the eastern end of Kent ideally situated to receive birds from the nearby Continent. Has a habit of producing rarish seabirds as well as a sometimes heavy passage of passerines. Good ringing programme operated by enthusiastic group. Hostel accommodation available for 14–20 visitors on a self-catering basis.

Spurn Head: At the southern tip of the Spurn Peninsula on the north side of the Humber and surprisingly isolated for a mainland site. Collects a good variety of migrants, including some really fine concentrations of seabirds on passage. Intensive ringing programme with rarities present from time to time. There is a resident warden and hostel accommodation throughout the year for up to 17 visitors.

Walney: Island on the northern side of the famous Morecambe Bay with excellent waders in season. Also the site of the largest colonies of Herring and Lesser Black-backed Gulls in Europe and a growing colony of Eiders. Migration and ringing important and accommodation available in a cottage and caravan throughout the year. There is a resident warden at all times.

trapped and ringed. Rarities turn up most seasons and the so-called 'Patch' of warm water produced by the power station attracts interesting seabirds. Accommodation is available on a self-catering basis for up to 11 visitors throughout the year and there is a resident warden.

Fair Isle: Classic bird migration centre with an unsurpassed history of adding new birds to the British List. Situated roughly halfway between Shetland and Orkney, and isolated from both, its drawing power is immense. Siberian waifs regularly make their landfall here, to the delight of a regular population of enthusiasts. Breeding birds include an excellent collection of northern seabirds with both skuas, but

autumn is *the* season. First-class purpose-built hostel offering full-board accommodation from March to November. Resident warden. The autumn season must be booked well in advance – demand is always heavy in September and October. Ideal for bird-watching holidays at other periods.

Gibraltar Point: Strategically situated at the northeastern corner of the Wash near Skegness on the Lincolnshire coast. The surrounding area is a local nature reserve, with a variety of habitats including large intertidal areas, that holds many different species. The coastal dunes attract considerable numbers of migrants and there is an extensive ringing project. Seabird passage is often dra-

matic. The observatory and field centre accommodates 25 visitors, with additional space for up to 6 individuals, and offers an excellent programme of natural history courses. Full board is available from March to September and self-catering throughout the year. Warden.

Man, Calf of: This small island at the southern tip of the Isle of Man has been administered as a nature reserve and bird observatory by the Manx National Trust since 1952. The island has always boasted an attractive population of breeding seabirds including auks and Kittiwakes as well as Choughs, but in its 30-year history the observatory has produced a string of rare birds as well as coverage of the important

Major Haunts of Rarities

Birds are the most mobile of all animals and their seasonal comings and goings have been remarked upon since Biblical times. The arrival of summer visitors – Swallows, warblers and flycatchers – is awaited with eager anticipation. Some arrive by the million, others are decidedly scarce. Inevitably, along the way, some birds get lost and make journeys that take them hundreds or even thousands of kilometres off course. Such birds, common enough perhaps in their natural range, then become rarities.

Britain and Ireland are ideally suited to gather such waifs and have, as a result, a higher percentage of rarities on their lists than any other area of the world. The reasons for this gathering power are discussed elsewhere (see *Range and Distribution*, p. 54), but the result has been to make the British watcher remarkably 'rarity conscious'. Unfortunately most bird-watchers are based in the south and east of England, with the result that more rarities are found in these parts of the country. Outside this region well-established rarity spots are overmanned every autumn while others are sadly neglected. Thus Fair Isle has for long been known as a special site and is thronged in season. More recently the Isles of Scilly have taken on a similar mantle. Akeragh Lough in Co. Kerry is noted for transatlantic waders and wildfowl and Cape Clear Island in Co. Cork for seabirds. Yet the whole northwestern coastline of Britain and Ireland has been sadly neglected, not because rarities do not occur but because no one has established regular watching.

The Major Haunts of Rarities are thus places where others regularly watch for rare birds, rather than places chosen by rare birds themselves. There are wonderful opportunities for those with a sense of adventure to select and work new sites for themselves. A glance at the map opposite will show the gaps that exist around our coastline.

Aberlady Bay: Fine estuarine bay on the south coast of the Firth of Forth with the benefit of nature reserve status and, together with nearby Gullane Point, a regular haunt of rare birds and their watchers. Waders, gulls and terns are most usual species, though all manner of rarities appear.
Akeragh Lough: Located on the Kerry coast north of Tralee, this attractive shallow marsh offers the first fresh water to transatlantic migrants. Between July and October the prevailing westerly winds aid the passage of American waders and wildfowl which occasionally appear here in small flocks. On several occasions American waders have outnumbered European birds and a small sandpiper is as likely to be a 'peep' as a Little Stint.
Cape Clear Island: Lying at the extreme southwest corner

of Ireland, Cape Clear is ideally placed for the observation of seabirds driven into the seas at the mouth of St George's Channel between Britain and Ireland. As they make their way out into the Atlantic huge numbers may pass close offshore. Passerine rarities may also appear from time to time.
Cley and Blakeney: Situated where the north Norfolk marshes narrow and terminate, this remarkable site has become the bird-watchers' Mecca. Huge list of rarities every year, but literally hundreds of watchers every weekend in spring and autumn so that few waifs escape detection. Also acts as an interchange centre for rarity information from all parts of the country.
Dungeness: Well-established area strategically situated to receive Continental migrants and birds wandering along the

coast of Belgium and northern France. Also manages to attract good numbers of rarities, though seldom the extreme vagrants that other, more isolated, sites produce.
Fair Isle: Lying approximately halfway between Shetland and Orkney and surrounded by featureless seas, the drawing power of Fair Isle is unsurpassed. No doubt birds lost in the northern part of the North Sea also alight in Shetland, Orkney and mainland Scotland, but they are then widely spread among the available cover. Fair Isle concentrates birds and is just small enough to be well covered by a small team of watchers. As a result really rare birds occur every autumn and birds new to Britain and Ireland are discovered every year or so.
Farlington Marshes: Area of grazing marshes on the south coast intersected by clumps of bushes and open pools situated in, and almost surrounded by, Langstone Harbour. Now a nature reserve, the marshes have always attracted a wide variety of birds including many of the waders and wildfowl that abound on the adjacent mud banks. Rarities turn up with some regularity.
Holkham: National Nature Reserve on the north Norfolk coast with a substantial belt of pines planted to stabilize the coastal dunes. The landward

side of the pines, as well as open clearings among them, has been colonized by birch and bramble scrub and it is here that the Norfolk rarity hunters find their birds. The site has produced the most extraordinary run of mainly Asiatic vagrant passerines and is hard to beat in September and October for these species.
Minsmere: RSPB reserve on the Suffolk coast renowned for Avocets and other East Anglian specialities. Also manages to attract off-course vagrants in some numbers every year, mainly to the 'Scrape' and to the bushy areas at the 'Sluice'. The variety of habitats ensures that any rarity will find a suitable niche and extended stays are regular.
Out Skerries: Group of small inhabited islands east of the Shetland mainland that produces a rarity or two for anyone prepared to spend some part of the autumn in splendid isolation. Regular manning would undoubtedly produce many more. Though the geographical position is, perhaps, not as favourable as that of Fair Isle, the pleasure of finding one's own rarities is adequate compensation.
Pagham Harbour: Small estuarine bay on the south coast just east of Selsey Bill that produces rarities, especially waders, with surprising regularity. No doubt the num-

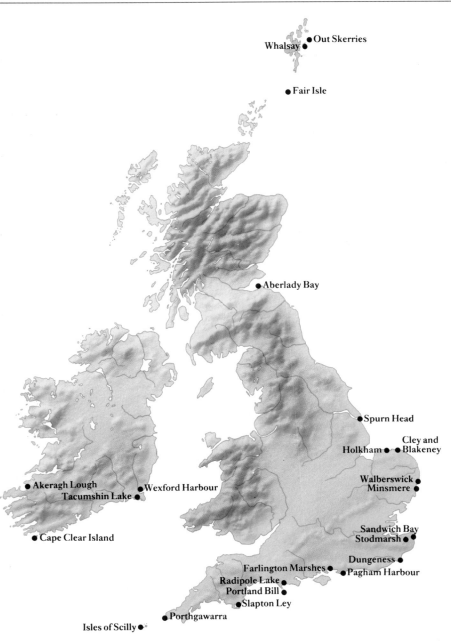

ber of watchers is a contributory factor, but the handy viewable size is a further advantage. Most rarities tend to concentrate at Sidlesham Ferry Pond on the north side adjacent to the best access road.

Porthgawarra: Handily situated on the Lizard Peninsula and frequented by many birders on their way to and from the Isles of Scilly in autumn. Regularly produces transatlantic passerine vagrants as well as waifs from other directions.

Portland Bill: Famous Dorset site of excellent bird observatory that protrudes into the Channel and has, as a result, considerable gathering power. Small walled fields with growths of brambles offer minimal cover so that most birds present can be seen. Has some excellent records to its credit and a bonus in the form of a regular passage of seabirds.

Radipole Lake: Unlikely site, virtually surrounded by seaside town of Weymouth, that holds rare birds at every season. Good variety of habitat with reeds, scrub, mud, open water and banks, and easily viewed from public paths. Nearby Lodmoor, though much degraded, is always worth a visit.

Sandwich Bay: Diverse area near Ramsgate, with intertidal sands, fresh marshes and areas of bushy cover near the coast, that regularly holds interesting birds. Being so near the Continent it often attracts unusual gulls and terns that sometimes spend extended periods off passage.

Scilly, Isles of: Splendidly situated, with nothing but ocean between them and America, these islands have become a place of autumn pilgrimage for hundreds of birders. Though transatlantic vagrants are the main attraction, rarities arrive from every direction including Siberia. It would be a poor autumn that did not produce at least a handful of American birds and there is always a chance of a new bird for Britain and Ireland. But this is no place for those seeking their birds in solitude.

Slapton Ley: Large, reed-covered coastal fleet south of Torquay that has a reputation for holding scarce marsh-type warblers in autumn. Aquatic Warblers are as regular as anywhere, but most are picked out of mist nets for ringing. Very difficult to observe such birds in the field.

Spurn Head: Long, narrow bar at the mouth of the Humber that has been the site of a bird observatory for many years and which produces good rarities most years. Birds are often difficult to see because of the heavy growth of bushes. The adjacent mud flats are always interesting and the area is sometimes particularly fine for seabird movements.

Stodmarsh: Kentish site east of Canterbury best known as the haunt of colonizing marsh-type warblers, but of proven attraction to a good range of rare vagrants. Reed beds and open water are the main habitats, but bushy areas may hold the odd bird. Being so close to the Continent all manner of birds may, and do, turn up.

Tacumshin Lake: Coastal lagoon in Co. Wexford, protected by a sand spit, that was tidal until 1974. Now much reduced, it is a haunt of ducks and waders that regularly attracts transatlantic birds. The White Hole, at the northwestern corner, is often favoured. Avocets bred here for the only time in Ireland in 1938.

Walberswick: Highly varied Suffolk coastal area, often overshadowed by more famous Minsmere to the south. Mostly a National Nature Reserve, but with good access along public rights of way. Lagoons, reed beds, heaths and woodland combine to offer the incoming vagrant a wide choice of habitat and many birds are undoubtedly overlooked as a result. All seasons are interesting, but late autumn is perhaps the best.

Wexford Harbour: Famous wildfowl haunt at southeastern corner of Ireland with regular large flocks of geese in winter. Waders too are· numerous. From a rarity viewpoint the almost-regular American Snow Geese are the main attraction, though other rare birds turn up from time to time.

Whalsay: Small, eastern island of the Shetland group that has rewarded those few watchers who have made the effort to visit it during a peak passage period. A single observer produced a whole string of rarities one season, showing the potential of this and any other strategically sited spot for attracting rarities.

Major Seabird Colonies

By virtue of their unique geographical position at the edge of a large landmass, and because they are surrounded by seas rich in marine life, Britain and Ireland are home to one of the most important populations of seabirds in the world. Many, such as the Manx Shearwater, literally roam the oceans of the world. Others are more confined and seldom venture far from our shores. All earn their living from the sea and come to land only to breed. Most spectacular are the cliff-breeding species that line the ledges of the most fearsome of cliffs. In some places thousands of birds can be seen at a glance, as spectacular a wildlife sight as any on earth.

The seabird cliff forms not only a remarkable spectacle: it is a complex and dynamic ecosystem in which each species picks out its own particular breeding niche.

With the cliff-nesting species the spectacle may be enjoyed from a cliff-top vantage point, or from below from a boat. Both methods require caution. Every year ornithologists are killed while studying cliff-nesting seabirds, and it is a foolish boatman who would bring his boat close in under cliffs without experience of local currents. Yet the cliffs are spectacular and worth visiting – but only with the greatest of care.

Ailsa Craig: Small precipitous island at the mouth of the Firth of Clyde holding 12 breeding species including over 13,000 pairs of Gannets that have bred since 1520. Good numbers of auks, though former huge Puffinry virtually deserted.

Alderney and Burhou: Best seabirds in the Channel with 10 breeding species including Storm Petrel on Burhou. Les Étacs, Alderney, has had a flourishing Gannetry since 1940.

Bardsey: Inhabited island off Lleyn Peninsula, north Wales, with 9 breeding species. Often overshadowed by better-known Welsh islands to the south.

Bass Rock: Splendid stack at mouth of Firth of Forth with renowned Gannet colony and 8 other breeding species. Nearly 9,000 pairs of Gannets breed annually.

Bempton Cliffs: Most spectacular seabird cliffs on English mainland with vast colonies of auks, Kittiwakes and Fulmars and a small Gannetry. Over 12,000 pairs of Guillemots.

Berneray and Mingulay: Southernmost islands of Hebridean chain with large numbers of auks, Kittiwakes and Fulmars and a total of 10 breeding species. Reached from Barra.

Berriedale: Cliffs extending southwards for several miles along the Caithness coast and holding 11 species including auks and Kittiwakes in good numbers.

Blasket Islands: Outstanding group of seldom-visited seabird islands off the Kerry coast with 13 breeding species including Manx Shearwater, Storm Petrel, possible Leach's Petrel and the usual auks including good numbers of Puffins.

Bull and Cow Rocks: Tiny islands off the Cork coast with 9 breeding species including 1,500 pairs of Gannets.

Clare Island: Substantial island off the coast of Co. Mayo holding 12 breeding species. Most of the usual species including good populations of auks.

Clo Mor: Northwestern corner of British mainland near Cape Wrath and the highest mainland cliffs. Eight species breed including all the usual auks. Gannets regularly pass by.

Copinsay: Island off the east coast of Orkney purchased as a memorial to the late James Fisher who loved both islands and seabirds. Boasts 12 breeding species including all the regular auks. Administered by RSPB.

Duncansby Head: Adjacent to John o'Groats. Seabird cliffs extending southwards for several kilometres with continuous movements of auks and gulls coming and going. Twelve breeding species may include both skuas. Nonbreeding Gannets present.

Dunnet Head: Most northerly point of British mainland. Easily viewed cliffs holding 11 breeding species including auks, Kittiwakes, Fulmars and passing skuas.

Farne Islands: Delightful, easily accessible islands off Northumberland coast with historical connections with St Cuthbert. Thirteen breeding species include usual gulls and auks, remarkably tame Eiders and best collection of British terns with regular Roseates.

Fetlar: Eighteen breeding species make this second only to Westray in numbers of seabirds. Huge auk, Kittiwake and Fulmar colonies along north coast together with one of the largest Shaggeries in Britain.

Flannan Islands: Isolated outposts of Outer Hebrides north of more famous St Kilda. Ten breeding species including Leach's Petrel and recently established Gannetry.

Foula: Western outpost of Shetland with 16 breeding species including Storm Petrel. Holds some of the largest concentrations of seabirds in these islands and over half of British Great Skua population.

Fowlsheugh: Extensive cliffs near Stonehaven, Kincardineshire, with usual auks and gulls. Administered by RSPB.

Grassholm: Though holding 9 breeding species, this flat-topped island off south Wales is best known for its huge, fast-growing Gannetry. Over 16,000 pairs breed, but landing is difficult and irregular.

Great and Little Skellig: Offshore islands on Kerry coast with 11 breeding species and no less than 20,000 pairs of Gannets. Also Manx Shearwater, Storm Petrel and possible Leach's Petrel.

Handa: Situated on the west coast of Sutherland and an accessible RSPB reserve. Spectacular seabird cliffs at their very best. Fifteen species breed, many in their tens of thousands.

Hermaness: Northern point of Britain with fearsome cliffs

Hermaness
Fetlar
Foula •
• Noss

Westray and Papa Westray
Sule Skerry and Sule Stack
Sula Sgeir and North Rona •
Marwick Head
Hoy • Copinsay
Clo Mor • Dunnet Head
Duncansby Head
Flannan Islands •
• Handa
St Kilda •
Berriedale
Shiant Isles •
Troup and Pennan Heads
Rhum •
Berneray and Mingulay •
Fowlsheugh
Treshnish Isles •
Isle of May
Bass Rock
St Abb's Head
Horn Head •
Rathlin Island
Farne Islands
Ailsa Craig
Scar Rocks
St Bee's Head
Bempton Cliffs
Clare Island •
Calf of Man
Cliffs of Moher
Lambay Islands
Loop Head
Puffin Island
Basket lands
Bardsey
eat and Little ellig
Bull and w Rocks
Saltee Islands
Skomer
Grassholm
Skokholm
Isles of Scilly •
Alderney and Burhou

St Kilda: Most famous seabird island in North Atlantic, but difficult access and no accommodation. Fifteen breeding species in amazing numbers with 52,000 pairs of Gannets, both petrels, and huge populations of auks, Kittiwakes and Fulmars.

Saltee Islands: Thirteen species of seabird breed on these islands off the coast of Co. Wexford including Gannet, Manx Shearwater and Storm Petrel. All the usual auks and gulls as well.

Scar Rocks: Situated off Galloway, these small islands hold a few hundred pairs of Gannets and 10 other species including auks, Kittiwakes and Fulmars.

Scilly, Isles of: Though lacking spectacular cliffs, the outer islands offer a wide range of seabird habitat and are home to auks as well as terns. Fourteen species breed, but without being spectacular in numbers or variety.

Shiant Isles: Small group of islands in the North Minch with 11 breeding species including all the usual cliff-nesting ones and possible Storm Petrel.

Skokholm: Classic seabird site off the Welsh coast with huge population of Manx Shearwater and usual breeding auks. Accommodation and access available via bird observatory.

Skomer: One of the richest and most accessible of all seabird islands. Coastline allows excellent viewing and photography of many of the 13 breeding species. Storm Petrel and Manx Shearwater both in strong numbers as well as auks.

Sula Sgeir and North Rona: Remote uninhabited islands off northwestern Scotland with 14 breeding species including Storm and Leach's Petrels, Great Skua, all 4 auks and nearly 9,000 pairs of breeding Gannets. Expedition access.

Sule Skerry and Sule Stack: Isolated, uninhabited islands off north Scottish coast with 12 breeding species. Probably both petrels, over 4,000 pairs of Gannets and very large Puffinry. Expedition access.

Treshnish Isles: Group of small islands cradled in the arms of Mull in the Inner Hebrides. Thirteen species of mainly cliff-breeding seabirds including all 4 auks and probable Manx Shearwater.

Troup and Pennan Heads: Good stretch of cliffs on Banffshire coast with 9 breeding species including usual auks, Kittiwake and Fulmar.

Westray and Papa Westray: With 19 breeding species, the top British and Irish site. Cliff colonies of auks and gulls in spectacular numbers.

holding 14 species of breeding seabird including fast-growing Gannetry. Stronghold of Great Skua last century.

Horn Head: Mainland cliffs on Donegal coast with 9 breeding species and a really substantial colony of Razorbills. Other auks and gulls easily viewed.

Hoy: Large island in Orkney with many spectacular cliffs and stacks full of birds. Fifteen species breed with good numbers of auks, both skuas and Manx Shearwater.

Lambay Islands: Ten species of seabird breed on these Irish Sea islands north of Dublin, including the usual auks in good numbers.

Loop Head: Southwestern corner of Co. Clare at the mouth of the River Shannon. Seven breeding species include Razorbill, Guillemot and Kittiwake. Leach's Petrel bred in the past and may still do so.

Marwick Head: Spectacular

cliffs on west coast of Orkney and easy to view RSPB reserve.

Man, Calf of: Small offshore island south of Isle of Man noted as the original home of the Manx Shearwater, which still breeds there. Ten other species include the usual auks.

May, Isle of: Famous bird island in Firth of Forth with 9 breeding species including usual auks. Formerly interesting tern population, but these birds now nest elsewhere.

Moher, Cliffs of: Mainland cliffs along the coast of Co. Clare with 8 breeding species including all 4 auks.

Noss: Easily accessible island near Lerwick in Shetland with daily boat trips in summer. With 16 breeding species one of the top sites in Britain and an exceptional spectacle, especially from boats. Birds include over 4,000 pairs of Gannets.

Puffin Island: Small offshore island off southeastern tip of Anglesey with auks and terns

among its 10 species of breeding seabird.

Rathlin Island: Beautiful, inhabited island off northeastern Ireland in Co. Antrim. Thirteen species of breeding seabird include Manx Shearwater and 3 species of auk.

Rhum: National Nature Reserve in Inner Hebrides best known, since 1716, for huge colony of Manx Shearwaters presently numbering some 70,000 pairs. Eleven other species include usual auks and possible Leach's Petrel.

St Abb's Head: Cliffs on Berwickshire coast with 9 breeding species including auks, Kittiwakes, Fulmars and non-breeding Gannets offshore.

St Bee's Head: Eight breeding species of seabird including auks and the only English Black Guillemots. Viewed via Whitehaven.

Major Estuaries

Estuaries are numbered among the richest of all habitats. Twice each day the tide covers the banks of mud and sand that line their lower reaches. As the water recedes millions of planktonic creatures are left behind, food for the innumerable molluscs and crustaceans that live among the ooze. Mussels, oysters, cockles and crabs are but the largest and most obvious of these animals; their numbers are dwarfed by other shellfish, shrimps and worms. A square metre of mud may hold several thousand such animals, making the estuary richer by far, in terms of what it produces, than, say, a field of cereals. So far man has found little way of exploiting this resource, but to wading birds and wildfowl these riches are the very stuff of life.

Britain and Ireland, with their wide range of tides, are particularly rich in estuaries, several of which are important even in global terms. The Wash, Morecambe Bay and the Ribble all hold upwards of 200,000 birds and are ranked among the top 10 such areas in Europe. In winter these huge flocks, particularly of Knot, Dunlin and Oystercatcher, are an awe-inspiring sight. During passage periods these same estuaries are of crucial importance to birds passing from their breeding grounds in the north and east to wintering grounds further south. While waders may be the most numerous birds to utilize the riches of estuaries, wildfowl also find ideal feeding and roosting grounds. Brent and Pink-footed Geese may be seen by the thousand and flocks of Wigeon may reach 10,000 or more.

Small numbers of these birds may be seen at virtually any river mouth, but spectacular conglomerations are confined to the larger estuaries. Here the problem is that birds may be scattered over huge areas, sometimes several miles away across the mud. Fortunately, as the tide rises the birds are pushed inland and concentrated into an ever smaller area. Eventually they are pushed off altogether and flight to a secure high-tide roost. This is the time to enjoy the shorebird spectacular. Sand banks are dangerous. Tides may flow faster than a man can run and, in any case, walking over the open ooze is a notoriously poor way to see birds. Stay on the shore, watch during the 2 hours before high tide, and do not disturb a roost.

Ballymacoda, Co. Cork: Estuary of River Womanagh with 1,000 Wigeon and huge flocks of Golden Plover and Lapwing.

Beauly Firth, Highland: Part of Moray Firth east of Inverness. Pink-footed and Greylag Geese, Whooper Swan, Goosander and good numbers of Redshank in winter.

Blackwater, Essex: Really good estuary with over 10,000 Dunlin and 2,500 Redshank, along with many other waders. Large flocks of Brent Geese, and Wigeon.

Bridgwater Bay, Somerset: Moulting ground for 3,500 Shelduck, and largest flock (500–1,000) of Whimbrel in Britain. Also usual wildfowl and wader concentrations.

Burry Inlet, West Glamorgan: Estuary of River Loughor with huge Oystercatcher flock of more than 10,000 birds. Equal numbers of Dunlin and Knot together with other waders. Many Wigeon and small flock of Brent Geese.

Chichester Harbour, Sussex: Up to 10,000 Brent Geese and 5,000 Shelduck, with huge (20,000) flock of Dunlin. Other waders reach 4 figures: Grey Plover, Lapwing, Redshank and both godwits.

Clyde, Firth of, Strathclyde: Good numbers of wildfowl and waders, but they tend to be scattered and difficult to see.

Cork Harbour, Co. Cork: Good numbers of wildfowl and large flock of Shelduck. Outstanding numbers of Golden Plover, Lapwing and up to 3,600 Black-tailed Godwit.

Dee, Cheshire: Monumental numbers of waders gather at Hilbre Island to roost: more than 25,000 Dunlin and Knot, up to 10,000 Sanderling, and 5,000 Lapwing, Bar-tailed Godwit and Curlew. Particularly large flock (5,000) of Pintail.

Dornoch Firth, Highland: Good populations of Teal and Wigeon together with decent numbers of waders.

Dublin Bay and Bull Island, Co. Dublin: Rich in variety and numbers, and a famous nature reserve. Over 10,000 each of Knot and Dunlin, 2,000 Bar-tailed Godwit and 3,000 Oystercatcher. Over 1,000 Brent Geese with larger numbers of Teal and Wigeon.

Dundalk Bay, Co. Louth: Autumn peak of 28,000 Oystercatcher – about 10,000 winter. Seven per cent (7,000) of west European Bar-tailed Godwits together with over 3,000 each of Golden Plover, Curlew, Redshank, Knot and 12,000 Dunlin. Large number of Wigeon, small flock of Brent Geese.

Exe, Devon: Workable estuary with Brent Geese and Wigeon in good numbers and 1,000 or more Oystercatcher, Dunlin, Redshank, Curlew and both godwits. Wintering Avocet, Greenshank and Spotted Redshank a feature.

Forth, Firth of, Lothians: Huge inlet with wonderful winter birds. Sea ducks in staggering numbers – Scaup 25,000; Eider 10,000; Scoter 3,500; Goldeneye 5,000; and lesser numbers of Long-tailed Duck, Merganser and Velvet

Map labels:
Dornoch Firth
Beauly Firth
Firth of Tay
Firth of Forth
Firth of Clyde
Lindisfarne
Solway Firth
Teesmouth
Morecambe Bay
Dundalk Bay
Ribble
Humber
Dublin Bay and Bull Island
Dee
Mersey
The Wash
Shannon and Fergus
Wexford Slobs
Stour
Blackwater
Foulness
Cork Harbour
Ballymacoda, Co. Cork
Burry Inlet
Swale and Medway
Bridgwater Bay
Langstone Harbour
Chichester Harbour
Exe
Poole Harbour

Knot; 25,000 Dunlin; 10,000 Black-tailed Godwit and Sanderling; and totals of over 1,000 for several other species. All round one of the top sites in Britain.

Shannon and Fergus, Limerick: Largest Irish estuary with up to 15,000 wildfowl and 67,000 waders. Wigeon by the thousand together with lesser numbers of Greylag and Brent Geese, Shelduck and Whooper Swan. Over 8,000 Black-tailed Godwit are half the Icelandic population.

Solway Firth, Dumfries and Galloway, and Cumbria: Massive estuary dividing England and Scotland with huge populations of wildfowl and waders. Pink-footed Goose 15,000 and Barnacle Goose 10,000 are of international importance. Waders include 10,000 Oystercatcher, Dunlin and Knot, along with 5,000 Redshank, Curlew and Golden Plover.

Stour Estuary, Essex and Suffolk: Over 1,000 each of Wigeon, Mallard, Shelduck and Pintail, and 500 Brent Geese. Dunlin 10,000 and Redshank 5,000 are most numerous waders but 1,000 Black-tailed Godwit are significant.

Swale and Medway, Kent: Outstanding areas on Thames Estuary. White-fronted and Brent Geese flocks together with good numbers of Shelduck, Wigeon and Mallard. Totals for over 1,000 for many waders.

Tay, Firth of, Tayside: Fine estuary with many good haunts. Pink-footed and Greylag Geese reach 4 figures and strong wader population includes Dunlin, Oystercatcher and Redshank.

Teesmouth, Cleveland: Steadily declining due to industrialization. Still good flocks of Shelduck and Mallard, together with 10,000 each of Dunlin and Knot, and 1,000 Redshank.

Wash, The, Norfolk and Lincs: Second only to Morecambe Bay in wader numbers with 50,000 Knot; 25,000 Dunlin; 10,000 Curlew and Redshank; and other species over 1,000. Grey Plover almost a quarter of British total. Huge wildfowl population includes thousands of Pink-footed and Brent Geese; Wigeon 10,000; Scoter 2,500; and many others.

Wexford Slobs, Co. Wexford: Principal wildfowl haunt in Ireland including half (5,000) world population of Greenland White-fronted Goose. Also Brent Goose, Pintail and Wigeon in good numbers. Bewick's Swans are regular and several waders reach 4 figures.

Scoter. Over 10,000 each of Knot and Dunlin and more than 1,000 Oystercatcher, Golden Plover, Lapwing, Turnstone, Redshank, Bar-tailed Godwit and Curlew. Pink-footed Goose and Whooper Swan regular.

Foulness, Essex: Up to a sixth (10,000) of world population of dark-bellied Brent Goose, and huge numbers of Wigeon, Dunlin, Knot, Redshank, Bar-tailed Godwit and Curlew. No access, owned by Ministry of Defence.

Humber, Humberside: Long estuary with concentrations of species at different points. Pink-footed Goose haunt, and thousands of ducks and some really large concentrations of waders.

Langstone Harbour, Hants: Fine approachable estuary with up to 5,000 Brent Geese and 2,500 Shelduck and Wigeon. Good collection of waders with 2,500 Redshank and 10,000 Dunlin. Greenshank winter.

Lindisfarne, Northumberland: Huge National Nature Reserve with Greylag and Brent Geese, Whooper Swan and more than 10,000 Wigeon. Regular Scoter, Long-tailed Duck and scarcer grebes. Fine wader population includes 5,000 Bar-tailed Godwit and thousands of other waders.

Mersey, Merseyside: Good populations of waders and wildfowl including several thousand Teal and Wigeon, together with all the usual waders.

Morecambe Bay, Lancs: Top wader estuary in Britain with over 200,000 birds in winter: Knot 50,000; Dunlin and Oystercatcher 25,000; Sanderling and Ringed Plover 10,000 are all best British totals. Also Curlew 25,000; Bar-tailed Godwit 10,000 and so on. Wildfowl less important, but 2,500 Pink-footed Geese are regular.

Poole Harbour, Dorset: Intricate estuary with several thousand ducks and small flock of Brent Geese. Several waders reach 4 figures.

Ribble, Lancs: Very rich estuary with 20,000 Pink-footed Geese and 2,500 each of Shelduck, Mallard, Teal, Wigeon and Pintail. Waders in staggering numbers including 50,000

Reservoirs

Reservoirs are a comparatively recent addition to our countryside. The earliest were constructed as feeders for the great canal boom of the eighteenth and early nineteenth centuries, and only later were they created for industrial and domestic water supplies. In the present century, mainly over the past 40 years, their number and size has grown immensely, particularly in the lowlands where rivers became quite unable to cope with the demands made upon them. This new habitat has enabled aquatic birds to spread into areas where they were once unknown and bird-watchers now keep an eye on every new reservoir with the certain knowledge that birds will soon start to use it. In general upland reservoirs are comparatively poor for waterbirds and in what follows only lowland waters in England and Wales have been covered.

Reservoirs vary from huge seminatural lakes to small concrete storage bowls. Most can be seen from public roads or rights of way, but some require special permission to enter, though this is usually available on request from the relevant water authority. Virtually all new reservoirs make some provision for wildlife, particularly birds, and there are many nature reserves associated with the larger waters.

Abberton: Near the Essex coast and Britain's top bird reservoir for many years. Large (up to 7,500 birds) and varied population of wildfowl, including genuine wild Red-crested Pochard in autumn. Good breeding population of terns and grebes, and excellent concentrations of migrants in spring and autumn including Black Terns and Little Gulls.

Ardleigh: North of Colchester near old A12 and a fine modern reservoir with good variety of birds at all seasons. Comparatively small size makes viewing easy.

Barn Elms: Four concrete-banked pools situated in the heart of London near Hammersmith Bridge. Winter home to large rafts of diving ducks and to the declining Smew. Grebes, gulls and passage terns and waders find a home here, but increasing angling pressure may well be a deterrent.

Barrow Gurney: Three small concrete-banked pools near Bristol that attract numbers of winter ducks, but which are overshadowed by the richer nearby Chew Lake.

Belvide: A natural-banked reservoir near Wolverhampton that has interesting birds throughout the year. Wildfowl are quite numerous in winter and regularly include a few of the scarcer species such as Goosander and Smew. Often has good waders in autumn.

Bewl Bridge: Near Tunbridge Wells on the Kent–Sussex border, this new reservoir has already attracted good numbers of ducks in winter and a variety of other species in season.

Blagdon: Outstanding reservoir near Bristol with up to 2,000 wildfowl in winter and interesting birds throughout the year. It is ranked ninth among reservoirs for wildfowl and up to 1,000 each of Wigeon, Teal and Pochard occur on occasion.

Blithfield: Flooded in 1952 near Rugeley in Staffordshire, this is the third most important reservoir for wildfowl with over 3,000 birds regularly present in winter. Teal and Wigeon are most numerous, but the scarcer species, such as Goldeneye, are present in good numbers. Grebes are also numerous.

Bough Beech: Nestling in the Weald near Sevenoaks, this attractive water has a good wildfowl population and an interesting passage of waders and terns.

Brent: Lying alongside London's North Circular Road, this is a popular spot among urban-based birders that has a variety of winter wildfowl, sometimes including Smew.

Cheddar: Large concrete bowl near Bristol with significant bird population, particularly of diving ducks, which raises it to eleventh place in the reservoir wildfowl league. In freeze-ups has open water after neighbouring waters are frozen solid.

Chew: Large, natural-banked reservoir near Bristol that is ranked fourth among wildfowl reservoirs, and which is a delight to visit. Has interesting birds throughout the year and a regular passage of waders and terns that has few equals among inland sites.

Covenham: Concrete-banked reservoir in Lincolnshire with large winter wildfowl population. Divers and grebes also occur and there is usually a good passage of waders and terns.

Cropston: Near Leicester with good winter wildfowl population, sometimes including Bewick's Swan. Passage birds may be interesting and nearby Swithland Reservoir should not be ignored.

Durleigh: Smallish, natural-banked reservoir near Bridgwater that is important for dabbling ducks and which has a good passage of waders.

Eccup: Natural-banked reservoir near Leeds with a winter wildfowl population that includes Goosander. Passage terns and waders in an area that is otherwise rather devoid of wetland habitat.

Eglwys Nunydd: Situated within the Margam steelworks at Port Talbot, this is a noted site of winter wildfowl including good numbers of diving ducks. Passage is varied, but rarities turn up with some frequency.

Eye Brook: Situated near Corby in Leicestershire. The natural and gently shelving banks make this a favoured haunt of dabbling ducks, Bewick's Swan, and a variety of passage waders and terns. Black Terns are as regular as anywhere inland in the country.

Farmoor: Two concrete-banked pools near Oxford. The older is heavily fished and sailed over, the newer has yet to settle down. Some ducks and grebes, a few waders, and often some good terns on passage.

Foxcote: A refuge of the Berks, Bucks and Oxfordshire

Map labels: Whittledene, Hurworth Burn, Leighton-Roundhill, Gouthwaite, Eccup, Covenham, Blithfield, Belvide, Cropston, Gailey, Rutland Water, Eye Brook, Stanford, Ravensthorpe, Grafham, Pitsford, Foxcote, Talybont, Tring, King George VI, Ardleigh, Abberton, Llandegfedd, Farmoor, Hanningfield, Eglwys Nunydd, Lisvane, William Girling, Walthamstow, Llanishen, Barrow Gurney, Brent, Staines, Stoke Newington, Blagdon, Chew, Queen Mary, Barn Elms, Cheddar, Queen Elizabeth II, Bough Beech, Durleigh, Bewl Bridge, Weir Wood, Tamar Lakes, Sutton Bingham

but Shoveler are particularly important. Regular passage of terns.

Queen Mary: Large concrete bowl west of London and a haunt of wildfowl, including rarities from time to time.

Ravensthorpe: Overshadowed by top-ranking neighbouring waters, but a good haunt of a variety of wildfowl.

Rutland Water: Largest man-made water in England, and since opening in 1975 has become the second-ranked wildfowl reservoir in the country. Easily worked despite its size, with a fine population of ducks, passage terns and waders.

Staines: Classic London bird-watching site, the causeway separating the 2 concrete-banked pools is a noted haunt of top birders. Good wildfowl, including Smew, with terns and grebes frequently interesting.

Stanford: Natural-banked water near Rugby with good winter wildfowl and some terns and waders on passage.

Stoke Newington: Two tiny concrete-banked pools in north London suburbs noted for diving ducks and Smew. Despite size and position still ranked seventh in wildfowl reservoir table.

Sutton Bingham: Natural-banked water near Yeovil with good numbers of surface-feeding ducks and ranked ninth among wildfowl reservoirs. Regular passage of waders and terns.

Talybont: Natural-banked water near Brecon with good wildfowl and passage waders and terns.

Tamar Lakes: Only major water in West Country and a haunt of winter wildfowl with all manner of species occurring. Declared a nature reserve in 1950.

Tring: Group of old canal reservoirs in Hertfordshire noted as first breeding site of colonizing Little Ringed Plovers. Regular winter wildfowl and passage terns and waders. Well frequented by bird-watchers.

Walthamstow: Twelve pools at southern end of Lea Valley in London. Many wooded islands support breeding birds, including Herons, and in winter there are wildfowl and grebes. Ranked in top 20.

Weir Wood: Sussex downland water with natural banks and good shallow areas for waders.

Whittledene: Good natural-banked reservoir near Newcastle with large wintering population of Tufted Duck.

William Girling: Important Lea Valley water near London with good wintering wildfowl population that merits a place in the top 20 list.

Naturalists' Trust and a significant haunt of winter wildfowl. Passage waders and terns.

Gailey: Three concrete-banked canal feeders near Wolverhampton that hold diving ducks in winter.

Gouthwaite: An attractive flooded valley near Harrogate with Whooper Swan and other winter wildfowl, and the odd tern on passage.

Grafham: Huge natural-banked reservoir near Huntingdon which was opened in 1966 and set the style for multi-use lowland waters. Ranked fifth on the wildfowl reservoir table with good variety and number of species present. Terns and waders sometimes numerous in season.

Hanningfield: Overshadowed by nearby Abberton, this is still a first-rate reservoir ranked in the top 20 and offering a variety of birds at all seasons. Ducks are plentiful in winter and wader passage is frequently outstanding for an inland site.

Hurworth Burn: Small reservoir near Teesmouth with some winter wildfowl, a few waders on passage, and a notable concentration of Little Gulls in autumn.

King George VI: Lying in the Lea Valley north of London, this is one of a series of waters that together hold one of the largest concentrations of birds in inland Britain. The present reservoir was constructed in 1947 and is ranked in the top 20 on the wildfowl reservoir table.

Leighton-Roundhill: The most important wildfowl reservoirs in northern England, these 2 waters were constructed in 1911 and 1929 and, despite being 250 m (800 ft) above sea level in the Yorkshire Dales, are ranked eighth among wildfowl reservoirs.

Lisvane and Llanishen: Small, adjacent concrete-banked pools in the Cardiff suburbs with good wildfowl populations and regular grebes and divers.

Llandegfedd: Large water near Pontypool with good variety and numbers of winter wildfowl and some grebes.

Pitsford: Large, natural-banked reservoir near Northampton with really outstanding numbers of diving ducks, regular Bewick's Swan and the occasional flock of geese. Passage of terns and waders usually interesting.

Queen Elizabeth II: Large reservoir west of London that is ranked in the top 20 on the wildfowl reservoir table. Numbers may not be outstanding,

Birds and the Law

The Wildlife and Countryside Act which came onto the Statute books in the autumn of 1981 encompassed and revised the provisions of the Protection of Birds Act of 1954, which was consequently repealed. The Act, of course, covers a whole host of subjects, including the protection of animals, plants, habitats and national parks, as well as the importation of endangered species. The following summary, however, covers the main aspects as far as bird protection is concerned. For more comprehensive information the RSPB's *Wild Birds and the Law* should be consulted.

Basic Provisions
The basic provision of the Act is that all birds, their nests and eggs are protected by law and it is thus an offence, with certain exceptions (see below), intentionally to:

1 kill, injure or take or attempt to kill, injure or take any wild bird,
2 take, damage or destroy or attempt to take, damage or destroy the nest of any wild bird whilst in use,
3 take or destroy or attempt to take or destroy the egg of any wild bird,
4 have in one's possession or control any wild bird (dead or alive), part of any wild bird or any egg or part of an egg which has been taken illegally since the passing of the Act,
5 disturb any wild bird listed on Schedule 1 while it is nest building, or on or near a nest containing eggs or young, or disturb the dependent young of such a bird,
6 have in one's possession or control any bird of prey or with certain exceptions any Schedule 1 birds unless they are registered and ringed or marked in accordance with the Secretary of State's regulations.

Sale of wild birds and their eggs
It is an offence to sell or exchange:
1 any live wild bird unless listed on Schedule 3 (Part I) and then only if aviary bred and ringed or marked in accordance with regulations laid down by the Secretary of State,
2 the egg of any British bird,
3 any dead wild bird other than a bird on Schedule 3 (Part II or III).

Exhibition of wild birds
It is an offence to show at any competition or in premises in which a competition is being held any live wild bird unless listed on Schedule 3 (Part I).

Methods of killing and taking birds
A number of methods of killing, injuring or taking birds are prohibited. These include gins, spring traps (normally in the form of pole traps), snares, nets, bird lime, electrical scaring devices and poisonous or stupefying substances. The use of decoys of live birds tethered, blinded or maimed in any way is also illegal.

Birds in captivity
It is illegal to keep any bird (excluding poultry) in a cage or other receptacle which is not of sufficient size to permit the bird to stretch its wings freely.

Exceptions
The most notable exception to the above provisions are:
1 an authorized person (a landowner or occupier) may kill birds on Schedule 2 (Part II) but not in Scotland on Sundays or Christmas Day,
2 a person charged with killing or attempting to kill a wild bird, other than one included on Schedule 1, shall not be guilty of an offence if he can show his action was urgently necessary for the purpose of preserving public health or air safety, preventing spread of disease or preventing serious damage to livestock, foodstuffs for livestock, crops, vegetables, fruit, growing timber or fisheries,
3 a person may take, kill or injure in attempting to kill a bird listed on Schedule 2 (Part I) outside the close season.

Licences
Licences may be issued to kill or take birds (or disturb Schedule 1 birds) for the following purposes:

scientific or educational   taxidermy
ringing or marking   photography
falconry or aviculture

to prevent serious damage to livestock, foodstuffs for livestock, crops, vegetables, fruit, growing timber or fisheries.

THE SCHEDULES

> Any species not listed on Schedule 1 or 2 is fully protected throughout the year

SCHEDULE 1: Part I
Birds and their eggs protected by special penalties at all times

Avocet	Garganey
Bee-eater	Godwit, Black-tailed
Bittern	Goshawk
Bittern, Little	Grebe, Black-necked
Bluethroat	Grebe, Slavonian
Brambling	Greenshank
Bunting, Cirl	Gull, Little
Bunting, Lapland	Gull, Mediterranean
Bunting, Snow	Harriers (all species)
Buzzard, Honey	Heron, Purple
Chough	Hobby
Corncrake	Hoopoe
Crake, Spotted	Kingfisher
Crossbills (all species)	Kite, Red
Divers (all species)	Merlin
Dotterel	Oriole, Golden
Duck, Long-tailed	Osprey
Eagle, Golden	Owl, Barn
Eagle, White-tailed	Owl, Snowy
Falcon, Gyr	Peregrine
Fieldfare	Petrel, Leach's
Firecrest	Phalarope, Red-necked

Plover, Kentish
Plover, Little Ringed
Quail, Common
Redstart, Black
Redwing
Rosefinch, Scarlet
Ruff
Sandpiper, Green
Sandpiper, Purple
Sandpiper, Wood
Scaup
Scoter, Common
Scoter, Velvet
Serin
Shorelark
Shrike, Red-backed
Spoonbill
Stilt, Black-winged
Stint, Temminck's
Stone-curlew
Swan, Bewick's
Swan, Whooper
Tern, Black
Tern, Little
Tern, Roseate
Tit, Bearded
Tit, Crested
Treecreeper,
 Short-toed
Warbler, Cetti's
Warbler, Dartford
Warbler, Marsh
Warbler, Savi's
Whimbrel
Woodlark
Wryneck
Jackdaw
Jay
Magpie
Pigeon, Feral
Rook
Sparrow, House
Starling
Woodpigeon

SCHEDULE 3: Part I
Birds which may be sold alive at all times if ringed and bred in captivity

Blackbird	Linnet
Brambling	Magpie
Bullfinch	Owl, Barn
Bunting, Reed	Redpoll
Chaffinch	Rook
Dunnock	Siskin
Goldfinch	Starling
Greenfinch	Thrush, Song
Jackdaw	Twite
Jay	Yellowhammer

SCHEDULE 1: Part II
Birds and their eggs protected by special penalties during the close season (1 February to 31 August)
Goldeneye
Goose, Greylag (in Outer Hebrides, Caithness, Sutherland and Wester Ross only)
Pintail

SCHEDULE 2: Part I
Birds which may be killed or taken outside the close season (1 February to 31 August) unless stated otherwise
Note: close season for duck and geese below high water mark is 21 February to 31 August

Capercaillie	Plover, Golden
Coot	Pochard
Curlew	Redshank
Duck, Tufted	Shoveler
Gadwall	Snipe, Common (close
Goldeneye	season 1 Feb. to
Goose, Canada	11 Aug.)
Goose, Greylag	Teal
Goose, Pink-footed	Wigeon
Goose, White-fronted	Woodcock (close season
(in England and	1 Feb. to 30 Sept.,
Wales only)	except Scotland
Mallard	where 1 Feb. to
Moorhen	31 Aug.)
Pintail	

SCHEDULE 3: Part II
Birds which may be sold dead at all times

Pigeon, Feral	Woodpigeon

SCHEDULE 3: Part III
Birds which may be sold dead from 1 September to 28 February

Capercaillie	Pochard
Coot	Shoveler
Duck, Tufted	Snipe, Common
Mallard	Teal
Pintail	Wigeon
Plover, Golden	Woodcock

The Game Acts
The Wildlife and Countryside Act does not cover gamebirds included in the Game Acts. These are listed below, together with the dates of the *close season* (when they may not be shot).

Pheasant 2 February to 30 September	Ptarmigan (in Scotland) 11 December to 11 August
Partridge 2 February to 31 August	Ptarmigan (in England and Wales is fully protected at all times)
Black Grouse 11 December to 19 August	
Red Grouse 11 December to 11 August	

SCHEDULE 2: Part II
Wild birds which may be killed or taken by authorized persons at all times

Crow	Gull, Lesser
Dove, Collared	Black-backed
Gull, Great	Gull, Herring
Black-backed	

Societies and Useful Addresses

NATURE CONSERVANCY COUNCIL
GREAT BRITAIN HEADQUARTERS
19/20 Belgrave Square, London
SW1X 8PY

ENGLAND
Headquarters for England
Calthorpe House, Calthorpe Street,
Banbury, Oxon OX16 8EX

Regional Offices:
East Anglia
60 Bracondale, Norwich, Norfolk NR1 2BE

East Midlands
PO Box 6, Godwin House, George Street,
Huntingdon, Cambs PE18 6BU

Northeast
Archbold House, Archbold Terrace,
Newcastle upon Tyne, NE2 1EG

Northwest
Blackwell, Bowness-on-Windermere,
Windermere, Cumbria LA23 3JR

South
Foxhold House, Thornford Road,
Crookham Common, Newbury,
Berks RG15 8EL

Southeast
Zealds, Church Street, Wye, Ashford,
Kent TN25 5BW

Southwest
Roughmoor, Bishop's Hull, Taunton,
Somerset TA1 5AA

West Midlands
Attingham Park, Shrewsbury, Shropshire
SY4 4TW

SCOTLAND
Headquarters for Scotland
12 Hope Terrace, Edinburgh EH9 2AS

Regional Offices:
Northeast
Wynne-Edwards House, 17 Rubislaw
Terrace, Aberdeen AB1 1XE

Northwest
Fraser Darling House, 9 Culduthel Road,
Inverness, IV2 4AG

Southeast
12 Hope Terrace, Edinburgh EH9 2AS

Southwest
The Castle, Loch Lomond Park, Balloch,
Dunbartonshire, G83 8LX

WALES
Headquarters for Wales
Plas Penrhos, Penrhos Road, Bangor,
Gwynedd LL57 2LQ

Regional Offices:
Dyfed–Powys
Plas Gogerddan, Aberystwyth, Dyfed
SY23 3EB

North
Plas Penrhos, Penrhos Road, Bangor,
Gwynedd LL57 2LQ

South
44 The Parade, Roath, Cardiff CF2 3AB

BRITISH MUSEUM
(NATURAL HISTORY)
Sub Department of Ornithology, Tring,
Herts HP23 6AP

BRITISH ORNITHOLOGISTS'
UNION
c/o Zoological Society of London,
Regent's Park, London, NW1

BRITISH TRUST FOR
ORNITHOLOGY
Beech Grove, Station Road, Tring, Herts
HP23 5NR

FAUNA AND FLORA
PRESERVATION SOCIETY
c/o Zoological Society of London,
Regent's Park, London, NW1

INTERNATIONAL COUNCIL FOR
BIRD PRESERVATION
219c Huntingdon Road, Cambridgeshire

INTERNATIONAL COUNCIL FOR
BIRD PRESERVATION (BRITISH
SECTION)
c/o British Museum (Natural History),
Cromwell Road, London, SW7 5BD

IRISH WILD BIRD CONSERVANCY
c/o Royal Irish Academy, 19 Dawson
Street, Dublin 2, Eire

PHEASANT TRUST
Great Witchingham, Norwich, Norfolk

ROYAL SOCIETY FOR NATURE
CONSERVATION
The Green, Nettleham, Lincolnshire

ROYAL SOCIETY FOR THE
PREVENTION OF CRUELTY TO
ANIMALS
The Causeway, Horsham, Surrey

ROYAL SOCIETY FOR THE
PROTECTION OF BIRDS
The Lodge, Sandy, Bedfordshire
SG19 2DL

Scottish Office
17 Regent Terrace, Edinburgh,
EH7 5BN

Northern Ireland Office
58 High Street, Newtownards,
Co. Down

SCOTTISH ORNITHOLOGISTS'
CLUB
21 Regent Terrace, Edinburgh EH7 5BN

SEABIRD GROUP
c/o British Ornithologists' Union
(see above)

WILDFOWL TRUST
Slimbridge, Gloucestershire

YOUNG ORNITHOLOGISTS'
CLUB
c/o Royal Society for the Protection of
Birds, The Lodge, Sandy, Bedfordshire
SG19 2DL

Bibliography

AUTHOR	BOOK	DATE
Atkinson-Willes, G. L.	*Wildfowl in Great Britain*	London, 1963
Bannerman, D. A.	*Birds of the British Isles* (10 vols)	Edinburgh, 1953–61
Brown, Leslie	*British Birds of Prey*	London, 1976
Campbell, B. and Ferguson-Lees, J.	*A Guide to Birds' Nests*	London, 1972
Chance, E. P.	*The Truth about the Cuckoo*	London, 1940
Cramp, S. and others	*The Seabirds of Britain and Ireland*	Oxford, 1971
Cramp, S. and others	*Birds of the Western Palearctic* (2 vols)	Oxford, 1978–80

Eastwood, E.	*Radar Ornithology*	London, 1967
Etchécopar, R. D. and Huë, F.	*The Birds of North Africa*	Edinburgh, 1967
Fisher, James	*Watching Birds*	Harmsworth, 1940
Fisher, James	*The Fulmar*	London, 1953
Fisher, James	*The Shell Bird Book*	London, 1966
Gooders, John	*Where to Watch Birds*	London, 1967
Gooders, John	*How to Watch Birds*	London, 1978
Gooders, John	*The Bird Seekers' Guide*	London, 1980
Harrison, Colin	*A Field Guide to the Nests, Eggs and Nestlings of British and European Birds*	London, 1975
Harrison, Colin	*An Atlas of the Birds of the Western Palearctic*	London, 1982
Heinzel, H., Fitter, R. and Parslow, J. F.	*The Birds of Britain and Europe*	London, 1972
Keith, Stuart and Gooders, John	*Collins Bird Guide*	London, 1980
Lack, D.	*The Life of the Robin*	London, 1943
Lack, D.	*Population Studies of Birds*	London, 1966
Lack, D.	*Natural Regulation of Animal Numbers*	Oxford, 1954
Mathews, G. V. T.	*Bird Navigation*	Cambridge, 1955
Murton, R. K.	*Man and Birds*	London, 1971
Nelson, J. B.	*The Gannet*	Tring, 1978
Nelson, J. B.	*Seabirds: Their Biology & Ecology*	London, 1980
Newton, I.	*Finches*	London, 1972
Parslow, J. F. (Ed.)	*The Status of Birds in Britain and Ireland*	Oxford, 1971
Parslow, J. F. (Ed.)	*Breeding Birds of Britain and Ireland*	Tring, 1973
Perrins, Chris	*British Tits*	London, 1979
Peterson, Roger Tory	*A Field Guide to the Birds*	Boston, 1934
Peterson, Roger Tory	*A Field Guide to Western Birds*	Boston, 1941
Peterson, Roger Tory and others	*A Field Guide to the Birds of Britain and Europe*	London, 1954
Peterson, Roger Tory	*A Field Guide to the Birds of Texas*	Boston, 1960
Porter, R. F. and others	*Flight Identification of European Raptors*	Tring, 1974
Sharrock, J. T. R. (Ed.)	*Atlas of Breeding Birds in Britain and Ireland*	Tring, 1976
Simms, Eric	*British Thrushes*	London, 1979
Snow, D. W.	*A Study of Blackbirds*	London, 1958
Sparks, John and Soper, Tony	*Owls: Their Natural and Unnatural History*	Newton Abbot, Reprinted 1978
Svensson, L.	*Identification Guide to European Passerines*	Stockholm, 1975
Thomson, A. Landsborough (Ed.)	*A New Dictionary of Birds*	London, 1964
Tinbergen, N.	*The Herring Gull's World*	London, 1953
Tuck, G. and Heinzel, H.	*A Field Guide to the Seabirds of the World*	London, 1978
Voous, K. H.	*Atlas of European Birds*	London, 1960
Voous, K. H.	*Lists of Recent Holarctic Bird Species*	London, 1977
Watson, Donald	*The Hen Harrier*	Berkhamstead, 1978
Williamson, K.	*Identification for Ringers:* 1 *Acrocephalus* and *Hippolais*; 2 *Phylloscopus*; 3 *Sylvia*	Tring, 1960–74
Witherby, H. F. and others	*The Handbook of British Birds* (5 vols)	London, 1938–42

INDEX

Figures in **bold** type give the main entry for each bird

Accentor, Alpine, 61, **349**
accidental species, 353
Accipiter gentilis, **132**, 135
    nisus, 35, 45, 48, 51, 132, **133**,
        134, 135, 141
Acrocephalus aedon, 353
    agricola, 13, 353
    arundinaceus, 56, **350**
    dumetorum, 13, **350**
    melanopogon, 277, 353
    paludicola, 277, **350**
    palustris, 13, 25, **278**, 279, 350
    schoenobaenus, 23, 25, 33, 275,
        277, 279, **350**
    scirpaceus, 26, 33, 42, 261, 274,
        276, 277, 278, **279**, 350
Actitis hypoleucos, 33, 172, 191,
    193, 345
    macularia, 68, 193, **345**
Aegithalos caudatus, 42, **292**
Aegolius funereus, **347**
Aegypius monachus, **356**
Aix galericulata, 62, **355**
    sponsa, **355**
Albatross, Black-browed, 60, 68,
    338
Alca torda, 32, 57, **217**
Alcedo atthis, 33, 42, **236**
Alectoris chukar, 62
    rufa, **149**, 150
Alauda arvensis, 24, 25, 28, 36,
    243, 244, 330
Alle alle, 55, **219**, 220
Alopochen aegyptiacus, **355**
Anas acuta, **112**
    americana, **340**
    clypeata, **114**
    crecca, 33, **109**, 113, 340
    discors, **340**
    falcata, **353**
    formosa, 353, **355**
    penelope, 28, 32, 53, **107**, 340
    platyrhynchos, 19, 25, 33, 36,
        51, 108, **110**, 114, 359
    querquedula, **113**, 340
    rubripes, **353**
    sibilatrix, **359**
    strepera, **108**
anatomy: body systems and
    forms, 18–19, 47–8, 52;
    brood patch, 44; jaws, 47, 50,
    52–3; sense organs, 48–9;
    tongue, 52–3; *see also* bills
Anser albifrons, **101**, 102, 107, 340
    anser, 33, 100, **102**, 359
    brachyrhynchus, 57, 70, 99, **100**
    caerulescens, **340**
    cygnoides, **359**
    erythropus, **340**
    fabalis, **99**
Anthropoides virgo, **360**
Anthus campestris, **348**
    cervinus, **349**
    godlewskii, 353
    gustavi, **348**
    hodgsoni, **348**
    novaeseelandiae, **348**
    pratensis, 17, 23, 24, 28, 33, 65,
        142, 248, **249**, 250, 348, 349
    spinoletta, 17, 23, 24, **250**
    trivialis, 17, 24, 38, **248**, 249
Apus affinis, **353**
    apus, 28, 36, 45, 50, 64, 66,
        134, 143, **235**, 347
    melba, **347**
    pallidus, **353**
Aquila chrysaetos, 12, 33, 40,
    42–4, 49, 52, 135, **138–9**, 311

clanga, 353
Ara ararauna, **360**
Ardea cinerea, 25, 33, 40, 63, **93**,
    231, 339
    purpurea, **339**
Ardeola ralloides, **339**
Arenaria interpres, 28, 170, 175,
    190, **196**
Argusianus argus, **360**
Asio flammeus, 33, 43, 232, **233**
    otus, 48, **232**
Athene noctua, 62, **230**, 347, 354
Auk, Great, 12
    Little, 55, **219**, 220
Avocet, 11, 37, 53, **160**
Aythya collaris, **340**
    ferina, **116**, 117
    fuligula, 116, **117**, 118, 340
    marila, **118**
    nyroca, **341**

Bantam, 360
Bartramia longicauda, **344**
Bee-eater, **348**
    Blue-cheeked, 353
bills: shapes and structures, 47–8,
    50–53; finches, 50–52, 327;
    Bewick's Swan, 97
Birds and the Law, 376–7
Bittern, 11, 17, 33, 37, **92**, 339
    American, **339**
    Little, **339**
Blackbird, 22–3, 25, 27–9, 35,
    36, 58, 268, **269**, 270, 271,
    304, 312
Blackcap, 22, 23, 32, 58, 283, **284**
Blackcock, *see* Grouse, Black
Bluetail, Red-flanked, 61, **353**
Bluethroat, 63, **262**
Bobolink, 353
Bombycilla garrulus, 59, 61,
    69–70, 219, **255**
Bonxie, *see* Skua, Great
Botaurus lentiginosus, **339**
    stellaris, 11, 17, 33, 37, **92**, 339
Brambling, 17, 48, 50, 66,
    316–17
Branta bernicla, 49, 64, 65, **105**
    canadensis, 62, 70–71, **103**, 104
    leucopsis, 57, **104**
    ruficollis, **340**
British Museum (Natural
    History), 378
British Ornithologists' Union, 378
British Trust for Ornithology,
    378
Bubo bubo, 353
Bubulcus ibis, **339**
Bucanetes githagineus, 61, **353**
Bucephala albeola, 353, **359**
    clangula, 63, **123**, 359
Budgerigar, 66
Bufflehead, 353, **359**
Bullfinch, 25, 48, 52, 327, **328**
Bulweria bulwerii, **353**
Bunting, Black-headed, **353**
    Chestnut, **357**
    Cirl, 17, 58, 332, **333**
    Corn, **336**
    Cretzschmar's, 353
    Indigo, **357**
    Lapland, 11, 63, **330**
    Little, **353**
    Ortolan, 56, 60, **334**
    Painted, **375**
    Pallas's Reed, 353
    Pine, 353
    Red-headed, **357**

Reed, 23, 33, 330, **335**, 353
Rock, 353
Rustic, **353**
Snow, 24, 58, **331**
Yellow-breasted, 61, **353**
Burhinus oedicnemus, 22, 27, 55,
    161
Bustard, Great, 12, 55, 62, **342**
    Houbara, 353
    Little, **342**
Buteo buteo, 127, 128, 132, 134,
    135, **136**, 137
    lagopus, 61, 70, 134, **137**
Butorides striatus, 353
Buzzard, 127, 128, 132, 134, 135,
    136, 137
    Honey, **127**, 135
    Rough-legged, 61, 70, 134, **137**

Cairina moschata, **359**
Calandrella cinerea, **348**
    rufescens, **348**
Calcarius lapponicus, 11, 63, **330**
Calidris acuminata, **344**
    alba, 17, **170**, 191
    alpina, 17, 18, 27, 28, 33, 58,
        170, 171, 172, 174, **176**, 187,
        190, 191, 194, 343, 344
    bairdii, **343**
    canutus, **169**, 187, 191
    ferruginea, **174**, 190, 343
    fuscicollis, **343**
    maritima, 11, 170, **175**, 196
    mauri, 353
    melanotos, **343**, 344
    minuta, **171**, 172, 191, 343, 348
    minutilla, **343**
    temminckii, 11, 60, 63, **171**,
        172, 191
Calonectris diomedea, **338**
camouflage, 41–2, 45
Canary, 357
Capercaillie, 35, 62, **148**, 337, 354
Caprimulgus aegyptius, 353
    europaeus, 47, 50, 51, **234**
    ruficollis, 353
Carduelis cannabina, 24, 50, **322**,
    323, 324
    carduelis, 48, 50, **320**, 327
    chloris, 24, 36, 50, **319**, 327
    flammea, 24, 28, 48, 50, 58, 70,
        321, **324**, 352
    flavirostris, 33, **323**, 324
    hornemanni, 60, **352**
    spinus, 24, 48, 50, **321**, 327
Carpodacus erythrinus, 61, **352**
Catharus fuscescens, 353
    guttatus, 353
    ustulatus, 353
Cepphus grylle, 32, **218**
Cercotrichas galactotes, **349**
Certhia brachydactyla, 353
    familiaris, 28, 58, 288, **300**
Ceryle alcyon, 353
Cettia cetti, 11, 63, **274**, 279
Chaffinch, 23, 27, 28, 35, 42, 48,
    50, 57, **316–17**, 327
Charadrius alexandrinus, 60, 164,
    165
    asiaticus, 353
    dubius, 11, 37, **162**, 164, 191
    hiaticula, 28, 32, 38, 41, 162,
        163, 164, 191, 343
    leschenaultii, 353
    morinellus, **165**
    semipalmatus, 353
    vociferus, **343**
Chettusia gregaria, 61, **343**
    leucura, 353
Chiffchaff, 22, 58, **286**, 287, 351

Chlidonias hybrida, 213, **346**
    leucopterus, 215, **347**
    niger, 11, 215, 346, 347
Chordeiles minor, 353
Chough, 37, **307**
Chrysolophus amherstiae, 62, **356**
    pictus, 62, **356**
Ciconia ciconia, 20, 71, **340**
    nigra, 339
Cinculus cinculus, 33, 54, 193, **256**
Circus aeruginosus, 37, **129**, 341
    cyaneus, 33, **130**, 131, 135, 233
    macrourus, 353
    pygargus, **130**, 131, 135
Cisticola juncidis, 11, 12, 13, 63,
    353
Clamator glandarius, **347**
Clamydotis undulata, 353
Clangula hyemalis, 32, **120**
climate, 54–7
close seasons, 376
Coccothraustes coccothraustes, 25,
    31, 48, 52, 327, **329**, 357
Coccyzus americanus, **347**
    erythrophthalmus, 353
Colaptes auratus, **357**
Colinus virginianus, 62, **356**
Columba livia, 36, **221**, 222, 360
    oenas, 42, 221, **222**
    palumbus, 26, 29, 35, 49, 71,
        132, 222, **223**
Coot, 33, 36, 41, **157**, 158
Coracias garrulus, **348**
Cormorant, 32, 58, **90**, 91
Corncrake, **156**
Corvus corax, 25, 33, 37, 40, 43,
    310, **311**
    corone, 25, 231, **308**, 310, 352
    frugilegus, 25, 32, 35, 40, 232,
        308, 309, 310
    monedula, 25, 35, 42, **309**
Coscoroba coscoroba, **358**
Coturnix coturnix, 59, **151**
Courser, Cream-coloured, 61, **342**
courtship, 40
Crake, Baillon's, **342**
    Little, **342**
    Spotted, **155**
Crane, 12, **342**
    Demoiselle, **360**
    Sandhill, 353
Crex crex, **156**
Crossbill, 9, 10, 31, 43, 48, 52,
    69, 219, **325**, 326, 327, 352
    Parrot, 9, 10, 57, 326
    Scottish, 9, 10, 29, 35, 57, 58,
        325, **326**, 327
    Two-barred, **352**
Crow, Carrion, 25, 231, **308**, 310,
    352
    Hooded, **310**
Cuckoo, 23, 26, 33, 42, 43, 45–6,
    226–7, 279, 347
    Black-billed, 353
    Great Spotted, **347**
    Oriental, 227
    Yellow-billed, **347**
Cuculus canorus, 23, 26, 33, 42,
    43, 45–6, **226–7**, 279, 347
    saturatus, 227
Curlew, 26, 33, 53, 58, 184, **185**,
    190, 191, 340
    Eskimo, 353
    Stone, *see* Stone-curlew
Cursorius cursor, 61, **342**
Cygnus atratus, **359**
    columbianus, 28, 95, **96–7**, 98
    cygnus, 26, 28, 95, **98**
    melanocoryphus, **359**
    olor, 33, 43, **95**, 96, 98

Dabchick, *see* Grebe, Little
Delichon urbica, 36, **247**
Dendrocopos major, 26, 31, 35, 36, 42, 50, 70, **240**, 241
    minor, 26, 63, **240**, **241**
Dendroica coronata, 353
    petechia, 353
    tigrina, 353
Diomedea melanophris, 60, 68, **338**
Dipper, 33, 54, 193, **256**
display, 26, 39–40, 44; ritual behaviour, 46; *see also* plumage
distribution, 54–63
Diver, Black-throated, 32, **75**, 76
    Great Northern, 32, 59, 63, 75, **76**, 338
    Red-throated, 33, **74**, 75
    White-billed, 60, **338**
Dolichonyx oryzivorus, 353
domesticated species, 358–60
Dotterel, **165**
Dove, Barbary, **360**
    Collared, 63, **224**, 360
    Rock, 36, **221**, 222, 360
    Rufous Turtle, 353
    Stock, 42, **221**, **222**
    Turtle, **224**, **225**
Dowitcher, Long-billed, **344**
    Short-billed, **344**, 353
drumming, 26
Duck, Aylesbury, **359**
    Black, **359**
    Domestic, **359**
    Ferruginous, **341**
    Harlequin, 353
    Khaki Campbell, **359**
    Long-tailed, 32, **120**
    Mandarin, 62, **355**
    Muscovy, **359**
    Ring-necked, **340**
    Ruddy, 62, **355**
    Tufted, 116, **117**, 118, 340
    Wood, **355**
Dunlin, 17, 18, 27, 28, 33, 58, 170, 171, 172, 174, **176**, 187, 190, 191, 194, 343, 344
Dunnock, 36, 38, 58, **258**, 266, 349, 351

Eagle, Golden, 12, 33, 40, 42, 43, 44, 49, 52, 135, **138–9**, 311
    Spotted, 353
    White-tailed, 12, 62, **341**
egg: calls from, **29**; and reproduction, 38; size, 38; colours, 38–9; laying patterns, 42–3; incubation and hatching, 43–6; *see also* nests
Egret, Cattle, **339**
    Great White, **339**
    Little, **339**
Egretta alba, **339**
    garzetta, **339**
Eider, 45, **119**, 341
    King, **341**
    Steller's, 60, **341**
Emberiza aureola, 61, **353**
    bruniceps, **357**
    caesia, 353
    cia, 353
    cirlus, 17, 58, 332, **333**
    citrinella, 17, 28, **332**, 333, 353
    hortulana, 56, 60, **334**
    leucocephalos, 353
    melanocephala, 353
    pallasi, 353
    pusilla, 353
    rustica, 353
    rutila, **357**
    schoeniclus, 23, 33, 330, **335**, 353

embryos: noises from, 28–9
Eremophila alpestris, 11, 63, **244**
Erithacus rubecula, 17, 22, 25, 28, 35, 36, 39, 58, 64, **259–60**, 262
eruptive species, 61, 69–70
escaped species, 354–7
Estuaries, Major, 372–3

Falco cherrug, 353
    columbarius, 33, 134, **142**
    eleonorae, 353
    naumanni, **341**
    peregrinus, 33, 37, 40, 134, **144**, 341
    rusticolus, 61, 63, **341**
    sparverius, 353
    subbuteo, 134, **143**
    tinnunculus, 16, 36, 58, 133, 134, 135, **141**, 143, 341
    vespertinus, **341**
Falcon, Eleonora's, 353
    Peregrine, 33, 37, 40, 134, **144**, 341
    Red-footed, **341**
    Saker, 353
Fauna and Flora Preservation Society, **378**
feeding, 47–53, 57; of young, 45–6
Ficedula albicollis, 291, 353
    hypoleuca, 16, 19, **290**, **291**
    parva, 351
Fieldfare, 11, 30, 63, 66, **270**, 273
finch bills, 50–52, 327
Finch, Citril, 353
    Trumpeter, 61, 353
Firecrest, 11, 58, 288, **289**
Flamingo, American, **358**
    Chilean, 355, **358**
    Greater, **355**, **358**
    Lesser, **358**
Flicker, Yellow-shafted, **357**
Flycatcher, Collared, 291, 353
    Pied, 16, 19, **290**, 291
    Red-breasted, **351**
    Spotted, 17, 31, **290**, 291
Food and Feeding, 47–53; *see also* feeding
Fratercula arctica, 32, **220**
Frigatebird, 60
    Magnificent, 353
Fregata magnificens, 353
Fringilla coelebs, 23, 27, 28, 35, 42, 48, 50, 57, **316–17**, 327
    montifringilla, 17, 48, 50, 66, **316–17**
Fulica atra, 33, 36, 41, **157**, 158
Fulmar, 46, 55, 63, 66, **83**
Fulmarus glacialis, 46, 55, 63, 66, **83**

Gadwall, **108**
Galerida cristata, 56, 243, **348**
    theklae, 348
Gallinago gallinago, 13, 17, 25, 26, 35, 48, 53, 179, **180**, 344
    media, 344
Gallinula chloropus, **157**, **158**
Gallinule, Allen's, 353
    American Purple, 353
Gallus gallus, **360**
Gannet, 28, 32, 40, 43–4, 55, 63, 68, **88–9**, 199
Garganey, **113**, 340
Garrulus glandarius, 25, 28, 35, 57, 61, 70, 232, **305**
Gavia adamsii, 60, **338**
    arctica, 32, **75**
    immer, 32, 59, 63, 75, **76**, 338
    stellata, 33, **74**

Gelochelidon nilotica, 210, **346**
Geothypis trichas, 353
Glareola nordmanni, **343**
    pratincola, **343**
Godwit, Bar-tailed, 11, 182, **183**, 190
    Black-tailed, 27, **182**, 183, 190
Goldcrest, 17, 20, 28, 31, 42, **288**, 289, 351
Goldeneye, 63, **123**, 359
Goldfinch, 48, 50, **320**, 327
Goosander, 33, 70, 125, **126**
Goose, Barnacle, 57, **104**
    Bean, **99**
    Black Brant, 105
    Brent, 49, 64, 65, **105**
    Canada, 62, 70–71, **103**, 104
    Chinese (Swan), **359**
    Dark-bellied Brent, 105
    Domestic, **359**
    Egyptian, **355**
    Greylag, 33, **100**, 102, 359
    Lesser White-fronted, **340**
    Pale-bellied Brent, 105
    Pink-footed, 57, 70, 99, **100**
    Red-breasted, **340**
    Snow, **340**
    White-fronted, **101**, 102, 107, 340
Goshawk, **132**, 135
Grebe, Black-necked, 81, **82**
    Great Crested, 33, 37, 63, **78–9**
    Little, 27, 37, 41, **77**
    Pied-billed, 353
    Red-necked, 59, 78, **80**
    Slavonian, 81, **82**
Greenfinch, 24, 36, 50, **319**, 327
Greenshank, 14, 17, 27, 58, 173, **188**, 344, 345
Grosbeak, Blue, **357**
    Evening, 353
    Pine, 353
    Rose-breasted, 353
Grouse, Black, 26, **147**
    Red, 9–10, 26, 33, 49, 57, 58, **145**, 146
    Willow, 9, 10, 57, 145
Grus canadensis, 353
    grus, 12, **342**
Guillemot, 28, 32, 38, 41, **216**, 217, 347
    Black (Tystie), 32, **218**
    Brünnich's, **347**
Guineafowl, Helmeted, **360**
Guiraca caerulea, **357**
Gull, Black-headed, 33, 81, 82, 200, **202**, 203, 345, 346
    Bonaparte's, **346**
    Common, 33, 200, **203**, 345, 346
    Franklin's, 353
    Glaucous, **207**
    Great Black-backed, 85, 207, **208**
    Great Black-headed, 353
    Herring, 46, 203, **204–5**, 206, 207
    Iceland, **207**
    Ivory, 60, **346**
    Laughing, 12, **345**
    Lesser Black-backed, 14, 57, 204–5, **206**, 208
    Little, 11, **201**
    Mediterranean, 11, **200**
    Ring-billed, 12, **346**
    Ross's, 60, **346**
    Sabine's, 60, **346**
    Slender-billed, 353
Gyps fulvus, 353
Gyrfalcon, 61, 63, **341**

habitat, 30–7, 40, 54–7; uplands, 33–4; woodland, 31, 34–5, 55; freshwater lakes, 31–2; coast, 31–2; fresh water, 31–3; farmland, 34–6, 37, 55; urban, 36
Haematopus ostralegus, 32, 41, 51, 58, **159**
Haliaeetus albicilla, 12, 62, **341**
Harrier, Hen, 33, **130**, 131, 135, 233
    Marsh, 37, **129**, 341
    Montagu's, 130, **131**, 135
    Pallid, 61, 353
Hawfinch, 25, 31, 48, 52, 327, **329**
Heron, Green, 353
    Grey, 25, 33, 40, 63, **93**, 231, 339
    Night, 92, **339**
    Purple, **339**
    Squacco, **339**
Hesperiphona vespertina, 353
Himantopus himantopus, **342**
Hippolais caligata, 13, **350**
    icterina, 60, **350**
    pallida, **350**
    polyglotta, **350**
Hirundapus caudacutus, 353
Hirundo daurica, 11, **348**
    rustica, 28, 30, 50, 66, 245, **246**, 247, 348
Histrionicus histrionicus, 353
Hobby, **134**, **143**
Hoopoe, 20, 59, **237**
Hydrobates pelagicus, 32, 67, **86**, 87
Hydroprogne tschegrava, **346**
Hylocichla minima, **350**

Ibis, Glossy, **340**
Icterus galbula, 353
Identification, 16–21
incubation, 43–6
International Council for Bird Preservation (British Section), 378
Introduced and Escaped Birds, 354–7
introduced species, 62–3
Irish Wildlife Conservancy, 378
irruptive species, 61, 69–70
Ixobrychus minutus, **339**

Jackdaw, 25, 35, 42, **309**
Jay, 25, 28, 35, 57, 61, 70, 232, **305**
Junco hyemalis, 353
Junco, Slate-coloured, 353
Junglefowl, Red, **360**
Jynx torquilla, 11, 28, 47, 63, **238**

Kestrel, 16, 36, 58, 133, 134, 135, **141**, 143, 341
    American, 353
    Lesser, **341**
Killdeer, **343**
Kingfisher, 33, 42, 49, **236**
    Belted, 353
Kite, Black, 56, 128, **341**
    Red, **128**, 135
Kittiwake, 32, 40, 63, 201, **209**
Knot, 64, **169**, 187, 191

Lagopus lagopus, 9–10, 26, 33, 49, 57, 58, **145**, 146
    mutus, 26, 33, **146**
Lanius collurio, 11, 25, 38–9, 63, **303**, 351, 352
    excubitor, 59, **304**, 351

isabellinus, 351
minor, 304, 351
senator, 352
Lapwing, 26, 33, 35, 41, 65, 67–8, 166, 168, 343
Lark, Bimaculated, 353
Calandra, 353
Crested, 56, 243, 348
Lesser Short-toed, 348
Shore, 11, 63, 244
Short-toed, 348
Thekla, 348
White-winged, 61, 353
Larus argentatus, 46, 203, 204–5, 206, 207
atricilla, 12, 345
canus, 33, 20, 203, 345, 346
delawarensis, 12, 346
fuscus, 14, 57, 204–5, 206, 208
genei, 353
glaucoides, 207
hyperboreus, 207
ichthyaetus, 353
marinus, 207, 208
melanocephalus, 11, 200
minutus, 11, 201
pipixcan, 353
philadelphia, 346
ridibundus, 33, 81, 82, 200, 202, 203, 345, 346
sabini, 60, 346
Limicola falcinellus, 57, 344
Limnodromus griseus, 344
scolopaceus, 344, 353
Limosa lapponica, 11, 182, 183, 190
limosa, 27, 182, 183, 190
Linnet, 24, 50, 322, 323, 324
Locustella certhiola, 353
fluviatilis, 353
lanceolata, 350
luscinioides, 11, 24, 275, 276, 279
naevia, 24, 275, 276, 277, 350
Lophura nyothemera, 360
Loxia curvirostra, 9, 10, 31, 43, 48, 52, 69, 219, 325, 326, 327, 352
leucoptera, 352
pytyopsittacus, 9, 10, 57, 326
scotica, 9, 10, 28, 35, 57, 58, 325, 326, 327
Lullula arborea, 11, 23, 27, 58, 242
Luscinia calliope, 353
luscinia, 349
megarhynchos, 23, 25, 261, 262, 284, 295, 349
svecica, 63, 262
Lymnocryptes minimus, 179

Macaw, Blue and Yellow, 360
Magpie, 25, 231, 232, 306
Mallard, 19, 25, 33, 35, 36, 51, 108, 110, 114, 359
Martin, House, 36, 247
Sand, 42, 245, 246, 313
Melanitta fusca, 121, 122, 341
nigra, 32, 115, 121, 122, 341
perspicillata, 341
Melanocorypha bimaculata, 353
calandra, 353
leucoptera, 61, 353
Merganser, Hooded, 353, 359
Red-breasted, 33, 125, 126
Mergus albellus, 124
cucullatus, 353, 359
merganser, 33, 70, 125, 126
serrator, 33, 125, 126
Merlin, 33, 134, 142
Merops apiaster, 348

superciliosus, 353
Micropalama himantopus, 344
migration, 30, 58–60, 64–71;
nomadism, 66–7, 70;
'invasion' migration, 69;
'moult' migration, 70; 'broad
front' migration, 71; 'narrow
front' migration, 71
Migration and Movements, 64–71
Miliaria calandra, 336
Milvus migrans, 56, 128, 341
milvus, 128, 135
Mniotilta varia, 353
Monticola saxatilis, 349
solitarius, 357
Montifringilla nivalis, 353
Moorhen, 33, 35, 36, 41, 45, 157, 158
Motacilla alba, 14, 19, 57, 65, 254, 349
cinerea, 28, 33, 54, 251
citreola, 349
flava, 14, 36, 57, 252–3
Muscicapa striata, 17, 31, 290, 291

National Nature Reserves, 362–3;
see also Nature Reserves
Nature Conservancy Council, 378
Nature Reserves, 15, 37, 362–5
Neophron percnopterus, 353
nests, 38–42, 49
Nests and Nesting, 38–46
Netta rufina, 115
nidicolous young, 44–5
nidifugous young, 45
Nighthawk, Common, 353
Nightingale, 23, 25, 261, 262, 284, 295, 349
Thrush, 349
Nightjar, 47, 50, 51, 234
Egyptian, 353
Red-necked, 353
Nucifraga caryocatactes, 61, 70, 352
Numenius arquata, 26, 33, 53, 58, 184, 185, 190, 191, 340
borealis, 353
phaeopus, 27, 59, 184, 185, 191, 199
Numida meleagris, 360
Nutcracker, 61, 70, 352
Nuthatch, 27, 31, 301
Nyctea scandiaca, 61, 63, 70, 72, 229
Nycticorax nycticorax, 339

Observatories, Bird, 366–7
Oceanites oceanicus, 67, 353
Oceanodroma castro, 353
leucorhoa, 29, 67, 87
Oenanthe deserti, 349
hispanica, 349
isabellina, 353
leucura, 353
oenanthe, 33, 34, 58, 267
pleschanka, 353
Oriole, Baltimore, 353
Golden, 59, 302
Northern, 353
Oriolus oriolus, 59, 302
Ornamental and Domesticated
Birds, 358–60
Osprey, 51, 52, 72, 134, 140
Ostrich, 38
Otis tarda, 12, 55, 62, 342
tetrax, 342
Otus scops, 347
Ouzel, Ring, 33, 34, 268
Ovenbird, 353

Owl, Barn, 36, 50, 228
Eagle, 353
Hawk, 61, 347
Little, 62, 230, 347, 354
Long-eared, 48, 232
Scops, 347
Short-eared, 33, 43, 232, 233
Snowy, 61, 63, 70, 72, 229
Tawny, 35, 36, 141, 231, 232
Tengmalm's, 347
Oxyura jamaicensis, 62, 355
Oystercatcher, 32, 41, 51, 53, 58, 159

Padda oryzivora, 357
Pagophila eburnea, 60, 346
Pandion haliaetus, 51, 52, 72, 134, 140
Panurus biarmicus, 33, 293
Parakeet, Rose-ringed
(Ring-necked Parakeet), 62, 356
Partridge, Chukar, 62
Grey, 36, 149, 150
Red-legged, 149, 150
Parula americana, 353
Parus ater, 23, 31, 36, 57, 70, 288, 296
caeruleus, 36, 38, 40, 42, 46, 49, 58, 298
cristatus, 35, 58, 297
major, 22, 25, 27, 28, 42, 296, 299
montanus, 47, 294, 295
palustris, 294, 295
Passer domesticus, 36, 39, 231, 241, 247, 314, 315, 319, 354, 357
hispaniolensis, 353
montanus, 314
Passerina ciris, 357
cyanea, 357
Pavo cristatus, 360
Peafowl, 360
Pelagodroma marina, 353
Pelecanus crispus, 55, 354, 355
onocrotalus, 354, 355
Pelican, Dalmatian, 55, 354, 355
White, 354, 355
Perdix perdix, 36, 41, 149, 150
Peregrine, 33, 37, 40, 134, 144, 341
Pernis apivorus, 127, 135
Petrel, Bulwer's, 353
Capped, 353
Leach's, 29, 67, 87
Maderian, 353
Storm, 32, 67, 86, 87
White-faced, 353
Wilson's, 67, 353
Phalacrocorax aristotelis, 90, 91
carbo, 32, 58, 90, 91
Phalarope, Grey, 60, 195
Red-necked, 44, 194, 195
Wilson's, 345
Phalaropus fulicarius, 60, 195
lobatus, 44, 194, 195
tricolor, 345
Phasianus colchicus, 26, 41, 62, 64, 152–3
versicolor, 153
Pheasant, 26, 41, 62, 64, 152–3
Golden, 62, 356
Great Argus, 360
Japanese, 153
Lady Amherst's, 62, 356
Reeves's, 356
Silver, 360
Pheasant Trust, 378
Pheuticus ludovicianus, 353

Philomachus pugnax, 11, 177–8, 187, 190, 343, 344
Phoenicopterus chilensis, 355, 358
minor, 358
ruber, 355, 358
Phoenicurus ochruros, 11, 263
phoenicurus, 16, 261, 264
Phylloscopus bonelli, 351
borealis, 61, 351
collybita, 22, 58, 286, 287, 351
fuscatus, 351
inornatus, 351
proregulus, 68, 351
schwarzi, 351
sibilatrix, 285
trochiloides, 25, 351
trochilus, 22, 286, 287, 351
Pica pica, 25, 231, 232, 306
Picus viridis, 32, 58, 239
Pigeon, 358
Feral, 36, 222
Fancy, 360
Pinicola enucleator, 353
Pintail, 112
Pipilo erythrophthalmus, 353
Pipit, Blyth's, 353
Meadow, 17, 23, 24, 28, 33, 65, 142, 249, 250, 348, 349
Olive-backed, 348
Pechora, 348
Richard's, 348
Red-throated, 349
Rock, 17, 23, 24, 250
Scandinavian Rock, 250
Tawny, 348
Tree, 17, 24, 38, 248, 249
Water, 250
Piranga olivacea, 353
rubra, 353
Platalea leucorodia, 12, 94
Plectrophenax nivalis, 24, 58, 331
Plegadis falcinellus, 340
Plover, Caspian, 353
Golden, 27, 33, 35, 57, 58, 166, 173, 343
Greater Sand, 353
Grey, 28, 167, 173
Kentish, 60, 164, 165
Lesser Golden, 343
Little Ringed, 11, 37, 162, 164, 191
Ringed, 28, 32, 38, 41, 162, 163, 164, 191, 343
Semipalmated, 353
Sociable, 61, 343
White-tailed, 353
plumage, 17–19
Pluvialis apricaria, 27, 33, 35, 57, 58, 166, 173, 343
dominica, 343
squatarola, 28, 167, 173
Pochard, 116, 117
Red-crested, 115
White-eyed, see Duck, Ferruginous
Podiceps auritus, 81, 82
cristatus, 33, 37, 63, 78–9
grisegena, 59, 80
nigricollis, 81, 82
Podylimbus podiceps, 353
Polysticta stelleri, 60, 341
Porphyrula alleni, 353
martinica, 353
Porzana carolina, 353
parva, 342
porzana, 155
pusilla, 342
Pratincole, Black-winged, 343
Collared, 343
Protection of Birds Act 1954, 376–7

Prunella collaris, 61, **349**
  modularis, 36, 58, **258**, 266, 349, 351
Psittacula krameri, 62, **356**
Ptarmigan, 26, 33, **146**
Pterodroma hasitata, 353
Puffin, 32, **220**
Puffinus assimilis, 85, **338**
  gravis, 55, 67, **84**, 338
  puffinus, 32, 59, **85**, 220, 338
Pyrrhocorax pyrrhocorax, 37, 72, **307**
Pyrrhula pyrrhula, 25, 48, 52, 327, **328**

Quail, 59, **151**
  Bobwhite, 62, **356**

Rail, Sora, 353
  Water, 33, **154**
Rallus aquaticus, 33, **154**
Range and Distribution, 54–63
Raptors in Flight, 14, 134–5
Rare Birds, 338–353
Rarities, Major Haunts, 368–9
Raven, 25, 33, 37, 40, 43, 128, 310, **311**
Razorbill, 32, 57, **217**
Recurvirostra avosetta, 11, 37, **160**
Redpoll, 24, 28, 48, 50, 58, 70, 321, **324**, 352
  Arctic, 60, **352**
Redshank, 16, 27, 32, 49, 173, 186, **187**, 188
  Spotted, 173, **186**, 187
Redstart, 16, 261, **264**
  American, 353
  Black, 11, **263**
Redwing, 11, 25, 28, 30, 63, 66, 270, **272**
Reedling, Bearded, *see* Tit, Bearded
Reeve, *see* Ruff
Regulus ignicapillus, 11, 58, 288, **289**
  regulus, 17, 20, 28, 31, 42, **288**, 289, 351
Remiz pendulinus, 353
reproduction, 38–46
reserves, *see* Nature Reserves
Reservoirs, 37, 374–5
Rhodostethia rosea, 60, **346**
ringing, 65–6, 376
Riparia riparia, 42, **245**, 246, 313
Rissa tridactyla, 32, 40, 63, 201, **209**
Robin, 17, 22, 25, 28, 35, 36, 39, 58, 64, **259**–60, 262
  American, **350**
  Rufous Bush, **349**
Roller, **348**
Rook, 25, 32, 35, 40, 232, **308**, 309, 310
Rosefinch, Scarlet, 61, **352**
Rostratula benghalensis, 13
Royal Society for Nature Conservation, 378
Royal Society for the Prevention of Cruelty to Animals, 378
Royal Society for the Protection of Birds, 378; Reserves, 364–5
Rubythroat, Siberian, 353
Ruff, 11, **177**–8, 187, 190, 343, 344

Saker, 353
Sanderling, 17, **170**, 191
Sandgrouse, Pallas's, 61, 70, **347**
Sandpipers in Flight, 173
Sandpiper, Baird's, **343**

Broad-billed, 57, **344**
Buff-breasted, **344**
Common, 33, 172, 191, **193**, 345
Curlew, **174**, 190, 343
Green, 173, **189**, 192, 345
Least, **343**
Marsh, **344**, 345
Pectoral, 343, **344**
Purple, 11, 170, **175**, 196
Sharp-tailed, **344**
Solitary, **345**
Spotted, 68, **193**, **345**
Stilt, **344**
Terek, **345**
Upland, **344**
Western, 353
White-rumped, **343**
Wood, 14, 27, 58, 173, 189, **192**, 344, **345**
Sapsucker, Yellow-bellied, 353
Saxicola rubetra, **265**, 266
  torquata, 265, **266**
Scaup, 117, **118**
Scolopax rusticola*, 24, 27, 32, 35, 48, 63, **181**, 344
Scoter, Common, 32, 115, **121**, 122, 341
  Surf, 121, **341**
  Velvet, 121, **122**, 341
Scottish Ornithologist's Club, 378
Seabird Colonies, Major, 370–71
Seiurus aurocapillus, 353
  noveboracensis, 353
Serin, 11, **318**, 319, 357
Serinus canaria, **357**
  citrinella, 353
  serinus, 11, **318**, 319, 357
Setophaga ruticilla, 353
Shag, 90, **91**
Shearwater, Balearic, 85
  Cory's, **338**
  Great, 55, 67, **84**, 338
  Little, 85, **338**
  Manx, 32, 59, **85**, 220, 338
Shelduck, 32, 45, 58, 70, **106**, 340, 355
  Ruddy, **340**
Shoveler, **114**
Shrike, Brown, 351
  Great Grey, 59, **304**, 351
  Isabelline, **351**
  Lesser Grey, 304, **351**
  Red-backed, 11, 25, 38–9, 63, **303**, 351, 352
  Woodchat, **352**
Siskin, 24, 48, 50, **321**, 327
Sitta europaea, 27, 31, **301**
Skua, Arctic, 57, 197, **198**, 345
  Great (Bonxie), 198, **199**
  Long-tailed, 60, **345**
  Pomarine, 60, **197**, 198
Skylark, 24, 25, 28, 36, **243**, 244, 330
Smew, 59, **124**
Snipe, 13, 17, 25, 26, 35, 48, 53, 179, **180**, 344
  Great, **344**
  Jack, **179**
  Pin-tailed, 13
Snowfinch, 353
Somateria mollissima, 45, **119**, 341
  spectabilis, **341**
Songs and Calls, 22–9; *see also* voice
Sparrow, Hedge, *see* Dunnock
Sparrow, Fox, 353
  House, 36, 39, 231, 241, 247, **314**, **315**, 319, 354, 357
  Java, **357**

Song, 353
Spanish, 353
Tree, **314**
White-crowned, 353
White-throated, **353**
Sparrowhawk, 35, 45, 46, 48, 51, 132, **133**, 134, 135, 141
Sphyrapicus varius, 353
Spoonbill, 12, **94**
Sprosser, *see* Nightingale, Thrush
Starling, 24, 28, 35, 50, 219, 255, **312**–13, 342, 352, 354
  Rose-coloured, 61, **352**
  Spotless, 313
Stercorarius longicaudus, 60, **345**
  parasiticus, 57, 197, **198**, 345
  pomarinus, 60, **197**, 198
  skua, 198, **199**
Sterna albifrons, 32 58, **214**
  anaethetus, 346, 353
  dougallii, 66, **211**
  forsteri, 353
  fuscata, **346**
  hirundo, 32, 37, 211, **212**, 213
  maxima, 353
  paradisaea, 28, 67, 211, 212, **213**
  sandvicensis, 28, 32, 66, **210**, 346
Stilt, Black-winged, **342**
Stint, Little, **171**, 172, 191, 343, 348
  Temminck's, 11, 60, 63, 171, **172**, 191
Stone-curlew, 22, 27, 55, **161**
Stonechat, **265**, 266
Stork, Black, **339**
  White, 20, 71, **340**
Streptopelia decaocto, 63, **224**, 360
  orientalis, 353
  risoria, **360**
  turtur, 224, **225**
Strix aluco, 35, 36, 141, **231**, 232
Sturnus roseus, 61, **352**
  unicolor, 313
  vulgaris, 24, 28, 35, 50, 219, 255, **312**–13, 342, 352, 354
Sula bassana, 28, 32, 40, 43, 55, 63, 68, **88**–9, 199
Surnia ulula, 61, **347**
Swallow, 28, 30, 50, 66, **245**, 246, 247, 348
  Red-rumped, 11, **348**
Swan, Bewick's, 28, 95, **96**–7, 98
  Black, **359**
  Black-necked, **359**
  Coscoroba, **358**
  Mute, 33, 43, **95**, 96, 98
  Whooper, 26, 28, 95, **98**
Swift, 28, 36, 45, 50, 64, 66, 134, 143, **235**, 347
  Alpine, **347**
  Little, 353
  Needle-tailed, 353
  Pallid, 353
Sylvia atricapilla, 22, 23, 32, 58, **283**, 284
  borin, 22, 25, **283**, 284, 350
  cantillans, **350**
  communis, 23, 24, 27, 280, 281, **282**, 350
  conspicillata, 353
  curruca, **281**, 282, 333
  hortensis, 353
  melanocephala, 353
  nana, 61, 353
  nisoria, **351**
  ruepelli, 353
  sarda, 280
  undata, 24, 58, **280**

Syrmaticus reevesi, **356**
Syrrhaptes paradoxus, 61, 70, **347**

Tachybaptus ruficollis, 27, 37, **41**, 77
Tadorna ferruginea, **340**
  tadorna, 32, 45, 58, 70, **106**, 340, 355
Tanager, Scarlet, 353
  Summer, 353
Tarsiger cyanurus, 61, **355**
Teal, 33, **109**, 113, 340
  Baikal, 353, **355**
  Blue-winged, **340**
  Falcated, 353
  Green-winged, 109
Tern, Arctic, 28, 67, 211, 212, **213**
  Black, 11, **215**, 346, 347
  Bridled, 346, 353
  Caspian, **346**
  Common, 32, 37, 211, **212**, 213
  Forster's, 353
  Gull-billed, 210, **346**
  Little, 32, 58, **214**
  Roseate, 66, **211**
  Royal, 353
  Sandwich, 28, 32, 66, **210**, 346
  Sooty, **346**
  Whiskered, **213**, 346
  White-winged Black, 215, **347**
territory, 39–41
Tetrao tetrix, 26, **147**
  urogallus, 35, 62, **148**, 337, 354
Thrasher, Brown, 353
Thrush, Black-throated/Red-throated, 353
  Blue Rock, **357**
  Dusky/Naumann's, 353
  Eye-browed, 353
  Grey-cheeked, **350**
  Hermit, 353
  Mistle, 23, 25, 28–9, 32, 35, 269, 271, **273**
  Rock, **349**
  Siberian, 353
  Song, 22, 25, 28, 29, 35, 65, 269, **271**, 273, **350**
  Swainson's, 353
  White's, **349**
Tichodroma muraria, 61, 353
Tit, Bearded (Bearded Reedling), 33, **293**
  Blue, 36, 38, 40, 42, 46, 49, 58, **298**
  Coal, 23, 31, 36, 57, 70, 288, **296**
  Crested, 35, 58, **297**
  Great, 22, 25, 27, 28, 42, 296, **299**
  Long-tailed, 42, **292**
  Marsh, **294**, 295
  Penduline, 353
  Willow, 47, **294**, 295
Towhee, Rufous-sided, 353
Toxostoma rufum, 353
Treecreeper, 28, 58, 288, **300**
  Short-toed, 353
Tringa erythropus, 173, **186**, 187
  flavipes, **345**
  glareola, 14, 58, 173, 189, **192**, 345
  macularia, 68, **193**, 345
  melanoleuca, **345**
  nebularia, 14, 17, 27, 58, 173, **188**, 344, 345
  ochropus, 25, 173, **189**, 192, 344, 345
  solitaria, **345**
  stagnatilis, **344**, 345